Techniques for Computer Graphics

Red Mirror Ball on a Field of Neon (Mike Muuss)

David F. Rogers   Rae A. Earnshaw

Editors

Techniques for Computer Graphics

With 274 Illustrations, 82 in Color

Springer-Verlag
New York Berlin Heidelberg London Paris Tokyo

David F. Rogers
Aerospace Engineering Department
U.S. Naval Academy
Annapolis, Maryland 21402, USA

Rae A. Earnshaw
University of Leeds
Leeds LS2 9JT
United Kingdom

Cover illustration: *Copper Apple with Columns* (Michael Kaplan, Eliot Feibush, and Paul Hughett)

Library of Congress Cataloging-in-Publication Data
Techniques for computer graphics.
  Papers for an International Summer Institute on the
State of the Art Computer Graphics, held at the
University of Stirling, Scotland, summer 1986,
sponsored by the British Computer Society Computer
Graphics and Displays Group
and the Computer Graphics Society.
  Includes bibliographies and index.
  1. Computer graphics—Congresses. I. Rogers, David
F., 1937–   II. Earnshaw, R. A. (Rae A.), 1944–
III. International Summer Institute on the State of the
Art in Computer Graphics (1986 : University of Stirling)
IV. British Computer Society. Computer Graphics and
Displays Group. V. Computer Graphics Society.
T385.T45   1987   006.6   87-9766

© 1987 by Springer-Verlag New York Inc.
Softcover reprint of the hardcover 1st edition 1987

9 8 7 6 5 4 3 2 1

ISBN-13:978-1-4613-8715-2   e-ISBN-13:978-1-4613-8713-8
DOI: 10.1007/978-1-4613-8713-8

Acknowledgments

The papers in this volume formed the basis of an International Summer Institute on The State of the Art in Computer Graphics held at the University of Stirling, Stirling, Scotland, United Kingdom.

We are very grateful to our co-sponsors: the British Computer Society (BCS), Computer Graphics and Displays Group, and the Computer Graphics Society (CGS). We also thank the Association for Computing Machinery (ACM) for their co-operation and support.

Our thanks and appreciation go to Mrs. Frances Johnson, Conference Officer at the University of Leeds, and to Brian Booker, for all their help and support with the practical arrangements for the Institute.

Our thanks and appreciation also to all those delegates who attended from many countries and contributed by their discussion, interaction and inspiration. The following countries were represented: Belgium, Canada, Denmark, Federal Republic of Germany, Finland, Iceland, Japan, Netherlands, Norway, Poland, the United Kingdom, and the United States.

A volume such as this is the result of many months of planning and preparation, and we thank all those who have assisted us. Colleagues, students, contributors, and publisher—we thank you all for your forbearance and patience, and for enduring our persistence in seeking to bring this project to a successful conclusion.

David F. Rogers   Rae A. Ernshaw
Annapolis, Maryland, USA   Leeds, UK

Contents

Introduction to Techniques
for Computer Graphics

Capturing the state-of-the-art in computer graphics is akin to attempting to photograph a fast moving target. The result, at best, is a synoptic snapshot. The current volume represents a snapshot of a number of topics in computer graphics. These topics include: workstations, graphics standards, image generation, computer-aided design (CAD), curves and surfaces, human-computer interface issues, electronic documents, integrated graphics and text, solid modeling, VLSI, and innovative applications.

Many of the papers first present a background introduction to the topic followed by a discussion of current work in the topic. The volume is thus equally suitable for non-specialists in a particular area, and for the more experienced researcher in the field. It also enables general readers to obtain an acquaintance with a particular topic area sufficient to apply that knowledge in the context of solving current problems.

The volume is organized into eight chapters as follows: Design, Modeling, Image Generation, Workstations, Hardware, Human-Computer Interface, Graphics Standards, and Documentation.

In the first chapter John Lansdown provides an overview of the design process in the context of computer graphics. In the first of two papers Lansdown points out that computer graphics has been used as a design tool for some thirty years. In most cases it has enabled the iterative design process to be performed more efficiently and quickly. However, one of the real problems is in the central area of design, viz, intuition and creativity. Modeling of these activities seems to be far more difficult than modeling objects. Lansdown presents an analysis of these issues and outlines a method of parametric variation for using computers to fine-tune a designer's proposals.

His second paper examines the relationship of visual literacy to the design process. Indeed, such a relationship is vital if effective images are to be produced. More attention needs to be paid to the classical form and content of images and pictures in order to better understand the use of color, texture and form. Increased understanding of these aspects of computer graphics will result in more effective composition and exploitation of inherent information.

The second chapter discusses the requirements and techniques for creating models. In particular, it provides a survey of current work in geometric modeling including curves and surfaces.

The first paper by Robin Forrest raises several key issues in the development and implementation of geometric models. He points out that the quality of rendering is now so good that deficiencies in the underlying models are clearly evident. Thus, more attention needs to be paid to the rigor and quality of the model definition and to the numerics associated with the model.

The second paper by John Woodwark and Peter Quarendon provides an introduction to solid modeling. Solid modeling enables real objects (e.g. buildings, engineering components, organs of the human body, etc.) to be represented in a complete form such that ultimately quantitative information can be extracted during the design process. Picture generation techniques are outlined and anticipated developments for future advanced architectures capable of dealing with more complex models are summarized.

The abstract of Brian Barsky's elegant lectures summarizing the concepts and application of the beta-spline, a mathematical technique for curve and surface representation, appears next. Dr. Barsky pointed out that the underlying geometric nature of the technique combined with local control through shape parameters forms a powerful tool for computer graphics and computer-aided geometric design and modeling. These aspects of the technique are amply illustrated in a highly recommended forthcoming book by Professor Barsky entitled 'Computer Graphics and Geometric Modeling Using Beta-splines'. The book is to be published by Springer-Verlag.

The next paper by computer graphics pioneer Tosiyasu Kunii briefly discusses several examples of modeling systems. These include an apparel pattern making system, a constructive solid modeling system, an animation system for engineering models, a system for generating, manipulating and managing the many tables required in engineering and manufacturing, a scheme for region detection for rasterized data, a device independent model driven system for accessing local area network facilities, and finally a system for generating and managing user friendly interactive menus.

The final paper in the chapter is by Mike Muuss. Muuss presents an excellent review of the origins and basic principles of solid modeling. In contrast to many papers on solid modeling, he discusses, in detail, the mathematics of typical solid primitives, including their mathematical definitions, the mathematics of Boolean operations as applied to these primitives and the mathematics of ray (line) - primitive intersections. As an example of a modern geometric solid modeler he describes MGED—a fully implemented production engineering design solid modeler currently in daily use at the U.S. Army Ballistic Research Laboratory. MGED is capable of representing models composed of in excess of 5000 objects. The modeler is fully integrated with critical engineering analysis programs. The paper also provides an excellent introduction to ray tracing including a discussion of the general data structures, code organization and space partitioning algorithms. In MGED, ray tracing provides critical analysis as well as rendering capability.

The third chapter contains two papers on image synthesis. First, Mike Kaplan provides a very complete description of a modern space partitioning ray tracing algorithm. The algorithm, which for a given resolution, operates in nearly constant time independent of the number of objects in the scene, is more than two orders of magnitude more efficient than the naive algorithms of less than ten years ago.

Next, Roy Hall discusses illumination models and color in the context of illumination models. Hall first provides a physical model for a nearly complete general illumination model. He then shows, in detail, how the traditional illumination models used in computer graphics, including Bouknight, Gouraud, Phong, Blinn, Whitted, Cook, Hall and the radiosity method, approximate the general model. Each model is illustrated by a specially generated comparative color image. Finally, he discusses a number of image display considerations, particularly with respect to video, required for optimal presentation.

These first three chapters basically address the questions of how do we model a design and effectively and realistically render it. In the fourth chapter Zsuzsanna Molnar discusses the characteristics and capabilities of a modern engineering/scientific professional graphics workstation. The workstation described by Molnar uses VLSI hardware technology to achieve increased graphics performance. Using a current 32 bit super-microprocessor makes the workstation suitable for a wide range of applications requiring both high compute power and fast image generation.

In the fifth chapter three authors discuss current state-of-the-art research using VLSI based hardware to further enhance graphics performance. In the first of these papers Henry Fuchs discusses the origins of todays graphics systems from a hardware viewpoint. He outlines the generic organization of several types of systems. Historically, three kinds of graphics systems have been optimized for different requirements: the high-performance 3-D system, the color frame buffer, and the general workstation display. With increasing power and flexibility, it is now becoming common for a workstation to satisfy two or more of these requirements.

Next, Adrian Thomas presents a series of interrelated concepts for a display and modeling system based on the use of Boolean expression models to represent shape. This display system, which transforms models into pictorial form, is implementable in VLSI hardware. A prototype system is outlined. A further area of interest is the reverse process of capturing shape information by generating the corresponding Boolean model from TV camera input. This simple form of machine vision is capable of extension and improvement. Thus, Boolean models provide the common baseline linking together real-time object display and real-time image processing techniques.

Finally, in this section Alistair Kilgour discusses a practical requirement in the generation of VLSI circuits: the merging of different polygons in the description. He describes the formulation, implementation, and performance of an efficient and secure algorithm for processing such polygons.

Chapter 6 turns to the popular area of human-computer interaction with two papers by current researchers in the field. Brian Shackel addresses the issues of hardware; Tom Stewart outlines current research and development in the field.

The human interface is concerned with all those features that characterize the interaction of the user with the machine. It consists not only of hardware but also any relevant software and documentation. Interaction may consist of a sequence of communications based on response to messages produced by the system. These messages may be alphanumeric, graphical, or both. Brian Shackel's paper is concerned with the hardware aspects of the human interface, including input and output devices such as terminals, VDUs, displays, printers, workstations, and the characteristics of the environment in which they are used. The relative merits of input devices such as the keyboard, lightpen, trackball, mouse, touchscreen, touchpad, and voice are discussed. Characteristics of output devices are analyzed and the issue of visual versus auditory response/cues is examined. Finally, the ergonomic issues of screen size, use of color, and terminal design are presented.

Tom Stewart examines Human-Computer Interface (HCI) design and surveys research and development in User Interface Design. The features and facilities of the interface govern the quality of the HCI: Good user interface design promotes good HCI–it has to be designed in, it cannot be bought in. Usability and acceptability are user and task specific. The results of numerous studies of user/task combinations are outlined in the paper. User interfaces in graphics systems are reviewed as is the incorporation of AI techniques to create adaptive user interfaces. Some reasons for poor interfaces are outlined. In the main these are due to too little attention being paid to human factors at an early stage in the design. Finally, current developments in HCI and user performance are reviewed, and prospects for the future summarized.

In the next chapter, Jose Encarnacao reviews current progress in graphics standards, including PHIGS, GKS, and the new PHI-GKS proposal. Computer graphics metafile standards, GKSM and CGM, along with the WSI, CGI and GDS device and workstation interface standards are also reviewed. A number of application areas in which on-going research and development is taking place are summarized. These include documentation systems (an interface to SGML), presentation graphics, window management and user interface management systems. The relationship to expert systems (e.g. GKS and functional languages), robot programming and simulation is discussed. Work on embedding GKS functionality in silicon is also reviewed.

The final chapter contains two papers on documentation issues. Peter Brown's paper analyzes methods for displaying documentation and describes a new approach for attractive presentation and user-interaction. These techniques can be applied to any form of documentation, whether computer hardware and software manuals, office procedures, encyclopedias, or timetables. Utilizing workstation facilities, the user is able to tailor what is displayed to what he wishes to see. In addition, the use of graphics and multiple fonts can make the documentation more readable and attractively presented.

Methods for combining text and graphics are outlined by Heather Brown. This task is a subset of a larger problem, viz, the combination and integration in one document of several different forms of input such as images, voice, tables, spreadsheets, text and graphics. The emergence of international standards for documentation description and interchange (e.g. Office Document Architecture (ODA)) is beginning to provide a framework for formally combining these different elements. This paper outlines the exploitation of these features for combining text and graphics.

Computer graphics pioneers looked to the time when computer graphics would come of age, when anticipated developments would become the reality of today. This has now happened. The contributors to this volume have made it very clear that computer graphics is not just a potential tool, it is a real tool. Many of the powerful methods and techniques that are encapsulated in the body of knowledge called computer graphics are increasingly being embedded in silicon. Consequently they are now available on the desk top, under the workstation keyboard at affordable prices. Images can be generated, rendered and displayed in real time; interaction and modification of reasonably complex images is almost instantaneous. In the future, desk-top systems will have even greater power and performance than today's mainframe. In the meantime, current functionality will move to down-market systems that provide greater flexibility and attractiveness. Graphics standards are already producing greater uniformity of software interfaces - the key to greater transportability and to greater migration of programs and data across high-speed networks. Engineering design and manufacture has benefited substantially from the modeling systems currently in use. Quantitative design information can now be output from the computer model and sent directly to the manufacturing plant. Finally, the human-computer interface has been the subject of increased scrutiny and rigorous experiment. All this is to the benefit of the user. It enhances his problem-solving capability and capacity. We look to even greater developments in the future in the areas of image and print generation, adaptive user-interfaces, the modeling of the design process, and the rendering of images. The computer is an information processing machine, and in the context of computer graphics is processing pictorial information in one form or another. In order to fully exploit this capability, greater attention needs to be paid to visual input, image handling, the utilization of parallel processors, effective links to data bases, and the efficient display of the resulting image.

Acknowledgements. The papers in this volume formed the basis of an International Summer Institute on The State of the Art in Computer Graphics held at the University of Stirling, Stirling, Scotland, United Kingdom. We are very grateful to our co-sponsors: the British Computer Society (BCS) Computer Graphics and Displays Group, and the Computer Graphics Society (CGS). We also thank the Association for Computing Machinery (ACM) for their cooperation and support. Our thanks and appreciation go to Mrs. Frances Johnson, Conference Officer at the University of Leeds, and to Brian Booker, for all their help and support with the practical arrangements for the Institute. Our thanks and appreciation also to all those delegates who attended from many countries and contributed by their discussion, interaction and inspiration. The following countries were represented: Belgium, Canada, Denmark, Federal Republic of Germany, Finland, Iceland, Japan, Netherlands, Norway, Poland, the UK, and the USA.

Our special thanks and appreciation go to Gerhard Rossbach of Springer-Verlag, Computer Science Editor, USA West Coast Office, Santa Barbara, California who organized the typesetting and production.

A volume such as this is the result of many months of planning and preparation, and we thank all those who have assisted us. Colleagues, students, contributors, and publisher—we thank you all for your forbearance and patience, and for enduring our persistence in seeking to bring this project to a successful conclusion.

David F. Rogers
Annapolis, Maryland, USA

Rae A. Earnshaw
Leeds, United Kingdom

1   Design

Computer Graphics in Design:
Parametric Variation as a Design Method

JOHN LANSDOWN

Abstract

A way of using computers in visual design by means of an exploratory process which the author calls procedural or parametric variation is outlined and discussed. In this methodology, a model of some aspects of visual appearance (colour, dimension, shape and so on) is set up and the parameters to the model are modified in a systematic way under computer control. In particular, the discussion centres on the way in which the attributes of colour may be manipulated to home-in on factors which the designer might consider to be significant. Parametric variation is seen as an appropriate way of using computers to fine-tune a designers proposals.

Introduction

Computers have been used in design almost since they first came into commercial existence about thirty years ago. However, their current use generally tends to copy the techniques of pre-computer times and they are usually employed to do things more efficiently or quickly that were previously done in a similar way by hand.

This phenomenon of a new technology initially copying the one it finally replaces is not restricted to computing. It seems to be a general characteristic of innovation. Early cars, to give just one example, were horseless carriages: they looked like it, and were expected to behave like it. The phenomenon, too, is not restricted to new technology. Oppenheimer [OPPE56] reminds us that even new scientific theories also exhibit the characteristic:

We cannot, coming into something new, deal with it except on the basis of the familiar and the old-fashioned . . . At each point the first scientists have tried to make a theory like the earlier theories, light, like sound, as a material wave; matter waves like light waves, like a real, physical wave; and in each case it has been found that one had to widen the framework a little, and find the disanalogy which enables one to preserve what was right about the analogy.

As yet, there has been little use of computers to tackle design in a new way but we can just begin to see how this might be done in a manner which broadens the designers scope and more fully exploits the computers potential.

This paper introduces a method of designing which might be called *procedural* or *parametric variation*. It is, I think, one of the possible new ways of designing. It owes little or nothing to previous methods and could not have been proposed as a possibility before computers were available to exploit it. It is a computer-aided design technique for making systematic and exploratory alterations to the parameters of the artifact being designed. By the word, parameters, I mean such attributes as dimension, material composition, shape, colour and so on - all items under the control of designers and which, if varied, produce changes in the performance or appearance of the artifact.

The basis of the technique is to create a computer-based mathematical, logical or graphical model of the object being designed and then to modify appropriate elements of the model in a regulated way. For our purposes here, the model can be thought of as a black box whose inputs are the design parameters and whose outputs are aspects of performance. Thus, for example, given a model of the thermal characteristics of a building, its design parameters would be such things as the building geometry, its insulation, plant operation, air flow, shading and so on. Note that these are the parameters under the designers direct or indirect control: there are other necessary inputs to this model that are not within the designers ambit. Climate and occupancy are examples of these. Such parameters should be accommodated in the model: they would then resemble, and have the same restrictions as, the exogenous variables familiar to simulation model builders [EMSH70].

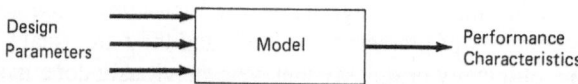

Figure 1. Parametric Model

The purpose of this form of working is to try to isolate the currently important features of a design in progress and to study the effects of changes to these independently, as far as possible, of others. Because of the essentially *interdependent* nature of many design variables, creating models for parametric variation is not always easy. It is, though , a worthwhile task for three reasons:

1. Once a suitable model has been devised, it can be applied generally to other tasks of the same type.
2. Designers are provided with a powerful tool for investigating and homing-in on the characteristics of a design which they believe to have the most significance.
3. A new way arises of teaching and learning about design.

The ABACUS Unit at Strathclyde has devised a number of models able to be used for procedural variation of *functional* factors such as thermal performance and space allocation [LANS84]. It is not my intention here to cover models dealing with such functional characteristics. What I want to do is to suggest how parametric variation of graphical models might be applied to *visual* aspects of design and, in particular, to colour.

Designing Conventionally and With Computers

When we design in the conventional way with pencil and paper we tend to work intuitively, gradually moving towards a satisfactory outcome by a process of trial and error. Since time is limited, in any practical case we have sometimes to terminate the trial and error process prematurely before we are completely satisfied with the results of our endeavours. Of course, even if we had all the time in the world, we could not be certain that a particular line of approach would ultimately prove successful. Often a given line turns out to be unfruitful but we find this out too late to make fundamental changes. Thus any tool that, if nothing else, makes it easier and more speedy to run through a range of possible design options is likely to be of value.

I have pointed out elsewhere [LANS85] that the progression towards the final outcome of a design is not a totally continuous one. Discontinuities arise as we develop our ideas. It has to be said immediately that parametric variation will not work across these discontinuities. It cannot replace genuinely new and intuitive ideas. In an excellent critique of Knuths [KNUT82] parametrisation of letter forms, Hofstadter [HOFS82] shows that the approach is not sufficient to deal with all possible design variations for typefaces:

Clearly there is much more going on in typefaces than meets the eye - literally. The shape of a letterform is a surface manifestation of deep mental abstractions. It is determined by conceptual considerations and balances that no finite set of merely geometric...[parameters]...could capture. Underneath each instance of A there lurks a concept, a Platonic entity, a *spirit.*

This is accepted but, within the continuous stages and for a large range of outcomes, the method is valid. For we can think of the continuous stages as ones where we are fine tuning the ideas rather than conceiving new ones. Parametric variation works well for fine tuning - indeed, I believe it to be one of the most powerful ways we have of fully exploiting the inevitably limited numbers of ideas we can have.

Computer Graphics

There are, essentially, two forms of computer graphics system for visual design: *paint systems* and *modelled systems*. With a paint system we sketch our ideas into the computer using it as a more-or-less sophisticated drawing board. The paint system gives us aids in drawing straight lines in a variety of styles, circles, ellipses, pattern-filled areas and so on. Mistakes are easily rectified; for example, by asking the computer to undo our last action, and we can modify parts of drawings and save them for later re-use. Paint software can be purchased for almost every form of graphics system and many of the best allow full-colour working.

The alternative to painted computer graphics is *modelled* graphics. In this case, we do not sketch the images we want to realise; what we do here is to give the machine a mathematical model of the objects we wish to create and have the computer make its images from this. As might be anticipated, this is quite a different way of working. A painted image is nothing more than a picture. A paint system knows nothing about the objects it depicts. Thus, for example, if we are dissatisfied with the perspective viewpoint we have chosen for a painted drawing, we cannot ask the computer to give us another view from a slightly different angle. If we want a different view, we must sketch it ourselves. With a modelled system on the other hand, the computer has sufficient information about the scene (and, if needed, the laws of perspective) to be able to give us different views of it. Visual procedural variation requires the use of modelled graphics - either in 2-D or 3-D. Paint systems can only be used in a limited way for parametric variation. The technique essentially requires the use of a modelled system.

Visual Procedural Variation: an Example

In the Museum of Modern Art, New York is a model of a table lamp designed in 1924 by the Dutch architect, Gerrit Rietveld. It stands roughly 380mm high and is made from metal and glass. Despite its age, it has a quality that makes one feel that it was designed only yesterday. As an experiment, we can examine some variations of its parameters: say, its overall height, the height to the centre of the globe, the diameters of the globe and the housing tube, as well as the dimensions of the supporting and balancing tubes. Obviously, the dimensions of such objects cannot be varied absolutely independently — although it is always worth trying to do so to see whether new ideas result. In addition, there are upper and lower limits on the permissible dimensions. All these constraints can be built into a simple computer program. Figure 2 shows some examples of output from a Macintosh Pascal program to designed to allow easy manipulation of the relationships. Incidentally, those familiar with Rietvelds design should note that one of its most important and characteristic features is not taken into account in the program. This is the way in which the whole lamp is physically balanced. Rietveld achieved this by use of the bottom tube and setting the lamp housing assymetrically on a vertical support. This feature and its parameters could easily be accommodated and the necessary calculations needed to ensure physical balance performed. The demonstration program, however, does not do this.

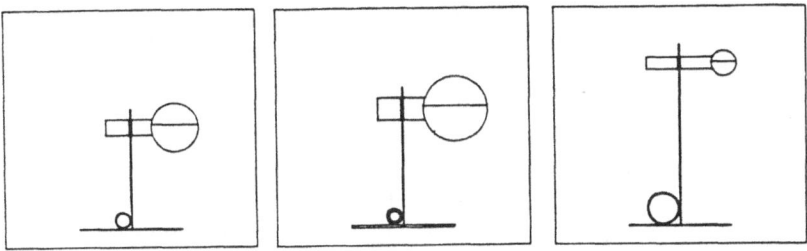

Figure 2

The significance of these examples is two-fold. Firstly, as in the case of a musical theme and variations, the general feeling of the proposals is similar despite extremes of variation. Secondly, the variations can be examined at great speed — each drawn to the same standard as the original. This examination can be carried out either intuitively, changing parameters as the mood dictates, or systematically, by computer program. In the latter case, care must be taken to avoid combinatorial explosion — just 5 parameters each varied over 10 steps produces 100,000 options. Viewing each for only one second would take nearly 28 hours! This fact, and others, has led me to propose the use of knowledge-based filters in design. These are aimed at limiting the number of variations whilst guiding the model towards desirable outcomes. The way in which these filters might be accommodated is outlined in Lansdown [LANS86].

Colour

Transformations of dimensions and shape are fairly easy to carry out and to understand. With computing, though, we can also transform other, less obviously manipulatable, attributes of an object and can do so using essentially the same procedures as those for physical dimension. In particular, colour can be procedurally varied.

Since 1853, when the scientist, Grassman, expounded his laws, it has been accepted that as far as colour is concerned, the human perceptual system is responsive to just three attributes. These are hue, brightness (or lightness), and saturation. Hue is what we normally call the colour. Red, green, magenta and so on are hues. Hue is determined by the dominant wavelength of the light emitted: reds, for instance, have dominant wavelengths between 620 and 670 nanometetres. Brightness is the variation from darkness to lightness. Saturation is determined by the purity of the colour, that is, the amount by which the colour differs from grey of the same lightness. Strictly, the most saturated colours have the least number of different wavelengths contributing to them. As it happens, Swedish research carried out since the 1950s and largely incorporated into the Swedish Natural Colour System, suggests that we are actually sensitive to rather different things than hue, lightness and saturation [HESS84]. The principles of what I am saying, though, are not undermined by these findings and the Natural Colour System can also be used as the basis for procedural variation.

At the device level, colours are set in graphics systems by giving the computer appropriate percentages of red, green and blue. If we assume that these percentages are represented on a three-dimensional graph by decimal numbers between 0 (for zero percent) and 1 (for 100 percent), we have a cube as shown in Figure 3. All the colours that the system can produce sit within or on the surface of this cube and we can think of this as the RGB normalised colour space. The range of greys from black to white lie on the diagonal line running between (0,0,0) and (1,1,1). The fully saturated colours are at the corners away from the black and white corners. Particular RGB values can be transformed to their HLS (Hue, Lightness, Saturation) equivalents and back again by the application of simple computer procedures [FOLE82] [ROGE85]. To facilitate these transformations, it is customary to assume that the HLS colour space is a double cone as shown in Figure 4. Hues are represented in this space by their position around the horizontal colour circles. The most saturated colours are at the circumference. Lightness varies along the axes of the cones. Using these, or other, colour spaces we can easily explore variations based on mathematical transformations.

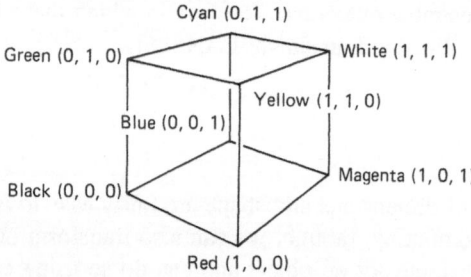

Figure 3 RGB Colour Model

Imagine, for example, that we have chosen three colours in HLS space. These are situated on the colour circle at, say, 0 degrees (blue), 25 degrees (reddish violet), and 150 degrees (deep yellow). On this group we can perform a rigid transformation which would be the equivalent of translation in geometry. We can do this simply by adding a constant value to these positions. By adding, say, 40 degrees to the numbers, we transform them to 40 degrees (purple), 65 degrees (violet red), and 190 degrees (yellowish green). The effect of this transformation is to maintain the same *relationships* between the colours but to move them bodily around the colour circle. Adding 180 degrees (mod 360) to the numbers specifies their complements. This much could be done without the aid of a computer. What would be more difficult by hand, however, would be to perform more complex variations such as non-rigid, but proportional, transformations. For example, we can map the numbers into a smaller arc, thus narrowing the differences between the hues, or we can map them to a larger arc, thus widening the differences. In both cases, we would maintain something of the relationships previously possessed. These mapping transformations can be compounded by translations around the circle as well as by changes to lightness and saturation. Importantly, too, the effect of the transformations, however complex they turn out to be, can be viewed almost immediately.

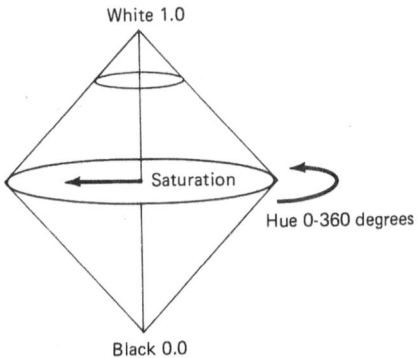

Figure 4. HLS Colour Model

In the RGB colour space, transformations can be thought of as being directly analogous to geometric transformations in normalised 3-D space. Thus the usual rigid transformations of translation, rotation and regular scaling can be applied to groups of points representing colours in this space. These transformations directly maintain the relationships between the colours. In addition, the non-rigid transformations of shearing and differential scaling [COXE61] are also available. With these, the colour relationships are modified in subtle and unusual ways.

As with geometric variations, alterations to colour parameters can also be made intuitively or by systematic method. However, because of the difficulties in imagining the type of changes that are likely to be profitable, (especially when working in the RGB colour space where all sorts of spatial manipulations are possible), I believe systematic working to be preferable. The initial experiments I have carried out on procedural variation at the level of visual design suggest that this approach is likely to prove a fruitful one. Coupled with the computers ability to relate the formal variations to performance ones too, procedural variation represents a powerful new tool to assist in that most difficult of human endeavours, designing.

Acknowledgements. The ideas in this paper were first presented to the Construction Industry Computer Conference in early 1986. The ideas partly arose out of meetings and discussions with Bill Mitchell on an extended visit he and I made in the Summer of 1985 to the Department of Architectural Science, Sydney. I am grateful to Bill and the students there for these discussions and to John Gero, Professor of the Department, for making them possible.

References

[COXE61] Coxeter H. S. M. (1961) Introduction to Geometry. John Wiley & Sons, New York 1961

[EMSH70] Emshoff J. R. and Sisson R. L. (1970) Design and Use of Computer Simulation Models. The Macmillan Company, London 1970

[FOLE82] Foley J. D. and van Dam A. (1982) Fundamentals of Interactive Computer Graphics. Addison-Wesley, Reading, Mass 1982

[HESS84] Hesselgren S. (1984) Why colour order systems? Colour Research and Applications. Winter 1984 (9) 4 pp220-228

[HOFS82] Hofstadter D. R. (1982) Meta-Font, Metamathematics and Metaphysics Visible Language. Autumn 1982 (XVI) 4 pp309-338

[KNUT82] Knuth D. E. (1982) The concept of a Meta-Font. Visible Language. Winter 1982 (XVI) 1 pp3-27

[LANS84] Lansdown J. and Maver T. (1984) CAD in architecture and building. CAD Journal 1984 (16) 3 pp148-154

[LANS85] Lansdown J. (1985) Requirements for knowledge-based systems in design Proceedings. CAAD Futures Conference, Delft 1985

[LANS86] Lansdown J. (1986) Notes on Knowledge-Based Filters in Procedural Variation. System Simulation Ltd., London 1986

[OPPE56] Oppenheimer J. R. (1956) Analogy in science. American Psychologist 1956 (11) pp127-135

[ROGE85] Rogers D. F. (1985) Procedural Elements for Computer Graphics. McGraw-Hill Book Company, New York 1985

Design in Computer Graphics:
A Plea for Visual Literacy

JOHN LANSDOWN

Abstract

Starting from the premise that the making and understanding of images requires as much training as any other aspect of literacy, this paper suggests some of the important texts on visual understanding that might be of value to computer graphics workers.

Introduction

It comes as something of a shock to computer scientists specialising in computer graphics when they first learn that the products of their labours are not always received with approbation by graphic designers. Examples of computer-produced graphics that might have been accorded a standing ovation at a SIGGRAPH conference are sometimes regarded with indifference — or even downright disdain — by those trained in art and design. Why should this be?

I think the main reason is that most published computer graphics are nothing more than experiments to test whether or not something can be done. Conventional artists and designers are constantly making such studies. However, unlike computer graphics workers, they rarely publish these tentative efforts except to illustrate some educational or polemical point. At an early stage in the development of a new medium there is obvious value in showing studies of this nature but we must be careful to see these illustrations as what they are: explorations of technique. That they do not particularly impress trained artists and designers unfamiliar with computer graphics is, in this light, not surprising. Technique is only one aspect of a picture. (Admittedly, the public often thinks otherwise. Many people find it hard to accept modern art because it does not often seem to exhibit the same degree of technical craftsmanship as that featured in pre-Twentieth century art. My children could do paintings like that, they say. Conversely and perversely, they find it hard to understand the piano music of, say, Pierre Boulez — where exceptional technical virtuosity is a prerequisite for performance. I cannot explain this contradiction.)

Furthermore, to be impressed by virtuoso technique, you must know something about the difficulties involved. We marvel at brilliant violin playing or gymnastic prowess or accomplished pencil sketching because we know how hard it is. We know that our fingers cannot move sufficiently fast; that our bodies cannot act with such coordination; and we have seen the results of our own attempts at pencil sketching. And, strangely, the better we are at such things the more we can appreciate the problems of doing them well. Most graphics designers do not understand the problems of making computer pictures. But even if they did, they would say that technique in itself is insufficient. A picture needs something more.

Visual Literacy

We make pictorial images in order, among other things, to convey information. That information has to be encoded into graphic form and then decoded in order to be understood. In this process, some extra information is gained, some is lost

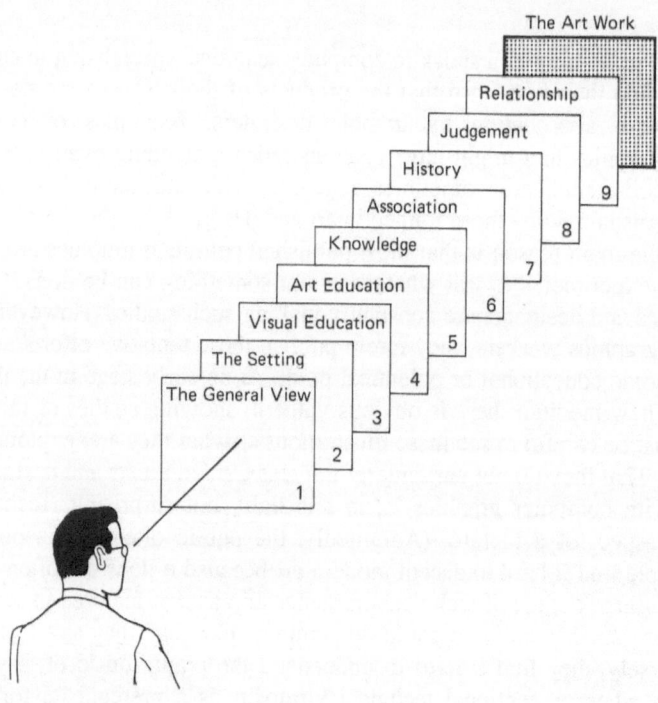

Figure 1 Filters that influence our viewing of an image

and there is considerable potential for ambiguity. Since the mid-1970s we have come to call the ability to encode and decode images, *visual literacy* and one of the things we have learned by studying the subject is that we have to view images through many filters which influence the way we interpret what we see.

Dealing with visual literacy, Boughton [BOUG86] introduces the work of Vincent Lanier [LANI82] and follows his suggestion that there are nine filters (or screens as he calls them) which, as it were, stand between an art object and the viewer (Figure 1). Some or all of these screens are present in any viewing of a piece of graphics and their presence determines what the viewer sees in the image. The screens that Lanier suggests are:

1. What other people say about art and the particular work in question.
2. The setting of the art work.
3. How we have learned to see.
4. How much we know about the elements and principles of design.
5. What we know about the particular symbols used in the work.
6. What the art work reminds us of.
7. How much we know about the history of the work.
8. How we judge the work.
9. What relationship the work has to our life.

Most artists and designers would agree that some or all of these interfering elements seem to be present when they make or view a picture. For my part, I think it important that we visualise these elements not as *screens*, which simply obscure or distort our view like sheets of patterned or coloured glass, but as sort of *active band-pass filters* which restrict some aspects and amplify others — thus enabling us to see what we want to see. For, even at the physical level, perceiving is not a passive activity: we only see what we attend to [LANS85] and the filters give us aid in doing this. (From this, it will be clear that I do not believe that removing the filters would help us see the object better. On the contrary, the filters are there to enable us to see the object at all.)

Like conventional literacy or numeracy, visual literacy has to be learned. It is surprising that this has to be said. But many computer scientists, highly numerate and literate (more or less) in the conventional sense, fail to realise it. They seem to believe that, unlike numbers and words, the understanding of images is somehow innate; that we are born with an ability to encode and decode information in pictures without training. (Of course, they appreciate that the *craft* of making pictorial images has to be learned; that skilled painting, drawing, etching, airbrushing and so on needs extensive training. They do not seem to see, however, that the principles of encoding and decoding are also in this position). Eisner [EISN77] quoted by Broughton, puts the point succinctly:

The codes that are used in reading, in the conventional sense of the term reading, are referred to as syntax. But syntax is not limted to the written word. The arts, for example, possess what might be called qualitative syntax. Qualitative syntax is the form within which a particular work is created. Abstract expressionism, surrealism, cubism, romanticism, and classicism exemplify the construction of different syntaxes in the arts. We call these syntaxes or codes in the arts style. Each has its own logic and each logic must be understood if the form is to be meaningfully read ....

The reason for our inability to recover meanings from such expressive forms as works of modern art is not because we are unintelligent, but because we are ignorant. We have not learned to read the syntax the artist has used. When this syntax is understood, we are able to put to the work appropriate questions. We cease expecting the messages of Matisse to be the same as those of Massachio.

As form and content — syntax and semantics — are difficult, if not impossible, to separate in works of art and design, I think there is a danger in pressing the analogies of syntax and reading too far, but Eisners quotation does encapsulate something noteworthy: that images are coded messages: that to understand an image we must know the forms and codes in which it was created: in short, that visual literacy is important. This paper is, in part, a plea for computer graphics workers to extend their visual literacy.

Improving Visual Literacy

It would be unrealistic to suggest that computer graphics students should follow the same course of training as professional artists and designers even when, as many of them finally do, they will spend most of their working hours creating art-related images. It is not unreasonable though to ask that the education they receive in colleges and universities should take on board some of the concerns of visual literacy. These include: an understanding of how people respond to images; an understanding of the ways in which aesthetic value is assigned to visual imagery; the role of signs and symbols in conveying information. I have already suggested that, whether or not the filtering process talked of earlier in fact occurs, a persons response to visual imagery is governed by a number of determinants that really have little to do with the intrinsic properties of the object being viewed. These determinants are in the provinces of Perception, Psychology, Sociology and Cultural Anthropology and it is important that those who produce images have some appreciation of these subjects.

To give just one example: the cultural role that colour plays in our appreciation of images is not straightforward. Indeed, the noted — if controversial — American authority on perception, James Gibson [GIBS68] tells us that even,

'the meaning of the term colour is one of the worst muddles in the history of science'.

Umberto Eco [ECO85] shows that some languages of the past, Latin for instance, did not have words to distinguish between, say, blue and green, and hence, when dealing with colour, linguistically grouped together items which we would consider to be different. This is a point of some significance. We no longer know why the Romans felt it unnecessary to distinguish clearly between blue and green, but this must have made a difference to how they *saw* these colours. (Eco might have mentioned, too, that the Welsh word, *glas*, can also mean blue or green in historical writings. This is still the case in current Welsh but, nowadays, *glas* and *gwyrdd* are usually distinguished). Apparently, Hindus consider red and orange to be essentially the same — although it is unlikely that they cannot actually see the difference between them. However, the untrained European or North American can distinguish and name only about 7-10 colours seen in isolation from one another. When seen together, so that one colour can be directly compared with another, of course, many more are coped with, but it is interesting to note that most people find it very difficult to arrange comparatively small numbers of colours, say between 20 and 100, in a graduated scale and certainly have no names by which to categorise these hues. On the other hand, it is said that Maoris can recognise and name different 3000 colours! (Note that 24 bits of colour — fairly common and always considered desirable in graphics devices — produce 16.7 million different colours. No human being can distinguish more than 10 million colours and most can cope with only about 2 million).

In computer graphics, particularly in graphics used to convey quantitative information, colour is used both to differentiate and to emphasise. But the wide cultural differences in colour categorisation — differences which seem to be more significant than those between normally sighted and colour-defective persons — might well militate against these ends. An understanding of the Cultural Anthropology and Semiology of colours is thus essential.

Design and Information Graphics

Nowhere in computer graphics does the lack of visual literacy appear so strikingly than in the production of images for business information: so-called business graphics [LAN82]. In this domain, charts and graphs are prepared mainly to assist managers to come to decisions but also to illustrate to the public aspects of business performance. Two forms of output pertain: online, where information is relayed to VDUs for immediate viewing and, possibly, interactive decision-making; and offline, where information is conveyed in the form of 35mm slides, overhead transparencies or hardcopy graphics. It appears to me that much of this output is poorly designed: some of it so poorly designed as to be misleading and counter-productive. You will note that Im not saying here that such graphics are necessarily ugly or visually displeasing: many are not. What I am saying is that they do not properly perform their intended functions.

Although it is difficult to lay down hard and fast principles in any area of graphic design, it is in the field of business graphics that some useful rule of thumb guidance can be given so that, at the least, some of the worst problems arising from visual illiteracy can be alleviated. There are a number of texts that can help. Marcus [MARC80] and Paller, Szoca and Nelson [PALL81] are steps in the right direction but Tufte [TUFT83] is probably the most useful work with which to start. Although it is not aimed specifically at computer graphics, Tuftes excellent book is full of examples of all sorts of different ways of visually displaying quantitative information. He is especially good at exposing what he calls chartjunk. Some other noteworthy texts are Bertin [BERT83], to which Tufte is a good introduction; White [WHIT80] for all manner of inventive ideas; and Holmes [HOLM85], which shows something of the ways in which an imaginative designer works with charts and graphs. A companion volume covering the design of symbols and logos is Holmes [HOLM85a]. Herdeg [HERD76] is essential reading. No one who wishes to present graphical information effectively should embark on the project without first absorbing the contents of these important documents. They are the foundation for visual literacy in the area.

Design and General Image-making

In the more general domain of image-making, visual literacy is harder to come by. Only a highly selective and personal sprinkling of possible texts can be suggested. Maurice de Sausmarez [SAUS83] gives a useful introduction to Basic Design whilst two books by Gyorgy Kepes [KEPE56] [KEPE61], give a broader view, as does Maier [MAIE77] . Booth-Clibborn and Baroni [BOOT80] deal excellently with the language of graphics : their book is full of well-conceived examples of the best in graphic design. Thompson and Davenport [THOM80] is also replete with instructive visual examples. Meggs [MEGG83] covers the history of graphic design. More theoretical, but nonetheless, essential works are Arnheim [ARNH56] and Gombrich [GOMB82]; in fact anything and everything by these two giants must be read. A quite different sort of book to the others is Goldsmith [GOLD84]: in fact it is a review of research into pictorial representation and creation. This contains many useful elements.

Given the grounding in the subject that the foregoing texts can present, the only other thing to do is to keep looking at pictures. When Gauss was asked why hed become such a great mathematician, he replied that hed learned from the masters and not their pupils. Following his example we can do no better to improve our literacy of visual things than to look at great art. Works by the masters abound. We must simply look and learn from them.

References

[ARNH56] Arnheim R (1956) Art and Visual Perception. Faber, London 1956

[BERT83] Bertin J (1983) Semiology of Graphics: Diagrams, Networks, Maps. (A transanslation by W T Berg of Bertins 1967 Semiologie Graphique), University of Wisconsin Press, Madison 1983

[BLON85] Blonsky M (ed) (1985) On Signs: A Semiotics Reader. Basil Blackwell, Oxford 1985

[BOOT80] Booth-Clibborn E and Baroni D (1980) The Language of Graphics. Thames and Hudson, London

[BOUG86] Boughton D (1986) Visual Literacy: Implications for Cultural Understanding Through Art Education. Journal of Art & Design Education 1986 (5) 1&2 pp125-142

[deSA83] de Sausmaurez M (1983) Basic Design: The Dynamics of Visual Form. The Herbert Press, Huntingdon 1983, (first published 1964)

[EARN85] Earnshaw R A (ed) (1985) Fundamental Algorithms for Computer Graphics. Springer-Verlag, Berlin 1985

[ECO85] Eco U (1985) How Culture Conditions the Colours We See. in Blonsky, (1985) pp157-175

[EISN77] Eisner E (1977) Address to Art and Reading Conference. New York 1977, quoted in Boughton, (1985)

[GIBS68] Gibson J J (1968) The Senses Considered as Perceptual Systems. Allen and Unwin, London 1968

[GOLD84] Goldsmith E (1984) Research into Illustration: An Approach and a Review. Cambridge University Press, Cambridge 1984

[GOMB82] Gombrich E (1982) Mirror and Map: Theories of Pictorial Representation., from the Image and the Eye, Phaidon, Oxford 1982

[HERD76] Herdeg W (ed) (1976) Graphis / Diagrams. Second Edition, Graphis Press, Zurich 1976

[HOLM85a] Holmes N (1985) Designers Guide to Creating Charts and Diagrams. Watson-Guptill Publications, New York 1985

[HOLM85b] Holmes N (1985a) Designing Pictorial Symbols. Watson-Guptill Publications, New York 1985

[KEPE56] Kepes G (1956) The New Landscape in Art and Science. Paul Theobald and Co., Chicago 1956

[KEPE61] Kepes G (1961) Language of Vision. Paul Theobald and Co., Chicago 1961

[LANI82] Lanier V (1982) The Arts We See: A Simplified Introduction to the Visual Arts. Teachers College Press, New York 1982

[LANS82] Lansdown J (ed) (1982) Business Graphics : State of the Art Report. Series 10, Number 3, Pergamon Infotech Ltd., Maidenhead 1982

[LANS85] Lansdown J (1985) Visual Perception and Computer Graphics. in Earnshaw, (1985), pp1005-1026

[MAIE77] Maier M (1977) Basic Principles of Design: The Foundation Programme at the School of Design. Van Nostrand, Reinhold, New York 1977

[MARC80] Marcus A (1980) Computer-assisted chart making from the graphic designers perspective. Computer Graphics, 1980 (14) 3 pp247-253

[MEGG83] Meggs PB (1983) A History of Graphic Design. Allen Lane, London 1983

[PALL81] Paller A, Szoca K and Nelson N (1981) Choosing the Right Chart. Integrated Software Systems Corp., San Diego 1981

[THOM80] Thompson P and Davenport P (1980) The Dictionary of Visual Language. Bergstrom and Boyle Books Ltd., London 1980

[TUFT83] Tufte E R (1983) The Visual Display of Quantitative Information. Graphic Press, Cheshire, Conn. 1983

[WHIT80] White J J (1980) Graphic Idea Notebook. Watson-Guptill Publications, New York 1980

2 Modeling

Computational Geometry and Software Engineering:

Towards a Geometric Computing Environment

A. R. FORREST

Abstract

Computational Geometry has made rapid strides in recent years in the two related areas where the term is employed: the development and analysis of algorithms and the geometric modelling of complex shapes. However, building large geometric systems is still largely a black art, with software engineering techniques sadly lacking or not applied and the problems arising from real geometric computation seldom being addressed by theoreticians. The paper discusses challenging problems for both theorists and implementors which arise when attempts are made to construct large, complex, reliable, accurate and consistent geometric systems, and suggests that the development of geometric computing environments is a fruitful endeavour for all computational geometers.

Introduction

The term computational geometry seems to have been coined independently at least three times with the unfortunate result that there appear to some to be two rather different communities, both claiming to be the true adherents. One of the aims of this paper is to reconcile the two camps by reviewing achievement and lack of achievement and by discussing areas which need attention from both factions.

The earliest reference to computational geometry is the sub-title of Minsky and Paperts pioneering book Perceptrons [MINS69]. Unfortunately, the term is undefined and is not mentioned in the rest of the book, but clearly they had in mind computation involving shapes, mainly from the point of view of image understanding and recognition. My own definition [FORR71], the computer definition, representation, analysis and synthesis of geometric information, followed from a conviction that new geometric techniques were necessary if computers were to be used in a geometric context and that the simple application of classical geometric techniques was totally inappropriate. I was working in the field of computer-aided geometric design and computer graphics, and the term rapidly gained currency in those circles from the early 1970s. Perhaps because at that time my published papers were mainly concerned with curves and surfaces, there has arisen the incorrect assumption that this definition was intended to apply only to curves and surfaces [LEE84, PREP85], whereas I intended the term to apply to geometry *in general*. Computational geometry relates to graphics, geometric modelling, and CAD/CAM, as classical geometry relates to engineering drawing.

As a result of a second paper in 1974 presented at the Computer-Aided Geometric Design Conference in Salt Lake City [FORR74], I was made aware of the work of Dobkin and Shamos at Yale University who independently had introduced the term computational geometry [SHAM74a,b,c], this time in the context of complexity theory and the analysis and design of algorithms. Since then I have endeavoured to bridge the gap between the two cultures, believing them to represent two aspects of the same subject: theoretical and applied. Both cultures have made remarkable strides but there is still a gap, albeit of diminishing size. Each has much to learn from the other and it is no service to computing science to maintain the gulf by pretending otherwise.

In this paper we highlight the problems which arise in attempts to build practical systems for computational geometry and geometric modelling and suggest that a software engineering approach to the construction of geometric systems is essential if those systems are to exhibit the desirable properties of accuracy, reliability, consistency, maintainability, and robustness in addition to efficiency. Before discussing such topics we will review — hopefully in an even-handed manner — the achievements and failures of the state-of-the-art in computational geometry, both from a theoretical and from a practical standpoint.

Successes of Theoretical Computational Geometry

The proliferation of papers on computational geometry testifies to the existence of a fruitful field of research, starting with the work of Shamos and others at Yale [SHAM74a,b,c,] [SHAM78]. Computational geometry appears to be particularly amenable to complexity analysis: worst case space and time characteristics of many problems are now established. Sometimes this has led to novel approaches to geometric problems, and in many cases to more efficient algorithms. Advances in data structures, both for static problems and for dynamic problems [OVER83], have been particularly notable. Rigour, theorems, and proofs, usually missing in practical computational geometry, suggest that at some future date a comprehensive theory of computational geometry, probably based on a restricted and idealistic model of computation, may emerge. Currently, the most common model of computation is the random access machine [AHO74] with the addition of real arithmetic [LEE84] (indeed, as we shall see later, it is generally assumed that this real arithmetic is *exact* real arithmetic, in the sense of Sproull [SPRO82]).

Already certain computational paradigms such as plane sweep and divide and conquer are well-established, and exploitation of the Voronoi diagram and variations of tree structures are common. Triangulation, range searching, point location, and intersection problems have all yielded important results [LEE84], sometimes carrying over into ostensibly non-geometric problems such as database queries. The importance of convexity in reducing computation or simplifying problems has been highlighted by Chazelle [CHAZ80a] who, with Dobkin, has also pointed out the general principle that detection is easier than computation [CHAZ80b]. Note in passing that hidden *surface* removal, which involves the question of whether or not a point is visible (detection), is in general rather easier than hidden *line* removal where we need to evaluate where visibility changes (computation).

Successes of Applied Computational Geometry

Applied computational geometry has met with considerable success in the representation of complex shapes, particularly curves and surfaces, motivated by the needs of industry. In the early days of computer graphics, when equipment was expensive, the problems encountered in designing and manufacturing the doubly curved shapes associated with cars, aircraft and ships were sufficiently important to attract heavy investment. There was thus an early emphasis not only on more complex geometries than straight lines, but also on three-dimensional problems. Only those who have had experience with three-dimensional computational geometry can fully appreciate the folly of attempting to generalise from two-dimensional problems!

More recently, there has been considerable progress in the representation and design of three-dimensional solids, under the various guises of volume modelling, solid modelling, and even geometric modelling. Initially in this area the shapes were rather simple — rectangular parallelepipeds, prisms, cylinders, cones, spheres, and tori — and the intention was to be able to model the complex assemblies of relatively simple shapes which are commonly found in mechanical engineering design (e.g., in the case of cars, the parts under the body shell rather than the body shell itself). In this work, a great deal of emphasis was placed on the *legality* of the models constructed so that, for example, a polyhedron would always be tested for self-intersection. Curiously, legality seldom seems to have been a concern for implementors of surface design systems, perhaps because these were intended to be used by highly trained personnel who would be well aware if, for example, they caused the top surface of a wing to penetrate the lower surface. In a sense, therefore, developments in solid modelling were less concerned with geometric representation (approximation theory is the underpinning of much of the work in curves and surfaces) than with data structures, geometric computations such as intersection, and geometric legality (in theory, at least).

Two rival methods emerged: constructive solid geometry [REQU78] and boundary representation [BRAI75] [BRAI78] [BRAI79]. The former is based on the theory of closed regular sets, solids being represented by tree structures in which the leaves are half-spaces and the nodes are the regularised set operators of union, intersection, and difference. This representation has many desirable properties but does not explicitly contain a representation of the faces, edges, and vertices bounding a solid, these having to be derived by further computation. Regular set theory guarantees legality of the CSG model, but once an attempt is made to evaluate the model, accuracy and hence legality, is at the mercy of real arithmetic. Nevertheless, many applications of solid modellers, in particular the generation of shaded images, do not need accurate evaluation of the model and can be implemented straightforwardly using CSG. Boundary representation, by contrast, models solids by building the relevant face-edge-vertex graph, using the so-called Euler operators to maintain Eulers rule for polyhedra, and checking that the geometric parameters for the faces, edges, and vertices are consistent with the graph. A full complement of intersection evaluation algorithms must be provided for a boundary representation modeller, making implementation a more difficult task but providing, in the basic modeller, more facilities than are present in the minimal CSG modeller. After several years of controversy, there is now some agreement that a blend of the two approaches is desirable.

Remarkable advances have been made in the field of image synthesis. Hidden line and hidden surface removal are among the classical problems of computer graphics, with a great deal of emphasis placed on efficiency of execution. One of the pioneering works on computational complexity (little recognised as such and probably not to the taste of theoretical computational geometers) was the paper by Sutherland, Sproull and Schumacker analyzing the structure and performance of a variety of solutions to the problem [SUTH74]. The plane sweep paradigm for some classes of computational geometry problem is little more than scan conversion, and the algorithms of Watkins [WATK70] and Archuleta [ARCH72] illustrate this convincingly, predating the methods popularity in theoretical circles [LEE84] [NIEV82].

More recently, there has been a tendency in rendering towards realism at the expense of efficiency (previous work was to an extent driven by the flight simulator business where speed is of the essence), a prime example being ray tracing [ROTH82]. The standards achieved by rendering techniques are now so high that fundamental limitations of many of the underlying geometric models are now revealed. It is no longer adequate to approximate curved objects by planar-faced polyhedra, nor are simple approximations to the physics of reflection and illumination sufficient. We can anticipate future concentration on better modelling techniques and a greater emphasis on understanding the physics of natural phenomena in creating realistic images of natural scenes [FOUR86].

Computer-aided design techniques have had considerable practical success in the field of integrated circuit design. VLSI masks pose the problem of highly complex two-dimensional assemblies of relatively simple shapes (mainly paraxial rectangles). Here we cite in particular the work of McCreight [MCCR80] where a practical algorithm has attracted theoretical interest as well.

Kilgour describes some of the issues elsewhere in this volume [KILG86].

The author contends, however, that the main contribution of successful practical computational geometry has been the development of *systems* rather than algorithms in isolation: this raises issues of a rather different nature to which we shall later return. They may not be as efficient as is theoretically possible, they may not be 100% reliable, they may lack rigour and a sound theoretical basis, but these systems *do* work most of the time and are in daily use.

Limitations of Theoretical Computational Geometry

A practically oriented computational geometer can find much to argue about as far as the theoretical approach to his subject is concerned. Ignoring the very real contributions to what is, after all, a relatively new field, the practitioner complains of over-much emphasis on worst-case complexity analysis, and too little work on average-case complexity. We lack realistic estimates for the constants of proportionality, giving rise to the suspicion, often justified in practice, that simplistic $O(n^2)$ algorithms out-perform sophisticated $O(n \log n)$ algorithms for all values of n that are of practical concern. Average case analysis is, of course, rather hard, but determination of constants of proportionality by implementation and experimental testing is seldom carried out.

Indeed, actual implementation of geometrical algorithms is by no means straightforward. Special cases, the bugbear of real computational geometry [SEDG83], are often ignored or brushed aside. As an example, we quote from Lee and Preparata [LEE84]: let us assume that no lines of the input define half-planes that are vertical. (This can always be done by rotating the coordinate axes). In practice this is an unreasonable assumption since numerical accuracy effectively makes it impossible, in the general case, to ensure that no lines are *computationally* vertical. A practical implementation could not afford to treat this special case by a dodge such as rotation, but would have to tackle the special geometric case as it stands, or restrict the class of half planes to be treated to, say, those defined by integers. There appears to be no systematic way to ensure that all special cases have been identified. Even if we can identify these cases, we are still at the mercy of computing on a real machine with all the perils of *real* real arithmetic — our theoretical model of computation is unrealistic in a field such as geometry where configurations which give rise to inaccuracy and numerical instability are surprisingly common and far from avoidable.

A valid criticism of much of the theoretical work is that it has considered only a rather restricted geometric domain — largely two-dimensional, with the added restriction of the simple geometry of points and straight lines. Three-dimensional geometry is considerably harder than two-dimensional geometry (the rough rule of thumb in graphics is that 3-D is an order of magnitude more difficult than 2-D), and many two-dimensional algorithms do not extend naturally to three and higher dimensions. For example, whereas the vertices of a planar polygon are intrinsically ordered, the vertices of a three-dimensional polyhedron are not: this leads to more complex data structures and algorithms for threading these data structures in a systematic manner [BRAI78].

Mention has been made earlier of the importance of convexity in reducing the complexity of problems. We find in Preparata and Shamos [PREP85] much concerning the intersection of planar polygons. It is known, for example, that given two polygons with, respectively, m and n sides, their intersection can be found in $O(m+n)$ time if both polygons are convex, but in $O(mn)$ time if they are general polygons. Preparata and Shamos give an algorithm for the convex intersection case, but not for the general case, a serious omission for the practically oriented reader. That there is a reluctance to tackle the harder problems is perhaps a sign that the subject is still young. Unfortunately, the justification for many practical computational geometry systems is based on their ability (in potential at least) to handle the more difficult problems which cause problems for humans. The lack of theoretical computational geometry results for the more complex geometries is rather less of a concern since much has already been learnt elsewhere in practice. As a case in point, the complexity of curve-curve intersection is known, but reliable evaluation is difficult, and algebraic or numerical considerations outweigh the geometric [GEIS83] [PRAT86].

Many papers in computational geometry appear to achieve optimal algorithms by devising new and more complex data structures, each new problem requiring a fresh twist to the data structure. Sometimes, because of the way in which the problem is posed, this is inevitable. If, for example, we are concerned with identifying and counting all the intersections of a set of random line segments in the plane, then the first step is to impose some order, and hence structure, on the line segments. Triangulation and the Voronoi diagram [SHAM78] [GREE78] [GUIB85] seem to provide appropriate structures for random point sets, and to be applicable to a wide range of problems, but we await other general structures for random line segments, random polygons, etc. Since the construction of data structures, whether from scratch or by transforming other existing structures, is a major overhead, and since it is often required in practice to perform several different analyses for a particular set of data, general structures have their attractions, even if some theoretical reduction in efficiency for a particular analysis results. Guibas and Stolfi [GUIB85] have suggested a general structure for two-dimensional subdivisions, akin to the more general structures which arise in higher dimensions from the applications of Eulers rule [BAUM74] [BRAI78] [MANT82] [WEIL85].

Related to the general data structure issue is the question of assemblies of objects. Whereas much is known about optimal algorithms for random points, lines or polygons, there has been little work on algorithms concerned with complex structured assemblies of such geometric primitives. This is really a manifestation of the lack of a systems approach to theoretical computational geometry: problems have been tackled in a one-off manner, rather than in the context of a system, or what we might term a geometric computing environment.

Limitations of Applied Computational Geometry

Practical computer-aided geometric design systems tend to be very large, slow, and difficult to build. As a result, many systems are ad hoc in nature, and have evolved with little benefit of theory. Whilst a great deal has undoubtedly been learnt, little has been published for two reasons: firstly, commercial pressures inhibit publication, and secondly practice and experience papers tend to carry little academic weight. Heavy investment in code militates against re-writing systems with the benefit of hindsight, so many systems do not bear close scrutiny. More rigour and discipline in implementation and a better understanding of algorithm design is called for.

Overall, there has been too much emphasis on image generation (you can justify anything provided the picture looks good) at the expense of sound implementation of geometric algorithms. Generation of shaded images is not a particularly demanding process from the computational geometry point of view since, as we have observed, it involves a detection operation (is this point visible?) and perhaps the evaluation of a surface normal. Given the low resolution of graphical devices, the precision of computation required is not high, and there is an attitutde in some quarters that the end justifies the means, or paraphrased, the quality of the image justifies many short cuts and geometric deceptions. As mentioned earlier, this attitude may change due to the increasing standards of realism in rendering now expected.

There is also a tendency to believe that what you see on the screen represents the truth. Again, this is dangerous, since sampling the geometry at a relatively low resolution is no guarantee of absolute correctness but merely enables the user to filter out gross errors. Given the increasingly high tolerances demanded by todays engineering industry, it is no longer sufficient to say that a design *looks* right; rather, we need to be able to *prove* that the design is right. Industrial contracts in the U.K. now tend to require designs to be signed off as correct by chartered engineers, and one wonders how many implementors of practical geometric design systems would be prepared to sign off designs produced by their systems. Guarantees and proofs of performance are required but not yet deliverable.

We have alluded to an emphasis on representation, particulary of curves and surfaces. Whilst there are many papers describing the pros and cons of various representations, there are too few papers which deal with the fundamental geometric interrogation operations of intersection, proximity, etc.. Reliable and robust algorithms for curve and surface intersections seem to be available, to a certain extent, for polynomial and B-spline forms [LANE80] [GEIS83,] [PRAT86], but not for more exotic representations. Given the emphasis in solid modelling on intersections and legality, it is strange that this emphasis is not found in surface modelling systems.

Despite salesmens talk, geometric modellers are far from robust. In some cases known to the author, this lack of robustness manifests itself in an apparently random manner, and since it is often possible to avoid the problem by using a slightly different sequence of commands, the breakdown is seen as a quirk of the computer and not a fundamental fault of the implementation. Again, through lack of published information, each implementor seems to learn the hard way and to evolve a personal set of rules to minimise unreliability. There are two major sources of unreliability: special cases, and numerical problems. One modeller is said to have failed when a designer chose to place the vertex of a cone tangentially on the surface of a torus. This special case had not been provided for since such a configuration was thought to be physically un-realisable, as indeed it is; but the designer was using this configuration as a *construction* for a legal object, so the special case was entirely reasonable. The first object we attempted to construct using the BUILD modeller [BRAI79] [HILL82], once we had implemented the modeller on our PR1ME 550 at the University of East Anglia, caused numerical overflow despite our setting the default floating point precision to 64 bits! Surprisingly, many of us seem to over-look numerical analysis (if we have ever learnt any) in the context of computa-tional geometry, but as we shall see, application of numerical analysis principles could avoid, or at least minimise, many problems. Once again, our remarks on signing off designs are relevant.

Systems and Software Engineering

One common thread running through the criticisms of both theoretical and ap-plied computational geometry is the lack of consideration of system issues. Theoretical computational geometry approaches problems, by and large, in isola-tion rather than in the context of systems, and applied computational geometry has developed no real computational geometry flavour in its use of software en-gineering techniques. However, computational geometry raises systems en-gineering issues which need both theoretical and practical attention. We must be able to develop efficient, robust, reliable, accurate, consistent systems which are documentable and maintainable. For this we require attention to certain problems which are often overlooked.

We require an understanding of the theoretical and practical possibilities and limitations of computational geometry. We have already mentioned that numeri-cal analysis should play an important rôle. Consider one issue of concern to the author [FORR85b]: the intersection of line segments. Lee and Preparata [LEE84] suggest that computing the intersection of two straight lines can be considered as a primitive operation, but can we actually implement this primi-tive correctly in practice? Despite raising this issue at several recent conferences and workshops, I have yet to discover any correct *general* algorithm, and suspect that although reliability is possible for limited cases, it is not achievable in general.

Mathematically, the problem is simple: two line segments intersect if there ex-ists a non-null set of points common to both segments. Note that this definition covers the special case, sometimes overlooked or left as an exercise for the reader [SEDG83], where the two segments *overlap*. If we consider lines computed on an integer grid, then this condition is no longer applicable and we need a different definition of intersection. As Bresenham shows [BRES87], two integer line segments may cross without sharing a common integer point, and two line segments may share common points whilst mathematically they do not *intersect*. If we restrict line segments to those defined by rational end points, then the intersection point or intersection interval can be expressed exactly in terms of rationals and hence computed exactly given adequate precision. If, however, we wish to use real arithmetic, because, for example, an end point lies on a circular arc, thus introducing irrational numbers, then the vagaries of floating point arithmetic enter the scene, and the remarks concerning integer lines apply, but in a more complex manner: the true intersection point may not be exactly representable in terms of floating point numbers and we need to be able to handle the resulting approximations and roundings in a reliable way [RAMS82].

Mathematically, the intersection of two lines can be found by solving two simultaneous linear equations. Elementary numerical analysis texts will tell the reader that accuracy is highest when the two equations are orthogonal, i.e., the lines are perpendicular, and thoroughly unreliable when the lines are nearly parallel. In a geometric context, both cases are equally likely, and we must be able to handle coincidence and near-coincidence robustly. Thus not only do we have a representation problem in terms of floating point, but we have an accuracy problem which can be severe.

Continuing in the numerical vein, we consider other aspects of accuracy. Solomon's thesis [SOLO85] is a good source of numerical wisdom in the context of geometry. It contains, for example, the remark that "...ideally the origin should be near the centre of the object being modelled." After a moment's thought we realise that this is simply another way of saying that the subtraction of large floating point numbers can cause considerable loss of significance. How many system implementors consider the possibility that their systems will produce different results for similar operations on similar objects, depending on where these operations are carried out?

The use of tolerances is often advocated as a solution to problems of inaccuracy, for example in testing for proximity. Solomon points out that tolerances become insignificant far from the origin, again for floating point reasons. Consider a further problem with floating point arithmetic which can arise with the use of tolerances. Suppose we agree that two points are to be considered functionally identical if they lie within a certain radial distance of each other. In Figure 1, points A and B could be considered identical, as could points B and C, but, clearly, points A and C are distinct. Depending on the order of evaluation, we will come to different conclusions for the same set of points! This lack of consistency is a pervasive problem in practical computational geometry. Since detection is generally cheaper than computation, we might wish to detect whether two line segments intersect before embarking on evaluating the point of intersection. As the detection and evaluation procedures are computationally distinct, it is quite possible that detection will return a positive answer,

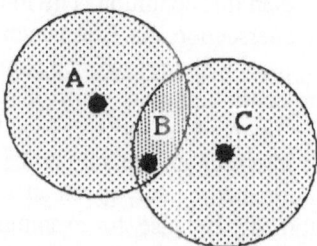

Figure 1: Positional Tolerance

whereas evaluation will not return a point of intersection on either segment, or vice versa. Perhaps, because complete accuracy probably cannot be achieved, we ought to strive instead for consistency. Can we build systems which are consistent?

To overcome numerical problems, it has been suggested that rational arithmetic might be used. This has the advantage of being closed under simple arithmetic operations, and hence exact, but only for a restricted geometry. A major disadvantage, as pointed out by Thomas [THOM84], is that rational arithmetic tends to be rather slow. Mudur and Koparkar have advocated the use of interval arithmetic [MUDU84] which reduces some of the problems but is also slow unless hardware assistance is available. Ramshaw [RAMS82] suggests careful tuning of the arithmetic evaluation sequence, and certainly we ought to design systems with this very much in mind. Postponing, or if possible eliminating, floating point arithmetic is an obvious tactic. Both Geisow [GEIS83] and Thomas [THOM84] have used algebraic manipulation to this end, and algebraic manipulation offers the possibility of reducing expressions to a canonical form and hence ensuring consistency in the order of arithmetic evaluation if arithmetic cannot be avoided.

We might question whether this care with arithmetic is really necessary, but numerous horror stories from practice testify to the need for action. Painstaking efforts with arithmetic will undoubtedly lead to performance penalties and one approach worth considering is to provide alternative options for evaluation: quick-and-dirty for rapid response, and thorough for proof of correctness and final checking. Conceivably, both could co-exist in a manner similar to the author's quality hierarchies for raster graphics software [FORR85a] with quick-and-dirty evaluation being employed initially, but when the user pauses for contemplation, thorough re-evaluation automatically absorbing otherwise unused workstation cycles.

One basic problem of computational geometry is the fundamental mismatch between the dimensionality of the problems and the dimensionality of the tools used for their solution. We are attempting to solve two-, three- or higher-dimensional problems by mapping them on to one-dimensional processors with one-dimensional memories and writing our algorithms in terms of conventional serial languages. Most geometric modelling systems are slow and large, and could benefit from some form of hardware assistance, but what form should this take? Considerable effort has been invested in attempting to provide hardware for one particularly pressing problem - the generation of shaded images from contructive solid geometry trees. CSG trees, as we have earlier mentioned, contain all the information necessary for image generation implicitly (one might cite CSG as a prime example of lazy evaluation!), and given that the accuracy required for shaded image rendering is not particularly high, hardware solutions are possible. Boundary representation modellers, on the other hand, absorb a great deal of computation simply in chasing pointers and threading complex data structures; an architecture which somehow adapted to match a given data structure to give rapid access would seem to be required.

More directly, it is tempting to consider what a true geometric processor might implement in additional to data structuring support. Operations such as line segment intersection are obvious candidates for the basic geometric machine operations, but as we have seen high accuracy is required. Parallelism of some form is indicated, but a rigid parallel architecture such as an array processor does not seem to be the answer. Since many geometric algorithms map naturally into divide and conquer trees, a tree-oriented architecture has many advantages, but I believe we should really be considering a multiprocessor architecture which is more flexible and dynamically configurable. What is certain is that a good geometric computing environment would undoubtedly contain some element of special geometric hardware.

In practice, most computational geometry algorithms are implemented, one suspects, in Pascal, C or FORTRAN, whilst many theoretical algorithms are described in English or pseudo-English. What form should a true geometric language take? The current implementation languages do not make for easy expression or understanding of geometric algorithms. In recent years there has been little talk of graphical languages, and the emphasis in graphics has shifted to graphics *packages* such as GKS and PHIGS, implemented as subroutine or procedure libraries. Perhaps as an interim step we ought to be considering a similar approach for geometry. Whatever the approach, we must be able to build powerful data structures, both specific and general, and to implement efficient algorithms in a maintainable way, preferably based on general rather than specific data structures; current languages do not fit the bill.

Conclusions

Construction of systems for computational geometry requires not only the conventional wisdom of software engineering but an awareness of fundamental issues affecting the implementation of geometric algorithms on real machines. Current tools for geometric computation are far from ideal; we need to develop languages, hardware, and in general a congenial computing environment in which to build practical, reliable, correct, efficient, and robust geometric systems. To do this, we need a sound theory for the systems issues raised by computational geometry as opposed to the theory of algorithms in isolation; but we also need a more disciplined and better educated approach by practitioners to the implementation of systems.

Acknowledgements. I am grateful to many colleagues with whom I have had valuable discussions on the issues raised in this paper. In particular I would like to thank Martin Newell of Cimlinc, Menlo Park; Frank Crow and Eric Bier of the Xerox Palo Alto Research Center; Leo Guibas and Lyle Ramshaw of DEC Systems Research Center, Palo Alto; Charles Lang and Ian Braid of Three-Space, Cambridge; past and present members of the Computational Geometry Project at the University of East Anglia; and Dick Laue of the Office of Naval Research who first suggested bridging the gap.

References and Selected Bibliography

[AHO74] A.V. Aho, J.E. Hopcroft and J.D. Ullman. The Design and Analysis of Computer Algorithms. Addison-Wesley, 1974

[ARCH72] M. Archuleta. Hidden Surface Line Drawing Algorithm. University of Utah, Department of Computer Science, UTEC-CSc-72-121, June, 1972

[BAUM74] B.J. Baumgart. Geometric Modeling for Computer Vision. Stanford Artificial Intelligence Laboratory Memo AIM-249, STAN-CS-74-463, October 1974

[BOWY83] A. Bowyer and J. Woodwark. A Programmer's Geometry. Butterworths, 1983

[BRAI75] I.C. Braid. The Synthesis of Solids Bounded by Many Faces. Communications of the ACM, Volume 18, Number 4, April 1975

[BRAI79]I.C. Braid. Notes on a Geometric Modeller. University of Cambridge, Computer-Aided Design Group, Document 101, June 1979

[BRAI78] I.C. Braid, R.C. Hillyard and I.A. Stroud. Stepwise Construction of Polyhedra in Geometric Modelling. University of Cambridge, Computer-Aided Design Group, Document 100, October 1978

[BRES87] J.E. Bresenham. Ambiguities in Incremental Line Rastering. In "Theoretical Foundations of Computer Graphics and CAD" Ed. R. A. Earnshaw, Springer-Verlag, to be published

[CHAZ80a] B.M.Chazelle. Computational Geometry and Convexity. Carnegie-Mellon University, Department of Computer Science, CMU-CS-80-150, July 1980

[CHAZ80b] B.M. Chazelle and D.P. Dobkin. Detection is Easier than Computation. Proceedings of the 12th Annual ACM Symposium on the Theory of Computation, Los Angeles, 1980

[COHE83] E. Cohen. Some Mathematical Tools for a Modeler's Workbench. IEEE Computer Graphics and Applications, Volume 3, Number 7, October 1983

[DOBK78] D.P. Dobkin. Steps Towards a Language for Computer Geometry. Department of Computer Science, University of Arizona, 1978

[FAUX79] I.D. Faux and M.J. Pratt. Computational Geometry for Design and Manufacture. Ellis-Horwood, 1979

[FOLE82] J.D. Foley and A. van Dam. Fundamentals of Interactive Computer Graphics. Addison-Wesley, 1982

[FORR71] A.R. Forrest. Computational Geometry. Proceedings of the Royal Society of London, Series A, Volume 321, 1971

[FORR74] A.R. Forrest. Computational Geometry - Achievements and Problems. In "Computer-Aided Geometric Design", Eds. R.E. Barnhill and R.F. Riesenfeld, Academic Press, 1974

[FORR85a] A.R. Forrest. Antialiasing in Practice. In "Fundamentals Algorithm for Computer Graphics", Ed. R.A. Earnshaw, Springer-Verlag, 1985

[FORR85b] A.R. Forrest. Computational Geometry in Practice. In "Fundamental Algorithms for Computer Graphics", Ed. R.A. Earnshaw, Springer-Verlag, 1985

[FOUR86] A. Fournier and W. Reeves. A Simple Model of Ocean Waves. ACM SIGGRAPH Computer Graphics, Volume 20, Number 3, August 1986 (SIGGRAPH '86 Proceedings)

[GEIS83] A.D. Geisow. Surface Interrrogations. University of East Anglia, Ph.D. Thesis, 1983

[GREE78] P.J. Green and R. Sibson. Computing Dirichlet Tesselations in the Plane. Computer Journal, Volume 21, Number 2, April 1978

[GUIB83] L.J. Guibas, L. Ramshaw and J. Stolfi. A Kinetic Framework for Computational Geometry. Xerox PARC and Stanford University, 1983

[GUIB82] L.J. Guibas and J. Stolfi. Computational Geometry. Stanford University, Lecture Notes for CS445, 1982

[GUIB85] L.J. Guibas and J. Stolfi. Primitives for the Manipulation of General Subdivisions and the Computation of Voronoi Diagrams. ACM Transactions on Graphics, Volume 4, Number 1, April 1985

[HILL82] R.C. Hillyard. The BUILD Group of Solid Modelers. IEEE Computer Graphics and Applications, Volume 2, Number 2, March 1982

[KILG86] A.C. Kilgour. Polygon Processing for VLSI Pattern Generation. This Volume

[LANE80] J.M. Lane and R.F. Riesenfeld. A Theoretical Development for Computer Generation and Display of Piecewise Polynomial Surfaces. IEEE Transactions on Pattern Analysis and Machine Intelligence, PAMI-2, pages 35-46, 1980

[LEE84] D.T. Lee and F.P. Preparata. Computational Geometry - A Survey. IEEE Transactions on Computers, Volume C-33, Number 12, December 1984

[LEE82a] Y.T. Lee and A.A. Requicha. Algorithms for Computing the Volume and Other Integral Properties of Solids. I. Known Methods and Open Issues. Communications of the ACM, Volume 25, Number 9, September 1982

[LEE82b] Y.T. Lee and A.A. Requicha. Algorithms for Computing the Volume and Other Integral Properties of Solids. II. A Family of Algorithms Based on Representation Conversion and Cellular Approximation. Communications of the ACM, Volume 25, Number 9, September 1982

[MANT82] M. Mantyla and R. Sulonen. GWB: A Solid Modeler with Euler Operations. IEEE Computer Graphics and Applications, Volume 2, Number 7, September 1982

[MCCR80] E.M. McCreight. Efficient Algorithms for Enumerating Intersecting Intervals and Rectangles. Xerox Palo Alto Research Center, Technical Report CSL-80-9, 1980

[MINS69] M. Minsky and S. Papert. Perceptrons: An Introduction to Computational Geometry. M.I.T. Press, 1969

[MORT85] M.E. Mortenson. Computational Geometry. Wiley, 1985

[MUDU84] S.P. Mudur and P.A. Koparkar. Interval Methods for Processing Geometric Objects. IEEE Computer Graphics and Applications, Volume 4, Number 2, February 1984

[NEWM79] W.M. Newman and R.F. Sproull. Principles of Interactive Computer Graphics. Second Edition, McGraw-Hill, 1979

[NIEV82] J. Nievergelt and F.P. Preparata. Plane-Sweep Algorithms for Intersecting Geometric Figures. Communications of the ACM, Volume 25, Number 10, October 1982

[OVER83] M.H. Overmars. The Design of Dynamic Data Structures. Lecture Notes in Computer Science 156, Springer-Verlag 1983

[PAVL82] T. Pavlidis. Algorithms for Graphics and Image Processing. Springer-Verlag, 1982

[PRAT86] M.J. Pratt and A.D. Geisow. Surface Intersection Problems. In "Mathematics of Surfaces", Ed. J.A. Gregory, Proceedings of the IMA Conference, Manchester, September 1984, Oxford University Press, 1986

[PREP85] F.P. Preparata and M.I. Shamos. Computational Geometry: An Introduction. Springer-Verlag, 1985

[RAMS82] L.H. Ramshaw. The Braiding of Floating Point Lines. Xerox Palo Alto Research Center, CSL Notebook Entry, October 14, 1982

[REQU78] A.A.G. Requicha and R.B. Tilove. Mathematical Foundations of Constructive Solid Geometry: General Topology of Closed Regular Sets. Production Automation Project, University of Rochester, Report TM-27, March 1978

[RIES83] R.F. Riesenfeld. A View of Spline-Based Modeling. Proceedings of Autofact 5, American Society of Mechanical Engineers, 1983

[ROTH82] S.D. Roth. Ray Casting for Modeling Solids. Computer Graphics and Image Processing, Volume 18, Number 2, February 1982

[SEDG83] R. Sedgewick. Algorithms. Addison-Wesley, 1983

[SHAM74a] M.I. Shamos. Problems in Computational Geometry. Ph.D. Thesis outline. Yale University, Department of Computer Science, June 1974

[SHAM74b] M.I. Shamos. Introduction to Computational Geometry. Yale University,

Department of Computer Science, October 1974

[SHAM74c] M.I. Shamos. Results in Geometric Complexity (extended abstract). Yale University, Department of Computer Science, November 1974

[SHAM78] M.I. Shamos. Computational Geometry. Yale University, Ph.D. Thesis, 1978

[SOLO85] B.J. Solomon. Surface Intersections for Solid Modelling. University of Cambridge, Ph.D. Thesis, 1985

[SPRO82] R.F. Sproull. Using Program Transformations to Derive Line-Drawing Algorithms. ACM Transactions on Graphics, Volume 1, Number 4, October 1982

[SPRO68] R.F. Sproull and I.E. Sutherland. A Clipping Divider. Proceedings of the Fall Joint Computer Conference, 1968. Thompson Books, 1968

[SUTH74] I.E. Sutherland, R.F. Sproull and R.A. Schumacker. A Characterization of Ten Hidden Surface Algorithms. ACM Computing Surveys, Volume 6, Number 1, March 1974

[THOM84] S.W. Thomas. Modelling Volumes Bounded by B-Spline Surfaces. University of Utah, Department of Computer Science, Ph.D. Thesis, June 1984

[TILO80] R.B. Tilove. Set Membership Classification: A Unified Approach to Geometric Intersection Problems. IEEE Transactions on Computers, Volume C-29, Number 10, October 1980

[TILO81] R.B. Tilove. Line/Polygon Classification: A Study of the Complexity of Geometric Computation. IEEE Computer Graphics and Applications, Volume 1, Number 2, April 1981

[TILO84] R.B. Tilove. A Null-Object Detection Algorithm for Constructive Solid Geometry. Communications of the ACM, Volume 27, Number 7, July 1984

[WATK70] G.S. Watkins. A Real-Time Visible Surface Algorithm. University of Utah, Department of Computer Science, UTEC-C-Sc-70-101, June 1970

[WEIL85] K. Weiler. Edge-Based Data Structures for Solid Modeling in Curved-Surface Modeling Environments. IEEE Computer Graphics and Applications, Volume 5, Number 1, January 1985

[WOOD86] J.R. Woodwark. Computing Shape. Butterworths, 1986

The Model for Graphics

P. QUARENDON AND J. R. WOODWARK

Abstract

The techniques of solid modelling were developed to provide a precise and complete computer-based representation of component geometry for engineering application. While obtaining pictures from such representations was originally considered very difficult, progress in this direction has been such that solid models are now appropriate for many "pure" computer graphics applications

Introduction

If one puts oneself in the position of a painter in the Middle Ages, without even a camera obscura, it is not too difficult to see that the problem of creating, on canvas, a realistic representation of people and objects from the world about was a daunting one. Many early paintings do indeed show very curious versions of perspective projection. During the Renaissance, these problems were essentially solved, and even if the subjects chosen were sometimes unrealistic, in the sense of being fanciful or allegorical, most pictures were, technically, representations of a photograph that might have been

In computer graphics, we are just emerging from the medieval stage, inasmuch as the programming of basic elements of realistic scene synthesis such as perspective projection and hidden surface elimination is essentially understood. Faster versions of such algorithms must now be seen as technical improvement, rather than movement forward. It is interesting to compare the current fascination with topics such as light sources with the painting of candlelit subjects, or to observe that many real-world objects which still give difficulty in computer graphics, such as clouds, have often perplexed painters as well.

Today, we see that abstract types of data are often presented via representations of realistic scenes, albeit extremely stylized ones. For instance, diagrams for "business graphics" may be in the form of blocks, or a "solid" pi-chart. This can be seen as the computer graphics equivalent of the allegorical painting. Just as such a painting may exhibit great sophistication of effect, the presentation of data is usually considered to be enhanced, rather than otherwise, by the provision of "realistic" features, such as lighting models and shadows, even though the whole picture is purely diagrammatic!

It took, say, three centuries and the invention of photography for artists in general to tire of realism and for the freer use of graphical media to become usual. Although the problems still to be overcome in the computer generation of truly realistic pictures are considerable, why should one doubt that the production of such pictures will eventually become routine? Surely, computer graphics will continue beyond that point, to the synthesis of unrealistic pictures which, like impressionist paintings, are (allegedly) capable of communicating more in terms of emotion than the corresponding photographic rendering. While abstract computer-generated pictures have appeared, they are not currently the mainstream of computer graphics work. However, such developments need not be wholly outside the technical sphere. False-colour is already widely used to enhance the readability of images. Again, there are problems (such as the visualization of data in greater than three dimensions) that have been addressed by computer graphics, but never convincingly solved. Existing developments in this direction would seem hardly to have started to explore the potential of the computer to tell us things that the camera cannot.

If the course of art was (possibly) changed by the invention of photography, there is no similar external technology likely to make computer graphics obsolete. But, nevertheless, there are elements within computer graphics, developed (predictably) by engineers, which are making the hand-crafting of realistic pictures obsolete. A particular technique we have in mind is called *solid modelling*, and its application within computer graphics is the subject of this paper. It affects, not the production of the picture, but the creation of the data representing the scene. Not only is the creation of scenes made much easier, but the objects in a scene can now automatically be guaranteed to correspond to real solid shapes, rather than that correspondence only existing as a result of the care taken by the model creator. Doesn't that sound something like the difference between painting and photography?

Types of Model for Computer Graphics

Let us first examine the classical data structure for representing objects for computer graphics: the *face model* [WOOD86a]. This consists of polygonal tiles positioned in space. The number of edges per tile, and whether strict planarity must be maintained, varies between implementations, but this is of only marginal importance. From face models, pictures can be produced with different degrees of realism using such classically important techniques as hidden-surface elimination [SUTH74] [WILL85]. It is surprising what a wide range of visual effects can be produced, or rather simulated, by applying various processes to such a simple data structure.

Face models were a logical basis for computer graphics work on the assumption that only *visible* surfaces needed to be modelled. While their potential was first being exploited, other systems were being developed for engineering applications, in which the primary purpose was to provide data in a form suitable for application programs of many different sorts. It was envisaged that applications would initially be a range of engineering analyses but, ultimately, the computer-based synthesis of components and assemblies. There is, if anything, an even wider range of computer-based shape representations originally developed for engineering applications than for graphics. They range from two-and-a-half-dimensional schemes designed especially to support machining processes to sculptured surface patches. In general, representations initially intended for engineering applications have a greater range of shape elements (their *domain*) than representations intended for graphics, because adequate pictures can often be obtained from models which are not exact, whereas engineering components must meet more stringent criteria. As well as producing a wider domain, work on engineering shape representations has also focused on the *completeness* of shape models. Face models can be constructed which are incomplete: the set of faces does not correspond to the faces of a possible solid object. In engineering, the wish to perform analysis functions on the resulting models excludes representations of this form, and it is generally felt to be better to have a shape modelling technique which is intrinsically geared to producing representations of solids, rather than to rely on the user to create the required set of faces.

Most of these *solid models* [REQU80] [WOOD86a] are based on one of two data-structures, and often both are present. The *set-theoretic* (or CSG) solid model is defined as a combination of simple, or primitive, solids using operators derived from set theory. The boundary model, on the other hand, is much more like the face model, except that the faces, edges and vertices of a model are linked together into a structure which assures its topological consistency; that is to say, the numbers of faces, edges and vertices are constrained to obey Euler's rule. However, this does not prevent models corresponding to unrealizable objects from being created. For instance, a concave vertex could be allowed to protrude through the "far side" of a model. Luckily, set-theoretic models can be converted into boundary models, and boundary models can be combined using set-theoretic operators. These methods of construction are the only way to make boundary models which are guaranteed to represent solids.

In the present context, the important thing is that these more complete models are also very suitable for supporting picture generation processes. Indeed, it has been a continuing thorn in the side of people interested in using solid models for engineering analysis and synthesis, that (excepting mass property calculations) graphics has actually been the only process widely implemented so far. However, intelligent application of computer graphics techniques to engineering, and other disciplines, can lead to pictures which, while not realistic in the usual sense, are capable of conveying information about a structure in ways which would never have been considered as economic using purely manual techniques [JARE84a] [QUAR84] [WOOD83] (Figures 1,2,3).

Solid models are of value even when the only product being manufactured is a picture [BOWY83]. The boundary model can quite easily be converted into a face model, essentially by removing some of the linking information, and in this

way boundary models, once created, allow pictures to be produced using existing programs. This has been happening for quite some time. Set-theoretic
models can also form the basis for picture production, using a technique called
ray-casting. This technique, which was invented quite some time ago, is intrinsically very slow. In this paper we discuss the use of solid models in graphics,
and show how more recently developed techniques exploit the structure of solid
models to generate many different sorts of pictures with the ease of face models
but from a much better organized input.

Differences in Domain Between Face and Solid Models

As mentioned in the introduction, face models consist of collections of
polygonal faces. In most systems, these are essentially flat, although, where a
polygon is permitted to have an arbitrary number of edges, it can be difficult to
ensure that its edges are actually coplanar, especially if they may be specified
directly by the person using the system. One solution to this problem is to permit
only triangular faces. This guarantees planarity, and can also make programs
using the faces easier to write. However, the amount of data corresponding to a
given scene is then increased, and the smaller triangular faces are much more
fiddly to input. Of course, the user could be permitted to input more complicated
polygons, which would then be triangulated by the program. In practice, the
"classical" system handles arbitrarily complex polygons directly, and non-con-
vex polygons are usually permitted. The responsibility for avoiding crossing
edges devolves upon the user, in addition to his other duties in maintaining the
consistency of the model. Even allowing arbitrary polygons, planarity could be
assured (to within machine accuracy) by constraining the user to input each
polygon in two dimensions, and then transforming it into position. In practice
this can be inconvenient, and in fact many picture producing algorithms are
tolerant of deviations from planarity in the sets of edges bounding a "polygon".
No attempt is made to decide what actual shape non-planar edges define; calculations are performed using samples of the edge data, with the assumption
that, if the "polygon" is not too far from planar, the results will not be noticeably
inconsistent.

This approach, of fostering illusion about a shape, is raised to new heights in
the simulation of curved surfaces. Instead of adding curved faces to the model,
the flat faces of face models are "shaded" in such a way as to give an illusion of
a continuous surface. This is achieved by interpolating either colours (Gouraud
shading [GOUR71]) or surface normals (Phong shading [PHON75]) across each
face. A picture produced in this way can be identified from the shape of the
horizon of the object. It will follow the original faces, and thus have a "faceted"
appearance (Figure 4). Within the silhouette of the object, however, the illusion
of smoothness is remarkably effective.

Some solid modelling systems are also restricted to planar surfaces. For many
engineering purposes, however, it is essential to have an exact representation of

curved surface types. Early solid modelling systems included cylindrical as well as planar surfaces, and the plane, cylinder, cone, sphere and torus are a common standard for today's commercial systems (e.g. NONAME [WICK83]). Producing line drawings of such curved-surfaced models is demanding, because of the algebraic complications in determining edges where primitives intersect. The number of types of intersection curve increases as the square of the number of surface types implemented. Other techniques of picture production, such as ray-casting, can be used on models with curved surfaces, but must also be modified to take account of their high-order equations. However the problem of finding intersections between a simple geometric entity, such as a ray, and a number of different complicated ones is far less demanding then that of finding all the mutual intersections between the latter.

In order to avoid the difficulties associated with high-order surfaces, it is possible to construct a system with an exact representation that is used for analysis purposes, from which is derived a faceted model for producing pictures. This approach is fast, but techniques for constructing accurate pictures from curved-surfaced models are better in computer graphics terms, because the resulting pictures exhibit geometrically correct variation of colour, and smooth horizon lines.

Models with simple curved surfaces which correspond to machining operations have widespread applicability in engineering. However, the ability to generate superior pictures from them is of little value in computer graphics work in which more general curved surfaces, such as organic forms, are required. But flowing, curved surfaces are also important in engineering; the development of sculptured surface techniques, based on bi-parametric patches, antedates almost all other work in computer-aided design. As with simpler curved surfaces, an easy way to render patched surfaces is to convert the patches into a large number of small facets, and then to use Gouraud or Phong shading to produce the pictures. This is in many ways a more satisfactory way of producing an illusion of smoothness than by shading handmade face models, because we can create a much larger number of much smaller facets than would be feasible from manual input. The number of such facets can be varied to give "draft" and "final" quality pictures during the development of a model. As with the more standard primitives, work has been done in rendering patched surfaces directly [GRIF84]. These techniques are currently more expensive than faceting but offer a guarantee of accuracy.

There are very considerable difficulties in integrating "classical" sculptured surfaces with set-theoretic solid modelling techniques (although they may relatively easily contribute to the same *picture* - Figure 4). Essentially, the problem is that there is no natural way to define the inside and outside of a parametric surface. Parametric surfaces may however be incorporated directly into boundary models [JARE84b] [ROCK83], by including them in simple models in *ad hoc* ways, and combining these small models set-theoretically into the final model. However, the presence of parametric surfaces will add to the difficulty of many processes of model maintenance and application. Alternatively, parametric surfaces may *theoretically* be converted into implicit surfaces, but this leads to

great algebraic complication [SEDE84] and also unpredictable effects which occur when the bounding imposed by the parametric intervals, over which a patch
is defined, is removed. For instance, distant parts of the implicit surface can intersect the part of the surface corresponding to the original patch, spoiling the
creation of a neat "inside" and "outside."

It has been known for some time that there are alternative methods of describing curved surfaces that are suitable for set-theoretic systems. The earliest technique [RICC73] used a replacement of the set-theoretic operators by algebraic
approximations to make parts of a model flow into one another (Figure 5).
However, the forms generated by this approach are insufficiently localized for
most engineering applications. What are often required are *blend* surfaces,
suitable for the description of small regions of curved surface on castings and
forgings. It has recently been shown possible to construct implicit surfaces
capable of meeting constraints on position and slope and thus suitable for such
applications. One favoured approach [TOR84] [WOOD86b] based on the
generation of two-dimensional quadratics to meet constraints of position and
slope by a method originally used in the cross-sectional design of aircraft
[LIMI44]. These types of surfaces require display techniques considerably different from those applicable to face models (Figure 6).

Solid models are also able to incorporate transformation operations in their
descriptions, and this forms a very convenient and powerful way to describe
bent and twisted shapes. It has been performed on quadric surfaces [BARR84]
and, more recently, with set-theoretic solid models: in this case by integrating
bends into a subdivision technique (Figure 7). There are considerable problems
with displaying bends. With ray-casting, for example, the transformations must
be applied to the ray, and curved rays are difficult to deal with.

Overall, solid models provide the opportunity for a much superior rendering
within the now considerable domain that they cover. Furthermore, in many
cases, curved surfaces are easier to create consistently than a face model sufficiently finely faceted to look reasonable after shading. However, it has to be said
that the techniques of Gouraud and Phong shading, although illusory, do provide
the opportunity to "hand craft" a wider range of shapes than any one solid
modelling techniques has yet shown itself able to cover.

Input

Creating a face model entirely by hand is very time-consuming. It is necessary
to determine and input the coordinates of every vertex. An elementary level of
assistance can be provided by facilities for coordinate transformation, to allow
faces to be created in a convenient position and orientation and then moved into
position. More sophisticated facilities are provided by using graphics equipment
interactively. Devices are available that allow digitization in three dimensions,
and it is possible to create shape models in this way. Difficulties in control and
with accuracy make this an uncommon technique. It has been shown possible to

recreate solid models from wire frames [PREI80] or from a set of projections [WESL81]. At present these approaches are limited in application and, as far as wire frames are concerned, ambiguity is endemic in the representation. A more usual but more limited technique is based on creating pieces of object of limited complexity from two-dimensional input. A single sketched line can be interpreted as a shape of constant cross-section (engineers think of it as an extrusion) by erecting a wall of edges upon it. Alternatively, it can form the basis for a (faceted) solid of revolution (or "turned part") by forming edges to join copies of the line segment rotated about an axis.

In solid modelling, the same techniques are used. In one well known system (Medusa) the extrusions and rotations are built into a single engineering drawing-like interactive program, an approach which is popular with draughtsmen. Using boundary models, there is little more work in building a solid rather than a face model from a sketch. The sketched curve must be constrained to be closed, the appropriate links must be created and top and bottom faces added. With set-theoretic models, the problem is rather more difficult, but recent work [PETE86] [TOR84] [WOOD82] has shown that it is possible to determine the set-theoretic representation of a plane figure from the curve segments that make it up. Once having created the two-dimensional set-theoretic representation, it is a simple matter to convert it into a three-dimensional model.

In the above respects, there are few differences between face and solid models. However, when it comes to combining small models that have been created in the ways mentioned above, the face model offers no help. It is necessary manually to modify the sets of faces that have been constructed, or add extra faces to connect them to the rest of a model, or both. Because set-theoretic and boundary models (almost all) support set-theoretic operations, these can be used to join small models automatically. Because face models do not have to be complete, there is no inside and outside on which set-theoretic operations could be based. If one tried to implement them on face models, they would produce unpredictable results as missing and extra faces were encountered.

Graphics Techniques Based on Solid Models

We have already stated that boundary models may be stripped of surplus data and supplied to existing types of computer graphics software. If the boundary models contain exactly represented curved surfaces, then there is the choice of faceting the model, or adapting existing graphics techniques to the surface types being used. Curved surfaces raise a number of problems. They require horizons to be determined. They make hidden-line and hidden-surface techniques more complicated. For instance, algorithms often use what are called boxing tests to cut down the work necessary in deciding whether two geometric elements intersect. If, for example, it is required to determine whether two faces intersect, a boxing test can be done by creating cuboids around each face and comparing these cheaply before undertaking an exact comparison of the faces themselves.

With plane faces, the extend of the boxes can be determined from the vertex coordinates. With curved surfaces, this is not possible.

Originally, pictures were most commonly obtained from set-theoretic models via conversion to boundary models. The authors have been among those concerned in recent years with developing efficient techniques to obtain pictures directly from set-theoretic models. Their approach revolves around the spatial segmentation of the space occupied by a model, and the pruning of the model to produce smaller sub-models in each of the sub-spaces created. This is used to overcome the poor performance engendered by the global nature of the set-theoretic model. In some implementations [QUAR82] [WOOD84], division has been used as a *technique* with which to construct a picture (Figures 8 and 9). The division pattern is aligned with the plane of projection, and the division structure is related to Warnock's hidden surface technique [WARN69] with the addition of divisions in the direction of depth from the viewer. Results from programs based on this technique show a better-than linear performance over a range of practical models, and one that therefore competes with face models for the display of scenes of higher complexity.

By saying that, in the past, pictures of set-theoretic models were largely obtained via boundary models, we have omitted the technique of *ray-casting*, which was mentioned in the introduction. It was originally implemented in the Synthavision system [GOLD79]. Ray-casting, which can also be used with face models, starts with the calculation of many "rays" into the scene, each ray corresponding to the viewer's line of sight through a pixel on the graphics display. The intersection is then found between each ray and every surface in the scene, and the colour of the nearest surface is written into the pixel. Using a set-theoretic model, programming this technique is very straightforward, but somewhat time-consuming, because the set-theoretic relationship between the parts of the model must be considered instead of simply noting the first object struck. In this case, recursive division and pruning can be used to make a divided model *structure* [QUIN82] [WALL84a] [WOOD80] and, more recently, [WYVI85]. Ray-casting into this, each ray is quickly compared with the tree of sub-spaces, and only subsequently with the pieces of model that they contain. This technique was first implemented in a computer-aided engineering context [WALL84b] and has more recently been used in "pure" computer graphics [WOOD86b] [WYVI86]. Picture generation times are dramatically shortened by this approach and, moreover, the rate of increase of picture generation time with model complexity is much better than linear. Once ray-casting into a divided model can be supported, subsequent rays to simulate shadows and reflections are as easily added as with the simplest ray-casting system (Figures 10 and 11).

The unbounded nature of the set-theoretic model looks at first sight unfriendly for many of the advanced graphics techniques that have been developed for face models. In particular, it is difficult to see how the Gouraud and Phong shading techniques that we have already mentioned could be applied to a set-theoretic model. However, the appropriate route to overcoming this problem is clearly not through shading, but to model curved surfaces exactly, using implicit equations.

Another problem that would seem to be difficult with the set-theoretic model is texture simulation. In particular, if texture mapping is to be used and the edges of the object are not known, then how can texture patterns be matched where surfaces meet? This problem turns out to be quite easy to solve, by defining texture throughout a three-dimensional space, but only evaluating it at the surface of the object. The authors have been concerned with the development of such *solid texturing* techniques, based either on Fourier transforms of real textures acquired photographically, or on pseudo-fractals [WOOD86b] (Figure 12). While these techniques were being developed, a paper [PERL85] was published which described a similar solid-texturing technique (but not, in fact, based on either of the above approaches) which was being advocated as more efficient in general, rather than just to overcome problems with set-theoretic solid models.

In the future we may well see further extensions in the use of set-theoretic modelling techniques for graphics purposes.

We see that the spatial segmentation techniques developed for set-theoretic models are now starting to being used to speed up operations on boundary models [AYAL85]. It seems likely that a more general spatial indexing technique could be developed which was capable of supporting more than one representation. (The pseudo-fractals texturing already alluded to uses two spatial divisions. The model is stored in one segmented space, and the pseudo-fractal generation uses another. In this case, however, it was convenient to separate the two structures, and that used in creating the fractals is generated on the fly, rather than being stored.) In this way other types of model, such as particle models, could be integrated into a single framework. More efficient spatial access should accelerate the implementation of beam-tracing [HECK84], which is a more general form of ray-casting capable of producing refractions and soft shadows. We would also hope to see inroads into the expense of other parts of picture production, for instance the development of a better-than-linear way of implementing large numbers of light sources.

Conclusions

The main development in computer graphics over the next five years is almost certain to be the wide adoption of parallel processors of various forms to accelerate picture generation. In the debate that has already started about the relative suitability of different architectures and algorithms other issues may take a back seat. The casting of favoured algorithmic approaches into silicon may well have a blighting effect on the width of development of computer graphics techniques in general. It will be difficult to justify experimenting with a program on a serial machine in order to obtain some small increase in algorithm performance or picture quality, when an "adequate" picture can be obtained in a ten-thousandth of the time on a "standard" parallel architecture. Such an effect can already be seen in the use of modified depth buffers capable of Gouraud and Phong shading. The existence of these is one of the reasons for the display of curved surfaces via facets, and militates against the development of exact algorithms acting on the curved surface equations directly.

However, the desire to model a scene at the highest possible level will continue. The use of solid models will become common, and it will become more frequent for large parts of the geometry of a model to be determined automatically, using numerical or AI techniques. For instance, we may expect to see animations of springy structures move from the diagrammatic stage at which they are currently employed by stress engineers to a state where they can be routinely used in film production. In turn, this will put more emphasis on the availability of models with versatile and easily created geometric elements. Furthermore, models will need to be compatible with other kinds of computer graphics structure, such as fractals and particle models.

Like multiprocessor architectures, new types of solid models are expensive to create and to equip with features already available in older schemes. Hence, in computer graphics, we may well see models sandwiched between two layers of software. Above, the model will be programs which convert high-level specifications of the scene into geometry. Below it, there will be code to change the model's data into a form appropriate for the fastest picture production machine available. It is regrettable not to be able to postulate a new and universal shape modelling tool. But this has not been the trend of recent events, and there is no immediate breakthrough in sight. The future for modelling techniques in graphics is one of coping with a steady increase in both model complexity and expected performance.

Acknowledgements. In this paper, the authors have tried to present a flavour of some of the graphics-oriented work in solid modelling being done in the UK in general, not just at the IBM UK Scientific Centre. The authors are therefore very grateful to Dr. A. Bowyer, Mr. A. F. Wallis & Mr. Zhang, D.Y. of the School of Engineering, University of Bath, Mr. G. E. M. Jared of the Department of Mathematics, Cranfield Institute of Technology, and Mr. R. G. Oliver of the Geometric Modelling Project, University of Leeds for allowing them to use examples of their work. Thanks are also due to Mr. S. J. P. Todd, who wrote the SLED program, and to Mr. R. Q. Wright, for providing an example of his work in computer art.

References

[AYAL85] D. Ayala, P. Brunet, R. Juan & I. Navazo "Object Representation by Means of Nonminimal Quadtrees and Octrees", ACM Trans. on Graphics 4,1 (pp 41-59), 1985

[BARR84] A.H. Barr "Global and Local Deformations of Solid Primitives" Computer Graphics 18,3 (pp 21-31), 1984

[BOWY83] A. Bowyer, A.F. Wallis & J.R. Woodwark "The Artist's Model", Proc. CG-83 Conf., London (pp 233-245), 1983

[CARL85] I. Carlbom & I. Chakravarty "A Hierarchical Data Structure for Representing the Spatial Decomposition of 3-D Objects", IEE Comput. Graphics and Appl. (pp 24-31), April 1985

[GOLD79] R. Goldstein & L. Malin "3-D Modelling with the Synthavision System", Proc. First Annu. Conf. on Comput. Graphics in CAD/CAM Sys., Cambridge (US) (pp 244-247), 1979

[GOUR71] H. Gouraud "Continuous Shading of Curved Surfaces", IEE Trans. on Comput., C-20 (6), (pp 623-628), 1971

[GRIF84] J.S. Griffiths "A Depth-Coherence Scanline Algorithm for Displaying Curved Surfaces", Comput. Aided Des. 16,2 (pp 91-101), 1984

[HECK84] P.S. Heckbert & P. Hanrahan "Beam Tracing Polygonal Objects", ACM Comput. Graphics 18,3 (Proc. SIGGRAPH 84 Conf.) (pp 119-127), 1984

[JARE84a] G.E.M. Jared "Shape Features in Geometric Modeling", in "Solid Modelling - from Theory to Applications" (Proc. GM Research Laboratories Symp., Detroit, 1983) Plenum (pp 121-133), 1984

[JARE84b] G.E.M. Jared & T. Varady "Synthesis of Sculptured Surfaces and Volume Modelling in BUILD", Proc. CAD-84 Conf., Brighton (pp 481-495), 1984

[LIMI44] R.A. Liming "Practical Analytical Geometry with Applications to Aircraft", Macmillan, New York, 1944

[MIDD85] A.E. Middleditch & K.E. Sears "Blend Surfaces for Set-theoretic Volume Modelling Systems", ACM Comput. Graphics 19,3 (Proc. SIGGRAPH 85 Conf.) (pp 161-170), July 1985

[PERL85] K. Perlin "An Image Sysnthesizer", ACM Comput. Graphics 19,3 (Proc. SIGGRAPH 85 Conf.) (pp 287-296), 1985

[PETE86] D.P. Peterson "Boundary to Constructive Solid Geometry Mappings: a Focus on 2-D Issues", Comput. Aided Des. 18,1 (pp 3-14), 1986

[PHON75] B.-T. Phong "Illumination for Computer-generated Pictures", Commun. of the ACM 18,6 (pp 311-317), 1975

[PREI80] K. Preiss "Constructing the 3-D Representation of a Plane-faced Object from a Digitized Engineering Drawing", Proc. CAD-80 Conf., Brighton (pp 257-265), 1980

[QUAR84] P. Quarendon "A General Approach to Surface Modelling Applied to Molecular Graphics", J. Mol. Graphics 2,3 (pp 91-65), 1984

[QUIN82] K.M. Quinlan & J.R. Woodwark "A Spatially-segmented Solids Database - Justification and Design", Proc. CAD-82 Conf., Brighton (pp 126-132), 1982

[REQU80] A.A.G. Requicha "Representations of Rigid Solids: Theory Methods and Systems", ACM Comput. Surv. 12,4 (pp 437-464), 1980

[RICC73] A. Ricci "A Constructive Geometry for Computer Graphics", Comput. J. 16, 2 (pp 157-169), 1973

[ROCK83] A.P. Rockwood "Introducing Sculptured Surfaces into a Geometric Modeler", in "Solid Modeling - from Theory to Applications" (Proc. GM Research Laboratories Symp., Detroit, 1983) Plenum (pp 237-253), 1984

[ROTH80] S.D. Roth "Ray Casting as a Method for Solid Modeling", GM Research Laboratories Computer Science Department Res. Publ. GMR-3466 (1980)

[SEDE84] T.W. Sederberg, D.C. Anderson & R.N. Goldman "Implicit Representation of Parametric Curves and Surfaces", Comput. Vision, Graphics and Image Process. 28,1 (pp 72-84), 1984

[SUTH74] I.E. Sutherland, R.A. Sproull & R.A. Schumacker "A Characterization of Ten Hidden-surface Algorithms", ACM Comput. Surv. 6,1 (pp 1-55), 1974

[TOR84] S.B. Tor & A.E. Middleditch "Convex Decompositions of Simple Polygons", ACM Trans. on Graphics, (pp 244-265), October 1984

[WALL84a] A.F. Wallis & J.R. Woodwark "Creating Large Solid Models for NC Toolpath Verification", Proc. CAD 84 Conf., Brighton (pp 455-460), 1984

[WALL84b] A.F. Wallis & J.R. Woodwark "Interrogating Solid Models", Proc. CAD-84 Conf., Brighton (pp 236-243), 1984

[WARN69] J.E. Warnock "A Hidden-surface Algorithm for Computer-generated Halftone Pictures", Univ. of Utah Computer Science Department Report TR4-15, 1969

[WESL81] M.A. Wesley & G. Markowsky "Fleshing Out Projections", IBM J. Res. Dev. 25,6 (pp 938-954), 1981

[WICK83] L.P. Wickens "Presentation of Leeds University Modelling System (BOXER)", Proc. CAM-I Geometric Modelling Seminar, Cambridge (UK) (CAM-I Docu. P-83-GM-01) (pp 113-135), 1983

[WILL85] P.J. Willis "A Review of Recent Hidden-surface Removal Techniques", Disp. 6,1 (pp 11-20), 1985

[WOOD80] J.R. Woodwark & K.M. Quinlan " The Derivation of Graphics from Volume Models by Recursive Subdivision of the Object Space", Proc. CG-80 Conf., Brighton (pp 335-343), 1980

[WOOD82] J.R. Woodwark & K.M. Quinlan "Reducing the Effect of Complexity on Volume Model Evaluation", Comput. Aided Des. 16,4 (pp 285-291), 1982

[WOOD82] J.R. Woodwark & A.F. Wallis "Graphical Input to a Boolean Solid Modeller", Proc. CAD-82 Conf., Brighton (pp 681-688), 1982

[WOOD83] J.R. Woodwark "Solid Modelling of Fluid Power Components", Proc. I.Mech.E. Conf., "CAD in High Pressure Hydraulic Systems", London (UK) (pp 99-100), 1983

[WOOD86a] J.R. Woodwark "Computing Shape", Butterworths, 1986

[WOOD86b] J.R. Woodwark & A. Bowyer "Better and Faster Pictures from Solid Models", Comput. Aided Eng. J. 3,1 (pp 17-24), 1986

[WYVI85] G. Wyvill & T.L. Kunii "A Functional Model for Constructive Solid Geometry", The Visual Comput. 1,3 (pp 3-14), 1985

[WYVI86] G. Wyvill, T.L. Kunii & Y. Shirai "Space Division for Ray Tracing in CSG", Comput. Graphics & Appl. (pp 28-34), April 1986

[ZHAN86] Zhang, D.-Y. & A. Bowyer "CSG Set-theoretic Solid modelling and NC Machining of Blend Surfaces", Proc. ACM 2nd Symp. on Computational Geometry, Yorktown Heights, 1986

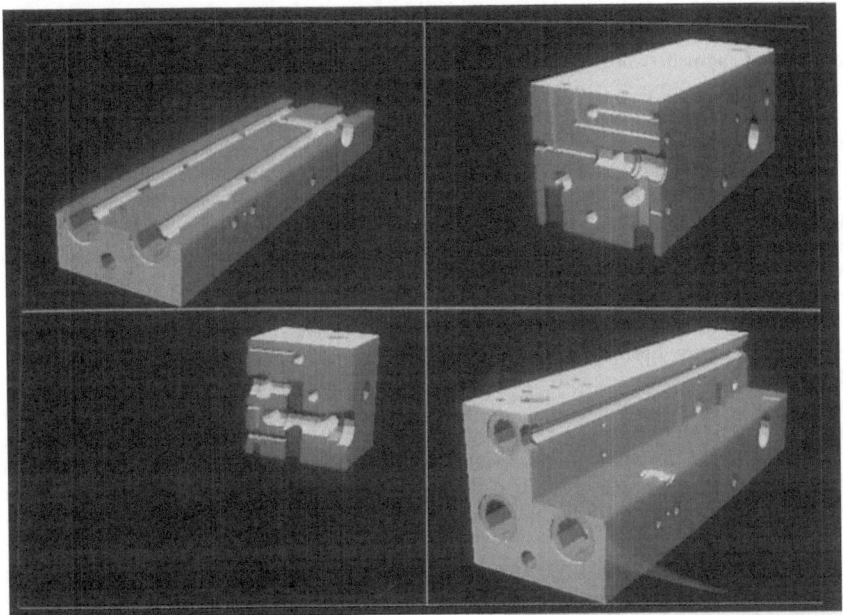

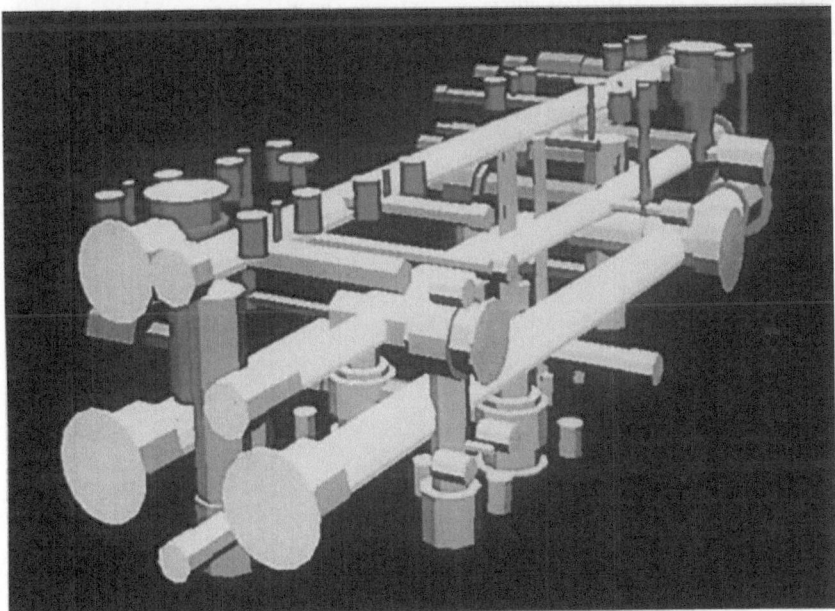

Figure 1. Visualization in engineering

A hydraulic manifold is a block of metal with a number of holes drilled in it, providing one or more hydraulic circuits. In an engineering drawing, it looks deceptively simple. The view on to each face consists of a rectangle enclosing a number of circles, representing the end views of the holes, each annotated with its depth. In practice it is not at all easy to visualize the manifold's internal structure from a drawing of this sort, and particularly to spot intersections between holes. It is not unknown for a drawing believed to be correct to include unwanted intersections between different hydraulic circuits which only manifest themselves after manufacture. More insidious are thin walls between holes which rupture when pressure is applied.

The set-theoretic operations available in solid modelling systems make the construction of a model of a manifold particularly easy [WOOD83]. Of course, one could write a special analysis program to look for defects in the layout of manifolds, but the simple ability to take arbitrary sections of a model, as in picture (a), is a valuable design aid in its own right. Additionally, pictures like (b) may be prepared showing the holes as positive volumes, by intersecting them with the block, rather than differencing them from it.

Whatever type of picture is chosen, its readability may be enhanced by using a range of unrealistic colours. Indeed, for the purpose of understanding the shape of a component of this sort, it would be particularly stupid to display it in the uniform grey of the actual alloy, and the height of folly to spend time computing shadows, thus obscuring a lot of the internal detail. Even if a range of colours is applied to the parts of the model more or less at random, there is likely to be a considerable advantage in discriminating between various features. A number of more logical artificial colouring schemes are possible. Each hydraulic circuit could be coloured diffently. An alternative, as shown in picture (a), is to colour the holes according to the machining processes to be used to make them. In this case, drilled holes are shown grey, tapped ones blue, spotfaced ones yellow, and the holes to be reamed with a special valve seat cutter are shown green. In picture (b), a third possibility is shown; the holes are coloured depending on the face from which they were drilled. If an error is suspected, this allows easy reference back to the appropriate view on the drawing. With all of these colouring schemes, the abandonment of "realism" as a goal adds to the value of the picture as an informative medium

(The manifold shown in this figure is part of an experimental dynamometer developed at the University of Bath, where the pictures were produced)

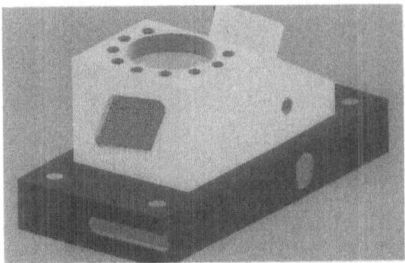

Figure 2. Labelling component features

Picture (a) is an isometric of a model created with the BUILD system, while picture (b) shows the result of processing that model using a program designed to recognize "features" [JARE84a]. In this case they are bosses, coloured blue, through holes, coloured red, pockets, coloured yellow, and slots, coloured green. Similar techniques can be applied to identifying parts of a model which can be made by a particular machining process, and this is important in the automation of process planning. BUILD is a boundary modeller, and it is not obvious how this sort of feature recognition could be applied to set-theoretic models.

Simply being able to display the results of such recognition, rather than incorporate them into, say, a process planning system, is a possible way to make engineers see a component they have designed in a different light, and perhaps remind them of manufacturing and other implications of the design, depending on the types of feature which can be recognized.

(Pictures produced at Department of Mathematics, Cranfield Institute of Technology.)

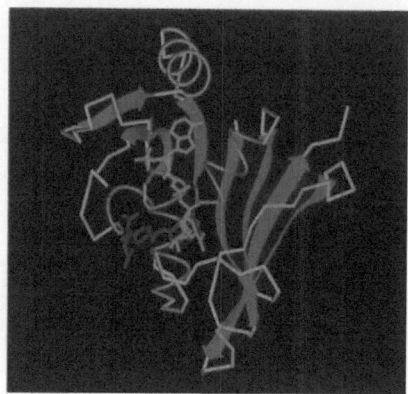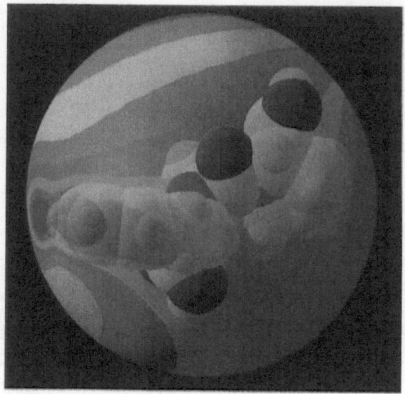

Figure 3. Molecular models

The laws of physics make a nonsense of the idea of "seeing" molecules in detail. However, it is convenient to represent molecules as solids, and such molecular models can simply be constructed from plastic spheres and wire. However, there are many advantages to modelling molecules, especially large ones, on the computer. Most molecular graphics systems are configured for vector refresh graphics displays, in order to achieve fast interaction. Because of the limitations of that technology the wires of a physical model are represented as lines, and the surfaces of the spheres representing the atoms are approximated by a dot surface. On raster graphics, different views are slower to produce, but are much less ambigious. Bespoke molecular modelling systems have been written based on spheres alone, and this makes many display algorithms simple to write. However, where a more versatile solid modelling system is available, the readability of pictures can be enhanced by representing parts of a molecule whose structure is well understood as a large aggregate shape. Picture (a) was produced by the WINSOM system [QUAR74], which boasts a helix primitive primarily for this purpose (rather than for modelling springs!).

As molecular modelling develops, there is pressure to be able to model more than just the arrangement of atoms and groups of atoms. One example of such extra data is the electric field around a molecule. (This information is important in determining how two molecules are likely to combine.) It is possible to model a field as a number of discrete solids, for instance as arrows (each one a cone unioned to a cylinder). In picture (b), however, the field is represented by its intersection with a sphere around the molecule, with different potentials shown as different transparent colours. While it is not too difficult to produce such a picture of a field, integrating techniques for doing that with an efficient method of rendering the molecule is more challenging.

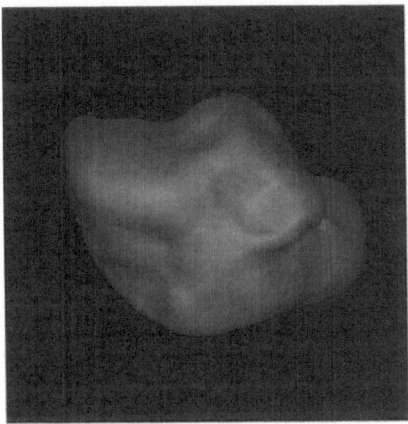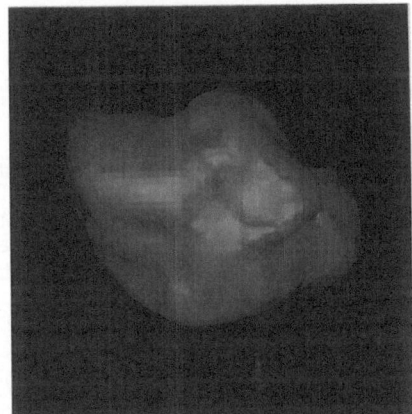

Figure 4. Combining surfaces and solids

This figure shows a geometric model of the human heart. It is designed to be animated as a medical aid, and a beating heart video has in fact been made. The model is an interesting mixture of a number of techniques. The heart itself is constructed from bicubic patches fitted to measured data obtained from x-ray information. The grid of patches is essentially spherical, and this does give rise to some slight problems at the poles.In displaying the heart, the patches are faceted and then Phong shaded. Pictures (a) and (b) show a deliberately rather coarse faceting, and even after shading the polygonal horizon of the model is noticeable. Picture (c) shows a still from the film. Here arteries defined as cylinders and spheres combined set-theoretically have been added to the patched surface of the heart. That could have been achieved using a depth buffer, but this picture was produced by integrating the two structures within an experimental recursive division system.

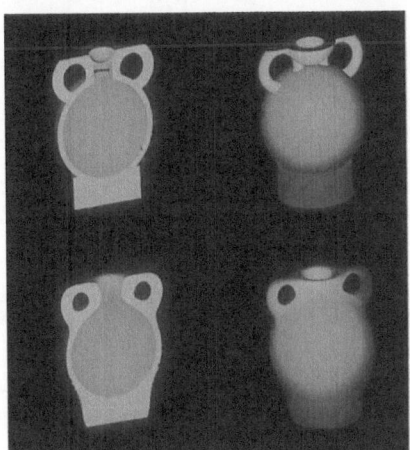

Figure 5 Ricci blends (left)

This picture illustrates a form of blending originally put forward by Ricci [RICC73]. A model is constructed incorporating the union and intersection operators, but these are replaced by numerical approximations as follows:

$$(S_1 \cup S_2 \cup \ldots \cup \dot{S}_n \Rightarrow (S_1^{-p} + S_2^{-p} + \ldots + S_n^{-p})^{-1/p}$$
$$(S_1 \cup S_2 \cup \ldots \cup S_n \Rightarrow (S_1^{p} + S_2^{p} + \ldots + S_n^{p})^{2/p}$$

(p is positive)

If the value of p is very large, then the real set-theoretic operators are nearly exactly implemented, and the resulting model has almost sharp edges at the intersection between primitives. As the value of p becomes smaller, the two solids being combined flow more into each other. As stated in the text, the problem with this technique is that the composite object differs from its components to some extent over its entire surface, even though, far from their intersection, these deviations may be very small. In the implementation by which the picture was produced, the rate of decay is increased by approximating the operators by logarithms of exponents, rather than raising them to powers.

The figure shows two views of a vase, before and after blending the primitives together, and a section through each. For objects of this sort, the very small amount of data to be supplied by the user may be an advantage, and the small changes of shape just referred to are not significant. Ricci's original implementation of these blends included only the production of section lines, although these could be displayed with hidden lines removed (the algorithm used for this was not disclosed in [RICC73]). The pictures here were obtained from an implementation of Ricci blends within the WINSOM solid modelling system, which uses recursive subdivision as a strategy for picture generation.

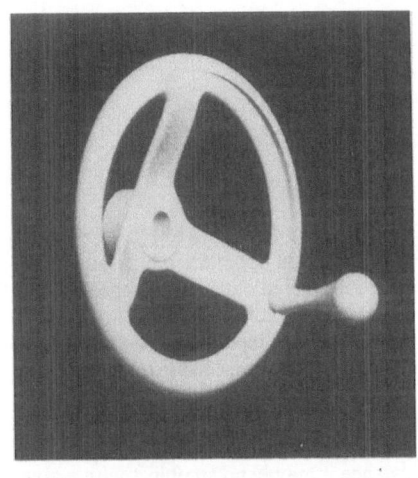

Figure 6 Liming blends

This figure shows a model of a handwheel casting, which has been generated using Liming blends [LIMI44]. It has been found possible [MIDD85] [WOOD86b] to extend Liming's technique to three dimensions, and also to allow blends to be blended to each other. Blends are created from surfaces with which smooth joints are to be made, and other surfaces which limit the extent of the blend. The "fatness" of the blends can be controlled by a weighting factor.

Applying the process of recursive division to a set-theoretic model relies on being able to prune the set-theoretic expression by eliminating parts of the model that do not contribute to a given sub-space. With planar half-spaces, this is very straightforward. With a range of "conventional" primitives, such as those in WINSOM or NONAME [WICK83] there are not too many problems. It can be performed exactly, but it has been found more efficient to compare primitives with a sphere surrounding each cuboid sub-space, and accept that some sub-models will be more complex than necessary, rather than to perform the exact tests. With the Liming blend surfaces, it is not possible to attack the problem directly in any way. Instead, interval arithmetic is employed to generate limits on the distance of the blend surface from the sub-space. In this way, a spatially segmented model can be created, although some of the sub-models that it contains will clearly be larger than necessary. Ray-casting is performed by traversing the division structure as with other models, and then finding intersections between the ray and the components of the model numerically. Use of the segmented model is not, however, limited to graphics: one additional application that is not trivial is the generation of cutter paths for numerically controlled machining. A pattern for cutting the handwheel shown has been produced in this way [ZHAN86].

(Picture produced at the School of Engineering, University of Bath)

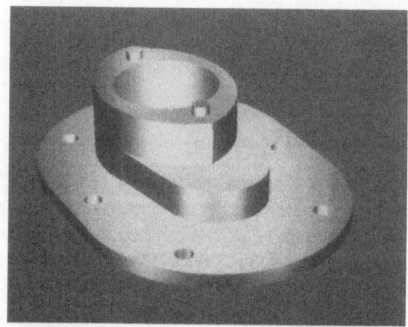

Figure 7 Bends

Barr [BARR84] suggested the introduction of deformation operators into solid modelling as a convenient way to represent certain geometric objects which are difficult to model in other ways. Examples are chairs made from laminated and bent wood.

A deformation operator converts an undeformed shape into a deformed one. For instance it may bend an object with a given bending radius, or twist an object through a given angle. The deformation is specified by means of a transformation which maps points in the original object to equivalent points in the deformed object.

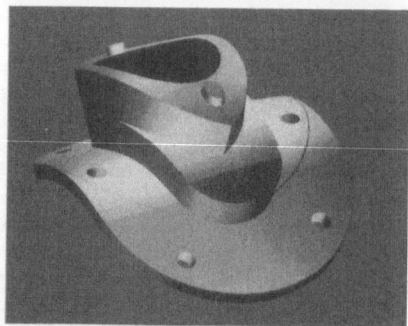

Operations of this type have been incorporated into WINSOM. This has been done in a general way so that deformed objects can have the normal set operations applied between them, and can themselves be blended and so forth. It is possible to simulate operations which are quite difficult to perform in real life, such as drilling a bent hole in a rectangular block. Deformed objects can be re-deformed if necessary

Picture (a) illustrates a cover plate from a small pump. Picture (b) shows the result of bending it through a 45 degree angle, while picture (c) shows the result of applying a violent twist along its longer axis.

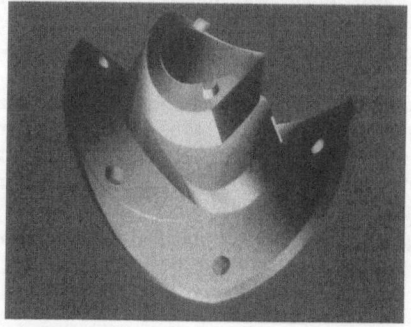

Figure 8 Editing lighting models

In many ways, lighting models are independent of the data structure of the object representation being used. This figure illustrates that sophistication in lighting design is possible with solid, as well as with face, models. The picture shows two of the primitives available in the WINSOM system. The SLED lighting editor is a piece of software that allows (shadowless) lighting to be set up quickly for a particular view of a model. A picture is created which contains depth and surface normal information, as well as colour, at each pixel; it is effectively a bas-relief. As lights are moved and altered in direction and intensity, the effect can be shown in the picture much more quickly than by recomputation from the whole model. More unusually, it is possible to use the graphics cursor to describe where one would like highlights to appear and how sharp they should be, and the program will work backwards to determine what type of light should be used, and where it should be placed. This facility can save a lot of time spent in trial and error.

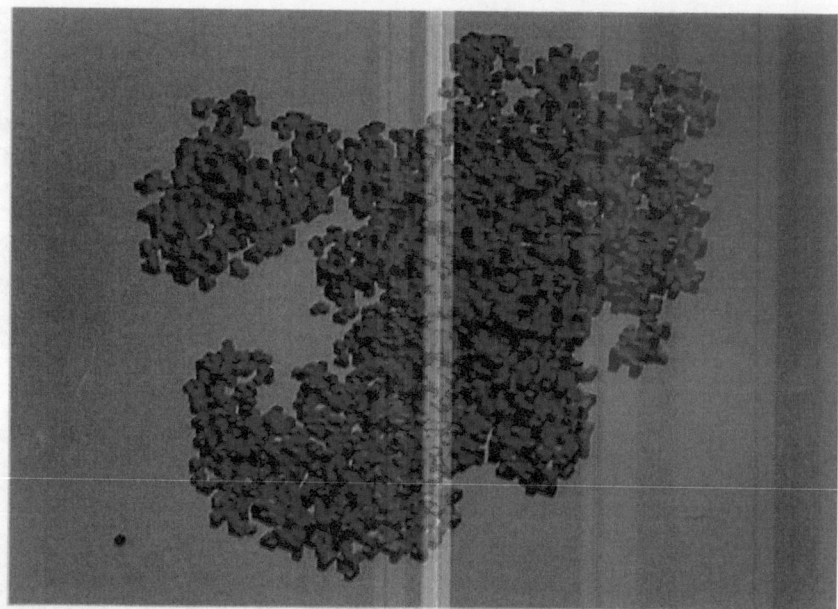

Figure 9 Solid modelling as art

This picture was produced by an artist using the WINSOM modeller as a processor to
display solids generated by his own software. He describes his program as: "a prototype
mathematically-based language for visual art. It works by taking the central cube in the
picture and repeating it through space according to a set of symmetry transformations
chosen by the artist. These simple operations allow a vast number of different images to
be defined, many of them resembling organic forms and other complex structures able to
be exploited for artistic purposes".

Figure 10 Shadows by ray-tracing

This figure shows one of a sequence of views of a solid model of the temple of Sul Minerva, and its associated precinct (including the present-day King's Bath). The model was prepared for the BBC, and this is one of a sequence of views shown on the "Chronicle" programme in March 1984. The pictures were produced by the DORA program [WOOD86b], which performs ray-casting into a spatially-segmented solid model. In this program, the segmentation is optimized for the ray-casting process. A ray is created corresponding to each pixel on the screen, and these are followed "backwards" into the model to determine the surface nearest the viewer. The colour to illuminate the pixel is obtained from the colour of the surface struck by the ray, and its orientation to the light.

It is very easy to include a number of visual effects with a ray-casting system. Shadows enhance this picture, and are calculated by constructing a further ray from the point struck by the first ray, and towards the light. It is then determined whether this second ray strikes another part of the model. If it does, the first point is in shadow, and a reduced lighting intensity is used. Of course, the computation of the second ray also benefits from the spatial segmentation. In this picture, a parallel lighting direction was used to correspond to natural illumination. Shadowing may be performed in the same way for point and multiple light sources, but when multiple light sources are involved a corresponding number of rays must be cast. In picture (b), the human figures have been added using a pixel painter.

(Pictures produced at the School of Engineering, University of Bath)

Figure 11 Reflections by ray-tracing

Once a ray-casting algorithm has been implemented, it is relatively easy to generate sub-sequent rays to model shadows and reflections. The model shown in this figure was originally created using the NONAME system. NONAME itself is a large modeller capable of handling the curves generated by the intersection of curved primitives, and producing various styles of line drawing output for engineering use. This picture was computed by ray-casting into a spatially-segmented model produced by an experimental program from the original model's NONAME definition. This segmentation is not op-timized for ray-casting, but is intended to support a number of operations: in particular to be updated *in situ*.

The ray-casting software includes an adaptive anti-aliasing facility. If adjacent pixels have colours differing by a certain amount, further rays are cast at sub-pixel pitch, to determine an average colour at the pixels in question, and to avoid jagged edges to parts of the picture. The picture was computed at 512 x 512 pixel resolution, and this technique can be seen to have been very effective.

(Picture produced at the Geometric Modelling Project, University of Leeds)

Figure 12 Pseudo-fractal texture

As mentioned in the text, the generation of textured surfaces on set-theoretic models is somewhat more problematic than on boundary models. This figure shows a pseudo-fractal texturing technique which is based on an even binary division of the space occupied by the object [WOOD86b]. Values of the "fractal" are associated with the corners of the original object space and, as division proceeds, new values are calculated for the mid-points of the edges which are cut by the division plane. These values are based on the original corner values, a random number, and the fractal dimension. The random number is seeded from the coordinate values at the mid-point, to ensure that subsequent regeneration of the value during other phases of the division produces the same result.

The division of the space could not, of course, be constructed to an acceptable depth over the entire object space. Instead, the divisions are created only when fractal values are required. Because the ray-casting process that is used to produce the picture is coherent in its access to the model, it is not necessary to rebuild the entire tree of fractal values, but just to create sufficient new branches to "home in" on each new point at which a fractal value is required. The resolution of this process may be fixed, or varied with distance to the viewpoint, so as to avoid unnecessary divisions. In this picture, the fractal values have been used to perturb the colour of the "metal" surface of the casing of a motor car air filter to give the illusion of rust.

There is no difficulty in producing a number of separate "fractal fields", with the same or different characteristics, and to use these to produce textured objects. The fractals can be used to do more than simply change the surface colour. One possibility is to use the values to vary the surface normal, so as to give an illusion of roughness.

(Picture produced at the School of Engineering, University of Bath)

The Beta Spline:
A Curve and Surface Representation for Computer Graphics and Computer Aided Geometric Design

BRIAN A. BARSKY

The Beta-spline is a new curve and surface representation that has been developed expressly for computer graphics and computer aided geometric design and modelling. Its graphical and geometrical orientation is reflected in the replacement of the traditional *parametric* continuity, C^2 with *geometric* continuity, G^2. From a user standpoint, the Beta-spline can be specified in an intuitive manner through the use of *shape parameters* beta1 and beta2 called *bias* and *tension*, respectively. The shape parameters have an intuitive connection to the "flatness" of the curve and surface, and thus can be used to provide further control of shape.

In addition to the shape parameters, a Beta-spline is also controlled by the positions of an arrangement of control vertices. The Beta-spline representation has the important advantage of *local control*; that is, the capability of modifying one portion of the shape by moving a vertex without altering the remainder of the shape. The combination of the geometric nature of this technique with shape control via the shape parameters as well as the presence of the local control property forms a powerful representation.

For a detailed description of the Beta-spline representation, the reader is referred to the forthcoming Springer-Verlag book entitled *Computer Graphics and Geometric Modelling Using Beta-splines* by the same author.

A Model-Driven Approach to CAD and Graphic Communication Networks

Tosiyasu L. Kunii

I Introduction

Objects are represented in a computer in a variety of forms. A model abstracts the forms. For example, the study of programming languages has been centered around modeling varieties of computational procedures. The models of "formal languages" and "semaphores" constitute the theoretical basis of constructing numerous compilers and operating systems. The data models of database systems are the result of modeling complicated and large amounts of data in terms of entities and their relationships.

Generally speaking, more than one model is used in a given system , and the combination of the models is not unique. The performance of the system depends largely on the choice of relevant models, and to guide system designers, builders, and users, appropriate selection of models really helps to speed up their tasks. This article introduces a new approach to the modeling and construction of CAD and graphics communication network systems. This approach is called a "model-driven" approach and it is used in contrast to a "presentation-oriented" approach concerned mainly with how to render images and what tools to use. A "model-driven" approach is described in section II. From section III to section IX, several examples of models are shown. Section X concludes this article.

II Model-Driven Approach

2.1 The Hierarchy of Models

When the number of models used in a CAD system is greater than one, a hierarchical structure is often formed. A parent and child pair is decided from a certain set of rules. The followings are examples of such rules:

1) Inclusion Rule

When a model A is composed of models $B1, B2, ..., Bn$, A is a parent of $B1, B2, ..., Bn$, and $B1, B2, ..., Bn$ are children of A. For example, when an engineering drawing model is composed of a picture model and a table model, the engineering drawing model is a parent and the picture model and the table model are children.

2) Abstraction Rule

When models A and B represent the same object and A is more abstract than B according to a given measure, A is a parent of B and B is a child of A. For instance, a picture model represented by regions, lines, and points is more abstract than another model represented by pixels.

Note that an instance of a parent model can deterministically produce that of its child models.*

From the discussions above, the deterministic identification of data of all the models in the system is equivalent to that of data of the highest models in the system. Therefore, the human interaction with CAD systems for data input and data manipulation needs to take place at the highest level of the models.

2.2 Presentation-Oriented Approach

Before explaining what a "presentation-oriented" approach is, let us look at a two-dimensional drafting system. Before the appearance of computer-aided design, a design is manually drafted on a paper as a two-dimensional (2D) drawing.

This traditional method has two problems:

1) When the design is modified, the drawing must be manually redrawn. Thus, drawing maintenance requires significant man power, and hence is not cost effective.

2) The drawing does not correspond to the entity. For example, a solid object shape is manually interpreted and represented by several projections and a set of symbols. To reproduce the solid object shape, projections are interpreted back by utilizing the symbols (Figure 1).

The earlier CAD systems changed a drafting paper into a graphic display and a plotter. Although they have reduced the redrawing cost significantly, the double interpretation is still required.

This double interpretation originates from the selection of models, especially, the highest model. Here, the highest model does not reflect the shapes of the solids (such as mechanical parts) but corresponds to the drawing itself.

In other words, a "presentation-oriented" approach is defined such that the highest models of the system directly control the presentation.

---

*In many cases, the data conversions from a child model to its parent model are also popular research topics in computer science, for instance, in image processing and computer vision.

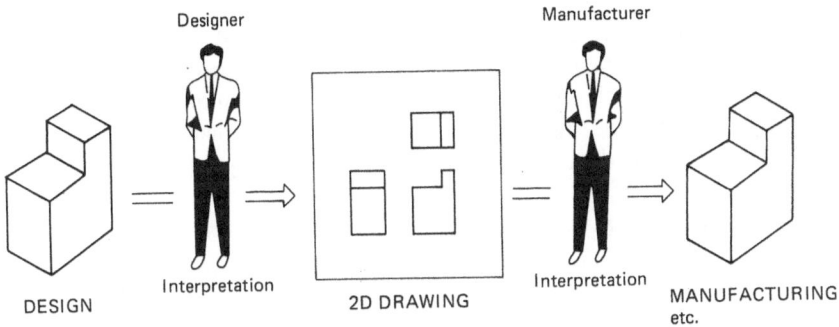

DESIGN   Interpretation   2D DRAWING   Interpretation   MANUFACTURING
etc.

Figure 1

2.3 Model-Driven Approach

To solve the second problem in the above example, we propose another approach, a "model-driven" approach. In this approach, the highest model is set at a level higher than the "presentation" model. The displayed image must always reflect the data in the system database which is defined based on the highest model (Figure 2). What users do is not to change the image presentation, but change the database instance which corresponds to the presentation.

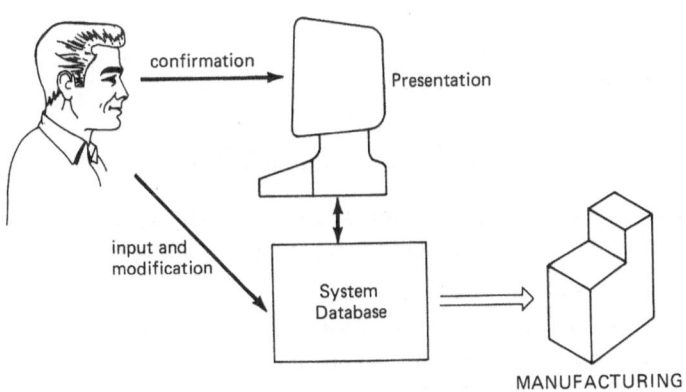

MANUFACTURING

Figure 2

If, in the example of a 2D drafting system, the highest model is an adequate solid model, the double interpretation in Figure 1 becomes unnecessary. This is the most remarkable advantage of a "model-driven" approach.

Other advantages of a "model-driven" approach over a "presentation-oriented" approach are summarized in the following two points:

1) Navigated Data Input

The models serve as frameworks of data input. Instead of specifying all the details of data, as in the case of the system designed by a presentation-oriented approach, users need to input only a portion of the data, which is necessary for the models to select a few out of many possibilities for elaborating the data, following a series of input requests prompted by the models.

2) Verifiable Data Generation

The models restrict the data in data types, ranges and relationships. Instead of conducting exhaustive checking of data validation and consistency, only a limited data check remains necessary at the portion which goes beyond the restriction.

In a model-driven approach, the system is designed as follows:

1) Definition of Model

The model abstracts the objects to be represented, and the system database is defined based on the highest models.

2) Definition of Manipulation

The manipulation operations should include all the basic manipulation functions used in the system.

3) Definition of Integrity

This decides the verification method, which judges the correctness of the input data.

4) Navigated Data Input Design

The model serves as the framework of data input. Good navigation enables users to input data easily and effectively.

2.4 Models for CAD and Graphics Communication Networks

The number of models used in a single system is not always one. Here we introduce examples of models for CAD and graphics communication networks.

1) Geometric Models

In the case of CAD, geometric models are often used for representing object shapes. They are usually a higher model than a presentation model.

Section III describes a computer-aided apparel pattern-making system VIRGO as a geometric model for two-dimensional objects which, in this case, are flat patterns. This system handles all the information on flat patterns and on guide lines or points separately from patterns. It is also a good example of notation for higher models.

For three-dimensional solid objects, geometric models are called solid models. There are two kinds of solid models, that is, Constructive Solid Geometry (CSG) and Boundary Representations (B-reps). In section IV, a functional CSG model is introduced. It is a procedural model which describes geometric properties. Section V explains an engineering animation system, ANIMENGINE. ANIMENGINE is an assembly verification system for solids in B-reps.

2) Table Models

Practical drawing and engineering information usually contains tables of data as well as pictures. The relational data model is well-known for managing unnested tables of data. In Section VI, a nested table data model, which is used for handling a variety of traditional and commonly used table forms, is proposed.

3) Lower Models

In CAD/CAM (CIM), we have to treat models lower than those described above. In many cases, one of the lowest models is a pixel array model. In finding the location of robot arms from digital images and the shape of 3D objects from images or drawings, it is important to convert data from lower models to higher models. Section VII introduces two examples of such conversions, that is, region detection from pixel arrays and top-down construction of 3D object shapes from drawings.

4) Network Models

If we think of a "model-driven" approach as modeling the essential structure of objects, this approach is also applicable to the design of more complex and distributed objects such as graphics communication network systems. CrossoverNet, described in section VIII, is a local area network operating system to handle and transfer both digital and analog information, including graphics, video, and voice data, efficiently. In this system, logical objects are grouped into three levels forming a hierarchical structure which reflects the original structure of the environment where the system is used.

5) Menu System Models

To enhance control of graphics communication network systems, an interactive and user-friendly menu is developed. To eliminate complicated manual programming for menu systems, an automated menu generator called InteractiveProto is designed and implemented, and is shown in section IX. For the design and implementation of InteractiveProto, the models of menu systems, Menu Transition Tree and MacroMenu, have been developed. InteractiveProto adopts a visual or graphical programming language and enables end-users to program menu systems easily. InteractiveProto is a good example of navigated data input.

III VIRGO: A Computer-Aided Apparel Pattern-Making System

This section introduces VIRGO, a new computer-aided apparel pattern-making system based on flat pattern-making. In particular, a flat pattern model in VIRGO is discussed. The details of VIRGO are described in [NOMA86].

Currently, apparel design and manufacturing is heavily dependent upon human labor. To save manpower in the apparel (or garment) industry, it is important to develop a computer-aided data input system, that is, a pattern-making system, and that system has to be interfaced with manufacturing processes, such as marking and cutting.

To interface design processes with manufacturing processes, a pattern-making system should model and manage the entire information on two-dimensional real objects, namely, flat patterns.

3.1 Pattern and Part

Kopp et al. [KOPP81] define a pattern as that which represents a piece of a garment developed in sections. Here a pattern is defined as a set of pieces which form a garment, and each piece is called a part of the pattern. All patterns within their shapes include seam and hem allowances, grainline, size, notches, and placement for buttons, buttonholes, pockets, etc. [KOPP81].

In VIRGO, a part is a standard unit of pattern-making. Each part belongs to a pattern, and consists basically of several loops, none of which intersect itself. Some loops are called "seam loops", where the part is sewn or the outline of the garment exists. Others are called "allowance loops", where the part is cut out of cloth. We will informally explain the topological restriction of the seam and allowance loops of a part.

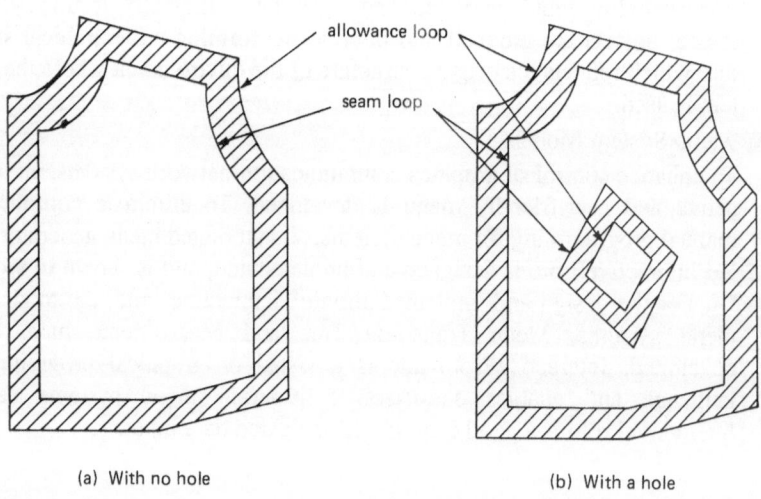

(a) With no hole   (b) With a hole

Figure 3

When a part has no hole, it has one seam loop and one allowance loop. Let SA be an area surrounded by the seam loop. Let AA be an area surrounded by the allowance loop. Then $AA - SA$ is seam allowances. It is obvious that the allowance loop encloses the seam loop (Figure 3a).

A hole in a part is also formed by two loops, but here the seam loop encloses the allowance loop (such a hole represents either an actual hole or a closed dart). The two types of loops never cross each other (Figure 3b), and part connectivity implies that a hole will never contain an "island" within itself. Formally we can restate the topological restriction of a part as follows:

Definition

> $sur(x)$ = the area surrounded by loop x;
> $x > y \Leftrightarrow sur(x) \supset sur(y)$:
> $\Leftrightarrow$ loop x encloses loop y;
> $x = y \Leftrightarrow x > y$ and $y > x$;
> S : a set of seam loops of a part;
> A : a set of allowance loops of the part;

Restriction

> (1) $\exists | \, so \in S, \forall s \; \forall S, so > s$;
>
> $\exists | \, ao \in A, \forall a \forall A, ao > a$;

so and ao are called a seam outer loop and an allowance outer loop, respectively.

> (2) $\forall s, s' \in S - \{so\}, s \not> s'$;
> $\forall a, a' \in A - \{ao\}, a \not> a'$;
>
> (3) $ao > so$;
> $\forall s \in S - \{so\}, \forall a \in A - \{ao\}, a \not> s$;
>
> (4) $\forall p, q \in S \cup A, p > q$ or $p < q$ or $sur(p) \cap sur(q) = \phi$.

Although both loops must be treated separately, we cannot assume that each part has seam loops and allowance loops. For example, a sloper has no seam allowance, since seam allowances can sometimes interfere with the proportioning and developing of design variations [KOPP81]. Some of the patterns used in the apparel industry have only allowance loops.

3.2 Flat Pattern Model

To make the system reliable and compact, actions in VIRGO are divided into two levels, a "data manipulation level" and a "command level". Actions at the data manipulation level directly manipulate the database in VIRGO. Actions at the command level call actions at the data manipulation level. Only those at the command level are available to users.

In VIRGO, the models of objects and relations are defined as a group of sets and functions. Actions at the data manipulation level are defined as procedures composed of operations on the sets and the functions. They are described in detail in [NOMA86].

Here we show the definitions of parts and actions on part seam as an example of data definitions and actions at the data manipulation level. Parts are defined as follows:

Definition (Parts)

A part of a pattern p is given by:

$p = ($ *PSV, PSL, pslf, pscf, so, PAV, PAL, palf, pacf, ao, PNP, PNS, pnsf, pncf, PM, pmaf, pmcf, pmdf, PIP, psif, paif, pnif, picf* $)$

where

(1) *PSV* : a set of part seam vertices;

(2) *PSL* : a set of part seam loops;

(3) *pslf* : part seam loop function:

$pslf : PSL \rightarrow \bigcup_{n} PSV^n;$

(4) *pscf* : part seam coordinate function:

$pscf : PSV \rightarrow R^2;$

(5) *so* : a part seam outer loop;

(6) *PAV* : a set of part allowance vertices;

(7) *PAL* : a set of part allowance loops;

(8) *palf* : part allowance loop function:

$palf : PAL \rightarrow \bigcup_{n} PAV^n ;$

(9) *pacf* : part allowance coordinate function:

$pacf : PAV \rightarrow R^2;$

(10) *ao* : a part allowance outer loop;

(11) *PNP* : a set of part nonloop points;

(12) *PNS* : a set of part nonloop segments;

(13) *pnsf* : part nonloop segment function:

$pnsf : PNS \rightarrow PNP \times PNP;$

(14) *pncf* : part nonloop point coordinate function:

$pncf : PNP \rightarrow R^2;$

(15) *PM* : a set of part marks;

(16) *pmaf* : part mark attribute function:

$pmaf : PM \rightarrow PMA;^*$

(17) *pmcf* : part mark coordinate function:

$pmcf : PM \rightarrow R^2;$

(18) *pmdf* : part mark direction function:

$pmdf : PM \rightarrow R;$

(19) *PIP* : a set of part interpolation points;

(20) *psif* : part seam interpolation function:

$psif : PSV \rightarrow \bigcup_{n} PIP^n;$

(21) *paif* : part allowance interpolation function:

$paif : PAV \rightarrow \bigcup_{n} PIP^{n};$

(22) *pnif* : part nonloop segment interpolation function:

$pnif : PNS \rightarrow \bigcup_{n} PIP^{n};$

(23) *picf* : part interpolation coordinate function:

$picf : PIP \rightarrow R^{2}.$

To manipulate the data of a part seam, we need seven actions. "Create" and "delete" change the number of part seam loops. "Divide" and "connect" insert and delete a vertex of a part seam loop, respectively. These four actions alter the topology a of part seam. "Move" moves a vertex of a part seam loop. "Add" and "remove" transform an edge of a part seam loop. The latter three actions change the geometry of a part seam.

Definition (Actions on Part Seam)

(1) *create(l)*   : create a part seam loop *l*:
{

       $PSL \leftarrow PSL + \{l\};$

       $pslf(l) \leftarrow (\ );$

}

(2) *delete (l)*   : delete a part seam loop *l*:
{

       for all $v \in PSV$

          $pslf(l) = (.., v, ..)$

            $\Rightarrow PSV \leftarrow PSV - \{v\};$

       $PSL \leftarrow PSL - \{l\};$

}

(3) *divide (l,v,x,y)*   : divide a part seam edge associated with a part seam vertex *v* in loop *l* into two part seam edges and insert a part seam vertex *v'*:
{

       (* suppose *pslf(l)* is (v1, v2, .. ,v, v", .. ,vn) *)

       $PSV \leftarrow PSV + \{v'\};$

       $pslf(l) \leftarrow (v1, v2, .. ,v, v', v", .. ,vn);$

       $pscf(v') \leftarrow (x, y);$

       $psif(v) \leftarrow (\ );$

       $psif(v') \leftarrow (\ );$

}

---

*Part Mark Attribute: Part mark attributes, such as grainline, notches, and placement of buttons, have to be also defined.

Definition (Part Mark Attribute)

  PMA : a set of part mark attributes;

(4) *connect (l,v)*   : connect two part seam edges and delete a part seam vertex *v* in loop *l*:
{
       (* suppose *pslf(l) is (v1, v2, .. ,v', v, v", .. ,vn)*)
       pslf(l) ← *(v1, v2, .. ,v', v", .. ,vn);*
       PSV ← *PSV - {v};*
       psif(v') ← *( );*
}

(5) *move (v,x,y)*   : move a part seam vertex *v*:
{
       pscf(v) ← *(x, y);*
}

(6) *add (v,n,p[])*   : add the part interpolation points *p1,.., pn* to a part seam edge associated with a part seam vertex *v*:
{
       psif(v) ← *(p1, .., pn);*
}

(7) *remove (v)*   : remove the part interpolation points from a part seam edge associated with a part seam vertex *v*:
{
       psif(v) ← *( );*
}

In VIRGO, such mathematical notations help specify the system clearly . Hence, system verification tasks become easier.

IV A Functional Model for CSG

This section introduces an experimental CSG system [WYVI85] which models solid objects by functions which are represented in the computer as procedures [KAJI83]. We are using a space division technique, based on the octree, to combine our functional definitions and enable the set operations of CSG.

4.1 Motivation

Constructive Solid Geometry (CSG) systems allow the user to describe a solid shape as a combination of other simpler shapes. The object in Figure 4 is a block from which one cylinder has been subtracted and one has been added. Its description in a directed acyclic graph (DAG) is also shown in the figure. Each vertex represents either a primitive object or a combination of other objects. A DAG is used rather than a tree structure because the same sub-object can be used many times in a particular description.

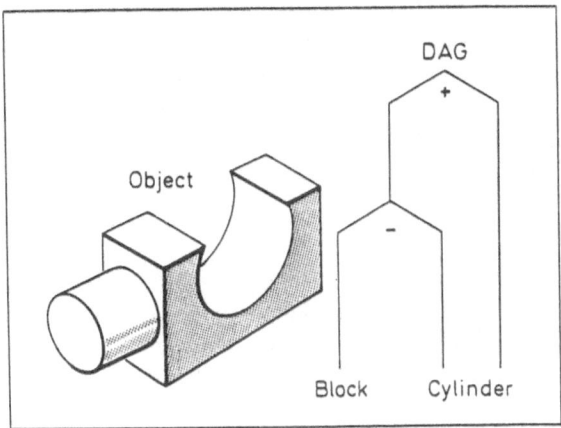

Figure 4

The DAG, however, only provides a description of the object. There must also be a means of extracting useful information from the structure. Most systems do this by converting the solid description into a boundary representation.

Ideally, we would like to represent solid objects in a way which inherently describes their properties as solids. Then we could extract any information we wanted about the solid from its definition.

For example, we would like to:

1) construct models for each application without radically changing the structure,
2) know the rules for sketching the objects, and
3) represent infinite sets of points defined by set operations with sufficient accuracy in a computer of modest size.

There is one way to handle all these tasks with a single structure: the procedure. A procedure can provide a functional definition of an almost infinite set of points or describe the rules for sketching an object, like a cylinder. If all our solid objects are represented by a set of procedures, we can describe any of their properties using the full power and flexibility of a programming language. In addition, we can extend our definitions easily and systematically if extra properties are needed for particular applications.

To combine and manipulate objects described by procedures, in our experimental system, we have defined the interface required to match a procedure to a purpose, and then written procedures conforming to the required pattern for each of our 'primitive objects'. This means that other parts of the system use the same code to extract information from a structure whether that structure represents a cylinder, a sphere or any other primitive shape. The calling routine 'knows' only that a primitive has been encountered. The detail is left to the routine which belongs to the particular primitive.

Now the primitive procedures associated with a cylinder, for example, do not include solving equations of intersection with other primitive shapes. This would make our primitive procedures interdependent. Instead we use a system of space division analogous to the octree to separate our primitive components into different compartments. Only one primitive is allowed in one compartment. This device enables us to use a truly 'solid' representation for our objects.

4.2 DAGs and Descriptions

Our first data structure is the DAG. When a designer creates a description of an object, it is stored here. In our experimental system, the DAG is built from a text description. The following describes the crankshaft shown in Figure 5.

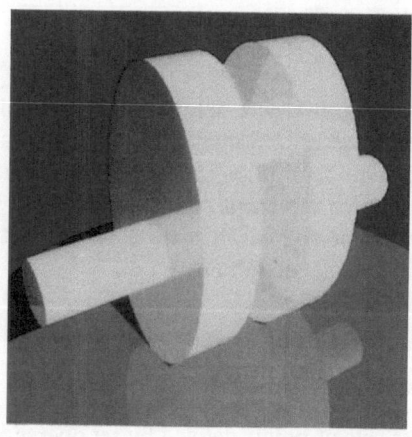

Figure 5

```
slab = new(plane);
LINK(slab, MINUS, shift(0.0, 0.0, 1.0, new(plane)));
tool = slab;
    LINK(tool, MINUS, new(cylinder));
crank = stretch (1.0, 1.0, 14.0, new(slab));
    LINK(crank, MINUS, shift(-1.0, 0.0, -1.0,
                            stretch(5.0, 3.0, 16.0,new(tool))));
    LINK(crank, MINUS, shift(0.0, 0.0, 10.0,
                            stretch(1.0, 1.0, 5.0, new(tool))));
    LINK(crank, MINUS, shift(0.0, 0.0, -1.0,
                            stretch(1.0, 1.0, 5.0, new(tool))));
    LINK(crank, MINUS, shift(-3.0, 0.0, 6.0,
                            stretch(1.0, 1.0, 2.0, new(tool))));
```

Units are arbitrary, as scaling takes place later. This description creates three objects: "slab", "tool", and "crank" from the primitives* "plane" and "cylinder". The object "plane" represents a universe in which all points below the x,y plane are empty and everywhere else is full. The object "cylinder" represents a solid cylinder of unit radius and infinite length whose center coincides with the z axis.

To understand the rest of this notation, it is necessary to understand the structure of the DAG in some detail. This DAG is shown in Figure 6. Each of the named objects: "slab", "tool", and "crank", points to a definition which is a list of DAG elements. In the Figure, this list is shown linked by broken, horizontal arrows. Each DAG element in the list represents an instance of some object. An instance is best thought of as a request to put a copy of the object in the current definition. In the DAG, instances are represented by pointers to definitions. In the Figure, these are the solid, vertical pointers.

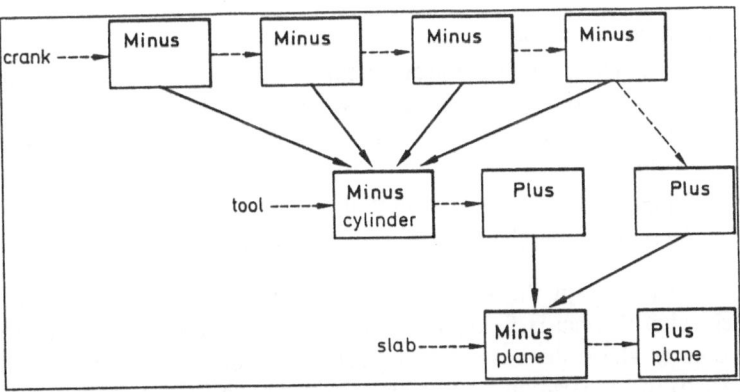

Figure 6

The LINK command (above) links a DAG element as an instance, into an existing definition. Thus four LINK commands connect four copies of "tool" to "crank". The keyword "MINUS" tells us that the set subtraction operation is to be used. The alternative is "PLUS", indicating set addition. We use the word addition in preference to union because our system does not permit conventional set union. If two objects overlap after an addition, this is flagged as an error.

The DAG elements also contain information about the position in space of the instance to which they refer. This information is a position and orientation with

---

*The simplest objects are called "primitives".

respect to the current definition. It is represented in the DAG element by a matrix of real numbers e.g.:

$$
\begin{bmatrix}
a & b & c & d \\
e & f & g & h \\
i & j & k & l \\
0 & 0 & 0 & 1
\end{bmatrix}
*
\begin{bmatrix}
x \\
y \\
z \\
1
\end{bmatrix}
=
\begin{bmatrix}
ax + by + cz + d \\
ex + fy + gz + h \\
ix + jy + kz + l \\
1
\end{bmatrix}
$$

This matrix transforms the point $<x,y,z>$ into some other coordinate system. The elements d,h,l describe a translation of $<x,y,z>$ and the other elements describe rotation and magnification. For reasons of efficiency, we also store the inverse matrix in each DAG element and we shall return to this point later. The detailed structure of a DAG element is as follows:

Mode : PLUS or MINUS

Trans : A pair of matrices which describe the position of this instance in the current definition.

This : A pointer to another object's definition. (This instance.) This can alternatively point to a structure which contains the procedures which describe a primitive object. In that case we say the DAG element is 'primitive'.

Next : A pointer to the next element of this definition.

Props : A pointer to another structure containing properties of this instance.

Now we can explain the rest of the description. The functions "shift" and "stretch" alter the matrix fields of the DAG element on which they act: shift (x, y, z, object) alters the matrices in "object" so that the instance is shifted (translated) to the position $<x,y,z>$; similarly, stretch (x, y, z, object) alters the matrix, magnifying the instance by x, y and z in the three coordinate axes. This operation is very useful. It converts cubes into brick shapes and cylinders into ellipsoids. There is also a "rotate" function and a "new" function which creates a copy of a DAG element.

4.3 The Octree Structure

An octree [JACK80] [MEAG82] is a tree structure which describes the division of a cubic region of space into smaller cubes (Figure 7). Each cube can be 'full' or 'empty' or further divided into smaller cubes ('partial'). In the tree structure, a 'full' or 'empty' cube is represented by a leaf-node and a 'partial' cube is represented by pointers to nodes which represent the eight sub-cubes into which it is divided. This structure can represent any solid shape, approximately, and the operations of set union and subtraction can be performed with very simple algorithms. Unfortunately, octree structures are fairly large and some of the information in the original structure is lost when conversion to octree takes place. For example, if you want to display such an object by ray-tracing, how do you find the surface normal?

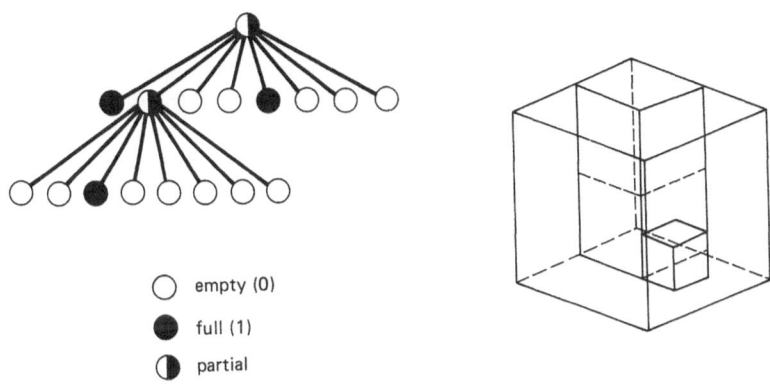

○ empty (0)

● full (1)

◑ partial

Figure 7

Another related structure has been suggested by Yamaguchi, Kunii et al. [YAMA84] and independently by Carlbom [CARL85]. Space is divided, recursively, as for an octree, but the leaves of the tree are also allowed to represent cubes which contain a single plane, edge, or vertex of the original object's boundary. This structure is more compact than an octree and it may prove very suitable for some applications. But it is essentially an efficient way to handle a boundary representation.

In our functional CSG model, we use an octree-related structure for separating the primitive components of a solid described by a DAG so they can be accessed, in arbitrary sequence, by display or other routines. More precisely, we construct a tree in which each node corresponds to a cubical region of space. If the node is not a leaf of the tree, then the region of space is 'partial' and further divided into eight sub-cubes which correspond to the eight sub-nodes of the tree. If the node is a leaf of the tree, then it represents a cube which:

1) is Full,
2) is Empty,
3) contains boundaries between empty space and one primitive object,
4) contains boundaries between full space and one primitive object (In this case the object is being subtracted from full space), or
5) represents a volume of space less than the limit of system resolution.

Note that the leaf nodes in Figure 7 above would also be partial and have 'children,' with no limit on resolution. We refer to these cells as "nasty" as there is no easy way to extract information from them. Surprisingly, the presence of nasty cells is quite acceptable. They occur along edges where primitive objects meet. Provided the resolution is reasonably high, the volume occupied by the nasty cells is a vanishingly small proportion of the total and we can ignore it even in exacting applications like ray tracing. The resolution used to create Figure 5 was about one thousand. This corresponds to ten levels of octree division. The relationship between the tree and the corresponding area of space is shown in Figure 8. Note that this structure differs from [YAMA84] and [CARL85] in that the leaf nodes refer to a primitive solid object and not to part of a plane, edge, or vertex. Further details of our octree structure creation are described in [WYVI85].

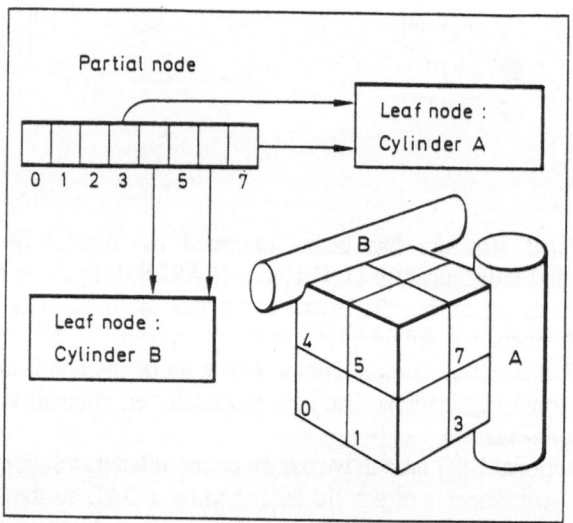

Figure 8

V ANIMENGINE: an Engineering Animation System

In the area of computer integrated manufacturing (CIM), an animation is very useful for engineering design, and especially, manufacturing design, and for verifying movement of designed objects during assembly process. ANIMENGINE, introduced in this section, is an engineering animation system, and it aims to help designers find and solve the problems encountered in the design process with a superior man/machine interface.

5.1 Requirements

In contrast with costly, realistic, image-oriented entertainment animation, an engineering animation system needs to meet the following requirements:

1) Exact and Unambiguous Display of Objects:

Objects to be animated in engineering applications are parts, modules, units of production, and assembly machines such as robots. They must be displayed exactly and unambiguously with a solid appearance.

2) High-speed and Automatic Production of Engineering Animations:

An engineering animation needs to be produced as fast as possible to encourage communication between designers, engineers, and workers. In addition, engineering animations should be produced automatically.

3) Lower Host Dependency and Cost Saving:

Typically, several work stations will share a central host computer and these must not put too heavy a load on the host computer. The system must be constantly available during the design process, and the work stations should be inexpensive.

5.2 Design Decisions

Based on the previous three requirements, we made the following design decisions for ANIMENGINE.

1) From the first requirement:

We selected a raster display, because we needed to display solid areas of color and patterns to make the components of our pictures identifiable.

2) From the second requirement:

A real-time animation system is ideal, but hardware for a real-time raster graphics animation system is expensive. Instead, we decided to use an interactive video display combined with a video recorder. The designer can see his or her animation a frame at a time and record each frame for later display as a smooth animation. This system configuration produces frames fairly quickly, several frames per minute, and the designer can get a good impression of what the animation will look like as it is produced. We call this "pseudo real-time animation".

3) From the third requirement:

In order to achieve the lower host dependency, we need to utilize an intelligent graphic device.

5.3 Projection

For the internal data of the intelligent graphic device, three dimensional data are preferable, but two-dimensional, intelligent graphic devices are useful, too. This comes from the fact that much of the motion we wish to display is parallel motion combined with simple rotation and this can be done with a two-dimensional display.

If the movements of the displayed objects are parallel and the projection is a parallel or oblique projection, then we can treat shifting (translation) of an object in the three-dimensional object space as shifting in the two-dimensional projected plane. The case of parallel projection is shown in Figure 9. The projection of an object M which is shifted by (x,y,z) in the object space is the same as the projection of M shifted $xP_x + yP_y + zP_z$ in the projected plane, where P_x, P_y, P_z are projections of unit vectors in the object space. Accordingly, we decided to employ a two-dimensional graphic device and to adopt parallel projection, especially, axonometric projection. This means that for parallel motion we need only transmit a projection of an object's shape to the work station once, and the animation can be produced locally. Of course, in the case of rotating objects we have to transmit a different projection for each frame. As a matter of fact, most of the rotations can be treated easily by "template models" described later.

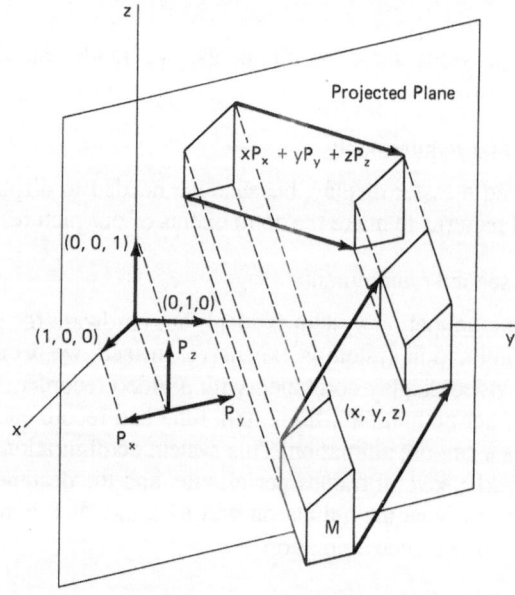

Figure 9

5.4 Cartographic Display Technics and Drawing Edges

As is the case with cartographic displays, colors of each object need not be realistic, just unique to each object. Of course, the color of each face varies within certain limits depending on the shading effect. This makes identification of each object easier. Characteristic textures are also used for the same purpose.

ANIMENGINE can display symbolic marks and/or additional lines. Symbolic marks are used to express the positions of small holes or unseen points. Additional lines can represent the directions of movements or the center lines of shafts. These are called "cartographic" display technics.

To make the hidden surfaces recognizable, ANIMENGINE can display edges of hidden surfaces together with visible surfaces and edges enabling us to recognize the whole shape of a given object.

These display rules are modeled as a presentation model in ANIMENGINE, and the system converts the data in B-reps into the data in this presentation model.

5.5 Hidden Surface Problem in a Dynamic Environment

Hidden surface removal is usually done with a static environment and a static view-point. If we apply it to an animation it takes a lot of time because it is necessary to repeat the calculation for each picture.

We, therefore, wish to remove hidden surfaces of several frames at the same time. Our algorithm is based on the painter's algorithm, and currently can deal with objects only in parallel and uniform motion. The algorithm is described in [NOMA85] in detail.

5.6 Template Model

ANIMENGINE adopts boundary representation as its figure model and is a general and advantageous model for animation. It is not always appropriate to have boundary representation data for all objects. For example, shafts, rings, bolts, nuts, and screws appear quite frequently in an engineering animation. They have the same shape within a particular type and only their sizes differ.

Just as a template is used when drafting, to draw figures which often appear but are hard to draw, so ANIMENGINE enables us to specify regular parts as "template models".

A template model is a kind of presentation model. It consists of the the part name and a list of numbers to specify its size, and when the template model is drawn, drawing information in Template Database is used. Generally, the drawing information does not include solid models or full specifications of the shape in three-dimensional space, but only rules for drawing. Therefore invisible 'back' surfaces can be omitted.

Two examples of template rules for drawing a cylinder are shown in Figure

10. Figure 10 (a) has shading effects on the curved surface and Figure 10 (b) is without shading. Note that the back faces are not considered. Whether Figure 10 (a) or (b) is adopted is determined by the entry in Template Database.

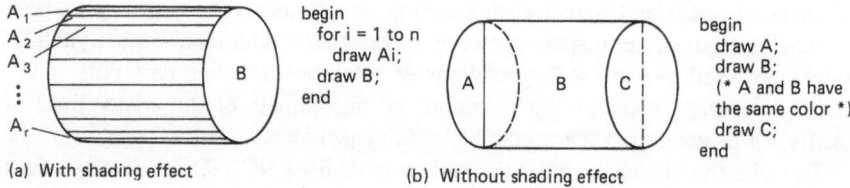

(a) With shading effect

(b) Without shading effect

Figure 10

Template models have another advantage, which is for handling object rotation. For example, when a shaft, specified as a "template model", rotates around its center line, it need neither be redrawn nor does it require its shape data transferred from the host computer. This is because its rotation does not change the way it is drawn. Note that the way in which the template is designed is important here. Suppose a shaft is defined by an inappropriate boundary representation, say a polygonal approximation, then the view of its boundary differs after rotation (Figure 11). It then becomes necessary to redraw its shape repeatedly during its rotation. What is worse is that, in this case, the shape data would be transmitted from the host, repeatedly.

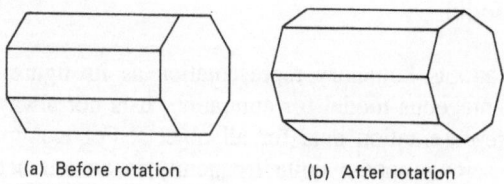

(a) Before rotation   (b) After rotation

Figure 11

5.7 Examples

Figure 12 is a simulation of assembling a copier. Each module is identified with its characteristic colors, and a robot hand and its arm gripping a drum module are identified with a texture. Two sets of three red triangles are symbolic marks. The right-hand set represents the positions of screws on a drum module and the left-hand set is the corresponding positions on a base module. Edges of hidden surfaces help to represent the whole shape of each module.

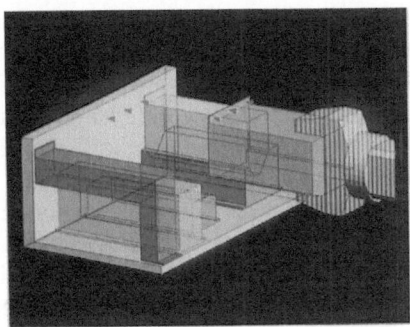

Figure 12

Figure 13 is a simulation of setting rings onto a shaft. The shaft and the rings are defined as template models. Additional lines indicate the center line of the shaft.

Figure 13

VI Nested Table Data Model

This section introduces a nested table data model (NTD) as a powerful data modeling tool for the manipulation of business and engineering (including graphics) data.

6.1 Table Model

Business data are usually in business forms as well as text forms. The real draw-ing and engineering information is also accompanied by data in table form such as part/supplier tables and stock/order tables. As for the management of tables of data, the relational data model is well known [CODD70]. One of its remarkable features is its logical simplicity based on data-independent flat structure. However, relations in the model are often too primitive to handle actual business and engineering-form data. Our model is required to handle more complex struc-tures, to accommodate diverse views of the application data, and to represent more varieties of semantic relationships.

A Nested Table Data model *(NTD)* is introduced as a straightforward, uniform data representation form [KITA82]. In 6.2 we define nested tables. 6.3 defines four fundamental operators, which are called form transformers on nested tables. 6.4 illustrates table transformation through a simple example.

6.2 Nested Tables

A nested table *(NT)* is a table with nests of columns and rows. Some ter-minology is introduced as follows.

field: a column in an *NT*;

root: the top level field in NT hierarchy;

components: child fields of the given field;

occurrences: data values actually appearing in the table contents;

tuple: a row in an *NT*;

simple/group fields: fields of at least one component are called group fields, and otherwise simple;

(non-)repeating fields: fields which have set of tuples are called to be repeat-ing, and otherwise non-repeating.

Let us look at the example in Figure 14. Repeating fields are tagged with as-terisks. We observe that fields of nested table *PART-SUPPLY-FORM are clas-sified as follows.

1) non-repeating simple fields : SID, PID, TYPE, QTY, YEAR, MONTH, DAY,

2) repeating simple fields: none,

3) non-repeating group fields: PART, DATE,

4) repeating group fields: *PART-SUPPLY-FORM, *SLIST.

Each field F has a domain *dom(F)* of its occurrences. Domains have to obey the following constraints:

1) if F is a non-repeating simple field, *dom(F)* is a set of atomic data items (e.g., integers, character strings, texts, and images),

*PART-SUPPLY-FORM						
SID	PART		*SLIST			
	PID	TYPE	QTY	DATE		
				YEAR	MONTH	DAY
1	1	A	50	80	MAY	15
			60	80	JUN	3
1	2	A	30	80	JUN	3
1	3	B	20	80	MAY	24
2	3	B	100	80	MAY	15
			50	80	JUN	3
3	2	A	10	80	MAY	24
			50	80	JUN	3
⋮	⋮	⋮	⋮	⋮	⋮	⋮

Figure 6.14 Nested Table *PART-SUPPLY-FORM

2) If F is a repeating simple field, $dom(F)$ is the power set of a set of atomic data items,

3) if F is a non-repeating group field, and $C1,...Cn$ are its components, then
$$dom(F) \subseteq C1 \times C2 \times ... \times Cn, \text{ and}$$

4) if F is a repeating group field, and $C1,...Cn$ are its components, then,
$$dom(F) \subseteq 2(C1 \times C2 \times ... \times Cn),$$
(the power set of $C1 \times C2 \times ... \times Cn$))

Here $C1 \times C2 \times ... \times Cn$ denotes the Cartesian product of sets $dom(C1),..$ $dom(Cn)$. An occurrence of filed Ci in a tuple t is denoted by $t[Ci]$. This notation is also used for a group field.

6.3 Form Transformer Operators

Next, four operators on NT's for 'ennesting' and 'denesting' columns and/or rows are defined. They are Column Ennest (CE), Column Denest (CD), Row Ennest (RE), and Row Denest (RD). Those are referred to as FT (form transformer) operators. Here let $F1,...Fn$, and H be components, F be a non-repeating component, and $*F$ be a repeating component of some group field G, respectively.

1) **Column Ennest : $CE[F1,...Fn$ INTO $H]$**
This operator creates a new non-repeating group field H as a component of G and changes $F1,..., Fn$ into components of H.

2) **Column Denest : $CD[H]$**
This operator erases field H from G, and component $F1,..., Fn$ of H is changed into those of G.

3) **Row Ennest :** *RE[F]*

This operator changes non-repeating field *F* into a repeating field **F* according to occurrences of fields other than *F*.

4) **Row Denest :** *RD[*F]*

This operator changes repeating field **F* into non-repeating field *F*.

The above four *FT* operators' functions are illustrated in Figure 15.

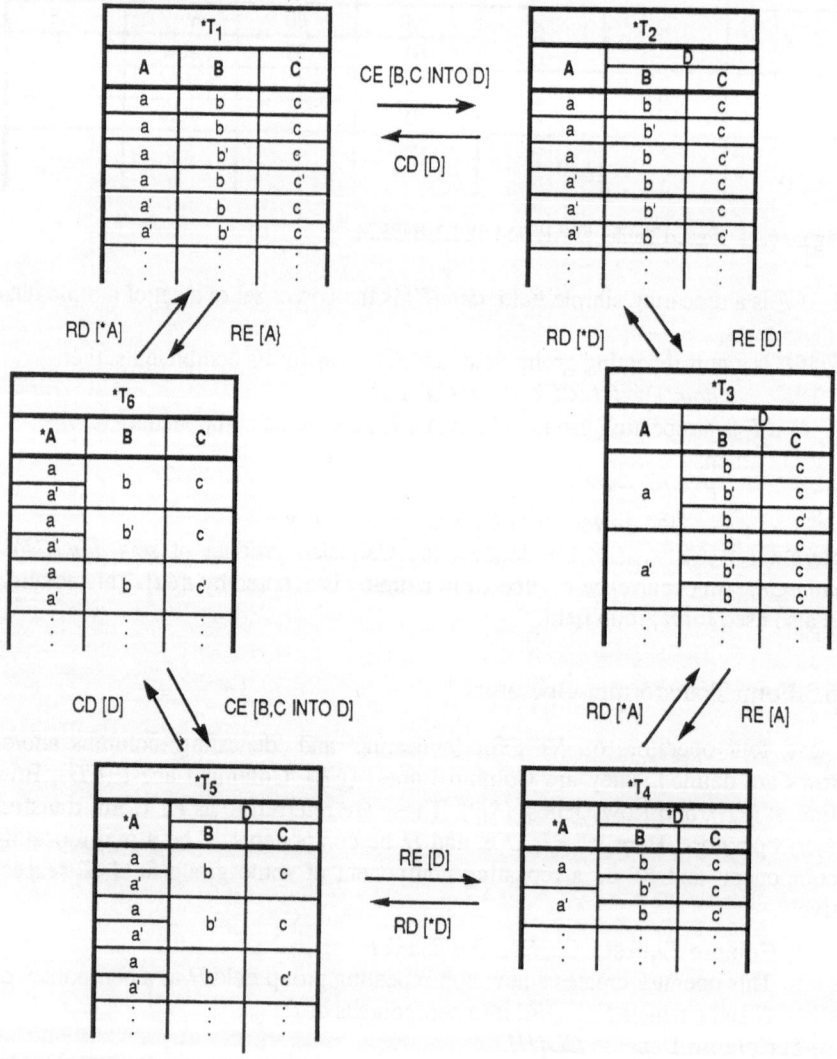

Figure 15

6.4 Transformation Example

The *FT* operators are used to reform a given *NT* into another one that is most appropriate for application data use in information retrieval, report generation, etc. An *NT* *PART-SUPPLY-FORM in Figure 14 fits data usage such as:

(usage 1) find the date(s) when the supplier *X* supplied the part *Y*,

(usage 2) find the combination(s) of a supplier and a part such that the supplier has supplied the part more than *X* times, and

(usage 3) find the combination(s) of a supplier and a part such that the quantity of parts supplied is always greater than *X*.

Those queries are easily formulated as the selection operator applied to *PART-SUPPLY-FORM. However, it is not well-suited both for a user view on which queries are formulated and for a report form:

(usage 4) for each day, find the part supply of each supplier,

(usage 5) find the date(s) when each supplier supplied all kinds of parts, and

(usage 6) find the date(s) when the total quantity of parts supplied by each supplier is greater than *X*.

To evaluate these queries more easily, we can construct another *NT* *YET-ANOTHER-PART-SUPPLY-FORM as shown in Figure 16. This NT can be derived from the original *NT* *PART-SUPPLY-FORM by the following sequence of *FT* operators:

*RD[*SLIST];*

CD[SLIST];

CE[PART, QTY INTO SLIST-PER-SUPPLIER];

CE[SID, SLIST-PER-SUPPLIER INTO SLIST-PER-DATE];

RE[SLIST-PER-DATE];

RE[SLIST-PER-SUPPLIER].

Note that there are some other sequences of the *FT* operators which get the same result.

6.5 Discussions

In [KITA82], functional dependency and multivalued dependency in *NT*'s are formalized to examine the assurance of the reversibility and commutability of *FT* operators. Furthermore [KITA84] proposed the architecture of a form-based graphics data base workbench system named Formgraphics. The system has a three-layer model-hierarchy. The two higher layers are form management layers, where the user handles data as well-organized sets of form documents, and

*YET-ANOTHER-PART-SUPPLY-FORM						
*SLIST-PER-DATE				DATE		
	*SLIST-PER-SUPPLIER					
SID	PART		QTY	YEAR	MONTH	DAY
	PID	TYPE				
1	1	A	50	80	MAY	15
2	3	B	100			
1	3	B	20	80	MAY	24
3	2	A	10			
1	1	A	60	80	JUN	3
	2	A	30			
2	3	B	50			
3	2	A	50			
:	:	:	:	:	:	:

Figure 6.16 Nested Table *YET-ANOTHER-PART-SUPPLY-FORM

data processing layers, where several types of data including diagrams, text, and images are manipulated individually. *NTD* is a model of the lowest data management layer and plays a key role as a database processor in uniform data management and dynamic, flexible data handling.

VII Lower Models

7.1 A Graph-Theoretical Approach to Region Detection

This section presents a simple scheme for region detection from pixel arrays using a graph-theoretical model [OHBO79]. First, suppose that a digital picture is modelled as a connected graph in a matrix format, where each node represents a pixel, and each edge has a weight which is defined as the difference of brightness values between adjacent pixels (Figure 17a). There are two criteria to be satisfied for efficient picture segmentation:

1) to traverse the spatially adjacent graph, and

2) to maintain the structural organization of an image.

A data structure which satisfies the criteria is a Minimal Spanning Tree (MST). MST is one of many spanning trees of the graph for which the sum of weights of its edges is minimum. Figure 17(b) shows an MST of the picture graph in Figure 17(a). MST can be constructed by some existing algorithms, for example, Kruskal's Algorithm [KRUS56].

Now we can show a general outline of the MST Traversing Merge (MSTTM) algorithm as follows:

Input: A set of edges of a given MST $ST = <V, A>$ of PG. PG is a partial graph of the given graph $G = <V, E>$, where V is a set of vertices, and E is a set of edges. $A \subset E$.

Output: a partition of A into A_s and $(A-A_s)$.

Algorithm:

Step1: Set $A \leftarrow \phi$.

Step2: Remove an edge (i,j) from A.

Step3: (Let $PST_s = <V, A_s>$ be a partial MST.)
If $P(i, j, PST_s) =$ true then $A_s \leftarrow A_s \cup \{(i,j)\}$.

Step4: Repeat Steps 2-3 until all edges have been removed from A. Then connected component of PST_s of ST represents homogeneous region obtained by the MSTTM.

Here, $P(i,j,PST_s)$ is a merging function which determines whether two homogeneous regions $R(i)$, $R(j)$, PST_s including the vertices i,j in V, should be merged. A candidate of $P(i,j,PST_s)$ is Piece Constant Approximation.* Let $MAX(R(i))$ and $MIN(R(i))$ be a maximal and a minimal value of brightness levels in $R(i)$, respectively. Then $P(i,j,PST_s)$ is defined as follows: ·

$$P(i,j,PST_s) = \begin{cases} \text{true if } |max\{, MAX(R(i)), MAX(R(j))\} - \\ \quad min\{MIN(R(i)), MIN(R(j))\}| < \theta \\ \text{false otherwise} \end{cases}$$

where θ is a specific threshold.

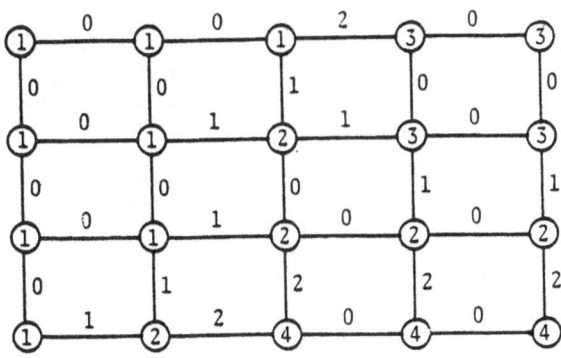

Figure 17(a) A graph representation of picture. Associated with each pixel is a brightness value placed in a circle. Each number above an edge represents a weight value.

---

*We have also defined a preliminary version of a simple biregional merging function $P(i,j,PST)$. See [OHBO79] for more details.

Since MSTTM can traverse edges in the MST in non-decreasing order of weight to take advantage of the Kruskal algorithm property, MSTTM can conceptually be expressed as moving up branches of that decomposition tree of the given image, which is composed of i-thresholded regions. The tree is equivalent to the one constructed by Kirsh's algorithm [KIRS70]. Figure 17c illustrates i-thresholded regions ($i = 0,1,2$) and Figure 17d is the corresponding decomposition tree.

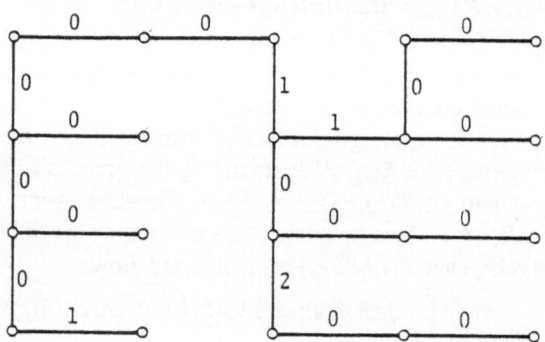

Figure 17(b) MST of the graph in Figure 17(a)

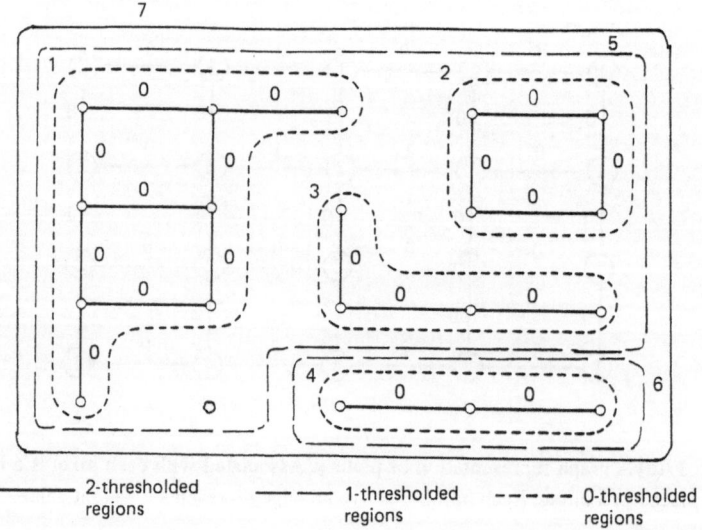

Figure 17(c)

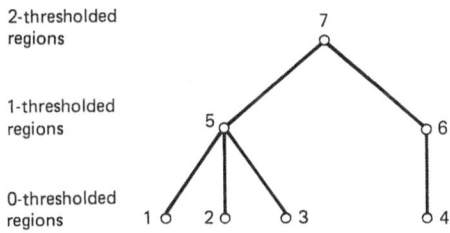

2-thresholded regions

1-thresholded regions

0-thresholded regions

Figure 17(d)

Finally, we show an example of the scene analysis. Figure 18a is the original image, which has 128 x 755 pixels whose brightness ranges from 0 to 127.

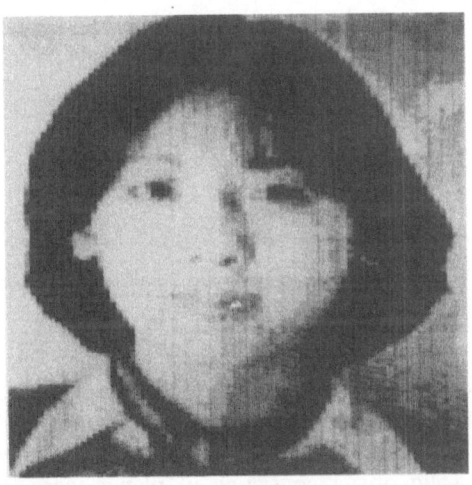

Figure 18(a)

An MST for the image is shown in Figure 18b.

Figure 18(b)

Figure 18c plots boundaries representing the segmentation by MSTTM employing Piecewise Constant Approximation, where θ is 12. As a result, the number of homogeneous regions equals 94.

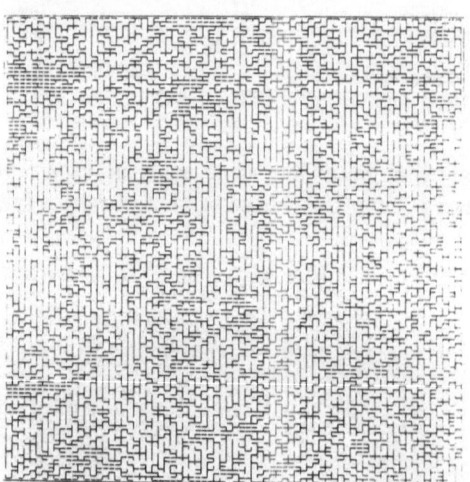

Figure 18(c)

7.2 Top-Down Construction of 3D Mechanical Object Shapes from Engineering Drawings

This section introduces a model of building three-dimensional (3D) objects from engineering drawings with abbreviations and comments [YOSH84].

Markovsky and Wesley [WESL81] developed a procedure for automatic generation of a solid object consisting of planar faces from its projections. Sakurai and Gossard [SAKU83] expanded this method so as to treat non-planar objects such as cylinders.

Both approaches are 'bottom-up', that is, given projections, they start with the simplest elements, which are vertices, and then construct edges and surfaces. These elements are combined to create blocks and finally objects are assembled.

However, these approaches have not been practical so far for the following reasons:

1) They can only handle standardized input, i.e., each projection must be perfect and consistent. However, almost all engineering drawings have some form of abbreviations, following design rules and conventions. These abbreviations make it difficult to enter the drawings directly.

2) They create a large computational load on the host computer, because of the heavy use of combinatorial calculations.

Based on these considerations, we propose a new procedural model for automatically generating 3D objects from engineering drawings, using natural language processing. The following steps summarize this model:

1) A scanner reads everything on an original sheet, that is, the engineering

drawing together with the comments, and digitize them into a binary image.

2) The captured binary image is analyzed to separate the drawing part and comment-character part. At this stage, additional lines and arrows used for pointing to some part of the figure should not be misinterpreted as being part of the projections.

3) Character parts are analyzed using character recognition techniques to form comments.

4) Drawing parts are vectorized, i.e., line patterns in a binary image are recognized to be a line segment in a drawing, and circle patterns are interpreted as a circle, and so on. Furthermore, numbers which indicate edge lengths are interpreted to form an internal data representation of the 2D projection.

5) The edges, circles, and vertices are formed into a 2D geometrical structure.

6) The comments are analyzed using natural language processing techniques.

7) The meaning of the comments and stored knowledge about engineering drawings is used in conjunction with the 2D structure to extract the 3D elements from the projections.

8) The projections are passed to the bottom-up procedure to build a final 3D object. Internally, conventional knowledge is stored in frames, and quad-trees are used to represent drawings. This method is a top-down approach because it mitigates the computational task by denoting the parts of an object in a natural language.

VIII CrossoverNet: A Computer Graphics/ Video Crossover LAN System

In the area of computer integrated manufacturing (CIM), there exists an increasing demand for a network system interconnecting offices and factories. In order to transmit data between the central host computer and local work stations effectively and efficiently, we have developed a local area network (LAN) operating system called CrossoverNet that can handle both digital and analog data. CrossoverNet helps managers, designers, and manufacturers share and control such data. The details of CrossoverNet are shown in [KUNI86b].

8.1 Device-Independent Design

Here we focus on audio-visual (AV) devices for analog data. In a CIM system, they are utilized for communications and monitoring. Most of current AV device control systems have a problem concerning device-dependency of the control programs.

In CrossoverNet, this problem is solved by a model-driven approach. There are two layers of software, a LogicalLayer and a PhysicalLayer, and at each layer, there exists a device model, a LogicalDevice and a PhysicalDevice. A LogicalDevice is an abstract, device model with functions that are characteristic of its type (e.g. a video casette recorder, a TV display). A PhysicalDevice is the device model which reflects an actual device.

In CrossoverNet, most of control software packages are developed in the LogicalLayer. The software in the LogicalLayer controls only LogicalDevices. The software in the PhysicalLayer maps the above functions onto their corresponding low-level descriptions to control the PhysicalDevice. This model-based approach enables us to design and develop generalized and device-independent control software packages.

For example, the LogicalDevice of a TV display may be represented by the combination of the following five items:

1) **source** = {broadcasting, video, RGB};

2) **channel** = {1, 2, ... , n };
   n is the maximum channel number.

3) **sound_mode** = {stereo, sub, mono};
   In case of a bilingual broadcasting program, the "sub" sound_mode switches into subvoice from mainvoice.

4) **sound_volume** P = { 0, 1, ... , m };

5) **power** P = {on, off}.

A user can utilize his/her programs to drive even recently purchased new AV devices by changing only portions of mapping information in the PhysicalLayer. Consequently, the device-independent design prolongs the lifetime of the software beyond that of the individual devices connected to the network.

8.2 Three-Level Hierarchical Structure

The logical structure of CrossoverNet is illustrated in Figure 19. It reflects an original structure of the environment where the system is used. In CrossoverNet, any object in the logical structure is called a LogicalObject. The CrossoverNet LogicalObjects are grouped into the following three levels:

1) a NetworkLevel;

2) a WorkstationLevel;

3) a DeviceLevel
   consisting of

   3.1) a DeviceManagerLevel,

   3.2) a DeviceDeviceLevel.

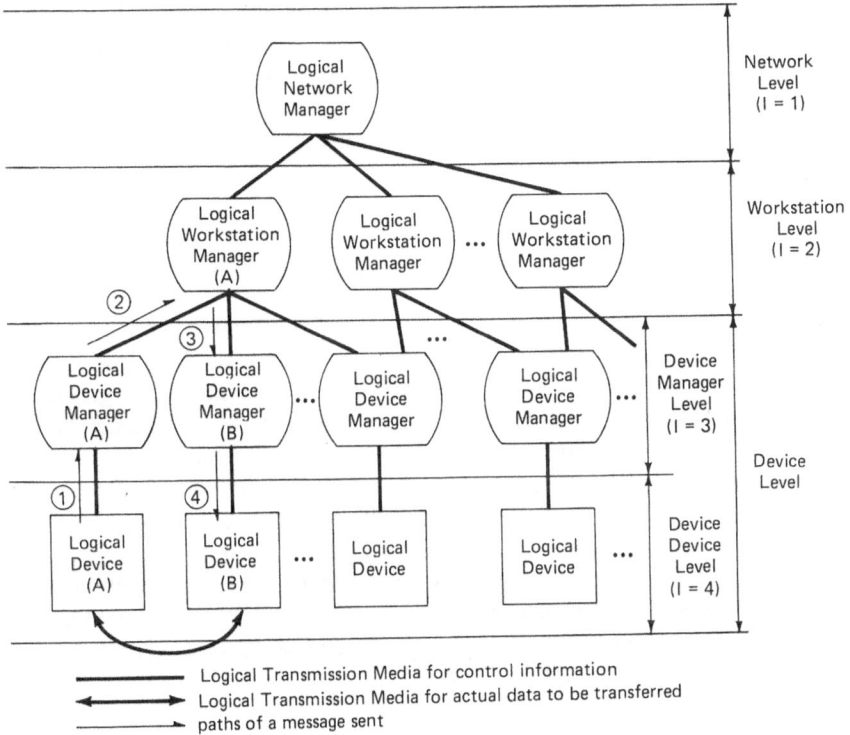

Figure 19

At the DeviceLevel, each LogicalDeviceManager controls a LogicalDevice which is under its supervision. At the next WorkstationLevel, each Logical-WorkstationManager coordinates all the LogicalDeviceManagers in the logical workstation area assigned to it. Finally, at the highest NetworkLevel, all the LogicalWorkstationManagers are supervised by one LogicalNetworkManager.

LogicalObjects are connected by bidirectional, logical, transmission media. These logical transmission media connect LogicalObjects at the different levels, and construct a LogicalObject hierarchical structure. Note that these logical transmission media are hierarchically structured, and that the information whose transmission is restricted by the logical hierarchy of CrossoverNet is not the information contents but the control information. In other words, the logical transmission of the information contents is not restricted by the LogicalObject hierarchy. Suppose, in Figure 19, LogicalDevice(A) wishes to send some control information to LogicalDevice(B). The control information from Logical-Device(A) must reach LogicalDevice(B) via LogicalDeviceManager(A), LogicalWorkstationManager(A), and LogicalDeviceManager(B).

In CrossoverNet, a parent LogicalObject and its child LogicalObject communicate directly. In general, a message from a LogicalObject to another LogicalObject must be sent up to the closest common ancestor LogicalObject first, and then down to the destination LogicalObject. When the message is actually sent, its physical route is decided dynamically at the PhysicalLayer level, and it is independent of the logical route.

IX InteractiveProto: a Menu System Generator

CrossoverNet can enhance its controllability by an interactive and user-friendly menu system through which a user issues commands to control devices. With an automated menu-generator called InteractiveProto, users can easily generate a menu system by their specification based on the menu system model Macro-Menu. This is a good example of a model-navigated data input.

In this section, we limit our attention to a formal definition of MacroMenu. Other aspects are described in [KUNI86a]. MacroMenu is a menu-driven, finite-state transition system. At first, we define a menu-transition graph by which most general-purpose, menu-driven systems can be described. Very often, a menu-driven system is organized in the form of a tree of menus. Therefore, we define a MacroMenu that has a tree structure by imposing some restrictions on a general menu-transition graph.

9.1 Definition of a Menu-Transition Graph

A menu-transition graph is defined as a directed graph. Each node, except an end node, corresponds to a status that holds a menu, and each arc represents a transition which causes an action. At end nodes, the running process is killed and the program is terminated.

Definition (Menu-Transition Graph)

A menu-transition graph G is given by:

$G = (N, T, tf, s, E, M, LB, NA, menu, button, act)$
where

(1)	N	:	a set of nodes;
(2)	T	:	a set of transition arcs;
(3)	tf	:	a transition arc function:
			$tf : T \to N \times N;$
(4)	$s(\in N)$	:	the start node;
(5)	$E(\in N)$	:	a set of end nodes, having no menus;
(6)	M	:	a set of menu images displayed on the screen;
(7)	LB	:	a set of LogicalButtons;
(8)	NA	:	a set of actions;
(9)	$menu$	:	a menu function:

$$menu \quad : \quad N\text{-}E \to M;$$

(10)   *button*   :   a button function mapping a transition arc to a LogicalButton:

$$button \quad : \quad T \to LB;$$

(11)   *act*   :   an action function mapping a transition arc to an action to be taken in the transition:

$$act \quad : \quad T \to NA.$$

A menu-transition graph G has to satisfy the following conditions to maintain the consistency of the system:

1) $\forall n \in N, \exists\, path(s, ..., n)$;

2) $\forall e \in E, \forall n \in N, (e, n) \notin tf(T)$;

3) $\forall n \in N\text{-}E, \exists n' \in N$ such that $n \neq n', (n, n') \in tf(T)$.

4) $\forall n \in N\text{-}E, \forall t, t' \in T, tf(t) = (n, l)$ and
$tf(t') = (n, m)$, and $t \neq t' \Rightarrow button(t) \Rightarrow button(t')$.

Here we define an 'active' arc and an 'active' button of a node as follows:

Definition (Active Arc)

     A transition arc $t \in T$ is an active arc of a node n.
$\Leftrightarrow \exists n' \in N, tf(t) = (n, n')$.
The set of active arcs of a node n is represented by $AA(n)$.

Definition (Active Button)

     A LogicalButton $b \in LB$ is an active button of a node n.
$\Leftrightarrow \exists t \in AA(n), button(t) = b$
The set of active buttons of a node n is represented by $AB(n)$.

In short, the fourth condition for system consistency is that a function *button* is injective when its domain is restricted to the set of active arcs. Then the range is limited to the set of active buttons of the node, and the bijection depending on the node n can be defined as follows:

$$bt_n \quad : \quad AA(n) \to AB(n).$$

So the inverse of bt_n

$$bt_n^{-1} \quad : \quad AB(n) \to AA(n)$$

is also defined. Here we define a destination function *dest* that maps an arc to the node where the arc terminates.

$$dest \quad : \quad T \to N.$$

Definition (Transition Rule of Menu-Transition Graph)

     The n-th node of a menu-transition graph, node(n), is defined as follows:

(1) $node(1) = s$;

(2) Suppose the system is in the node$(n\text{-}1)$ and

$b \in AB(node(n\text{-}1))$ $(n \geq 2)$:

(2i) If $dest(bt_{n-1}^{-1}(b)) \in E$, then $node(n) =$
$dest(bt_{n-1}^{-1}(b))$:

(2ii) If $dest(bt_{n-1}^{-1}(b)) \in E$, then the system terminates and $node(n)$ is undefined.

Consider the state transition of a system represented by a menu-transition graph. Initially, the system is in the "initial state", depicted by the start node of the graph. When the system is in a state represented by a node n^*, the menu (n) is displayed on the screen. When an end-user chooses one of the 'active' buttons, the state of the system changes according to the arc associated with the Logical-Button chosen. The action associated with the transition arc is carried out, and the new state is represented by the node where the arc terminates. Then the image of the new node is displayed. When the button associated with an arc directed to an end node is selected, the system halts after the ending action is executed.

9.2 Definition of MacroMenu

Although the menu-transition graph of the previous section gives a full description of a general-purpose, menu-driven system, the use of a directed graph sometimes complicates menu specification, verification, and operation. A more restricted graph simplifies the task of describing a menu-driven interface program for casual users. Thus, MacroMenu is defined as a restricted menu-transition graph.

In MacroMenu, the LogicalButtons displayed on the screen are called cell icons. Therefore, a set LB and a function $button$ are replaced with a set C of cell icons and a cell function,

$$cell : T \to C$$

respectively. Furthermore, a set M and a function $menu$ are changed into a set B of background menu images and a background menu function bgm

$$bgm : N\text{-}E \to B.$$

In the rest of the paper, an image of the menu on the screen is called a menu frame. A menu frame is defined as follows:

Definition (Menu Frame)

Menu frame $F(n)$ of n is given by:

$$F(n) = (bgm(n), cell(AA(n))).$$

Figure 20 shows an example of a menu frame.

---

*Here, "a state of the system" and "a node of the corresponding menu-transition graph" are used interchangeably, i.e., "the system is in a node n" means "the system is in the state represented by a node n."

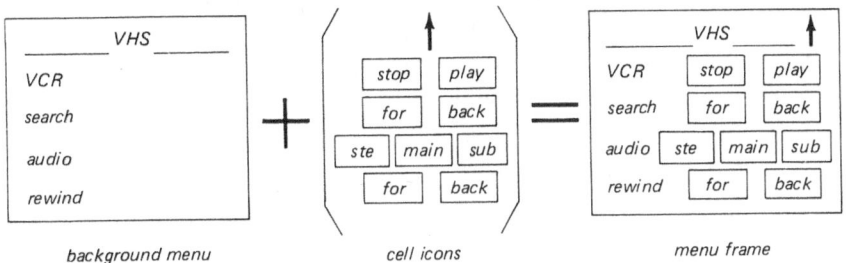

background menu   cell icons   menu frame

Figure 20

Restrictions for MacroMenu.

There are the following five restrictions for *MM*.

Restriction 1

The number of transition arcs mapped to the same image by a function *tf* is at most one, i.e.,

$$\forall t, t' \in T, tf(t) = tf(t') \Rightarrow t = t'.$$

Therefore, an arc is identified with an ordered pair of nodes.

Restriction 2

A 'loop' arc is not permitted:

$$\forall n \in N, (n, n) \notin tf(T).$$

Restriction 3

If there is a transition arc, the corresponding 'reverse' arc must also exist:

$$\forall n, n' \in N, (n, n') \in tf(T) \Rightarrow (n', n) \in tf(T).$$

Then a pair of 'directed' arcs can be treated as one 'undirected' arc, which has a pair of actions to be executed depending on the direction of transition.

Restriction 4

There exists exactly one simple path from a start node to any other node. A simple path is a path on which no node is visited more than once. Consequently, the structure of *MacroMenu* is in the form of a tree. A start node is defined as the root of a tree and each arc can be associated with its 'tacit' direction from a parent node to a child node. To take the full advantage of its tree structure, an up-action function, *uact*, a down-action function, *dact*, an up-cell function, *ucell*, and a down-cell function, *dcell* are defined in place of an action function, *act*, and a cell function, *cell*. The domain of functions *act* and *cell* is a set of arcs. The domain of functions *uact*, *dact*, *ucell*, and *dcell* is a set of nodes.

Restriction 5

When arcs point to the same parent node, their associated actions are identical. That is, control returns to the parent node, the action is executed so that the environment can return to its former state. So the definition of a function *ucell* requires a slight modification. First of all, an equivalent relation E on T is defined by:

$t E t' \Leftrightarrow \mathrm{parent}(t) = \mathrm{parent}(t')$.

Then the quotient set T/E is defined. Then a function g of $n \in N - L$ which maps its argument to an equivalence class $\bar{t}$, the representative of which is an arc t with the parent node n, the given argument. L is a set of leaf nodes of the tree. Thus

$g \quad : \quad N - L \to T/E$.

Next, a function $\bar{\bar{act}}$ is defined. Although *act* is a function of an arc, $\bar{\bar{act}}$ is a function of an equivalent class $\bar{a}$ with the representative t:

$\bar{a} \quad : \quad T/E \to NA$.

Then the function *uact* is defined as follows:

$uact = \bar{a} \circ g$.

It can be easily shown that *uact* is well-defined. The behaviors of the functions are shown in Figure 21.

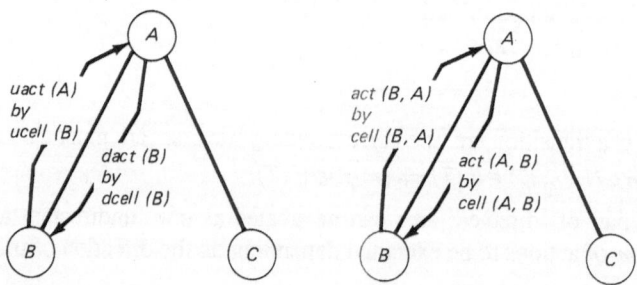

Figure 21

Lastly, an action leaf and an end leaf deserve some explanation. As stated in the second restriction, a loop arc is prohibited and an action without a menu change cannot be incorporated. Therefore, it is necessary to define an action leaf that has no menu frame. When a transition arc connected with an action leaf is picked by means of an icon, the action is executed and the system returns to the parent node of the action leaf. An end node is one sort of action leaf in *MacroMenu*, but in this case, the action is carried out and the system terminates. In what follows, a node which is not an action leaf is a menu node.

Definition (MacroMenu)

MacroMenu M is a tree and it is given by:

$$M = (N, T, A, r, E, B, C, NA, bgm, ucell, dcell, uact, dact)$$

where

(1)　　　　N　:　a set of nodes;

(2)　　　　T　:　a set of unordered pairs of nodes, called transitionarcs;

(3)　$A(\subset N)$　:　a set of action leaves which correspond to actions without menus;

(4)　$r(\in N\text{-}A)$　:　the root of the tree (start node);

(5)　$E(\subset A)$　:　a set of end leaves;

(6)　　　　B　:　a set of background menu images on thescreen;

(7)　　　　C　:　a set of cell icons (areas for interaction on thescreen);

(8)　　　NA　:　a set of actions which is defined below;

(9)　　bgm　:　a background menu function:
　　　　bgm　:　$N - A \rightarrow B$;

(10)　　$ucell$　:　an up-cell function mapping a non-root node to an icon which is associated with a trigger for the transition to its parent node:
　　　　$ucell$　:　$N - \{r\} \rightarrow C$;

(11)　　$dcell$　:　a down-cell function mapping a non-root node to an icon which is associated with a trigger for the transition from its parent node:
　　　　$dcell$　:　$N - \{r\} \rightarrow C$;

(12)　　$uact$　:　an up-action function mapping a non-leaf node to an action to be taken in the transition from ts child node:
　　　　$uact$　:　$N - L \rightarrow NA$;
　　　　where
　　　　L　:　a set of leaf nodes

(13)　　$dact$　:　a down-action function mapping a non-rootnode to an action to be taken in the transition from its parent node:
　　　　$dact$　:　$N - \{r\} \rightarrow NA$.

Conceptually, the transition rule of MacroMenu is identical to that of a menu-transition graph.

Conclusions

A model-driven approach to computer graphics and graphics communication networks has been proven to be superior to a currently popular presentation-oriented approach which tends not to be based on models. Various examples in this article show a spectrum of models from higher to lower levels.

Future research includes clarification of the basic common architecture of model-driven graphics, and of the measure to evaluate the levels of the models from high to low.

Acknowledgements. This work has been sponsored in part by Software Research Center (SRC) of Ricoh Co., Ltd. Special thanks are due to Dr. Hideko S. Kunii, the SRC Director, and Mr. Takao Nawate, General Manager of the Technology Division, Ricoh Co., Ltd. Members of Kunii Laboratory of Computer Science at the University of Tokyo have been helpful in preparation of the manuscript. Mr. Tsukasa Noma's contribution is unforgettable. Mr. Issei Fujishiro has added further help.

References

[CARL85] Carlbom, I. Chakravarty, I., and Vanderschel, D., "A Hierarchical Data Structure for Representing the Spatial Decomposition of 3-D Objects." IEEE CG&A, Vol. 5, No. 4, April 1985, pp. 24-31

[CODD70] Codd, E. F., "A Relational Model for Large Shared Data Bank." CACM, Vol. 13, No. 6, June 1970, pp. 377-387

[JACK80] Jackins, C. L. and Tanimoto, S. L., "Oct-Trees and Their Use in Representing Three Dimensional Objects." Computer Graphics and Image Processing, Vol. 14, No. 3, Nov. 1980, pp. 249-270

[KAJI83] Kajiya, J. T., "New Techniques for Ray-Tracing for Procedurally Defined Objects." Computer Graphics, Vol. 17, No. 3, July 1983, pp. 91-99

[KIRS70] Kirsh, R. A., "Computer Determination of the Constituent Structure of Biological Images." Computers and Biomedical Research, Vol. 4, 1970, pp. 315-328

[KITA82] Kitagawa, H. and Kunii, T. L., "Form Transformer - Formal Aspects of Table Nests Manipulation." in Proc. 15th Ann. Hawaii Int'l Conf. System Sciences, Jan. 1982, pp. 132-141

[KITA84] Kitagawa, H. Kunii, T. L. Azuma, M., and Misaki, S., "Formgraphics: A Form-Based Graphics Architecture Providing a Database Workbench." IEEE CG&A, Vol. 4, No. 6, June 1984, pp. 38-56

[KOPP81] Kopp, E., Rolfo, V., Zelin, B., and Gross, L., Designing Apparel through the Flat Pattern (5th edn.). Fairchild, New York, 1981

[KRUS56] Kruskal, J. B., "On the Shortest Spanning Subtree of a Graph and the Traveling Salesman Problem." in Proc. Amer. Math. Soc., Vol. 7, 1956, pp. 48-50

[KUNI86a] Kunii, T. L. Shirota, Y., and Noma, T., "A Menu Generator for Audio Visual Networks." The Visual Computer, Vol. 2, No. 1, Jan. 1986, pp. 15-30

[KUNI86b] Kunii, T. L. and Shirota, Y., "CrossoverNet: A Computer Graphics/Video Crossover LAN System - Architecture, Design, and Implementation." The Visual Computer, Vol. 2, No. 2, 1986, in press

[MEAG82] Meagher, D., "Geometric Modeling Using Octree Encoding." Computer Graphics and Image Processing, Vol. 19, No. 2, June 1982, pp. 129-147

[NOMA85] Noma, T. and Kunii, T. L., "ANIMENGINE: An Engineering Animation System." IEEE CG&A, Vol. 5, No. 10, Oct. 1985, pp. 24-33

[NOMA86] Noma, T., Terai, K., and Kunii, T. L., "VIRGO: A Computer-Aided Apparel Pattern-Making System." in: Kunii, T.L., (ed.), Advanced Computer Graphics, Springer-Verlag, 1986, pp. 379-401

[OHBO79] Ohbo, N. Shimizu, K., and Kunii, T. L., "A Graph-Theoretical Approach to Region Detection." in Proc. IEEE COMPSAC, Chicago, Nov. 1979, pp. 751-756

[SAKU83] Sakurai, H. and Gossard, D. C., "Solid Model Input Through Orthographic View." Computer Graphics, Vol. 17, No. 3, July 1983, pp. 243-252

[WESL81] Wesley, M. A. and Markovsky, G., "Fleshing Out Projections." IBM J. Research and Development, Vol. 25, No. 6, Nov. 1981, pp. 934-954

[WYVI85] Wyvill, G. and Kunii, T. L., "A Functional Model for Constructive Solid Geometry." The Visual Computer, Vol. 1, No. 1, July 1985, pp. 3-14

[YAMA84] Yamaguchi, K. Kunii, T. L. Fujimura, K., and Toriya, H., "Octree-Related Data Structures and Algorithms." IEEE CG&A, Vol. 4, No. 1, Jan. 1984, pp. 53-59

[YOSH84] Yoshiura, H. Fujimura, K., and Kunii, T. L., "Top-Down Construction of 3-D Mechanical Object Shapes from Engineering Drawings." IEEE Computer, Vol. 17, No. 12, Dec. 1984, pp. 32-40

Understanding the Preparation and Analysis of Solid Models

MICHAEL JOHN MUUSS

Origins and Principles of Solid Modeling

Brief history of design

When prehistoric man began fashioning tools and adapting his surroundings to suit him, the history of design began. Driven by his desires, prehistoric man made plans in the form of ideas and mental images. Whether the implementation of these plans was successful or unsuccessful, the plan and goal remained as private mental images, locked within the mind of the individual.

The limitations of this elegant and simple design process were reached when prehistoric man encountered à stone or tree too massive to be dealt with by a single individual. A new dimension was introduced as he attempted to share his ideas and goals with his peers, and organize their aid. Most likely he communicated his ideas by arranging small stones and sticks to form a miniature representation of the initial state of things, and then to manually manipulate his model step by step (no doubt accompanied by grunts, wild gestures, and significant glances) until the desired final configuration was achieved. Then the group went off to implement the plan in full scale. Variations of this design metholodgy persist into the present.

As evolution progressed and the fashionings of man became more and more complex, the necessity for constructing a physical model to communicate ideas grew cumbersome. Detailed models could require substantial effort to construct, and could be difficult to transport. The time required to construct a model might be a substantial fraction of the time to construct the actual object. Furthermore, insight into the construction process could be difficult without disassembling and reassembling the model. Considerations such as these motivated the next level of abstraction: the drawing. The first drawings were probably simple scratchings in earth or sand, depicting the outlines of the objects involved: a two-dimensional wireframe.

With the passage of time, drawings evolved beyond simple engineering representations into recordings of significant events, and art. Drawings were enhanced with color and shading in an attempt to more accurately convey the three-dimensional nature of reality. As the field of engineering progressed further, draftsmen began explicitly providing indications of the three-dimensional nature of their subjects by representing hidden and false edges as light or broken lines, [REQU82], such as in Figure 1. Subsequent to this development, drafting advanced very little, and has persisted nearly unchanged up to the present.

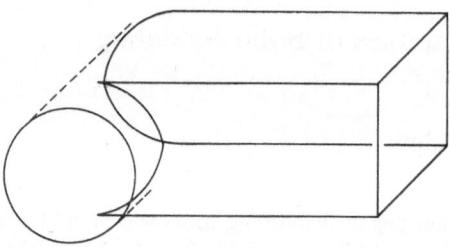

Figure 1 - Wireframe Ambiguity

The digital computer provides the opportunity for nearly infinite variety in the representation of information within it. Improving the design of complex, expensive objects is always an area ripe for technological improvements, and with the emergence of graphics displays, computer-aided design (CAD) packages began to appear. Designers of early CAD packages focused their efforts on the most tedious, time-consuming, and unrewarding aspect of conventional design: the process of converting a designer's sketches and notes into finished engineering drawings suitable for use by a manufacturing facility—the drafting process. Thus, while computers offered the ability to create arbitrarily powerful mathematical representations for objects, initial CAD systems replicated traditional two-dimensional drafting techniques. Only modest gains in efficiency were made in creating the first version of a design, but tremendous gains were made when design modifications were needed, because the computer retains and redraws the unchanged portions of the drawing.

Once a computer-aided drafting system has been used to create a computer representation of a design, the designer (and his management) is often tempted to expect more out of the computer system than simply drawings. One would expect that a representation that depicted the boundaries of an object from several views would provide sufficient information for computing a whole variety of useful facts about the model, such as center of mass, volume, cross-sectional area, etc. Two-dimensional drafting systems were poorly prepared for this sort of interrogation. With the addition of appropriate connectivity and material property information, these capabilities became possible, giving rise to 2.5-dimensional drafting systems, which are frequently called 3-dimensional wireframe systems. For limited analysis, 2.5-dimensional models may provide all the required information.

Four major types of difficulties have plagued wireframe systems. First, the user is required to supply a large amount of information, often at a very low level. Because of the drafting heritage, some of this information may be "construction lines" that do not actually contribute to the ultimate shape of any object. Second, because the user is providing such low-level information, objects can easily be defined which can not be physically realized due to non-closed faces and dangling lines. Third, it is possible to construct a wireframe which might represent several different solid objects; additional information is needed to disambiguate the description. Finally, wireframe models may include lines representing false edges such as profile lines and silhouettes, leading to ambiguous interpretations [REQU82]. These issues have driven the refinement of drafting-type systems, but have also focused attention on the quiet evolution of an entirely different approach to representing objects: solid models.

What is a solid model?

A solid model is a computer description of closed, solid, three-dimensional shapes represented by an analytical framework within which the three-dimensional material can be completely and unambiguously defined [DIET83]. Solid models differ from drafting-type systems in several important ways: objects are composed of combinations of primitive objects (some quite complex), each of which is complete, unambiguous, physically realizable, and modifiable. Because these properties hold for the primitive objects, they hold for any Boolean combinations as well.

Completeness is assured because the representation contains a full description of a piece of solid matter; there is no view-specific information. Because the solid matter is completely described, there is no possibility for ambiguity. For primitive solids defined by specifying parameters to an analytic function, there is no possibility of having missing faces, loose edges, or other similar defects. Systems which offer boundary representations as primitive solids must carefully validate each such solid when it is created. Because solid modeling systems generally do not attempt to compute an exact analytic representation of the surfaces of all the objects, but instead derive the actual surfaces by evaluating the Boolean combination expressions in the model interrogation process (such as by ray-tracing), a solid model is always amenable to further modification by Boolean combination with other shapes.

These properties guarantee that all the spatial information necessary for any subsequent analysis is directly available from the model representation. Object structure and material properties can be computed at any arbitrary point in the model or along all points of an arbitrary directed ray at any time. Therefore, solid modeling technology is particularly suited to the automation of many manufacturing and analysis tasks.

The Design Loop

Solid models are very useful for generating drawings or pictures of the modeled object, from any viewpoint. The power of this capability alone usually pays for the cost of developing the model. However, the solid model has a much larger role in the design process than simply automating the production of pictures and engineering drawings. Properly utilized, the solid model becomes the central element in the iterative process of taking a design from idea to prototype design to working design to optimized design. This iterative process is termed the "design loop", and is illustrated in Figure 2.

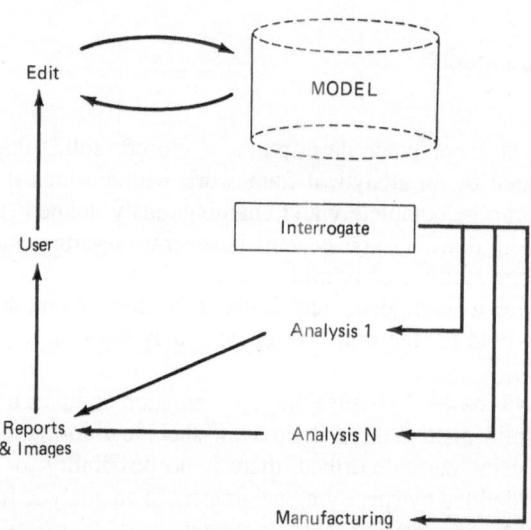

Figure 2 - The Design Loop

In a full scale solid modeling system, there is no need for initial drawings; the designer expresses the initial structures directly into the modeling system's editor, just as a modern author creates his "rough draft" directly into a word processor. At the completion of each version of the design, the model is subjected to a battery of analyses appropriate to the function of the object being designed. Strength, volume, weight, level of protection, and other similar evaluations can be reported, along with the production of a variety of images and/or drawings. These automated analyses help identify weaknesses or deficiencies in a design *early in the design process*. By detecting flaws early, the designer has the opportunity to correct his plans before having invested too much time in a bad design, or the designer can switch to an entirely different approach which may seem more promising than the original one. In this way, the solid modeling system allows the designer to concentrate on the important, creative aspects of the design process. Freeing the designer of routine analysis permits designs to be finished in less time than previously required, or allows much more rigorously optimized designs to be delivered in comparable timeframes and at the same cost as unoptimized designs created using older techniques [DEIT85].

A highly interactive modeling system can allow full designs to be completed in a matter of days, where weeks or months may have previously been required [DEIT82]. Furthermore, the modeling system allows sweeping design changes to be made quickly and cheaply, allowing great flexibility in the face of ever changing requirements and markets. The time needed to create a new product can be further decreased by re-utilizing elements of earlier models and then modifying them as appropriate. If such an existing component is entirely suitable for use in a new design, manufacturing and inventory savings should also be realized.

Yet another benefit of developing a solids model is the opportunity to exploit computer-aided manufacturing (CAM). In the design evaluation process, numerically controlled (NC) milling machines can be used to produce small quantities of prototype parts with a limited amount of human planning or supervision. When the design is ready for full-scale production, optimization of the automatically produced NC programs can result in maximum production rates from factory automation equipment with minimum waste.

In summary, allowing the designer the opportunity to explore and analyze more design options will allow the development of the highest quality product, while also improving the work environment of the designer by eliminating boring, repetitive tasks.

Model representations

Two major families of solid model representations exist, each with several unique advantages. The first representation, developed by MAGI under contract to BRL [MAGI67] in the mid 1960s, is the combinatorial solid geometry representation (CSG-rep). Solid models of this type are expressed as Boolean combinations of primitive solids. Each primitive solid is a geometric entity described by some set of parameters that occupies a fixed volume in space; the choice of primitive solid types available varies from system to system. The simplest solid that can be used is the halfspace [REQU82], defined by the infinite plane $a x + b y + c z + d = 0$ plus all points on one side of that plane. Systems which defined all objects in terms of Boolean combinations of halfspaces include SHAPES [LANI67] [LANI69] from Draper Laboratories and TIPS-1 [OKIN73a] [OKIN78] [OKIN73b] [OKIN74] [OKIN76] from Hokkaido University. While this choice of representation limits these systems to modeling objects with planar faces, and excludes smooth objects (or forces them to be approximated), the simplicity of this representation lends itself to very natural processing by VLSI hardware [KEDE85a] [KEDE85b]. Most CSG-rep systems in use today offer quite a variety of primitive solids, ranging from various types of spheres and ellipses, boxes and cones, and solids defined by swept or extruded curves. Some examples of CSG-rep systems which use primitive solids include GDP/GRIN (IBM) [FITZ81], PADL-1 [VOEL74] [VOEL78], PADL-2 [BROW82], Series 7000 SMS (Auto-Trol), GMSolid [BOYS82] [ROTH80], SynthaVision (MAGI) [GOLD71] [GOLD79], (SynthaVision is also marketed as ICEM by CDC, and Solids Modeling II by Applicon), MGED (BRL) [WEAV80] [MUUS83], and ProSolid (CAEtec).

The alternative to describing solids with primitives is to adopt a boundary representation (B-rep), of which there are two sub-types, the *explicit* and *implicit* boundary representations. In an explicit boundary representation, each solid is described by an explicit specification of all the points on the surface of the solid, typically by exhaustively listing the vertices of many planar facets. Alternatively, there are implicit boundary representations, where the surface of the solid is described by an analytic function such as Coons patches [COON67], Bezier patches [BEZI74], splines [deBO78], etc. Some examples of B-rep systems (not all of which qualify as solid modelers) are: Alpha_1 (U. Utah) [COHE83], Build-2 (U. Cambridge) [BRAI78] [BRAI80], CADD (McAuto), CATIA (Dassault/IBM), Compac (Technical U. Berlin) [KRAU76] [SPUR76a] [SPUR76b] [SPUR75] [SPUR78], Euclid (Matra Datavision) [BERN75], Euklid (Fides Co.) [ENGE74a] [ENGE74b], Glide (CMU) [EAST77] [EAST79], Medusa (Cambridge Interactive Systems, Ltd.), PATRAN (PDA Engineering), Romulus (Shape Data Ltd, Evans&Sutherland) [VEEN79]. and Solidesign (Computervision).

Representation Issues

Boundary representations offer the advantage of being able to naturally model solid objects with arbitrarily shaped surfaces, but can require a large amount of information to achieve acceptable results. Both CSG-reps and B-reps have certain advantages. With pure CSG representation, it can be exceedingly difficult and non-intuitive to attempt to describe sculptured, free-form surfaces. But similarly, implementing operations like Boolean intersection and Boolean differences on the fundamental representation itself can be difficult with pure Boundary representations. Many current B-rep modelers implement Boolean operations as an external procedure, because current brute-force schemes to evaluate Boolean operations are not closed. As an example of this, B-spline $\cap$ B-spline results in polygons rather than another B-spline. In a boundary representation closed under the set of Boolean operations, B-rep $\cap$ B-rep $\rightarrow$ B-rep. Thus, pure B-rep systems may be difficult to use for some types of objects, especially those with sculptured surfaces pierced by sharp rectangular gouges [THOM84].

Even though existing systems were listed earlier as being either CSG-rep or B-rep, the reality is that many of these systems are actually hybrids of the two approaches, offering the designer the choice of primitive solids or boundary representations, as appropriate for each task. In practice, the implementation of the CSG-rep and B-rep portions of the software may be quite different, but at the highest level of abstraction each representation is just a different way of viewing the other. Faceted primitives such as boxes and wedges can be thought of as explicit B-reps, and smooth primitives such as spheres and cones can be thought of as implicit B-reps defined by analytic functions. Until one uniform representation can be found, hybrid systems seem both inevitable and desirable.

Mathematical Descriptions of the Primitive Solids

There are differences between the primitive solids offered by any given modeling system. However, common primitives which are likely to be offered by most systems include the half-space, ellipsoid, truncated general cone, torus, convex polyhedra with small numbers of vertices (typically four to eight), faceted polyhedra, sets of closed B-spline surfaces which taken together define the bounds of a solid object, and curves swept through space. Examples of many of these types of primitives are shown hovering over a mirror in Plate 1.

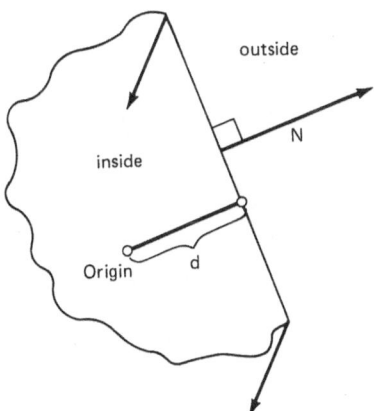

Figure 3 - Definition of a Halfspace

Halfspace (HALF)

The simplest solid that can be used is the halfspace, defined by the infinite plane $a x + b y + c z + d = 0$ plus all points on one side of that plane. Referring to Figure 3, another way to define a halfspace is to specify a vector $\vec{N}$ to the surface of the plane with unit length (i.e. $|\vec{N}| = 1$) and to specify the minimum distance d from the origin to the plane. If $d \geq 0$ then the origin is inside the halfspace, otherwise the origin is outside. More rigorously, any point $\vec{X}$ is contained within the halfspace if $\vec{N} \cdot \vec{X} \geq d$. Points lying on the surface of the plane are considered to be inside the halfspace.

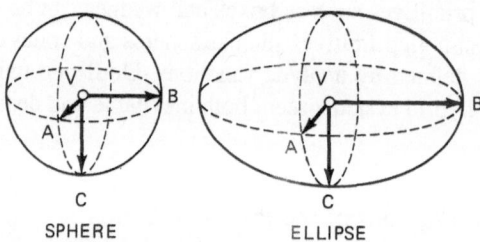

SPHERE   ELLIPSE

Figure 4 - Ellipsoid

Ellipsoid (ELL)

Referring to Figure 4, an ellipsoid can be defined by specifying a vector $\vec{V}$ from the origin to the center of the ellipsoid, and by specifying three vectors $\vec{A}, \vec{B}, \vec{C}$ which are mutually perpendicular, and whose magnitudes define the eccentricity of the ellipse.

Thus, $|\vec{A}| = |\vec{B}| = |\vec{C}|$ defines a sphere.

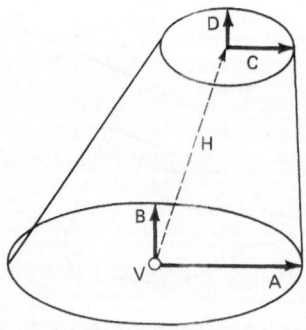

Figure 5 - Truncated General Cone

Truncated General Cone (TGC)

Referring to Figure 5, a truncated general cone can be defined by specifying a vector $\vec{V}$ from the origin to the center of the "lower" ellipse, two perpendicular vectors $\vec{A}$ and $\vec{B}$ which define the orientation and eccentricity of the lower ellipse, a vector $\vec{H}$ which defines the height and slant of the cone, and two more perpendicular vectors $\vec{C}$ and $\vec{D}$ which define the orientation and eccentricity of the upper ellipse.

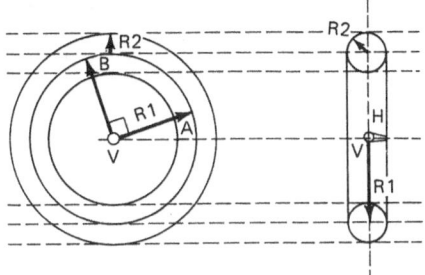

Figure 6 - Torus

Torus (TOR)

Referring to Figure 6, a torus can be defined by specifying a vector $\vec{V}$ from the origin to the center of the torus, three mutually perpendicular vectors $\vec{A}$ and $\vec{B}$ and $\vec{H}$ which specify the plane containing the torus and the normal to the plane, plus two radii, R_1 which specifies the overall radius of the torus, and R_2 which specifies the radius of the swept circular section of the torus. Some systems may allow the torus to have non-circular cross-section, in which case more parameters would be required.

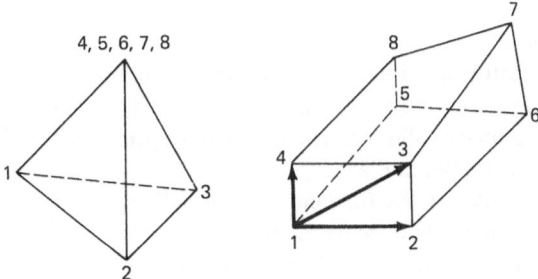

Figure 7 - Convex Polyhedron (ARB8)

Convex Polyhedron with 4 to 8 vertices (ARB8)

Referring to Figure 7, a convex polyhedron can be defined in absolute form by specifying the points which represent the vertices of the faces, or in relative form by specifying a vector $\vec{V}$ from the origin to the first vertex and seven additional vectors $\vec{R}_i|_{i=1..7}$ from $\vec{V}$ to the other vertices. Vectors $\vec{R}_i$ may coincide or have length = 0, $|\vec{R}_i|_{i=1..7} \geq 0$. Examples of this type of solid are the wedge, box, pyramid, etc.

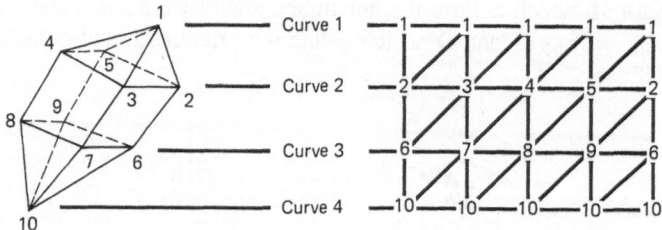

Figure 8 - Faceted Polyhedron (ARS)

Faceted Polyhedron (ARS)

Referring to Figure 8, any faceted polyhedron with logically rectangular structure can be defined by listing N points on each of M curves. In order to make this type of solid more useful, points may overlap, and points are taken in triples to form planar facets. Degenerate facets (lines and points) are discarded.

One can think of this type of polyhedron as representing data obtained by measuring "waterlines", i.e., by placing the object into a basin, adding some water, and measuring N points where the water touches the object. This procedure would be repeated M times to define the whole object. This type of solid is really an explicit boundary representation.

B-spline Solids (SPLINE)

A spline solid is composed of one or more spline surfaces (also called spline patches), which in combination completely enclose some region in space. This type of solid is really an implicit boundary representation. It is important that the model editor ensures that there are no gaps between the spline surfaces so that the primitive is actually solid. An example of one spline surface that might make up a spline solid is shown in Plate 2.

A clear explanation of the fundamentals of spline surfaces can be had from deBoor [deBO72] [deBO78], while a basis for good computer implementations can be found in Riesenfeld [REIS80] and Forrest [FORR78], so they will not be described further. Details of implementations to design sculptured surfaces using the B-spline representation can be found in Cobb [COBB84] and Stay [STAY84].

The Boolean Math of Combination

Boolean set operations are a natural way to combine shapes. The union operator gives the combined volume of two input shapes, while the intersection operator gives the common volume of two input shapes, and the difference (subtraction) operator acts like a "cookie cutter", giving the volume of the first input shape with the common volume of the two subtracted out. These familiar concepts are illustrated in 4 pairs of plates generated from three primitive solids: a box A, a cylinder B, and a wedge C. The wireframe and shaded image of $A \cup B \cup C$ are Figures 11 and 12, the wireframe and shaded image of $A - B - C$ are Plates 3 and 4, the wireframe and shaded image of $(A - B) \cap C$ are Plates 7 and 8, and the wireframe and shaded image of $C - A - B$ are Plates 9 and 10. Note that the wireframe approximations are for visualization purposes only; while the wireframe outlines are only approximate, the actual solids (e.g., the cylinder) are smooth. For a rigorous treatment of Boolean operations in CSG systems, consult Tilove [TILO80].

Model Structure

Most projects have a natural organization. Similarly, geometric models which are constructed need to have a good, logical structure which is easy to work with and reflects the natural structure of the project. Larger structures should be formed from sub-elements, facilitating top-down design of the overall structure, and bottom-up design of highly detailed subassemblies. This dual strategy allows detail to be added to sub-elements only when needed. Replicated components should not have to be re-described, but instead should be modeled as translated instances of the prototype assembly. Finally, there needs to be a mechanism to easily utilize "model parts bins". This allows elements of other models to be incorporated into the current model, either as an exact duplicate, or as a point of departure for further editing.

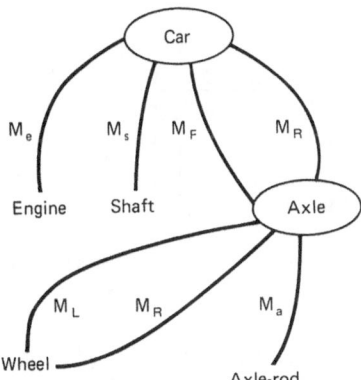

Figure 9 - Directed Acyclic Graph for Simple Car

A directed acyclic graph (DAG) is a good structure to choose to represent this type of structure in a model. A directed acyclic graph is composed of a collection of *nodes* connected by directed *arcs* without cycles (loops). Each node in the directed acyclic graph has a name. *Leaf nodes* contain a single piece of geometry (a single primitive solid), and *Non-terminal nodes* have one or more departing *arcs*, each *arc* referring to some other node by name. In addition to the referenced name, each *arc* contains a Boolean operator and a 4-by-4 transformation matrix. Refer to Figure 9 for an example of a directed acyclic graph used to express the relationships between various parts of a car.

As the directed acyclic graph is traversed from top to bottom, the total effect is accumulated by multiplying the matrices together. If $\vec{v}$ is some vector in a solid at a leaf node, and it is transformed by the matrix in a single arc, the transformed vector is

$$\vec{v}' = \vec{v} * \vec{M}.$$

When traversing the graph from top to bottom, the matrix on the first arc is considered $\vec{M}_1$, and the matrix on the final arc is $\vec{M}_n$. Thus, the final value of a vector is found by

$$\vec{v}' = \vec{v} * \vec{M}_n * \cdots * \vec{M}_1$$

In the example of the car in Figure 9, a vector in the left wheel on the front axle would be

$$\vec{v}'_{wheel} = \vec{v}_{wheel} * \vec{M}_L * \vec{M}_F$$

Each matrix is a 4-by-4 Homogeneous Transform Matrix, which may represent any combination of rotation, scaling (uniform or affine), or translation.

$$\bar{v} = [x \quad y \quad z \quad w]$$

$$\bar{v}' = [x' \quad y' \quad z' \quad w'] = \left[\frac{x'}{w'} \quad \frac{y'}{w'} \quad \frac{z'}{w'} \quad 1 \right]$$

$$\bar{v}' = \bar{v} * \bar{M} = [x' \quad y' \quad z' \quad w'] \begin{bmatrix} \alpha r & r & r & 0 \\ r & \beta r & r & 0 \\ r & r & \gamma r & 0 \\ \Delta x & \Delta y & \Delta z & \frac{1}{s} \end{bmatrix}$$

Here, the nine r elements specify the rotation, α, β, and γ specify the single-axis scaling factors (affine transformation), s specifies the uniform scaling factor, and Δx, Δy, and Δz specify the translation distances. Note that the three elements usually used for perspective transformations are zero. Perspective transformations are used for viewing only, and should not be part of a model matrix. For more details on homogeneous coordinates and homogeneous transform matrices, consult pp. 491-501 in Newman and Sproul [NEWM79], and also see pp. 46-88 in Rogers and Adams [ROGE76].

References

For reviews of the solid modeling field in general, see Requicha [REQU82], Johnson [JOHN85], and Baer [BAER79]. For more information on current solid modelers, the interested reader is referred to Wyvil [WYVI85], Boyse [BOYS82], Muuss [MUUS83], and Brown [BROW82].

History of Solid Modeling at BRL

The Ballistic Research Laboratory has a long history of innovation in computer science, starting with the world's first electronic digital computer, ENIAC, built for BRL by the Moore School of Engineering. In the early 1960s, BRL retained the Mathematical Applications Group, Inc. (MAGI) to develop a geometric description technique suitable for computer analysis of the survivability of armored military vehicles. This culminated in the development of the MAGIC solid modeling system and shotline (ray-tracing) code in 1966 [MAGI67], which was adopted and documented by a tri-service Joint Technical Coordinating Group for Munitions Effectiveness [JOIN70] [JOIN71] and also resulted in a number of other papers being published [GOLD71]. Further development at BRL evolved the MAGIC ray-tracing code into the GIFT (Geometric Information from Targets) ray-tracing code [BAIN75] [KUEH79], while MAGI pursued in-house developments which eventually resulted in the commercial Synthavision system [GOLD79] [GOLD81].

At BRL, the original GIFT models were prepared laboriously by hand. Each solid was described by dozens of parameters entered on punched cards. In GIFT descriptions, only one level of model structure is available, so good model structure was difficult to achieve. These difficulties notwithstanding, BRL built approximately 150 models for the GIFT system over a span of 14 years. With the exception of simple line drawings of the models, none of these models had ever been seen, and no graphical tools for viewing or manipulating them existed.

In late 1979, the author began an independent, unfunded research effort to investigate the use of three-dimensional graphics display hardware to assist in the development of combinatorial solid geometry descriptions of military vehicles. The success of this effort prompted the development in early 1980 of a special database to describe the hierarchical relationships between the sub-systems of the vehicles being modeled. Geometry so described could be viewed and modified using a special graphics editor called GED [WEAV80], documented in a monochrome movie which demonstrated the capabilities of the GED software.

In 1981, BRL initiated an industry-wide search for computer-aided design systems capable of meeting BRL's expanding requirements. Many systems were evaluated, but none met BRL's complex needs, and the decision was made to enhance the in-house software. The result was a state-of-the-art software package capable of meeting BRL's needs for vehicle assessment. In early 1982, the first dedicated DEC PDP-11/70 and associated graphics displays were installed, creating BRL's first production interactive CAD facility [MUUS83]. An early rendering produced by this system is shown in Plate 11. Later, GED was extended to have multi-display capability; the new version, MGED, went into production in 1984.

In April 1984, a "fast prototype" for a new ray-tracing code was designed and implemented in one week; the team effort to develop the full implementation continued through 1984. In July 1985, the results of recent research in techniques for decreasing the computational expense of ray-tracing [KAPL85] were extended in several simple but significant ways, resulting in substantially higher performance for the RT library. In summer 1985, RT reached production status.

The RT library has permitted other BRL researchers to implement capabilities that were not possible using earlier software, including bi-static lighting models, and models of laser illumination. A project to redesign all of BRL's applications codes around the power of the RT library was begun.

In mid 1985, the RT code was extended for fully parallel operation for execution on the BRL HEP Supercomputer. In late 1985, BRL began to experiment with ray-tracing fractal clouds and frequency-controlled random terrain, and began experiments in motion control and animation. Coupling this animation capability with the fully parallel HEP version of the RT code culminated in a 3-minute medium-resolution computer generated animation titled: "A Quick Run Through The M-2 Bradley".

Since the adoption of GED, BRL has been building models of 15 to 20 vehicles annually, usually producing between 3 and 12 variations of each. Most of these models have more than 2000 components, with the larger models often having in excess of 5000 components.

BRL's Solid Modeling Editor MGED: A Case Study

There are a significant number of solid modeling systems, each developed for different purposes by different groups. In this paper, details of the design of BRL's solid modeling system [MUUS83] will be presented. This presentation both documents some of the specific capabilities of the BRL system, and also serves as a good case study of the features and functionality that should be present in every solid modeling system. Most features are comparable to those found in commercial systems.

Philosophy

The role of CAD models at BRL differs somewhat from that of CAD models being built in the automobile and aerospace industries, resulting in some different design choices being made in the BRL CAD software. Because BRL's main use for these models is to conduct detailed performance and survivability analyses of large complex vehicles, it is required that the model of an entire vehicle be completely contained in a single database, suitable for interrogation by the application codes. This places especially heavy demands on the database software. At the same time, a somewhat more modest level of detail is required for these analysis codes than if direct NC machining was the primary goal.

At BRL, there are only a small number of primary designers responsible for the design of a vehicle, and for the construction of the corresponding solid model. Together they decide upon and construct the overall structure of the model, then they perform the work of building substructures in parallel, constantly combining intermediate results into the full model database. Because of the need to produce rapid prototypes (often creating a full design within a few weeks), there is no time for a separate integration stage; subsystem integration must be an ongoing part of the design process.

Once an initial vehicle design is completed, there is usually the need for exploring many alternatives. Typically, between 3 and 12 variations of each design need to be produced, analyzed, and optimized before recommendations for the final design can be made. Also, there is a constantly changing definition of performance; based on new developments it may be necessary to rapidly reevaluate all the designs of the past several years for trouble spots.

The user interface is designed to be powerful and "expert friendly" rather than foolproof for a novice to use, much like UNIX. However, it only takes about two days for new users to start doing useful design work with MGED. True proficiency comes with a few months practice.

Finally, it is vitally important that the software offer the same capabilities and user interface across a wide variety of display and processor hardware. Government procurement regulations make single-vendor solutions difficult. The best way to combat this is with highly portable software.

Displays Supported

It is important for a CAD system to have a certain degree of independence from any single display device in order to provide longevity of the software and freedom from a single equipment supplier. The MGED editor supports serial use of multiple displays by way of an object-oriented programmatic interface between the editor proper and the display-specific code. All display-specific code for each type of hardware is thus isolated in a separate display manager module. High performance of the display manager was an important design goal. Existing graphics libraries were considered, but no well established standard existed with the necessary performance and 3-dimensional constructs. By having the display manager modules incorporated as a direct part of the MGED editor, the high rates of display update necessary to deliver true interactive response are possible, even when using CPUs of modest power.

An arbitrary number of display managers may be included in a copy of MGED, allowing the user to rapidly and conveniently move his editing session from display to display. This is useful for switching between several displays, each of which may have unique benefits: one might have color capability, and another might have depth cueing. The "release" command closes out MGED's use of the current display, and does an implicit attach to the "null" display manager. This can be useful to allow another user to briefly examine an image on the same display hardware without having to lose the state of the MGED editing session. The "attach" command is used to attach to a new display via it's appropriate display manager routines. If another display is already attached, it is released first. The null display manager also allows the MGED editor to be run from a normal alphanumeric terminal with no graphic display at all. This can be useful when the only tasks at hand involve viewing or changing database structures, or entering or adjusting geometry parameters in numerical form.

Creation of a new display manager module in the "C" language [RITC78a] generally takes an experienced programmer from one to three days. The uniform interface to the display manager provides two levels of interactive support. The first level of display support includes the Tektronix 4014, 4016, and compatible displays, including the Teletype 5620 bit-mapped displays. However, while storage-tube style display devices allow MGED to deliver the correct functionality, they lack the rate of screen refresh needed for productive interaction. The second level of support, including real-time interaction, is provided by the Vector General 3300 displays, the Megatek 7250 and 7255 displays, the Raster Technologies Model One/180 display, the Evans and Sutherland PS300 displays with either serial, parallel, or Ethernet attachment, and the Silicon Graphics IRIS 2400 workstation family.

Portability

Today, the half-life of computer technology is approximately two to three years. To realize proper longevity of the modeling software, it needs to be written in a portable language to allow the software to be moved readily from processor to processor without requiring the modeling software or users to change. Then, when it is desirable to take advantage of the constantly increasing processor capabilities and similarly increasing memory capacity by replacing the installed hardware base, there are a minimum of ancillary costs. Also, it may be desirable to connect together processors from a variety of vendors, with the workload judiciously allocated to the types of hardware that best support the requirements of each particular application program. This distribution of processing when coupled with the fact that users are spread out over multiple locations makes networking a vital ingredient as well.

BRL's strategy for achieving this high level of portability was to target all the software for the UNIX operating system [RITC78b], with all the software written in the "C" programming language [RITC78a]. All communications software is based upon the TCP/IP protocol suite developed by DARPA [FEIN85] and now formally designated MIL-STD-1777 and MIL-STD-1778. The CAD software is currently running on all UNIX machines at BRL, under several versions of the UNIX operating system, including Berkeley 4.3 BSD UNIX, Berkeley 4.2 BSD UNIX, and AT&T System V UNIX. In addition, there has been a limited subset of the software ported to the Digital Equipment Corporation VAX/VMS operating system, using the VMS C compiler.

The list of manufacturers and models of CPUs that support the UNIX operating system [DEIT84] is much too lengthy to include here. However, BRL has experience using this software on DEC VAX 11/750, 11/780, 11/785 processors, Gould PN6000 and PN9000 processors, Alliant FX/8 processors (including systems with 8 CPUs), Silicon Graphics IRIS 2400, 2400 Turbo, and 3030 workstations, and the ill-fated Denelcor HEP H-1000 parallel supercomputer.

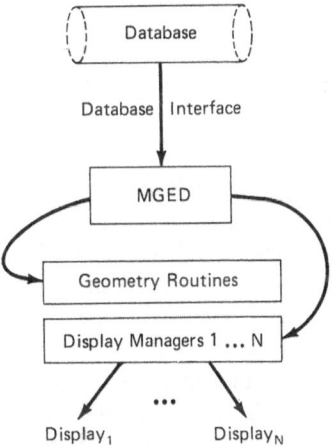

Figure 10 - Object-Oriented Design

Object-Oriented Design

The central editor code has four sets of object-oriented interfaces to various subsystems, including database access, geometry processing, display management, and command parser/human interface. In each case, a common interface has been defined for the set of functions that implement the overall function; multiple instances of these function sets exist when a multiplicity of support exists. The routines in each instance of a function set are completely independent of all the routines in other functions sets, making it easy to add new instances of the function set. A new type of primitive geometry, a new display manager, a new database interface, or a new command processor can each be added simply by writing all the routines to implement a new function set. This approach greatly simplifies software maintenance, and allows different groups to have responsibility for the creation and enhancement of features within each of the function sets.

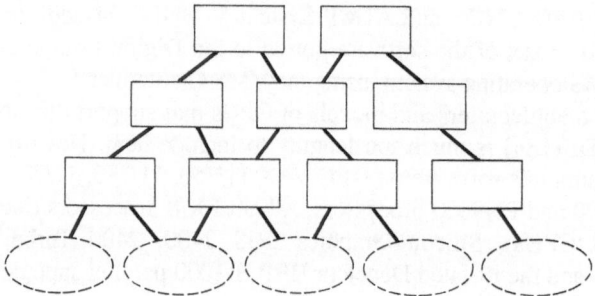

Figure 12 - Hierarchy

Directed Acyclic Graph and Database Details

The database is stored as a single, binary, direct-access UNIX file for efficiency and cohesion, with fixed length records called database granules . Each object occupies one or more granules of storage. The user sees and manipulates the directed acyclic graphs like UNIX paths (e.g., car/chassis/door), but in a global namespace. There can be many independent or semi-independent directed acyclic graphs within the same database, each defining different models, as depicted in Figure 12. The figure also makes heavy use of the instancing capability. As mentioned earlier, the leaves of the graph are the primitive solids.

Commands exist to import sub-trees from other databases and libraries, and to export sub-trees to other databases. Also, converters exist to dump databases in printable form for non-binary interchange. Within the database, all points are stored as floating point numbers, in millimeters. However, it is important to note that the user edits in his choice of arbitrary working units.

Interaction Forms

Textual and numeric interaction with the MGED editor is the most precise editing paradigm because it allows exact manipulation of known configurations. This works well when the user is designing the model from an existing drawing, or when all dimensions are known (or are computable) in advance.

The use of a tablet or mouse, knob-box or dial-box, buttons, and a joystick are all simultaneously supported by MGED for analog inputs. Direct graphic interaction via a "point-push-pull" editing paradigm tends to be better for prototyping, developing arbitrary geometry, and fitting together poorly specified configurations. Having both types of interaction capability available at all times allows the user to select the style of interaction that best meets his immediate requirements.

The Faceplate

When the MGED program has a display device attached, it displays a border around the region of the screen being used along with some ancillary status information. Together, this information is termed the editor "faceplate". In the upper left corner of the display is a small enclosed area which is used to display the current editor state; this is discussed further in the Editor States section, below.

Underneath the state display is a zone in which three "pop-up" menus may appear. The top menu is termed the "button menu" as it contains menu items which duplicate many of the functions assigned to the button box. Having these frequently used functions available on a pop-up menu can greatly decrease the number of times that the user needs to remove his hand from the pointing device (either mouse or tablet puck) to reach for the buttons. An example of the faceplate and first level menu is shown in Plate 12. The second menu is used primarily for the various editing states, at which time it contains all the editing operations which are generic across all objects (scaling, rotation, and translation). The third menu contains selections for object-specific editing operations. The choices on these menus are detailed below. It is important to note that while some display hardware that MGED runs on has inherent support for pop-up menus included, MGED does not presently take advantage of that support, preferring to depend on the portable menu system within MGED instead. It is not clear whether the slight increase in functionality that might accrue from using display-specific menu capabilities would offset the slight nuisance of a non-uniform user interface.

Running across the entire bottom of the faceplate is a thin rectangular display area which holds two lines of text. The first line always contains a numeric display of the model-space coordinates of the center of the view and the current size of the viewing cube, both in the currently selected editing units. The first line also contains the current rotation rates. The second line has several uses, depending on editor mode. Normally it displays the formal name of the database that is being edited, but in various editing states this second line will instead contain certain path selection information. When the angle/distance cursor function is activated, the second line will be used to display the current settings of the cursor.

It is important to mention that while the database records all positions in terms of millimeters, all numeric interaction between the user and the editor are in terms of user-selected display units. The user may select from millimeters, centimeters, meters, inches, and feet, and the currently active display units are noted in the first display line.

The concept of the "viewing cube" is important. Objects drawn on the screen are clipped in X, Y, and Z, to the size indicated on the first status line. This feature allows extraneous wireframes positioned within view in X and Y, but quite far away in the Z direction to not be seen, keeping the display free from irrelevant objects when zooming in very close to a particular part of the model.

Changing the View

At any time in an editing session, the user may add one or more subtrees to the active model space. If the viewing cube is suitably positioned, the newly added subtrees are drawn on the display. (The "reset" function can always be activated to get the entire active model space into view). The normal mode of operation is for users to work with wireframe displays of the unevaluated primitive solids. These wireframes can be created from the database very rapidly.

On demand, the user can request the calculation of approximate boundary wireframes that account for all of the Boolean operations specified along the arcs of the directed acyclic graph in the database. This is a somewhat time consuming process, so it is not used by default, but it is quite reasonable to use whenever the design has reached a plateau. Note that these boundary wireframes are not stored in the database, and are generally used as a visualization aid for the designer. Plate 13 shows an engine connecting rod. On the left side is the wireframe of the unevaluated primitives that the part is modeled with, and on the right side is the approximate boundary wireframe that results from evaluating the Boolean expressions.

Also, at any time the user can cause any part of the active model space to be dropped from view. This is most useful when joining two complicated subsystems together; the first would be called up into the active model space, manipulated until ready, and then the second subsystem would also be called up as well. When any necessary adjustments had been made (perhaps to eliminate overlaps or to change positioning tolerances), one of the subassemblies could be dropped from view, and editing could proceed

The position, size, and orientation of the viewing cube can be arbitrarily changed during an editing session. The simplest way to change the view is by selecting one of nine built in preset views, which can be accomplished by a simple keyboard command, or by way of a button press or first level menu selection. The user is given the ability to execute a "save view" button/menu function that attaches the current view to a "restore view" button/menu function. The rate of rotation around each of the X, Y, and Z axes can be selected by knob, joystick, or keyboard command. Because the rotation is specified as a rate, the view will continue to rotate about the view center until the rotation rate is returned to zero. Similarly, the zoom rate (in or out) can be set by keyboard command or by rotating a control dial. Also, displays with three or more mouse buttons have binary (2x) zoom functions assigned to two of the buttons. Finally, it is possible to set a slew rate to translate the view center along X and/or Y in the current viewing space, selectable either by keyboard command or control dial. In VIEW state, the main mouse button translates the view center; the button is defined to cause the indicated point to become the center of the view.

This assignment of zoom and slew functions to the mouse buttons tends to make wandering around in a large model very straightforward. The user uses the binary zoom-out button to get an overall view, then moves the new area for inspection to the center of the view and uses the binary zoom-in button to obtain a "close up" view. Plate 14 shows such a close up view of the engine connecting rod. Notice how the wireframe is clipped in the Z viewing direction to fit within the viewing cube.

Model Navigation

In order to assist the user in creating and manipulating a complicated hierarchical model structure, there is a whole family of editor commands for examining and searching the database. In addition, on all keyboard commands, UNIX-style regular-expression pattern matching, such as "*axle*" or "wheel[abcd]", can be used. The simplest editor command ("t") prints a table of contents, or directory, of the node names used in the model. If no parameters are specified, all names in the model are printed, otherwise only those specified are printed. The names of solids are printed unadorned, while the names of combination (non-terminal) nodes are printed with a slash ("/") appended to them.

If the user is interested in obtaining detailed information about the contents of a node, the list ("l") command will provide it. For combination (non-terminal) nodes, the information about all departing arcs is printed, including the names of the nodes referenced, the Boolean expressions being used, and an indication of any translations and rotations being applied. For leaf nodes, the primitive solid-specific "describe yourself" function is invoked, which provides a formatted display of the parameters of that solid.

The "tops" command is used to find the names of all nodes which are not referenced by any non-terminal nodes; such nodes are either unattached leaf nodes, or tree tops. To help visualize the tree structure of the database, the "tree" command exists to print an approximate representation of the database subtree below the named nodes. The "find" command can be used to find the names of all non-terminal nodes which reference the indicated node name(s). This can be very helpful when trying to decide how to modify an existing model. A related command ("paths") finds the full tree path specifications which contain a specified graph fragment, such as "car/axle/wheel". In addition to these commands, several more commands exist to support specialized types of searching through the model database.

Editor States

The MGED editor operates in one of six states, with a state transition diagram as shown in Figure 13. Either of the two PICK states can be entered by button press, menu selection, or keyboard command. The selection of the desired object can be made either by using illuminate mode, or by keyboard entry of the name of the object.

Illuminate mode is arranged such that if there are n objects visible on the screen, then the screen is divided into n vertical bands. By moving the cursor

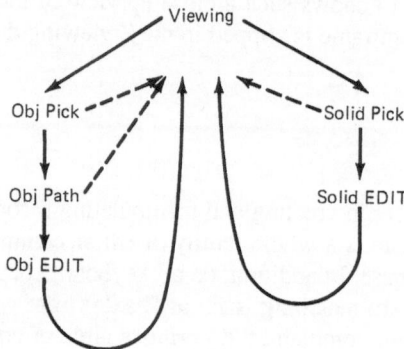

Figure 13 - Editor State Transitions

(via mouse or tablet) up and down through these bands, the user will cause each solid in turn to be highlighted on the screen, with the solid's name displayed in the faceplate. The center mouse button is pressed when the desired solid is located, causing a transition to the next state (Object Path, or Solid Edit).

Illuminate mode offers significant advantages over more conventional pointing methods when the desired object lies in a densely populated region of the screen. In such cases, pointing methods have a high chance of making an incorrect selection. However, in sparsely populated regions of the screen, a pointing paradigm would be more convenient, and future versions of MGED will support this.

Add Primitive

Another family of commands exists to allow the user to add more actual solids (leaf nodes) to the model database. To obtain a precise duplicate of an existing solid (presumably to be changed by a subsequent editing command), the copy ("cp") command can be used. It is important to note that the copy operation is different from creating an instance of an existing solid; there are occasions to use both operations. If the precise configuration of the solid desired is not important, the "make" command can be used to create a stock prototype solid of the desired type with the given name, which can then be edited to suit. The "mirror" command makes a duplicate of an existing solid reflected about one of the coordinate axes.

If the actual numeric parameters of a solid are known, then the "in" command can be used. In addition to prompting for the descriptions of the full generic primitive solids, this command also accepts abbreviated input formats. For example, a wedge or an RPP can be entered with a minimum of parameters, even though a database ARB8 is created. Similarly, the parameters for a right circular cylinder can be given, resulting in a truncated general cone (TGC) being stored.

This is not a very sophisticated way to build solids, but it receives a surprising amount of use.

A number of commands also exist to create new solids with some higher level description. For example, the "inside" command creates a new solid inside an existing solid, separated from the existing solid by specified tolerances. This is quite useful for creating hollow objects such as fuel tanks. It is possible to create a piece of metal plate with a specified azimuthal orientation and fallback angle, or to create an ARB8 (plate) by specifying three points and a thickness, or to create an ARB8 given one point, an azimuthal orientation, and a fallback angle.

Edit Primitive

There are two classes of editing operations that can be performed on leaf nodes, the primitive solids. The first class of operations are generic operations which can be applied to any type of solid, and the second class of operations are those operations which are specific to a particular type of solid. Generic operations which can be applied to all primitive solids are all those transformations that can be specified by a 4-by-4 homogeneous transformation matrix; each type of transformation can be performed through several types of user direction. Primitives can be rotated around the center of the viewing cube; this rotation can be specified in degrees via keyboard command, or can be controlled by the rotation of a set of control dials or the motions of a three-axis joystick. Translation of a primitive can be specified in terms of a precise new location via keyboard command, or by adjustment of a set of control dials. The primitive can also be moved to a designated position by pointing and clicking with the mouse or tablet. Uniform and single-axis (affine) scaling of a primitive can be controlled by a numeric scale factor via keyboard command, or through repeated analog scaling by pointing and clicking with the mouse or tablet.

Finally, the numeric parameters which define the actual primitive solid can be edited using the user's choice of UNIX text editor (specified by the EDITOR environment variable). The "tedit" command forms a printed representation of the solid's numeric parameters in a temporary file and forks a sub-process to allow the user to edit that file. When the text editor exits, MGED regains control, parses the file back into the internal representation of the primitive, and remains in the SOLID EDIT state to allow further modifications.

Each primitive solid also has a variety of editing operations available that are specific to the definition of that solid. Many of these operations are detailed below, but all fall into one of two classes. First, simple scalar parameters such as a radius can be entered numerically via a single parameter keyboard command ("p"), or they can be adjusted in analog form by pointing and clicking with the mouse or tablet. Secondly, defining vectors can be made to pass through a specified point, or changed to terminate at a given point. The particular point can be specified by entering three parameters to the "p" command, or by pointing and clicking with the mouse or tablet to "drag" the vector.

Ellipsoid Parameter Edit

Refer to Figure 4 for an example of the parameters that control the ellipsoid. Most interesting transformations on an ellipsoid can be accomplished by changing it's orientation in space using the generic operations such as rotation and translation. The shape (eccentricity) of the ellipsoid is controlled by varying the relative lengths of the *A, B,* and *C* vectors; these modifications are controlled by this solid-specific menu:

ELLIPSOID MENU
Scale A
Scale B
Scale C
Scale A, B, C

Truncated General Cone Parameter Edit

Refer to Figure 5 for an example of the parameters that control the truncated general cone. It is possible to change the length of the *H, A, B, C,* or *D* vectors, resulting in a change in height or eccentricity of the end plates. The overall size of the *A,B* or *C,D* end plates can be adjusted, or the size of both can be changed together, leaving only the H vector constant. The H vector can be rotated in space, either with the end plates remaining in the same plane, or with the end plates reorienting to be perpendicular to the H vector as it changes. These functions are selected from this menu:

TGC MENU
scale H
scale A
scale B
scale c
scale d
scale A, B
scale C, D
scale A, B, C, D
rotate H
rotate A x B
move end H (rot)
move end H

Torus Parameter Edit

Refer to Figure 6 for an example of the parameters that control the torus. While the internal representation of the torus allows for elliptical cross-sections and an elliptical overall shape, those sorts of tori are rarely needed, and this editing menu only permits changing the two radii of a torus with circular cross-section and circular overall shape.

TORUS MENU
Scale r1
Scale r2

ARB8 Parameter Edit

Refer to Figure 8 for examples of an ARB4 and ARB8. ARBs are defined by their vertices, but the placements of the vertices are not entirely free, as each face must be planar. When an ARB is being edited, the user must specify which edge is to be moved. Then the user specifies a point in space through which the line containing the edge must pass; this is done either by numerically specifying the parameters with the "p" command, or by pointing and clicking with the mouse or tablet. When editing an ARB with 8 distinct vertices, here is the solid-specific menu that the user would see:

ARB8 MENU
move edge 12
move edge 23
move edge 34
move edge 14
move edge 15
move edge 26
move edge 56
move edge 67
move edge 78
move edge 58
move edge 37
move edge 48

Plate 15 shows the wireframe of a box modeled as an ARB8, just after entering SOLID EDIT state but before any editing has taken place. Plate 16 shows the solid after edge "1-4" has been moved to a new location.

As the number of distinct vertices in the ARB decreases, the number of menu choices decreases as well, with more and more edge motion choices turning into point motion choices. Consider the ARB4 as an example of this; an example of one is provided in Figure 7. When editing an ARB with only 4 distinct vertices, here is the solid-specific menu that the user would see:

ARB4 MENU
move edge 12
move edge 23
move edge 13
move edge 14
move edge 24
move edge 34
move point 4

There are several keyboard commands that apply only to ARB solids which are being edited in SOLID EDIT state. Once such command is "mirface", which replaces a designated face of the ARB with a copy of an original face mirrored about the indicated axis. Another such command is "extrude", which projects a designated face a given amount in the indicated direction.

Creating Non-Terminal Nodes

Non-terminal nodes in the directed acyclic graph stored in the database are also called combinations . It is possible to extend the definition of a non-terminal node by adding an instance of an existing node to the non-terminal node with an associated Boolean operation of union; this is done by the "i" (instance) command. To start with, such an instance has an identity matrix stored in the arc; the user needs to separately edit the arc to move the instance to some other location. If the non-terminal node being extended does not exist, it is created first.

The instance command provides the simplest way to create a reference to a another node. Instances of a whole list of nodes can be added to a non-terminal node by way of the group "g" command. If instances of a list of nodes with non-union Boolean operations is to be added to a non-terminal node, the region "r" command accepts a list of (operation, name) pairs, where the single lower case character "u" indicates union, "–" indicates subtraction, and "+" indicates intersection. The first operation specified is not significant. An example of this command might be:

   r non-terminal *u* node1—node2 + node3

For historical reasons, there is no explicit grouping possible, occasionally forcing the user to create intermediate non-terminal nodes to allow the realization of the desired Boolean formula. It is also important to note that for the same reasons there is an implicit grouping between union terms, ie.,

$$u\ n1 - n2 + n3\ u\ n4 - n5$$

is evaluated as

$$(n1 - n2 + n3)\ \text{union}\ (n4 - n5)$$

rather than

$$((((n1 - n2) + n3)\ \text{union}\ n4) - n5)$$

MGED contains a few high-level operations implemented as built-in commands; the most interesting one of these makes an articulated track for a vehicle given the locations of the drive, idler, and road wheels. It is straightforward to create similar domain-specific built-in capabilities as desired, merely by adding another function to the command processor.

Edit Non-Terminal

Before being able to enter the OBJECT EDIT state (i.e., edit non-terminal), it is necessary to pass through two intermediate states in which the full path of an object to be edited is specified, and the location of one arc along that path is designated for editing. It is possible to create a transformation matrix to be applied above the root of the tree, affecting everything in the path, or to apply the matrix between any pair of nodes. For example, if the full path /car/chassis/door is specified, the matrix could be applied above the node "car", between "car/chassis", or between "chassis/door".

The transformation matrix to be applied at the designated location can be created by the concatenation of operations, each specified through several types of user direction. Trees can be rotated around the center of the viewing cube; this rotation can be specified in degrees via keyboard command, or can be controlled by the rotation of a set of control dials or motions on a three-axis joystick. Translation of trees can be specified in terms of a precise new location via keyboard command, or by adjusting a set of control dials. Tree translation can also be accomplished by pointing and clicking with the mouse or tablet. Uniform and single-axis (affine) scaling of a tree can be controlled by a numeric scale factor via keyboard command, or by way of repeated analog scaling by pointing and clicking with the mouse or tablet.

Miscellany

MGED has a substantial number of commands which defy easy categorization; some of these commands will be described in this section. The "analyze" command is used to obtain a simple analysis about a single primitive object, including the plane equations, surface area, azimuth and fallback angles of each face, plus the lengths of each edge and the volume of the enclosed space, both in terms of cubic user units, and also in terms of fluid capacity.

Given that the current view is of the evaluated boundaries of the solids, one can obtain a reasonable estimate of the presented area of the components from the current viewing direction by using the "area" command.

It is possible to view, specify, and text-edit information pertaining to the material type and color of various parts of the model tree. This is an interim capability intended to provide enough material properties information for current rendering and analysis purposes until the design of a full material properties database can be finalized.

In addition to a variety of usual database manipulation and status commands, there are commands to compare the current database for name overlap (conflicts) with another database, as well as commands to import and export subtrees to/from the current database. If name conflicts between the two databases do exist, there are commands to rename an individual node without changing any of the references to it ("mv"), or to rename a node and change all the references to it ("mvall"). Another command which is useful for preparing to move subtrees between databases is the "push" command, which adjusts the transformation matrices from the indicated point down to the leaves of the directed acyclic graph, leaving the higher level arcs with identity matrices.

Output Features

The "plot" command can store an exact image of the current (non-faceplate) display on the screen, either using the System V standard 2-D monochrome UNIX-Plot (plot(4)) format, or the BRL 3-D color extended-UNIX-Plot format. These plots can be sent to a disk file, or "piped" directly to a filter process. This can be useful for making hard copies of the current MGED view for showing to others, using a local pen plotter or laser printer.

An important capability even beyond the ability to generate an evaluated boundary wireframe is the ability of MGED to initiate a quick ray-trace rendering of the current view on any nearby framebuffer! This is implemented by using the MGED "rt" command to fork off an instance of the RT program, and sending the RT program a description of the current view with any user-specified options. This allows the designer to use the power of MGED to select the desired view, and then to quickly verify the geometry and light source placement. A 50 by 50 pixel rendering of the current view can usually be done in less than a minute (on a DEC VAX-780 class processor), and allows for general verification before the designer uses the "saveview" command to submit a batch job for a high resolution ray-trace of the same view.

Animation

The MGED editor includes a number of features which are useful for developing animation tools and scripts. The full description of the current viewing transformation and eye position can be saved in a file, and such a previously saved view can be read back at any time, immediately changing the editor's view. In addition, the current viewing transformation and eye position can be appended to a file containing a collection of keyframes. Most importantly, a file full of keyframe information, either raw keyframe positions or smoothly interpolated keyframe sequences, can by "played" in real time using MGED, providing a powerful and fast animation preview capability.

As a separate animation capability intended for developing demonstrations and instructional material relating to the use of the MGED editor, all user interactions with the editor can be recorded in a file, along with an indication of the time elapsed between user actions. This file can be adjusted using a normal text editor to remove any errors, or to eliminate dead time where the user stopped to think. Once created, this session script can be replayed through the editor at any time, either to provide a smooth "canned" demonstration before a live audience, or to create a film or videotape.

Model Building Philosophy

The power of a full directed acyclic graph structure for representing the organization of the database gives a designer a great deal of flexibility in structuring a model. In order to prevent chaos, most designers at BRL choose to design the overall structure of their model in a top-down manner, selecting meaningful names for the major structures and sub-structures within the model. Actual construction of the details of the model generally proceeds in a bottom-up manner, where each sub-system is fabricated from component primitives.

The first sub-systems to be constructed are the chassis and skin of the vehicle, after which a set of analyses are run to validate the geometry, checking for unintentional gaps in the skin or for solids which overlap. The second stage of model construction is to build the features of the main compartments of the vehicle. If necessary for the analysis codes that will be used, the different types of air compartments within the model also need to be described. The final stage of model construction is to build the internal objects to the desired level of detail. This might include modeling engines, transmissions, radios people, seats, etc.. In this stage of modeling, the experienced designer will draw heavily on the parts-bin of model components and on pieces extracted from earlier models, modifying those existing structures to meet his particular requirements.

Throughout the model building process it is important for the model builder to choose part names carefully, as the MGED database currently has a global name space, with individual node names limited to 16 characters. In addition, BRL has defined conventions for naming the elements in the top three levels of database structure so that people will be able to easily navigate within models prepared at different times and by different designers, facilitating the integration of design changes into old models with a minimum of difficulty.

Interrogating the Model: Ray-tracing

What Applications Want and Need

The objective of a given application will to a large degree determine the most "natural" form in which the model might be presented. For example, extracting just the edges of the objects in a model would be suitable for a program attempting to construct a wire-frame display of the model. Another family of applications exists which needs to be able to find the intersection of small object paths (eg., photons) with the model. Generally, these alternatives are motivated by the representation of a physical process being simulated, and each alternative is useful for a whole family of applications. By choosing the ray sampling density within the Nyquist limit, these applications are well satisfied by extracting ray/geometry intersection information, the well known "ray-tracing" algorithm. However, a mathematical ray has as its cross section a point, while physical objects have significant cross-sectional area. This lack of cross-sectional area can result in sampling inaccuracies, and has lead some applications developers to try to minimize these difficulties. Applications which simulate particles or small rocks approaching the model might benefit from cylinder/geometry intersection capability, and applications which shine beams of light on the model such as spotlights or even highly collimated light such as laser light might benefit from cone/geometry intersection capabilities [AMAN84] [KIRK86]. Applications which are attempting to simulate wave effects might be well expressed in terms of plane/geometry intersection curves, and structural analysis routines would probably prefer to obtain the geometry as a collection of connected hyper-patches.

While very recent research has begun to explore techniques for intersecting cylinders, cones, and planes with geometry [KAJI83], ray-tracing is by far the most well developed approach. Fortunately, most applications can function well with approximate, sampled data about the model, rather than needing a precise representation. Data with statistical validity can be obtained by sampling the model with an adequate number of rays and computing the ray/geometry intersections. This approach is also by far the easiest one to implement, as the one-dimensional nature of a mathematical ray makes the intersection equations relatively straightforward.

Given that one has decided to force all applications to interrogate the model strictly by computing ray/geometry intersections, there are still several implementation strategies that could be adopted. The most traditional approach has been batch-oriented, with the user defining a set of "viewing angles", turning loose a big batch job to compute all the ray intersections, and then post-processing all the ray data into some meaningful form. However, the major drawback of this approach is that the application has no immediate control over ray paths, making another batch run necessary for each level of reflection, etc.

In order to be successful, applications need: (1) interactive control of ray paths, to naturally implement reflection, refraction, and fragmenting into multiple subsidiary rays, and (2) the ability to fire rays in arbitrary directions from arbitrary points. Nearly all non-batch implementations have closely coupled a specific application (typically a model of illumination) with the ray-tracing code, allowing efficient and effective control of the ray paths. The most flexible approach of all is to implement the ray-tracing capability as a general-purpose library, and make the functionality available as needed to any application.

References

The origins of modern ray-tracing come from work at MAGI under contract to BRL, initiated in the early 1960s. The initial results were reported by MAGI [MAGI67] in 1967. Extensions to the early developments were undertaken by a DoD Joint Technical Coordinating Group effort, resulting in publications in 1970 [JOIN70] and 1971 [JOIN71]. The detailed presentation of the fundamental analysis and implementations of the ray-tracing algorithm found in these two documents forms an excellent and thorough review of the principles of solid modeling.

More recently, interest in ray-tracing developed in the academic community, with Kay's [KAY79] thesis in 1979 being a notable early work. One of the central papers in the ray-tracing literature is the work of Whitted [WHIT80]. Model sampling techniques can be improved to provide substantially more realistic images by using the "Distributed Ray Tracing" strategy [COOK84]. For an excellent, concise discussion of ray-tracing, consult pages 363-381 of Rogers [ROGE85].

Ray -vs- Geometry

The process of intersecting one ray with the model geometry can be decomposed into two distinct tasks. First, the ray must be intersected with each and every primitive solid in the model. Each successful intersection will result in a set of line segments being returned. Secondly, the Boolean combinations expressed in the model's directed acyclic graph must be evaluated over this collection of line segments.

We will examine the details of intersecting a ray with a halfspace, a generalized ARB, and an ellipsoid. These three analyses provide all the information necessary to enable one to intersect a ray with any solid possessing a quadratic surface. For example, a truncated general cone can be dealt with as an infinite cylinder (a quadratic) bounded by two planes. The extension to surfaces of higher order is straightforward, and depends only on having a reliable root-finding algorithm. Information about ray-tracing of spline objects can be found in a recent paper by Sweeny [SWEE86].

Rays begin at a point $\vec{P}$, and proceed infinitely in a given direction $\vec{D}$. Any point $\vec{X}$ on a ray may be expressed as a linear combination of $\vec{P}$ and $\vec{D}$:

$$\vec{X} = \vec{P} + k * \vec{D}$$

where valid solutions for k are in the range $[\,0,\,\infty)$. ($\vec{D}_x$, $\vec{D}_y$, $\vec{D}_z$) are the *direction cosines* for the ray, being the cosine of the angle between the ray and the appropriate axis. While not necessary, in this analysis it is assumed that $\vec{D}$ is of unit length, i.e., $|\vec{D}| = 1$.

Ray/Halfspace Intersection

Consider a plane with arbitrary orientation. This plane partitions space into two half-spaces. Define $\vec{N}$ to be an outward-pointing unit-length vector which is normal to the plane. Let point $\vec{A}$ lie anywhere on the plane. Let the ray in question be defined such that any point $\vec{X}$ on the ray may be expressed as $\vec{X} = \vec{P} + k\vec{D}$.

Determine if the ray is parallel to the surface of the plane, and if not, determine if the ray is entering or exiting the half-space by comparing the direction of the ray with the direction of the normal $\vec{N}$:

$$\vec{N} \cdot \vec{D} \;=\; \begin{cases} 0 & \text{parallel, no solution} \\ > 0 & \text{exiting half-space, segment } t \;=\; [0, k] \\ < 0 & \text{entering half-space, segment } t \;=\; [k, \infty] \end{cases}$$

If a solution exists, i.e. $\vec{N} \cdot \vec{D} \neq 0$, find parameter k for intersection of ray and plane. To accomplish this, a useful form for the equation of the plane is $\vec{N} \cdot (\vec{X} - \vec{A}) = 0$, where the vector from any point on the plane ($\vec{A}$) is tested for perpendicularity with the normal $\vec{N}$. To find k, we substitute the parametric version of $\vec{X}$, giving:

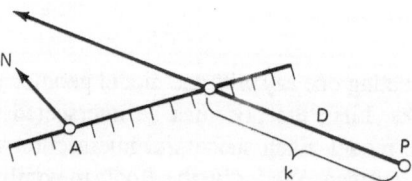

Figure 14 - Ray/Halfspace Intersection

Ray/ARB Intersection

An ARB is a convex volume bounded by 4 (pyramid), 5 (wedge), or 6 (box) planes. This analysis depends on the properties of objects with convex hulls. Let the ray in question be defined such that any point $\vec{X}$ on the ray may be expressed as $\vec{X} = \vec{P} + k\vec{D}$. Intersect the ray with each of the planes bounding the ARB as discussed above, and record the values of the parametric distance k along the ray. With outward pointing normal vectors, note that the ray *enters* the half-space defined by a plane when $\vec{D} \cdot \vec{N} < 0$, is *parallel* to the plane when $\vec{D} \cdot \vec{N} = 0$, and *exits* otherwise. Find the entry point farthest away from the starting point $\vec{P}$, i.e., it has the largest value of k among the entry points. The ray enters the solid at this point. Similarly, find the exit point closest to point $\vec{P}$, i.e., it has the smallest value of k among the exit points. The ray exits the solid here.

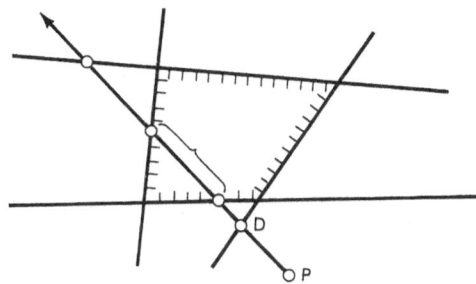

Figure 15 - Ray/ARB Intersection

Ray/Ellipse Intersection

Let the point W belong to the set of points on the surface of an ellipsoid which is defined by $\vec{V}, \vec{A}, \vec{B}, \vec{C}$, where $\vec{V}$ is the center of the ellipsoid, and $\vec{A}, \vec{B}$, and $\vec{C}$ are mutually perpendicular and define the orientation and shape of the ellipsoid. By affine transformations, map the points on the original ellipsoid into the set of points $\hat{W}$ in the "hat" space which lie on the surface of a unit sphere, located at the origin. For any point X, the corresponding point in the "hat" space is $\hat{X} = S(R(X{-}V))$, where

$$R(X) = \begin{bmatrix} \bar{A} / (|\bar{A}|) \\ \bar{B} / (|\bar{B}|) \\ \bar{C} / (|\bar{C}|) \end{bmatrix} \qquad \text{and} \qquad S(X) = \begin{bmatrix} \frac{1}{|\bar{A}|} & 0 & 0 \\ 0 & \frac{1}{|\bar{B}|} & 0 \\ 0 & 0 & \frac{1}{|\bar{C}|} \end{bmatrix} * X$$

Intersect this ellipse with a ray; points on the ray L are of the form $P + k * D$. This can be be expressed as the intersection of the ray in "hat" space with the unit sphere, where points on the ray $\hat{L}$ are of the form $\hat{P} + \hat{k}\hat{D}$. The mapping between regular and "hat" space for vectors is:

$$\hat{D} = S(R(D))$$

and for points is:

$$\hat{P} = S(R(P{-}V))$$

With W defined to be the point where ray L intersects the ellipsoid, and $\hat{W}$ is the point where $\hat{L}$ intersects the unit sphere, then

$$\hat{W} = \hat{P} + \hat{k} * \hat{D}$$

and

$$\hat{W} = S(R(W{-}V))$$

In order to find the point $\hat{W}$, we refer to the definition for a sphere with unit radius located at the origin

$$x^2+y^2+z^2 = 1$$

and substitute in the parametric definition of $\hat{W}$, giving

$$(\hat{P}_x+\hat{k}*\hat{D}_x)^2 + (\hat{P}_y+\hat{k}*\hat{D}_y)^2 + (\hat{P}_z+\hat{k}*\hat{D}_z)^2 = 1$$

Regrouping terms as a polynomial in $\hat{k}$ gives

$$(\hat{D}_x^2 + \hat{D}_y^2 + \hat{D}_z^2)\hat{k}^2 + 2*(\hat{D}_x\hat{P}_x + \hat{D}_y\hat{P}_y + \hat{D}_z\hat{P}_z)\hat{k} + \hat{P}_x^2 + \hat{P}_y^2 + \hat{P}_z^2 - 1 = 0$$

$$(\hat{D}\cdot\hat{D})\hat{k}^2 + 2(\hat{D}\cdot\hat{P})\,\hat{k} + [(\hat{P}\cdot\hat{P}) - 1] = 0$$

Solving the quadratic equation for $\hat{k}$ yields 0, 1, or 2 roots

$$\hat{k} = \frac{-2(\hat{D}\cdot\hat{P}) \pm \sqrt{[2(\hat{D}\cdot\hat{P})]^2 - 4(\hat{D}\cdot\hat{D})[(\hat{P}\cdot\hat{P})-1]}}{2(D^\wedge\cdot D)}$$

$$\hat{k} = \frac{-(\hat{D}\cdot\hat{P}) \pm \sqrt{(\hat{D}\cdot\hat{P})^2 - (\hat{D}\cdot\hat{D})[(\hat{P}\cdot\hat{P})-1]}}{(\hat{D}\cdot\hat{D})}$$

If a solution for $\hat{k}$ exists, these values of $\hat{k}$ define the intersection point(s) $\hat{W}$. In order to determine W, the relationship between $\hat{k}$ and k needs to be found.

$$\hat{W} = \hat{P} + \hat{k}*\hat{D}$$

$$\hat{W} = S(R(W - V))$$

Can be rearranged in terms of W

$$W = V + R^{-1}(S^{-1}(\hat{W}))$$

Then, substituting in the parametric form of $\hat{W}$

$$= V + R^{-1}(S^{-1}[\hat{P} + \hat{k}*D])$$
$$= V + R^{-1}(S^{-1}[S(R(P - V)) + \hat{k}*S(R(\hat{D}))])$$
$$= V + R^{-1}(S^{-1}(R(P - V)) + \hat{k}*R(D))$$
$$= V + (P - V) + \hat{k}*D$$
$$W = P + \hat{k}*D$$

but,

$$W = P + k*D$$

so $k = \hat{k}$. This useful result is not surprising because affine transformations applied to straight lines yield straight lines, and R and S are both affine transformation matrices. The fact that k is constant for both W and $\hat{W}$ means that the solution for $\hat{k}$ can be determined from $\hat{D}$ and $\hat{P}$ without needing to transform the results out of the "hat" space.

Given that we can find the point $\hat{W}$ where ray $\hat{L}$ intersects the unit sphere and the point W where ray L intersects the ellipsoid, what is the vector normal to the tangent plane at that point? The tangent plane on the unit sphere at $\hat{W}$ has normal vector $\hat{N} = \hat{W}$. (The vector from the origin to any point on the surface of the - sphere is pointing in the direction of the tangent at that point).

$$\hat{N} = \hat{W} = S(R(W - V))$$

The tangent plane at $\hat{W}$ transforms back to the tangent plane at W, with normal vector $\hat{N}$:

$$\hat{N} = [(R^{-1} * S^{-1})^T]^{-1}(\hat{N})$$

because if $\hat{H}$ is perpendicular to plane Q, and matrix M maps from Q to $\hat{Q}$, then $[M^T]^{-1}(\hat{H})$ is perpendicular to $\hat{Q}$.

$$\hat{N} = [(S^{-1})^T * (R^{-1})^T]^{-1}(\hat{N})$$

Because $(R^{-1})^T = R$ and $S^T = S$,

$$\hat{N} = [S^{-1} * R]^{-1}(\hat{N})$$
$$= R^{-1} * S(\hat{N})$$
$$= R^{-1}(S(S(R(W - V))))$$

Note that $|\hat{N}| \neq 1$.

Boolean Evaluation

In the context of the three-dimensional model, each ray passes through zero or more objects, but the objects are defined in terms of a Boolean combination of primitive solids. The first part of the task is to intersect the ray with each and every primitive solid in the model. For each solid, either the ray will miss, in which case nothing further need be done, or the ray will intersect the solid in one or more line segments. When all of the primitive solids have been intersected, the segments have to be sorted, and "woven" together into intervals. The original ray is broken into a new interval at each point where a primitive solid was entered or exited; the list of primitive solids intersected is constant within each interval. Note that the correct entry and exit normals must be selected each time a segment is broken into an additional interval.

After all the segments are woven together into intervals, each interval needs to be applied to the Boolean expression tree. For all primitive solids in the expression tree, if a segment is present within an interval, the expression tree sees a TRUE input, otherwise a FALSE input is presented. For all intervals in which the expression tree returns a TRUE output, the ray has passed through an actual solid object, and that interval is added to the solution list for this ray/model intersection. Note that by keeping the interval list sorted front-to-back in increasing k, and by incrementally weaving new segments into the interval list as they are computed, applications such as lighting models which are only interested in the first intersection with a solid object can be processed much more efficiently by stopping the intersection process after the first hit.

Bounding Volumes & Space Partitioning

Part of the computational expense of ray-tracing derives from the statement that "the first part of the task is to intersect the ray with each and every primitive

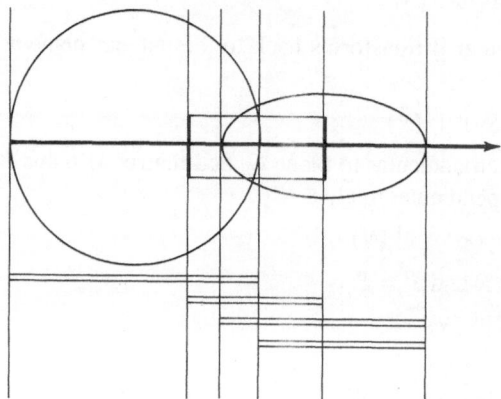

Figure 16 - Boolean Evaluation

solid in the model" results in an enormous amount of computation. Much of the
recent research in ray-tracing techniques has focused on strategies for reducing
the the amount of computation required. Overall, the goal is to develop methods
to avoid computing the actual ray/solid intersections when the ray does not pass
near the solid.

The first method for eliminating unnecessary ray/solid intersections involves
enclosing the solid within a *bounding solid*. Before computing the intersection
of a ray with the actual primitive solid, the ray is first intersected with the bounding solid to reject obvious misses. This is only effective if the cost of computing
the intersection with the bounding solid is significantly less than the cost of intersecting the ray with the primitive solid. Spheres, axis-aligned right-parallel-
pipeds (RPPs), and boxes are the three most popularly used bounding volumes.
An important issue is the measure of the quality of a bounding volume. The
desire is to minimize $VOL_{bound} - VOL_{geom}$, but each bounding volume is a poor
fit for some objects. The sphere is a poor bound for any object which is long and
thin. Axis-aligned RPPs are poor bounds for any object where the greatest width
is not axis aligned. The torus represents a solid that is very hard to bound well at
all.

The best bounding sphere has its center located at the centroid of the primitive
solid, with the radius r set to the smallest possible value that encloses the entire
primitive solid. Then, to determine if a ray needs to be intersected with the
primitive solid, it is merely necessary to determine if the distance from the -
sphere center $\hat{V}$ to line $\hat{P} + k * \hat{D} \leq r$, i.e.

$$\left| (\bar{V} - \bar{P}) \times \frac{\bar{D}}{|\bar{D}|} \right| \leq r$$

When $|D| = 1$, this can be quite fast to compute. Another way to speed the cal-
culation of this would be to compare the magnitude squared to the radius

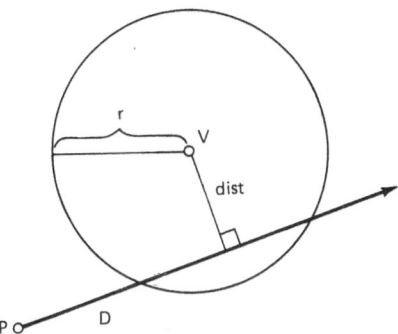

Figure 17 - Bounding Sphere

squared, eliminating the necessity for taking a square root in finding the distance.

A bounding RPP is defined by six numbers giving the extent of the RPP along each of the three axes, i.e., $MIN_{x,y,z}$ and $MAX_{x,y,z}$. Cyrus and Beck [CYRU77] provide an efficient algorithm for intersecting the ray with the six planes of the RPP. By taking advantage of the fact that all six planes are axis-aligned, the plane intersection equations are greatly simplified, and the following algorithm (written in pseudo-C) provides the fastest possible ray/RPP intersection, with a computational cost very close to the cost of computing the distance from a bounding sphere. (Assuming that the division by D_i is replaced with a multiplication by the inverse, which is calculated once per ray).

```
for( i = x, y, z ) {
    if( D_i == 0 ) {
        if(MIN_i > P_i) return(MISS);
        if(MAX_i < P_i) return(MISS);
    } else if(D_i > 0 ) {
        / * Heading toward larger numbers */
        if(MAX_i < P_i ) return(MISS);
        k = (MAX_i – P_i) / D_i;
        if(maxK > k) maxK = k;
        k = (MIN_i – P_i) /D_i;
        if(minK < k ) minK = k;
    } else {
        / * D_i < 0, heading to smaller numbers */
        if(MIN_i > P_i) return(MISS);
        k = (MIN_i – P_i) / D_i;
        if(maxK > k) maxK = k;
        k = (MAX_i – P_i) / D_i;
        if( minK < k ) minK = k;
```

        }
    }
    if($minK > maxK$) return(MISS);

If the ray intersects the RPP at all, it does so in the range ($minK, maxK$).

Space partitioning is an efficiency strategy which only intersects rays with bounding volumes that are "near" the path of the ray, and avoids finding intersections in irrelevant areas of the model [GLAS84] [FUJI85] [FUJI86].

Bin-trees enclose all of model space with 6 axis-aligned planes (an RPP), and split the RPP with a single plane carefully chosen to reduce complexity of at least one side of the tree by one solid. Lists of the contents of both new RPPs are made, and then both new RPPs are recursed into until the list of contents is "small". When a ray is to be fired, find the first RPP the ray enters by walking the tree, making binary decisions at each node. When a leaf node is found in the space partitioning tree, fire rays at solids listed (or their bounding volumes).

Oct-Trees operate similarly, except that at each node space is uniformly split by planes in X, Y, and Z.

RT Library Interface

In order to give all applications interactive control over the ray paths, and to allow the rays to be fired in arbitrary directions from arbitrary points, BRL has implemented its second generation ray-tracing capability as a set of library routines. The RT library exists to allow application programs to intersect rays with model geometry. There are two parts to the interface: preparation routines and the actual ray-tracing routine. Three "preparation" routines exist; the first routine which must be called is dir_build(), which opens the database file, and builds the in-core database table of contents. The second routine to be called is get_tree(), which adds a database sub-tree to the active model space. get_tree() can be called multiple times to load different parts of the database into the active model space. The third routine is rt_prep(), which computes the space partitioning data structures, and does other initialization chores, prior to actual ray-tracing. Calling this routine is optional, as it will be called by shootray() if needed. rt_prep() is provided as a separate routine to facilitate more accurate timing of the preparation and ray-tracing phases of applications.

To compute the intersection of a ray with the geometry in the active model space, the application must call shootray() once for each ray. Ray-path selection for perspective, reflection, refraction, etc., is entirely determined by the applications program, and passed as a parameter to shootray() in the RT "application" structure, which contains five major elements: the vector a_ray.r_pt ($P^\rightarrow$) which is the starting point of the ray to be fired, the vector a_ray.r_dir ($D^\rightarrow$) which is the unit-length direction vector of the ray, the pointer *a_hit() which is the address of an application-provided routine to call on those rays where some geometry is hit by the ray, the pointer *a_miss() which is the address of an application-provided routine to call on those rays where the ray does not hit any geometry, the flag a_onehit which is set non-zero to stop ray-tracing as soon as the ray has intersected at least one piece of geometry (useful for lighting models), plus various locations for applications to store state (recursion level, colors, etc.). Note that the return from the application provided a_hit()/a_miss() routine is the formal return of the function shootray(). The shootray() function is prepared for full recursion so that the application provided a_hit()/a_miss() routines can themselves fire additional rays by calling shootray() recursively before deciding their own return value. In addition, the function shootray() is fully prepared to be operating in parallel with other instances of itself in the same address space, allowing the application to take advantage of parallel hardware capabilities where such exist. This has actually been successfully demonstrated on the Denelcor HEP H-1000 machine and on the Alliant FX/8.

Sample RT Application

A simple application program that fires one ray at a model and prints the result is included below, to demonstrate the simplicity of the interface to the RT library.

```
struct application ap;
main() {
        dir_build("model.g");
        get_tree("car");
        rt_prep();
        ap.a_point = [ 100, 0, 0 ];
        ap.a_dir = [ -1, 0, 0 ];
        ap.a_hit = &hit_geom;
        ap.a_miss = &miss_geom;
        ap.a_onehit = 1;
        shootray( &ap );
}
hit_geom(app, part)
struct application *app;
struct partition *part;
{
        printf("Hit %s", part->pt_forw->pt_regionp->reg_name);
}
miss_geom(){
        printf("Missed");
}
```

RT Shootray

To show the simplicity of the overall ray-tracing algorithm, and to provide the reader with enough information to be able to implement a full ray-tracing package, the RT shootray() function is presented.

```
shootray(app)
struct application *app;
{
        if( ray outside model RPP ) return( a_miss() );
        do "push" from box to box {
                for all solids in box {
                        check bounding RPP
                        invoke SHOOT on solid, collect segment list
                }
                bool_weave(): add segs to interval list
                if( app->a_onehit > 0 ) {
                        bool_final()
                        if( any geometry hit ) break;
                }
        }
        bool_final();
        if( any geometry hit )
                call a_hit();
        else
                call a_miss();
}
```

The overall strategy here is simple, and only the addition of the space partitioning "box" (voxel) notion adds any complexity. If the ray does not even intersect
the model RPP, then call a_miss(). Otherwise, examine every box (voxel) that
the ray pierces, in increasing distance from the starting point $\vec{P}$. For every
solid inside each voxel, call the SHOOT routine appropriate for that type of
solid, and collect the resultant lists of intersection segments. After processing all
the solids in the voxel, call bool_weave() to sort the segments into the interval
list, creating additional intervals where segments overlap. If the a_onehit flag is
set, call bool_final() to evaluate the Boolean expressions on the sorted interval
list; if any interval evaluates as TRUE, then break the loop and call a_hit().
When all voxels have been examined, call bool_final(), and call a_hit() or a_-
miss() as appropriate.

It is important to note that the BRL MGED and RT software is available from
BRL at no cost by writing to the author. In this way, the author hopes to prevent
the implementation of more ray-tracers, and focus attention onto more fruitful
areas of research, such as developing more sophisticated algorithms for the
analysis of solid models.

Analysis of the Model

At any stage of the design, the model can be used to make realistic images and
engineering drawings. This capability is so powerful that it ordinarily justifies

the construction of the model. However, the real payoff from building a geometric model comes when it is time to analyze it. The model can be subjected to numerous engineering analyses, allowing the effects of varying many parameters to be studied in a controlled way.

Image Rendering

Many phenomena that are difficult to model with the more traditional scan-line-order rendering of faceted objects can be handled simply and elegantly with ray-tracing, although with a much greater cost in processing time. For example, in most conventional rendering packages, shadows are implemented by way of a subterfuge: computing the shadow volumes cast from the light source by each object as a set of "neutral density" polygons, and using them to influence the shading decisions for the actual surfaces underneath them. On the other hand, an illumination model based on ray-tracing merely needs to fire a ray at each light source to determine the total light energy at each point. While the computational requirements of this strategy can be explosive in a model with multiple light sources and many reflective objects, the ease and accuracy of using ray-tracing to model the laws of optics to create very realistic renderings has not yet been surpassed by other techniques.

By dithering the location of the light sources, this can also give a statistically good rendition of shadow penumbra effects. Unlike conventional rendering packages, ray-tracing also makes it easy to deal with objects that are partly or entirely reflective, and with transparent objects that have varying refractive indices. Furthermore, by applying the proper sorts of dither [COOK84], motion-blur, depth-of-field, translucency, and other effects are easily achieved. The ease and flexibility of modeling point-sampled optics with the ray-tracing paradigm is demonstrated by the lighting model code supplied with RT, which implements all of the features listed above (reflection, refraction, perspective views, penumbras, texture maps translucency, etc.) in less than 400 lines of heavily-commented "C" code.

An example of these features is shown in Plate 17. Plate 18 shows the outside and inside (skin removed) views of a BMP vehicle, and Plate 19 depicts an M109 with glass armor. Using simple techniques such as making selected parts of the model invisible or transparent, a designer can create powerful images for communicating the design.

Animation

Given that lighting model code exists for making static images, it is a relatively straightforward matter to develop code which can animate the position of the "eye" (camera) and light sources within the model, and only a modest additional effort to develop the capability of articulating the model geometry itself. Using animation can be very beneficial when trying to gain comprehension of complex geometry, especially when the object being modeled has never actually been physically built before. There is nothing that communicates complex structures more clearly than observing them passing by smoothly. In addition to assisting the design engineers understanding the geometry that they are developing, an animation capability is also very useful as a sales tool, both for aiding management understanding of the design project, and also to convey a strong message to potential customers.

In addition to being a valuable visualization tool, animation capabilities can be used to experimentally verify that moving assemblies do not interfere with each other, and that adequate clearances exist. This can be extended still further by explicitly modeling the presence of humans as part of the geometry, allowing pre-prototype testing and evaluation of the "human factors" portions of the design. Verification that the design provides adequate space to move around in, easily accessible operating controls, proper provisions for seating, and doorways that are convenient for non-contortionists can be achieved through animation studies.

Lens Design

The power of the lighting model code can further extended by making a provision to record the paths of all the rays followed when computing the light intensity for each pixel, and recording them in an auxiliary file. In addition to being a fantastic debugging tool, this capability allows one to follow the path of the light rays passing through lenses and being reflected by mirrors while performing image rendering. All these calculations are necessary simply to obtain a rendering of the scene, but if one is actually attempting to use the solid modeling system to study optics, the effects on the actual light ray paths can be obtained with no additional computation.

Studying the paths of light rays as they are repeatedly bent by passing from air to glass and back again has traditionally been a painstaking manual procedure for lens designers. By developing a solid model of some set of optics under consideration, it becomes possible to predict lens behavior, including making a determination of the exact focal length, finding the precise influence of spherical distortions and edge effects, determining the amount of image distortion due to internal reflection and scattering, and finding the level of reflections from the lens mounting hardware. Furthermore, experiments can be conducted to determine the effects of adding or removing baffles, irises, special lens coatings, etc.. This is an unusual but highly profitable coupling of solid models and analysis codes.

Property Calculations

In the design of vehicles, moments and products of inertia play a central role. Particularly when designing aircraft, weights, the center of gravity, and parameters related to inertia are vital aspects of creating a stable design with high performance. For ground vehicles and fixed structures these figures are quite significant, providing a good first estimate of structural loading, and allowing transportation costs to be assessed. Moments of inertia are important in determining what conditions a vehicle may be overturned by maneuvering or impact, and can also help predict the vehicle's handling when maneuvering over rough terrain [DEIT83].

By applying the Fundamental Theorem of integral calculus and performing spatial integration of the geometry as sampled by the ray-tracing process, it is possible to compute the presented areas and profile shapes from a given viewpoint, important information to have both for styling and functional design [LEE82]. By combining this spatial integration procedure with a knowledge of the properties of the various materials involved (density, etc.), it becomes possible to compute the mass, center of gravity, moments of inertia, overturning moments, and other similar engineering assessments [THOM72]. Plate 20 shows one planar set of material property samples from the ray-tracing analysis of an M48 tank. Such material samples comprise the input information for the codes which make the property calculations.

The mass of an object distributed over a region V and having a density $\delta(x, y, z)$ at the point (x, y, z) of V is given by the integral

$$M = \iiint \delta(x, y, z) dV$$

In the case of sampled geometry, this can be expressed as

$$M = \sum_x \sum_y \sum_z \delta(x, y, z).$$

Similarly, the center of gravity is

$$\left(\frac{\iiint x \delta(x, y, z) dV}{M}, \frac{\iiint y \delta(x, y, z) dV}{M}, \frac{\iiint z \delta(x, y, z) dV}{M} \right),$$

or for sampled geometry

$$\left(\frac{\sum_x \sum_y \sum_z x \delta(x, y, z)}{M}, \frac{\sum_x \sum_y \sum_z y \delta(x, y, z)}{M}, \frac{\sum_x \sum_y \sum_z z \delta(x, y, z)}{M} \right).$$

The moments of inertia I can be found as

$$I = \left(\iiint (y^2 + z^2) \delta(x, y, z) dV, \iiint (x^2 + z^2) \delta(x, y, z) dV, \right.$$

$$\left. \iiint (x^2 + y^2) \delta(x, y, z) dV \right).$$

These computational techniques can be extended [BLAS62] to provide the principle second moments and cross products of inertia. Due to the computational complexity of evaluating these mechanical design parameters, they have typically been unavailable to engineers using traditional design approaches.

Drafting

When a design created on a CAD system is to be produced in traditional manufacturing facilities rather than using a fully automated NC plant, clear and detailed drawings are a necessity. Thus, the production of engineering drawings, including orthogonal views, orthographic projections, and "exploded views" from the solid models is an important, if unglamorous, capability [LAMI86]. Once the model is constructed, the designer may define drawings containing an unlimited number of views, either standard orthogonal views or views from an arbitrary azimuth and elevation. While tolerance specification, fully automatic dimensioning, and tolerance indication is a difficult area [REQU82], recent research is beginning to provide strategies for implementing them [HASH86], and future CAD systems should demand less human intervention than current ones. BRL does not have a well developed capability in this area because of its heavy reliance on color shaded images to communicate final designs.

Numerical Controlled Milling

Direct numerical control (NC) of a milling machine provides the ultimate in "hard copy" output [VOEL81]. NC milling can be very useful for generating prototypes for initial testing, where the goal is to produce correct toolpath computation in a short amount of elapsed time, but requiring minimal human intervention.

However, NC milling is also very important in the mass production of final versions of the design. In this case, the objective is to compute toolpaths which result in maximum efficiency of the milling machine. A man/machine team effort with human-directed optimization of the automatically produced NC programs can result in maximum production rates from factory automation equipment with minimum waste.

Automatic toolpath generation is still difficult due to the complexity of tool/block interference testing, but various researchers are currently investigating using a ray-tracing paradigm for toolpath planning.

Structural Analysis

Currently, most structural analysis and hydrodynamics analysis is done using finite element mesh (FEM) techniques. FEM data is normally pre-processed by packages like PATRAN to develop inputs for NASTRAN, EPIC, ANSYS and other similar programs to to actually process the mesh data, including stress testing, computing loading factors, etc..

An automatic interface from the modeling system to a finite element representation is a very important capability. G. Moss at BRL is currently developing a post-processor program which converts CSG-rep solid models into a boundary form suitable for input to PATRAN-G, but this is still an active research effort.

Vulnerability Assessments

An important extension to simple static and dynamic loading of structures is to consider unexpected dynamic stress caused by a high-energy source impacting the object being designed. This could be as ordinary as a rock striking a car traveling at 80 kilometers per hour, hailstones falling from the sky, or a collision with another vehicle. On the other hand, if the object being designed is intended for use in a military setting, the range of threats which must be considered is greatly enlarged. Not only do designers have to worry about airplanes impacting with large birds, hail, and rain, they also need to design airplanes to withstand the buffeting from nearby explosions, flying shrapnel, and various projectiles [WEAV82]. When designing tanks and other ground vehicles, the designer needs to consider the effects of small arms fire, land mines, projectiles, and missiles. Similarly, designers of ocean-going vessels need to concern themselves with the effects of torpedoes, projectiles, and missiles; spacecraft designers need to contend with high-velocity particles, laser beams, and other similar challenges. For all designs, nuclear effects need to be considered.

To conduct a ballistic analysis of point burst effects, BRL has developed a model for lethality and vulnerability estimation which is used to evaluate the effects of antiarmor weapons used against ground vehicles, based upon a ray-tracing approach [BROW81] [RING81]. Following perforation of a vehicle armor shell by a penetrator, this code evaluates behind-armor spall cloud effects, described by a cone of debris extending from the point of armor penetration. This process is illustrated in Plate 21, where the red rods depict the path of the main penetrator, and the blue cone represents the extent of the debris. Soft components located within the spall cone are considered to be destroyed by the debris, while hard components survive unless they are impacted by the main penetrator. This code runs interactively and generates a color display to provide immediate feedback into the design process [OZOL82], an example of which is shown in Plate 22.

Nuclear Survivability

When a nuclear weapon is detonated, blast effects, thermal radiation, electromagnetic pulse, initial nuclear radiation, and fallout all pose threats to equipment and personnel. The initial nuclear radiation has three main components: prompt neutrons, neutron-induced secondary gamma particles, and prompt gamma particles [DEIT83]. The Vehicle Code System (VCS) [RHOD74a] [RHOD74b] considers total dose effects by first deterministically calculating the transport of radiation to an envelope that surrounds the vehicle, and then making a stochastic relationship between the radiation at the source envelope and at the detection point inside by using ray-tracing to track each particle through the vehicle. Plate 23 shows a rendering of a Tank Test Bed (TTB) concept vehicle, and a version displayed with a false coloring scheme, depicting the proportions of radiation leakage that reached the detection point inside. A surprising result of this test was the unexpectedly high proportion of radiation that entered the vehicle through the narrow front plate; examination of the model did not suggest that it was inadequate. The ability to find and correct this type of deficiency early in the design process is extremely important, and can result in huge cost savings.

Signatures by "Geometric Sampling"

In the next several sections the topic of predictive signature analysis will be examined for a variety of wavelengths using several slightly different approaches. The development of predictive signature analysis is like a double-edged sword; it can be useful both for developing techniques for reducing the signatures of existing vehicles by guiding product improvement plans, as well as ensuring that new vehicles being designed have an acceptably low signature for frequency ranges of interest, but this kind of analysis can also be used to guide testing and optimize designs for new or improved sensing systems.

It is very important to note that point-sampled geometric optics only bears a statistical relationship to the effects actually obtained from a wave optics analysis (or experiment), and that accounting for phase-related effects is difficult at best. Thus, developing predictive models does not relieve the designer of the responsibility for conducting tests with scale and full-size physical models of the prototype, but having these predictive models should make the possibility of unexpected behaviors in the prototypes quite small.

Vision Assessments

An interesting application for inside-out ray-tracing is to determine the view from within a vehicle through the vision ports or windows. This gives the designers the opportunity to adjust the shape, orientation, and placement of the vision elements of each vehicle so as to optimize the exterior field of view for the vehicle occupants.

Some modern weapons utilize a forward observer to designate a target by laser illumination, with a missile-borne sensor homing in on the reflected beam. This scenario is illustrated in Plate 24. In order to determine how such a sensor might perform, it is necessary to calculate the laser energy reflected from a variety of candidate targets [DEIT84]. A related assessment is to determine the amount of optical radiation that might enter a vehicle through each vision port when irradiated with the light from a laser designator. The result of this type of study is usually a cardioid shaped plot showing the energy transmitted as a function of azimuth angle [DEIT83].

Infrared Modeling

In the design of smart munitions, it is important to know the nature of vehicle signatures over a range of detection bands and for a variety of signal-processing schemes [RAPP83]. Actual predictive infrared modeling is possible based on solid modeling, using finite element techniques. To make predictions about the patterns of heat radiation, it is necessary to calculate a complete internal heat budget for the entire vehicle which accounts for all the sources and radiators of heat, such as engines and cooling fins, and then to take into account external thermal loading due to such factors as the surface of the earth and solar radiation. Heat flow is calculated from node to node in the model, with links between mesh elements characterized by thermal coupling coefficients. The methodology for performing this type of predictive modeling was developed at BRL [RAPP76], but has never been implemented.

Millimeter Wave Signatures

Dihedral and trihedral metal elements act as particularly efficient reflectors for millimeter wavelength radio transmissions, to the extent that the return from such elements represents the great majority of the return from vehicles [DEIT84]. BRL has developed a predictive millimeter wave signature model [LACE84] which concerns itself strictly with processing the dihedral and trihedral elements that compose a vehicle. G. Moss at BRL has developed a post-processor program which extracts these features, regardless of size and orientation, from the existing CSG-rep solid models to drive this analysis. An example of the result of this type of processing is shown in Plate 25.

Because there is a strong correlation between the quantity of dihedral vehicle surface topology and the intensity of the millimeter wave reflection, this feature extraction program can be used by itself without running the full deterministic millimeter wave reflection model to obtain initial estimates of the magnitudes of the millimeter wave signature of a given structure.

Synthetic Aperture Radar

Synthetic aperture radar (SAR) is a technique with which a variety of image information about a distant object can be obtained by correlating multiple radar samples taken from various positions [TOOM82]. While standard radars only report target backscatter and range information, SAR techniques can resolve distinct scattering regions of a target [DEIT84]. In 1984, BRL merged the Simulated Radar Image Modeling (SRIM) predictive SAR model from the Environmental Research Institute of Michigan (ERIM) with BRL's ray-tracing capability. The choice of ray density is based on the frequency of the radar being simulated and the cross-range resolution of the process. Any ray can reflect up to some preset number of times or until it leaves the vicinity of the target. An example of the ray paths for the first and subsequent reflections is shown in Plate 26. The actual results of the SAR calculation with an M48 vehicle using a single transmit/receive polarization is shown in Plate 27. These calculations were made in high-resolution mode unconstrained by practical frequency or coherence considerations of realizable radar systems. The radar signal is propagating from left to right.

Tradeoff Analysis

The philosophy adopted at BRL has been to develop a broad set of analyses which are supported from the same geometry database [DEIT84]. These analyses cover the spectrum from engineering decision aids, to design validators, to drafting and milling interfaces, to the generation of manufacturing drawings, to image generation for management comprehension and sales advantage. Key analysis capabilities have been developed to assess the strength, weight, and "protection" levels offered by the structures represented by a solid model. Using this analysis information and additional domain-specific applications tools makes it possible to produce highly detailed vehicle designs constructed with a philosophy of *system optimization* right from the start. This should allow the rapid development of vehicles with the desired levels of performance at the best attainable price.

Acknowledgements. The author would like to thank Bob Reschly for his assistance in creating the drawings using PIC and CIP, his supervisors Dr. Stephen Wolff and Dr. Paul Deitz for their unflagging support, Harry Reed for providing an environment that makes good research possible, and Professor David F. Rogers for persuading me to write it all down.

References

[AMAN84] J. Amanatides, Ray Tracing with Cones, Computer Graphics (Proceedings of Siggraph '84), V 18, N 3 (July 1984).

[BAER79] A. Baer, C. Eastman, M. Henrion, Geometric modelling: a survey, Computer-Aided Design, V 11, N 5, pp 253-272 (September 1979).

[BAIN75] L. W. Bain Jr., M. M. Reisinger, The GIFT Code User Manual; Volume I, Introduction and Input Requirements (U), BRL Report No. 1802, AD #A078364 (July 1975).

[BERN75] J. Bernascon, J. M. Brun, Automated Aids for the Design of Mechanical Parts, Tech. Paper MS75-508, Society of Manufacturing Engineers (1975).

[BEZI74] P. E. Bezier, Mathematical and Practical Possibilities of UNISURF, Academic Press, New York (1974).

[BLAS62] G. A. Blass, Theoretical Physics, p 102, Appleton-Century-Crofts, New York (1962).

[BOYS82] J. W. Boyse, J. E. Gilchrist, GMSolid: Interactive Modeling for Design and Analysis of Solids, IEEE Computer Graphics and Applications, V 2, N 2, pp 27-40 (March 1982).

[BRAI78] I. C. Braid, New Generations in Geometric Modeling, Proceedings of Geometric Modelling Project Meeting, P-78-GM-01, CAM-I, Inc., St. Louis MO (March 14-16, 1978).

[BRAI80] I. C. Braid, R. C. Hillyard, I. A. Stroud, Stepwise Construction of Polyhedra in Geometric Modelling, Mathematical Methods in Computer Graphics and Design, K. W. Brodie, Academic Press, London, pp 123-141 (1980).

[BROW81] F. T. Brown, D. C. Bely, D. A. Ringers, The Simple Lethality and Vulnerability Estimator (SLAVE) User's Manual, BRL Technical Report ARBRL-TR-02282, NTIS AD# B05527 (January 1981).

[BROW82] Brown, PADL-2: A Technical Summary, IEEE Computer Graphics and Applications, V 2, N 2, pp 69-84 (March 1982).

[COBB84] E. S. Cobb, Design of Sculptured Surfaces using the B-spline Representation, PhD dissertation, University of Utah (June 1984).

[COHE83] E. Cohen, Mathematical Tools for a Modelers Workbench, IEEE Computer Graphics and Applications (October 1983).

[COOK84] Cook, Porter, Carpenter, Distributed Ray Tracing, Computer Graphics (Proceedings of Siggraph '84), V 18, N 3, pp 137-145 (July 1984).

[COON67] S. A. Coons, Surfaces for Computer-Aided Design of Space Forms, Tech. report MAC-TR-41, Project MAC, MIT, NTIS AD# 663-504, Cambridge MA (June 1967).

[CYRU77] M. L. Cyrus, J. Beck, Computer Graphics: Two- and Three-Dimensional Clipping, Air Force Report AFHLR-TR-77-14, NTIS AD# A043017 (May 1977).

[deBo78] C. deBoor, A Practical Guide to Splines, Applied Mathematical Sciences 27, Springer-Verlag, New York (1978).

[deBo72] C. deBoor, On Calculating with B-splines, Journal of Approximation Theory, V 6, N 1, pp 50-62 (July 1972).

[DEIT82] P. H. Deitz, Solid Modeling at the US Army Ballistic Research Laboratory, Proceedings of the 3rd NCGA Conference, V 2, pp 949-960, (13-16 June 1982).

[DEIT83] P. H. Deitz, Solid Geometric Modeling - The Key to Improved Materiel Acquisition from Concept to Deployment, Defense Computer Graphics 83, Washington DC (10-14 October 1983).

[DEIT84a] P. H. Deitz, Modern Computer-Aided Tools for High-Resolution Weapons System Engineering, DoD Manufacturing Technology Advisory Group MTAG-84 Conference, Seattle WA (25-29 November 1984).

[DEIT84b] P. H. Deitz, Predictive Signature Modeling via Solid Geometry at the BRL, Sixth KRC Symposium on Ground Vehicle Signatures, Houghton MI (21-22 August 1984).

[DEIT85] P. H. Deitz, The Future of Army Item-Level Modeling, Army Operations Research Symposium XXIV, Ft. Lee VA (8-10 October 1985).

[EAST77] C. Eastman, M. Henrion, GLIDE: A Language for Design Information Systems, Computer Graphics (Proceedings of Siggraph '77),V 11, N 2, pp 24-33 (July 1977).

[EAST79] C. Eastman, K Weiler, Geometric Modelling Using the Euler Operators, Proc. First Annual Conference on Computer Graphics in CAD/CAM Systems, Cambridge MA, pp 248-259 (April 9-11 1979).

[ENGE74a] M. Engeli, A language for 30 graphics applications, International Computer Symposium '73, North-Holland Press (1974).

[ENGE74b] M. Engeli, V. Hrdliczka, EUKLID: eine Einfuhrung, Fides Co., Zurich (1974).

[FEIN85] E. J. Feinler, O. J. Jacobsen, M. K. Stahl, C. A. Ward, DDN Protocol Handbook, NIC 50004, DDN Network Information Center, Menlo Park CA (December 1985).

[FITZ81] W. Fitzgerald, F. Gracer, R. Wolfe, GRIN: Interactive Graphics for Modeling Solids, IBM Journal of Research and Development,V 25, N 4, pp 281-294 (July 1981).

[FORR78] A. R. Forrest, A Unified Approach to Geometric Modelling, Computer Graphics (Proceedings of Siggraph '78),V 12, N 3 (August 1978).

[FUJI85] A. Fujimoto, et al., Accelerated Ray Tracing, Proceedings of CG Tokyo '85, Tokyo (April 1985).

[FUJI86] A. Fujimoto, C. G. Perrott, K. Iwata, Environment for Fast Elaboration of Constructive Solid Geometry, pp 20-33, T. L. Kunii, Advanced Computer Graphics, Springer-Verlag (1986).

[GLAS84] A. S. Glassner, Space Subdivision for Fast Ray Tracing, IEEE Computer Graphics and Applications,V 4, N 10 (1984).

[GOLD71[R. Goldstein, L. Malin, 3-D Visual Simulation, Simulation,V16,N 1, pp 25-31 (1971).

[GOLD79] R. Goldstein, L. Malin, 3D Modelling with the Synthavision System, CAD/CAM Systems (Proceedings of the First Annual Conference Computer Graphics), Cambridge MA, pp 244-247 (9-11 April 1979).

[GOLD81] R. Goldstein, Defining the Bounding Edges of a Synthavision Solid Model, Proc. 18th Design Automation Conference,Nashville TN, pp 457-461 (June 29-July 1 1981)

[HASH86] J. Hashimoto, H. Fukushima, W. Kowaguchi, High Performance CAD System with Full Automatic Dimensioning and Multi-Modeling Features Based on Engineering Workstation, pp 358-378, T. L. Kunii, Advanced Computer Graphics, Springer-Verlag (1986).

[HILL82] R. C. Hillyard, The Build Group of Solid Modelers, IEEE Computer Graphics and Applications, V 2, N 2, pp 43-52 (March 1982)

[JOHN85] R. Johnson, Capabilities of Solid Modeling, Computer Graphics World, pp 50-64 .

[JOIN70] Joint Technical Coordinating Group for Munitions Effectiveness, MAGIC Computer Simulation, Vol. 1, User Manual, 61JTCG/ME-71-7-1 (July 1970).

[JOIN71] Joint Technical Coordinating Group for Munitions Effectiveness, MAGIC Computer Simulation, Vol. 2, Analyst Manual, 61JTCG/ME-71-7-2-1 (May 1971).

[KAJI83] J. T. Kajiya, New Techniques for Ray Tracing Procedurally Defined Objects, Transactions of Graphics, V 2, N 3, pp 161-181, (July 1983).

[KAPL85] M. R. Kaplan, Space-Tracing, a Constant Time Ray-Tracer, Siggraph '85 Tutorial "State of the Art in Image Synthesis", San Francisco CA (July 22-26, 1985).

[KAY79] D. S. Kay, Transparency, Refraction, and Ray Tracing for Computer Synthesized Images, Cornell Univ. (Jan 1979).

[KEDE84] G. Kedem,A J. L. Ellis, The Ray-Casting Machine, Proceedings ICCD'84, pp 533-538 (October 1984).

[KEDE85a] G. Kedem, Computer Structures and VLSI Design for Curve-Solid Classification, Siggraph '85 Tutorial "VLSI for Computer Graphics", San Francisco CA (July 23, 1985).

[KEDE85b] G. Kedem, J. L. Ellis, Computer Structures for Curve-Solid Classification in Geometric Modeling, Siggraph '85 Tutorial "VLSI for Computer Graphics", San Francisco CA (July 23, 1985).

[KIRK86] D. B. Kirk, The Simulation of Natural Features Using Cone Tracing, T. L. Kunii, Advanced Computer Graphics, pp 129-144, Springer-Verlag (1986).

[KRAU76] F. L. Krause and Vassilakopoulos, A Way to Computer Supported Systems for Integrated Design and Production, IFIPS CAD Working Conference, Austin TX (February 1976).

[KUEH79] G. G. Kuehl, L. W. Bain Jr., M. M. Reisinger, The GIFT Code User Manual; Volume II, The Output Options (U), US Army ARRADCOM Report No. 02189, AD #A078364 (September 1979).

[KUNI85] G. Wyvil, T. L. Kunii, A Functional Model for Constructive Solid Geometry, The Visual Computer,V 1,N 1, pp 3-14 (July 1985).

[LACE84] J. Lacetera, Deterministic Modeling of Tank Targets for MMW Radar Systems, Sixth KRC Symposium on Ground Vehicle Signatures, Houghton MI (21-22 August 1984).

[LAMI86] L. G. Lamit, V. Paige, The Influence of CADD on Teaching Traditional Descriptive Geometry and Orthographic Projection,T. L. Kunii, Advanced Computer Graphics, pp 473-484, Springer-Verlag (1986).

[LANI73] J. H. Laning, D. A. Lynde, V. Moreggia, SHAPES User's Manual,Charles Stark Draper Laboratory, Inc., Cambridge MA (May 1973).

[LANI79] J. H. Laning, S. J. Madden, Capabilities of the SHAPES System for Computer Aided Mechanical Design, Proc. First Annual Conference on Computer Graphics in CAD/CAM Systems, Cambridge MA, pp 223-231 (April 9-11, 1979).

[LEE82] Y. T. Lee, A. A. G. Requicha, Algorithms for Computing the Volume and Other Integral Properties of Solid Objects, Communications of the ACM, V 25, N 9, pp 635-650 (September 1982).

[MAGI67] MAGI Inc, A Geometric Description Technique Suitable for Computer Analysis of Both Nuclear and Conventional Vulnerability of Armored Military Vehicles, MAGI Report 6701, AD847576 (August 1967).

[MUUS83] M. J. Muuss, K. A. Applin, R. J. Suckling, G. S. Moss, E. P. Weaver, C. Stanley, GED: An Interactive Solid Modeling System for Vulnerability Analysis, BRL Technical Report ARBRL-TR-02480, NTIS AD# A-126-657, (March 1983).

[NEWM79] W. M. Newman, R. F. Sproul, Principles of Interactive Computer Graphics, 2nd ed.,McGraw-Hill, New York (1979).

[OKIN73a] N. Okino, Y. Kakazu, H. Kubo, TIPS-1: Technical Information Processing System for Computer-Aided Design, Drawing, and Manufacturing, Computer Languages for Numerical Control, pp 141-150, J. Hatvany, North-Holland Publishing Co, Amsterdam (1973).

[OKIN73b] N. H. Okino, H. Kubo, Y. Kakazu, TIPS-1: practical approaches for an integrated CAD/CAM System, Proceedings SME Conference on CAD/CAM, Detroit MI (1973).

[OKIN74] N. H. Okino, et al., TIPS, Graphics processor for computer-aided design, Proceedings of International Conference on Precision Engineering, pp 366-371 (1974).

[OKIN76] N. H. Okino, H. Kubo, Y. Kakazu, An integrated CAD/CAM system: TIPS-2, Proceedings Prolomat Conference, UK (1976).

[OKIN78] N. Okino et al., TIPS-1, '77 Version, Institute of Precision Engineering, Hokkaido University, Sapporo Japan (March 1978).

[OZOL82] A. Ozolins, D. A. Ringers, ISLAVE: Interactive Simple Lethality and Vulnerability Estimator, Proceedings of the Second Joint Technical Coordinating Group for Aircraft Survivability Workshop on Survivability and Computer-Aided Design, USAF Museum, Wright-Patterson AFB, OH, V 1 pp 91-99 (18-20 May 1982).

[RAPP76] J. R. Rapp, A Computer Model for Predicting Infrared Emission Signatures of An M60A1 Tank, BRL Report No. 1916, NTIS AD# B013411L (August 1976).

[RAPP83] J. R. Rapp, A Computer Model for Estimating Infrared Sensor Response to Target and Background Thermal Emission Signatures, BRL Memorandum Report ARBRL-MR-03292 (August 1983).

[REQU82] A. A. G. Requicha, H. B. Voelcker, Solid Modeling: A Historical Summary and Contemporary Assessment, IEEE Computer Graphics and Applications,V 2,N 2, pp 9-24 (March 1982).

[RHOD74a] W. A. Rhodes et al., Vehicle Code System (VCS) User's Manual, Oak Ridge National Laboratory Report ORNL-TM-4648, Oak Ridge TN (August 1974).

[RHOD74b] W. A. Rhodes, Development of a Code System for Determining Radiation Protection of Armored Vehicles (the VCS Code), Oak Ridge National Laboratory Report ORNL-TM-4664, Oak Ridge TN (October 1974).

[RIES80] R. F. Riesenfeld, E. Cohen, T. Lyche, Discrete B-splines and Subdivision Techniques in Computer Aided Geometric Design and Computer Graphics, Computer Graphics and Image Processing, V 14, N 2, pp87-111 (October 1980).

[RIES83] R. F. Riesenfeld, A View of Spline-Based Solid Modelling, Proceesings of Autofact 5, SME, Computer and Automated Systems Association of SME (1983).

[RING81] D. A. Ringers, F. T. Brown, SLAVE (Simple Lethality and Vulnerability Estimator) Analyst's Guide, BRL Technical Report ARBRL-TR-02333, NTIS AD# B059679 (June 1981).

[RITC78a] D.M. Ritchie, K. Thompson, The UNIX Time-Sharing System, Bell Sys. Tech. J.,V 57, N 6, pp 1905-1929 (1978).

[RITC78b] D.M. Ritchie, S.C. Johnson, A.E. Lesk, B.W. Kernighan, UNIX Time-Sharing System: The C Programming Language, Bell Sys. Tech. J.,V 57, N 6, pp 1991-2019 (1978).

[ROGE76] D. F. Rogers,A J. A. Adams, Mathematical Elements for Computer Graphics, McGraw-Hill, New York (1976).

[ROGE85] D. F. Rogers, Procedural Elements for Computer Graphics, McGraw-Hill, New York (1985).

[ROTH80] S. D. Roth, Ray Casting as a Method for Solid Modeling, Research Publication GMR-3466, General Motors Research Laboratories, Warren M (October 1980).

[SPUR75] G. Spur, J. Gausemeier, Processing of Workpiece Information for Producing Engineering Drawings, Proceedings 16th International Machine Tool Design and Research Conference, pp 17-21, Manchester UK (1975).

[SPUR76a] G. Spur, J. Gausemeier, G. Muller, COMPAC — The Use of Computer Internal Workpiece Models for Design and Manufacturing, Rep. Technische Universitat Berlin, Lehrstuhl und Institut for Werkzeugmaschien und Fertigungstechnik (1976).

[SPUR76b] G. Spur, F. L. Krause, Stages of Integration for Computer Supported Design and Manufacturing Process Planning, IFTOMM, Italy (October 1976).

[SPUR78] G. Spur, Status and Further Develoment of the Geometric Modelling System COMPAC, Proceedings Geometric Modelling Project Meeting, P-78-GM-01, CAM-I, Inc., St. Louis MO, pp 1-35 (March 14-16 1978).

[STAY84] P. R. Stay, Rounded Edge Primitives and their Use in Computer Aided Geometric Design, MS dissertation, University of Utah (August 1984).

[SWEE86] M. A. J. Sweeny, R. H. Bartels, Ray Tracing Free-Form B-spline Surfaces, IEEE Computer Graphics (February 1986).

[THOM72] G. B. Thomas Jr., Calculus and Analytic Geometry, Addison-Wesley (February 1972).

[THOM84] S. W. Thomas, Modelling Volumes Bounded by B-spline Surfaces, PhD dissertation, University of Utah (June 1984).

[TILO80] R. B. Tilove, A. A. G. Requicha, Closure of Boolean Operations of Geometric Entities, Computer Aided Design,V 12, N 5, pp 219-220 (September 1980).

[TOOM82] J. C. Toomay, Radar Principles for the Non-Specialist, Lifetime Learning Publications, London (1982).

[VEEN79] P. Veenman, ROMULUS — The Design of a Geometric Modeller, Geometric Modelling Seminar, W. A. Carter, P-80-GM-01, CAM-I, Inc., Bournemouth UK, pp 127-152 (November 1979).

[VOEL74] H. B. Voelcker, A. A. G. Requicha, E. E. Hartquist, W. B. Fisher, J. E. Shopiro, N. K. Birrell, An Introduction to PADL: Characteristics, Status, and Rationale, Tech. Memo. No. 22, Production Automation Project, University of Rochester (December 1974).

[VOEL78] H. B. Voelcker, A. A. G. Requicha, E. E. Hartquist, W. B. Fisher, J. Metzger, R. B Tilove, N. K. Birrell, W. A. Hunt, G. T. Armstrong, T. F. Check, R. Moote, J. McSweeney, The PADL-1.0/2 System for Defining and Displaying Solid Objects, Computer Graphics (Proceedings of Siggraph '78),V 12, N 3, pp 257-263 (August 1978).

[VOEL81] Voelcker, H.B., W.A. Hunt, The role of Solid Modelling in Machining-Process Modelling and NC Verification, Proceedings of the 1981 SAE International Congress and Expositio, Detroit MI, pp 1-8 (February 1981).

[WEAV80] E. P. Weaver, M. J. Muuss, Interactive Construction of COM-GEOM Targets, BRL Spring Technical Conference (1980).

[WEAV82] E. P. Weaver, P. H. Deitz, Solid Modeling in Survivability/Vulnerability, Proceedings of the Second Joint Technical Coordinating Group for Aircraft Survivability Workshop on Survivability and Computer-Aided Design, USAF Museum, Wright-Patterson AFB OH, V 1 (18-20 May 1982).

[WHIT80] J. T. Whitted, An Improved Illumination Model for Shaded Display, Communications of the ACM, V 23, N 6, pp 343-349 (June 1980).

Figure 18 ComGeom Primitive Solids

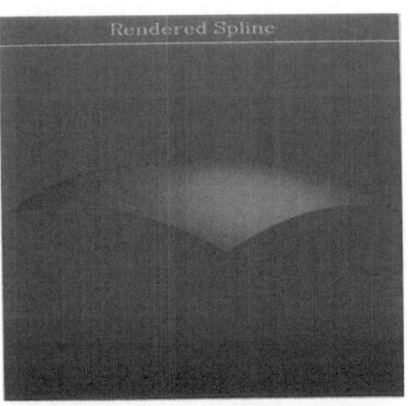

Figure 19 Rendered Spline Surface

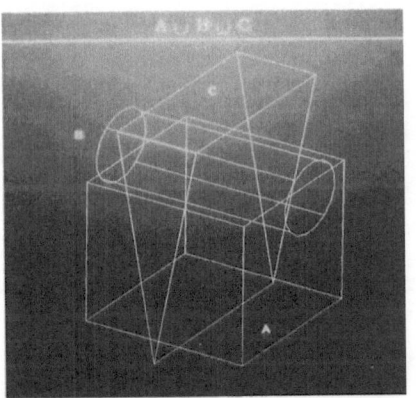

Figure 20 AuBuC Wireframe

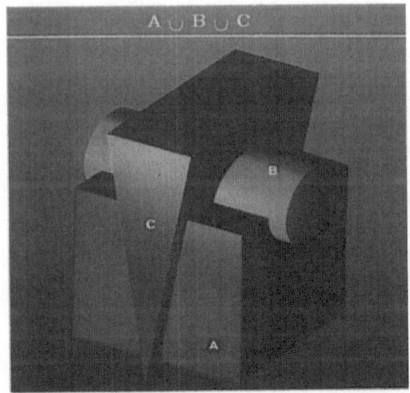

Figure 21 AuBuC Rendering

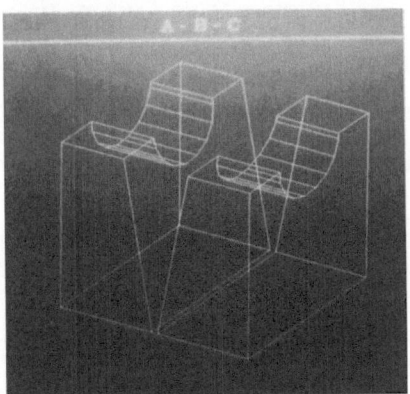

Figure 22 A-B-C Wireframe

Figure 23 A-B-C Rendering

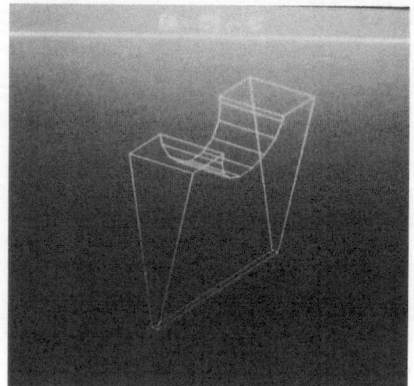

Figure 24 (A-B)+C Wireframe

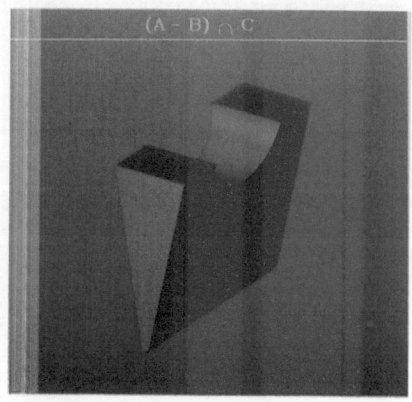

Figure 25 (A-B)+C Rendering

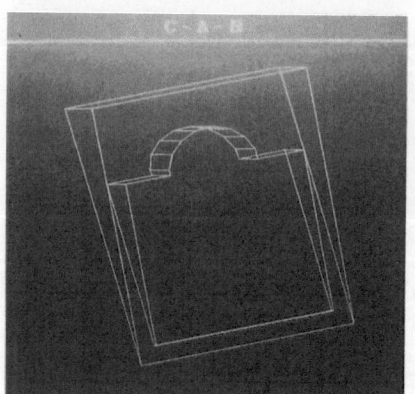

Figure 26 C-A-B Wireframe

Figure 27 C-A-B Rendering

Figure 28 Early Rendering of Vehicle

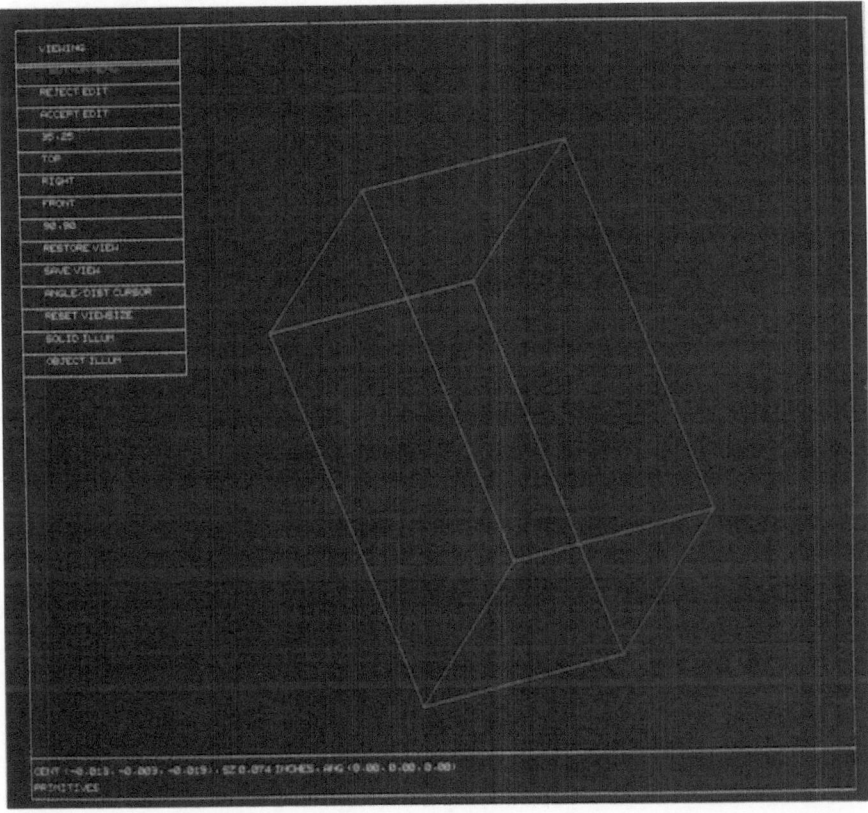

Figure 29 MGED Faceplate with First-level Menu

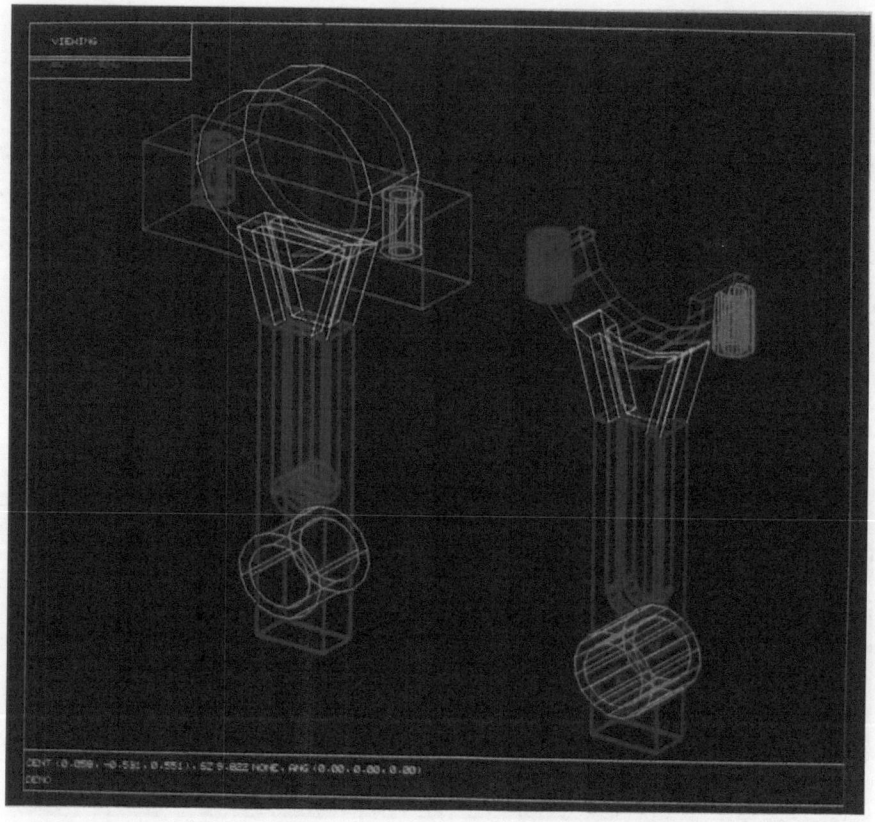

Figure 30 Engine Connecting Rod. Unevaluated and Evaluated Wireframes

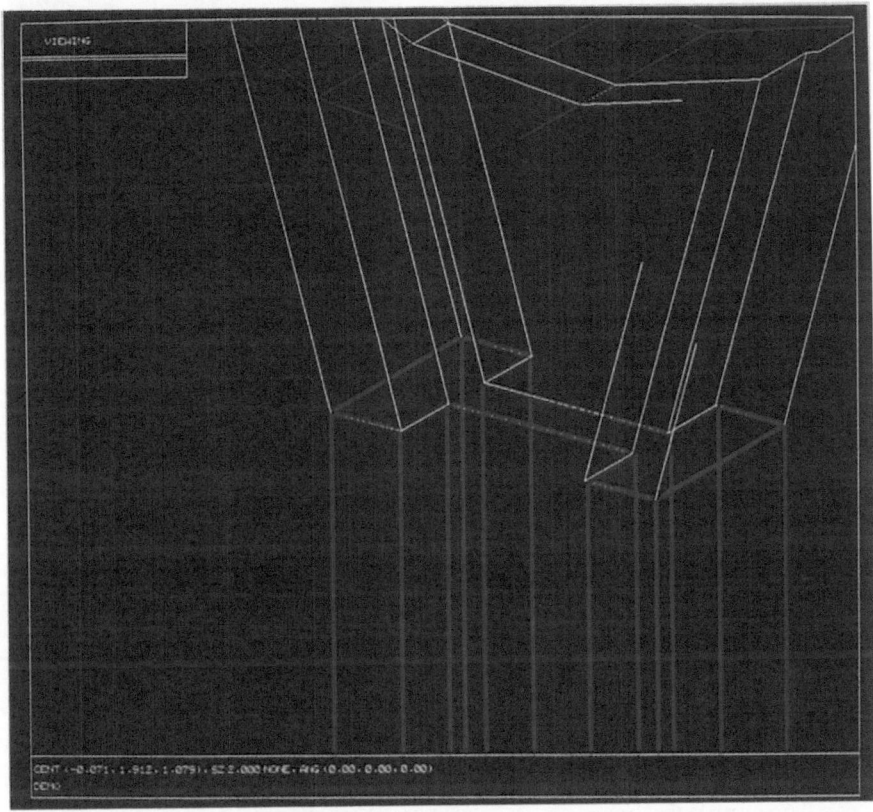

Figure 31 Close-up of Connecting Rod Joint

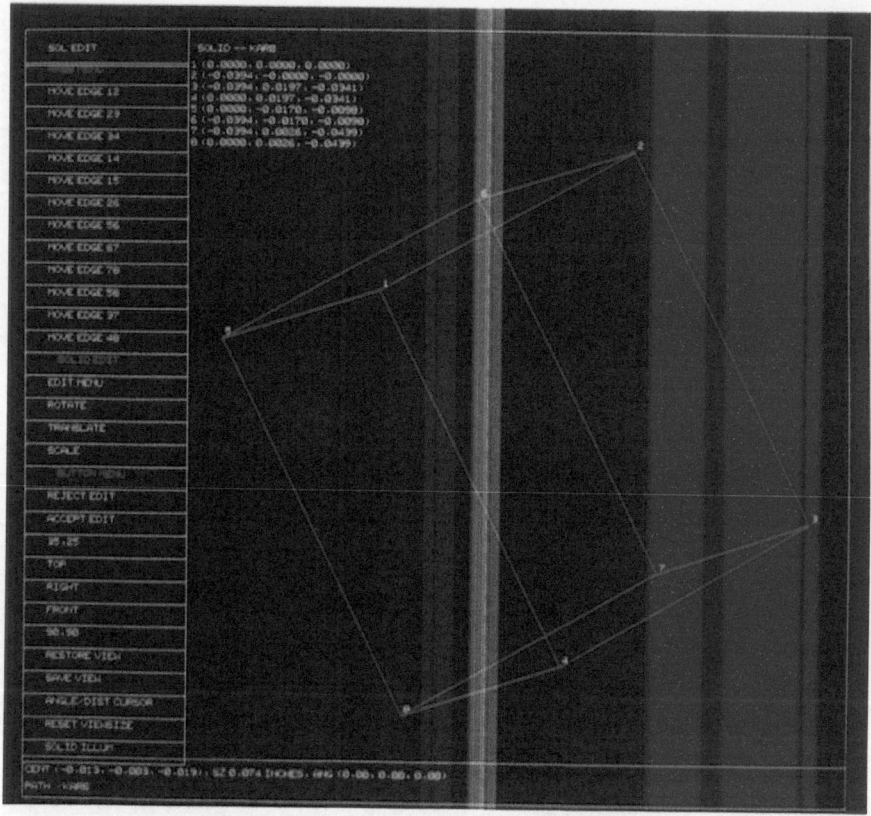

Figure 32ARB8 Before Editing

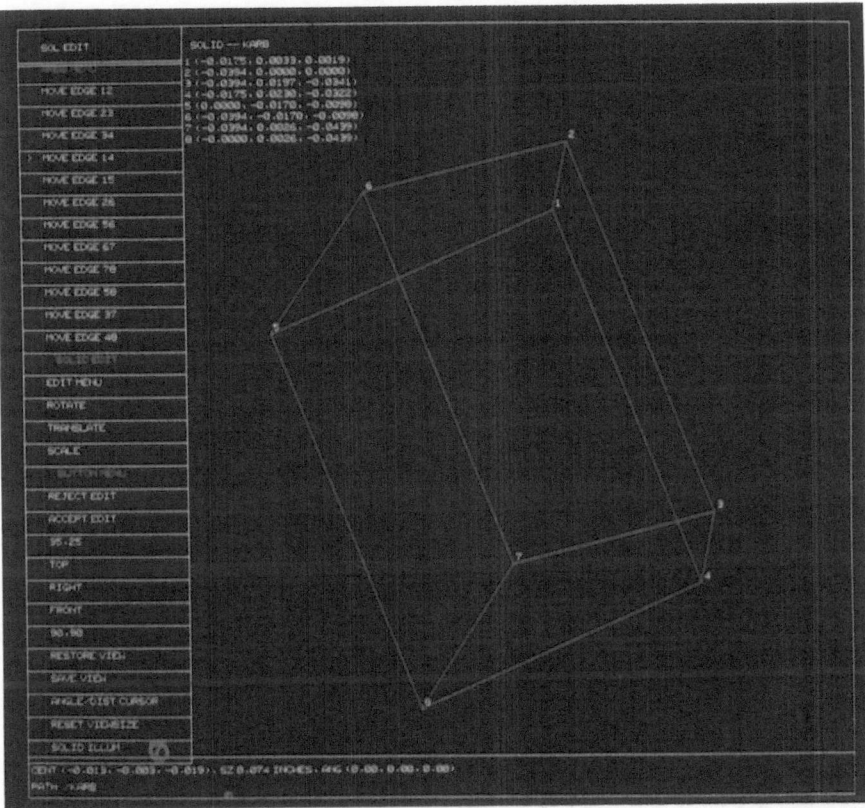

Figure 33 ARB8 After Editing Edges 1-4

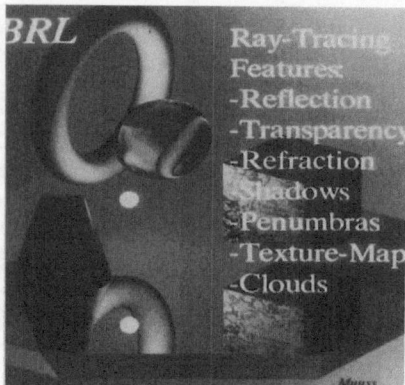

Figure 34 Ray-Tracing Features

Figure 35 Inside and Outside Views
of BMP

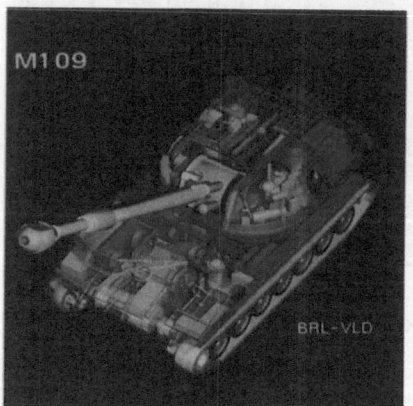

Figure 36 M109 with Transparent Armor

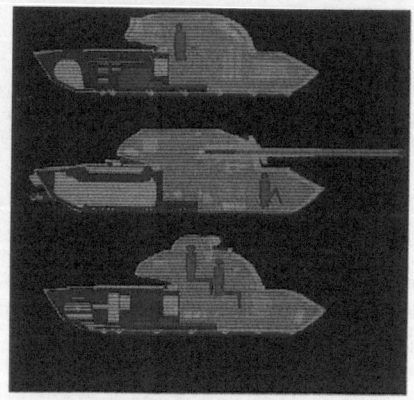

Figure 37 M48 Ray-Tracing sample,
w/Materials Colored

Figure 38 Main Penetrator and Spall Cone

Figure 39 Output of Vulnerability
Evaluation

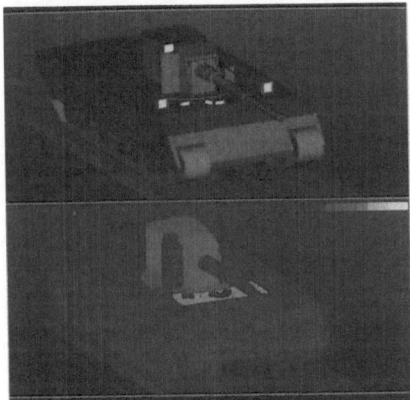

Figure 40 Neutron Study of Testbed Vehicle

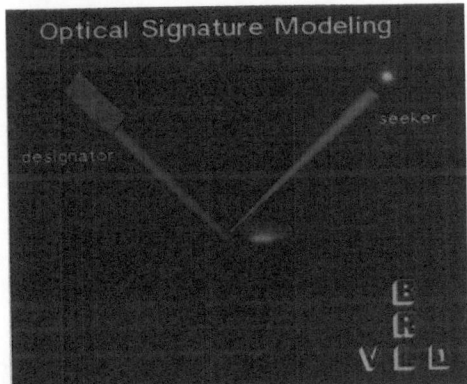

Figure 41 Optical Signature Modeling

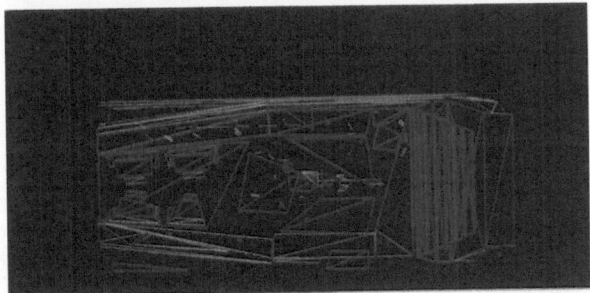

Figure 42 Dihedral and Trihedral Plates

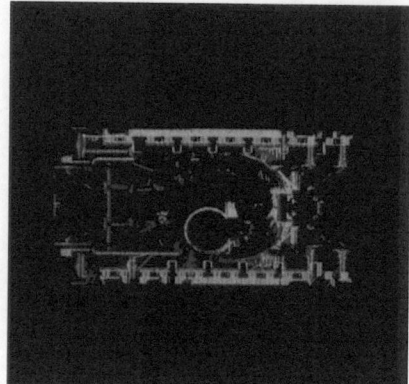

Figure 43 Ray Path of Radar Bounces

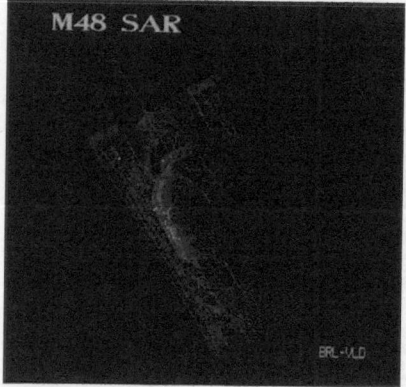

Figure 44 Ultra-high Resolution M48 SAR Image

3 Image Generation

3 Image Generation

The Use of Spatial Coherence in Ray Tracing

MICHAEL R. KAPLAN

Abstract

Although ray tracing has proven to be a valuable technique in realistic image synthesis and a variety of other disciplines, it traditionally has not been viable in highly complex, unstructured environments. Spatial coherence algorithms for ray tracing are proposed as a solution to this problem, and the tradeoffs between various spatial coherence schemes are discussed.

Introduction

In the most general sense, the synthetic generation of realistic shaded images can be viewed as an attempt to reproduce real-world optical phenomena in an imaginary environment. The majority of techniques that have been developed in this area have been based on the discipline of geometric, rather than physical, optics. Physical optics takes into account the inherent wave nature of light. Geometric optics assumes that diffraction and other wave effects are negligible with respect to large objects in the environment, and models light as a straight line phenomenon in a homogeneous media.

Image generation involves both hidden-surface and shading computations. The hidden-surface computation determines which objects in the simulated environment are visible, and which are obscured. The shading computation determines the appearance of the visible objects. Image generation algorithms in the "ray tracing" or "global shading" class generally provide the highest levels of realism and extensibility, as they provide a more complete simulation of geometric optics. The fundamental operation found in these algorithms is the tracing of rays (straight lines) in a three-dimensional environment, in order to determine their interaction with the objects, surfaces, fields, and other elements that are contained in it. This fundamental operation is frequently referred to as "ray tracing" or "ray casting". In this paper, these terms are taken to be synonymous.

The ray tracing operation is used in a number of different parts of the image generation process. These are summarized on the following page:

1. In the hidden-surface computation, rays are traced from the viewer, through the viewer's picture plane, and into the three-dimensional environment in order to determine the frontmost visible objects. These rays are often called viewer rays, hidden-surface rays, or first level rays.
2. In the shading computation, a number of effects can be simulated through the use of ray tracing:
   a. Shadow rays are traced from the visible surface in the direction of light sources in order to determine whether the surface is in shadow with respect to the lights.
   b. Reflection rays are traced from the surface in the mirror-reflection direction to model the perfect reflection contribution to the surface shade.
   c. Transmission rays are traced through the surface of a translucent object. These rays may also be refracted by the object, in which case they are called refraction rays.

Ray tracing is also a useful technique in a number of other disciplines; simulation of real-world phenomena for vision research, medical (radiation treatment planning), seismic (density calculations along a ray), mechanical engineering (interference checking), plant design (pipeline interference checking), hit-testing in geometric applications, and impact and penetration studies.

Recent algorithms have expanded both hidden surface and shading computations to include the concept of statistical sampling. This technique involves computing values based on the integration of multiple, distributed samples, rather than a single one. In the hidden surface computation, distributed samples can be used to simulate lens focus, depth of field, and motion blur. In the shading computation, shadows with penumbras, diffuse reflections and other effects can be simulated using distributed samples. When ray tracing is used as the fundamental operation for these computations, distributed samples can easily be obtained through the tracing of multiple, distributed, rays.

Although ray tracing provides the most elegant, easily extensible, and powerful basis for realistic image computation, there have been a number of barriers to its general use in this application. The two most important are the enormous computational complexity of the naive ray tracing algorithm, and the inherent point sampling nature of ray tracing.

Ray tracing has become increasingly viable in image generation thanks to recent solutions to the latter, anti-aliasing, problem. Briefly stated, any point sampling technique has the property that certain repetitive object elements will cause the false appearance of high spatial frequencies as visible lower frequencies. These are known as "aliasing" effects. Recent research has shown that the computation of sample values as the integration of statistically distributed subsamples solves this problem by trading off visible aliasing for uncorrelated noise, to which the human visual system is much less sensitive. Ray tracing techniques provide a straightforward way of computing these statistically distributed samples, a computation that is harder to perform with less general hidden surface and shading algorithms.

A large body of work has revolved around the solution of the former problem, that of the computational complexity of ray tracing. The use of ray tracing for realistic image synthesis in highly complex environments (those containing complex objects, or a large number of objects) has generally involved an enormous number of floating-point computations. Efforts to reduce the magnitude of this computation have succeeded in some cases, but until recently no general solutions have been proposed. These solutions form the chapter's major topic.

In order for ray tracing to be practical in a wide variety of image generation and other applications it should meet the following criteria:

1. Computation time should be relatively independent of scene complexity (number of objects in the environment, or complexity of individual objects), so that scenes having realistic levels of complexity can be rendered.
2. Per ray time should be relatively constant, and not dependent on the origin or direction of the ray. This property guarantees that overall computation time for a shaded image will be dependent only on overall image resolution (number of first level rays traced) and shading effects (number of second level and higher level rays traced). This guarantees predictable performance for a given image resolution and level of realism.
3. Computation time should be "rational" (say, within an hour) on currently available minicomputer processors, and should be "interactive" (within a few minutes) on future, affordable, processing systems.
4. The algorithm should not require the application to supply hierarchical objects descriptions or object clustering information. The user should be able to combine data generated at different times, and by different means, into a single scene.
5. The algorithm should deal with a wide variety of primitive geometric types, and should be easily extensible to new types.
6. The algorithm's use of coherence should not reduce its applicability to parallel processing or other advanced architectures. Instead, it should be amenable to implementation on such architectures.

In summary, in order to be really usable, it must be possible to trace a large number of rays in complex environments in a rational, predictable time, for a reasonable cost.

Historical Attempts to Speed Ray Tracing

The earliest ray tracing algorithms were based on a brute force technique. These naive algorithms solve the ray-environment intersection problem (finding the closest point of intersection between an arbitrary ray and the objects in the environment) in the following manner; an attempt is made to intersect the ray with each of the objects in the environment, the resulting intersections are then sorted to determine the closest one. The computations involved in this algorithm grow linearly with the number of objects in the environment, and it is thus unusable in applications which require the tracing of a large number of rays in a complex environment.

Early attempts to reduce overall ray tracing time focused on decreasing the computation necessary to compute an individual ray-object intersection. The basic principle is that, although each ray must still be tested against each object in the environment, the time for each ray-object intersection test will be reduced, making the ray tracing process more efficient. A number of algorithms were developed based on this principle, including individual object bounding volumes [Roth82] [CLAR86] [WHIT80] [WEGH84], procedural object descriptions [KAJI83], and composite or hierarchical objects descriptions [ROTH82] [CLAR76] [RUBI80].

Unfortunately, these schemes exhibit a number of properties which make them unacceptable as general solutions to the ray tracing problem. None of them meet all of the criteria listed above. First, each of the algorithms contains some dependence on the number of objects in the scene, since rays must still traced against the topmost bounding volumes in object hierarchies, or against the objects themselves. Thus, ray tracing still has as its fundamental computation the intersection of a ray against each of the objects in the scene. To the extent that the objects are described hierarchically, the efficiency of this step can be dramatically increased. However, all objects must still be considered, at least at the top level of description, and the ray-object intersections must still be sorted to find the closest intersection, since they are not found in order of distance from the ray's origin. Thus, these algorithms do not really succeed in making ray tracing independent of scene complexity. Rubin and Whitted's hierarchical algorithm, however, comes close to the new spatial coherence algorithms when it decomposes spatial areas into (possibly void) octants.

Secondly, most of the composite object schemes depend on the objects in the environment being described in some sort of hierarchical manner. This may require special user assistance in the preprocessing of the data, or a semiintelligent clustering step. Some of the schemes (like the procedural object description scheme of Kajiya) work only for specific object types.

Attempts to speed up ray tracing of complex scenes have included the use of special purpose processors. Most schemes of this sort capitalize on the fact that in standard ray tracing, ray to-ray coherence is not used. Thus, rays can be cast in parallel, without loss of performance. Unfortunately, the number of rays to be traced in a naive ray tracing algorithm is so high that even processing systems with current supercomputer performance are not fast enough to render highly complex scenes in "interactive" time.

New Approaches to the Use of Spatial Coherence in Ray Tracing

Historically, the inner loop of the ray tracing operation has involved an intersection test between the ray and each of the objects in the environment. Even if these ray-object intersection tests are computed efficiently, the computation in the inner loop, and hence the overall amount of computation in any application having ray tracing as its fundamental operation, will still be dependent primarily on the number of objects in the environment. In scenes which contain more than a trivial number of objects, statistics show that up to 95% of the computations during image generation involve the ray-object intersection tests in this inner loop [WHIT80]. Thus, in order to efficiently ray trace in complex environments, it is necessary to reduce the size of this inner loop to a predictable and manageable value.

A number of recent developments have concentrated on the solution to this problem, and the creation of ray tracing algorithms which meet the criteria of practicality described above. These developments have centered around the utilization of both object and spatial coherence to significantly reduce the dependence of the ray tracing computation on scene complexity. A number of theoretical considerations underly these new methods.

First, previous work has shown that the hidden-surface problem may be categorized as one of sorting; consisting of searching, culling, and merging steps [SUTH73]. Ray tracing is generally used in algorithms where a very large number of rays are traced in a static environment. If the naive ray tracing algorithms are used, each of these ray traces involves a similar set of searching, culling, and merging steps. Objects are culled from consideration as the ray is tested for intersection with them. The intersection points that are found must then be sorted with respect to distance from the ray's origin. Finally, in cases involving objects defined using the operations of constructive solid geometry, these intersections must be merged to obtain a geometrically correct result. These sorting steps are performed repetitively for each ray traced in the environment. The new ray tracing algorithms attempt to reduce the total number of individual ray-object intersection tests by moving some of the most frequently performed of these sorting operations out of the inner, per ray, loop and into a series of preprocessing steps, which are performed only once per scene.

A similar set of computational demands to those in ray traced image generation can be found in flight simulators, where a large number of views of a relatively static environment must be computed in real time. Approaches to obtaining reasonable and predictable performance in flight simulation applications have concentrated on preprocessing the environment in order to take the most time consuming sorting steps out of the per pixel or per polygon inner loops. This has been achieved through schemes such as the cluster priority and slicing plane algorithms of Schumacker [SCHU80]. Indeed, Schumacker was one of the first to suggest that image generation can be simplified in situations where the world model changes less frequently than the viewpoint or direction of view of the observer [FUCH80].

Another algorithm which attempts to speed up object space hidden-surface image generation for relatively static scenes is Fuchs' BSP algorithm [FUCH80]. This algorithm preprocesses the entire scene, classifying the objects in the en-

vironment into a binary space partitioning tree. Traversal of the resultant data
structure in an order dependent on the viewpoint of the observer produces a list
of scene elements in a visually consistent back to front ordering. Since each ray
trace performed as part of the generation of a single image is essentially a new
view of a static environment, it is reasonable to conjecture that similar techniques can be applied to speeding up all of the rays traced for a given image
generation. If sorting steps could be moved out of the per ray inner loop by some
kind of preprocessing of the environment, overall ray tracing time would be significantly reduced.

Traditional image space algorithms for non-global image generation make use
of object coherence in projected image space to provide, for highly complex
scenes, significantly increased efficiency over pure object space algorithms. The
two-dimensional character of the operations performed in these algorithms allows their initial sorting steps to be tailored to the resolution of the image raster,
and to the type of processing that will be performed during the actual per scanline and per pixel rendering computations.

Similarly, we would like to be able to exploit object coherence in local
regions of three-dimensional space to tailor the initial sorting steps to the actual
per ray operations performed in repetitive ray traces in a static environment, and
thus provide a significant advance over the naive ray tracing algorithm. Object
coherence is the property of connected three-dimensional surfaces and solids
which essentially states that if an object occupies an area of three-dimensional
space, it is also likely to occupy the nearest connected spatial areas in its
vicinity.

A major bar to utilization of object coherence has been the lack of a well defined method for classifying random searches of rays in three-dimensional space.
Unlike in projected image space algorithms, whose rendering order (usually
scanline) is well defined and inherently two-dimensional, rays can originate
anywhere in the scene and can have arbitrary direction. This has the tendency to
"randomize" accesses to the environment in such a manner as to negate the positive effects of object coherence within searched space. If searches to the data
produced during initial sorting steps cannot be keyed efficiently for each ray
trace, such data cannot be used effectively to reduce ray-environment intersection computations.

Recent developments have centered around methods of spatial organization
which allow such preprocessing to be effective. The new algorithms all have as
a central focus the fact that space itself is regular and connected. When a ray is
projected through space, it follows a coherent and predictable path. Through the
use of an auxillary three-dimensional structure superimposed over all space, rays
can be tracked through it in a coherent and predictable manner. Spatial
coherence is used in conjunction with ray tracking in these auxillary data structures to identify, in distance order, the spatial regions which lie along the ray's
path. The search through previously sorted data can thus be keyed directly on
the path of the ray, and object coherence can be utilized to reduce ray-environment intersection times.

Space-Tracing - A Constant Time Ray-Tracer

One algorithm illustrative of this method is the authors "space tracing" algorithm for ray environment intersection calculations [KAPL85]. This algorithm utilizes an auxillary data structure to adaptively subdivide all of three-dimensional space based on the objects in the scene. Rays are then tracked through space with the aid of this data structure, being intersected with objects only when they lie along the immediate path of the ray. A more detailed description of this algorithm follows.

The Fundamental Concept of Space Tracing

Since ray tracing attempts to simulate geometric optics, its fundamental operation is that of searching space for the intersections of a ray with objects in the environment. A ray of light (or a viewer line of sight, or other ray) in the physical world does not "know" about the objects in its path until it encounters one of them. When asked to draw a picture of a chair in the corner of a room, an artist will rarely scan every object in the environment before proceeding to draw each line of his picture. The fundamental concept of space tracing is thus simply, that ray tracing should be performed against known space, rather than the objects it contains. Only when a ray enters an area of space which is known to contain objects, and furthermore, where a ray-object intersection is highly likely, are any intersection tests performed.

The Algorithm and its Implementation

The space tracing algorithm may be broken up into two distinct steps; preprocessing and ray casting.

Preprocessing. The first step in the space tracing algorithm is the construction of a data base which will allow arbitrary ray-environment intersections to be computed as quickly as possible. This data base divides all of known space (all space within the world coordinate system which contains objects) into a hierarchical structure of cubic boxes aligned with the cartesian axes of the world coordinate system. It contains the information necessary to speed up the following operations:

1. Given a point in known space, obtain a reference to the box and its data which contains the point. Since space is divided adaptively and unevenly, this cannot be performed simply by indexing into a three-dimensional table of box references.
2. Given a ray, with origin point within a given box, determine the next box which the ray will pierce, or determine that the ray will leave known space.

3. Given a box, obtain a list of all of the objects in the environment whose surfaces intersect the subspace described by the box, and which must therefore be tested for intersection with each ray which pierces it.

This data base is organized as a binary tree (a tree where each non-terminal node can have exactly two child nodes directly attached to it), whose non-leaf nodes are called slicing nodes, and whose leaf nodes are called box nodes and termination nodes. Each slicing node contains the identification of a slicing plane, which divides all of space into two infinite subspaces. The slicing planes are always aligned with two of the cartesian coordinate axes of the primary space being subdivided. The child nodes of a slicing node can be either other slicing nodes, box nodes, or termination nodes. A box node, which is always a leaf node, describes the cubic area of known space which is bounded by all of the slicing planes of the slicing nodes which were traversed to reach it. A termination node, which is also always a leaf node, indicates an area which is entirely outside of known space. This entire data structure will be henceforth referred to as the BSP (binary space partitioning) tree.

The slicing nodes of the BSP tree are used to implement operation (1) above. The box nodes are used to implement operations (2) and (3). In order to accomplish this, each box node contains a list of the objects whose surfaces intersect it, in addition to a spatial description of the cubic subspace which it defines. The objects referenced in the box nodes are called intersection objects, because they contain all of the information necessary for the ray-object intersector to function. This information includes:

1. A reference to the intersection method, which is a procedure that the object uses to intersect its surface with a ray. In this way, the ray-object intersections can be performed in an object-oriented fashion, and each object can test for ray intersections using an algorithm which is particularly suited to its geometric type.
2. A reference to the instance data, which describes the particular instance of the geometric data type whose surface pierces the box.

Building the BSP tree proceeds in the following manner:

1. Generate a list of intersection objects for the environment. This list may be created directly by the user of the software, or may be procedurally generated from higher-level object descriptions as the following steps are performed.
2. Ask each intersection object to return its spatial limits in the world coordinate system. This information is used to determine the limits of known space. Note that the rays will be allowed to originate outside of known space, primarily so that the synthetic cameras for ray traced image generation may be positioned at a large distance from the objects in the scene, without increasing the size of known space. If distant cameras were included in known space, more levels of subdivision would be needed to subdivided the space into cubic areas of a certain size, thereby potentially increasing computation during the ray casting step.

3. Starting with a box which encompasses all of known space, and which is aligned to the world coordinate system's cartesian axes, ask each intersection object whether its surface intersects the box. Obtain in this manner a list of all of the intersection objects whose surfaces intersect the box. If this list contains more than a previously specified minimum number of elements (usually one or two), and the box is larger than a previously specified minimum size, then subdivide the box into eight subboxes, create the slicing nodes necessary to describe them, and recursively call the box subdivision algorithm with each of these subboxes. When the top level box recursion exits, the entire BSP tree has been constructed. When a box is subdivided, only those objects which intersected it are passed to the subdivision calls for its subboxes, thereby culling from consideration all of the other objects in the environment. Thus, the spatial subdivision step is not of linear complexity with respect to the number of objects in the environment, but more approximately depends (as Kunii has pointed out) on the overall surface area of the objects in the scene [KUNI85].

Ray-casting - Calculating Ray-Environment Intersections. Once the preprocessing step has been completed, the data base it generates can be used to quickly determine the intersections which a ray makes with the objects in the environment. The intersection points found in this manner will be exactly the same as if they had been computed using the naive ray tracing method of intersecting the ray with every object in the environment. Ray-environment intersection in space tracing is performed as follows:

1. First, determine the in-space origin of the ray. For rays which must originate inside of known space (ie., second or higher level rays projected as part of shaded picture generation), this point is merely the ray's origin. If the ray is one which could originate outside of known space (ie., first level rays in rendering) we must find an origin point for the ray inside of the limits of known space. This is done by intersecting the ray with the outermost bounding box of known space. If no ray-bounding box intersection is found, then the ray does not pierce known space and the ray casting step for it is complete, no intersections with objects in the environment are possible. If the ray does intersect the bounding box, determine its in-space origin by pushing along the ray a small amount from the point of intersection.

2. Traverse the BSP tree, comparing the (x,y,z) values of the ray's world coordinate system origin with each of the slicing nodes encountered in the tree. Decide at each slicing node whether to branch to the left or to the right child, depending on the relationship between one of the origin's coordinates and the location of the slicing plane. Eventually a leaf node will be reached. This may be a box node, which describes the cubic spatial area containing the ray's origin, or it may be a terminating node, indicating that the ray has left known space. In the latter case, ray tracing may be terminated, or the ray may be traced for reflection mapping outside of the world environment.

3. Ask each of the intersection objects to find the intersection point between the ray and its surface. Note that the intersection routine also knows the spatial coordinates of the box being processed, and can limit its intersection processing using this information, if such information is useful to the particular intersection method. If an intersection point is found, make sure that the point is within the box under consideration. This may not be true.
4. Sort the list of intersections from step 3, and find the closest intersection of the ray against the objects in the box. This point is the closest intersection point of the ray with any object in the environment.
5. If no intersection point was found in step 3, then the ray did not intersect any objects within the current box. Find the point where the ray leaves the box by intersecting it with the boundaries of the box. Since we know the spatial bounds of the box, that the box is aligned with the cartesian coordinate axes, and that the ray origin is inside the box, this test can be performed using a special, extremely efficient series of intersection tests. Now, push the ray just past the boundary of the box to obtain a new origin point for the ray, and proceed with step 1 above.

Performance Results

The space tracing algorithm for ray-environment intersection computation has been incorporated as a fundamental part of a large image computation software package [KOBR], designed to operate across a wide variety of systems, and in a wide variety of applications. Results have shown the algorithm to be extremely effective in achieving the criteria of practicality set forth above. Specifically, given the proper level of subdivision for a particular scene, the algorithm can be made to operate with approximately the same level of performance as a naive ray tracer would in an environment containing as few as five primitive objects, regardless of the number of objects present in the original scene. Tests with 6,000 objects in the environment run almost as quickly as those with 20, in some cases even faster. Thus, on a DEC VAX 11/780 class system, with floating point accelerator (approximate performance, 1 mips integer arithmetic, .2 mflops floating point arithmetic), a 512 by 512 non-antialiased image takes in the range of 45 to 60 minutes to compute. This computation time is roughly independent of the number of objects in the scene, but is dependent on the scene's visible complexity. Roughly stated, visible complexity in this case is a measure of the proportion of the rendered pixel elements which contain shaded surface points.

Thus, the performance improvement of space tracing over conventional ray tracing is roughly proportional to the ratio of the number of objects in the scene being rendered to five objects. If the scene contains 100 objects, space tracing is approximately $100/5 = 20$ times more efficient. If the scene contains 1000 objects, it is 200 times more efficient, and so on. Obviously, cases involving hundreds of thousands of objects may strain the memory capabilities of even a large virtual memory system, although the actual working set of the algorithm is under a megabyte. Provided these difficulties can be overcome, however, the performance improvement of space tracing for such scenes would be roughly proportional to the number of objects that they contain.

Analysis of Performance

Empirical evidence has demonstrated the performance of the space tracing algorithm against the naive ray tracing algorithm. The reasons for this are fairly obvious; because the objects are presorted into a spatial structure keyed directly by the path of a ray, rays are intersected with only a very small number of objects, regardless of the complexity of the scene. The sorting steps necessary to achieve this result are performed only once during preprocessing, and are thus moved out of the per ray loop. The sorting performed during preprocessing also ensures that the closest intersection point along the path of a ray is found first (except for the case where multiple objects intersect the same low-level spatial box, where some sorting must still be performed). Ray tracing can be continued past each intersection point, resulting in the discovery of all of the ray's intersections with objects in the environment, in the presorted order of closest to most distant. This means that the spatial coherence of the objects in the scene is implicitly utilized to sort the ray-object intersections, as well as to find these intersections quickly.

As mentioned above, it is visible complexity, more than geometric complexity, which determines the performance of the space tracing algorithm. Since it is generally true that, as the number of objects in a scene increases, the average portion of a single object which is visible from a given view point decreases, the visible complexity of a scene will tend to remain relatively constant as the number of objects that it contains increases. In no case will more initial rays be traced for non-antialiased image generation than the resolution of the viewplane raster grid.

The relatively constant and predictable performance of the space tracing algorithm over a large range of scene complexity, despite increased preprocessing requirements, and the necessity of moving rays through the more highly subdivided spatial data structure required for complex scenes, is a little more difficult to explain. An attempt is made in the following paragraphs.

Space tracing would not be as attractive if the preprocessing step had the same linear complexity with number of objects as ray tracing itself, although, since the preprocessing step is performed only once, versus potentially millions of times for the ray casting step, it might still be feasible. Fortunately, the rapid culling of objects during the subdivision process reduces this problem. Furthermore, bounding volume checks can be used to rapidly cull objects in the object-box intersection tests. Space tracing would also be less efficient, especially for highly subdivided scenes, if the movement of a ray through the space boxes was substantially slower than the intersection of a ray with an object. Operation counts, however, show that, in the time for a single ray-object intersection test (ie., with a sphere), approximately seven ray box pushes can be performed. This is mainly due to the fact that the boxes are aligned with the world coordinate system's axes, and that no 4x4 matrix transformation need be applied to the ray to transform it into the coordinate system of the boxes, as is often the case for intersection with geometric primitives.

One underlying reason for the constancy of performance is the fact that the only areas of known space which are heavily subdivided are those which contain a high density of objects. Areas containing a low density of objects remain more or less undivided, so that rays pass quickly through them. Once a ray enters a high density region of space, it has the potential of encountering a large number of small boxes. This could be a costly situation. Fortunately, the probability that the ray will soon strike a surface is also much higher in such areas, and the ray travel is quickly terminated, not by leaving the area, but by intersecting an object within it. Secondary (ie., shadow and reflection) rays emanating from these high density areas are also more likely to intersect a surface close to their origin, so that ray travel is again quickly terminated. Therefore, the mean path of ray travel, as measured by the amount of computation performed between one ray intersection and the next, remains relatively constant. A similar situation arises in the case of mean molecule travel between collisions in a gas, and in many other cases found in statistical physics and thermodynamics.

Application of Space Tracing to Shaded Picture Generation

Like any other algorithm for ray tracing, space tracing can be used in both the hidden surface and shading computation steps of image generation. In addition, there are a number of aspects of the algorithm which make it particularly well suited to the generation of realistic images.

One of the primary applications of ray tracing in shaded picture generation is in the simulation of shadows, particularly when light sources are in the scene, or the shadows being computed are for surface points not directly visible to the viewer (ie., reflective surfaces). In order to test whether a particular light source is shadowed for a given surface, a ray is traced from the surface point in the direction of the light source. If the ray intersects another object before the light source is encountered, then the surface is in shadow with respect to the light source. Standard ray tracing algorithms do not generate the list of ray object intersections in sorted order by distance from the ray origin, so all of the intersections must be determined before the closest intersection distance can be compared with the distance to the in-scene light source. Since space tracing always find the closest intersection first, only one intersection test and one distance comparison need to be performed to determine if the surface is in shadow with respect to a particular light source in the scene. If the first intersection found is not closer than the light source, then the surface is not in shadow.

Schemes for intersecting rays directly against high-order primitives like bicubic surface patches typically involve one of two approaches. Either the ray primitive intersection is calculated analytically, through solution of a set of equations for each intersection, or an iterative solution is used to converge onto the ray-primitive intersection point. One iterative scheme for bicubic patches works by recursively subdividing the patch and intersecting the ray with a bounding volume for each subpatch. When the subpatch which the ray intersects is flat to within some criteria, then it is approximated by a flat polygonal area, and the ray-polygon intersection is found. Another scheme works by recursively subdividing the patch until the bounding volume for the subpatch which is intersected by the ray is smaller than a pixel. This intersection point is taken to be the ray-patch intersection. Although these are elegant and powerful solutions to a number of ray-primitive intersection problems, they have the disadvantage of subdividing the overall patch until some criteria is met for each ray intersection. Some algorithms move this step outside of the per ray loop by presubdiving each patch into subpatches which cover a smaller area of three-space and which are closer to or at the termination criteria. Unfortunately, this type of preprocessing is antithetic to the naive ray tracing algorithm, which intersects each ray with every object in the environment, since it significantly increases the number of primitives in the environment. However, since space tracing may actually perform better with a larger number of smaller primitives, the presplitting of patches combines well with this algorithm.

Alternative Approaches to the Use of Spatial Coherence

The space tracing algorithm described in detail above is only one of a number of algorithms which take advantage of spatial coherence to improve ray tracing performance. Although developed independently, these algorithms are strikingly similar in their approach to the problem. As Fujimoto points out, all of the algorithms use an auxillary data structure imposed upon three-dimensional space in order to track a ray's path and identify the objects that it is likely to intersect [FUJI85]. The major differences among these algorithms appear in the types of auxillary spatial data structure that they utilize, and in their methods for tracking rays through these structures. The choices of auxillary data structure and of tracking method are intimately related, as will become evident when alternative approaches are considered.

Spatial coherence schemes for ray tracing can be classified by the type of auxillary data structure that they impose on space. The largest number of schemes, and historically the earliest group, involve the use of an octtree spatial organization, either directly encoded in the auxillary data structure, or implied by the ray tracking method. An octtree is a data structure where each node can point to one parent node and eight leaf nodes. In spatial coherence ray tracing algorithms, each node of the octtree represents a spatial area. If the spatial area represented by a node is simple (ie. empty, contains a minimum number of objects, or meets some other termination criteria), then it has no children, and instead references a list of objects whose surfaces intersect the spatial area. If it is not simple, then the children of the node represent the eight equally sized subareas of the parent's spatial area. Fujimoto states that the use of an octtree hierarchy as an auxillary data structure was first proposed by Fujimura, et. al., and almost simultaneously by Matsumoto and Murakami [FUJI85]. Glassner and Goldsmith also use this structure [GLAS84] [GOLD]. Kaplan's space tracing technique is also based on an octtree spatial representation [KAPL85].

The major differences among these techniques involve the manner in which the data structure is stored, in conjunction with the methods used to track rays through space. Glassner, for example, does not store the octtree explicitly, but encodes the spatial hierarchy in a combination of hash table and linked list data structures. His method for finding the node which contains a given three-space location involves generating a name through a numerical manipulation of the point's (x,y,z) coordinates. Space tracing, on the other hand, encodes the octtree in the form of a binary space partitioning tree, which is directly traversed to find the node containing a given point. Tracking of the ray in the octtree method generally involves some floating point multiplications and divisions in order to intersect the ray with the bounds of the space boxes and to push it into adjacent spatial areas.

The other predominate spatial representation is probably best exemplified by the SEADS (Spatially Enumerated Auxillary Data Structure) organization proposed by Fujimoto [FUJI85]. This organization is basically a three-dimensional decomposition of space into equally sized voxels. Fujimoto has developed a method of ray tracking which he calls 3DDDA. This method, which is well matched to the SEADS spatial organization, is a three-dimensional form of the two-dimensional digital differential analyzer algorithm commonly used for line drawing in raster graphics systems. The major advantage of the enumerated data structure over an octtree representation is related to ray tracking. The efficiency of ray tracking using the 3DDDA algorithm in the spatial enumeration scheme lies mainly in the fact that no floating-point multiplications or divisions are needed in track the ray from spatial area to area, once an initialization step for the ray has been performed. Claims of an order of magnitude improvement in ray tracking speed over the octtree methods have been made [FUJI85]. It is also possible to improve the performance of octtree traversal by utilizing the 3DDDA method to traverse horizontally in the octtree, but vertical level changes must still be traversed explicitly.

Other spatial enumeration, or cellular, techniques exist, and differ from SEADS in either the shape or the cell, the distribution of processing and objects in the cells, or the method of tracking rays through them. Cleary, et. al., have proposed a cellular scheme with equal sized voxels, with particular emphasis on processing by either a cubic or a square array of parallel processors [CLEA83]. Dippe has also proposed a parallel processor based algorithm, with variably sized cells [DIPP84]. In his scheme, the size and shape of the spatial cells adapt to the complexity and density of objects in local spatial areas in order to help equalize the distribution of work in a parallel processing environment.

Spatial Coherence Schemes: Issues and Future Directions

Work performed to date has only touched the surface of the research issues involved in the use of spatial coherence in ray tracing. As in the case of image space hidden surface algorithms, there is undoubtedly no "best" spatial coherence ray tracing scheme for all applications, and the area open to research is probably at least as large. In general, the following research areas seem particularly promising:

1. Increasing the overall efficiency of spatial coherence based ray tracing. Although spatial coherence algorithms provide significant improvements in computational efficiency over historical ray tracing algorithms in a wide variety of applications, there is still substantial room for improvement. Increased efficiency may be found in an analysis of the new "inner loops" found in spatial coherence ray tracing algorithms. The first "inner loop", or most highly intensive area of computation, involves the tracking of rays through space. The second "inner loop" involves the intersection of rays with the objects located in the spatial areas in proximity to their path.

2. The application of special processing structures, especially parallel processing, to provide "interactive" ray traced image generation. Even though spatial coherence algorithms have proven to be much more efficient than those previously available, they are still not capable of providing "interactive" reponse when executed on currently available general purpose processors. An analogy may be drawn to the development of the image space algorithms. These algorithms have also not performed quickly enough on general purpose processors to provide "interactive" response. However, one of them, the z-buffer, does have certain characteristics which make it particularly suitable for implementation on special purpose hardware. First, its performance is fairly predictable and constant over a wide range of scene complexity. Second, its basic operations are relatively easy to implement in hardware. Thus, the past five years have seen increasing use of hardware z-buffer implementations to provide "interactive" shaded picture generation.

   Unlike most historical ray tracing algorithms, those based on spatial coherence also provide relatively predictable and constant performance over a range of scene complexity. They also have basic operations which are amenable to implementation with special purpose hardware. Thus, it is likely that these algorithms will provide our "best bet" for affordable, interactive ray traced image generation.

3. The application of spatial coherence based ray tracing techniques outside of image generation. The basic operation of tracing a ray in an environment is fundamental to many applications outside of image generation. In geometric modeling, it provides a method of performing various analyses on objects defined through constructive solid geometry operations. It can be used for penetration analysis, interference checking, hit testing, and medical beam treatment planning. Some of these applications can directly benefit from the techniques discussed above, while some will require their integration into other algorithms.

Improving the Efficiency of
Spatial Coherence Based Ray Tracing

There are a number of tradeoffs involved in the overall efficiency of spatial coherence based ray tracing algorithms. Two of the most important are discussed below.

The Tradeoff Between Ray Tracking and Object Intersection.

One of the fundamental computational tradeoffs which appears in all ray tracing schemes based on the use of spatial coherence involves trading ray tracking computation for object intersection computation. The determination of the optimal spatial subdivision for a given scene is extremely important to the efficiency of ray tracing. Ray tracking time generally increases with increased spatial subdivision, while the average number of objects which must be intersected with a ray within each spatial area correspondingly decreases. The naive ray tracing algorithm can be viewed as a spatial subdivision scheme in which all of space is classified into a single, undivided, spatial area. Each ray must therefore be tested for intersection with every object in the environment. If space is too finely divided, however, ray tracking time may grow until the advantage gained by decreasing the average number of ray-object intersections per spatial area is offset by the cost of tracking a ray through a large number of areas, and the possibility that the ray will be repeatedly tested against the same primitive object in different areas.

In octtree based methods, ray tracking time is directly related to the average depth of the octtree data structure. The subdivision parameter which most closely governs this value is the maximum level of subdivision allowed during preprocessing. The maximum depth of the octtree can be no larger than the value of this parameter. On the other hand, the optimal subdivision level for the octtree may also depends on the average number of objects per spatial area in the environment. This value in turn depends on another parameter of the subdivision process, the minimum number of objects allowed per spatial area. This parameter specifies the upper bound on the number of objects that an area can contain before it must be further subdivided during preprocessing. The optimal choice of these parameters seems to be related to the structure and contents of the scene. Optimal cell size must also be considered in the case of the enumerated data structure.

The Tradeoff Between Object Coherence
and Spatial Coherence

The octtree is a spatial data structure which is a function of object shape and scene topology. This allows it to efficiently utilize object coherence. In a scene in which objects are not randomly distributed, the subdivision of the octtree will adapt to the nonuniform density of objects. Rays tracked through this structure will encounter fewer spatial areas on the average before intersecting an object than when space is evenly divided in a regular three-dimensional grid of boxes. On the other hand, the spatially enumerated spatial structure encodes none of the object shape or scene topology information, but is easier to track by a ray. It thus trades off the use of object coherence for a simpler, and more coherent, spatial data structure which can more effectively utilize spatial coherence. Where should the line be drawn between object coherence and spatial coherence for maximum efficiency? More research is needed to discover an answer to this question, but the choice of tradeoff point is probably tied to the characteristics of the types of environments most likely to be encountered in a particular application.

A Modest Proposal. Although previous efforts have concentrated on improving ray tracking efficiency in spatial coherence schemes, it is not clear that the next major improvement is to be found along these lines. As mentioned above, there are two "inner loops" to the new ray tracing calculations. The first involves only ray tracking, but the second involves the calculation of individual ray-object intersection tests. Current spatial coherence algorithms for ray tracing concentrate on speeding up this second "inner loop" by reducing the average number of objects per spatial box along with the average number of spatial boxes encountered per ray. Previous ray tracing algorithms have concentrated on improving the efficiency of each ray-object intersection calculation. A third method for improving this computation may, however, be possible in the context of spatial coherence schemes. Since these schemes generally reduce the number of objects per spatial area to a very small number, these spatial areas may be so simple that the visibility of the objects within them can be predetermined independently of point of view. In other words, many of the spatial areas may have the characteristics of what are referred to as "clusters" in flight simulator data bases [SCHU80]. If the preprocessing step, in addition to subdividing the environment into spatial areas, also detected areas which had the properties of clusters, and predetermined the visibility of the objects within them, then the operation of intersecting a ray with these spatial areas could be considered as an indivisible, single operation, independent of the number of objects within the areas. This might not only increase the efficiency of the ray-spatial area intersection step, but could also reduce the level of spatial subdivision necessary for efficient ray tracing, and thereby move the tradeoff point towards higher performance ray tracking.

References

[CLAR76] Clark, J.H., Hierarchical Geometrics Models for Visible Surface Algorithms. Communications of the ACM (Oct.1976)

[CLEA83] Cleary, J.G., Wyvill, B., Birtwistle, G.M., and Vatti, R., Multipro- cessor Ray Tracing. Research Report No. 83/128/17, The University of Calgary (1983)

[COOK84] Cook, R., Porter, T. and Carpenter, L., Distributed Ray Tracing. SIGGRAPH 84 Conference Proceedings (July 1984) 137-145

[DOCT81] Doctor, L. and Torborg, J., Display Techniques for Octree-Encoded Objects. IEEE Computer Graphics and Applications (July 1981) 29-38

[DIPP84] Dippe, M. and Swenson, J., An Adaptive Subdivision Algorithm and Parallel Architecture for Realistic Image Synthesis. SIGGRAPH 84 Conference Proceedings (July 1984) 149-158

[FUCH80] Fuchs, H., On Visible Surface Generation by A Priori Tree Structures. SIG-GRAPH80 Conference Proceedings (July 1980) 124-133

[FUJI85] Fujimoto, A., Tanaka, T. and Iwata, K., ARTS: Accelerated Ray-Tracing System. IEEE Computer Graphics and Applications, April, 1985

[GLAS84] Glassner, A. S., Space Subdivision for Fast Ray Tracing. IEEE Computer Graphics and Applications (Oct.1984) 15-22.

[GOLD] Goldsmith, J. and Salmon, J., A Ray Tracing System for the Hypercube. California Institute of Technology (CCP).

[KAJI83] Kajiya, J. T., New Techniques for Ray Tracing Procedurally Defined Objects. SIGGRAPH83 Conference Proceedings (July 1983) 91-102

[KAPL85] Kaplan, M.R., Space-Tracing, a Constant Time Ray-Tracer. SIGGRAPH 85 tutorial, San Francisco, July, 1985

[KOBR] Display Workbench Reference Manual, KOBRA Graphics, Inc. 820 No. Delaware St. #307, San Mateo, CA 94401

[KUNI85] Kunii, T.L., and Wyvill, G., A Simple But Systematic CSG System. Proc. Graphics Interface 85, Montreal, May 27-31, 1985

[ROTH82] Roth, S.D., Ray Casting for Modeling Solids. Computer Graphics and Image Processing 18 (1982) 109-144

[RUBI80] Rubin, S. and Whitted, T., A Three-Dimensional Representation for Fast Rendering of Complex Scenes. Computer Graphics 14 (1980) 110-116

[SCHU80] Schumacker, R. A., A New Visual System Architecture. Proc 2nd Interservice/Industry Training Equipment Conf. (Salt Lake City, Utah, Nov. 18-20, 1980)

[SUTH73] Sutherland, I.E., Sproull, R.F., and Schumacker, R.A., Sorting and the Hidden Surface Problem. in Proc, AFIPS 1973 National Computer Cong., vol. 42,1973

[VATT84] Vatti, R., Multiprocessor Ray Tracing. Master's Thesis, The University of Calgary (1984)

[WEGH84] Weghorst, H., Hooper, G., and Greenberg, Donald P., Improved Computational Methods for Ray Tracing. ACM Transactions on Graphics, Vol. 3, Number 1, Jan., 1984

[WHIT80] Whitted, T., An Improved Illumination Model for Shaded Display. Communications of the ACM 23 (June 1980) 343-349

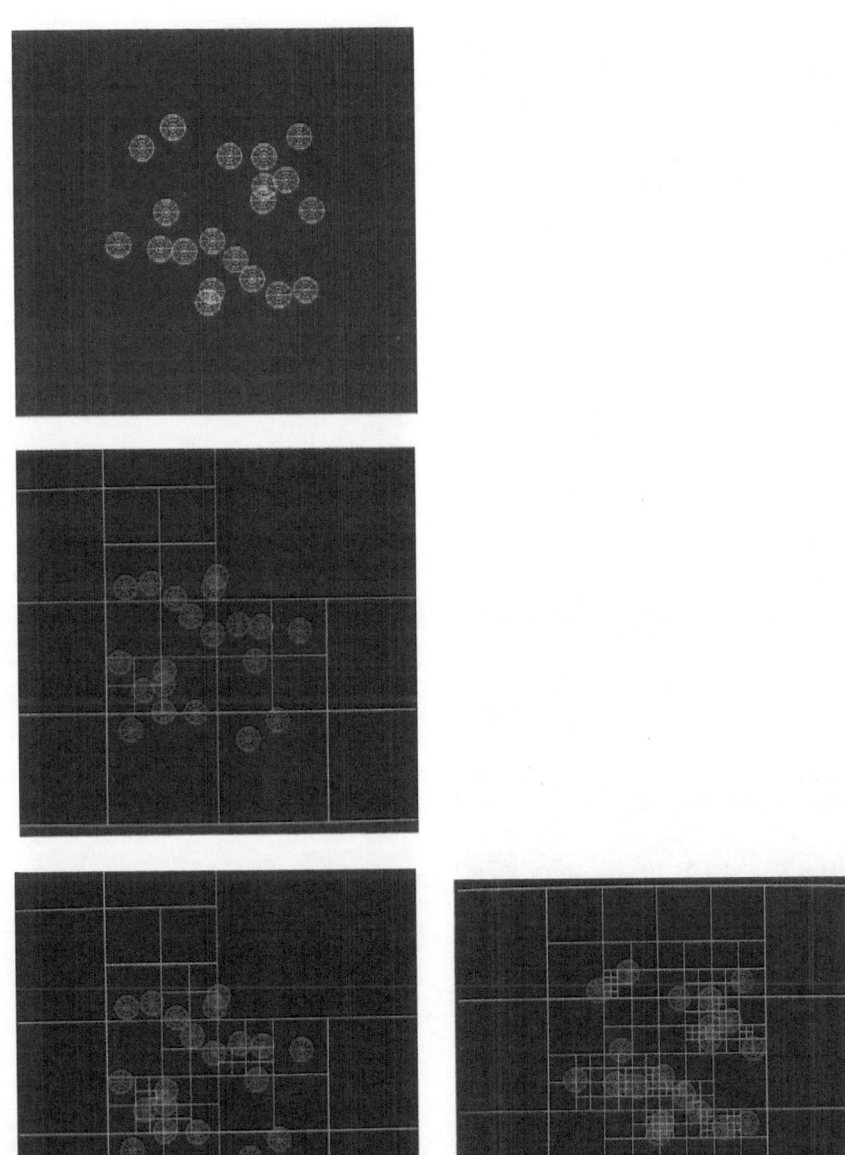

Figures 1 - 4

Figure 1 illustrates a two-dimensional slice through a three-dimensional space, showing a simple scene consisting of a small number of spheres. Figures 2 through 4 illustrate increasing levels of spatial subdivision.

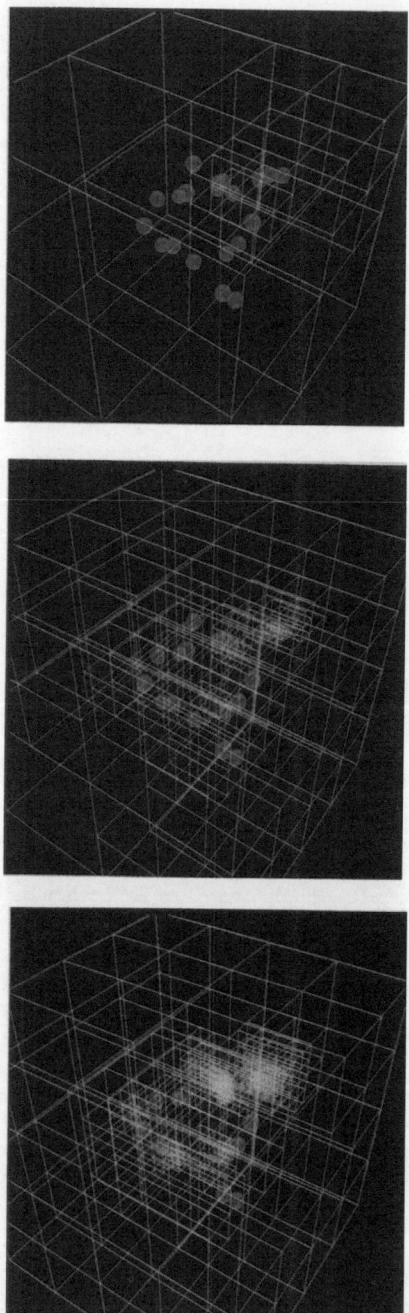

Figures 5 - 7

Three-dimensional images showing increasing levels of spatial subdivision for a simple scene containing a small number of spheres.

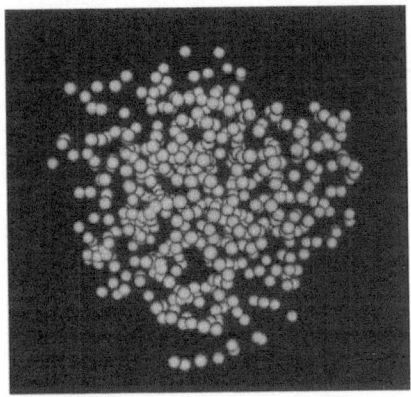 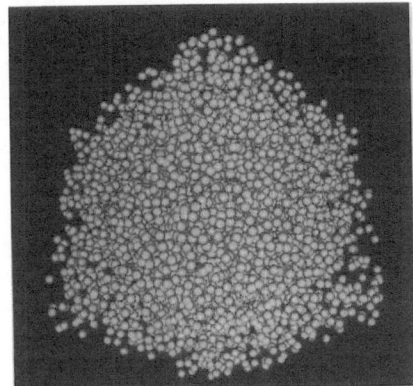

Figures 8 - 9

Space-tracing test images, containing 500 and 5000 randomly distributed spheres, respectively. Each of the images took approximately 1 hour to compute on a VAX 11/780 class system.

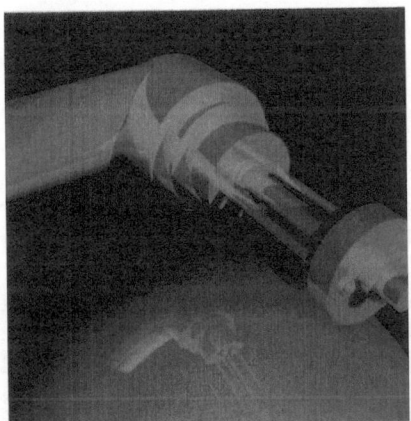 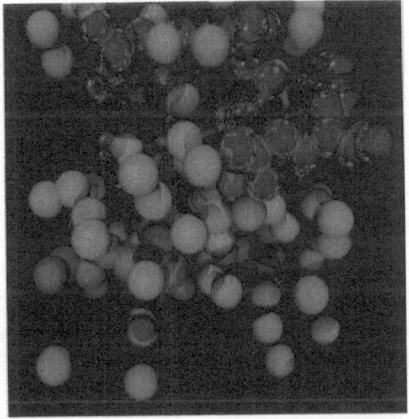

Figures 10 - 12

Images produced using the space tracing algorithm, as embedded in Visual Engineering Corporation's Visual:Genesis software package. The images are of scenes containing, respectively, 20, 200, and 2000 objects. Each of the images computed in approximately 1 hour on a VAX 11/780 class system, except the last, which took 10 hours due to a tenfold increase in secondary rays used to simulate multiple levels of reflectivity and translucency.

Color Reproduction and Illumination Models

ROY HALL

Abstract

A comprehensive analysis of previous research related to color computation and image display is presented. Physical, optical, and perceptual background references are described relative to color determination and display. Illumination models are cast into similar terms for a comparative analysis of visual and computational compromises. Finally, image display issues are discussed and illustrated.

Introduction

Realism is often a primary goal in the creation of computer generated imagery. A key element in creating the illusion of realism is displaying the correct colors for the objects in an image. Thus, a method for determining the correct color and a method for generating the color on a display device are needed.

Both color determination and color display are based upon an understanding of the nature of light and the perception of color. Physics and optics provide the required appreciation of the nature of light. Colorimetry provides the required background for exploring the color reproduction process. The first section of this discussion is a tutorial presentation of key elements in the understanding of light and color. This tutorial is intended to refresh the memory of those familiar with optics and colorimetry and to provide pointers to relevant references for those new to this material.

The second section of this discussion traces the evolution of illumination models and shading techniques up to the most current methods in use. Determining the correct color for display utilizes a mathematical model of how light illuminates a surface. Using this illumination model requires a variety of information such as the properties of the illuminated material, the roughness characteristics of the surface, the geometry of illumination and viewing, and details about the character of the illumination. This information is provided by the visible surface and shading techniques used in the generation of an image. There is a coincident evolution of illumination models and shading techniques to meet the increasingly demanding standards for image realism.

The third section of this discussion addresses image display considerations specifically for video display. Display media, whether video, film, or print, have been developed to provide the most visually acceptable color reproduction. Effectively using these media to provide the best possible rendition of color and intensity requires careful consideration of the properties and limitations of the display media.

Light and Color

The wave model of light is generally sufficient for the purposes of conventional image generation. Light is transverse electromagnetic radiation which travels through a vacuum at roughly 3.0×10^8 m/s. The effects of reflection and refraction at interfaces between different materials describe the events that are most often displayed in computer graphics. The speed of light propagation varies for different materials. The effects of diffraction, absorption, and scattering describe the events that occur as light travels through a material.

The visible range of light is generally agreed to be within the wavelengths 380nm to 770nm. Maintaining wavelength or 'spectrally' dependent information throughout the visible range is required for accurate modeling of color. Note that while the visible spectrum is normally used for image generation, the principles and procedures described are not limited to the visible spectrum.

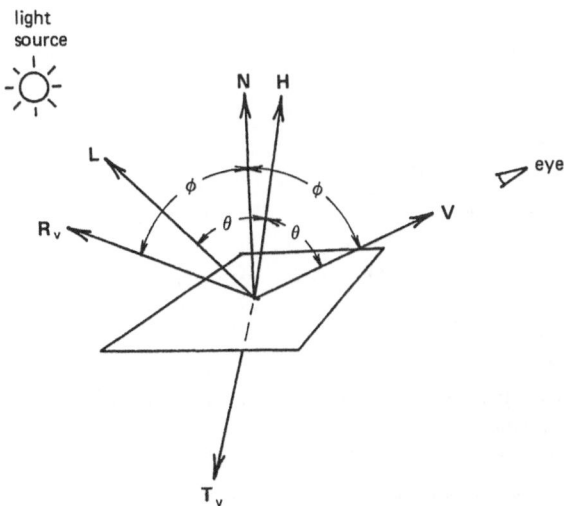

Figure 1

Terminology

The terminology used to describe light propagation and illumination models varies from reference to reference. For consistency and clarity a uniform terminology and notation will be used throughout this discussion and all illumination models will be cast into this notation.

All vectors describing directional information are normalized vectors that originate at the surface being considered and will be represented as boldfaced letters. **N** is the surface normal, **V** is the view vector, **L** is a light vector, **R** is a reflection vector and is subscripted indicating to which vector it is referenced, **H** is the vector bisector of the angle between **L** and **V** vectors, and **T** is a transmission vector and is subscripted indicating to which vector it is referenced (Figure 1). Figure 2 provides a table of terminology for the remainder of this discussion. Where applicable the parameters that a function is dependent upon are noted.

variable	description	functional dependence
V	Unit view vector from surface to eye	
L	Unit light vector from surface to light	
N	Unit surface normal	
H	Vector bisector of **L** and **V** (required **N** for mirror reflection) .	**L,V,N**
R	Reflected vector, mirror direction	**N**
T	Transmitted vector, by Snell's law	**N**, n
H'	Required **N** for Snell transmission of **L** to **V**	**L,V,N**, n
$d\omega$	Differential solid angle	
σ	Surface roughness	
λ	Wavelength	
I	Intensity	
Φ	Energy	
n	Index of refraction	
k	Coefficient of extinction	
F	Fresnel function	**V,L,N**,λ, n, k
R_{bd}	Bidirectional reflectance	**V,L,N**,σ,λ
T_{bd}	Bidirectional transmittance	**V,L,N**,σ,λ
K_a	Ambient reflectance	λ
K_d	Diffuse reflectance	λ
K_s	Specular reflectance	λ
Ns	Specular exponent	σ
D	Slope distribution function	**V,N,L**,σ
G	Geometric attenuation function	**V,N,L**,σ
A	Attenuation within a material	λ

Figure 2   Table of variables and functions

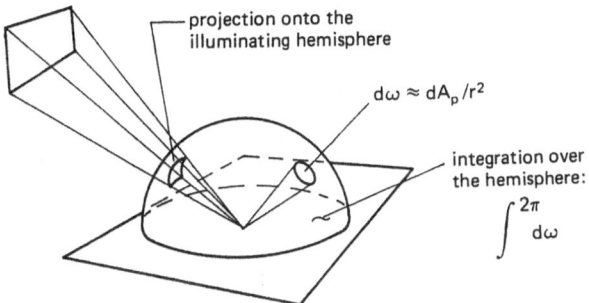

projection onto the
illuminating hemisphere

$d\omega \approx dA_p/r^2$

integration over
the hemisphere:
$$\int^{2\pi} d\omega$$

Figure 3

Figure 3 describes the concept of an illuminating hemisphere. The illuminating hemisphere is a notational convenience for describing the events above or below a surface. The events such as light sources, or other reflecting surfaces are projected onto this hemisphere. A differential solid angle, $d\omega$ describes the cone from the surface that subtents an area of the illuminating hemisphere. A small solid angle may be approximated as the projected area divided by the radius squared; $d\omega \approx dA_p/r^2$ (eq. 1) . Integrating over the hemisphere means considering all events above the surface weighted by the solid angle of their projections onto the hemisphere.

The terms intensity and energy are often used interchangably, however, they are distinctly different. Energy flux, Φ, is the energy per unit time and is often measured in watts. Intensity, I, is the energy flux per unit projected area, dA_p, of the source per solid angle, $d\omega$:

$$I = \frac{d^2\Phi}{dA_p \, d\omega} = \frac{d^2\Phi}{(\mathbf{N}\cdot\mathbf{L}) \, dA \, d\omega}$$

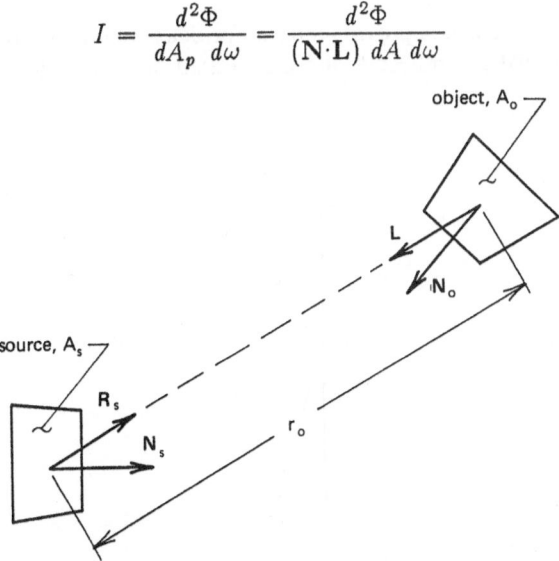

Figure 4

The energy is the intensity integrated over the solid angle through which it acts. Thus, for a source of area A_s and intensity I illuminating a surface patch of area A_o, (Figure 4), the energy reaching the patch is:

$$\Phi = I \ (\mathbf{N}_s \cdot \mathbf{R}_s) \int^{A_s} \int^{\omega_o} dA \ d\omega$$

Using the approximation for a small solid angle, eq (1), and integrating, the received energy becomes:

$$\Phi = \frac{I \ (\mathbf{N}_s \cdot \mathbf{R}_s) \ A_s \ (\mathbf{N}_o \cdot \mathbf{L}) \ A_o}{r_o^2}$$

Note that the intensity of a light source does not change as a function of distance from the source, but the energy decreases as the inverse square of the distance due to the decrease in solid angle as the inverse square of the distance.

Reflection and Refraction

Reflection and refraction result when light waves encounter the interface between materials. The index of refraction and coefficient of extinction of these materials are used to predict reflection and refraction phenomena. The law of reflection and Snell's law of refraction explain the directions of reflection and refraction using wave theory. This explanation may be found in any standard optics reference text, [DITC76] [HECH79] and [JENK76]. The geometry of reflection and refraction is shown in Figure 5. Given a view vector, $\mathbf{V}$, and a surface normal, $\mathbf{N}$, the reflection vector, $\mathbf{R}$, and the transmitted vector, $\mathbf{T}$, can be determined using the algorithm given in Example 1.

The Fresnel relationships provide a basis for determining the fractions of the incident energy that are reflected and transmitted at a material interface. The

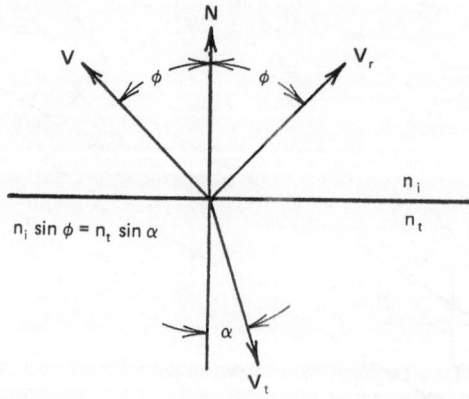

Figure 5

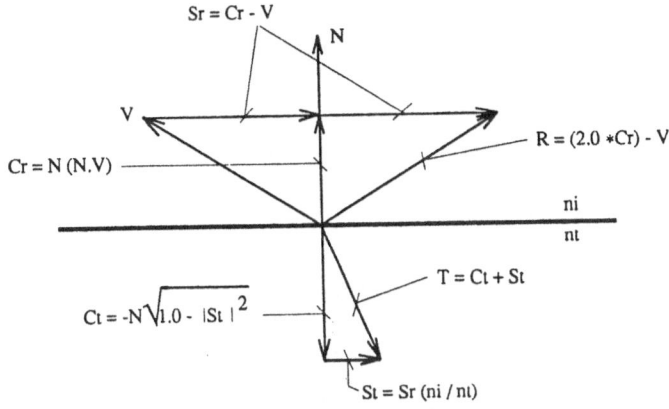

$$Sr = Cr - V$$

$$R = (2.0 *Cr) - V$$

$$Cr = N (N.V)$$

$$ni$$
$$nt$$

$$T = Ct + St$$

$$Ct = -N\sqrt{1.0 - |St|^2}$$

$$St = Sr (ni / nt)$$

```
typedef struct UNIT_VECTOR {float     i,j,k};

get_R_and_T (V, N, ni, nt, R, T)
UNIT_VECTOR      *V;    /* incident vector */
UNIT_VECTOR      *N;    /* surface normal */
float            ni;    /* index of refraction-incident */
float            nt;    /* index of refraction-transmission */
UNIT_VECTOR      *R;    /* reflected ray */
UNIT_VECTOR      *T;    /* transmitted ray */
{
    float        N_dot_V;    /* N·V */
    float        N_dot_T;    /* N·T */
    UNIT_VECTOR     Cr;    /* see illustration */
    UNIT_VECTOR     St;    /* see illustration */

    /* compute the reflected vector */
    N_dot_V = (N→i * V→i) + (N→j * V→j) + (N→k * V→k);
    Cr.i = N.i    * N_dot_V;
    Cr.j = N.j    * N_dot_V;
    Cr.k = N.k    * N_dot_V;
    R→i  = (2.0   * Cr.i) - V→i;
    R→j  = (2.0   * Cr.j) - V→j;
    R→k  = (2.0   * Cr.k) - V→k;

    /* compute the transmitted vector */
    St.i = (ni/nt)    * (Cr.i - V→i);
    St.j = (ni/nt)    * (Cr.j - V→j);
    St.k = (ni/nt)    * (Cr.k - V→k);
    if ((N_dot_T = 1.0 - ((St.i * St.i) + (St.j * St.j)
         + (St.k * St.k))< = 0.0)
            return FALSE;  /* transmitted internal reflection */

    N_dot_T = sqrt  (N_dot_T);
    T→i  = St.i - (N.i* N_dot_T);
    T→j  = St.i - (N.j* N_dot_T);
    T→k  = St.i - (N.k* N_dot_T);
    return TRUE;   /* transmitted vector generated */
}
```

Example 1 Computing the reflected and transmitted rays

Fresnel relationships are dependent upon the indices of refraction of the two materials, the polarization of the incident light, and the angle of incidence. The ratio of the amplitude of the reflected wave to the incident wave, r, for light polarized parallel and perpendicular to the plane of the N and L vectors is given by the Fresnel equations:

$$r = \frac{n_t(\mathbf{N \cdot L}) + n_i(\mathbf{N \cdot T})}{n_t(\mathbf{N \cdot L}) - n_i(\mathbf{N \cdot T})}$$

$$r = \frac{n_i(\mathbf{N \cdot L}) + n_t(\mathbf{N \cdot T})}{n_i(\mathbf{N \cdot L}) - n_t(\mathbf{N \cdot T})}$$

These equations are for a dielectric (nonconducting) media interface. A similar set of equations exists for an interface between conducting media. The derivation of the Fresnel equations is available available from many texts, [DITC76] [HECH79] and [JENK76], and will not be repeated here.

The energy in a wave is proportional to the square of the amplitude, thus the ratio of reflected energy to incident energy may be expressed as the square of r, and is termed the Fresnel reflectance, F_r. For the purposes of image synthesis, it is convenient to assume light is always circularly polarized, and that interactions may be characterized as the average of the perpendicular and parallel polarized light. Thus the reflectance may be expressed as:

$$F_r = 0.5 \left(r^2 + r^2 \right) = \frac{\Phi_r}{\Phi_i}$$

As a consequence of the law of conservation of energy, the transmittance, F_t, may be expressed as $F_t = 1.0 - F_r$.

Reciprocity relationships state that the reflective and refractive relationships are independent of the direction of energy propagation in the system. Specifically, this means that the reflectivity for light reaching a surface in the L direction and reflecting in the V direction is identical for light reaching the surface from the V direction and reflecting in the L direction. Similarly, the transmissivity for light reaching the surface from the L direction and transmitting in the T direction is identical for light reaching the surface from the T direction and transmitting in the L direction.

The Surface Illumination Process

The fundamental requirement for a physically valid model of an illuminated surface is the maintenance of energy equilibrium, i.e.,the energy reflected from the surface plus the energy transmitted through the surface boundary must be equal to the energy that illuminates the surface. If the material is opaque then the energy transmitted through the surface boundary is absorbed.

The reflection and transmission can be broken into two components, a coherent component and an incoherent or scattered component [BECK63]. The coherent component is reflected in the mirror direction and transmitted in the direction given by Snell's law. The incoherent component is reflected and transmitted in all directions based upon a statistical probability function of surface properties.

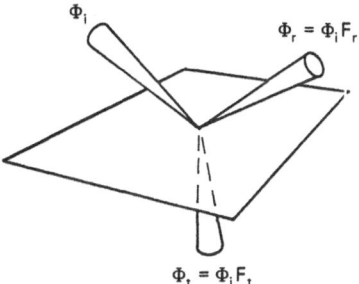

Figure 6

At an optically smooth interface only coherent reflection and transmission occur (Figure 6). Fresnel equations provide coefficients, F_r and F_t, that relate
reflected and transmitted energy to the incident energy. The resulting illumination model takes the form:

$$\dot{\Phi}_i = \Phi_r + \Phi_t = F_r \Phi_i + F_t \Phi_i; \qquad F_r + F_t = 1.0$$

Since the incident, reflected, and transmitted energy act through the same solid
angle, the intensity is proportional to the energy, and this expression can be written in terms of intensity or energy.

A rough surface produces incoherent reflection and transmission in addition to
the coherent reflection and transmission. The coherent reflection and transmission are attenuated by some functions of roughness, r_σ and t_σ. Bidirectional
functions, R_{bd} and T_{bd}, describe the incoherent reflection and transmission as a
function of the geometry of the N, V, and L vectors, of the surface roughness
characteristics, and of the wavelength and intensity of the incident light. In order
to maintain energy equilibrium, these functions must be integrated for incident
energy from the illuminating hemispheres above and below the surface (Figure
7). The resulting expressions for reflection and transmission of light energy at a
differential area of the surface boundary:

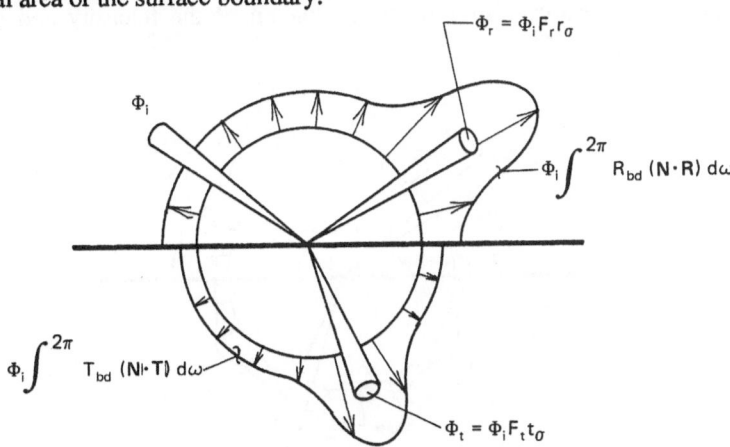

Figure 7

$$\Phi_r = r_\sigma F_r \Phi_i + \frac{\Phi_i}{dA} \int^{2\pi} R_{bd}(\mathbf{N \cdot R}) \, dA \, d\omega$$

$$\Phi_t = t_\sigma F_t \Phi_i + \frac{\Phi_i}{dA} \int^{2\pi} T_{bd}(\mathbf{N \cdot T}) \, dA \, d\omega$$

Substituting these into the basic energy equilibrium equation, eq. (8) and dividing by the incident energy results in the expression:

$$1.0 = r_\sigma F_r + t_\sigma F_t + \int^{2\pi} R_{bd}(\mathbf{N \cdot R}) \, d\omega + \int^{2\pi} T_{bd}(\mathbf{N \cdot T}) \, d\omega$$

This relationship is useful in examining the validity of analytic models for the illumination of a material interface. Satisfaction of this equality assures that the intensity functions and attenuation factors being used conform to the requirement for energy equilibrium.

By applying the reciprocity relationships, (eq. 11) can be rewritten to describe the intensity leaving a surface in a given direction as a function of surface illumination:

$$I = r_\sigma F_r I_r + t_\sigma F_t I_t + \int^{2\pi} I_i R_{bd}(\mathbf{N \cdot L}) \, d\omega + \int^{2\pi} I_i T_{bd}(\mathbf{N \cdot L}) \, d\omega$$

I_r and I_t are the intensity from the $\mathbf{R_v}$ and $\mathbf{T_v}$ directions and I_i represents the incident intensity over the illuminating hemisphere as required for the evaluation of the integral (Figure 8).

The application of this relationship requires a tremendous amount of information. Illumination models typically rely on gross approximations that capture the essence of this relationship to provide visually acceptable detail.

Note that the reflected intensity, I, is a wavelength dependent function as are most of the other terms in eq. (12). Computer graphics is typically concerned with the visible wavelengths only, however, the same relationships apply regardless of wavelength. The relationships described are independent of the color reproduction process. Specifically, evaluation of the intensity and color of a

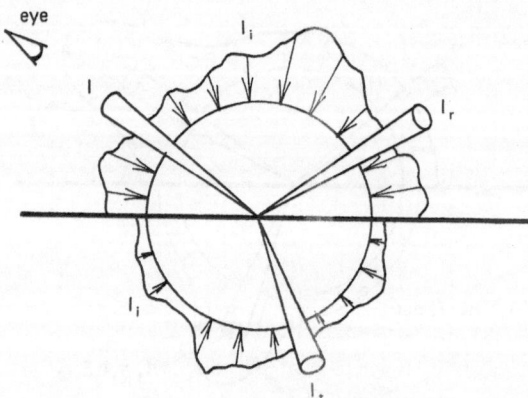

Figure 8

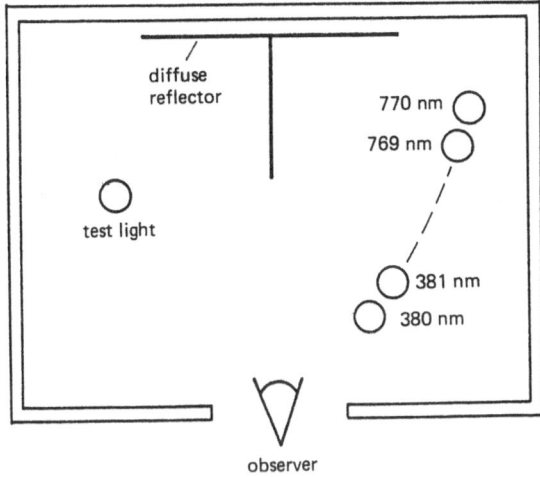

diffuse
reflector

770 nm

769 nm

test light

381 nm

380 nm

observer

Figure 9

point on an image can be performed regardless of the method that will be used for image display.

Notes on Colorimetry Section

Colorimetry is a perceptual science; that is, it studies and attempts to quantify how the human visual system perceives color. This study of perception has resulted in an empirically and statistically derived system of standards that can be applied to computer graphics with desirable and predictable results.

Imagine an experimental setup where a test light can shine on one half of a viewer's field and a set of control lights shine on the other half (Figure 9). The control lights are sources at 1nm wavelength increments throughout the visible spectrum with an intensity control for each source. When a test light is shown on half the field, the viewer matches the color of the test field by adjusting the intensities of the control lights illuminating the other half of the field. This is an idealization of the types of color matching experiments that were performed in colorimetry research.

For most colors, there are limitless different combinations of control source intensities that provide a match. This leads to speculation that the visual system does not have a receptor for each wavelength. Studies of the eye observe three types of color receptors called cones. Thus, by selectively exciting the types of cones it is possible to produce any color sensation. With three correctly selected control lights in the short, medium, and long wavelength range most test colors can be matched. Cornsweet [CORN70] presents a detailed discussion of these physiological aspects of color perception.

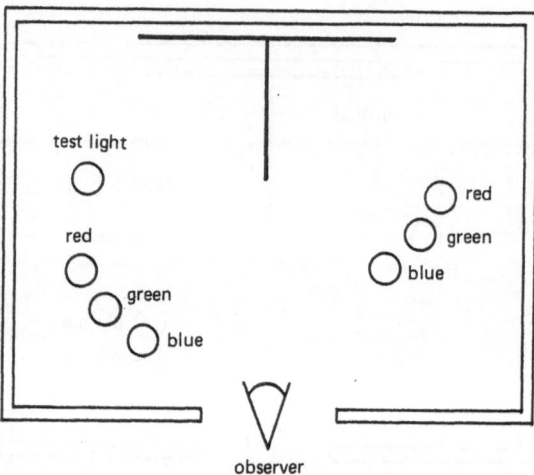

Figure 10

Matching a test color with some combination of intensities of three control lights becomes useful if the required intensities can be predicted given the spectral curve of the test color. The spectral curve for the test light is a graph of the intensity as a function of wavelength. The test color sensation is a summation of sensations produced by the intensity at every wavelength in the visible range. If the required control light intensities to match every wavelength are known, then the spectral curve for the test light can be multiplied by the curves that match the control lights to every wavelength. The areas under the resulting three curves are the required intensities of the control lights to produce a perceptual match to the test light.

To determine the curves that match the control lights to any given wavelength, three control lights are first chosen. For example, lights matching the red, green, and blue phosphors of a video monitor may be used. The observer attempts to match the color of spectral lines at 1nm increments with these control lights. In attempting to match the single wavelength test lights, none of them can be matched exactly by a combination of the three control lights. The test lights can be matched in hue by a combination of two of the control lights, but the observer needs to subtract some of the third control light color in order to match saturation. Obviously, negative color cannot be added to the control side, however, adding some of the third control color to the test side should produce the same result. Meyer [MEYE83] provides a discussion of the validity of this approach for simulating negative color addition. The color matching setup now looks like Figure 10. This experiment is performed with a representative sample of observers and a statistical analysis performed to generate the average human response.

Once the matching has been performed, the resultant graph of the matching curves for the red, green, and blue phosphors curves can be plotted (Figure 11).

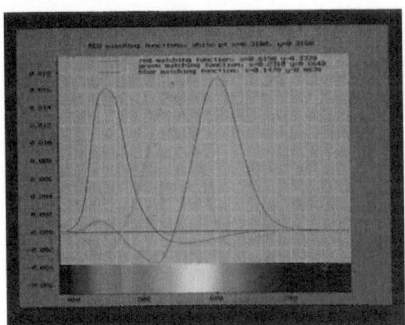

Figure 11 Graph of the spectral matching curves for three typical monitor phosphors

A more commonly used representation is created by a 2-D projection of a plot of these values in 3-space. Each orthogonal axis represents one of the control sources, L (low wavelength, blue), M (medium wavelength, green), and H (high wavelength, red). For each wavelength the vector LMH is plotted and extended until it intersects the plane $L+M+H = 1.0$. The coordinates of this intersection, LMH' are found by dividing each of L, M, and H by the sum $L+M+H$ (Figure 12). The curve defined by the intersection points of the vectors and the plane is then projected into 2-D by looking down the $-L$ axis (Figure 13).

This representation is a plot of hue and saturation is called the chromaticity diagram. The triangle created by intersections of the three axis and the plane describes all of the colors that can be reproduced by the three primaries. The in-

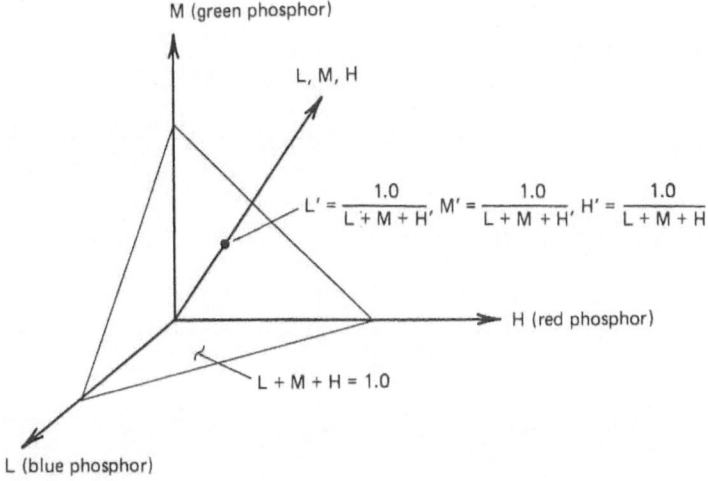

$$L' = \frac{1.0}{L + M + H}, \quad M' = \frac{1.0}{L + M + H}, \quad H' = \frac{1.0}{L + M + H}$$

Figure 12

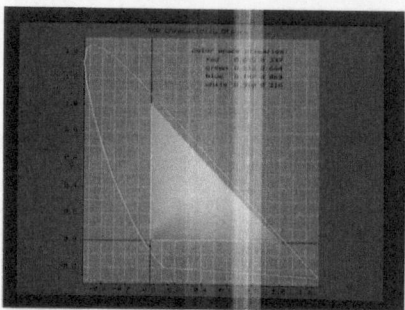

Figure 13 Chromaticity diagram for a typical monitor with reference to the RGB axis.

tensity of the color is not represented in this projection. The curve describes the pure spectral colors and all of the visible colors are represented by the interior of the curve.

The primaries that are used by RGB monitors vary. To use the results of color perception studies, they must be cast in terms of the primaries being used for color reproduction. Given the spectral curves for the other RGB phosphors, the intensities of *LHM* required to match each phosphor are determined as:

$$R = a\mathbf{L} + b\mathbf{M} + c\mathbf{H}$$
$$G = d\mathbf{L} + e\mathbf{M} + f\mathbf{H}$$
$$B = g\mathbf{L} + h\mathbf{M} + i\mathbf{H}$$

Which can be written in matrix form as:

$$\begin{bmatrix} \mathbf{L} & \mathbf{M} & \mathbf{H} \end{bmatrix} \begin{bmatrix} a & d & g \\ b & e & h \\ c & f & i \end{bmatrix} = \begin{bmatrix} \mathbf{L} & \mathbf{M} & \mathbf{H} \end{bmatrix} \begin{bmatrix} T \end{bmatrix} = \begin{bmatrix} \mathbf{R} & \mathbf{G} & \mathbf{B} \end{bmatrix}$$

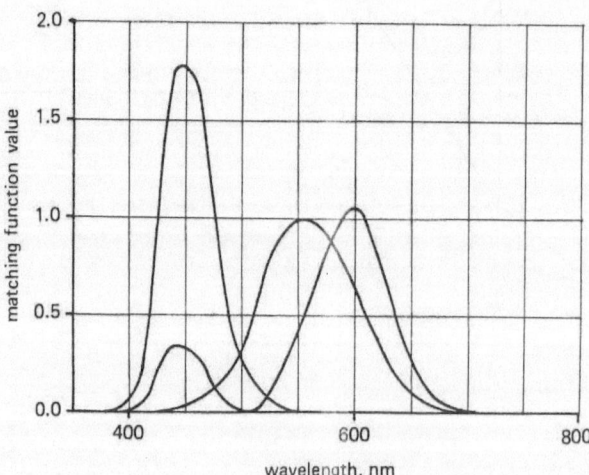

Figure 14

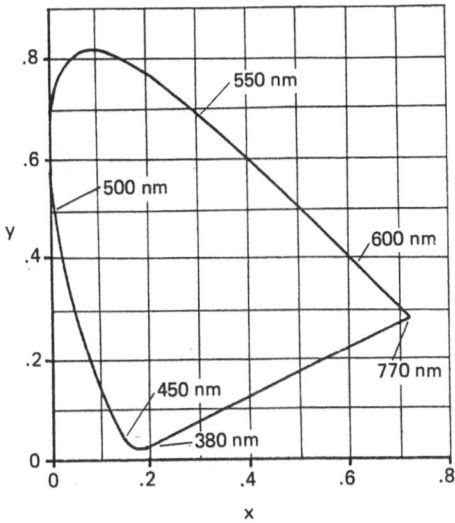

Figure 15

Using this relationship, the matching curves can be transformed for any set of primaries.

The CIE (Commission Internationale d'Eclairage) set up a standard hypothetical primary set, XYZ, that resulted in all visible colors being in the positive octant and whose integrated matching functions are of equal area. These primaries are hypothetical in that they are a convenient mathematical abstraction that do not exist in reality. Figures 14 and 15 provide the CIEXYZ matching curves and the CIEXYZ chromaticity diagram. The implication of equal area matching functions is that a flat spectral curve (equal intensity at all wavelengths) is represented by equal XYZ values. Additionally, the selection of XYZ primaries was made so that the Y matching curve is identical to the perceived intensity function (luminous efficiency function). The values for the CIEXYZ tristimulus matching functions are available in [JUDD75] and will not be repeated here.

This has been a very simplified and idealized discussion of colorimetry. In depth information can be obtained from [CORN70], [HUNT75], [JUDD75], and [MEYE83].

The Relationship of Colorimetry to the RGB Monitor Section

Proper display of a color on a monitor requires either the spectral curve or the CIEXYZ chromaticity of the color to be displayed. Additionally the transformation from CIEXYZ to the RGB primaries of the monitor must be known. The spectral curve of the color is sampled into CIEXYZ by multiplying the curve by the CIEXYZ tristimulus matching functions and integrating the resulting curves. The CIEXYZ color is then transformed into the RGB values for display.

The CIEXYZ to RGB matrix is generated using chromaticity data for the monitor phosphors. This can usually be obtained from the monitor manufacturer, otherwise, the chromaticities can be measured using an incident light chromaticity meter. Given the chromaticities of the monitor phosphors and the white point for the monitor, the following relationships are used:

red phosphor: r_x r_y $r_z = 1 - r_x - r_y$

green phosphor: g_x g_y $g_z = 1 - g_x - g_y$

blue phosphor: w_x w_y $b_z = 1 - b_x - b_y$

white point: w_x w_y $w_z = 1 - w_x - w_y$

$$\begin{bmatrix} \mathbf{R} \ \mathbf{G} \ \mathbf{B} \end{bmatrix} \begin{bmatrix} S_r(r_x) & S_r(r_y) & S_r(r_z) \\ S_g(g_x) & S_g(g_y) & S_g(g_z) \\ S_b(b_x) & S_b(b_y) & S_b(b_z) \end{bmatrix} = \begin{bmatrix} \mathbf{X} \ \mathbf{Y} \ \mathbf{Z} \end{bmatrix}$$

In this relationship, Sr, Sg, and Sb are scale factors for red, green, and blue, that set the correct white point for the transformation. Select RGB and XYZ values corresponding to the white point and then solve for Sr, Sg, and Sb. Note the RGB white point is 1,1,1; and the XYZ white point is wx, wy, and wz. The transformations are typically normalized so that Y for the white point is 1.0. Refer to example 2 for details of generating this matrix for a set of monitor primaries.

The RGB to CIEXYZ matrices are also useful for displaying images generated for a given monitor on a monitor with different phosphors. This requires a transformation of the image data from RGB of the first monitor to $R'G'B'$ of the second monitor. This transformation is expressed as:

$$\begin{bmatrix} \mathbf{R} \ \mathbf{G} \ \mathbf{B} \end{bmatrix} \begin{bmatrix} \mathbf{RGB} \\ \text{to} \\ \mathbf{XYZ} \end{bmatrix} \begin{bmatrix} \mathbf{R'} \ \mathbf{G'} \ \mathbf{B'} \\ \text{to} \\ \mathbf{XYZ} \end{bmatrix}^{-1} = \begin{bmatrix} \mathbf{R'} \ \mathbf{G'} \ \mathbf{B'} \end{bmatrix}$$

Example 3 provides details of generating this transformation between two monitors with dissimilar phosphors.

Color Spaces for Color Computation

This section addresses the use of spectral data in evaluating and displaying color. Although there has been a great deal of attention given to illumination models and color reproduction in computer graphics, arbitrary RGB triplets are normally plugged into these models in the hopes of generating realistic images. Accurate illumination models and color calibrated equipment will not produce realistic images unless the data supplied to the illumination model is accurate and the computation method does not distort this data.

Find the transformation between CIEXYZ and an RGB monitor with the following chromaticities:

	x	y
red	.615	.337
green	.231	.664
blue	.147	.063
white	.310	.316

Using eq. 14 and a CIEXYZ white point scaled to $Y = 1.0$

$$[1.0\ 1.0\ 1.0] \begin{bmatrix} Sr\,(.615) & Sr\,(.337) & Sr\,(.048) \\ Sg\,(.231) & Sg\,(.664) & Sg\,(.105) \\ Sb\,(.147) & Sb\,(.063) & Sb\,(.790) \end{bmatrix} = [.981\ 1.00\ 1.18]$$

Solving this equation set yields $Sr = .9400$, $Sg = .9036$ and $Sb = 1.3210$ resulting in the transformation:

$$[R\ G\ B] \begin{bmatrix} .578 & .317 & .045 \\ .209 & .600 & .095 \\ .195 & .083 & 1.044 \end{bmatrix} = [x\ y\ z]$$

The transformation from CIEXYZ to RGB is found by inverting the RGB to CIEXYZ matrix:

$$[x\ y\ z] \begin{bmatrix} RGB \\ to\ xyz \end{bmatrix}^{-1} = [x\ y\ z] \begin{bmatrix} 2.134 & -1.128 & .010 \\ -.688 & 2.052 & -.157 \\ -.342 & .046 & .969 \end{bmatrix} = [R\ G\ B]$$

Example 2 Computing transformations between CIEXYZ and an RGB monitor

Material and light source spectral curves are available from many sources such as [JUDD75] [PURD70], light and material manufacturers, etc.

Illumination models are generally expressed without specific reference to the wavelength of the light used. The implicit assumption is that the calculation is repeated for every wavelength. The general interpretation is repetition of the color calculation in red, green, and blue. While illumination calculations are normally performed this way, it is questionable whether this is the best method.

Several potential causes for error in computing colors using RGB values include: first, loss of information when the spectral curve is reduced to RGB

Find the transformation between the RGB monitor of example 2 and an RGB monitor with the following chromaticities:

	x	y
red	.590	.347
green	.322	.560
blue	.145	.070
white	.310	.316

Use the procedure of example 2 to generate the transformation for the RGB' monitor:

$$[R\,'G\,'B\,']\begin{bmatrix} .412 & .242 & .044 \\ .384 & .669 & .141 \\ .184 & .089 & .999 \end{bmatrix} = [x\ y\ z]$$

$$[x\ y\ z]\begin{bmatrix} 3.653 & -1.328 & .026 \\ -1.996 & 2.250 & .229 \\ -.497 & .045 & 1.017 \end{bmatrix} = [R\,'G\,'B\,']$$

The transformation from RGB to RGB' is found by substituting the computed transformations into eq. (15):

$$[R\ G\ B]\begin{bmatrix} RGB \\ to \\ xyz \end{bmatrix}\begin{bmatrix} R\,'G\,'B\,' \\ to \\ xyz \end{bmatrix} = [R\ G\ B]\begin{bmatrix} 1.457 & -.053 & -.012 \\ -.482 & 1.077 & -.036 \\ 0.025 & -.024 & 1.047 \end{bmatrix} = [R\,'G\,'B\,']$$

Example 3 Computing transformations between two RGB monitors

---

values; second, additional distortion of color values when computations are performed in the RGB colorspace; and third, since the RGB colorspace is specific to the monitor primaries, computation in different RGB colorspaces may produce different results.

Information about sharp features in a spectral curve is lost when the curve is sampled into RGB values. If the RGB values are going to be used in color computations, then important information may be lost. An example of this is shown in Figures 16 and 17.

Two filter materials with very sharp cutoff frequencies overlap each other in this image. The spectral curve of the light that passes through the first filter is found by multiplying the spectral curve of the light by the spectral curve of the filter. This is then multiplied by the spectral curve of the second filter to get the color that passes through when the filters overlap. Note that there are no overlapping non-zero values in the curves of the two filter materials. Thus, the overlay area should be essentially black. Figure 17 shows the results of computation

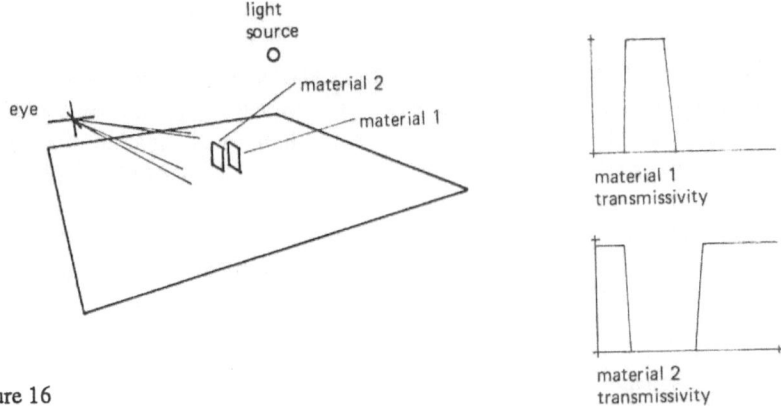

Figure 16

material 1
transmissivity

material 2
transmissivity

performed in the RGB colorspace, in the CIEXYZ color space, using 9 sample points, and at 1nm increments. The 1nm increment image is correct. Note the result of sampling information loss in the XYZ and RGB images.

Consider a perfect mirror surface, that is, a surface that reflects all of the incident light at every wavelength with no absorption. The spectral reflectivity curve for this material has a value of 1.0 at all wavelengths. Any light source, such as a D6500 source will be reflected with an unchanged spectral curve, the reflected color will be identical to the incident color. Using the primaries for a typical monitor and the NTSC white point, the RGB for the perfect mirror is 1.103, 0.970, 0.822 and the RGB for the D6500 light source is 0.956, 1.019, 0.898. The resultant calculated RGB is 1.055, 0.988, 0.738 which differs a great deal from the original light source color. This demonstrates distortion in color as a result of performing computations in the RGB colorspace.

A possible solution is to use the CIEXYZ values for computation and to transform to RGB after computation. Remember that the CIEXYZ curves are normalized to equal area and can therefore be scaled so that the perfect mirror samples to an XYZ of 1,1,1. However, there is still the problem of loss of infor-

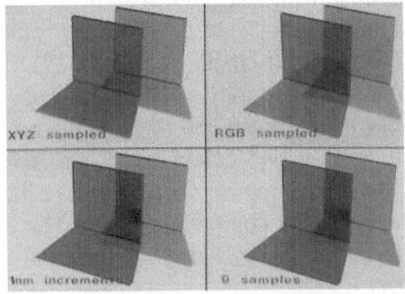

Figure 17 Comparative images for environment of Fig. 16 computed in RGB and CIEXYZ colorspaces, using 9 spectral samples, and using samples at 1nm increments

mation due to the reduction of spectral information to three sample values as demonstrated previously.

There is very little literature that describes alternate approaches to color computation. A method that has been used with very good results by the author divides the visible wavelength range into a number of smaller ranges. The spectral curve is averaged for each sub-range to produce a set of sample values for the spectral curve. All computations are performed on the sample values. After completing computations, a resulting spectral curve is reconstructed from the sample values. This spectral curve is then sampled into RGB for display. This approach has been used to create the 9 sample image of Figure 17.

This approach may sound complicated, however, its use is very straightforward (Figure 18). A sampling subroutine reduces the spectral curve data to sampled data. The illumination model computations are repeated for the number of samples used instead of the typical RGB repetition. Step functions are then used for reconstruction of the final spectral curve. Note that the step function can be presampled into RGB or CIEXYZ values allowing the generation of a matrix that transforms from the sampled values into the RGB or CIEXYZ colorspace for image storage and/or display. Details of this approach may be found in [HALL83b].

Areas that require additional research and investigation are the method of determining the appropriate subranges for sampling, the required number of samples for most applications, and the appropriate sampling and reconstruction functions. In spite of the unanswered issues surrounding spectral sampling techniques for color computation, it is clear that this methodology is preferable to the use of RGB or CIEXYZ values during color computation.

Illumination Models

The application of the results of research in physics and optics to computer graphics constitutes an evolution governed by the current visible surface algorithms, by what is considered computationally reasonable, and by the level of realism that is acceptable. The illumination models used fall into three general classifications: empirical, transitional, and analytical. The shading techniques that evolved with these models fall into three corresponding classifications: incremental, ray tracing, and radiosity methods (Figure 19).

Early illumination models are empirical in nature. They are evaluated within the perspective geometry of the scene and through the use of incremental techniques to exploit notions of image coherence. These models and application techniques are an adjunct development to scanline visible surface algorithms within the limits of the available computing power. The empirical models and incremental shading techniques are exemplified by the work of [BOUK70], [GOUR71], and [PHON75].

Transitional models use prior work in physics and optics to improve the earlier empirical models. Texture mapping [CATM75] [BLIN76], reflection

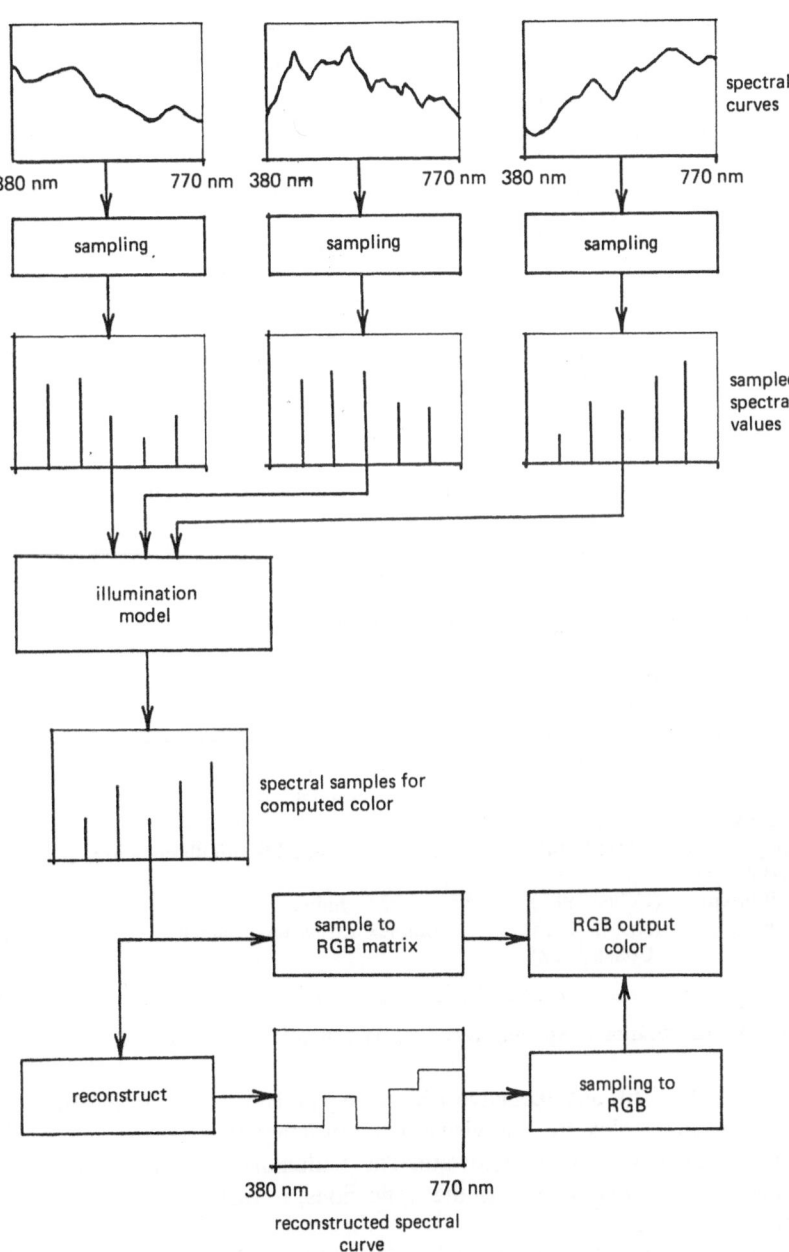

Figure 18

Rendering Technique	Reference	Shading Additions	Figure
	(Bouknight 1970)	Constant color	24
Incremental: perspective geometry, empirical illumination models	(Warnock 1969) (Ronmney 1970)	Distance attenuation functions	
	(Gouraud 1971)	Color interpolation across polygons	25
	(Newell 1972)	Psuedo transparency	
	(Phong 1975)	Normal interpolation across polygons	26
Ray Tracing: true geometry, empirical and theoretical illumination models	(Catmull 1975) (Blinn 1976)	Texture mapping .... Reflection mapping	27
	(Blinn 1977)	Incoherent reflection	
	(Kay 1979)	Distance attenuation and refraction in transparent materials	
	(Whitted 1980)	Recursive coherent reflection and refraction	28
	(Hall 1983)	Incoherent transmission	
	(Cook 1984) (Amanatides 1984)	Distributed sampling and area sampling ...	29
Radiosity: Analytic energy equilibrium model	(Cook 1982	Spectral character of highlights, energy formulation	
	(Goral 1984)	Diffuse energy equilibrium illumination	
	(Cohen 1985) (Nishita 1985) (Cohen 1972)	Improved technique for complex diffuse environments	30

Figure 19 Classification of Shading Technique and Illumination Models

mapping [BLIN76], and recursive ray tracing [WHIT80] reflect an increasing concern for color, shading, and visual detail in imagery supported by increased computational power of the hardware. These illumination models use the true geometry of the environment so that reflections, refractions, and shadows are geometrically correct.

Analytical approaches by [COOK82], [GORA84], [COHE85], and [NISH85], make the illumination model the driving force for the application of radiosity or energy equilibrium techniques to computer imagery. In addition to maintaining true geometry, the movement of light energy through the environment must be modeled to provide the information required to evaluate the illumination model. Although the results of these illumination models is greatly improved realism, the complexity and computational demands suggest that widespread use of these models is dependent on advances in application algorithms and hardware speed.

These three classifications describe a shift in research from solving the hidden surface problem to creating realistic appearance to simulating the behavior that creates the appearance.

Incremental Shading Techniques and Empirical Illumination Models

The illumination models originally implemented with scanline rendering systems use incremental shading techniques. These shading techniques use coherence information in the same fashion as the scanline method of visible surface determination. The key point of these shading techniques is incrementally updating illumination information from the previous scanline or pixel instead of repeated calculation.

A simple idealized scanline visible surface algorithm (Figure 20), will be used for this discussion. The process of incremental parameter updating is diagramed in Figure 21.

The parameter to be updated is evaluated at the vertices of each polygon and loaded into the edge database along with the rate of change per scanline. When an edge becomes active, the start value of the parameter is used as the value at the edge. For each subsequent scanline during which the edge is active, the parameter is updated by adding the rate of change per scanline. When the scanline is processed, a visible span for the polygon is created. A start pixel for the span is determined and the parameter value at the start pixel is computed. Additionally, the rate of change of the parameter per pixel is determined. When the span becomes active, the parameter start value is used. For each pixel during which the span is active, the current parameter value is incremented by the rate of change per pixel.

The illumination models used for scanline applications are subsets of an illumination model of the form:

$$I(\lambda) = f(d) \times (\text{ambient} + \text{diffuse} + \text{specular})$$

$$I(\lambda) = f(d) \times \left[K_a(\lambda)I_a + K_d(\lambda)\sum_{j=1}^{ls}(\mathbf{N} \cdot \mathbf{L}_j)I_j + \right.$$
$$\left. K_s \sum_{j=1}^{ls} f(\mathbf{V}, \mathbf{L}_j, \mathbf{N}, \sigma, \lambda)I_j \right]$$

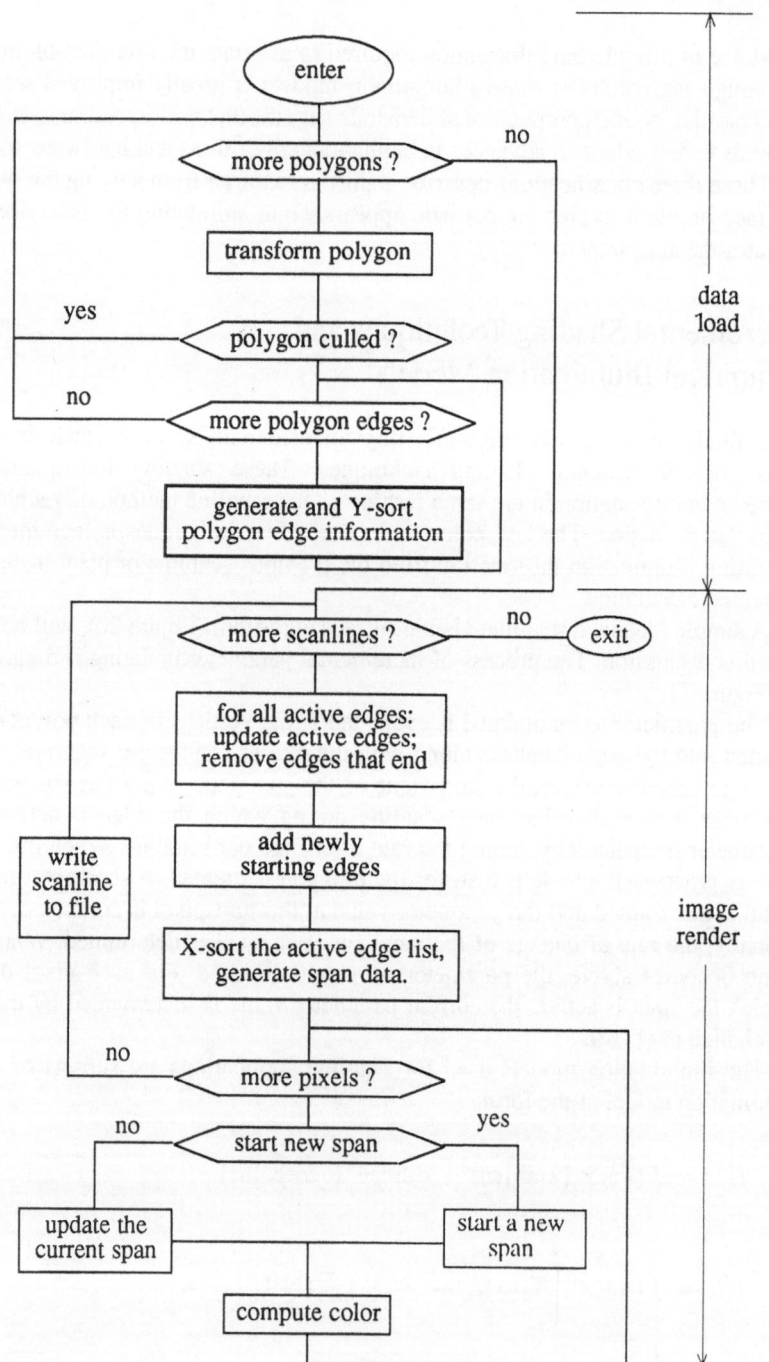

Figure 20 Idealized Scanline Visible Surface Algorithm

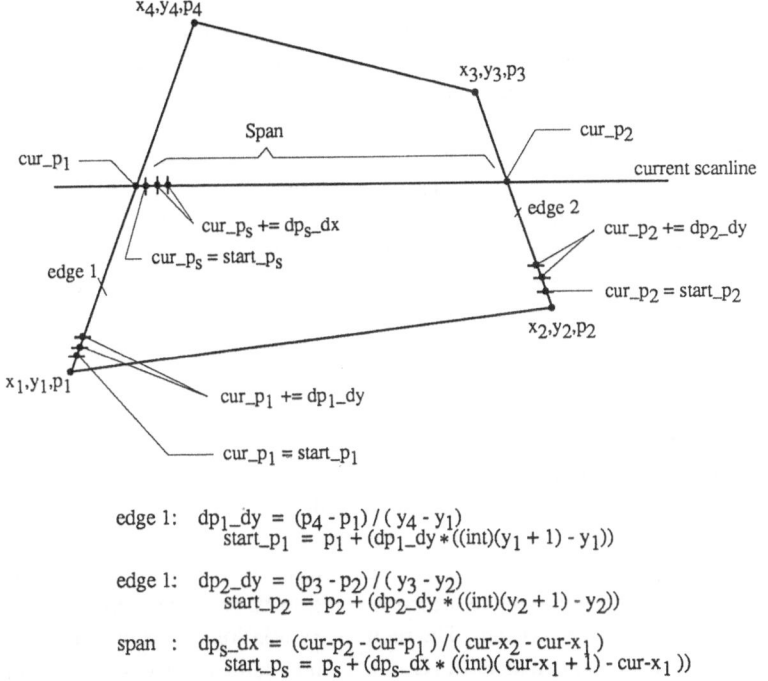

$$\text{edge 1:} \quad \begin{aligned} dp_1\_dy &= (p_4 - p_1) / (y_4 - y_1) \\ start\_p_1 &= p_1 + (dp_1\_dy * ((int)(y_1 + 1) - y_1)) \end{aligned}$$

$$\text{edge 1:} \quad \begin{aligned} dp_2\_dy &= (p_3 - p_2) / (y_3 - y_2) \\ start\_p_2 &= p_2 + (dp_2\_dy * ((int)(y_2 + 1) - y_2)) \end{aligned}$$

$$\text{span :} \quad \begin{aligned} dp_s\_dx &= (cur\text{-}p_2 - cur\text{-}p_1) / (cur\text{-}x_2 - cur\text{-}x_1) \\ start\_p_s &= p_s + (dp_s\_dx * ((int)(cur\text{-}x_1 + 1) - cur\text{-}x_1)) \end{aligned}$$

Figure 21 Incremental parameter updating in scanline algorithms

This is an approximation of the incoherent reflection term of eq. (12). In this expression $f(d)$ is an attenuation as a function of the distance, d, between the viewer and the object, and $f(V,L,N,\sigma,\lambda)$ is a directional reflection function for the specular highlight which is a function of V, L, N, and the surface roughness characteristics, σ.

The model described by [BOUK70] is representative of the first illumination models. The task of determining visibility was paramount and little computation time was devoted to image shading. This model uses the ambient and lambertian diffuse terms only, no distance attenuation, one light source which is placed at infinite distance in the direction of the eye, and ambient and light source intensities of unity. The model is then reduced to the form:

$$I(\lambda) = K_a(\lambda) + K_d(\lambda)N_z; \qquad (K_a + K_d) < 1.0$$

The eye is considered to be at infinite distance, thus L and V are constant at 0,0,1, and the $(N \cdot L)$ dot product is reduced to N_z. The model is evaluated once per polygon and the visible area of the polygon is filled with the color. During the scanning, pixel color changes if visibility changes, otherwise the current pixel is the same color as the last pixel.

Immediate improvements to this model provide an attenuation function so parallel planes have a reduced intensity when further from the viewer. A $1/d$ attenuation function is suggested by [WARN69], and a $(1/d)^4$ attenuation function is suggested by [ROMN70]. In these functions d is a measure of distance. These functions account for the decrease in incident light energy as distance from the source increases and for atmospheric attenuation due to fog or haze. The selection of this function and the measure of distance used is an empirical process.

Scanline algorithms generally use polygonal data and represent curved surfaces as a collection of approximating polygons. The result is facetted appearance. Gouraud [GOUR71] suggests curved surfaces can be shaded by interpolating color across the polygons. The curved surface normal instead of the approximating polygon normal is used to compute the color at each vertex. The color is then interpolated across the polygons using incremental updating as the image is scanned. The illumination model used does not change but the method of application results in better visual quality with minimal added computation expense.

Phong provides a specular or highlight reflection term for the illumination model. The $f(\mathbf{V}, \mathbf{L}_j, \mathbf{N}, \sigma, \lambda)$ term of eq. (17) is replaced by a constant specular reflectance coefficient K_s and a directional reflectance function $(\mathbf{V} \cdot \mathbf{R}_l)^{Ns}$ where Ns is a measure of surface roughness. Note that K_s is not a wavelength dependent function, thus the highlights are always white. In the original implementation, the eye and the light source are considered to be at infinite distance so that the $\mathbf{V}$ and $\mathbf{L}$ vectors are constant. The reciprocity relationship is used to write an alternate form of the specular term $(\mathbf{R}_v \cdot \mathbf{L})^{Ns}$. The vector $\mathbf{R}_v$ is easier to compute than $\mathbf{R}_l$ because the $\mathbf{V}$ vector has two zero components. The illumination model used is:

$$I(\lambda) = K_a(\lambda) + K_d(\lambda)(\mathbf{N} \cdot \mathbf{L}) + K_s(\mathbf{R}_v \cdot \mathbf{L})^{Ns}$$

Phong observes that interpolation of color across polygons creates discontinuities in the first derivative of color at polygon intersections; that is, the rate of color change is constant across each polygon but changes abruptly at polygon edges. This condition causes mach banding or perceptual amplification of the discontinuity. He also notes that specular highlights are sensitive to local geometry and that evaluating color only at vertices often results in misrepresentation of highlights.

Phong interpolates the surface normal across the polygon and repeats the color calculation for each pixel. The surface normal is incrementally updated during scanning of the image. For each pixel the interpolated normal is normalized, then the color calculation is performed. Computation time is greatly increased due to repeated illumination model evaluation at the pixel level.

The illumination models and incremental shading techniques described thus far treat only primary light sources in a limited geometric context. The models are created as empir- ical attempts to capture the observed behavior of light and have little theoretical basis. These illumination models are easily extended for multiple light sources. In this case the reflection coefficients and light intensities must be carefully selected so that the computed intensity does not exceed the displayable range. Figures 22 and 23 describe the intergation of the Bouknight,

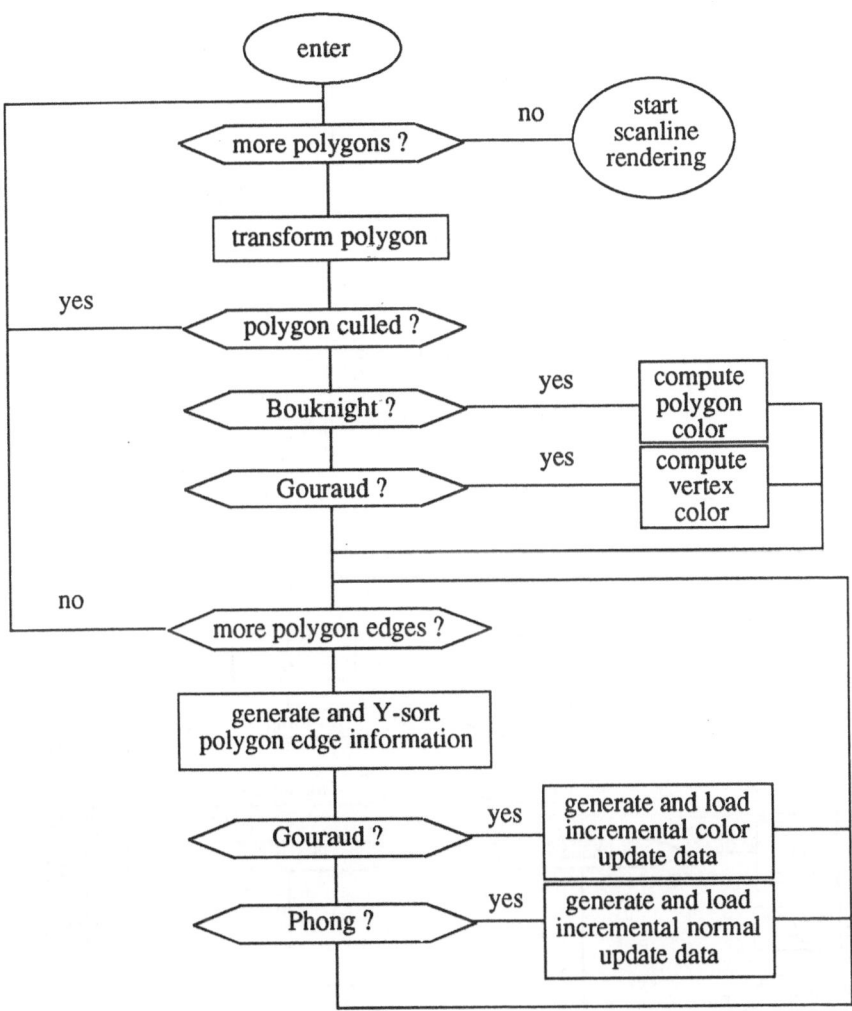

Figure 22 Revision to data load for the incremental shading techniques

Gouraud, and Phong shading techniques into the simple scanline visible surface algorithm.

The incremental shading techniques described are applied in perspective (screen) coordinates. As a result of the nonlinearity of the perspective transform, the shading interpolations are not invariant with screen position resulting in visual anomalies if these shading techniques are used in animated sequences. Ray tracing provides a solution to this problem by performing

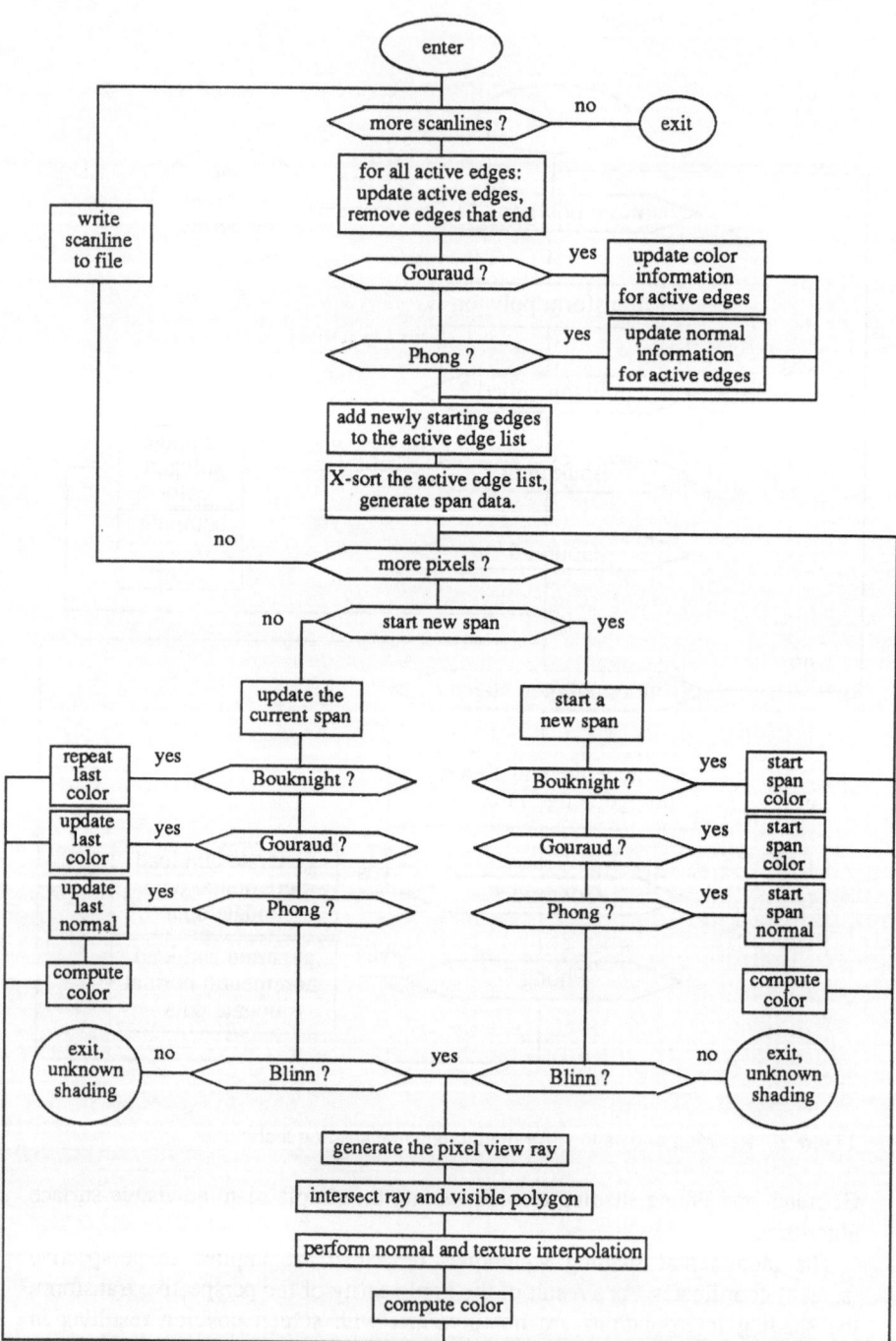

Figure 23 Revision to image render for the incremental shading techniques

illumination computations relative to the real geometry of objects, viewer, and light sources.

Ray Tracing and Transitional Illlumination Models

Rendering techniques that maintain true geometry information can be grouped as ray tracing rendering techniques. The key aspect of ray tracing techniques is that geometric information as well as color information must be calculated for each pixel.

The illumination models used for ray tracing applications are subsets of an illumination model of the form:

$$I(\lambda) = \text{ambient} + \text{diffuse} + \text{specular} + \text{transmitted}$$

$$I(\lambda) = K_a(\lambda)I_a + K_d(\lambda)\sum_{j=1}^{ls}(\mathbf{N}\cdot\mathbf{L}_j)I_j +$$

$$K_s(\lambda)\left[I_r + \sum_{j=1}^{ls}f_r(\mathbf{V},\mathbf{L}_j,\mathbf{N},\sigma)I_j\right]$$

$$+ K_t(\lambda)\left[I_t + \sum_{j=1}^{ls}f_t(\mathbf{V},\mathbf{L}_j,\mathbf{N},\sigma)I_j\right]$$

The I_r and I_t terms represent illumination from the reflected and transmitted direction and account for coherent reflection and transmission. Note that an incoherent transmission function, $f_r(\mathbf{V},\mathbf{L}_j,\mathbf{N},\sigma)$, has also been added.

Blinn [BLIN77] explores alternate forms for the reflectance function, f_r, based on the work of [TORR66], [TORR67], and [TROW75]. Integration of incident energy over the illuminating hemisphere is addressed; however, the point sampling technique of ray tracing provides insufficient information for this approach. An approximation with theoretically justified functions and empirically determined coefficients results.

Blinn [BLIN76] also uses the coherent reflection term by computing a reflection vector for the view vector and determining I_r through the use of a reflection lookup table. The illumination model used by Blinn is:

$$I(\lambda) = K_a(\lambda)I_a + K_d(\lambda)\sum_{j=1}^{ls}(\mathbf{N}\cdot\mathbf{L}_j)I_j +$$

$$K_s\left[I_r + \sum_{j=1}^{ls}\text{DFG}I_j/(\mathbf{N}\cdot\mathbf{V})\right]$$

Where D is a function of surface roughness, G is an attenuation function due to self-shading of rough surfaces, and F is a Fresnel reflectance function (refer to "Reflection and Refraction"). Addition of the Blinn shading technique to a simple scanline visible surface algorithm is given in Figures 22 and 23.

The microfacets of a rough surface mask and shade each other. A geometric attenuation factor, G, accounts for this shading. This function is expressed as:

$$G = \min\left[\, 1, \frac{2(\mathbf{N \cdot H})(\mathbf{N \cdot V})}{(\mathbf{V \cdot H})}, \frac{2(\mathbf{N \cdot H})(\mathbf{N \cdot L})}{(\mathbf{V \cdot H})} \,\right]$$

Details of the derivation of this expression may be found in [TORR67] and [BLIN77] and will not be repeated here. It should be noted that this function exhibits sharp discontinuities that can produce banding.

Three roughness functions, D, are suggested by Blinn. The first is an adaptation of the Phong specular term that considers the angle between $\mathbf{N}$ and $\mathbf{L}$ instead of $\mathbf{R}_v$ and $\mathbf{L}$. The rationale is that the specular function describes the probability that surface microfacets will deviate from the surface normal in the direction required for mirror reflection. Since $\mathbf{R}$ is the microfacet orientation required for mirror reflection, the angle between $\mathbf{N}$ and $\mathbf{H}$ is a more meaningful reference into the roughness function than the angle between $\mathbf{R}_v$ and $\mathbf{L}$. This roughness function has the form:

$$D = (\mathbf{N \cdot H})^{N_s}$$

The second roughness function is based upon the a Gaussian distribution used by [TORR67]:

$$D = e^{-(C_1 \mathrm{acos}(\mathbf{N \cdot H}))^2}$$

The constant C_1 controls the rate of fall-off for this roughness function.

A third function is based upon the work of [TROW75]:

$$D = \left(\frac{C_2}{(\mathbf{N \cdot H})^2(C_2^2 - 1) + 1}\right)^2$$

The constant C_2 controls the rate of fall-off for this roughness function.

To the author's knowledge, no definitive comparative study has been performed with these models. Thus, it is not possible to present any information about the the realism and computation time compromises between these roughness functions.

Catmull [CATM75] and Blinn [BLIN76] describe mapping parameter textures such as roughness, color, and normal perturbation onto surfaces prior to performing the color computation. This provides greater visual detail and complexity for a subjectively more realistic appearance. The mapping relates a location on the object to a location on the texture and requires determination of the true intersection between the view ray and surface for proper evaluation of the texture coordinates. Mapping does not change the illumination model; it provides the illumination model with different input data as a function of position on the surface.

Whitted [WHIT80] performs recursive visible surface and illumination calculations to determine the incident light from the reflected and refracted directions. This technique captures repeated reflections and refractions for greater realism. Additionally, the path from each light source to the object is checked for blockage by shadowing objects. The remarkable realism of this method results primarily from the recursive shading technique. Changes in the illumination model to accommodate this technique are minimal. The resultant illumination model is similar to the Blinn model of eq. (20) with a simplified incoherent specular function and an added coherent transmission term:

$$I(\lambda) = K_a(\lambda)I_a + K_d(\lambda)\sum_{j=1}^{ls}(\mathbf{N}\cdot\mathbf{L}_j)I_j +$$

$$K_s\left[I_r + \sum_{j=1}^{ls}I_j(\mathbf{N}\cdot\mathbf{H}_j)^{Ns}\right] + K_t I_t$$

Kay [KAY79] addresses attenuation of light passing through a material while traveling between intersections, thus extending the coherent reflection and refraction terms to $K_s I_r A_r^d$ and $K_t I_r A_t^d$ respectively. The A_r and A_t factors are the attenuation per unit length of travel and d is the distance that I_r or I_t has traveled from the previous intersection. The result is better representation of transparent objects.

Hall [HALL83a] adds a term for incoherent transmission and relates K_s and K_t to the Fresnel relationships. The incoherent transmission term provides better representation of light sources seen through transparent objects. The specular function suggested by [PHON75] is used in this model and adapted for incoherent transmission. The Fresnel relationships provide better representation of metals and glints from near grazing light sources. The Fresnel approximation suggested by [COOK82] is used to account for wavelength and incident angle dependencies of the reflection and transmission terms.

This model collects previously disjointed work into a single expression of the form:

$$I(\lambda) = \text{ambient} + \text{diffuse} + \text{specular} + \text{transmitted}$$

$$I(\lambda) = K_a(\lambda)I_a + K_d(\lambda)\sum_{j=1}^{ls}(\mathbf{N}\cdot\mathbf{L}_j)I_j + K_s F_r\left[I_r A_r^d + \sum_{j=1}^{ls}I_j(\mathbf{N}\cdot\mathbf{H}_j)^{Ns}\right]$$

$$+ K_s F_t\left[I_t A_t^d + \sum_{j=1}^{ls}I_j(\mathbf{N}\cdot\mathbf{H'}_j)^{Ns}\right]$$

Note that the wavelength dependency of the specular reflection and transmission terms is embodied in the Fresnel factors, F_r and F_t. Also note that K_t of eq. (25)

is replaced by using the Fresnel factors to determine the ratio of reflected and transmitted contribution.

Cook et al. [COOK84] uses a method of pseudorandom perturbation of many of the vectors in the model to provide greater information for the final evaluation of color. Amanatides [AMAN84] traces cones into the environment for greater information retrieval. These approaches begin a transition towards the energy equilibrium rendering techniques. The distribution of point samples or the area sampling of traced cones attempts to quantify what is happening in the illuminating hemisphere. The results relevant to this discussion are soft shadows and soft reflections. Additional benefits include motion blur and depth of field effects.

The transitional models and ray tracing techniques described attempt to model actual behavior of light but are still constrained by lack of information. In addition to the primary sources, contributions from the reflected and transmitted directions are considered, but this is still a very limited description of the illumination incident on the surface. The methods work well for very smooth reflective surfaces. However, with the exception of distributed ray tracing, the results are disappointing when the techniques are used for semi-gloss surfaces. Although the results of research into the nature of the interaction between light and matter have been incorporated into these models, their use still requires empirical determination of a large number of the coefficients.

Analytical Models and Radiosity Techniques

The energy equilibrium illumination models are subsets of the general illumination expression of eq. (12). The development of these models has been limited by the inability of the existing rendering techniques to provide sufficient information for evaluation of the model. Research in the area of improved energy equilibrium illumination models is forcing the development of new rendering techniques.

Cook and Torrance [COOK82] propose an energy formulation for the illumination model. This model uses the energy that reaches the illuminated surfaces from the light sources instead of the intensity. As with previous models, the illumination is divided into ambient, diffuse, and specular contributions. The resulting model is:

$$I(\lambda) = K_a(\lambda)I_a + K_d \sum_{j=1}^{l_s} R_d I_j (\mathbf{N} \cdot \mathbf{L}_j) d\omega_j +$$

$$K_s \sum_{j=1}^{l_s} R_{bd} I_j (\mathbf{H} \cdot \mathbf{L}_j) d\omega_j$$

The R_d function is the measured material spectral curve. K_s plus K_d equals one. The bidirectional reflection function is a combination of a Fresnel term, a roughness function, a geometric attenuation function, and some additional factors to satisfy energy equilibrium requirements. The Fresnel term accounts for wavelength dependency of the highlight. The bidirectional reflectance function, R_{bd}, is adapted from the work of [BECK63].

The images created using this model are particularly striking due to the inclusion of the spectral characteristics of highlights. However, the range of images produced is extremely limited because existing rendering techniques could only provide the required information for the primary light sources.

Goral et al. [GORA84] adapts radiosity techniques used in thermal engineering to model the movement of light energy through an environment. This technique assumes all surfaces are rough and the materials are opaque reducing the complete expression of eq. (12) to the incoherent reflection only. Additional simplification is achieved by assuming the surfaces are ideal diffuse (lambertian) reflectors. The reflection model used is then:

$$I(\lambda) = \frac{K_d(\lambda)}{\pi} \int^{2\pi} I_i(\mathbf{N} \cdot \mathbf{L}) \, d\omega$$

In application the integral is evaluated by summing the contributions of light reflected from the polygons in the illuminating hemisphere for the surface. The radiosity method describes the creation and solution of the equation set that describes the energy interrelationships of all of the polygons in the environment. Since all of these relationships are considered, the ambient illumination is explicitly evaluated by this method and no empirical terms appear in the illumination model.

The radiosity technique provides for the intensity of each polygon independently of processing for display. The display processing is very similar to creating an image using Gouraud shading with the exception that vertex colors are determined by averaging the colors of adjacent polygons. It is particularly noteworthy that a real control environment was created so that comparative studies and measurements could be made to evaluate the effectiveness of these techniques in simulating reality.

Cohen [COHE85], [COHE86] and Nishita [NISH85] describe improved methods for building the radiosity equation sets. These methods account for occlusion of polygons as they are projected onto the illuminating hemisphere. Soft shadows and very subtle lighting details are produced, resulting in very realistic images of diffuse environments. Similarly to the work of Goral et al., the polygon intensities are computed prior to rendering and color interpolation techniques are used in the rendering.

The development of radiosity methods has concentrated on the difficult problem of modeling the movement of light energy through the environment. These techniques have separated the problem of determining the color and shading to a process that is independent of the technique used to render for display. This separation allows sequences of motion through a static environment to be generated by solving the radiosity problem once, and repeating only the display calculation for the sequence of frames. It is ironic that the rendering technique for display is most similar to that proposed by Gouraud nearly 15 years earlier.

Figure 24 Constant color for each polygon using the Bouknight illumination model

Figure 25 Gouraud color interpolation across polygons using the Bouknight illumination model

Figure 26 Phong shading used with the Phong illlumination model

Figure 27 Ray tracing with reflection mapping using the Blinn illumination model, note the addition of reflected environment information

Figure 28 Recursive ray tracing using the Whitted illumination model, note the addition of shadows and refraction

Figure 29 Distributed ray tracing using the Hall illumination model, not soft shadows and spectral character of the reflections

Figure 30 Radiosity using a diffuse illumination model, note the subtle shadow and shading (Courtesy M. Cohen, Cornell University Program of Computer Graphics)

Shading technique and illumination model	figure	visible surface	shading information	illumination model	Total
constant color polygons	24	.465	—	.001	.466
color interpolation across polygons	25	.465	.012	.001	.478
normal interpolation, Phong model	26	.465	.114	.421(1)	1.000
true geometry, texture reflection mapping	27	.465	.804(2)	.613	1.882
recursive ray tracing, Whitted model	28	1.614	1.689(3)	.860(4)	4.163
distributed ray tracing, Hall model	29	1.614	1.708(5)	1.524	4.827

(1) Note increase due to repeated illumination computation on a per pixel basis instead of a per polygon basis.

(2) Note increase due to determining true geometry and texture lookup.

(3) Note relative increase due to repeated visible surface testing. This is very sensitive to database complexity.

(4) Note increase due to recursive application of the illumination model.

(5) Only light sources were distributed.

Figure 31 Relative comparison of shading technique and illumination models

Summary

The approximations and idealizations made in early illumination models are well justified. Empirical techniques were employed to generate something that looked realistic within the constraints of rendering technique and available hardware. Recent work has focused on modeling the behavior that creates the reality and has replaced the empirical techniques with theoretical formulations.

Comparative images and computation statistics for a sample environment are given in Figure 34. The database used for this testing can hardly be considered representative; thus, as with most computation statistics the results are not representative but merely indicative of performance for similar database configurations. The timing information provided is based upon sampling at 2K resolution for 512 resolution display. The relative times for complete image generation as well as visible surface processing, shading information calculation, and illumination model evaluation are provided. The scanline method used is a modified Watkins algorithm. The ray tracing method for the non-recursive illumination models uses a scanline method for visible surface determination then traces a ray to the visible surface. The recursive ray tracing method used is exhaustive search without space partitioning or other presorting methods. The test programs for generating these images were written in C and run on a Ridge-32 computer.

Incremental and ray tracing techniques have reached a mature state of development. Radiosity techniques as applied to computer imagery are in their infancy. The current radiosity techniques apply only to diffuse environments, while incremental and ray tracing techniques handle diffuse environments very poorly. When the radiosity method is used, movement through a static environment requires only one solution for environment illumination, then display processing for the animation frames. The incremental and ray tracing methods require repeating the entire frame computation for every frame. These differences in maturity of technique, appropriate applications, and application methodology make it impossible to develop meaningful comparative data at this time.

Current analytical models are limited to diffuse environments. The advances traced in this characterization of illumination models and shading techniques point to continued emphasis on greater realism supported by more powerful computing equipment. It is clear that the analytical models will play a prominent part in directing the research effort towards even greater realism in computer generated imagery.

Effort has been made to represent the cited works as accurately as possible. The true evolution of technique is not nearly as straightforward as presented in this discussion. As with any evolution there are many digressions from what appears to be the primary path.

Image Storage and Display

This section discusses the selection of an appropriate image storage colorspace, compression or clipping of the computed color values to the displayable range, and correction for display nonlinearity. Once an image has been computed, it must be stored and/or displayed. As previously stated, all visible colors cannot be reproduced on typical video display devices. This is also true for photographic and print media. Additionally, all image display media impose limits on the dynamic range of the image. The method of image storage selected should preserve as much perceptually relevant information as possible in a form that can make full use of the display capabilities of the display media. There is little published reference material addressing these issues, thus this is a collection of information from personal experience and discussions with other computer graphics professionals.

Clipping and Compressing to the Displayable Gamut

The monitor gamut of displayable colors is limited by the chromaticities of the primaries of the monitor and upon the maximum intensity that can be displayed. As shown in the chromaticity diagram of Figure 13, the displayable colors represent a subset of the visible colors. The color gamut can be represented as a cube drawn on the RGB axis system. Any color can be plotted in this axis system, and any color outside the cube is not displayable (Figure 32).

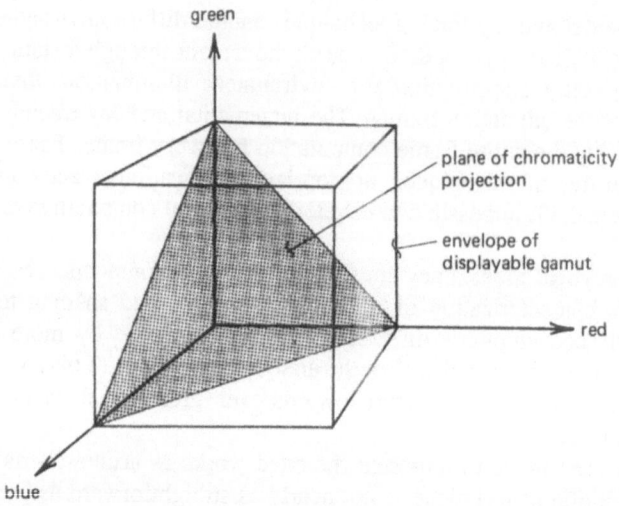

Figure 32

Any undisplayable color must be clipped or compressed into the displayable color space. The method of clipping or compressing should create a minimal perceptual distortion of the color and should not create any noticeable clipping anomalies in the image.

Cook [COOK81] breaks the problem into two cases. The first is colors that are within the positive octant of figure 32 but are outside the displayable gamut. The second is colors that are not in the positive octant. In the first case, the chromaticity of the color is reproducible, but not at the requested intensity. In the second case, the chromaticity of the color is not reproducible. He suggests that in the first case, all image values can be scaled until all values are displayable. This results in lowering the overall intensity and contrast of the image. In the second case, the hue or dominant wavelength of the color is maintained and the color is desaturated (white is added) until the color is in the displayable range.

Alternate solutions suggested for the first case are clipping any color value greater that 1 to 1, or scaling the length of the vector to the undisplayable color to the point where this vector intersects the surface of the color gamut cube. Clipping colors to 1, for example clipping an RGB of 1.0, 0.0, 2.0 to 1.0, 0.0, 1.0, results in a gross color shift from blue-violet to magenta. In the case of scaling the color, mach banding often results at the point in the image where clipping begins. The mach banding is due to a sharp discontinuity in the rate-of-change of the image intensity at the point where clipping starts.

An simple alternate solution is to draw an equal intensity vector from the undisplayable color to the neutral axis and to display the color at the intersection of this vector and the displayable gamut. This method attempts to maintain the intensity and hue of the requested color at the expense of saturation. Additionally, both undisplayable intensity and undisplayable chromaticity are treated in a consistent manner.

The neutral axis runs from black at 0,0,0 to white at 1,1,1. Planes perpendicular to this are considered to be equal intensity planes. Recognize however that this is only an approximation as planes perpendicular to the neutral axis are not necessarily equal intensity planes. The zero intensity plane is perpendicular to the neutral axis and passes through the RGB value 0,0,0, and has an equation of:

$$\frac{R}{\sqrt{3}} + \frac{G}{\sqrt{3}} + \frac{B}{\sqrt{3}} = d; \quad d = 0.0$$

The color value requiring clipping, rgb, is substituted into eq. (29) resulting is a perpendicular distance, d, from the zero intensity plane to the plane of equal intensity for rgb. Note that this also produces the plane equation for the plane through rgb. The point of intersection of this plane with the neutral axis, rgb', occurs where $r'=g'=b'$. The color that is displayed is the intersection of the vector from rgb' to rgb and the monitor gamut. Example 4 describes this clipping process.

This method preserves intensity and dominant hue. The saturation of the color is altered to pull the color into the displayable range. This method reduces the anomalies from color clipping but does not fully eliminate them. Discontinuities in the rate-of-change of a color still exist when clipping begins, but they have been shifted to the least objectionable color component. It may be argued that a roll-off curve should be used to compress rather than clip undisplayable colors into the gamut, thus further reducing or eliminating discontinuities. However, this introduces dominant hue shift anomalies which may may require very complex correction.

Color Correction for Multiple Monitors

Several frame buffers and monitors often comprise an image generation system. Often several monitors will be connected to a single frame buffer or video switchers will allow a monitor to be connected to one of several frame buffers. An image look the same no matter which monitor and frame buffer are used for viewing. More important, the image must look the same after recording as it did during design.

The calibrated studio monitor is the most representative monitor for video production. If more than one studio monitor at an installation, all should be the same type and be uniformly calibrated. This assures the phosphors and electronics are as similar as possible so that an image will look the same on all monitors.

As demonstrated in the previous discussion, the RGB colorspace is not an absolute color space. The chromaticities of the white point and RGB phosphors for the colorspace must be known to establish the true color of an RGB value. If

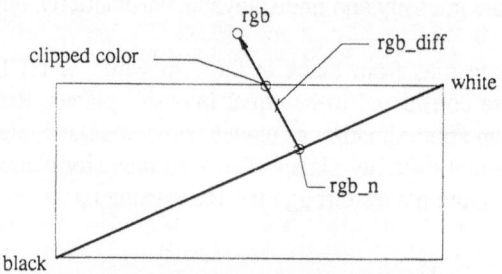

section through neutral axis of color gamut

```
typedef struct RGB {float  r,g,b}

clip_color (in_rgb, out_rgb)
RGB        *in_rgb;   /* pixel to be clipped */
RGB        *out_rgb;  /* clipped rgb values */
{
  RGB        rgb_diff;  /* diff vector */
  float          rgb_n;  /* rgb at neutral axis */
  float          len;   /* rgb_diff multiplier */
  float          tmp;   /* temporary length */
  /* neutral axis intersection */
  rgb_n = (in_rgb->r + in_rgb->g + in_rgb->b) / 3;

  if (rgb_n > 1)  /* beyond the clipping range */
  { out_rgb->r = out_rgb->g = out_rgb->b = 1.0;
  }
  else      /* inside clipping range */
  { len = 1.0
    rgb_diff.r = in_rgb->r - rgb_n;
    rgb_diff.g = in_rgb->g - rgb_n;
    rgb_diff.b = in_rgb->b - rgb_n;

    if (in_rgb->r < 0)
    { if ((tmp = (1-rgb_n) / rgb_diff->r) < len) len = tmp;
    }
    else if  (in_rgb -> r > 1)
    { if ((tmp = -(rgb_n) / rgb_diff->r) < len) len = tmp;
    }
    if (in_rgb->g < 0)
    { if ((tmp = (1-rgb_n) / rgb_diff->g) < len) len = tmp;
    }
    else if  (in_rgb->g > 1)
    { if ((tmp = -(rgb_n) / rgb_diff->g) < len) len = tmp;
    }
    if  (in_rgb -> b < 0)
    { if ((tmp = (1-rgb_n) / rgb_diff->b) < len) len = tmp;
    }
    else if  (in_rgb->b > 1){ if ((tmp = -(rgb_n) /
    rgb_diff->b) < len) len = tmp;
    }
    out_rgb->r = rgb_n + (len * rgb_diff.r);
    out_rgb->g = rgb_n + (len * rgb_diff.g);
    out_rgb->b = rgb_n + (len * rgb_diff.b);
  }
}
```

Example 4 Color Value Clipping

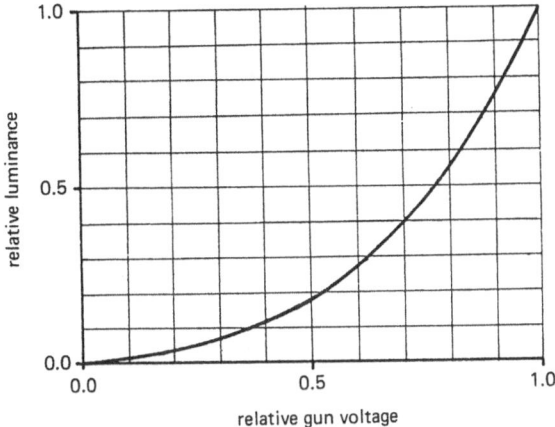

Figure 33

images are saved as RGB data, the chromaticities of the primaries of the RGB colorspace should be saved with the image. This allows transforming the image into the colorspace of any monitor, regardless of the monitor phosphors. Typically, the RGB colorspace for image storage will match the monitors used for production viewing and recording so that no color transformation is required for display. Color transformation often produces degradation in the color resolution of the image accompanied by color clipping, thus, should be avoided during display for recording.

The RGB to RGB transformation developed in section 2.5 in combination with the color clipping algorithm presented in section 4.1 provides the basis for a display program that will transform images from the storage RGB colorspace to the colorspace of the display. If all of the monitors at a site are identical this is not an issue. If a number of different monitors are used, it is critical that images appear the same on all of the monitors.

Gamma Correction for Image Files

Color computations are performed in a linear intensity color space. For example, an *rgb* color of .5,.5,.5 has half the intensity of an *rgb* color of 1,1,1. Traditionally, images produced for computer graphics are written into files of linear intensity byte data with one byte for each of red, green, and blue at every pixel. Thus pixel of a value of 127,127,127 has half the intensity of a pixel of value 255,255,255.

Unfortunately, the response of typical video color monitors and of the human visual system is non-linear and the storage of images in a linear format results in effective intensity quantization at a much lower resolution than the available 256 resolution per color. When a linear image is loaded into the frame buffer, a video lookup table (color map) is also loaded to correct for the non-linearity of the monitor. A typical monitor luminance curve is shown in Figure 33.

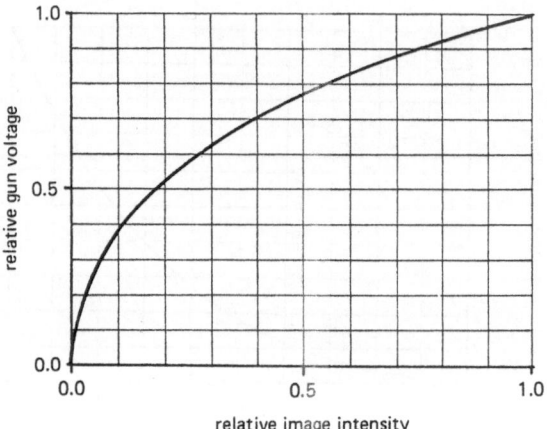

Figure 34   relative image intensity

Typical monitor response curve, relative luminance function relative gun voltage. The corresponding video lookup table curve to correct for monitor nonlinearity is shown in Figure 34. Typical video lookup table generate the correct gun voltage function image intensity.

The monitor correction function is an exponential function of the form:

$$\text{lookup value} \quad = \quad \text{intensity}^{1.0 / \text{gamma}} \tag{30}$$

Gamma represents the nonlinearity of the monitor. Monitors normally have a gamma value that is in the range 2.0 to 3.0. A gamma of 1.0 represents a linear device. Using an incorrect gamma value results in incorrect image contrast and chromaticity shifts. Figure 35 shows the chromaticity and contrast migration of the colors from the Macbeth ColorChecker* chart. If the gamma is too high, the contrast is decreased and the colors are desaturated. If the gamma is too low, the contrast is increased and the colors migrate toward the primaries. The black point in each color trace is at the correct chromaticity of the color.

The result of displaying an image through video lookup tables is that the lower 10% of the intensity range of the image is stretched into the lower 40% of the display resolution range. Another way to look at this is that an increment of 1 in the image file is mapped into a much larger increment for display. For example, using a monitor gamma of 2.5, the image value 4 is mapped into 48 and the image value 5 is mapped into 53. The displayable steps between 48 and 53 are never used. The observable result is that images tend to be banded in the low intensity regions due to intensity quantizing to a lower resolution than the available resolution of the display device. This banding is exhibited as both intensity bands and bands of shifted color.

The gamma function can be applied to the computed color values from the illumination model before they are converted to byte values for storage. The result

---

*ColorChecker is a trademark of Macbeth.

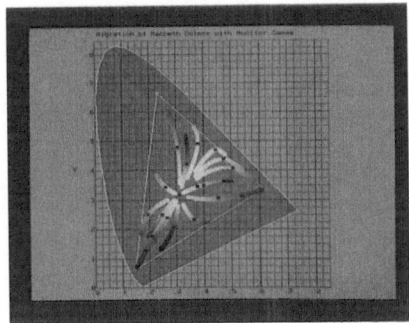

Figure 35 Migration of chromaticity of Macbeth Colorchecker colors as a result of incorrect gamma correction for the monitor. The black squares are the correct chromaticity.

is an image that can be displayed with linear video lookup tables thus taking advantage of the full intensity resolution of the display device. Although this discussion has been independent of visual perceptual issues, it should be noted that perceived linear brightness is logarithmic with respect to actual intensity and is similar to the monitor response curve, Figure 36. Thus, the typical monitor response provides roughly linear response in terms of perceived intensity. Human visual response curve, perceived brightness function relative luminance.

Figure 37 displays visual evidence of the banding that results from the use of video lookup table to correct for monitor nonlinearity. Limitations in the printing reproduction process mask these banding problems in the 8-bit resolution images. To assure that the nature of the banding problem is evident the image is also shown at 6-bit resolution in each of red, green, and blue.

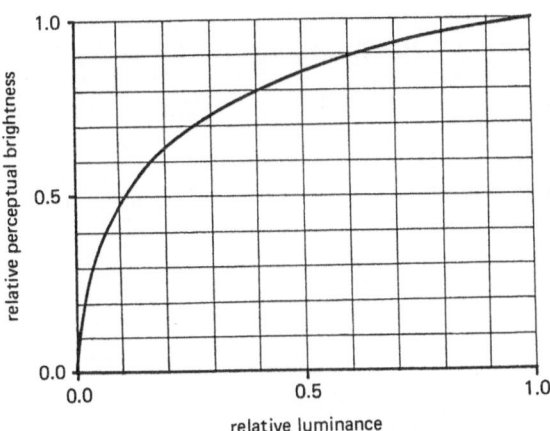

Figure 36

Figure 37

Conclusion

This discussion has reviewed the basics of light behavior, mathematical models for light behavior and color computation, and the color display process. The problem of computing and displaying the correct colors in computer graphics is not a trivial task. It is apparent that there are many areas in which are not fully addressed by the existing research. Hopefully this review will provide a reference to the work that has been done and will help highlight problems that are yet to be solved.

References

[AMAN84] Amanatides, John (1984) "Ray Tracing with Cones." ACM Computer Graphics, vol.18, no.3, pp129-135

[BECK63] Beckmann, Petr and Andre Spizzichino (1963), The Scattering of Electromagnetic Waves from Rough Surfaces. MacMillan, pp.1-33, 70-98, 1963

[BLIN76] Blinn, J. F. and M. E. Newell (1976) "Texture and Reflection in Computer Generated Images." Comm. of the ACM, vol.19, no.10, pp 542-547

[BLIN77] Blinn, James F. (1977) "Models of Light Reflection for Computer Synthesized Pictures." ACM Computer Graphics, vol.11, no.2, pp192-198

[BOUK70] Bouknight, W. J. (1970) "A Procedure for Generation of Three-dimensional Half-toned Computer Graphics Presentations." Comm. of the ACM, vol.13, no.9

[CATM75] Catmull, E. E. (1975) "Computer Display of Curved Surfaces." Proceedings IEEE Conference on Computer Graphics, Pattern Recognition and Data Structures, May 1975, pp 11-17

[COHE85] Cohen, Micheal F. and Greenberg, Donald P. (1985) "The Hemi-Cube, A Radiosity Solution for Complex Environments." ACM Computer Graphics, vol.19, no.3, pp 31-40

[COHE86] Cohen, Micheal F., D. P.Greenberg, D. S. Immel, and P.J.Brock (1986) "The Hemi-Cube, A Radiosity An Efficient Radiosity Approach for Realistic Image Synthesis." IEEE Computer Graphics and Applications, vol.6, no.3, pp26-35

[COOK81] Cook, Robert L. (1981) "A Reflection Model for Realistic Image Synthesis." Masters Thesis, Cornell University, Ithaca, NY

[COOK82] Cook, Robert L. and Kenneth E. Torrance (1982) "A Reflection Model for Computer Graphics." ACM Transactions on Graphics, vol.1, no.1, pp7-24

[COOK84] Cook, Robert L., Thomas Porter and Loren Carpenter (1984) "Distributed Ray Tracing." ACM Computer Graphics, vol.18, no.13, pp137-146

[CORN70] Cornsweet, T. N. (1970), Visual Perception. Academic Press, New York

[DITC76] Ditchburn,R. W. (1976), Light. Academic Press, London, vols.1 2

[GORA84] Goral, Cindy M, K. E.Torrance, D.P.Greenberg, and B.Battaile (1984) "Modeling the Interaction of Light Between Diffuse Surfaces." ACM Computer Graphics (SIGGRAPH 84), vol.18, no.3, pp213-222

[GOUR71] Gouraud, Henri (1971) "Continuous Shading of Curved Surfaces." IEEE Transactions on Computers, June 1971, pp623-629

[HALL83a] Hall, Roy A., and Donald P. Greenberg (1983) "A Testbed for Realistic Image Synthesis." IEEE Computer Graphics and Applications, vol.3, no.8, pp10-20

[HALL83b] Hall, Roy A. (1983), "A Methodology for Realistic Image Synthesis." Masters Thesis, Cornell University, Ithaca, NY

[HECH79] Hecht, Eugene and Alfred Zajac (1979), Optics, Addison-Wesley, Reading.

[HUNT75] Hunt, R. W. G. (1975) The Reproduction of Color. Third Edition, John Wiley and Sons, New York

[JENK76] Jenkins, Francis A. and Harvey E. White (1976) Fundamentals of Optics. Mc-Graw-Hill, New York

[JUDD75] Judd, D. B. and Wyszecki, G. (1975), Color in Business, Science, and Industry. John Wiley and Sons, New York

[KAY79] Kay, Douglas S. and Donald P. Greenberg (1979), "Transparency for Computer Synthesized Images. Computer Graphics, vol.13, no.2, pp158-164

[MEYE83] Meyer, Gary (1983), "Colorimetry and Computer Graphics." program of Computer Graphics, Report no. 83-1, Cornell university, Ithaca, NY

[NEWE72] Newell, M.; R. Newell and T. Sancha (1972), "A Solution to the Hidden Surface Problem." Proceeding of the ACM National Conference, 1972, pp433-450

[NISH85] Nishita, Tomoyuki and Eihachiro Nakamae (1985), "Continuous Tone Representations of Three-Dimensional Objects Taking Account of Shadows and Inter-reflection." ACM Computer Graphics, vol.19, no.3, pp23-30

[PHON75] Phong, Bui Toung (1975), "Illumination for Computer Generated Pictures." Comm. of the ACM, vol.18, no.8, pp311-317

[PURD70] Purdue University (1970), Thermophysical Properties of Matter.

[ROMN70] Romney,G. W. (1970), "Computer Assisted Assembly and Rendering of Solids." Dept. of Comp. Sci., University of Utah, Salt Lake City, Technical Report TR4-20

[TORR66] Torrance, K. E. and E. M. Sparrow (1966), "Polarization, Directional Distribution, and Off-Specular Peak Phenomena in Light Reflected from Roughened Surfaces." J. Opt. Soc. Am., vol.56, no.7, pp916-925

[TORR67] Torrance, K. E. and E. M. Sparrow (1967), "Theory for Off-Specular Reflection from Roughened Surfaces." J. Opt. Soc. Am., vol.57, no.9, pp1105-1114

[TROW67] Trowbridge, T. S. and K. P. Reitz (1967), "Average Irregularity Representation of a Roughened Surface for Ray Reflection." J. Opt. Soc. Am., vol.65, no.5

[WARN69] Warnock, John E. (1969), "A Hidden Surface Algorithm for Halftone Picture Representation." Dept. of Comp. Sci., University of Utah, Salt Lake City, Technical Report TR4-15

[WHIT80] Whitted, Turner (1980), "An Improved Illumination Model for Shaded Display." Communications of the ACM, vol.23, no.6, pp343-349

4 Workstations

Advanced Engineering/ Scientific Graphic Workstations

ZSUZSANNA MOLNAR

Abstract

The key to increased productivity is response time. Since an engineer typically performs several tasks in parallel, today's engineering workstations must be capable of running multiple tasks concurrently with each process displayed in a separate window on the monitor screen.

Advanced workstation technology: combining general purpose computing power, custom designed VLSI technology, standardized operating systems, and high-level graphics languages are discussed. The components of such a system provide fast execution of complex software as well as tools for accelerated program development. A new approach to a window management system with simultaneous, dynamic, real-time 2 or 3-D graphic displays as well as text and editing displays is discussed.

The high-performance graphics component of an engineering workstation capable of supporting transformations of solid 3-D objects in real-time, Gouraud shading or depth cuing and a host of input devices such as tablet, mouse, dials and buttons for interactive control of the system is discussed.

Major application areas, e.g., robotics, solid modeling, and scientific simulation, benefit from this type of workstation.

1. Difficult Problems Require Sophisticated Solutions

Today we face a revolution in the design and development of new products. The constantly accelerating race to bring a product to market is relentless. This development speed is coupled with a significant increase in product complexity. Electrical engineers are condensing more and more components into smaller and smaller spaces, while civil and mechanical engineers are approaching projects of massive scale. The traditional methods of research, conception, design, prototype and test are simply too time consuming and expensive. Together these factors mount a tremendous challenge to all the engineering disciplines to develop sophisticated solutions to difficult problems.

The graphics workstation has become an indispensable problem solving tool in the scientific and engineering environments. By joining analytical, computational and graphics capability, workstations enable the automation of design and research and the sharing of information by whole design teams. Only recently have computer systems been designed and marketed that are optimized for the special requirements of the typical engineering environment.

1.1 Basic Characteristics of an Advanced Graphics Workstation

- Runs standard operating system - UNIX
- Supports high performance graphics
- Supports graphics input devices such as tablet, mouse
- Supports graphics output devices such as color printers and plotters
- Provides optimizing native code C and FORTRAN compilers
- Has a reasonable amount of memory, mass storage and address space
- Ethernet network interface

1.2 Advanced Graphics Workstations
Start New Era in Geometric Computing

Advanced graphics workstations offer entirely new capabilities to an engineer. Real-time, three-dimensional graphics allows an engineer to work with a computerized model as easily as if it were a physical part. Increase in CPU performance allows the engineer to perform analysis and simulations using the geometry of the part and to obtain real-time visual output. This is not always possible with a physical model. The integration of three-dimensional graphics and computing into a single package is unique to the advanced graphics workstation. An integrated high speed network of workstations and terminals allows the engineering group to share information and to access data bases or more powerful computing resources when needed. This allows the work group to act in concert and reduce the effort required to communicate. By offering a standard operating system, such as UNIX, the engineer need learn only one set of commands to access all the computers in the network. Application vendors are using the power of advanced graphics workstations to improve performance and the man machine interface. Whenever the interaction of the engineer with the application program can be made faster the engineer can be more flexible in his or her efforts, more creative in designs, and more productive overall. Real-time, three dimensional graphics with integrated computing and with applications designed to take advantage of this architecture provide a revolution in mechanical engineering similar to the revolution caused by two-dimensional graphics in electrical engineering.

1.3 Computing and Graphics Trends

- Interactive computing - late 60's
- Interactive graphics - the early 70's
- Real-time, three-dimensional graphics - the early 70's
- Lower cost computing with 32 bit super minis - the late 70's
- Engineering workstations - 1981

Each of these trends has occurred because of the engineer's need to perform more work in less time. Any technological development which can make the design process more productive will very rapidly gain wide spread acceptance. The more cost effective this new technology is, the broader the target market is. Graphics workstations bring these trends together from a single source at a price which is acceptable. The price of this technology continues to fall rapidly and as a consequence a larger population of engineers will be able to justify these capabilities.

1.3.1 Response Time

Response time changes of as little as one second can significantly alter the productivity of an individual user. In a controlled study entitled "The Economic

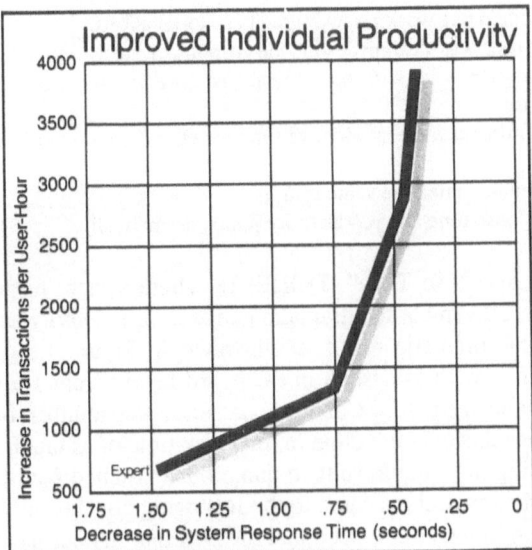

Figure 1 In a controlled study where system response time was the lone variable, IBM® recorded dramatic jumps in productivity as response time was reduced. A one second decline resulted in a quadrupling of hourly output.

The study results were confirmed in numerous unrelated facilities throughout the country. In each case, even fractional reductions in response time produced phenomenal reductions in total task time—more productivity.

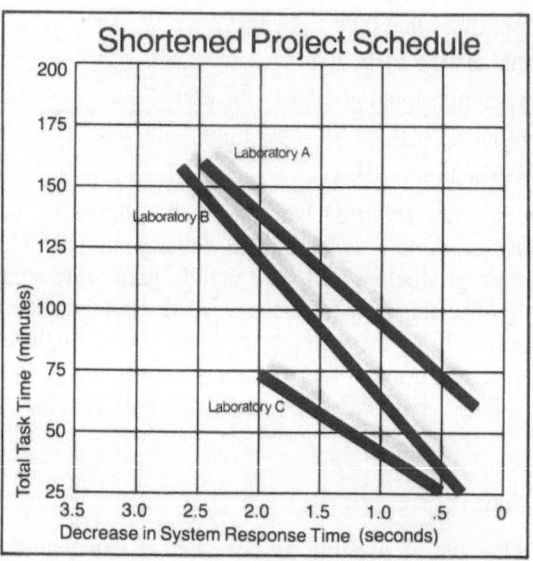

Figure 2 A study of systems designers at IBM's Product Systems Division measured the response time of engineers working with graphics workstations.

A card wiring task was designed with the response time as the sole variable; an 82 minute task on a system with a .6 second response time became a 66 minute task with a .25 second response time.

Result: Over 4 minutes more productive time for every .1 second of response time improvement.

More studies demonstrated the same results.

Shorten the response time and productivity jumps dramatically.

Value of Rapid Response Time" [DOHE82], where system response time was the lone variable, IBM recorded dramatic jumps in productivity as response time was reduced. This dramatic result is illustrated in Figure 1. By reducing the response time of a graphics system in PC board layout from 1.5 seconds to 0.5 second, users typically achieve about four times the number of transactions. Figure 2 translates this to a reduction in total task time of as much as 60%.

After confirming the study results in numerous unrelated facilities throughout the country IBM's researchers came to the following conclusion: "When a computer and its users interact at a pace that ensures that neither has to wait on the other, productivity soars, the cost of work done on the computer tumbles, employees get more satisfaction from their work, and its quality tends to improve. Few online computers systems are that well balanced; few executives are aware that such a balance is economically and technically feasible" [DOHE82].

The importance of system response time becomes more significant in the context of engineering tasks that require the display of a large amount of complex

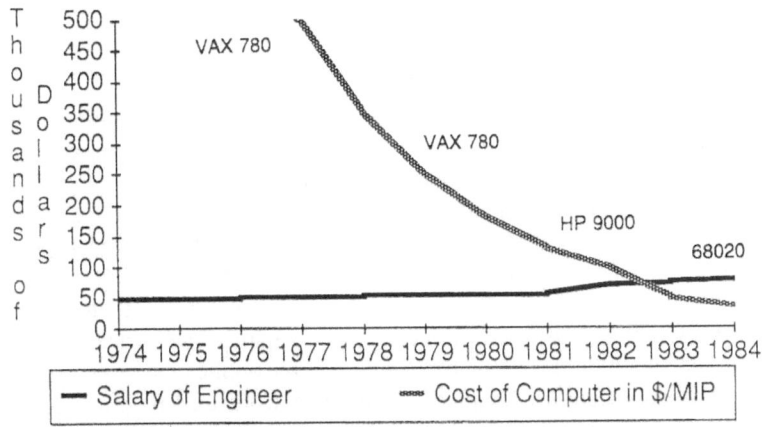

Figure 3

graphics. The productivity of engineers working with CAD/CAM and CAE has been hampered in the past by the serious shortcomings of traditional solutions to the graphics problem.

1.3.2 Computing Costs vs. Human Costs

A second factor driving the move to better productivity tools for engineers is cost. In the past ten years, the price/performance for a typical computer system has decreased from $1.5M/MIP in 1974 to about $40K/MIP in 1984. This corresponds to roughly a 43% per year compounded decrease, as shown in Figure 3. During the same period, the burdened salary of a typical engineer has risen from about $36k/year to roughly $75K/year. In the early 1980's, for the first time the computer user was more expensive than the computer. These trends indicated a need for both a personal/professional computer and an efficient interface to it.

Because it is such an essential part of engineering work, graphics has become this modern interface. Thus, the "graphics workstation", as it is discussed here, is minimally defined as a raster graphics system combined with an extensive set of tools for application software development, and a general-purpose computing environment in one physical package. The effectiveness of such systems is measured by their performance in the integration of three key areas: general purpose processing power; graphics capabilities; and, an interactive, user-friendly development environment. Only computer systems providing optimal performance on all three accounts can be expected to increase productivity by providing faster overall response time. We shall examine the details of a typical high-performance graphics workstation more closely.

2. Graphics: The Principal Computer Interface

2.1 Evolution of Graphics Systems

Vision is the most used human sense, so quite naturally graphics has become our most important form of computer interface. As with computer systems, however, graphics systems vary in their suitability for certain applications. The goal of the engineering or scientific workstation should be to provide a graphics system suitable for technical applications. Ivan Sutherland stated the problem we face today with prescience in 1963 when he said his sketch pad made "it possible for man and computer to converse rapidly through the medium of line drawing" [SUTH63]. Graphics has become increasingly sophisticated since then, but a graphics system still must be as closely suited to the application as possible.

Two basic approaches to graphics are used in workstations, bit-mapped and geometric. Bit-mapped graphics was developed for page imaging applications and has operations tailored for image manipulation of single bit images. It does not extend conveniently to color. Geometric graphics was developed as a tool to assist in the design and analysis of engineering problems. Geometric operations are tailored for the manipulation and display of geometric objects in the frame of reference of the designer.

2.1.1 Bit-mapped Graphics

Bit-mapped graphics was first developed in 1974 at Xerox PARC for the Xerox Alto. This was the first professional workstation. Because of the nature of Xerox's business, it was designed primarily for page layout and imaging applications — thus it used a bit-mapped raster display. The bit-mapped display is used in these applications because the image of a page to be produced on a laser printer is constructed from a large two-dimensional array of binary digits.

In the Alto, one microprogrammed processor did everything — it was the graphics processor, disk controller, ethernet controller and central processor all in one. High-level language compilers were written for the Alto, and most programmers used them, but when something had to run very fast, custom microprograms were implemented for it.

One of these custom microprograms was the "bit-blt", which means Bit Block Transfer. It was developed because of the relatively large amount of time required to draw, redraw and manipulate a page image on the Alto. With the bit-blt in microcode, one could more quickly modify a bit-image. Because construction of the bit-image was relatively time consuming and generalized, bit-blt operations allow the image to be "un"-altered with the logical "exclusive or", and the image was infrequently regenerated.

The focus of bit-blt or bit-mapped graphics systems is therefore in creating, manipulating and storing a bit-image, as in page layout systems. They are specialized for such applications and do not use specialized, higher-level processors to assist in manipulations of geometric objects, as required by most engineering applications. Their primary benefit is that they typically utilize a single processor for everything, thus reducing their costs. The Apple Macintosh and the Sun workstation are the best realizations of bit-mapped graphics workstations.

2.1.2 Geometric Graphics Systems

Geometric graphics originated with Sketchpad, in a graphics system implemented by Ivan Sutherland in 1964 on the TX-2 computer at MIT. As an engineer and scientist, Sutherland was interested in providing a graphical interface that allowed interactive, computer-assisted design of geometric engineering objects. In Sketchpad, objects were designed and manipulated in terms of the application's geometric coordinate system, or as we commonly say now, "user coordinates", "user space", or "world coordinates", The image created by a geometric graphics system is simply a rendering of the geometric objects being designed and manipulated — it is not an important entity in isolation, since it can easily be regenerated from the geometric description.

Fundamental geometric notions in use today were defined in Sketchpad. Because the geometric objects are described in one coordinate system (the user coordinates of the application) while the renderings of these objects are described in another (the image or screen coordinate system of the display), the notions of "windows" (user-space), "viewports" (screen-space), and a means for "mapping" from one to the other were defined. Likewise, because a window on the user's space might include only part of the whole drawing, "clipping" of information had to be performed before the mapping. Finally, because the user's application space is geometric, objects might be arbitrarily translated, rotated or scaled ("transformed") in the space and multiple "instances" of objects might be made before they are passed through the window, undergo clipping and so forth. Although Sketchpad was primarily a 2-D system, it defined these concepts in a general way that was applicable to 3-D design as well. (see Figure 8).

Design as envisioned by Sutherland was interactive and in real-time. Since the clipping and mapping functions defined in Sketchpad were very compute intensive, Sutherland concentrated on hardware to perform the functions as fast as possible. The "clipping-divider" designed by Bob Sproull with Ivan Sutherland at Harvard University in 1968 was the first hardware implementation of a system to implement the concepts defined in Sketchpad. This device used SSI semiconductor technology and by itself required four 19 inch racks.

2.2 Chip Based Graphics Performance or
Why Design Custom VLSI Circuits?

Why is speed so important in a graphics system, be it geometric or bit-mapped? Some applications, such as simulation, absolutely require it. Others simply may need it to improve productivity, since workstations are interactive systems, which implies that the user is waiting for a result to appear on the graphic display. If a graphics system cannot respond interactively, the user must do the task differently.

Fast geometric graphics makes no sense without special-purpose hardware to do the required computations. However, specialized hardware always adds extra cost. In the general-purpose computing area, microprocessors have ushered in the era of low-cost computing. In the geometric graphics domain, VLSI chips have ushered in a new era of low-cost geometric graphics.

The design of floating-point chip sets for graphics is increasing. For example, today we have the Geometry Engine, Weitek tiling chips, and the new Graphicon board from General Electric. Essential requirements for 3-D graphics accelerators are that they provide both clipping and 3-D perspective geometric graphics and incorporate the algorithms for processing graphical data or manipulating solid objects with shading.

Because technology has provided the ability to put very complex subsystems on a single integrated circuit, the modern system designer must be able to design her/his own integrated circuits. As systems get larger it becomes increasingly difficult for the semiconductor manufacturer to second guess what the system designer would like for building blocks. Moreover, the building blocks require small scale circuits to "glue" them together.

Gate arrays and standard cells only partially solve the problem. Gate arrays do not currently allow very high densities. Perhaps worse, they do not currently provide a means for integrating RAM and ROM with logic. On the other hand, standard cells, while allowing higher densities, impose a certain architectural style on the designer. Each of these techniques allows faster implementation than full custom design, however.

Perhaps the biggest advantage of full-custom integrated circuits is in the architectural freedom they provide. This freedom can be exploited to employ parallelism in ways that are rare or nonexistent in other integrated circuit techniques. The Geometry Engine is one of the better known examples, but other highly parallel architectures dedicated to various special problems are certain to be developed in the future. System design now implies integrated circuit design. The VLSI era is the era of the system designer[CLAR84].

2.3 Realism in Engineering Graphics

Scientists and engineers work mainly with two types of graphic images: wireframes and shaded or solid models. Wire-frame geometry is a gridwork of lines, while solid models are more realistic representations with surface contours, color, and shading.

Because shaded images have historically have been generated in software, which is very time consuming, wireframes have been most frequently used for engineering design work. This is changing as new workstations utilize architectures which produce shaded images in a fraction of the time required to produce software generated images. Improved graphics hardware and local processing of graphical data have made possible the manipulation of shaded models at speeds comparable to wireframes. Shaded images have become as easy to manipulate as wireframes. Changes are displayed almost instantly.

2.3.1 Dynamic Modeling

Until recent hardware advances, design engineers could not easily switch back and forth between shaded and wireframe models. Because of slow software operation, rotation, and transformation of models was difficult. This capability is particularly useful in animating a simulated scenario, for instance simulating the operation of a piston assembly. Designers can quickly determine in the shaded mode whether a design is working properly. Dynamic support of advanced geometry such as bi-cubic curves and surfaces patches is also important for advanced engineering applications. This kind of graphics flexibility in either shaded or wireframe versions, is a key advantage of the advanced graphics workstation.

2.3.2 Hardware Support for 3-D Viewing Techniques

Recent developments in VLSI design and fast processors have made real-time graphics operations, beyond the basic 3-D transformations such as rotation, translation, and scaling possible. Some of the advanced graphics features supported by a 3-D graphics workstation include:

- **perspective viewing**

This is perhaps the most common visualization aid on 3-D systems. Perspective transformations, as discovered by painters during the Renaissance, produce more realistic scenes by making objects which are further from the viewpoint appear smaller than those which are closer. This is a real-time operation on advanced graphics workstations.

- **clipping**

Clipping planes allow deletion of unnecessary details from the geometry. X, Y and Z clipping planes can be used to fit the model to view on the screen by clipping sections from the left, right, top, front and back of the image. Text and parts that block the user's view can be removed. Today's advanced workstations give the user immediate control over the depth of clipping.

- **depthcuing**

Determining depth in a wireframe has always been a 3-D viewing problem. Establishing which lines are in the front of an image and which are in back has been a laborious task for raster systems. Implementation of depth cuing on advanced graphics graphics workstations makes possible the use of brighter colors to indicate foreground objects, gradually changing to lower intensities for background objects. The systems accomplish this in real-time.

- **lighting models**

The perception of volume is enhanced by mathematically simulating light sources illuminating synthetic objects. Again, the trend is to move this task to hardware. Systems are appearing with built-in lighting models.

- **stereo-optic viewing**

There are several technologies which work on basically the same principle. Slightly different views are delivered to each eye to simulate true 3-D viewing. With some approaches, both images are on the screen simultaneously and color filtering is used to separate the views, while other approaches accomplish the same result by switching between eyes via shutters.

2.3.3 Shading Algorithms and Advanced Rendering Techniques

The generation of shaded images requires special processors integrated within the advanced workstation. Using a full 3-D geometric definition of the model, polygons are created which approximate the model. These polygons are shaded through manipulation of a simulated light source. New workstations offer a choice among the three main types of shading: flat faceted, Gouraud, or Phong smooth shading.

The simplest algorithm does flat faceted or planar shading. With faceted shading, a single intensity value is calculated, by the application, for shading an entire polygon. Each polygon is one color, and colors vary from polygon to polygon. This algorithm can be sped up using fast feedback routines and hardware support from VLSI graphics hardware. Flat faceted shading is very rapid, but polygon boundaries along the object are very obvious. Therefore it is primarily used for quick, interactive viewing or on relatively flat surfaces.

More advanced shading algorithms allow shading to vary within polygons. Gouraud shading is a smooth shading algorithm. With this algorithm, each polygon is shaded by linear interpolation of vertex intensities along each edge and then between edges along each scan line. Intensity discontinuities between polygons are reduced, producing a much smoother appearance. Gouraud shading's limitations are its lack of highlight rendering. Phong shading produces the most realistic shading effect— specular highlights on the surface of the model. Phong shading is a much more computationally costly smooth shading method because it interpolates the actual surface normals at each pixel and then calculates the color.

The animation field has pioneered advanced rendering algorithms to achieve a high level of synthetic realism. These techniques such as ray tracing, metallic reflections, transparency, and motion blur are extremely computationally expensive, often running on large Vaxes for hours to produce a single frame. For engineering applications, various types of shading and rendering can be used to improve the visual clarity of the model. The technique chosen, ranging from flat faceted to ray traced, depends on the type of part being designed and the quality of image required.

2.3.4 Animation and Image Quality

The graphics workstation should offer instant feedback while maintaining an optimal degree of both imaging flexibility and image complexity. Graphics image display memory should be expandable to 24 bits per pixel, and software configurable from eight to twenty-four bits per pixel, providing flexibility for the user's application needs.

Full color or RGB(full Red,Green,Blue) mode allows detailed, high quality renderings of full color displays with over 16.7 million colors. In RGB mode a total of 24 bits per pixel becomes available, 8 bits each for the red, green, and blue primaries. A second method, the use of color maps, is an economical way of using fewer bits per pixel. For instance, if only 8 to 12 planes are available, the system creates color via a colormap, so that between 256 and 4096 colors are selectable from a palette of 16.7 million different colors.

The availability of a double-buffer mode is important for animation. In double-buffer mode, the workstation splits the framebuffer into a front and a backbuffer for real-time animation of three-dimensional solids. While the image is drawn into the backbuffer, the frontbuffer is displayed. Then the buffers are switched in a rhythm of up to thirty frames per second.

2.3.5 Hidden Surface Removal

Hidden surface algorithms determine the visible sides of 3-D objects modeled from polygons. Given a 3-D object and a viewing specification defining the type of projection, the projection plane, etc., the visible edges and surfaces of the object must be determined. This involves the elimination of faces which intersect or overlap.

One technique to accomplish hidden surface removal is through the use of a Z-Buffer algorithm. Z-buffering is a general-purpose algorithm which will work for a scene of any complexity. A hardware Z-buffer or depth-buffer stores z-values for each pixel. Polygons are sorted by their relative Z coordinates, and the polygons closest to the eyepoint of the viewer are the ones finally drawn. Z-buffering, while rapid (5-15 seconds) is typically not a real-time operation.

Another technique for hidden surface removal, the Binary Space Partition algorithm (BSP) is primarily useful for rapid viewing of "rigid" bodies and for scenes where the world model changes less frequently than the viewpoint or direction of view of the observer. The BSP algorithm involves two steps: creation of the "BSP-tree" (i.e., the pre-sorting step); and display of the image. The pre-sorting step is not real-time. The actual length of time depends on the number of polygons and the complexity of the object or scene, but can take up to several minutes. However, once sorted, as long as the 3-D object or scene is not modified, the resulting BSP-tree lends itself to fairly fast display. If the object is modified or the scene changed (e.g., one object moves with respect to another), a new BSP-tree must be computed.

There are many applications which involve "flexing" bodies (e.g., robotics) or in which objects that are continually being modified (e.g., Mechanical CAD), or applications involving scenes in which several rigid objects interact with each other. For these applications, a more general-purpose algorithm like the z-buffer may be more appropriate.

2.4 Interactive Tools for Instantaneous Response

For many applications which depend heavily on accurate hand/eye coordination such as rendering and manipulation of objects, instant feedback is a necessity. In most graphics applications a three-button mouse furnishes a software controllable mechanism for pointing and selecting items from pop-up menus, positioning and drawing on the screen, and inquiring about the status of any displayed object. In conjunction with a real-time graphics display the mouse proves to be a quick and convenient decision making tool.

The issues surrounding 2-D interaction on a workstation have been exhaustively explored. Studies done during the 60's at Xerox PARC showed the mouse to be the most effective tool for manipulating objects on the screen. These findings have been subsequently borne out by the proliferation of systems which use the Xerox Star interface (mouse combined with popup/pulldown menus). The Apple Macintosh is a good example of such an interface. Text files, directories, and executable files are represented by icons displayed on the screen. The mouse in combination with pulldown menus is used to manipulate (move, copy, remove) files. Selecting an executable file's icon executes it. Once a program is started, other pulldown menus as well as new icons are available. Apple puts a great deal of effort into keeping its interface consistent. A minimum of typing is necessary. As an example of the power of this interface paradigm, Macpaint is so easy to learn that a child can work 'productively' within a few minutes.

However, there are applications where the mouse is not acceptable. For example, for freehand rendering or sketching a tablet is generally preferred. A tablet guarantees the highest degree of accuracy for digitizing engineering drawings. For such an application, the mouse may be uncomfortable for a number of reasons, the least subjective of which is that the orientation of the mouse on the table determines what direction a given mouse motion will translate to on the screen. This is not much of a problem for picking existing objects, which requires less precision, but for intuitive response in creating free hand images it is crucial. Although, as mentioned, the mouse and menu is a commonplace interface, there is much room for personal preference, and other devices, particularly the light pen and touch screen can be functionally substituted for the mouse.

Some applications benefit from a dial and button box, a standard graphics peripheral containing continuous turn dials and a set of function buttons. An LED alpha-numeric display is frequently used with dials and buttons to represent program status information. For instance, the Hollywood animation production house, Robert Abel and Associates, uses a dial and button box to individually specify transformation parameters for complex motions of multiple objects. In addition, previously created event sequences can be called up at the push of a button; a valuable feature for choreographing the animation.

2.4.1 3D Interactive Tools

The above techniques are helpful for viewing objects which already exist, but often fall short in the creation of new 3-D objects, (especially irregular ones), and in the modification of those objects. In the creation of objects programmers are often forced to use roundabout approaches to generate the required third dimension, such as slicing objects and entering them a slice at a time. Complex, curved objects which have no mathematical definition are also difficult to input.

Emerging technologies are addressing many of the problems posed by 3-D workstations. 3-D digitizers which allow one to model freely into 3-D space are now appearing. These devices aid in both the creation and examination of synthetic objects as well as in the digitization of existing objects. However, problems still exist in modifying synthetic objects because it is difficult to judge depth, even with the visualization aids listed above. Even stereo-optic glasses are not completely satisfactory because the image is displayed on a stationary screen. This makes it impossible for one to 'walk behind' an object facing away from the screen and still view the object. Ultimately it will be necessary for 3-D output devices to catch up with the evolution of 3-D input devices. Emerging technology in the form of 3-D helmets appears encouraging. In the next few years it should be possible to walk into a synthetic environment, and create, manipulate and view a synthetic reality.

Noninteractive acquisition of data is also an area of active growth. Digitizing cameras are available which will scan 2-D images. CAT scans can digitize 3-D tissue. Services are cropping up which allow one to send in an object (3-D) or image (2-D) and receive back its digital representation. Similarly, tapes of images can be sent out to services for printing. Furthermore, the objects digitized in this manner can be used for numerical control of equipment to generate physical copies of the objects digitized. Standardized image file and object files will have to be forthcoming for this to be of real universal use.

2.5 Cutting Development Time with a High Level Graphics Library

To provide an ideal applications development environment on an advanced graphics workstation, the quality of graphics software is important. The graphics software environment should include a high level graphics library callable from C, FORTRAN, or Pascal. An extensive set of subroutines should directly and completely exploit the speed and functionality of the graphics workstation hardware. Use of a graphics library assists applications programming, especially when compared to arduous micro coding or to incorporating a low-level instruction set into high-level programs. Even very complex graphics problems such as, coordinate transformations, interactive picking, curve and surface generation, hidden surface removal and smooth shading, should be invoked using a single subroutine from the library.

The types of graphics commands in a high-level graphics library can be broken into the following categories:

- *Primitive drawing* commands select characteristics for drawing lines, filling polygons, and writing text strings.

- *Coordinate transformation* commands map a user-defined world coordinate system onto the screen.

- *Display mode and color* commands determine how the image memory in the bitplanes is used and how objects are colored on the screen.

- *Input/output* commands initialize and read both polled and queued input-/output devices.

- *Object creation and editing* commands define complicated shapes from simple ones and provide tools for redefining those shapes.

- *Picking and selecting commands identify objects that are visible in a given area of the screen.*

- *Curve and surface* commands provide the means for constructing complex curved lines and surfaces from simple curve segments and surface patches.

- *Hidden surface* commands activate a mode in which hidden lines and surfaces are automatically removed from an image.

- *Shading* commands allow drawing of shaded surfaces and depth-cued lines.

- *Textport* commands reserve an area of the screen for writing text.

- *Window manager* commands create multiple concurrent windows or ports, for text and graphics output.

- *Feedback* commands provide direct access to the computing capabilities of the graphics hardware.

2.6 Graphics Standards

Establishing a graphics standard for today's computers has been elusive. The American Association of Computing Machinery's Special Interest Group in Graphics (ACM-SIGGRAPH), encouraged early work on graphics standards by publishing a proposal for a standard programmer interface known as the Core system in 1977. The GKS standard was adopted by the International Standards Organization (ISO), and American National Standards Institute (ANSI) in 1985. But both of these standards are based on older technology, for example GKS is a 2-D standard, and was defined before even bit-mapped displays were the dominant graphics display technology, not to mention 3-D geometric displays. A draft of the 3-D GKS standard is planned to be out in the spring of 1987.

More recently, the Computer Graphics Interface (CGI) standard has been gaining acceptance in the graphics community. Formally called the Virtual Device Interface (VDI), CGI is the lowest level standard interface for computer graphics programming. This standard, which is machine dependent, serves as the foundation for higher level standards such as GKS. The concepts of the most recent graphics standard, Programmer's Hierarchical Interactive Graphics System (PHIGS) stem from dissatisfaction with CORE and GKS limitations in application areas such as mechanical and electrical CAD and robotics. PHIGS was designed to be a high performance standard, offloading host computation to an intelligent graphics device. Among other performance attributes, it allows defining hierarchical graphic data. PHIGS capabilities include hierarchical data structures, dynamic editing of graphical entities, modeling coordinate systems, and primitive classes.

Hoping to create de facto standards for emerging applications, several companies are working on graphics interfaces. Regardless of the outcome, the range of computer graphics applications will involve flexible system design.

The acceptance of graphics standards is problematic because:

- Algorithms for rendering geometric objects are continuously evolving.

- Hardware is required to reduce the time necessary for repetitive calculations in rendering geometric images. Thus, graphics systems architectures that incorporate new algorithms change the software interface dramatically [CLAR85].

- Today's standards were designed to work with intelligent graphics terminals, but the close coupling of graphics and processor in a graphics workstation needs a fresh approach.

2.7 Window Managers for Advanced Graphics Workstations

Windows are the latest technique for increasing the information content of a CRT screen. A user-friendly window system provides integrated text and graphics systems with features not typically available in hard-wired systems. These features include the ability to clip information to fit within the dimensions of a window, magnification, overlapping of two windows, and independent control of graphics and text transformations.

2.7.1 The Popularity of Window Managers

Window managers have achieved their popularity because multiple windows are analogous to a desktop workplace. Tasks are divided among distinct screen regions (windows), much like papers are organized on a desk in an office. Attention can be focused upon a particular task, while the remaining work is readily

BIT-MAPPED GRAPHICS: (XEROX ALTO, 1974)

BIT-blt = THE PRIMARY OPERATION IN
BIT-MAPPED GRAPHICS

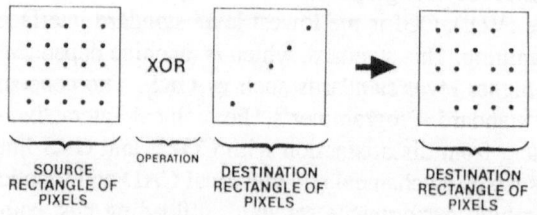

SOURCE   OPERATION   DESTINATION   DESTINATION
RECTANGLE OF   RECTANGLE OF   RECTANGLE OF
PIXELS   PIXELS   PIXELS

WRITTEN IN MICROCODE FOR SPEED ON THE ALTO

Figure 7

available. If work in another window becomes more urgent, the user can rapidly and flexibly refocus attention to a new project. Throughout a session, the windowing system must consume little computing resources while providing real-time response to a user.

With the addition of a mouse, tablet, or similar pointing device to a window manager, the user has more control of dialogue with the computer. A user points, rather than types, to a window to initiate or resume a task. With pointing devices, modules can be provide the window manager with a complete, consistent interface to applications. All application programs can use a similar set of scroll bars, menus, and other utilities. When interfaces between all applications become closely related, learning the operation of newly acquired programs is easier. By using available tools, the applications programmer can reduce project development time.

GEOMETRIC GRAPHICS: SKETCHPAD
(SUTHERLAND, 1964)

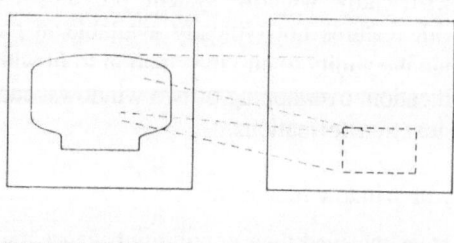

PAGE COORDINATES   SCOPE COORDINATES

Figure 8

2.7.2 A Historical Perspective on Window Management

The Smalltalk system developed at Xerox PARC (Palo Alto Research Center) pioneered personal, interactive, window environments [GOLD84]. Smalltalk is a windowing system designed for the single-user, monochrome, bit-mapped raster display of the Xerox Star. In Smalltalk, users can create several windows, each supporting text or graphics. Programs in windows have standard interaction techniques, such as menus and scroll bars. The user learns to expect visual cues, which prompt for action or inform the user of the status of the machine. For example, a common cue is the hourglass symbol which represents time consumption. The hourglass reassures the user that a lengthy job is underway, the system is not dead, and asks the user to be patient.

A large set of basic tools makes a system more flexible for the user. Instead of creating large, single-purpose programs, small single-purpose tools can be combined and recombined for different tasks. In a windowing environment, the tools can be graphics programs. For example, let's consider a hypothetical system with a drawing package and a pixel-based image editor. One can create a large drawing (in painterly terms, a canvas) using the drawing package. Then with the image editor tool, the canvas can be enlarged and touched up on an individual pixel level. With a windowing system, the user has both drawing package and image editor simultaneously available, and can work on one without losing sight of the other. From the application programmer's point of view, each tool can be written, debugged, and later enhanced separately.

The human factors principles of Smalltalk were the foundation for subsequent windowing interfaces (MacIntosh, Amiga and others), but the characteristics of the Xerox Star hardware heavily influenced the systems. Window managers must be developed around the capabilities of the hardware, particularly with respect to certain operations. For example, as windows are covered and uncovered, their contents are repeatedly drawn and redrawn. The Xerox Star hardware primarily handles text and documentation oriented functions. As sections of windows are covered up, the bit-block array of the covered section is saved in memory. When the window or a portion of the window is uncovered, it needs to recall the saved bit-block from memory and update the newly uncovered section.

2.7.3 New Technology Creates New Window Management Issues

The bit-blt is ideal for static, 2-D, monochrome images in window systems, but different issues are raised by technological advances. The location of a pixel in a bit-block can be saved as two integer values (x and y) and a single bit for the color (0 for black and 1 for white). However, a dynamic, 3-D, color geometric object is not so simply reduced to a bit-block. Dynamic objects undergo transformations which disorder the precise fabric of a bit-block. Geometric graphics are generally stored with three coordinates of data, specifying a location in *world coordinates*. Often a location is stored with floating point values and not restricted to the discrete integer values of pixels. A pixel with color information is several times more unwieldy than if it were monochrome. Advanced graphics workstations often have 24 bits of color information for each pixel, as compared to 1 bit per pixel for a monochrome display. For this reason alone, a bit-blt window manager runs several times slower on a color system than on a monochrome system. Clearly, the conventional desktop analogy supported by 2-D programs is inadequate to handle today's colorful 3-D world.

The advanced graphic workstation window manager must take a different approach. Multiple Exposure, the Silicon Graphics window manager, is unique. It allows the user to simultaneously view 2-D and 3-D dynamic graphics and text in separate, overlapping windows. An ideal modular tool set for a dynamic 3-D window manager is substantially different from the conventional 2-D tool set. Windows with color graphics, rather than monochrome bitmapped text, need to work in unison. Tools are needed to deal with geometry—to view and transform objects in 3-space, rather than for 2-D raster locations in image memory. For example, a color editing tool should allow the user to modify colors of chosen objects on the screen. Thus a user can experiment with the colors of objects in response to lighting conditions or personal taste without re-starting a program.

An innovative user tool kit is *Synergy*, a programming environment which runs under the IRIS Multiple Exposure window manager [HAEB86]. Synergy is a data-flow manager which enables the user to graphically patch together pathways into data networks and to interactively set the values of an object's coordinates and transformation matrices. In effect, the user can visually connect data files to be processed by the Geometry Engines and set the matrix values inside the VLSI chips used to display it.

The system offers a visual curve editor to create objects, curve data is routed to a sweep editor that controls how the initial curve is incrementally transformed to create a 3-D object (i.e., surfaces of revolution, or extrusion by translation). This object data can then be fed to a transformation matrix to set global viewing parameters. Ultimately, the user defines the hierarchical organization of a scene and its object's transformations by simply patching together a network of tools. The diagrammatic rules of Synergy simulate the paradigm of analog synthesizers which are programmed by patching processing modules together with cables. There is full interactive control over the data at all times. Changes applied to any one of the editors are propagated instantaneously throughout the network and simultaneously affect the real-time update of the display. The user is effectively relieved of writing programs to explicitly create data files and can operate exclusively in the visual domain of the graphics problem to be resolved.

To summarize the importance of this prototype, it attempts to facilitate a visually based dialogue between user and machine that far exceeds common menu-based systems. The user's commands are diagrammatically issued and interpreted as a series of data-driven processes [HAEB86].

Ultimately, real-time response is crucial in a multiple window environment. With many windows, overall machine speed is related to the sum of the time to update all displayed windows and the overhead of window management and its user interface. Only equipment with powerful underlying hardware for superior graphics performance leaves the 2-D desktop behind and provide true, real-time dialogue between the user and a 3-D world.

2.8 A Formula for a High Speed Graphics Workstation

One of the first engineering workstations to employ a specialized architecture for high-speed graphics was the Silicon Graphics IRIS. Dr. James Clark, Professor of Computer Science at Stanford University and founder of Silicon Graphics, realized that a typical workstation configuration would not be sufficient to generate the immediate visual response required by engineers. His solution led him to be the first to bring VLSI technology to graphics computation.

2.8.1 Graphics Performance and Custom VLSI Circuits

Starting in 1979, Dr. James Clark and co-workers at Stanford University began a research project with the goal of designing and implementing the first VLSI chip dedicated to real-time, 3-D geometric functions. This chip, called the Geometry Engine, is shown in Figure 4. "A convenient view of the system is as a hardware sub-routine to the IRIS processor/memory system." [CLAR82]. The most important and most time consuming geometric computations are now embedded in chips.

This additional geometric computing power is necessary to support instant response in demanding applications such as solid modeling, simulation, robotics, or molecular modeling. The advantages of a custom VLSI implementation are significantly higher performance and lower cost. Lower cost results from a lower component count, savings in board space, lower power requirements, and prolonged system reliability. Silicon is cheaper than gold, iron and PC boards. Increased performance derives from the integration of numerous ALU processors on a single chip and by reduced transmission delays.

"The Geometry System is a floating-point, geometric computing system for computer graphics constructed from a basic building block, the Geometry Engine." [CLAR82]. The Geometry Engine comprises approximately 75,000 transistors on a single chip. Each chip is a four component vector floating point processor and can be softly configured to perform basic computer graphics operations: matrix multiplication, clipping, perspective projection, and mapping to output devices. Twelve copies of the Geometry Engine arranged in a pipeline compose the complete system in its most general form. The first four Geometry Engines form the matrix subsystem, the next six form the clipping subsystem, and the last two a scaling subsystem. The matrix subsystem provides general two and three-dimensional transformations, including rotations, translations, scaling, and perspective projections. These four by four matrices also generate cubic and rational cubic splines. Each of the six clipping engines clip the object

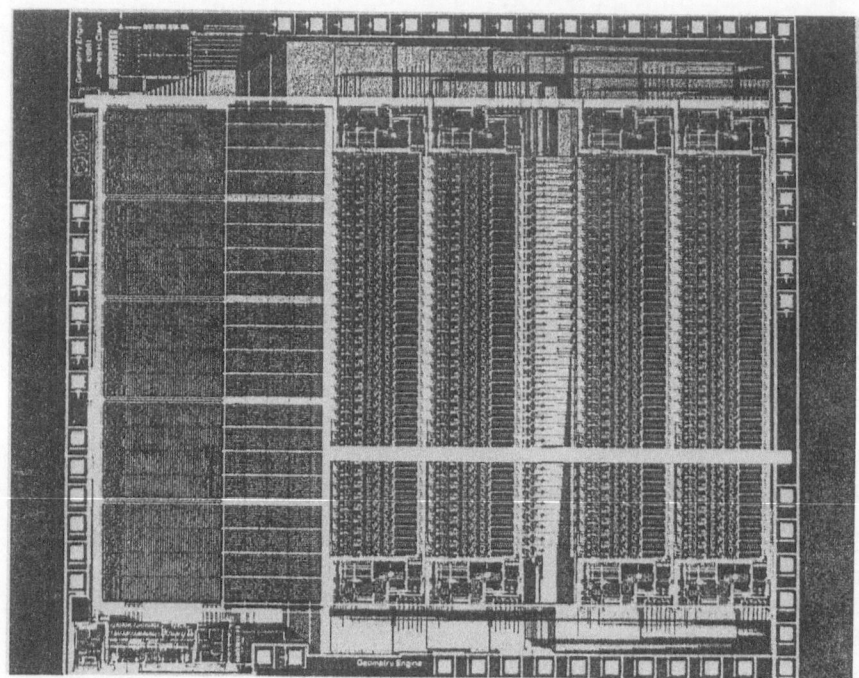

Figure 4

to a face of the clipping volume. The scaling subsystem finally converts the output of the pipeline to the physical coordinates of the display device. (see Figure
5).

The Geometry Engine is much more than a fast floating-point ALU. In addition to incorporating all of the processing necessary to perform each of the
geometric operations discussed previously, it also performs perspective division,
and in addition to processing vectors, it processes solid, colored, and shaded objects. Further, it generates parametric cubic curves and rational bicubic surfaces,
which are important in the design of automobiles and aircraft. It is a customized
floating-point array processor for graphics.

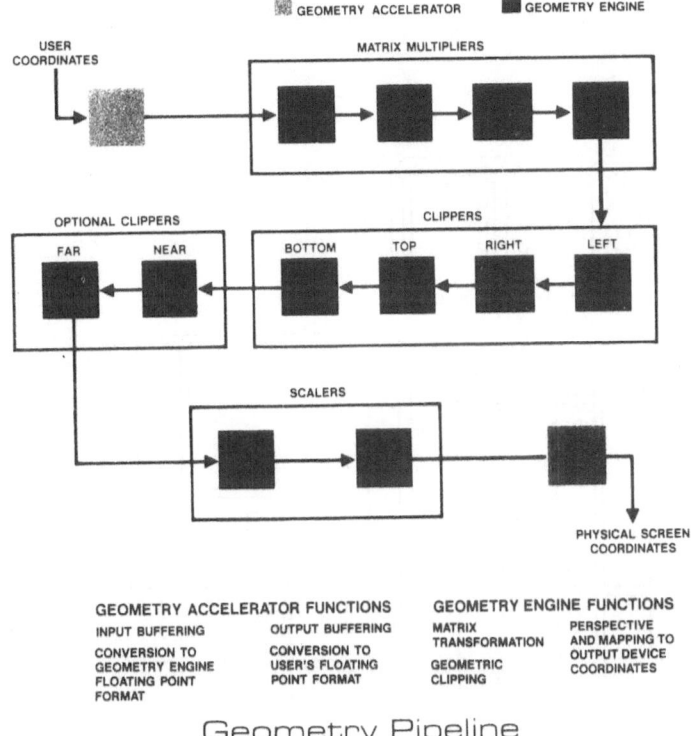

Geometry Pipeline

Figure 5

A second custom VLSI chip is the Geometry Accelerator. This IC provides buffering and floating-point conversion of the data stream at both ends of the pipeline to maximize throughput. The system can perform up to 86,000 3-D coordinate transformations per second.

2.8.2 System Performance

The IRIS graphics workstation combines custom VLSI graphics processors with a 32-bit CPU to provide fast response for graphics and applications processing. The workstation is divided into three sections linked by a proprietary bus: the central processing system, the geometry pipeline, and the raster subsystem. The Intel Multibus provides communication paths between the computer and the disk controller, optional floating point processors, Ethernet and other I/O devices. (see Figure 6).

A Motorola 68020 CPU executes application programs and interprets graphics commands. To accommodate today's large application programs the CPU can address up to 16 MBytes of main memory and 64 MB of virtual memory. The UNIX operating system supports multiple users in a multi-tasking environment.

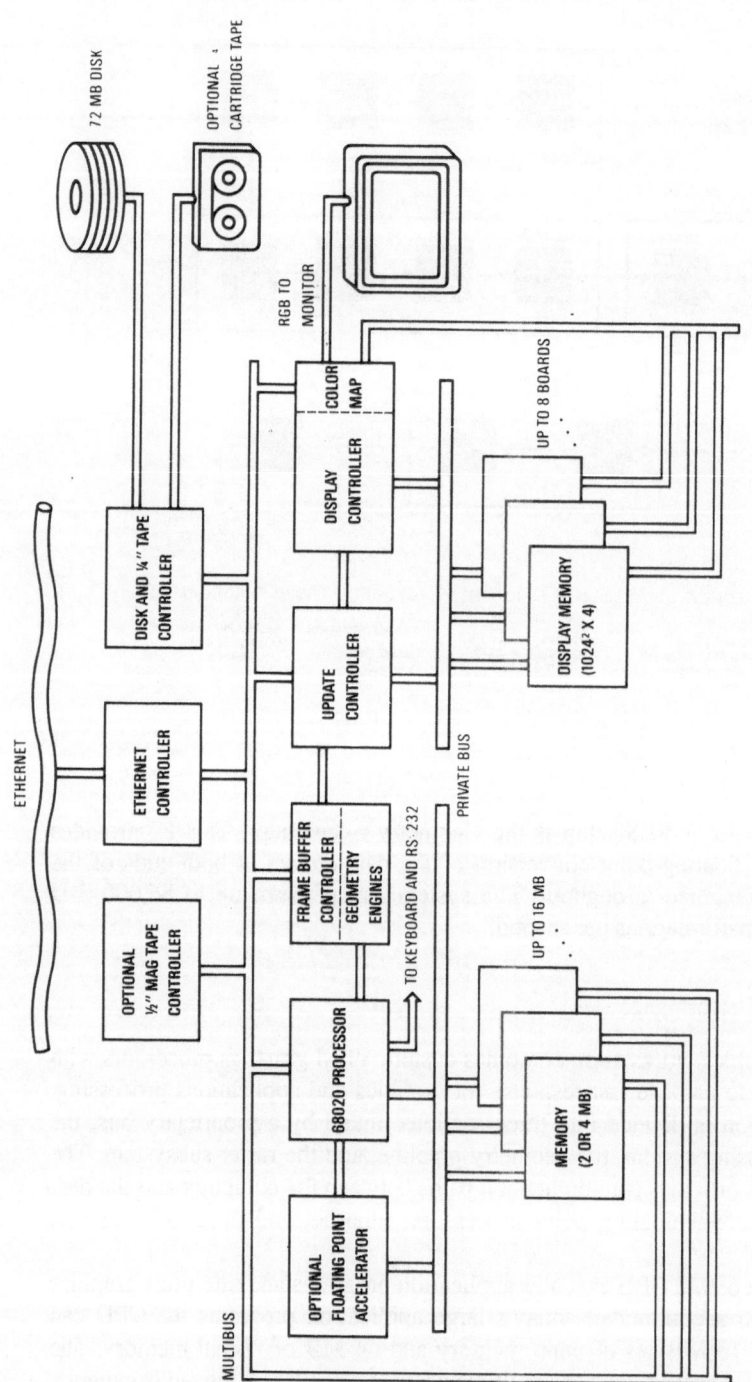

Figure 6

tandard UNIX System V has been enhanced to incorporate many Berkeley 4.2
JNIX features, such as demand paged virtual memory, the C-shell, the vi-editor
nd more. The FORTRAN 77, Pascal, and C compilers have also been tuned to
ie IRIS system to produce faster, more compact code. Each language is closely
oupled with an optional hardware floating point acceleration through kernel and
ompiler enhancements.

The raster subsystem takes information from the Geometry Engine pipeline,
rimarily absolute coordinates, and produces the screen display. A frame buffer
ontroller uses the pipelined coordinate data and computes coefficients for ren-
ering lines and polygons on the CRT. An update controller fills the frame buffer
iemory by performing scan conversion. Again, speed has been optimized to
ipport fast polygon fills at a sustained rate of 44 million pixels per second. The
isplay controller refreshes the display constantly and manages the bitmap
iemory. The IRIS features a high resolution display with 1024 by 768 pixels,
ach up to 24 pixels deep for a total of more than 16.7 million colors.

A Graphics Library provides a powerful and accessible real-time 3-D en-
ironment for the applications programmer. This set of library routines provides
oth high and low-level support for graphics programs with routines to support
-D and 3-D hierarchical object creation and viewing with constructs such as
oints, lines, polygons, arcs, circles, parametric cubic curves, and rational bi-
ubic surfaces. Other routines provide optimal links to hardware support
rovided by the Geometry Engines and bit-slice firmware for more advanced
raphics operations such as hidden surface removal, shading and collision detec-
on. The library directly accesses the system hardware to manage the transla-
on, rotation, scaling and clipping of objects.

An Ethernet local area network provides links to a network of other machines.
his allows the engineer to share information, access databases or more power-
il computing resources when needed.

Since interactive tools and a high-level software environment provide fast and
fficient control of the hardware, the combined power of the components of this
ystem can be fully utilized to speed up any given graphics application.

. A Professional Workstation Environment

.1 Workstation Evolution

he workstation era in computing has evolved from the availability of 32-bit
iicroprocessor CPU's, "portable" operating systems, programming language
evelopments, declining memory costs, low-cost graphics, and communications
etworking technology. More recent developments have enabled custom VLSI
chnology to inexpensively increase graphics speeds by factors of several
indred or more.

The major driving force behind this change is the 32-bit microprocessor. In the past, the introduction of the 8 and 16 bit microprocessors had a strong impact on the computer systems market, but the impact of the 32-bit microprocessor is even more of a milestone in the development of the microprocessor as a computing device. In 1984 samples of the first 32-bit processors were announced and during 1985 and 1986 these chips became widely available. In recent years, increased overlapping of capabilities has caused the lines of demarcation between microcomputers, minicomputers and mainframes to become less and less distinct. These lines were obliterated when full-featured, 32-bit microprocessors came into widespread use. For example, the MIP (million instructions per second) rating of a Motorola 68020 surpasses that of a Vax 11/780.

The professional workstation provides a general-purpose computer that may be either used alone or connected in a network with a wide variety of computing and support resources. A typical environment might consist of workstations, mainframe computers, terminals, hard copy media, database systems, and so forth as shown in Figure 9. Both high-speed computing and high-speed graphics are an integral part of this professional computing environment.

3.2 Computing Environment

3.2.1 General-purpose Computing

The computing capability of today's workstation is a result of numerous technological developments, including:

• Declining costs and increased speeds of microprocessor CPU's, semiconductor memory, and secondary storage media.
• Improved operating systems, compiler techniques, languages, and application development tools.

• Communications networking hardware and standard network software protocols.

3.2.2 General-purpose Hardware Developments

The 32-bit microprocessor available today has the computing speed of super-minicomputers of less than ten years ago. These microprocessors provide the foundation of most workstations' general-purpose computing capability. VLSI technology has moved the CPU from sets of discrete parts to custom integrated circuitry.

The Motorola 680X0 family of chips — initially the 68010 and now the 68020—have dominated the engineering workstation market from its 1981 beginnings. Although other 32 bit CPUs exist, (e.g., National Semiconductor's 32000 family of proprietary chips), according to International Data Corporation,

90% of the workstations installed in 1985 such as Sun, Silicon Graphics, Apollo, Hewlett-Packard, and Masscomp, were based on the Motorola microprocessor family. Recent engineering workstations, such as the IBM PC/RT the Hewlett-Packard Spectrum (both RISC-based), and the DEC MicroVaxII are based on proprietary chips. The segment of the market based on high performance proprietary architectures, especially the RISC architectures (Reduced Instruction Set Computing) will grow.

The 68020 is a full 32-bit microprocessor with 32-bit registers, 32-bit data path, 32-bit ALU and a 32-bit bus. Other advantages are:

- Pipelined architecture for efficient instruction execution.
- 256 byte prefetch cache.
- Support for 4 Gigabytes of virtual memory.
- Clock speed was designed to run at up to 28 MHz, though current units run at 16.67 MHZ

The preference in buses today is the VME bus, which has a 32-bit data path and is the standard bus for advanced workstations. Older industry standard buses are Intel's Multibus (16bit) or MultibusII (32bit).

Floating point performance can make a large difference in project productivity. To meet the modern engineering challenge, the advanced graphics workstation must use the highest performance floating point implementation possible. These features include: 32-bit read/write operations, full 64-bit arithmetic for each cycle, and single and double precision integer conversion. In most floating point implementations, traffic to and from the accelerator acts as a major impediment to fast system performance. The Motorola 68881 floating point chip is a commonly used option, but it is not the highest performance solution. The 68020/68881 interface is inherently slow, with delays resulting from the extensive handshaking required to pass data [SPEE86].

Another critical factor in any 68020 based workstation is how fast the processor can access memory. The speed of the 68020 makes it difficult for industry standard dynamic RAMS to keep up. One solution is to provide a relatively small cache of fast RAM, using slower but less expensive RAM to make up the bulk of the memory. This would allow the use of a 32-bit cache with older 16-bit memory boards. The performance of such a system would look very impressive when benchmark programs were implemented entirely within the cache. But users would soon discover that the actual throughput of the system wasn't as spectacular as it sounded. The key to a successful 68020 memory design is coupling memory and the processor tightly. Thus memory must be designed around a 32-bit data path.

Concurrent with microprocessor developments, Winchester disk technology is providing remarkable secondary storage capacities. Today's 5¼″ disks have capacities of 170 or 340 MB. In addition, improved and more dense semiconductor memories continue to lead the revolution in computing systems, with 1 MB chips allowing the packing of large amounts of memory on single boards.

These trends are expected to continue to yield more and more powerful general-purpose systems at very low cost.

3.2.3 UNIX

UNIX has become the de facto standard operating system for workstations and most minicomputers. All current graphics workstations run the UNIX operating system, even the DEC MicroVaxII and the new IBM PC/RT. It is the single most widely used operating system in universities — thus virtually every technical undergraduate in the country is familiar with it. UNIX was the first widely available "open" operating system. Developed in the early 1970's at Bell Labs, UNIX provides a rich and usable environment for applications development. The major question about UNIX in most people's minds is which version—System V and successors distributed by AT&T, or 4.2 BSD and successors implemented by the University of California at Berkeley.

The two systems have slightly different sets of utility programs, and each has features not in the other. The fundamental differences between them as they are distributed, and the effects on applications, are outlined below.

• **Demand Paging** - With demand paging, physical memory may be less than the logical memory required by an application. This is also referred to as virtual memory. Many engineering applications require a large virtual program and data space, and demand paging. In an engineering environment, this is the biggest shortcoming of System V as it is distributed by AT&T, and it is rectified in the upcoming System V.3 release.(Berkeley UNIX was developed primarily because of this shortcoming.)

• **File Structure** - The first UNIX file system used a simple minded layout of the physical disk. This structure can become fragmented over time. This will cause poor performance since the disk will have spend more time looking for each block. The later versions of AT&T UNIX use caching which increases file-system performance by reducing the number of disk accesses. At Berkeley, it was felt that a different system would provide faster file system performance than AT&T UNIX. The mechanism used to increase performance is most effective when the disk is less than 75% or more utilized. One of the reasons for this is that the implementation is very complex. When less than 25% of the disk is free, experience has shown that the system is not as fast as the standard UNIX file system. Both standard filesystem implementations could stand performance improvements. The Extent File System, written by Silicon Graphics, is a unique UNIX file structure handler that uses a larger block size and stores groups of blocks (extents) contiguously on the disk. When files are stored contiguously, only one seek is required to access a file, thereby reducing the access overhead. The larger block size also results in more data being transferred in a particular disk access. While compatible with the System V file system, the Extent File System provides a two-fold improvement in file handling performance over the standard System V architecture. The result is a truly faster system.

• **Network Protocols** - System V has no standard support for network communications nor for interprocess communications. 4.2 BSD incorporates a communications protocol defined for the ARPANET by the Department of Defense. (The development of 4.2BSD was funded by DOD.) These modules are easily ported to any UNIX version. Most vendors have implemented some sort of communications support for their system so there is no advantage for choosing one UNIX system over another.

• **Interprocess Communication** - Both systems have standard support for interprocess communication (IPC). Though these are accomplished in very different ways. The AT&T version of UNIX provides a queued message system, a semaphore passing system and shared memory. The Berkeley system also provides an IPC facility. Both versions of UNIX provide pipes between related processes.

The main point about any operating system feature is its effect on the application or its development. Demand Paging is essential to any engineering workstation and should be totally transparent to the application. The value of the reorganized file system is often debated, at least as implemented.

The ideal engineering UNIX system is one that incorporates demand paging and utilities of both System V and 4.2 BSD with expanded networking features that enable a distributed computing system. Thus an integration of the useful 4.2 features into AT&T distributed UNIX will eventually dominate the UNIX workstation market — it leaves the applications development and support environment least affected. In September 1985, AT&T and Sun Microsystems, Inc announced a major technology sharing agreement. Both companies will work together to facilitate convergence of System V and the 4.2 BSD-based Sun operating system. The resulting package will be available from both companies. The new package will continue to run the existing base of System V applications and will provide the networking services that previously have been available only in 4.2BSD [CHAN85].

3.3 Networking

Any distributed workstation environment must support a means for sharing data and resources on a network. Two basic technologies predominate:

3.3.1 Token Ring

This type of local area network (LAN) requires that all resources on the network be in a closed loop. Each node is allowed to send information to another in the ring after a token passes it — thus, messages are synchronized and require the active participation of all nodes on the network. A token, i.e., a special bit pattern, is sent around the network in a loop. As each node receives the token it

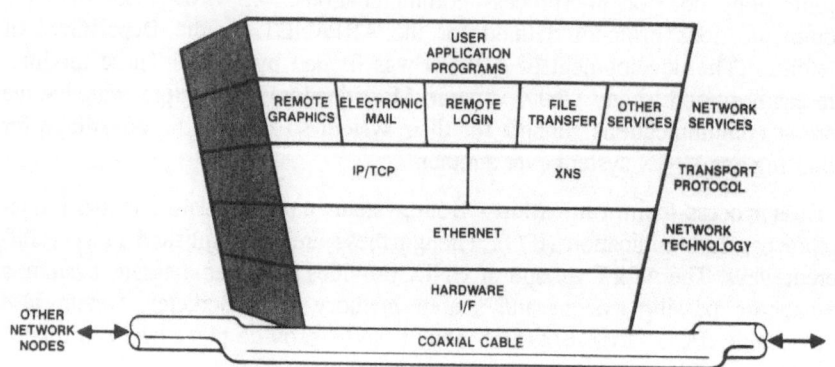

Figure 11

passes it to the next node (active repeaters). When a node wants to send a message it seizes the token and inverts it so that it becomes a connector. After inverting the token it then transmits its message. Each node can understand its address
and copy a message addressed to it. As the sending node recognizes the message
it has sent then it removes it from the ring. This net technology is straight forward. There are no contention problems since there is only one token on the net
at any time. A problem occurs if a node goes down. In this case the ring is not
complete and the entire net is unusable. Another problem occurs if a repeater
does not forward the token. If this happens, the net sits idle waiting for the
token. However, the main problem with this type of LAN is that the network is
not reconfigurable while it is running. The network must be disabled to install or
remove a node.

3.3.2 Ethernet

The Ethernet LAN is not a closed loop. An Ethernet module communicating
with another first "listens" to the network to see if it is in use. If not, it sends its
file or message to the recipient. A "collision" occurs if two different nodes
simultaneously sense that the network is quiescent and begin transmitting at the
same time. The message is garbled, so each must "back-off" and re-transmit its
message. If a collision occurs, each node waits a randomly chosen interval and
re-transmits. This lessens the likelihood that the collision will re-occur. Messages are asynchronous. Nodes are passive unless they are using the Ethernet, so
they may be removed and inserted at will. The main advantage here is that nodes
can be removed and inserted at any time without harm to the network.
Therefore, their network is easier to reconfigure. The most significant difference
between these two technologies is that the Ethernet LAN is an "open" architecture that has been adopted as a standard by Xerox, Intel, Hewlett Packard, Digital

THE GEOMETRY NETWORK

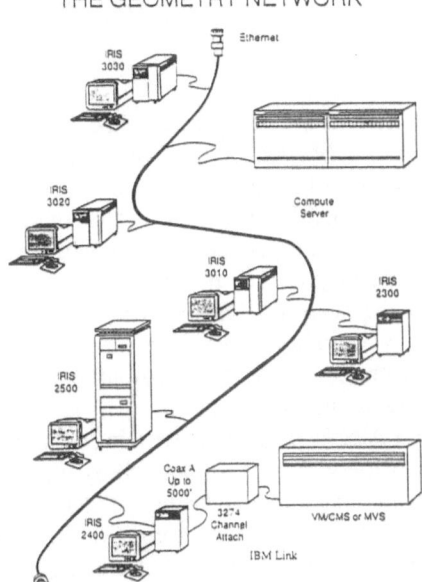

Figure 9

Equipment Corporation, Silicon Graphics, SUN Microsystems, and many others. All commonly used token ring approaches are "closed" or proprietary. No standard token ring approach has been widely adopted. No workstation environment is complete without the ability to share resources. The stand-alone workstation is not sufficient, nor is it even sufficient to have networked systems that simply allow file transfers. One of the principal advantages of a timesharing system is that a user may make use of the resources from any terminal, share and utilize data concurrently with others, connect to any working directory and so forth. A proper workstation environment allows these things as well.

3.3.3 Network Protocols

Both Ethernet and token ring LANs require a protocol, or "language", for message transmission. There are two published standards being used in most Ethernet installations, XNS and IP/TCP.

IP/TCP (or TCP/IP, Inter Net Transmission Control Protocol) was defined for the ARPANET and ARPA funded its development as a part of Berkeley 4.2 UNIX. IP/TCP is the most widely used Ethernet protocol. It has the advantage of being the industry standard. It can route messages to any point on the ARPANET, a nationwide network.

XNS (Xerox Network Software) is a simpler and sometimes faster local area network communications protocol defined at Xerox PARC, where incidentally

Ethernet was invented. It has the advantage of being tailored for local communications. Thus, it has no extra baggage associated with each message.

3.3.4 Distributed System

Distributed computer networks are becoming the backbone of office automation. A distributed system is a collection of predominantly autonomous machines, each controlled by its own user but able to communicate with other computers—such as in sending electronic mail or requesting data. An open network architecture requires facilities other than explicit file transfers between nodes and remote logins to other nodes and foreign hosts. It should allow any system user to refer to and use any file on the system implicitly, without explicit file copy. More generally, it should allow a virtual "system call" or shell command—where the command is actually executed should be transparent to the user. This encompasses the distributed file system notion and more.

NFS (Network File System) is Sun's networking concept which allows file system access among a variety of hosts, supported by the NFS protocol. NFS is both hardware and operating system independent, and is the first attempt to provide an industry standard solution for information transfer between systems at the applications layer, or Layer 7 of the ISO Reference Model for Open Systems Interconnection (OSI). Recent support for NFS has come from nearly 30 companies including DEC, Silicon Graphics, Gould, Pyramid, Convex, and Data General.

AT&T is promoting its own remote file sharing system (RFS), for general computing applications. It will shortly be released as part of UNIX System V Release 3.0.

4. Case studies:

4.1 Mechanical CAD/CAM

The major application for graphics workstations centers around the need to solve engineering problems such as finite element modeling, mass property calculations, and composite material modeling. PATRAN is a well-known and widely used finite element structural design and analysis package developed by PDA Engineering. It is one of many CAD/CAM packages implemented on the IRIS. In "An Overview of Analytic Solid Modeling" PDA engineers Malcolm Casale and Edward Stantoin point out the importance for CAD/CAM of several different graphics representations. "In engineering applications, graphics serves several important roles: an aid to model construction, a diagnostic tool for model verification, and a mechanism for rapid communication of engineering data." [CASA85]

"Geometric verification is possible through a variety of graphics display techniques. A simple wireframe plot, which is the least computationally expensive form of display, is useful to verify basic properties of shape and continuity of the model; but when a complex model is developed, wireframe displays soon become inadequate. Hidden-line algorithms remove unnecessary clutter from the screen and reveal much about the essential shape of the solid. Solid shading not only reveals the essential shape but much about smoothness in the sense of slope or first derivatives of the surfaces of the object as well. In this way a solid-shaded image may reveal a wrinkle or first-derivative discontinuity that would remain invisible in a wireframe or hidden-line display."

The IRIS can display an object in any of the forms mentioned above. In fact, running on the IRIS, PATRAN displays a dynamically updated 3-D wireframe model in one window, while simultaneously displaying a smoothly shaded version in another one. This is only possible because of a compiled hierarchical display list resident in the IRIS and the fast drawing speed the Geometry Engines support. The four-by-four matrices computed by the Geometry Engines are also traversed in reverse to support interactive picking to identify, select, and modify an object.

PATRAN prepares input data for and accepts output data from a number of well known software packages, including ANSYS, MSC/NASTRAN, and SAP. As preparation for an analysis run PATRAN compiles a stream of data for the analysis program. After the run is complete PATRAN graphically displays the results - perhaps showing a version of the model as deformed by the specified loads or a color-coded contour display of areas of equivalent temperature. Work is underway to integrate pre- and post-processing stages with the analysis computation. This single integrated package will be executed on workstations with increased processing power thus further reducing turnaround time.

4.2 Robotics

At SRI International in Menlo Park, California, research is being conducted in advanced robotics. Currently the scientists focus on better simulation and programming methods for robotic environments.

It is economically critical to reduce the overall costs necessary to train robots. Until now training is conducted online, requiring the availability of a robot. Typical prices today for the robot alone are in the $100,000 price range plus a whopping $1 Million for specialized surrounding environmental support. Second, time spent to train robots has been long and the programming cumbersome. And third, these classes of robots are not flexible enough to be easily adaptable to changing products, materials, etc.

The new approach is to introduce graphic simulation for visualizing complex spatial relationships between robots and the work area. Interactive programming of the task, combined with simulation, provides non-destructive "debugging" capabilities for the user. Future needs call for refining the program to accommodate spatial uncertainty. A solution for these complex problems is envisioned by SRI's research engineer Randall Smith in WORKMATE, an acronym for Workstation Modeling Analysis Training Emulator for robotic systems.

Various reasons prompted the researchers at SRI to select the IRIS graphics workstation for implementation of WORKMATE. A real-time, three-dimensional display is necessary to simulate the robot's motion. The IRIS not only features this but also allows the computation of the kinetic data with the same four by four matrix multiplications used to compute the geometric properties of the robot. This data is fed into the authoring part of the training emulator, which generates the program to control the actual robot. The "reach-ability" of objects in the robot's work-area can be determined visually by creating the "fuzzy" volume of all possible robot trajectories. Similarly the cycle time of robots can be calculated and optimized. Collision detection between the robot and obstacles is accomplished by using the clipping subsystems of the Geometry Engines.

Randall Smith considers this hardware feature of the IRIS a major advantage for his computations: "Algorithms and later VLSI chips have been designed to exploit the clipping process. The VLSI chips are arranged in a pipeline of clipping stages, with each individual clipper performing the clipping to its own plane. The clippers collectively define a "clipping polyhedron". Clippers not only determine whether interference occurred, but compute the intersection between the clipping volume and object as well. The extra information will be useful in collision avoidance once it is predicted along the path of a robot." [SMIT85].

Once a collision is detected it is indicated visually by blinking the colliding parts. The point of interference is marked for further investigation. In this particular application the IRIS' geometric computation capacity exactly matches the mathematical requirements needed to compute the robots' kinetic data. Furthermore, the visual feedback given by the real-time display enables the successful simulation of robotic motion. Finally, the existence of an extensive high-level graphics library helped the researchers to quickly develop their modeling software. For this application, where no software packages were commercially available, this was an absolute necessity.

4.3 Aeronautics

NASA, at NASA-Ames Research Center in Mountain View, California, recently started its most ambitious computing project yet, called the Numerical Aerodynamic Simulation Project (NAS). Its essence is to complement existing aeronautical test facilities such as wind tunnels, with computational aerodynamic simulators to improve aerospace vehicle design. CRAY- 1 and CRAY X-MP supercomputers are used as the centerpiece of the computing environment. They have one of the first CRAY-2s doubling the computing power to an aggregate peak rate of 2000 Mflops. These machines do the "number-crunching" for complex physical problems once considered insoluble. Twenty-five IRIS 2500 workstations are used to display the complex geometries involved.

Frank Bailey, Manager of the NAS project, outlines the tasks for the graphics workstations. The IRIS is "a microprocessor- based resource for the individual researcher, (it) will serve as a 'scientist's workbench' to perform text and data editing, to process and view graphics files, and to perform small-scale processing. Each individual workstation will have the appropriate memory, disk storage, and hard-copy resources to fit the local user's needs. Individual clusters of workstations will be networked through the High-Speed Data Network (HSDN) for use within local user groups." [BAIL85].

Communications between the super computers and individual workstations are carried via a 50-Mbit hyperchannel to several DEC-VAX computers. The later serve as the gateways and in turn communicate with the IRIS workstations over a conventional 10- Mbit Ethernet using the XNS protocol optimized for graphics. In addition, data communication links will be established for sites remote from Ames to ensure that the aerospace community can participate in research and testing via landlines and satellite.

The volume of data generated in applications like this can be staggering. The data resulting from increasingly refined approximations of aeroelastic distortions at near-sonic velocities, for instance, is so prolific that it can only be comprehended when displayed visually. Each solution is an array of thousands of points or vectors, and a presentation in the form of lists, tables, or even two-dimensional charts is unmanageable. The IRIS' Geometry Engines are idealy suited to solve the problem of fast three-dimensional visualization of large amounts of dynamically changing data. The workstation can also take on individual processing jobs involved in a project of the complexity described. The balance between general purpose processing power and specially designed graphics capabilities made the IRIS workstation attractive for this demanding application.

5. Evaluating Workstations

What distinguishes one workstation environment from another? In addition to cost, some pertinent issues are addressed by the following questions:

5.1 Applications Environment

Is the workstation general-purpose, allowing software for many applications on one machine?

What applications are available on the workstation?

How fast does it process an application?

5.2 Computing Environment

How are the workstations interconnected or networked?

What are the operating system, available languages, and applications development tools?

In the workstation's environment, can one do everything that is possible in a time-sharing system, such as share data transparently and work at any physical workstation?

5.3 Graphics Environment

Is the interface high-level, application (user-space) oriented, and conveniently coupled with the computing capability?

Is there support for 3-D wireframe and shaded pictures? How fast is it?

Is it color or B&W, high-resolution?

Is there multi-window support?

6. Conclusions and Summary

The technical workstation should be a balanced combination of general-purpose computing and either bit-mapped or geometric graphics, depending upon the application.

For the computing part, demand paged UNIX is the preferred operating system, and it should provide both System V and 4.2 BDS utilities. For compatibility with the widest variety of other systems, Ethernet provides a more open network architecture than a token passing scheme, and IP/TCP communications protocol is most desirable. The communications file sharing environment should be as transparent as possible, allowing a "virtual system call". The ability to fit into a larger network of other host computers, for example Cray supercomputers, is important.

For the graphics part, pure page imaging applications are perhaps better served with bit-mapped graphics systems. Most technical and engineering applications are better served with geometric graphics systems. The geometric graphics system, being much higher level, requires extensive software to make the graphics easily used by the application — drawing surfaces, curves and color, geometric objects in 3-D user space should be as simple as drawing a line in screen space or modifying a pixel. Since technical work requires documentation, the system should provide means to produce it, allowing a mixture of text and graphics. The graphics system should also provide a multiple window environment that allows the user to multiplex between several tasks. To enhance engineering productivity, speed in both computing and graphics are important to provide a graphics workstation that delivers subsecond response time.

In the next few years we will see further improvements in general-purpose computing, primarily through RISC technology with the possibility of 5 Mip workstations becoming available in 1986 and 10-20 Mip workstations in 1987. Graphics processing speeds will also increase through VLSI technology developments. In the next five years, we will see a revolution in what is currently considered "off-line" or batch computing. Major engineering analysis programs which currently run on large mainframes or super-minis will become "interactive on-line" programs running on super advanced graphics workstations. An engineer or scientist will be able to design, analyze and simulate their engineering problems on "simulation engines", i.e., new generation workstations, as quickly as you finish this sentence.

Acknowledgements. I wish to acknowledge valuable contributions and comments given to me by Jim Clark, Mason Woo, Paul Mlyniec and Al Casarez of Silicon Graphics, and Frank Dietrich of the University of Utah.

References

[BAIL85] Bailey, Frank R., Numerical Aerodynamic Simulation: Supercomputing Master Tool for Aeronautics. Aerospace America, January 1985, pp. 118-121

[CARD77] Card, S., W. K English, and B. Burr, Evaluation of Mouse, Rate-controlled Isometric Joystick, Step Keys, and Text Keys. for Text Selection on a CRT Xerox Research Center, Palo Alto, SSL-77-1, April 1977

[CASA85] Casale, Malcolm S./Stanton, Edward L., An Overview of Analytic Solid Modeling. IEEE Computer Graphics and Applications, February 1985, Vol. 5, No. 2, pp 45-56

[CHAN85] Chandler, David., The Monthly Report. UNIX Review, November 1985, Vol 3, No 11, pp. 8-15

[CLAR84] Clark, James, The Role of Geometry in the Workstation Marketplace. Unpublished

[CLAR82] Clark, James H., The Geometry Engine: A VLSI Geometry System for Graphics. Computer Graphics, Vol. 16, No. 3, 1982, pp. 127-133

[CLAR85] Clark, James H., Graphics Software Standards and Their Evolution with Hardware Algorithms. Fundamental Algorithms for Computer Graphics, NATO ASI Series, Vol. F17, edited by R.A. Earnshaw, Springer Verlag, 1985, pp. 619-629

[DIET86] Dietrich, Frank, Digital Media: Bridges Between Data Particles and Artifacts. Forthcoming in The Visual Computer

[DOHE82] Doherty, Walter J./Thadhani, Arvind J., The Economic Value of Rapid Response Time. IBM, White Plains, N.Y. 1982. IBM Pamphlet GE20-0752-0 (11-82)

[GOLD84] Goldberg, Adele, Smalltalk-80. Addison-Wesley Publishing, 1984, Reading, Massachusetts

[HAEB86] Haeberli, Paul E. A Data-Flow Manager for an Interactive Programming Environment. Usenix Summer 1986 Conference Proceedings, Usenix Association, El Cerrito, CA, 1986, pp 419-428

[MOLN84] Molnar, Zsuzsanna, Combining VLSI and Graphics. CAMP '84 Proceedings, AMK Berlin, Berlin 1984, pp. 448-453

[SMIT85] Smith, Randall, Fast Robot Collision Detection Using Graphics Hardware. Robotics Laboratory Note Project 7239, SRI, Menlo Park, CA. 1985

[SPEE86] Speelpenning, Bert, Graphics Terminal Reduces Dependence on External Host. Computer Design, January 1986, Volume 25, No 2, pp 87-91

[SUTH63] Sutherland, Ivan, Sketchpad, a Man-Machine Graphical Communications System. AFIPS Conference Proceedings, 1963, Volume 23, pp 329-334

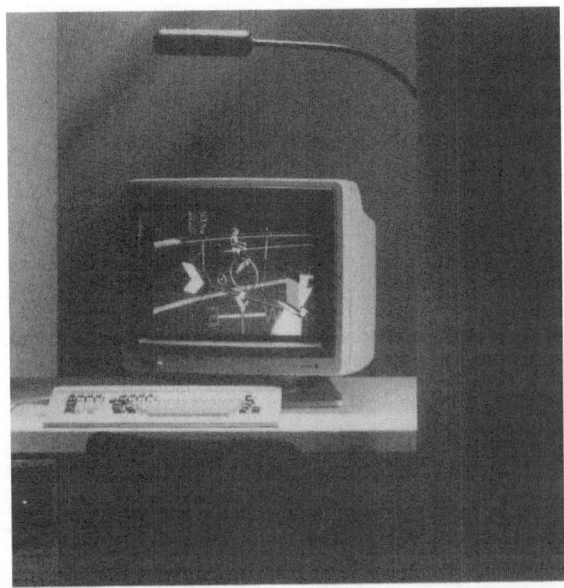

Figure 12 Example of an advanced graphics workstation, the Silicon Graphics IRIS.

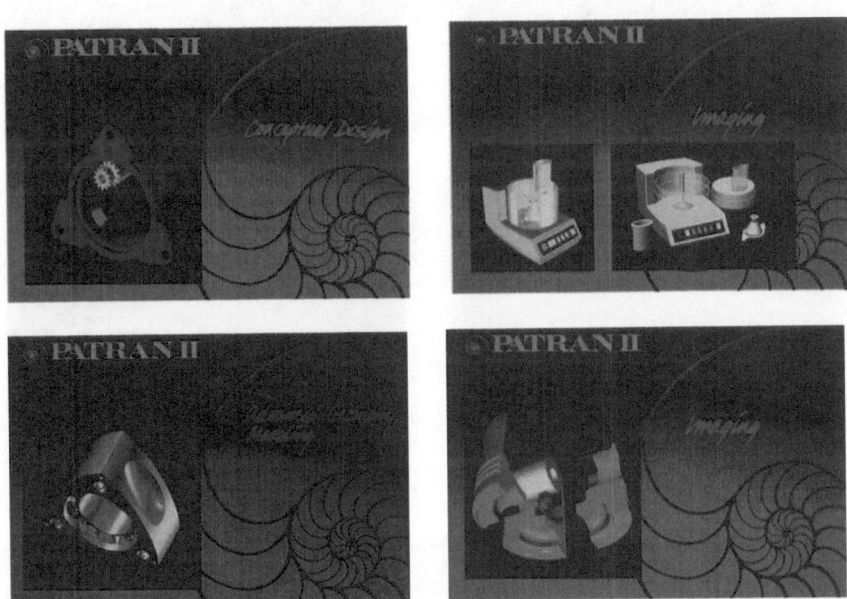

Figures 13, 14, 15, 16 Engineering analysis software, PATRAN finite element structural design and analysis package. Courtesy PDA Engineering.

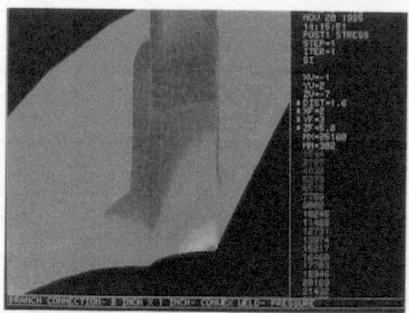 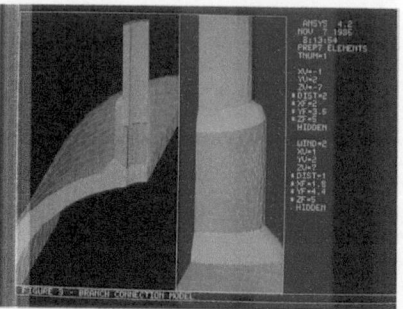

Figures 17 and 18 ANSYS analysis software, using Gouraud shading techniques to illustrate stress information. Courtesy Swanson Analysis.

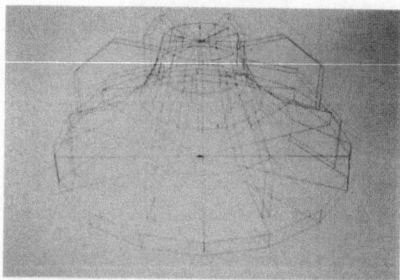 

Figures 19 and 20 Wireframe and flat facet shaded model of a rotor. Courtesy Silicon Graphics.

Figure 21 Flat facet shaded shuttle model. Courtesy PDA Engineering.

Figure 22 Rendered image of Corvette using Phong shading. Courtesy Alias Research.

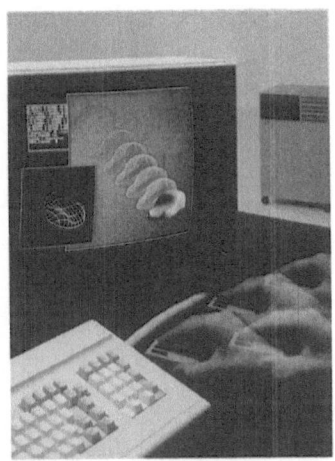

Figure 23 The key to engineering productivity is real-time response time.

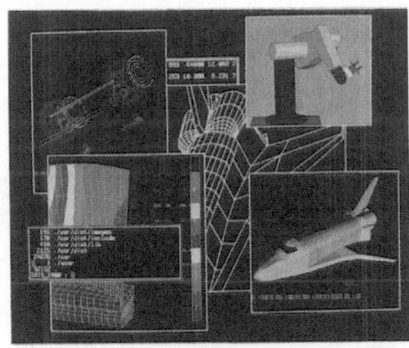

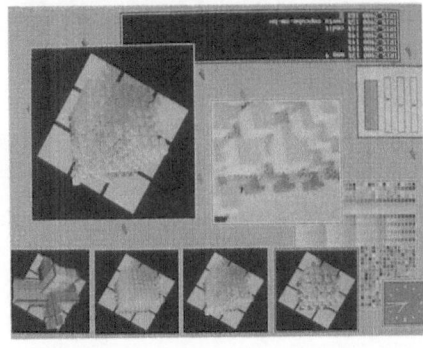

Figures 24 and 25 Multiple Exposure Window Manager features multiple over-lapping windows with dynamic 2-D and 3-D graphics. Courtesy Silicon Graphics.

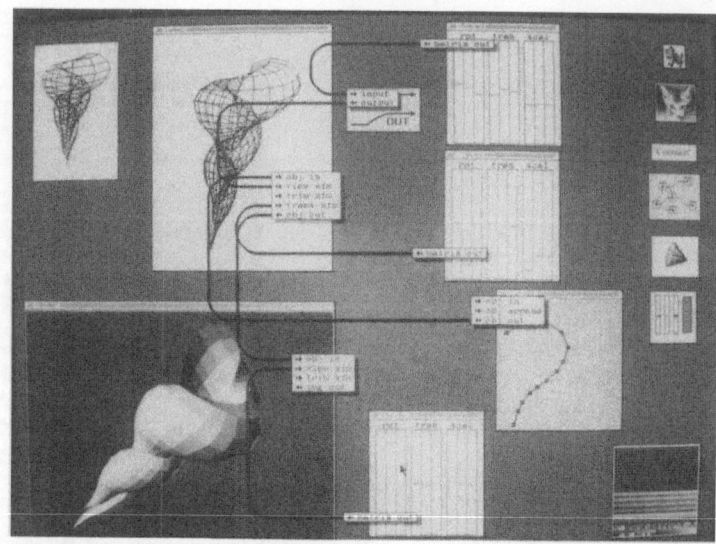

Figure 26 Synergy network manager, a surface design application. Courtesy Paul Haeberli, Silicon Graphics.

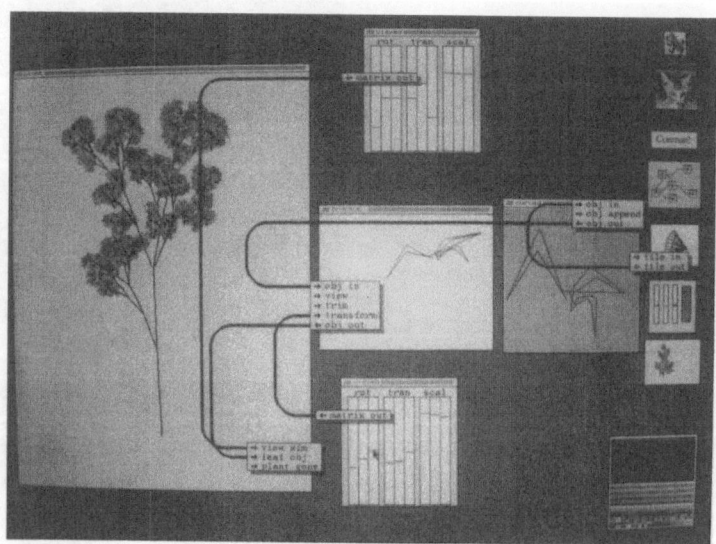

Figure 27 Synergy network manager, a plant design system. Courtesy Paul Haeberli, Silicon Graphics.

Figure 28 WORKMATE robotic simulation system. Courtesty Randall Smith, SRI International.

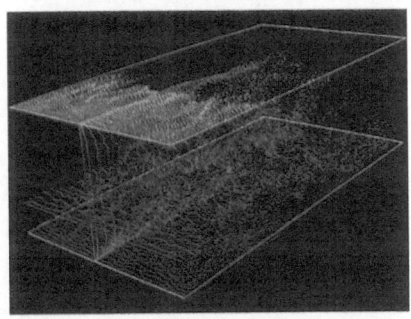

Figure 29 Fluid flow model. Courtesy NAS Project, NASA/AMES.

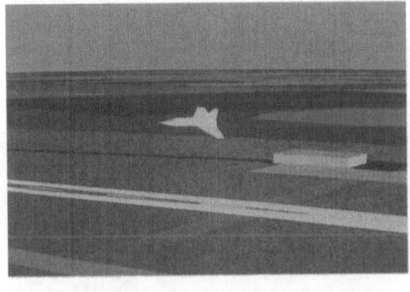

Figures 30, 31, 32 Flight simulation. Courtesy Silicon Graphics.

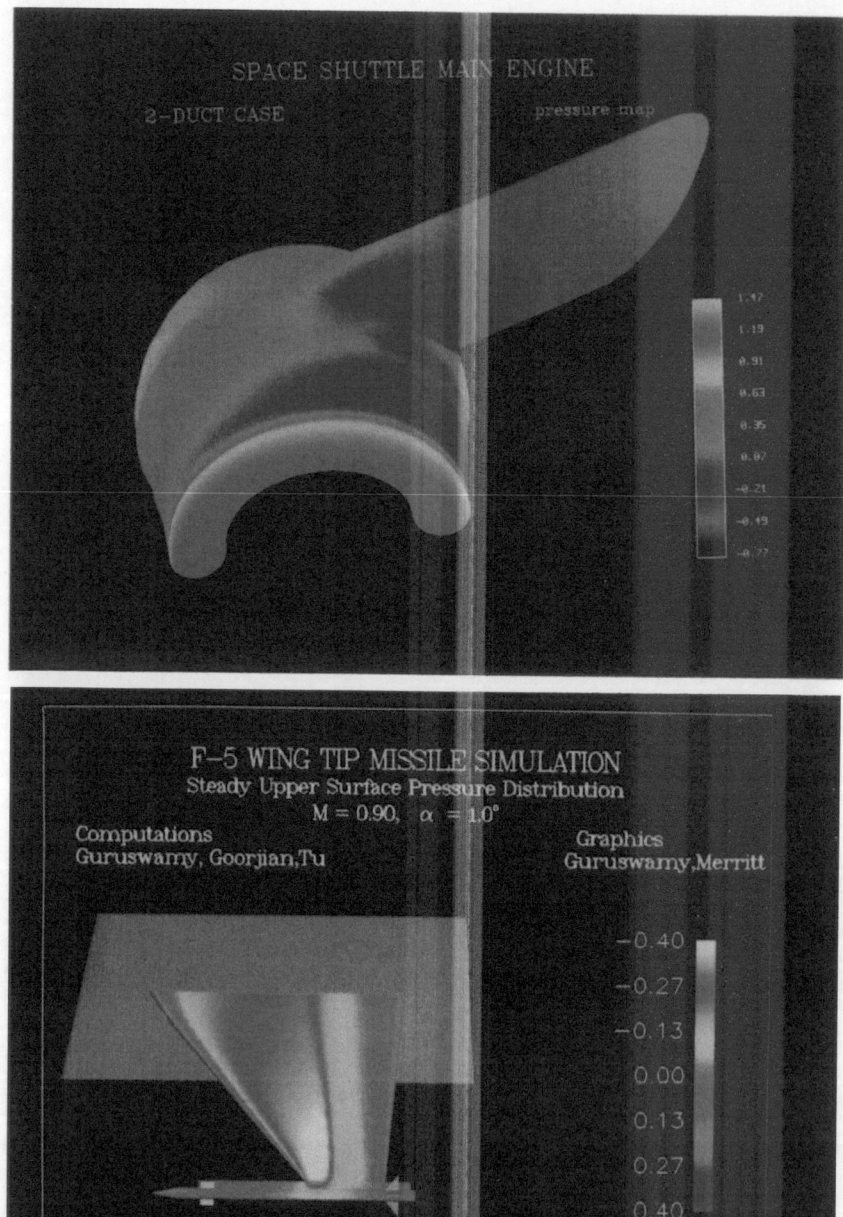

Figures 33 and 34 Space Shuttle stress analysis and F-5 Wing Tip Missle Simulation.
Courtesy NAS Project, NASA/AMES.

5 Hardware

VLSI for Graphics

HENRY FUCHS

Abstract

This paper reviews a personal sampling of research and commercial graphics systems and components that make intensive use of VLSI (Very Large Scale Integrated) circuits. The origins of today's graphics systems in the late 1960's and early 1970's are described, the generic organization of several types of systems are outlined, and some dozen systems are briefly described. The paper ends with a look to the future, suggesting a combination of trends that may merge in the coming decade to produce desktop systems with much higher performance than virtually any system today.

Introduction

Computer graphics has always been an expensive proposition and its users a demanding, unsatisfied lot–the picture never got onto the screen fast enough, or later, never moved fast enough once it got to the screen, and then, the picture was never sharp enough, never realistic enough. Many users have been tackling problems that could only be solved with highest performance graphics systems– the crystallographer trying to understand the structure of a complex protein from noisy data, the radiologist trying to detect a possible tumor amid the clutter of healthy tissues, an architect trying to "walk" the client through the still-unbuilt house with only the images on a video screen. This paper is fundamentally a compilation of how a number of graphics systems designers have responded to this need. Regrettably, because the internal details of commercial systems are often not published and are only revealed to outsiders on a non-disclosure basis, some systems that the author would like to have selected could not be described in this paper.

Historical Background and Overview

Graphics displays have been a part of computers since at least 1950 with the point-plotting CRT on MIT's Whirlwind 1 computer [EVER52]. The random-deflection CRT, driven by a refresh list of point locations, was the basis for virtually all graphics displays through the 1960's. By 1968, at least one system had general 4x4 matrix transformations, clipping, and perspective divide

[SUTH68], [SPRO68]. This paved the way for commercial systems with real-time manipulation of 3D wire-frame models with perspective [EVAN71]. These capabilities are the ones still found in today's high-performance random-scan vector systems.

The major drawback with all the random-scan vector systems has been their inability to produce realistically-rendered objects and scenes. Although algorithm development for generating continuous-tone renderings increased throughout the 1960's and early 1970's, the only output devices available were film recorders. These exposed a film image over many minutes in front of a CRT, on whose face was scanned out a sequence of hundreds of thousands of individual positions, each with a distinct intensity. Many users and system builders desired to speed up this realistic continuous-tone image generation, but until the mid-1970's, only very expensive systems, mostly visual subsystems of flight simulators, could afford the necessary expense [SCHU69], [WATK70], [SCHA81]. Systems for image processing applications were built that displayed continuously on a video monitor, the contents of an image buffer memory bank. However, these were of only limited use for computer graphics because their storage organization typically allowed only very restricted access to the pixel values. The medium was usually a disk track or a cyclical shift register that was only serially accessible. Thus, updating of random pixel values was unacceptably slow. In some systems, for example, it was only possible to change a pixel when its screen refresh time came around, once every 30 milliseconds.

The major turning point came when RAM's became sufficiently affordable so a bank big enough to store an entire video image could be built [KAJI74]. Once random-access frame buffers became affordable, in the late-1970's, they quickly became the system of choice for many users. They produced continuous-tone, often color images, and through various techniques with the color translation tables, these systems could produce a variety of useful effects–zooming, double buffering, simple animation, and moving overlays on a fixed background. Their prevalence has helped merge graphics and image processing. Combining flexible use of raster memory with built-in general processors, these frame buffer systems have steadily taken over areas previously dominated by the random-scan vector systems. A good example of such a flexible raster system is described in [ENGL81]; its successor is currently available as the Adage RDS 3000. These raster systems have been hindered by slower image generation speed and, to a lesser extent, lower quality ("jaggy") lines than the competitive random-scan systems. Overcoming these limitations has been the driving goal of many of the designs described in the following sections. These systems have typically been output devices on single-user or multiple-user host machines, in sharp contrast to the ALTO, which appeared in 1973.

A confluence of several people's varying interests in graphics, text processing, and flexible personal computers lead to the development in 1973 at the Xerox Palo Alto Research Center of the ALTO personal computer [KAY77], [THAC79]. Its basic design was a high-resolution B/W display (1 bit/pixel), dedicated processor, mouse for x,y input, and a high-speed interface to a local area network. It has been copied widely into successively newer technologies[BECH80] and has spawned the new industry of personal, professional workstations. Although these systems are used mostly for text display for multiple windows and flexible test fonts and styles, their flexibility allows the drawing of lined and some simple textures. The ALTO also pioneered the use of multiple, overlapping windows of arbitrary size, inside each of which could be any combination of text, graphics, and images. To facilitate rapid movement of text about the screen and between screen and off-screen memory, the machine included a BitBlt (for Bit-Aligned Block Transfer) instruction. Variations and generalizations of this instruction have been widely adopted, often under different names (Raster-Ops, Pix-BLT).

Each of these three kinds of graphics systems have been optimized for a different mix of tasks: a) the high-performance 3D interactive system, b) the color frame buffer display, and c) the personal workstation. While these three kinds of systems have blended together over the years, each has certain strengths that its designers have tried to bolster:

a) for the high-performance 3D system:
   • fast geometric transformation and clipping of primitives (typically, lines and polygons)
   • fast lighting calculations
   • fast rendering of primitives

b) for color frame buffers:
   • many bits per pixel and flexible ways of using them for multiple frames, background, overlays, etc.
   • fast, general processor for executing a variety of algorithms, the code often repeated for many or all pixels

c) for general workstation display:
   • high spatial resolution to display as many windows with as much information as possible
   • fast text generation of multiple fonts, sizes and styles
   • fast movement of text about the screen and to/from off-screen memory

As we shall see in the next section, with the increasing similarity between the three kinds of systems, manufacturers have started to offer systems that attempt to satisfy two and occasionally all three of these areas with a single system, or more often, a family of systems.

Taxonomy

Although the field of still too vague to arrange a definitive taxonomy, it may be useful to arrange the components around the simplified functional organization sketched in Figure 1. It should be noted that a number of the referenced systems

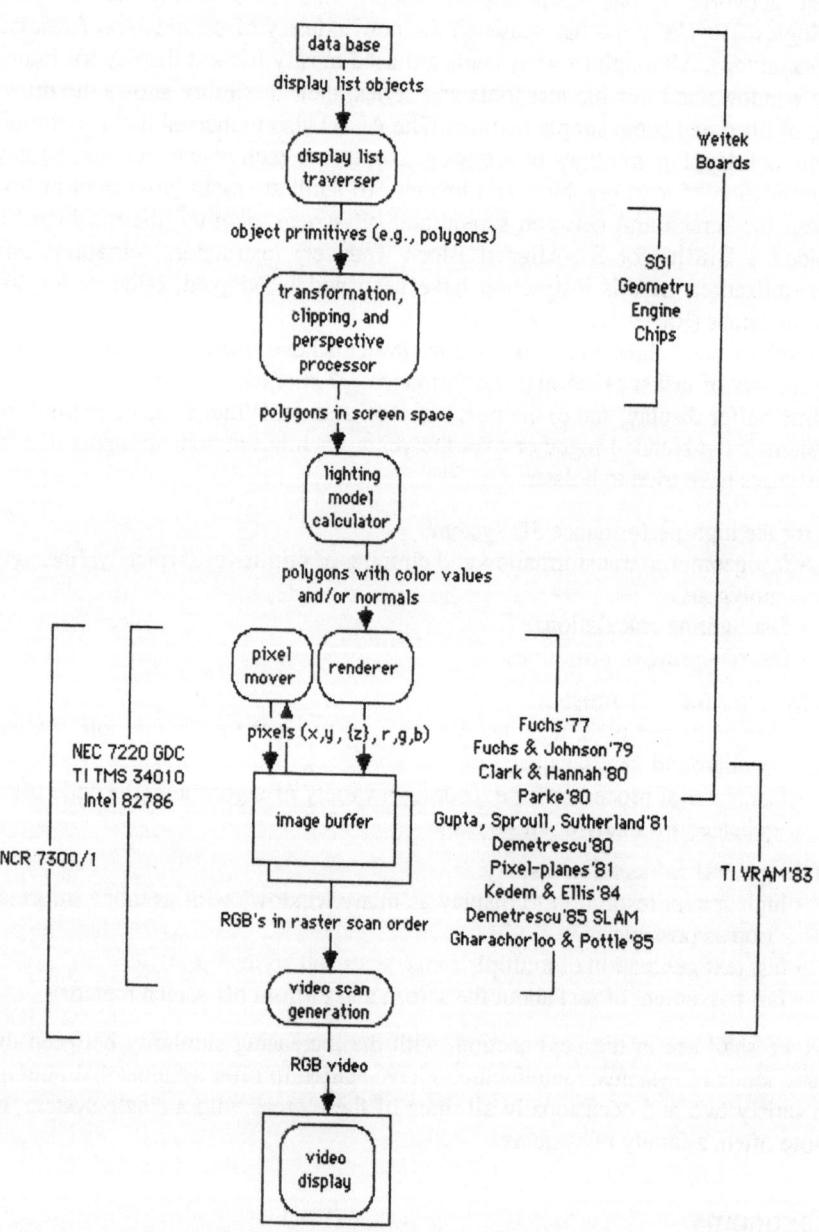

FIGURE 1: Generic Organization of 2D/3D Raster Systems

implement particular functions, such as rendering, with a totally different method than that indicated in the figure. They are listed in the figure to show the extent of their function in comparison to other systems. The brackets indicate the extent of each defined component; It is understood that a working system constructed from any of the referenced machines would include all the functional units from data base to video monitor.

A VLSI Sampler

The systems reviewed here are roughly in chronological order, but the order is occasionally modified for clarity of presentation.

Graphics Display Controllers

Probably the earliest custom chips for graphics were the various video timing chips that generated the complex synchronization and blanking signals needed to drive a video display. These also controlled the timing of the access to the frame buffer memories for refreshing the screen. As silicon structures shrank in size and more transistors could be integrated into the same chip, they increasingly took on tasks involved with the access to the frame buffer memories for image generation. The first generally available such chip that could also handle low level image generation, with help from some processor, was the NEC PD7220 GDC. It made possible the construction of frame buffers with much lower parts count and thus much lower cost. Among the first of the systems to use this chip, the Vectrix Corp. (Greensboro, NC) VX 128, contained a 480 x 672 pixel by 3 bits/pixel frame buffer, an internal 16-bit processor (Intel 8088), serial and parallel ports, separate package and power supply, for $2,000 in early 1983. The chip launched a flurry of under-$10,000 frame buffers and stimulated numerous "improved" versions from other chip vendors, some of which are described further below.

SGI's Geometry Engine

This chip, which performs arithmetic operations on 4-element vectors, was introduced in [CLAR80a] and fully described in [CLAR82]. It may have been the first custom VLSI chip for the 3D graphics market. The chip is the building block of a geometric transformation and clipping engine that is composed of a pipeline of a dozen of these chips. Each chip is configured to execute one part of the classic 3D processing pipeline as outlined in [SUTH68], [SPRO68], and [SUTH74]. The chip is basically a processor with four identical arithmetic units controlled by hardwired microcode that implements the various steps of matrix operations, clipping, and perspective divide. Each of the four units handles one of the elements of the 4-element vector in the commonly used homogeneous coordinate representation for handling 3D projective transformations. The arithmetic units handle 32-bit floating point representation, but due to silicon space limitations, many operations, such as multiply, take many clock cycles to perform. Nevertheless, with four arithmetic units per chip, and with a dozen chips in the pipeline, a 3D point is transformed in 15 microseconds. Improvements, made since 1982 in the commercial version of this chip from Silicon Graphics Inc., have improved its throughput considerably.

Transformations and Rendering with General Purpose Arithmetic Chips

The classic alternative to implementing a geometric transformation unit with custom chips is to implement it with general purpose standard arithmetic units. [WEIT86] describes the recommendations of one of the most popular suppliers of these fast arithmetic chips. Those who use these general chips expect that their faster inherent speed will allow them to use fewer units than those of the slower custom variety from Silicon Graphics. In addition, the general purpose chips allow coding of a wider variety of algorithms into the same unit. For example, the board-level products from Weitek not only perform geometric transformation, but also do rendering of planar and curved primitives. However, since the units have to transfer the pixels into an external frame buffer for screen refresh, their application to dynamically interactive systems has so far been limited. They do best on objects and scenes that take several seconds to transform and render.

Dividing Frame Buffer Among Multiple Processors

Several designs have aimed to speed up the rendering of primitives into the frame buffer by dividing the frame buffer among multiple, usually identical processors. The frame buffer can be divided in an interleaved fashion so that every eighth pixel in a row and every eighth pixel in a column is assigned to the same memory. In this way a geometric primitive such as a polygon or line segment is sure fall into many of the frame buffer sections and thus sure to be processed by many of the processing elements [FUCH77]. [FUCH79] describes an implementation of this scheme using 8-bit microprocesors for the processing elements. [CLAR80b] describes a variation of this scheme with an additional layer of eight processors , each responsible for all the processors in every eighth row. These higher-level processors could perform the set-up calculations so the startup costs for rendering a primitive is reduced.

[GUPT81] describe a system with similarly interleaved 64-piece frame buffer with processors optimized for data moving for workstation displays. In this system the processors are each connected to its 8 neighbors (up, down, left, right and four diagonals) plus 3 others far away. Movement of a rectangular region can be accomplished by reading a "footprint" of 64 pixels into the processors, transferring the pixels among the processors and having each processor write its newly acquired pixel back into its memory. A similar system is described in [SPRO83]. An alternative subdivision of the screen is suggested in [PARK80]. Here, the screen is successively subdivided in half. A memory portion and a rendering processor are stored at each leaf of a binary tree whose internals nodes each contain a "splitting" processor. A primitive travels down the tree, being steered to the region in which it is located and split if it straddles more than one region. The hope is that only a few of the primitives will end up at each root and thus the total rendering load will be shared among all the rendering processors. This interleaved scheme and the successive subdivision scheme are analyzed in [PARK82].

Processor-per-Polygon Pipeline

[DEME80]; [COHE81] describe a novel architecture for rapid rendering of many polygons using a distributed Z buffer algorithm. The system consists of a pipeline of processing chips, each responsible for a single polygon. Each chip has one input and one output port. It receives a packet of color and Z values through the input port and sends either the same packet or a new packet to the output port. The packets move through the pipeline in raster-scan order so each chip knows the X,Y address of the current pixel. To determine which packet a processor sends out, it first determines whether its polygon covers the current pixel at all–most of the time it will not. If it does, the processor compares its polygon's Z value with the Z value it received from its input and outputs the color and Z of whichever has the smaller Z. Thus, the polygon that is output, is the nearest one among all the ones in the pipeline. If the setup values can be loaded into all the polygons fast enough , and if each processor can complete its task relating to a pixel in one pixel's video refresh time, then the system might run in real-time. The chip was designed and built, but not debugged [DEME86].

An extension to handle anti-aliasing is proposed in [WEIN81]. In this scheme, the pipeline would not only pass color and Z values for a pixel, it would pass a sequence of polygon parts that would be visible within the pixel area. If a polygon processor found its polygon to be partially visible in the current pixel, it would add it to the sequence of inputs it received for the current polygon. Also, it would cull any polygon parts from the list that became obscured by its polygon and output all polygon parts still visible at that pixel. This enhancement significantly increases the amount of data passing through the pipeline and the amount of work required from each polygon processor. However, it allows a filter processor at the end of the pipeline to appropriately combine all visible portions of polygons for each pixel and therefore, calculate a reasonable anti-aliased image.

Processor-per-CSG-Primitive Tree Machine

[KEDE84] introduce a design for a machine that could render solid objects directly from their CSG (Constructive Solid Geometry) descriptions. A CSG tree consists of a primitive (such as cylinders and rectangular solids) at each leaf node and a set operator such as union and intersection at each internal node. The machine consists of a reconfigurable collection of processors onto which the CSG tree of the object is directly mapped. (It is assumed that the number of processors in the machine is typically larger than the nodes in the tree, although larger trees could be processed with multiple passes.) There are two kinds of processors, one to render a CSG primitive, such as a cylinder or a rectangular solid, and another to perform the set operation on the output stream from two renderers. Each rendering processor calculates the Z values and perhaps the shade, for its primitive in each pixel, in raster scan order. This stream of data is passed up the tree to a processor that performs the required set operation on this and another stream. The output at the root of the tree consists of a stream of packets, one for each pixel. The first color of each pixel packet is the color of the visible surface. These values are stored in a conventional frame buffer for screen refresh. The machine is currently under construction.

Pixel-planes Logic-enhanced Memory

A logic-enhanced frame buffer memory system was introduced in [FUCH81] and further developed in [FUCH82]. It can be programmed to perform polygon rendering, Z-buffer tests, Gouraud-shading, as well as more elaborate algorithms such as spherical display and shading, and shadow casting [FUCH85]. Detailed description of a working prototype can be found in [POUL85]. Its computational power comes from a novel tree structure that evaluates linear expressions for all pixels at its leaves when the linear coefficients are scanned in from its root. Extensions of this linear evaluation tree to evaluate full six-coefficient quadratic expressions is described in [GOLD86a]; algorithms to use the quadratic extensions to render solid models defined by Constructive Solid Geometry are described in [GOLD86b].

Rectangle-filling Memory Chip

A memory chip that rapidly fills axially-oriented rectangles of constant color is proposed in [WHEL82]. In this design, the addressing structures of both the row and column within a memory grid decode a Minimum and a Maximum address and propagate the enable signal to all cells rows (or columns) in between. Cells, whose row and column are both enabled, are changed to the new value.

Video RAM

Introduced by Texas Instruments in 1983, the video RAM TMS4161 elegantly solved the problem of accessing a high-resolution frame buffer memory for screen refresh [PINK83]. The 64Kb x 1 DRAM includes an internal 256 x 1 bit shift register which can be accessed independently from the rest of the chip. In one memory cycle, an entire row is transferred from the main memory to the shift register. Data can be shifted out of this register at up to 25MHz. During this read-out, the main memory is free to be accessed by the image generator. With standard DRAM's in a high-resolution frame buffer, up to 50% or more of memory cycles may go to screen refresh. This may significantly slow down the image generation system. The use of the VRAM can reduce this access rate to less than 2% [GUTT86]. To achieve a similarly low rate with standard RAM's, an elaborate memory organization with numerous extra parts may be needed. However, if dual frame buffers can be implemented, then one entire buffer can be devoted to screen refresh while the image generation system is creating the next image in the other one. This effectively eliminates the interference between the two systems, but at a substantial parts cost. (See [WHIT84] for a good discussion of this topic.)

Scan-Line Access Memory

[DEME85] describes a memory chip enhanced to allow reading or writing of an entire row of the memory in a single cycle. The memory grid in the chip is treated as a rectangular part of one bit-plane of the frame buffer. Access to the chip is via op-codes and values that allow setting of the Y row, the X-Left and the X-Right edges for writing a specific span of the row (via read-modify-write), and setting of a 16-bit fill pattern. When writing a sequence of spans, the chip assumes reasonable values for the parameters in order to minimize the number of cycles taken up specifying them: the Y register increments, the X registers remain constant. Thus, filling a rectangular area can be accomplished with a single read-modify-write cycle per scan line. For instance, in order to fill a polygon, it is sufficient to specify the starting row and thereafter only the left and right boundaries for each successive row. Characters are written one scan-segment at a time. As each successive horizontal segment is loaded and the write command invoked, the proper addresses will be already in place (Y incremented, X's remain the same). A small system consisting of some dozen chips has been built and demonstrated [DEME86].

Processor-per-pixel on a Scan-Line

[GARA85] describe a rendering system that is a combination of the classic Watkins scan-line processor [WATK70] and a variation on the processor-per-polygon design of [DEME80]. It sorts polygons by their top-most scan line and maintains an active queue of the polygons crossing the current scan line. For each of these, it calculates the left and right boundaries, and the starting and incremental Z values and colors. These are passed to a string of processors, one for each pixel on the scan-line. Each such processor performs a Z-buffer algorithm for its pixel on each data packet and passes the incremental values to its neighbor. The video data is scanned out of these pixel processors in the opposite direction of the packets: the packets travel right, the video data travels left.

TI's Programmable Graphics Processor

Texas instruments introduced early this year a graphics controller chip, the TMS34010, that is a fully programmable single-chip 32-bit CPU. Although it still handles video control and timing, the chip is expected to be programmed in C to perform a variety of image generating tasks more quickly than a general purpose 32-bit microprocessor. The processor contains 30 general purpose registers, stack instructions, a barrel shifter, field selection and control logic, and an instruction cache. It executes most instructions at 6MHz. Its instruction set has been enhanced with graphics-specific codes such as block-move-and-modify RasterOps, and such variants of arithmetic operations as Maximum and Add-with-Saturate for combining multiple image patterns. The chip's designers appear to emphasize text generation and movement. It is not yet clear how suitable the chip will prove to be for image generation tasks such as vector generation, polygon fill, and shading and lighting calculations. The approach is certainly reminiscent of the "wheel of reincarnation" effect described in [MYER68]. They note that designers tend to add more and more registers and functions to a display processor until it becomes essentially a CPU again, at which time it has become sufficiently slow and inefficient that the designer put on it a small, fast display processor, and thus the cycle starts again. It should be no surprise that there are so many functions implemented within this chip; with some 200,000 transistors, it is three times the size of the popular Motorola 68000 32-bit CPU that is the main processor in many professional workstations [GUTT86].

NCR Low Cost Integrated Controller

NCR recently announced its 7300 and 7301 chips set for the low-to-medium priced desktop personal computers [ELEC86b]. The system facilitates low parts count by including within the 7300 character generation for two complete fonts as well as a look-up table and four 4-bit DAC's. The chip set can also control up to 8 windows.

Intel 82786 Integrated Controller

Intel recently announced an integrated controller that is really three nearly separate processors on the same chip. In addition to the usual frame buffer refresh control, there is novel high-level control of virtually any number of windows and a separate graphics processor for drawing into those windows. The graphics processor can generate text, lines, circles, and other geometric primitives. To control multiple windows, the CPU supplies the display processor with a map of the parts of various windows it wants displayed on the screen. The display processor fetches the appropriate pixels from main graphics memory.

Other Systems

An early disclosure of a competitive graphics controller chip from American Micro Devices appeared in the June 27, 1985 issue of Electronic Design. A comprehensive new system from Hewlett-Packard will soon appear in [SWAN86]. [LINE86] claims that nearly a dozen new designs are being currently developed in various chip houses in England, USA and Japan.

Summary

The continuing decline of DRAM prices and the steady increase in capabilities that can be squeezed into a single chip are fueling an explosion of interest in graphics-specific chips among the chip design houses around the world. Most suppliers are aiming for general capabilities and low chip count in order to reduce parts cost to increase their market size. Except for Silicon Graphics and Weitek, most suppliers do not seem to be directed primarily at any specialty market, such as 3D, but are hoping to enhance the performance of general purpose workstations. Encouraging results continue to be reported from the research community, where working prototypes using custom chips are starting to appear.

Acknowledgements. The assistance of the following individuals is gratefully acknowledged: Dr. Rae Earnshaw of Leeds Univesity for providing the facilities to finish this paper; Mr. Julian Ball of Raven Computers, Bradford, Yorkshire, England, for providing Macintosh assistance at crucial times; Dr. Melanie Mintzer, for technical writing and editorial support; and Greg Abram and Andrew Glassner, for providing figures and text of earlier papers.

This research was supported in part by the (U.S.) Defense Advanced Research Projects Agency, (monitored by the U.S. Army Research Office, Research Triangle Park, North Carolina) under Contract DAAG29-83-K-0148, by the National Institutes of Health, under Grant R01-CA39060, and by the National Science Foundation, under Grant ECS-8300970.

References

[ABRA84] Abram, G. D. and H. Fuchs, VLSI Architectures for Computer Graphics. Proceedings of the NATO Advanced Study Institute on Microarchitecture for VLSI Computers, Urbino, Italy, Springer-Verlag, July 1984

[BECH80] Bechtolsheim, A. and F. Baskett, High-Performance Raster Graphics for Microcomputer Systems. Computer Graphics, Vol. 14, No. 3, (Proceedings of 1980 SIGGRAPH Conference), July 1980, pp. 43-47

[CLAR80a] Clark, J., A VLSI Geometry Processor for Graphics. IEEE Computer, Vol. 13, No. 7, July 1980, pp. 59-68

[CLAR82] Clark, J., The Geometry Engine: A VLSI Geometry System for Graphics. Computer Graphics, Vol. 16, No. 3, (Proceedings of 1982 SIGGRAPH Conference), July 1982, pp. 127-133

[CLAR80b] Clark, J. and M. Hannah, Distributed Processing in a High-Performance Smart Image Memory. Lambda (since 1981, called VLSI Design), Vol. 1, No. 3, 3rd Quarter, 1980

[COHE80] Cohen, D. and S. Demetrescu, Presentation at 1980 SIGGRAPH Conference Panel on Trends on High Performance Graphics Systems.

[DEME80] Demetrescu, S., Master's Thesis. Department of Computer Science, California Institute of Technology 1980.

[DEME85] Demetrescu, S., High Speed Image Rasterization Using Scan Line Access Memories. Proceedings of the 1985 Chapel Hill Conference on Very Large Scale Integration, Computer Science Press, May, 1985., pp. 221-244

[DEME86] Demetrescu, S., Personal Communication. June, 1986

[ELEC86a] Electronics, Intel Designs a Graphics Chip for both CAD and Business Use. Electronics, May 19, 1986, pp. 57-60

[ELEC86b] Electronics, NCR aims its Graphics Chips at PC instead of Work Stations. Electronics, May 19, 1986, pp.61-63

[ENGL81] England, N, Advanced Architectures for Graphics and Image Processing.. Proceedings of the IEEE, Vol. 301 August 1981, pp. 54-57

[EVAN71] Evans and Sutherland Computer Corporation, Line Drawing System Model I System Refernce Manual. Evans and Sutherland Computer Corporation, P.O. Box 8700, Salt Lake City, Utah, 84108, 1971

[EVER52] Everett, R. R., The Whirlwind I Computer. Joint AIEE-IRE Conference, 1952. Review of Electronic Digital Computers, February, 1952, p. 70

[FUCH77] Fuchs, H. Distributing a Visible Surface Algorithm Over Multiple Processors. Proceedings of 1977 ACM Annual Conference, October 1977, pp. 449-451

[FUCH85] Fuchs, H., J. Goldfeather, J. Hultquist, S. Spach, J. Austin, F. Brooks, J. Eyles, and J. Poulton, Fast Spheres, Shadows, Textures, Transparencies, and Image Enhancements in Pixel-planes. Computer Graphics, Vol. 19, No. 3, (Proceedings of 1985 SIGGRAPH Conference), July 1985, pp. 111-120

[FUCH79] Fuchs, H. and B. Johnson, An Expandable Multiprocessor Architecture for Video Graphics. Proceedings of the 6th Annual Symposium on Computer Architecture, ACM-IEEE, April 1979

[FUCH81] Fuchs, H. and J. Poulton, PIXEL-PLANES: A VLSI- Oriented Design for a Raster Graphics Engine. VLSI Design, Vol. 2, No. 3, 3rd Quarter 1981, pp. 20-28

[FUCH82] Fuchs, H., J. Poulton, A. Paeth, and A. Bell, Developing Pixel-Planes, A Smart Memory-Based Raster Graphics System. Proc. Conference On Advanced Research in VLSI, Massachussetts Institute of Technology, published by Artech House, Dedham, Mass., January 1982

[GHAR85] Gharachorloo, N., and C. Pottle, Super Buffer: A Systolic VLSI Graphics Engine for Real Time Raster Image Generation. Proceedings of the 1985 Chapel Hill Conference on Very Large Scale Integration, Computer Science Press, May, 1985., pp. 285-306

[GLAS85] Glassner, A. and H. Fuchs, Hardware Enhancements for Raster Graphics. Proceedings of the 1985 Advanced Study Institute on Fundamental Algorithms in Computer Graphics, Ilkley, Yorkshire, England, Springer-Verlag, April 1985

[GOLD86a] Goldfeather, J. and H. Fuchs, Quadratic Surface Rendering on a Logic-Enhanced Frame-Buffer Memory System. IEEE Computer Graphics and Applications, Vol. 6, No. 1, January 1986, pp. 48-59

[GOLD86b] Goldfeather, J., J. Hultquist, and H. Fuchs, Fast Constructive Solid Geometry Display in the Pixel-Powers Graphics System. to appear in Computer Graphics, Vol. 20, No. 3, (Proceedings of 1986 SIGGRAPH Conference), August 1986.

[GUTA] Gutag, K. and M. Asal, A VLSI 32-Bit Graphics System Processor. submitted for publication

[GUPT81] Gupta, S. and R. Sproull, and I.E. Sutherland, A VLSI Architecture for Updating Raster-Scan Displays. Computer Graphics, Vol. 15, No. 3, (Proceedings of 1981 SIGGRAPH Conference), August 1981, pp. 71-78

[GUTA86] Gutag, K., J. Van Aken, and M. Asal, Requirements for a VLSI Graphics Processor. IEEE Computer Graphics and Applications, Vol. 6, No. 1, January 1986, pp. 32-47

[IKED84] Ikedo, T., High-Speed Techniques for a 3-D Color Graphics Terminal. IEEE Computer Graphics and Applications, Vol. 4, No. 5, May 1984, pp. 46-58

[KAJI75] Kajiya, J. T., I.E. Sutherland, and E.C. Cheadle, A Random-Access Video Frame Buffer. Proceedings of the IEEE Conference on Computer Graphics, Pattern Recognition, and Data Structure, May 1975

[KAY77] Kay, A., Microelectronics and the Personal Computer. Scientific American, Vol. 237 No. 3, September 1977

[KEDE84] Kedem, G. and J. Ellis, Computer Structures for Curve-Solid Classification in Geometric Modelling. Technical Report TR137, Department of Computer Science, University of Rochester, May 1984

[LINE86] Lineback, J. R., The Scramble to Win in Graphics Chips. Electronics, May 19, 1986, pp. 64-65

[MYER68] Myer, T. H. and I. E. Sutherland, On the design of Display Processors. Communications of the ACM, Vol. 11, No. 6, June 1968, pp. 410-414

[PARK80] Parke, F., Simulation and Expected Performance Analysis of Multiple Processor Z-Buffer Systems. Computer Graphics, Vol. 14, No. 3, (Proceedings of 1980 SIGGRAPH Conference), July 1980, pp. 48-56

[PARK82] Parks, J. K., A Comparison of Two Graphics Computer Designs. M.S. Thesis, Computer Science Department, University of North Carolina at Chapel Hill, C.S. Tech Report TR82-001, 1982

[PINK83] Pinkham, R., M. Novak, and K. Guttag, Video RAM Excels At Fast Graphics. Electronic Design, Vol. 31, No. 17, August 18, 1983, pp. 161-172

[POUL85] Poulton, J. and H. Fuchs, J. Austin, J. Eyles, J. Heinecke, C.-H. Hsieh, J. Goldfeather, J. Hultquist, and S. Spach, Implementing a Full-Scale Pixel-planes System. Proceedings of the 1985 Chapel Hill Conference on VLSI, Computer Science Press, Rockville, Md., pp. 35-60

[SCHA81] Schachter, B., Computer Image Generation for Flight Simulation. IEEE Computer Graphics and Applications, Vol. 1, No. 4., 1981

[SCHU69] Schumacker, R., B. Brand, M. Gilliland, and W. Sharp, A Study for Applying Computer Generated Images to Simulation. AFHRL-TR-69-14, Air Force Human Resources Lab, Wright-Patterson AFB, Ohio, September 1969

[SPRO68] Sproull, R.F. and I.E. Sutherland, A Clipping Divider. Proceedings of the Fall Joint Computer Conference, Thompson Books, Washington, D.C., pp. 765-775

[SPRO83] Sproull, R. F., I. E. Sutherland, A. Thompson and C. Minter, The 8 by 8 Graphics Display. ACM Transactions on Graphics, Vol. 2, No. 1, January, 1983, pp. 32-56

[SUTH65] Sutherland, I. E., The Ultimate Display. (abstract only), Proceedings of the 1965 IFIP Congress, Vol. 2, North-Holland Publishing Co., Amsterdam, 1965

[SUTH68] Sutherland, I. E., A Head-Mounted Display. Proceedings of the Fall Joint Computer Conference, Thompson Books, Washington, D.C., pp. 757-764

[SUTH74] Sutherland, I. E. and G. W. Hodgman, Reentrant Polygon Clipping. Communications of the ACM, Vol. 17, No. 32, January, 1974

[SWAN86] Swanson, R. W. and L. J. Thayer, A Fast Shaded-Polygon Renderer. to appear in Computer Graphics, Vol. 20, No.3, (Proceedings of the 1986 SIGGRAPH Conference), August, 1986

[THAC82] Thacker, C. P., E. M. McCreight, B. W. Lampson, R. F. Sproull, and D. R. Boggs, ALTO: A Personal Computer. Xerox Corp., 1979, in Siewiorek, Daniel P., C. Gordon Bell, and Allen Newell, Computer Structures: Principles and Examples, McGraw-Hill, 1982, pp. 549- 572

[WATK70] Watkins, G. S., A Real-Time Visible Surface Algorithm. Ph.D. dissertation, University of Utah Computer Science, UTEC-CSc-70-101, June 1970, NTIS AD-762 004

[WEIN81] Weinberg, R., Parallel Processing Image Synthesis and Anti-Aliasing. Computer Graphics, Vol. 15, No. 3, (Proceedings of 1981 SIGGRAPH Conference), August 1981, pp. 55-61

[WEIT86] Weitek Corporation, Preliminary Data Documentation, Board Level Graphics Processors and Scientific Processors. Weitek Corporation, 1060 East Arques, Sunnyvale, California 94086, 1986

[WHEL82] Whelan, D., A Rectangular Area Filling Display System Architecture. Computer Graphics, Vol. 16, No. 3, (Proceedings of 1982 SIGGRAPH Conference), July 1982, pp. 147-153

[WHIT84] Whitton, M. C., Memory Designs for Raster Graphics Displays. IEEE Computer Graphics and Applications, Vol. 4, No. 3, March 1984, pp. 48-65

[WIEN86] Wientjes, B., K. Guttag, and D. Roskell, First Graphics Processor takes Complex Orders to Run Bit-Mapped Displays. Electronic Design, January 23, 1986, pp. 73-81

[WILL83] Williamson, R. and P. Rickert, Dedicated Processor Shrinks Graphics Systems to Three Chips. Electronic Design, Vol. 31, No. 16, August 4, 1983, pp. 143-148

Specialised Hardware
for Computer Graphics

A. L. THOMAS

Abstract

Boolean expression geometric models provide a powerful, formal way of defining shape and building up descriptions of solid objects. In this paper, various properties of these models are presented, along with a series of operations on them useful in design and graphics systems. A real time display system can be constructed to directly interpret these models into pictorial form. The hardware design for such a system is briefly outlined, and the different layouts of this hardware, in a form suitable for VLSI implementation, are discussed. Finally, the reverse operation of generating the boolean models for solid objects automatically from a series of TV images of the real objects, is outlined.

Introduction

In this paper a series of inter-related ideas for a display and modelling system is presented, which have been slowly evolving since the early seventies. The central theme of the work is the use of Boolean expression models to represent the shape of objects. This approach was initially adopted to provide a simple object description- building language for a design system. The particular advantage it offered came from the way it was able to support interactive work, and allow operations such as interference testing to be expressed and implemented in a direct and natural way.

The use of Boolean expressions with logical variables, with sets and with geometric objects considered as point sets, in a programming environment which supports abstract data types, permits a variety of important modelling and display facilities to be brought within the descriptive scope of the appropriate high level language in a very simple way. All that seems necessary to make this approach into a practical proposition is the implementation of a few key geometric operations in a fast enough form. With this idea in mind, the development of display algorithms to work directly with these models resulted in proposals to make hidden line and hidden area removal a hardware display primitive. This work in turn was extended and led to proposals for parallel: synchronous and systolic processors capable of supporting real time systems:

important in simulation and interactive aspects of CAD work. Finally, to make this approach economically practical, the design of these processors was undertaken as integrated circuits. This work is now at an advanced stage: the basic approach has been shown to be viable, and more advanced features are currently being explored.

In many applications using spatial models, the automatic capture of geometric shape information is an important objective. The possible relationship between Boolean expression, geometric models and the visual perception effects demonstrated by Kanizza's triangle led to a study of this modelling systems ability to support a simple form of machine vision, based of TV camera input. The combination of the real time manipulation of object models and real time image processing techniques has been shown to be an interesting area of study, and is being pursued in future work. Whether it will eventually prove possible to take advantage of the common base provided by the different uses and interpretations of Boolean expressions to develop a unified system linking relational data bases and knowledge subsystems, logic language based inference systems and the man-machine, world-machine interfaces which are discussed below-time will tell.

Object Models

The work presented in this paper was started in 1969 with the development of hidden line removal algorithms for use with block models of terrain. The importance of true solid modelling appeared in the treatment of contour line segments when they were generated for general cartographic use. The creation of self-crossing contour lines indicated the kind of problem which would arise if the process were not handled correctly. In 1970 this 2½ D work was extended to a full study of three dimensional models, starting with polyhedral objects. The polygon facet models of Appell were developed into a graph-matrix representation using the dual naming derived from GIMMS and the DIME system. Generating polyhedral models as graph matrices led to the development of the Boolean expression model as an input language statement. By 1972 an algorithm had been defined which, though primitive, could give a display directly from input expression models.

The goal of this early work was to provide an object modelling system for architects, urban planners, engineers and geographers. At the time there were two views of modelling systems. The first as a tool for the difficult analysis or problem solving functions required of the computer. The second as a vehicle for holding the spatial information needed in design work — usually in large quantities — in other words, more of a data management tool. The early work on sculptured surfaces for aircraft and car-body design, and on finite element methods came under the first heading, while work on cartographic and architectural design systems came under the second. Although both approaches are now recognised as essential in a integrated design system, there was in the early days an element of class distinction between the two. It was the introduction of the concept of solid modelling and the importance of geometric algorithm design by the latter group, to cope reliably with large quantities of data, which finally earned them respectability!

In a general purpose design system it seems likely that a variety of different kinds of modelling techniques will always be necessary. However, where interactive working is required, it seems essential to create or to maintain a very close relationship between the input form of a model definition and the output form required to generate a display. This has to be done to provide the necessary visual feedback to keep track of complicated geometrical commands while working in conversational mode. The consequence of doing this may well be that different models for analysis purposes have to be created as a secondary task once the initial input of shape information is correct. The reason for this is that special hardware and software is necessary to give the required feedback display speed. To make the best use of this hardware, input data has to be in a form which is capable of driving it in a fairly direct way.

Once it was realised that hardware support had to be developed for display purposes if new input models were being proposed, a desire grew to extend this special support to other geometrical operations which made object modelling and display systems slow. Not only was it necessary to solve the many technical aspects of such a development, it was also necessary to make an economic case for it.

Why Hardware

Answering the question "Why Hardware?", is not the simple task it first appeared. If a literalist position is taken, the question should probably be modified to "What Hardware?", because why hardware seems to give an option for having no hardware. Computer hardware can be reduced to the minimum of a Turing-like machine without losing its general purpose capabilities: but no hardware would mean no computing power. Simple engineering objectives such as a reasonable working speed, a physically small system, and practical construction costs generally require more than a minimum system of this kind. What hardware? implies an engineering choice among alternatives, where the suitability of a particular alternative depends on the application.

However, "Why Hardware?" can be interpreted in a different way: Implying that using a general purpose computer system is preferable to building dedicated machinery for Algorithmically Specialised Computers. Certainly the cost of designing and implementing a special purpose system can be programmed to carry out the same task. But where a specialised system provides a service which cannot be obtained from a general system, and there is a market for it, then production of the unit would seem to be fully justified.

Developing special purposes hardware is generally regarded as an expensive solution to any problem which employs computing facilities. In early systems it was an economic necessity to minimise hardware, because the technology was relatively large and very costly. Unnecessary duplication of components had to be avoided wherever possible. Current developments in VLSI circuit technology appear to be changing the importance of some of these early design rules. The development of the single chip microprocessor has already had a considerable effect on the distinction made between general purpose and special purpose systems. Hardware solutions can now be created by fixing the program in a microprocessor is cheap through mass production, so given the appropriate development system, this kind of design solution can cost very little more than the cost of developing the necessary software. Customised gate arrays can be prepared for a fraction of the cost differential between special purpose and general purpose hardware. The development of the silicon compiler promises to take this process several stages further, blurring even more the cost differences between hardware and software solutions to problems.

Two properties justify special hardware for display, apart from an ability to generate an image! The first is speed, the second is a small product, which is important where display units are required by each system user. The importance of real time speed is open to argument, depending on the application. However, if it can be provided in an economic way, it appears to be a facility like colour in displays which will make many applications easier to implement, even where it is hard to justify the step based on current practice. In the work described below the initial aim was the simulator market where real time is essential. The secondary aim was interactive CAD systems where real time facilities would be very useful. The long term aim, however, was to provide a more general interface to the computer system: extending the one main alternative to the currently language dominated forms of communication.

The geometric operations which make modelling systems slow still require general purpose computing facilities. Developing specialised hardware in the context of a general purpose system presents a difficult evaluation and design task. As already observed, simple hardware can be used to carry out most tasks. At the same time it is possible to improve the performance of the total system by including more sophisticated hardware in the right places. The selection of the most cost effective functions by keeping statistics of the system while it is running. Operations which are used very often, or are on critical paths can then either be implemented in more efficient software, or supported by new hardware. The only difficulty with this approach is estimating the ways of using a system which are impractical given a current level of service, but which would develop given an improvement to it.

A very real difficulty justifying new hardware for a particular task results from the speed with which general hardware has improved. The standard of systems has risen so fast that demands for many specific improvements have been possible to meet simply by waiting for the next generation of machines built with faster electronics. The problem which now seems to be emerging is that this approach is reaching a limit. It is not that equally great improvements in the supporting technology are not being made, but that the complexity of modern systems seems to dissipate the advantage provided by low level improvements. One reason suggested for this is that the limitation of the von Neumann architecture used in most systems has finally come to dominate their overall performance. If this is the case, then it is necessary to develop systems with a new structure in order to obtain major improvements. The difficulty with this approach is that the resulting improvements usually only apply for a restricted class of problems. To obtain an overall improvement it therefore becomes necessary to combine an appropriate collection of specialised units in some simple parallel architecture to give back a general system.

This would appear to be, at least in part, the kind of reasoning which lies behind the proposals being made for the Fifth Generation computer systems. In one way, this kind of development can be regarded as an extension of a system tuning exercise, with the migration of important function down a system's hierarchy. In another, it can be viewed as a continuation of the system's subdivision into parallel units which started in very early computer systems with the separation of the I/O functions to processors independent of the CPU, to ensure that data flow through the system was as efficient as possible. As computing facilities and services become more and more integrated with everyday aspects of life, it will not be surprising if this form of system partitioning should not be regarded as simple form of economic product differentiation, rather than a technical design choice. From this point of view a systems architecture will be important only in so far as it helps or restricts the scope for change. In this context the architecture becomes the network, or the communication framework, into which new components or products can be placed. Given a growing openness in basic systems there now seems to be a greater potential for the evolution of higher level units to satisfy specialised needs and their subsequent development into new and optimal forms.

Almost from an historical position the search for special hardware to support design work was considered under two separate headings:

1. Problem Solving and Analysis

2. Man Machine Communication

A survey of some of the possible analysis models used in different areas of design work showed that general purpose computing facilities were essential. Improvements would have to depend on the choice of system architecture and the selection of primitive hardware functions it would support. The man machine interface presented a different case. In this situation special purpose hardware was already well established. Also, the general requirements of the human perception system meant that a large market for the right hardware must exist. The development of the TV monitor/receiver and its success goes a long way in support of this assertion. The separation and development of an interactive interface unit, firstly as a graphics display unit, then as an intelligent display terminal, and finally as a work station in a network, represents a trend on which most of the work described below depends.

The Evolution Of Interactive Modelling Display Hardware

The adoption of the cathode ray tube as a display device marks the starting point for the development of interactive computer graphics, and the subsequent development of computer aided design systems. All real-time display facilities appear to fan out from this point. The first synthetic moving image is reported to have been generated in M.I.T., where it took the speed of the Whirlwind computer to cope with the display of a bouncing ball. The next development was also M.I.T. based. Ivan Sutherland in his Ph.D. research, designed the SKETCHPAD system which gathered together most of the main components necessary for an interactive draughting load on the computer, line interpolation hardware was developed. This permitted the display to be represented by list of line-segment, end-point coordinates. Marking the interpolation of lines a task of the display system, to be carried out repeatedly for each refresh cycle of the CRT, makes it possible to move a point in the display list and have the lines linked to it move like rubber bands, following the point on the screen to wherever it is finally placed. This gave a new interactive editing facility that it was clearly desirable to extend.

The next step in development was to allow whole objects to be moved around in a display as an editing operation. To do this it was necessary to identify an objects set of edges and then to transform the end point coordinates to give the required movement. Simple two dimensional translations were achieved using a form of base displacement addressing hardware which employed absolute and relative coordinates. However, because the system was based on point coordinates, it was possible to apply a range of geometrical transformations to an object: scaling, rotation, translation, reflection, etc. by using homogeneous coordinates and applying the appropriate matrix operation to the list of object coordinates. This general approach allowed three dimensional models to be used within the same scheme, the coordinates being projected onto the plane of the CRT screen for display purposes. Again, though the results were desirable a heavy computational load was placed on the host computer if continuous movement was required. This led to the development of specialised matrix processors to support real time display systems in simulators, but the same development had to wait for technology to advance before it was made available for editing applications. Other line based primitives were developed that were suitable for hardware implementation such as clipping and windowing. However, at this point a series of difficulties emerged which had to be solved before further steps in hardware development were worthwhile.

Although simple wireframe models were adequate for visualisation they had serious short-comings when used to represent solid objects. The problems encountered are illustrated by the well known set of drawings in Figure 1.

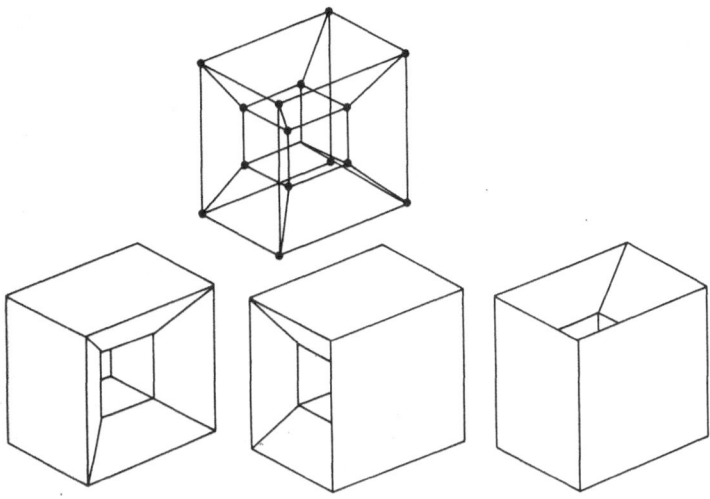

Figure 1 Wire Frame Ambiguity and Hidden Line Removal

Without further information the simple line model is ambiguous if meant to represent a solid object. The figure illustrates a further difficulty, that without removing the hidden lines the display is also ambiguous. Hidden line removal requires a non ambiguous representation, is necessary for comprehension when objects are complex, and is a computationally intensive operation. Including hidden line removal in the display process effectively destroyed the system response necessary for interactive work and lost much of the advantage gained by providing fast point transformation and line interpolation hardware.

In order to provide sufficient information for solid modelling and display purposes, it was necessary to define the surface of objects. This could be done implicitly—by structuring the list of coordinates in an appropriate way to support an accepted form of interpolation. Alternatively it could be done explicitly by giving the functional definition for each piece of an object's surface. In both approaches there were difficulties maintaining self consistency and accuracy when manipulating or displaying the object. Curving or sculptured surfaced objects were the most difficult to manage, but even simplified polyhedral approximations were not without their problems.

Better structures for modelling solid objects slowly evolved, but one important problem still remained. In interactive work it was necessary to be able to move objects round in a scene for object construction and editing purposes. In this process, objects could unintentionally be made to overlap. The consequence of this "placement" problem was that simple hidden-line removal strategies ceased to work. If two objects overlapped it was necessary to generate the edges where the surfaces of the two objects intersected in order to get a correct display. Finding whether objects interfered with each other added to the complexity of the display process. It was the attempt to resolve this problem which led to the use of the Boolean models described below. However, it was the adoption of an alternative display principle which eventually circumvented this particular difficulty.

As soon as images could be generated fast enough to drive a television then half-tone and even full colour display became a possibility. The task of generating realistic images fast enough to do this was undertaken by the General Electric Corporation for NASA. in the late sixties. The aim of this work was to develop electronic displays for pilot training simulators, which synthesised their images rather than televising them from scale models. Work started in the State University of Utah, about the same time, on a whole series of studies of raster graphics topics. For this work to succeed it was necessary to find faster and more efficient ways of structuring the large amount of calculation needed to produce a raster image of a high enough resolution to be acceptable. Alternatively, it was necessary to design special display hardware that could reduce the display work carried out by the host computer, in the same way that the specialised interpolation facilities succeeded in doing in the case of refreshed line displays.

The most important step taken in this direction so far was the introduction of the framestore. Memory, as it became cheaper and packaged in large enough volumes, finally became fast enough and densely packed enough to store a total TV image in a digital form. This information could then be accessed and converted into an analogue video signal at the rate required to drive a television Work in the CAD. Centre in Cambridge. It produced the "Bugstore", a two port block of memory which allowed information to be written to it from the computer while maintaining a constant flow of out put at the required video refresh rate to a TV monitor. The hidden area removal algorithm of Newell, Newell and Sancha [NEWE72] was designed to use this kind of memory based display hardware. Working with polygon facet models, this approach employed the overwriting of memory to model the way that nearer object facets obscured more distant object facets by entering the property or colour value of the more distant facets first. This operation required two supporting procedures. The first was the depth ordering of polygons; the second was a form of polygon shading or polygon fill needed to determine which memory locations to overwrite.

Polygon facets can be impossible to sort into a simple order, and more important, can intersect each other as a result of the placement problem caused by interactive editing. A simple hardware solution to this problem was provided by the depth buffer. A new polygon being painted into display memory was only entered at a particular pixel position if its depth value at that position was less than the depth value of the polygon already stored at the point. This approach was an ideal solution to the problem of preparing static displays, as no restriction was placed on the way that new depth or property values were generated. It permitted results from a large variety of different object modelling systems to be merged, whatever the speed and order the new data were prepared.

Both these approaches were beautifully simple, but had one drawback if speed was the ultimate objective. Every polygon has to be painted into memory, so in a complex scene every memory location would expect to be accessed several times per frame. Memory access time provides one limiting constraint on the resolution of raster displays. Since greater resolution can confidently be seen to be unsatisfied until wall sized images are easy to produce, it seemed unlikely that this approach in its simplest form could represent the ultimate solution, particularly where real time editing and moving synthetic images are the goal. For such an objective, greater speed in generating images had to be found. This was possible in one of two interrelated ways. Polygon data being entered into memory had to be preprocessed to remove hidden zones. Once resolution of this kind of system was high enough line displays could also be prepared using it. Once this was possible, line based procedures could be used. In particular, hidden line removal algorithms could be employed to reduce the number of accesses to memory described above. The average number of accesses to each memory location had to be reduced to one per frame.

Before the framebuffer, G. S. Watkins had outlined the design of a real-time, raster-based, hidden-area-removal system. It used a polygon-facet-boundary-model of objects. However, even though raster based, this system depended heavily on previous line based systems. Edges were created by interpolation between polygon vertices, onto a raster grid. The movement of edges was obtained by transforming vertex coordinates before interpolation. Polygons were tested for overlap by comparing section lines through the polygons, created by intersecting them with a section plane through the current raster line and the eye. Polygon section lines were generated by linking together corresponding boundary points on a raster line from the same polygon boundary. Hidden area removal was accomplished by selecting the nearest polygon section point at each pixel position. This process was based on a binary sub-division of polygon sections which overlapped in the raster line in a process designed to quickly select the nearer section. Segments were compared in a pair-wise manner in an ordered traversal of the raster line. Output was an ordered list of change points between different visible polygon sections.

Where two polygon sections intersected their crossing point had to be found. This point could be found to the nearest pixel position by the binary sub-division process used to select the nearer of two polygon sections. The two nearer segments of the crossing polygon sections were then selected and presented for display. This approach solved the display aspect of the placement problem by generating the union of any objects which had accidentally been made to overlap. It was by extending this process that a display algorithm was developed to handle Boolean expression models in a direct way. In his PhD thesis Watkins [WATK70] proposed a direct hardware implementation of his algorithm which Evans and Sutherland adopted in their simulator display system.

Once the difficulties associated with hidden-line and hidden-area removal algorithms became fully understood, further hardware developments started

to emerge. Before giving a more detailed account of the scheme based on
Boolean expression models and the hardware it made possible, a brief list of
some related proposals which have been made by people working in this area is
given below.

Display Algorithms and Display Processor Hardware

1963	SKETCHPAD	I. E.Sutherland
	Line Interpolation Rubber Banding	Ph.D. Thesis
1963	Hidden Line Removal Algorithm	L. Roberts.
1968	LDS 1 3D Vector Pipeline	Evans and
	4x4 Matrix Multiplication	Sutherland
1968	Clipper Divider	R. F. Sproull
		I. E. Sutherland
1968	Hidden Line Algorithm Halftone Pictures	J. E. Warnock
1969	Simulator Display System	R. Schumacker
	General Electric Company	
1969	OBLIX Profile Hidden Line Removal Algorithm	A. L. Thomas
1970	A Real Time Visible Surface Algorithm	G. S. Watkins
		Ph.D. Thesis
1972	Boolean Expression Model	A. L. Thomas
	Hidden Area Removal Algorithm	
1972	Painter's Algorithm	M. Newell
		R. Newell
		T. Sancha
1975	A Random Access Video Frame Buffer	J. Kajiya
		I. E. Sutherland
1976	Boolean Expression Engine	A. L. Thomas
	Polygonal & Polyhedral Processors:	Ph.D. Thesis
	1. Binary, Quad, Oct-Tree Processors (VLSI)	
	Pixel Plane Interpolator, Reconfigurable	
	Systolic Array Processor	
	2. Pipelined Pixel Processors	
	3. Pipelined Surface Processors	
	4. Pipelined Sorting Processor	
	5. Maximum/Minimum Seeking Bus	
1977	Multiple Processor Visible Surface Algorithm	H. Fuchs
1979	VLSI Pixel Processor Pipeline	A. L. Thomas
	Line, Area, Volume Scene-Coherence Processors	
1979	Zone Management Processor:	R. L. Grimsdale
		A. A. Hadjiaslanis
		P. J. Willis
1979	VLSI Triangle Pipeline	G. C. Roman
		T. Kimura
1980	Polygon Pipeline Processor	D. Cohen
		S. Demetrescu
1980	Smart Image Memory	J. Clark
		M. Hannah

1980	Object Space Recursive Subdivision Display Algorithm	J. R. Woodwark K. M. Quinlan
1981	Transformation Unit for Plane Half-Spaces	A. L. Thomas
1981	PIXEL-PLANES VLSI processor	H. Fuchs
1982	Geometry Engine	J. Clark
1982	Oct-Tree Display System	J. M. Meagher
1983	Recursive Scanline, Quad-tree Oct-tree Scene Coherence Processor	A. L. Thomas
1984	Multiprocessor Architecture for Viewing Solid Models	J. R. Woodwark
1984	Extension to Pixel Processor for Pattern Projections and Real Time Multiple Shadow Casting	A. L. Thomas
1984	Composite Solid Geometry Viewing Ray Processor	G. Kedem J. L. Ellis
1984	Distributed Ray Tracing	R. Cook T. Porter L. Carpenter
1985	Regularised Set Operation Boundary Expansion Rules	A. L. Thomas
1985	Scan Line Access Memory	S. Demetrescu
1986	PIXEL POWERS	H. Fuchs
1986	Quartic Surfaces Real Time?	A. L. Thomas

It can be seen from this list that there are a few common themes crystallising out, and the next few years should see a series of stable products emerging from this research work. One of the likely products will be a CSG or Boolean expression modelling and display system. One approach to this kind of system is described more fully below.

Boolean Expression Solid Modelling Display System

Watkins' algorithm was a solution to real-time display generation which was hard, in principle, to improve. There were four steps to producing a moving synthetic image:

1. Transformation Processing

2. Divide and Conquer Scan-Line, Scene Coherence Processing

3. Pixel Rendering or Value Interpolation

4. Illumination Calculations

What did seem open for improvement was the object modelling stage of the process. In a general interactive system the main flows of information will be those shown in figure 2. The close link between the display list used in vector graphics systems, and the way a draughtsman might describe the construction of a drawing gave the close coupling between the input and the output necessary for interactive work. The move to three dimensional, solid models made the in

put and output more remote from each other. The adoption of the frame buffer
provided a way of merging the displays from a variety of different models in the
way summarised in figure 3, but this did not provide an easy way to describe and
build three dimensional models which could then be quickly used to generate a
display. The fastest way depended on constructing a wireframe model and then
rendering its polygonal facets.

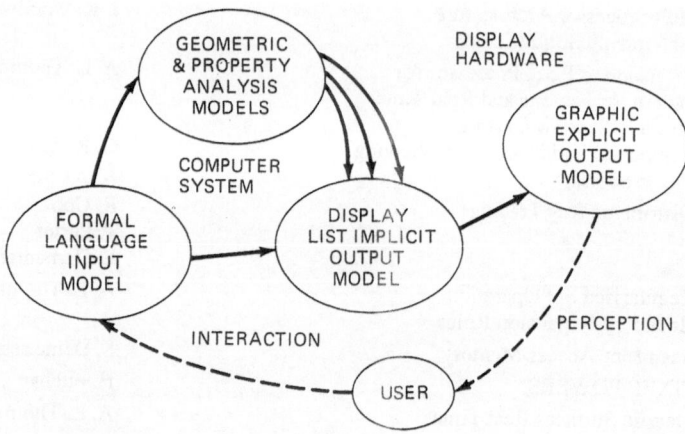

Figure 2. Models and Interactive Information Flow

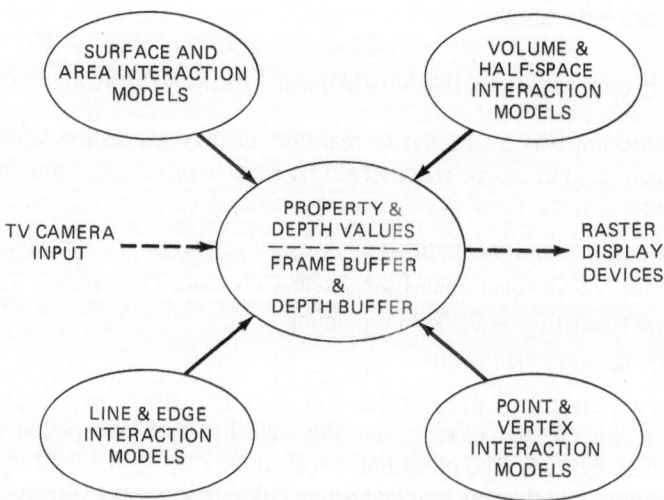

Figure 3. Merging Different Model Displays

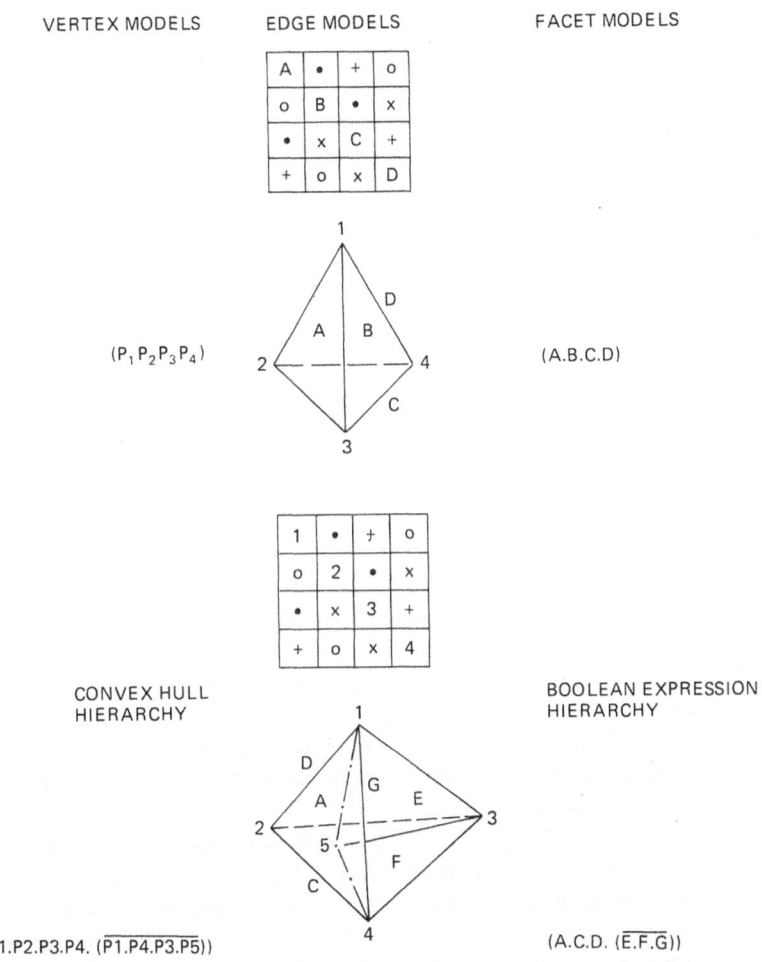

VERTEX MODELS   EDGE MODELS   FACET MODELS

$(P_1 P_2 P_3 P_4)$ (A.B.C.D)

CONVEX HULL   BOOLEAN EXPRESSION
HIERARCHY   HIERARCHY

(P1.P2.P3.P4. ($\overline{P1.P4.P3.P5}$))   (A.C.D. ($\overline{E.F.G}$))

Figure 4 Alternative Volume Models

Two main approaches to modelling emerged from a study of this part of the system. The first was based on a set of homogeneous vertex coordinates, (x,y,z,w), the second on a set of facet plane equation coefficients, (a,b,c,d). The vertex based approach consisted of different ways of setting up triangulated networks. A characteristic of this model was that shape changes could be most simply achieved by transforming vertex coordinates. Edges and facets depended on interpolation to complete the model. One way of implementing this system was to represent a set of tetrahedra as 4x4 graph matrices and then employ a series of operations to glue the tetrahedra together by adding together the appropriate matrices. A variation of this approach resulted in a hierarchy of convex hulls: a

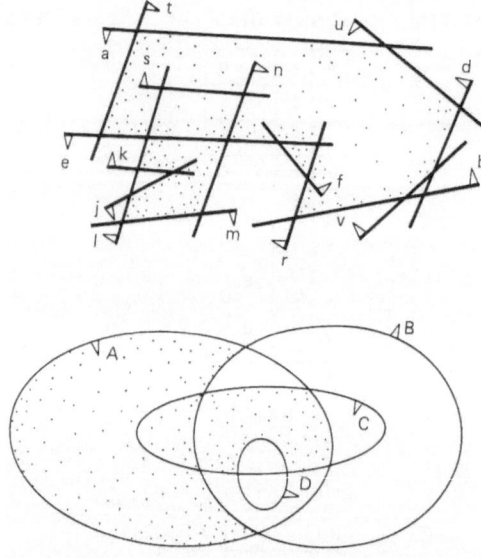

Figure 5 Boolean Expression Model Standard Form

system used in the automatic volume definition process described below. The second main method grew out of a study of overlap operations. The facets of the target volume were represented by a set of plane half-spaces. These planes partitioned the object space into a collection of convex blocks: the required volume was defined by writing down the Boolean expression which selected the appropriate collection of convex blocks. This expression model could be automatically converted into a graph-matrix or convex hull model if required, and vice versa. Shape modification following the second approach was achieved by transforming the surface plane equations. Each of these models was capable of being transformed using the same matrix multiplication hardware. If an object in the form shown in Figure 5 is entered into the computer system, defined as the interaction of a sequence of sub-models

> where the
> Target Volume $T = C.d. \ (!E+f). \ D;$

where the lower case names represent plane half-spaces but the capital letter names represent the other objects:

> $C = a.b;$
> $E = e.r. \ (l+m+! \ (k+j) \ +n+s);$
> $D = t.u.v;$

The first step is to substitute for the object names:

> $T = a.b.d. \ (!(e.r.(l+m+!(k+j) \ +n+s))+f).t.u.v;$

The next step is to apply De Morgan's theorem to all complemented sub-expressions to give:

$$T = a.b.d.(!e+!r+(!l.!m.(k+j).!n.!s)+f).t.u.v;$$

and the final step is to collect all the free plane half-spaces at each level into convex groups that can be renamed in the way shown in Figure 5.

$$T = \underbrace{a.\ b.\ d.\ t.\ u.\ v}_{(A}.\underbrace{(!\ e+!r+f}_{(B} + \underbrace{(!1.!\ m.!n.!\ s}_{(C}.\underbrace{(k\ +j}_{(D)}))));$$

This process is implemented using the tree structures which result from parsing the input expressions defining the various objects, and which are illustrated in Figure 6.

Boolean Expression Parsing & Processing

The use of Boolean expressions to define objects makes it possible to develop a computer language based on different ways of manipulating and interpreting the expressions. The input-output section of the language at a minimum requires four types of statement:

1. A plane half-space definition,
2. A boolean expression volume definition,
3. A property assignment statement, and
4. An output, display statement.

Transformations can also be included to allow one surface to be defined as a function of another, and to allow trajectories to be specified using a Boolean expression model will be of the form:

<statement>	::= NAME, '=' <rightname>.
<rightname>	::= <plane-definition>| <boolean-expression>.
<plane-definition>	::= '(', NUMBER, NUMBER, NUMBER, NUMBER,')'.
<boolean-expression>	::= <phrase>, '+', <boolean-expression>| <phrase>.
<phrase>	::= <factor>, '.', <phrase>| <factor>.
<factor>	::= <operand>| '!', <operand>.
<operand>	::= NAME| '(', <boolean-expression>, ')'.

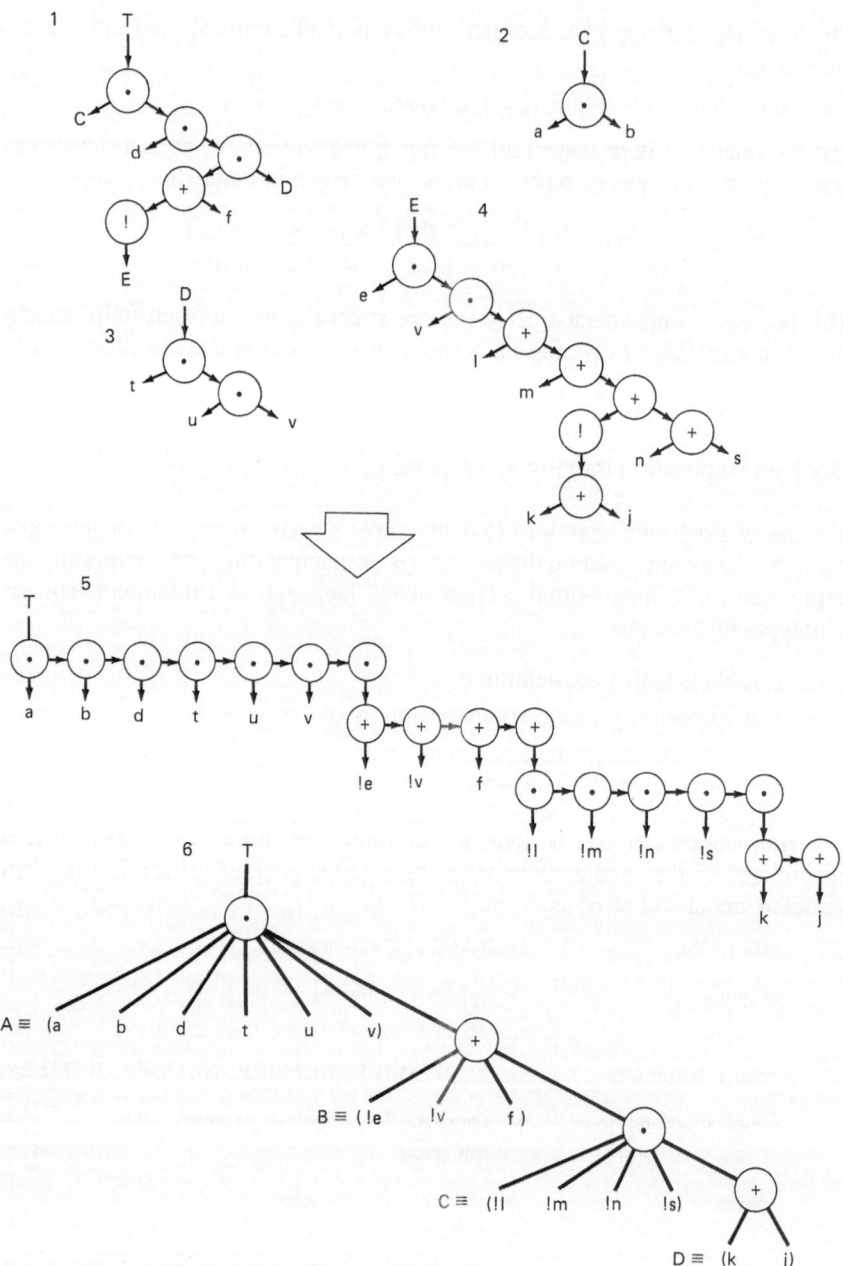

Figure 6 Boolean Expressions as Tree Structures

Figure 6 illustrates the input models which result from parsing the volumes labelled T,C, D and E in the trees numbered 1,2,3,4. The first step in processing these trees was to link incomplete references to the relevant trees. In this case the result is a single expanded tree for T. Applying De Morgan's theorem consists of switching all the operator nodes in the complemented sub-tree and complementing all the half-space references. This makes it possible to represent the expression by a Knuth tree where each alternative level corresponds to alternation union and intersection operators. The final step is to collect all the free half-space references together at each level in the Knuth tree at the beginning of each level row. Renaming these units allows the schematic representation using convex elements shown in Figure 5 to be used. This diagram corresponds to the tree labelled 6 in Figure 6, which would be implemented in the form of the tree labelled 5. The convex units in this example are $(a.b.d.t.u.v.)$, $(!e+!r+f)$, $(!l.!m.!n.!s)$ and $(k+j)$. Renaming these convex units results in an object defined as $A.(B+(C.(D)))$ or $A(B(C(D)))$ where the first level is known.

Once the convex components have been set up in this way it is possible to carry out a further series of operations on these trees which correspond to the algebraic manipulation of the original expression described below. The purpose of these operations is to generate a Boundary model from the simple expression form used for input. This process was initially developed to control the conversion of the expression model to the corresponding graphmatrix form.

Take as an example the triangular object $(A.B.C)$. It is a natural step to define the boundary of this object—expressed as $@(A.B.C)$—as made up from the three sides of the triangle. The first side of the triangle will be the boundary of the half-space A where it lies inside $(B.C)$, in other words $@A.B.C$. Similarly the second and third sides will be $@B.A.C$ and $@ C.A.B$ respectively, giving in total:

$$@(A.B.C) = @A.B.C + @B.A.C + @C.A.B$$

This idea can be extended by considering the triangle to be a hole rather than a solid. In which case the expansion becomes:

$$@(\overline{A \cdot B \cdot C}) \quad = \quad @(\overline{A} + \overline{B} + \overline{C})$$

$$= \quad @\overline{A} \cdot B \cdot C \quad + \quad @\overline{B} \cdot C \cdot A \quad + \quad @\overline{C} \cdot A \cdot B$$

From this example two swapping rules can be extracted:

$$@(A \cdot B) \quad \rightarrow \quad @A \cdot B \quad + \quad @B \cdot A \qquad @(A+B) \quad \rightarrow \quad @A \cdot \overline{B} \quad + \quad @B \cdot \overline{A}$$

If these swapping rules or productions are applied to the previous example, the results will be the set of boundary segments shown in Figure 7 as $B1$, $B2$, $B3$ and $B4$ where these elements are defined as follows:

$$@(A.(B + (C.(D)))) \rightarrow @ A.(B + C.(D)) + @(B + (C.(D))).A$$
$$@(B + (C.(D))).A \rightarrow @B.A.(\overline{C.(D)}) + @(C.(D)).A.\bar{B}$$
$$@(C.(D)).A.\bar{B} \rightarrow @ C.A.\bar{B}.(D) + @ D.A.\bar{B}.C$$

Renaming:

$$B1 = @A (B + (C.(D)))$$
$$B3 = @ C.(A.\bar{B}.(D))$$
$$B2 = @ B.(A.(\bar{C} + (\bar{D})))$$
$$B4 = @ D.(A.\bar{B}.C)$$

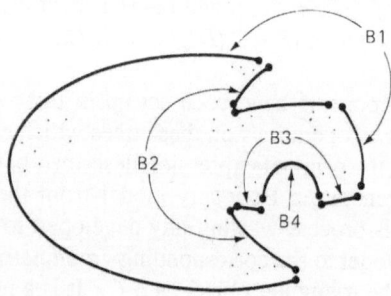

Figure 7 Boolean Expression Boundary Operator

An alternative expansion can be obtained by using a different swapping rule for the '+' operator.

$$@(A + B) \rightarrow @A + @B$$

Applying this rule to the previous example gives:

$$@(A.(B + (C.(D)))) \rightarrow @(A.(B + (C.(D))) + @(B + (C.(D))).A$$

$$@(B + (C.(D))).A \rightarrow @B.A + @(C.(D)).A$$

$$@(C.(D)).A \rightarrow @C.A.(D) + @D.A.C$$

renaming:

$$B1 = @A.(B+(C.(D)))$$
$$B3 = @C.(A.(D))$$
$$B2 = @B.(A)$$
$$B4 = @D.(A.C)$$

The alternative expansion makes use of the fact that pieces of surface which lie inside the solid interior of an object will not be seen. It was developed to handle the problem of hanging faces described below. This form of boundary expansion allows sheet like objects with no thickness to be handled by a display algorithm on one hand and, applying a different interpretation, it also allows regularised set operations to be implemented in the display process on the other.

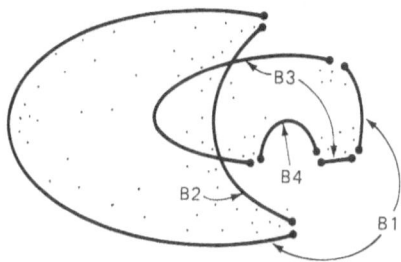

Figure 8 Alternative Boundary Expansion

The Display of Boolean Expression Models

The way that Watkins' algorithm generated the union of two overlapping boundary models, by selecting the surface which lay nearest to the picture plane, suggested the following algorithm. If selecting the minimum distance to a surface at each pixel position, along a viewing ray, generates the union of two objects then selecting the maximum should give the intersection of the two objects. This turned out to be true, with qualifications. Consider a convex solid defined as the intersection of a set of plane surfaced half-spaces. From any viewing point, this set will be partitioned into two sets: those facing towards the viewing position and those facing away from it. The front surface of the convex object can be defined by selecting the front plane which lies furthest away from the viewing position along a given viewing ray. Conversely the back surface of the same object will be given by selecting the back plane which lies closest to the viewing position along any viewing ray. These two surfaces, however, are infinite in extent, defined in this way, whereas the original object is not. The final step is to select that section of the front surface which lies in front of the back surface, as the visible surface of the convex object. Given a set of convex objects, then the nearest one to the eye will be the visible object in a particular viewing direction.

Viewing Ray Distances

The distance to a plane surface from a pixel position R can be evaluated in the way shown in Figure 9. The distances to two surfaces AA and BB are shown in the diagram as the lengths NR and MR.

$$\frac{MR}{ME} = \frac{CR}{PE} \qquad\qquad \frac{NR}{NE} = \frac{LR}{KE} \quad \text{Similar triangles}$$

$$MR.PE = CR.(MR+RE) \qquad NR.KE = LR.(NR+RE)$$

$$MR = \frac{RE.CR}{(PE-CR)} \qquad\qquad NR = \frac{RE.LR}{(KE-LR)}$$

Since *RE* will be a constant for any pixel position these relationships can be renamed to give the ratios

$$\frac{k_B^1}{k_B^2 - k_B^1} > \frac{k_A^1}{k_A^2 - k_A^1}$$

where k^1 and k^2 are the perpendicular distances from the plane to the raster point and the eye respectively. These distances can be obtained by calculating the dot product of the coefficients of the planes equation with the coordinates of the positions of R and E.

A Schematic Cellular Processor

There were two approaches open for developing the basic display algorithm. The first was in software, where it would be necessary to develop some way of using scene coherence in the manner of Warnock or Watkins. The second was to use specialised hardware and attempt to take advantage of the simplicity of the algorithm by using a highly repetitive structure. It must be observed that the classification of simple was based on a software rather than a hardware background! The diagrammatic repetitive processing unit shown in Figure 10 was set up in 1973/4 as an object for further study.

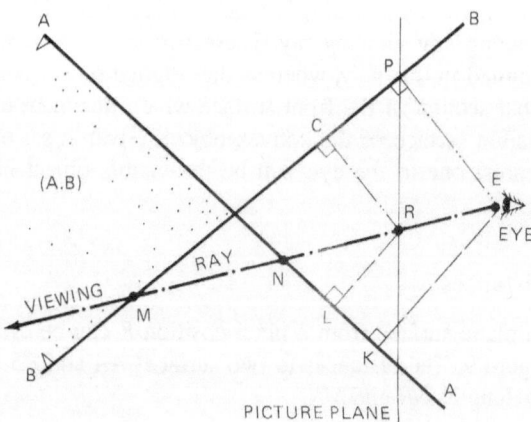

Figure 9 Viewing Ray Distances

As this system was examined in greater detail the many problems which it posed were not slow to emerge. The objective of this work, however, was and is still valid. It can best be summarised by giving the list of functions it was thought

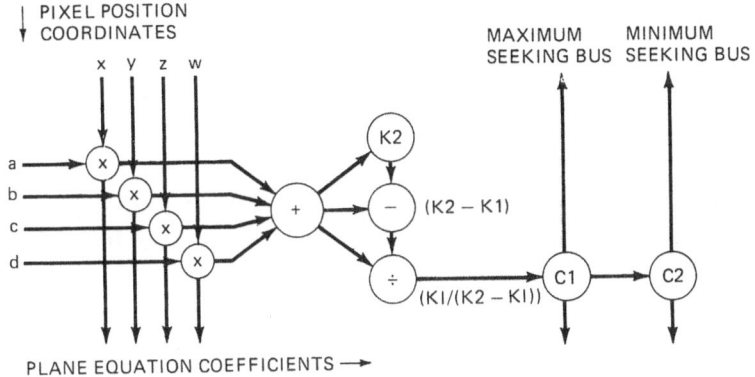

Figure 10 Schematic Parallel Processor

that an arrangement of this kind would be able to support, and which would justify special hardware. These are:

1. Matrix Multiplication
2. Sort a List of Numbers into Order
3. Point in Polygon Testing
4. Point in Polyhedron Testing
5. Raster Scan Display of Polygons
6. Line Shaded Polygon Displays
7. Nearest Neighbour Polygon Displays
8. Shaded Perspective Displays of Volumes
9. Line Drawing Displays of Volumes
10. Cross Section Displays of Volumes
11. Polyhedral Overlap Testing
12. Polygon Overlap Testing

The repetitive use of multipliers in the way shown was the first casualty of reality—though VLSI brings this approach back into the range of the possible, now, for ray casting machines. At the time, digital multipliers were too expensive, too large and too slow to use in this way. A possible solution to this practical difficulty was provided by the use of Multiplying Digital to Analogue Converters. Setting up the coefficients for each plane in a digital form and controlling the x,y,z, and w values as analogue signals still has an appealing structure to it. The main outcome of this exploration of hybrid computing was a redefinition of the distance of depth function. Because it was the order in which surfaces cut a viewing ray which was important, the ratios:

$$\frac{k_A^1}{k_A^2 - k_A^1} < \frac{k_B^1}{k_B^2 - k_B^1}$$

could be replaced by:

$$\frac{k^1_A}{k^2_A} < \frac{k^1_B}{k^2_B}$$

These ratios have the advantage that their values lie in the range O to 1, as well as preserving the order of surface intersections with a viewing ray. If this ratio is expanded to give

$$\frac{k^1}{k^2} = \frac{a . x^1 + b . y^1 + c . z^1 + d . w^1}{a . x^2 + b . y^2 + c . z^2 + d . w^2} = Z$$

where Z is the new distance value, then a new display space is defined, and the transformation from the object space to this new space can be summarised by rearranging (1) to give:

$$[a, b, c, d] \cdot \begin{bmatrix} 1 & 0 & -x^2 & 0 \\ 0 & 1 & -y^2 & 0 \\ 0 & 0 & -z^2 & z^1 \\ 0 & 0 & -1 & 1 \end{bmatrix} \cdot \begin{bmatrix} x^1 \\ y^1 \\ Z \\ 1 \end{bmatrix} = 0$$

This matrix defines the perspective transformation for the plane (a,b,c,d). The advantage of using this form is that this matrix can be concatenated with rotation and translation matrices in the same way that is done in point processing systems. The importance of this is that point, line, area and volume objects can all be transformed using the same hardware, more or less in the same way. Pipelining this operation: first passing a scene description through a matrix multiplier to transform it, then passing it through a hidden area removal and illumination processor, could provide a real time system if the second stage were fast enough.

If a plane (a, b, c, d) in the object space gives a new plane in the display space (A, B, C, D), then the depth value

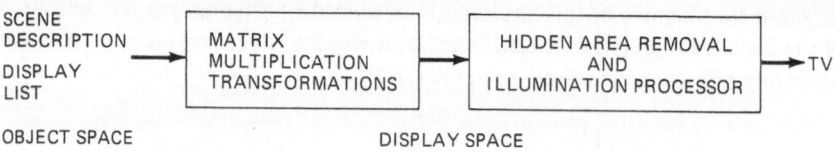

SCENE DESCRIPTION → MATRIX MULTIPLICATION TRANSFORMATIONS → HIDDEN AREA REMOVAL AND ILLUMINATION PROCESSOR → TV

DISPLAY LIST

OBJECT SPACE   DISPLAY SPACE

Figure 11 Display Pipeline

Z can be calculated at any pixel position (X,Y) by the equation:

$Z = (A.X + B.Y + D)/(-C)$

This distance is perpendicular to the display screen in the display space, and can be used to represent the plane in visibility tests at the given pixel position. An alternative distance which is important in several algorithms is the distance K from the pixel position to the plane, taken perpendicular to the plane itself.

$K = (A.X + B.Y + D)$

Working with a raster display it is possible to simplify the calculations of K and Z for each pixel by calculating an initial depth value at one pixel position and then calculating the size of the increments needed to modify this value, moving in regularly spaced steps over the display surface.

If the display transformation is set up so that the display space has its origin at the origin of the object space with the x and y axes corresponding to the X and Y axes and the direction of viewing being along the zaxis, then the following values can be calculated:

$Z = D/(-C)$

$\Delta Zx = A.\Delta X/(-C)$

$\Delta Zy = B.\Delta Y/(-C)$

where ΔX and ΔY are the pixel spacing dimensions, or the screen width increments—depending on the next stage. Where $C \to 0$ then there is a problem. This situation corresponds to the plane surface getting closer and closer to being perpendicular to the display screen. The perpendicular and near perpendicular plane can be processed in a different way, by using the value of K rather than Z. This value and its increments will already be available:

$K = D$

$\Delta Kx = A.\Delta X$

$\Delta Ky = B.\Delta Y$

$\Delta Kz = C.\Delta Z$

In other words, the intermediate result, before carrying out the division operation. The critical situation where the value of K replaces the value of Z will occur when either of the pixel level increments of Z exceeds 1.0. This corresponds to a surface which is not visible at one pixel position but has crossed the display screen to give a cross section cut at a neighbouring pixel position. Although there are a variety of ways in which this set of operation can be carried out, a simple pipelined arrangement is shown in Figure 12, where an approximation method of calculating the division is employed, which makes the test for perpendicularity easy to implement.

The division by multiplication is carried out in the following way. Consider D/C. Normalise C to be a fraction of form $0.xxxx$ and consider it to be the value

$(1-\Delta)$. Both D and C are then multiplied by $(1+\Delta)$ *which is* $(2-(1-\Delta))$ in other words $2-C$.

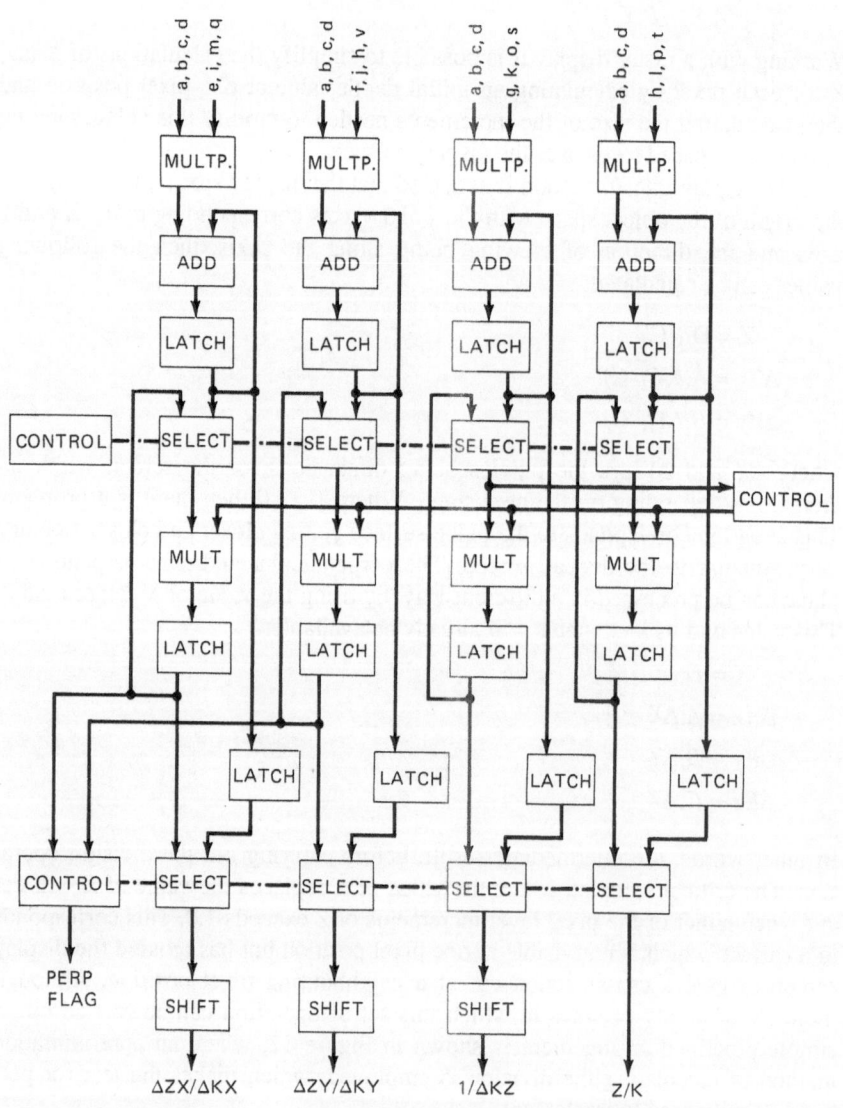

Figure 12 Schematic Layout of Plane Transformation Unit

$$\frac{D}{C} = \frac{D}{(1-\Delta)} = \frac{D \cdot (1+\Delta)}{(1+\Delta) \cdot (1-\Delta)} = \frac{D1}{C1}$$

$C1 = (1-\Delta^2)$ which permits the process to be repeated:

$$(1+\Delta^2) \;\; = \;\; 2 - C1$$

$$\frac{D1}{C1} = \frac{D1 \cdot (1+\Delta^2)}{(1+\Delta^2) \cdot (1-\Delta^2)} = \frac{D2}{C2}$$

$$C2 = (1-\Delta^4)$$

This process is continued until the error term is below some fixed value. At this point

$$\frac{Dn}{Cn} \rightarrow \frac{-Z}{1.0} = -Z$$

In the scheme shown in Figure 12 it has been estimated that 4 or 5 multiplies in series will give the required accuracy for the division operation. If multiplication time is 100 nsecs then 500 nsecs are required for each plane transformation. This will allow 80,000 planes to be transformed in the frame time of 1/25 sec. If the transformation time can be reduced to 400 nsecs then this figure goes up to 100,000 planes in a frame time.

Moving Images and Transformations

The selection of the front and back surfaces of a convex object at a particular pixel position can be achieved in one pass through the display list–list of plane half-spaces linked by intersection operators: $A.B.C.D.E.F$. It is necessary to hold two temporary values in registers during this process: the first holding the furthest away front surface encountered up to that point, the second holding the nearest back surface. In order to carry out this process it is necessary to know which are front surfaces and which are back surfaces. Clearly this is a classification task which has to be carried out after each plane transformation, if a moving scene is being generated.

Consider a plane defined relative to the origin by the value K. This distance will be positive where the origin lies inside the plane and negative where it lies outside:

$$K = a.x + b.y + c.z + d$$
$$K = d \qquad (x = 0, y = 0, z = 0)$$

The sign of d can consequently be used to indicate the inside-outside relationship between a plane and the origin. Backness or frontness depends on the intercept of the plane on the Z axis, combined with this inside-outside value.

From the diagrams in Figure 13 it can be seen that the *exclusive OR* of the sign bits of K and Z defined at the origin gives a simple and fast way of maintaining the classification of H.

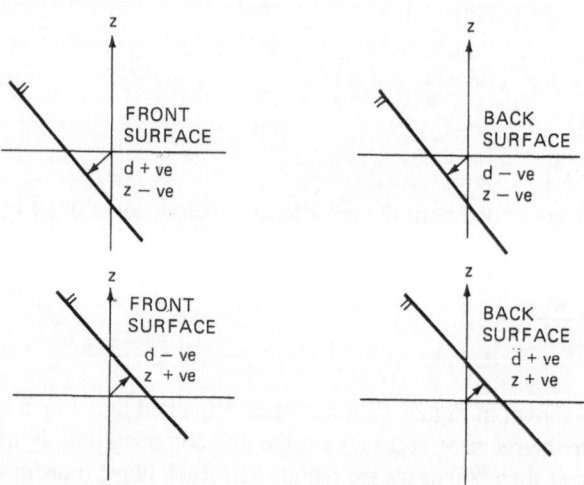

Figure 13 Front or Back Planes (H)

If display lists for convex units are pre-ordered so that all front surfaces are received for processing before the back surfaces in the same convex group, then only one temporary value needs to be stored carrying out the display algorithm. However, this requires a reordering of the elements in the display list after each transformation. If the length of each convex unit is held with each display list then a simple addressing operation can be used to achieve this reordering, before outputing the values to the hidden area removal processing unit, from the transformation unit.

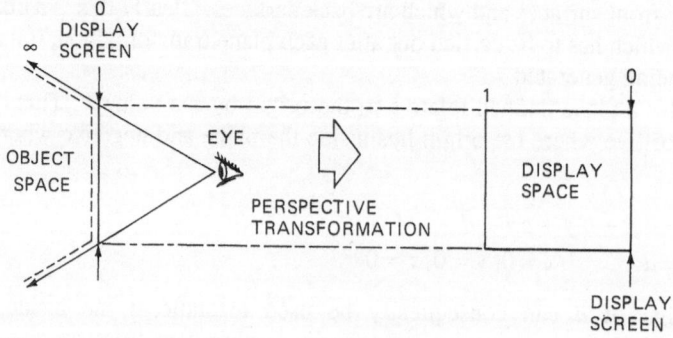

Figure 14 Object Space to Image Space Transformation

Figure 14 summarises the transformation operation implemented in the way described above. The result is a display space which can be thought of as a cube lying behind the display screen. Objects in the display space can be displayed by using a very simple parallel projection operation. The display algorithms used for Boolean expression models in this context are shown in Figure 15 for both convex solids and convex voids. The latter is described below, and is important in boundary expansion models.

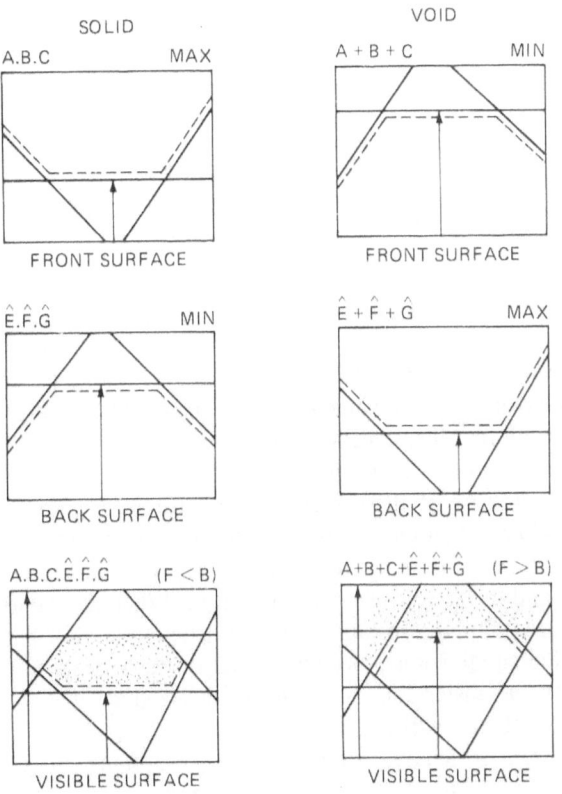

Figure 15 Display Operations: Convex Units

Hidden Area Removal Hardware

Given the ability to calculate depth values using a transformation unit not unlike that used for point based models, the next task was to develop matching hardware to implement the selection operations summarised in Figure 15 for hidden area removal. It was clearly possible to implement a Watkins style scan-line algorithm. An advantage which resulted from having surfaces spanning the whole display space was that binary sub-division, instead of being applied to

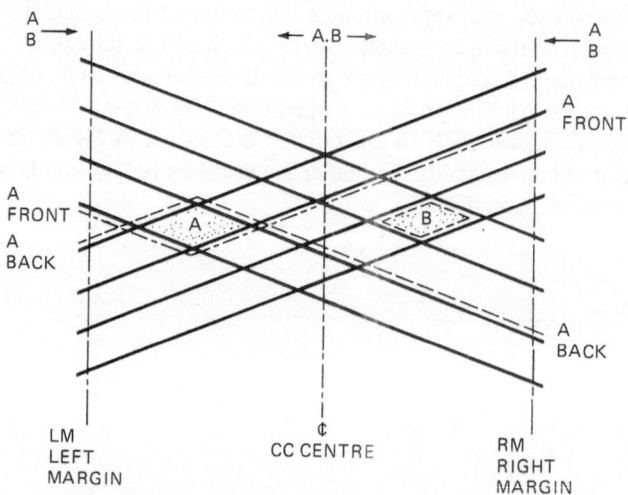

Figure 16 Binary Subdivision of a Raster Line Cross Section Plane

each polygon facet section, could in the manner of Warnocks algorithm be applied to the display space. The whole of a scan line could be sub-divided using a common framework for all surface-surface comparisons.

Consider the two volumes A and B in cross section in Figure 16. If the front surfaces and back surfaces of these two volumes are determined at the margin positions LM and RM, then their relative positions and orientations will indicate in which direction the objects lie. In this case both A and B exist to the right of the left margin and to the left of the right margin. When the same tests are applied at the centre point, the results show that A lies to the left but B lies to the right. A recursive subdivision procedure based on these tests will sort objects into order along the raster line and considerably reduce the work in finding visible sections of objects surfaces.

It appeared that if reasonably simple scenes were being processed then this approach would be adequate. All that was needed to obtain a display was a video-rate interpolator to fill in the pixels between the facet edges determined by the subdivision algorithm. However, where an image complexity was required which might demand changes every few pixels, then this subdivision process could not be carried out fast enough to support real time, without some form of parallel hardware implementation. At the time this seemed too difficult. What appeared much easier to implement was the simple hidden area algorithm of Figure 15, in an iterative form using repeating hardware units, and then to use it in partnership with a software subdivision or other scene coherence algorithm. It now seems fairly clear that to obtain the speed and complexity desired will need both stages, both implemented in hardware. The overall system structure being extended to that shown in Figure 17.

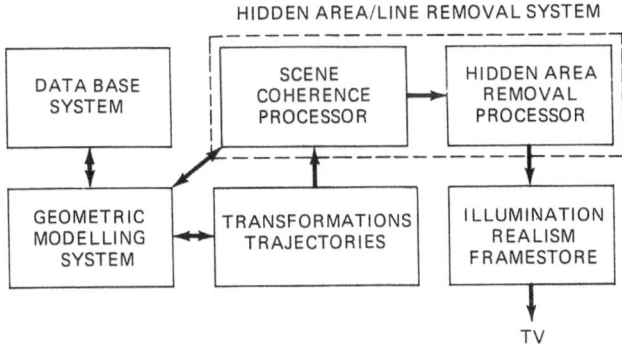

Figure 17 Display System Block Diagram

Parallel Schemes

There were two stages to the simple iterative implementation of the algorithm, which were:

1. Evaluating depth values at each pixel position for each plane half-space in the display list.
2. Comparing depth values to select visible surfaces, based on inside-outside or viewing ray priority tests.

It was found possible to construct two different parallel schemes. In the first, depth generating units from parallel processors were combined into a single entity. In the second the comparison and selection units were combined together as a single unit. Each of these combined units could be implemented using either pipelined — systolic — processing,or simultaneous — synchronous — processing.

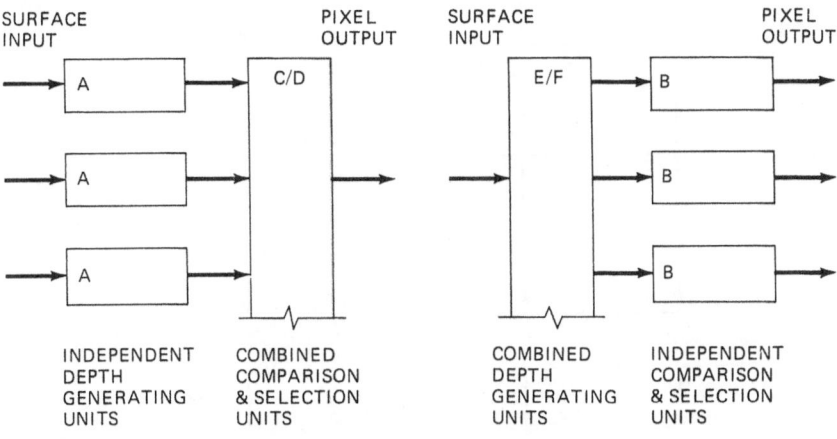

Figure 18 Parallel Processing Schemes

This gives four general schemes. The two main parallel implementations are shown in Figure 18. The labelled sub-systems: A, B, C, D, E and F are shown in Figures 19 to 24.

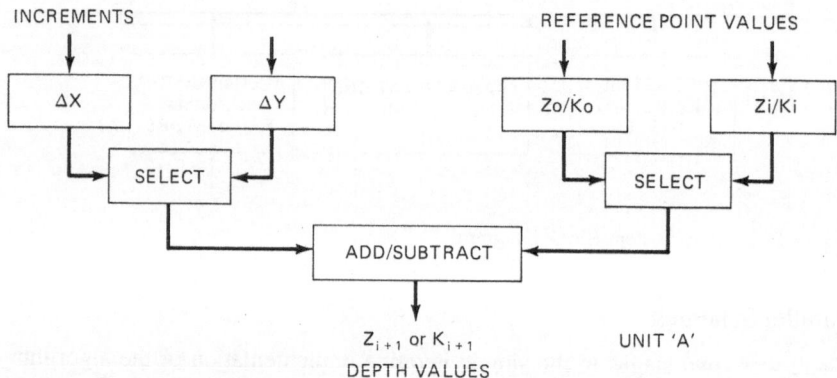

Figure 19 Independent Depth Generating Unit

The independent depth generating unit can be a microprocessor. However, the minimum arrangement for modelling a plane surface is given in Figure 19. The minimum unit can be combined in two ways to create a stream of depth values for neighbouring pixel positions. The first is a systolic solution, using a pipeline, the second is a synchronous solution, in this case using a binary, quad or oct tree of incrementing units, in the way shown. The advantage that independent units have over the combined units is that they can be implemented using general purpose microprocessors: as long as video rate output is not required, this arrangement provides the simplest scheme for exploring the modelling of curved surfaces.

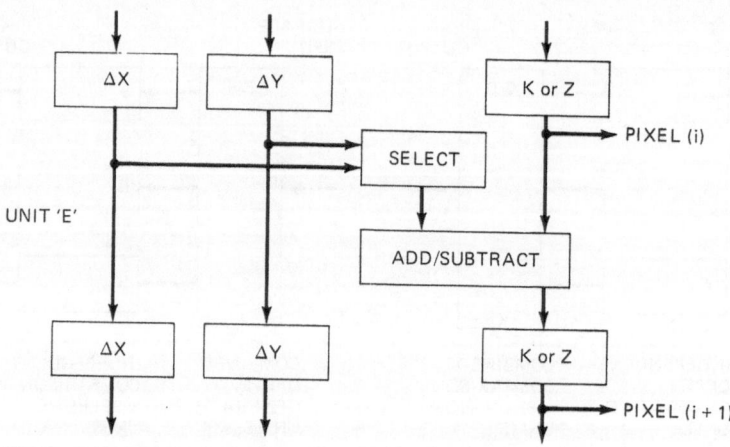

Figure 20 Pipelined Incrementing Unit

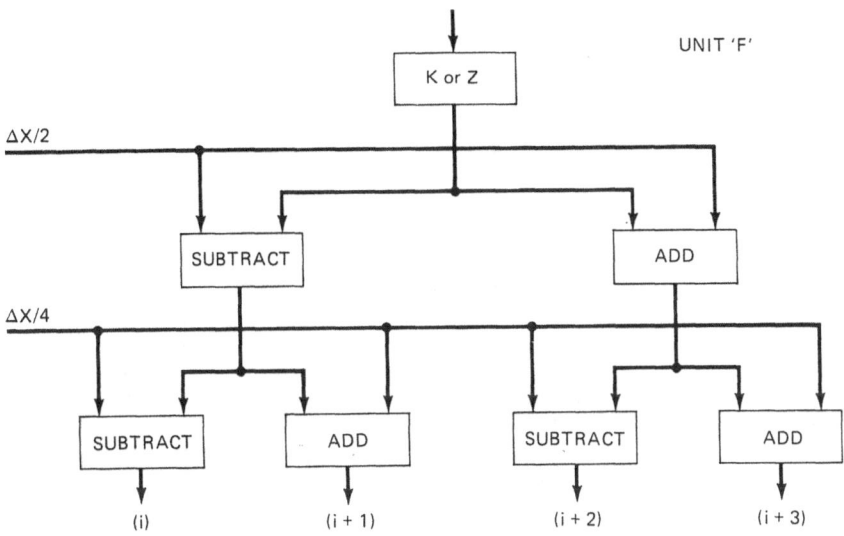

Figure 21 Synchronous Incrementing Unit

The combined depth generating units are shown in Figures 20 and 21. Figure 22 shows an independent comparison and selection unit. Figures 23 and 24 show the two combined units. In unit C depth values are passed from unit to unit in a pipelined system, in unit D values are compared with a broadcast value on a bus. An alternative to D is a tree structure made up from comparison units. In the example shown, a special bus driver was designed to maintain the maximum value on the bus from all the values being driven onto the bus, and to flag the units where this maximum value originated.

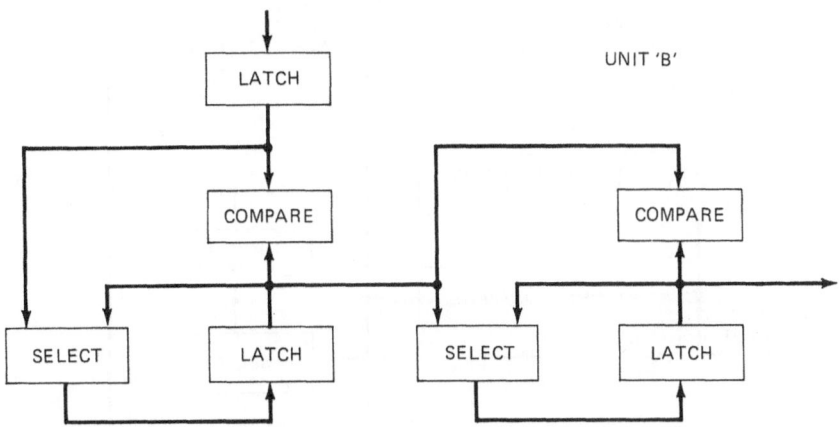

Figure 22 Independent Comparison and Selection Unit

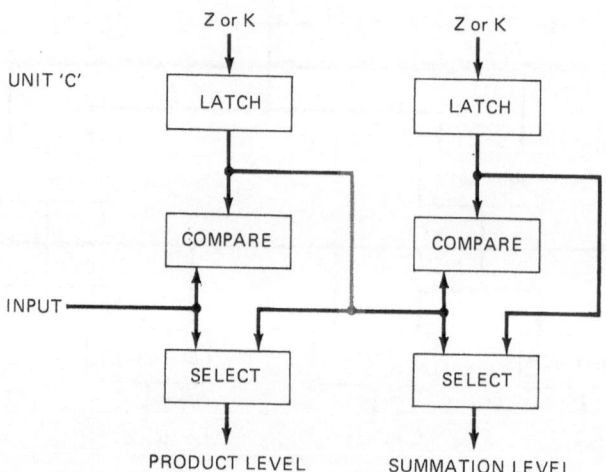

Figure 23 Pipelined Comparison and Selection Unit.

These comparison and selection units were initially designed in two stages corresponding to the product level and summation level of a simple Boolean expression. However, the structure of unit D suggested a way of implementing an array processor which would handle multiple level Boolean expression models. This approach also linked to a way of processing quadric surfaces.

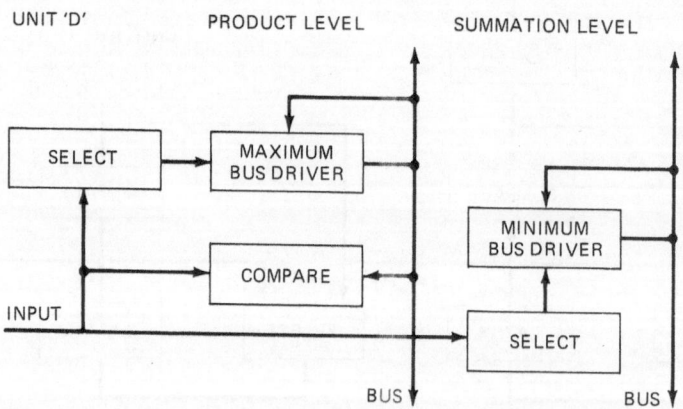

Figure 24 Synchronous Comparison and Selection Unit

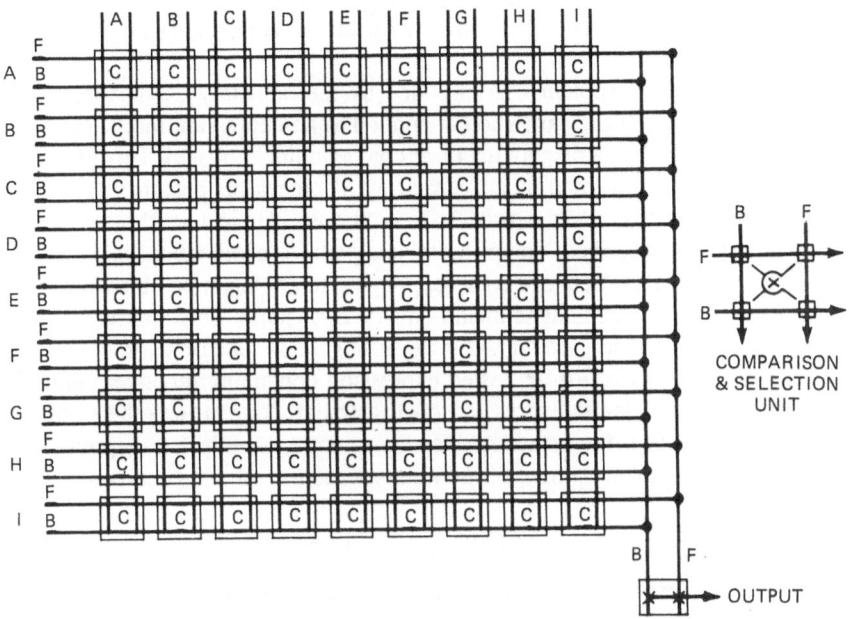

Figure 25 Comparison and Selection Array Processor

Quadric Surfaces, Convex Objects and Front and Back Pairs

A quadric surface can cut a viewing ray twice, and if it does it will intersect the ray with a front and back surface in much the same way that a product phrase made up from plane facets does. This means that the surface can be considered to be two variable surfaces called F for front and B for back. The hierarchical structure of a Boolean model allows a parallel scheme of the kind shown in Figure 25 to be constructed, which is capable of video rate output.

In this arrangement each of the comparison and selection units compares two sets of front and back depth values. Values passing from left to right in the array are either passed through or replaced by values on the vertical lines, depending on their relative location in the Boolean expression hierarchy and their relative values. This system generates the set of viewing ray spans which define where the viewing ray pierces solid objects in a particular line of sight. The final stage in the array represents a sorting bus or a sorting pipeline of the form described above.

A general solution to this problem requires a square array of $n.n$ comparison and selection units, because the worst case expression of the form $(A(B(C(D(E(F(G(H(I))))))))))$ requires (n^2) comparisons. The array processor can be implemented using either a synchronous or a systolic sorting process. In the latter case the data wave front has to flow diagonally across the array to maintain a continuous pixel refresh rate of output. The problems arise with this system when the worst case does not occur—many of the comparison and selection units become redundant.

A solution to this problem was provided by the boundary expansion. If the first form of the boundary expansion is applied to an expression model containing n convex units then a display list of n^2 convex units is created. This modified display list can be processed by a linear array of processors designed to handle boundary expressions. Such a processor is almost identical to the two stage processor already described. The primary data path for depth values is the same. Only the control is a little more complex, having to contain a one bit wide push down stack to hold intermediate inside-outside test values. This approach to the display problem seemed more versatile because given a pipe of n^2 processors. It was possible to process a fully nested expression containing n convex units, at one extreme, and a simple expression of n^2 elements long at the other: both in real time both in the same processor. There was not a complicated mapping task setting up an array in an optimal fashion, in order to use all of its components.

The Boundary Expansion and Clipping Volumes

The boundary expansion of the model shown in Figure 5 was:

$$@ (A.(B + (C.(D)))) \;=\; @A.[B + (C.(D))] + @B.[A.(A.(\overline{C} + (\overline{D}))]$$
$$+\; @C.[A.\overline{B}.(D)] + @D.[A.\overline{B}.C]$$

Each phrase in the expansion consists of a convex element, nominally a surface, followed by a volume definition inside a pair of square brackets. The phrase represents the section of the surface which lies inside the volume. In the expression shown there are four pieces of surface making up the boundary of the total object. The visible section of each convex surface can be determined in the same way used to display simple convex solids. Since these convex boundary pieces can be voids, in other words concave surfaces, this process has to be extended in the way summarised in Figure 15 to include convex voids.

The visible surface at each pixel position will be represented by a distance along the viewing ray. It is possible to test this distance against the front and back surface distances of the convex units making up the clipping volume in the square brackets. The inside outside results of these tests can be combined using the Boolean operators in the clipping expression, to determine whether the surface point is within the clipping volume and should be retained or whether it is outside and should be discarded. If the convex surface is processed first, and its visible surface distance is held in the first stage register of the comparison and selection unit, and then the half-spaces in the clipping expression are passed through the input register of the same unit, it is then possible to implement the clipping operation using a one bit wide push-down stack to hold intermediate inside outside results. The operation is illustrated in Figure 26 for the simple object $A+B$.

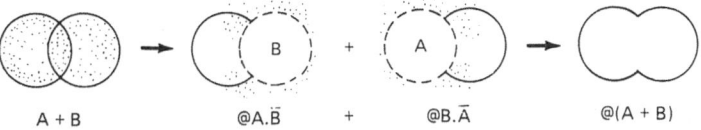

$A + B$ @A.$\bar{B}$ +   @B.$\bar{A}$ @(A + B)

Figure 26 Boundary Operator

A Prototype Display Processor

Of the four schemes outlined above the two processors with combined pipelined units appeared the easiest to implement in an efficient way, using the minimum of hardware. The one being investigated in current work is the one with a pipelined, combined depth generating unit. In this system depth values are established for a reference pixel point for all the plane half-spaces in a scene model. These depth values are then passed to the first comparison and selection unit, on one hand, and through an incrementing unit to the next processor on the other. In this way the depth values received by the second processor represent the planes at the next pixel position, so that the identical process can be repeated by each processor in the line, the difference being that the values operated on by neighbouring processors are for neighbouring pixel positions.

Block diagrams of a processor which can be used in a pipeline of this kind are given in Figures 27, 28 and 29. If the arrangement in Figure 27 allows increments to be subtracted as well as added, then these units can be made to follow any linear sequence of steps on the display screen, as an alternative to following a regular raster pattern. In Figure 28 the results of the comparisons I and J are combined with control data to give the select signals P, Q and the output enable signal R.

There are two comparison and selection stages. In the first one the visible front surface facet for each convex volume is selected for a pixel position by

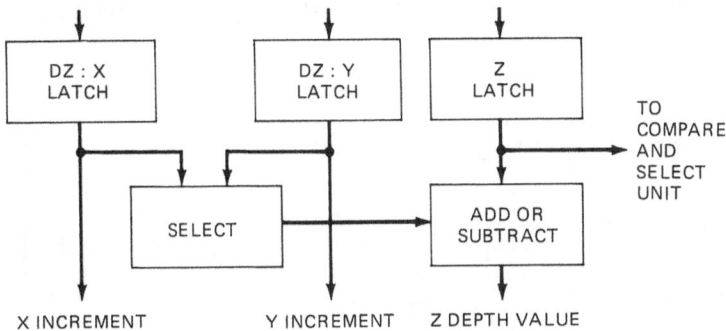

Figure 27 Incrementing Stage

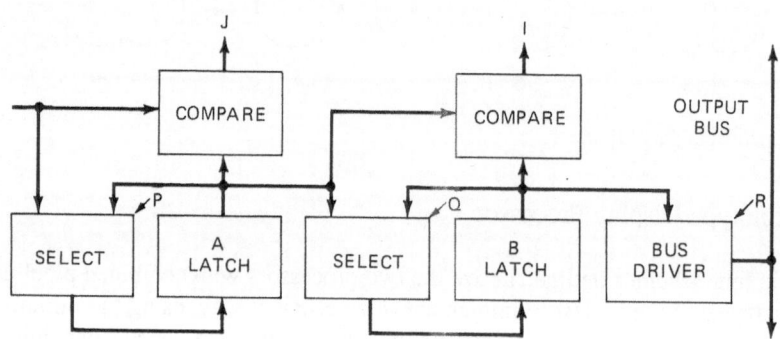

Figure 28 Comparison and Selection Stage

retaining the front surface with either the maximum depth value for solids or minimum depth value for voids. These front surface values are then clipped either by back surface values or by an explicit clipping expression. The second comparison stage selects the minimum visible front surface value from the values passed from the first stage.

It is necessary to select the depth value of the visible surface, but it is also necessary to select the name or some property of the visible surface for later reference. This is done using a slave selection unit controlled by the same signals P,Q and R shown in Figure 28. The property selection unit is shown in Figure 29. Outputs are driven onto a bus. Since only one unit contains the end of a display list there is no contention on the bus, as the last element in the list triggers the output.

The output from a simulation of this kind of system is given in Figure 30, where a single convex box and the union of two convex boxes are shown.

To obtain the subtraction of a convex box from another convex box in the way shown in Figure 31 can be achieved in two ways. Either the initial expression

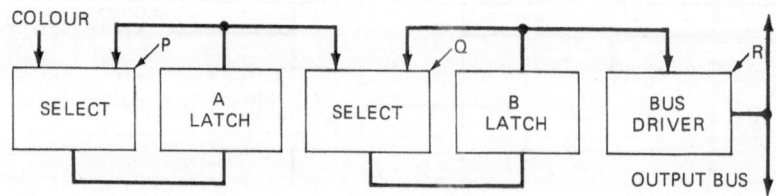

Figure 29 Property Value Selection Unit

Figure 30 Simple Convex Solids

Figure 31 Boolean Subtraction: Boundary Expansion

can be multiplied out in the following way:

$$A.B.C.D.E.F.(\overline{G.H.I.J.K.L}) =$$

$$\overline{G}.A.B.C.D.E.F + \overline{H}.A.B.C.D.E.F$$
$$\overline{I}.A.B.C.D.E.F + \overline{J}.A.B.C.D.E.F$$
$$\overline{K}.A.B.C.D.E.F + \overline{L}.A.B.C.D.E.F$$

(As a general approach this is clearly not an acceptable method. Two spheres subtracted from another sphere where each sphere is approximated by 200 intersecting half-spaces, will generate a display list of 8,080,000 elements using this form of expansion.) Or the boundary expansion can be used to give:

$$A.B.C.D.E.F.(\overline{G.H.I.J.K.L}) = @(A.B.C.D.E.F).[\overline{G.H.I.J.K.L}]$$
$$+@(\overline{G.H.I.J.K.L}).[A.B.C.D.E.F]$$

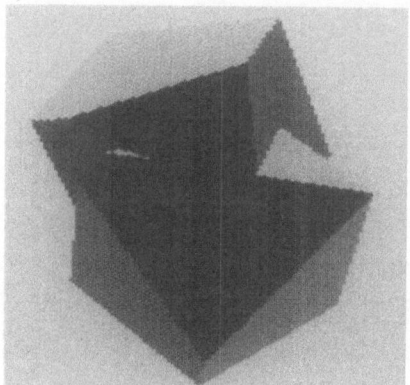

Figure 32 Cross Sections: Pixel Inside Outside Tests

This approach would give a display list of 1,800 elements for the three spheres. Figure 31 illustrates the subtraction of two boxes showing the way the image is made up from convex surface pieces. This method is not a total solution to the problem, but is is a major step in the right direction, given the combinatorial nature of the original model. Only the subdivision algorithms described below start to tame this form of display list explosion, which is inherent in the method of representation, and is essential for interference testing, in the general case.

It is possible to implement the algorithm so that objects are automatically clipped by the display plane in the way shown in Figure 32. Both the union of simple solids and the boundary model behave in the same way, giving a cross section cut. A prototype system to implement this display algorithm was built using eight processors constructed from TTL components. Real-time moving displays were obtained for simple objects, demonstrating the principle. A problem emerged, however, connected with the number of bits representing some of the depth values used in selecting visible surfaces.

Resolution, Accuracy and Depth Values

The display scheme is based on the cubic display space shown in Figure 33. The depth values for each plane are the Z values corresponding to different pixel positions, which satisfy the equations of the plane.

$$A.X + B.Y + C.Z + D = 0$$

In order to analyse the accuracy with which it is necessary to represent these depth values to obtain accurate images it is useful to define a dimension called the resolution unit. The idea is clear enough in the case of pixel positions and corresponds to the spacing between pixels. The aspect which is less clear is that

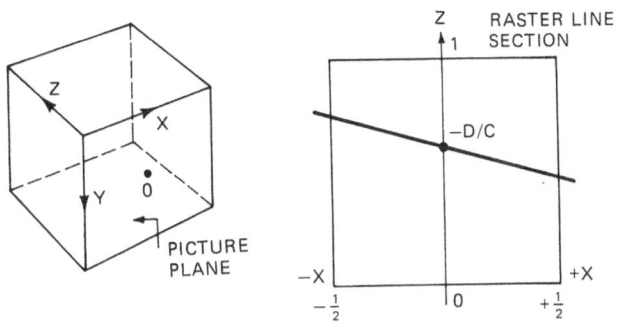

Figure 33 Display Cube

a spacing of the same dimension needs to be specified in the Z direction. For simplicity consider the unit cube as the display space and consider the same sized resolution unit being used in each of the X, Y and Z directions. The advantage of this approach is that for a resolution of 1:1024, three ten bit integer numbers will define any point in the display space.

It is possible to apply perspective transformations to points in a real object space and convert values which can range in size from 0 to effectively infinity, to integer values in the range of the cube's size in the way indicated in Figure 14. This makes it possible to design hardware which is set up to handle a specific range of integer values: the objective being speed and simplicity.

Following the same reasoning, when it was necessary to define a plane in the display space the first step seemed to be to restrict the plane's surface points so that they lay on a three dimensional grid with resolution unit spacing. This meant that the minimum non zero slope that could be represented across the cube would be one where a single step in the surface values took place in the way shown in Figure 34. This, however, posed problems for the simple incrementing scheme outlined above for defining plane surface depth values at neighbouring pixels. If only one resolution unit step was to be made traversing the cube, but increments were to be added on at each pixel position across the cube, then increments had to be a small fraction of the resolution unit size. If the resolution is given in powers of two in order to indicate the number of bits necessary to represent the value. Then if the resolution is n bits then an $n+1$ bit fractional increment is necessary to define a plane surface which only steps by one resolution unit across the main diagonal of the display cube. This requires a depth value of at least $2n+1$ bits in the way shown in Figure 34.

Even though the total object space viewing pyramid can be mapped into the display cube, and points on the rear surface of the cube represent an infinite distance in object space, it is still possible to have planes which are orientated in the way shown in Figure 35.

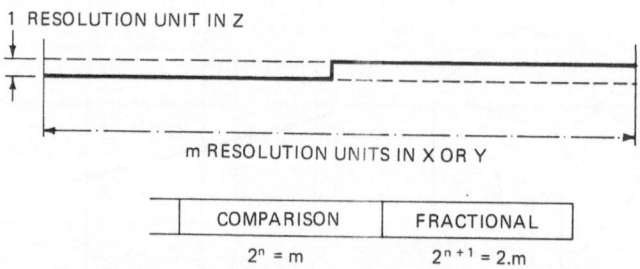

Figure 34 Representing Minimum Slope

Again, this raises problems generating depth values for such planes using the simple value and incrementing scheme outlined above. The limiting case will be a surface which enters the rear of the display cube at one pixel position and leaves the front of the display cube at the neighbouring pixel position. Any surface which is steeper than this has to be treated as a plane perpendicular to the display surface. Other planes which leave the rear surface of the display cube have to have an initial depth value greater than the $2n+2$ bit value already described. In the limiting case either or both the X and Y increments will be the depth of the display cube. The worst case is the virtually perpendicular plane in the corner, which is diagonal to the starting point, in the way shown in Figure 35. Again, the number of increments between these two points is twice the resolution, in other words $n+1$ bits. To hold a depth values of the required range needs a word size of $3n+3$ bits, as shown in Figure 35 for a resolution of n bits.

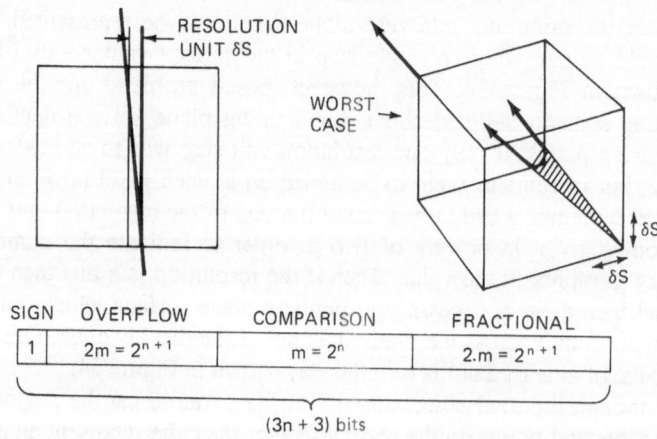

Figure 35 Depth Values and Word Size

Figure 36 Edge Effects

Intersection Boundaries: The Comparison Stage

Although the incrementing unit required depth values of $3n+3$ bits, there seemed no reason initially why the comparison and selection operation should not be carried out on the truncated values made up from the "comparison field" shown in Figure 35. The difficulties which resulted from this approach are shown in Figures 36 to 37. In Figure 36 the contrast between using the full comparison and fractional fields together and the comparison field alone are shown. The edges of the cubes break up in the latter case. In the former case edges are defined in the way that a line interpolator would define them, given the pixel grid as its framework.

Figure 37 illustrates an alternative approach to the problem of edge definition. Each facet of the objects is modelled by a plane surface which is clipped by a pyramidical volume with its apex at the eye and each of its sides passing through the edge of the facet. When this volume is transformed in perspective into the display cube, it becomes a prism with its sides perpendicular to the display screen. These perpendicular planes can only be used in inside-outside tests. Although the distances to these planes have to be generated accurately by the incrementing unit, it is only the signs of these distances which are needed in inside-outside tests, and which therefore affect the comparison and selection operation. This is illustrated by Figure 37 where all the original edges of the two overlapping cubes which modelled in this way, are correctly defined. It is the boundary between the cubes which indicates the lack of accuracy with which the depth values are being compared. Figure 37 compares the two approaches using the same size comparison values.

It is the "placement" problem where objects are either intentionally or accidentally made to overlap during interactive volume building that make this set of examples important. They show that edge modelling, although attractive, does not make it possible to reduce the accuracy with which depth values have to be

Figure 37 Edge Modelling and Interference Edges

represented if all edges are to be defined as exactly as the resolution of the display permits. The facets in the examples in Figures 36 and 37 meet at angles greater than 45 degrees. It seemed likely that the problems encountered with these examples would be substantially worse if they had more acutely angled edges. In Figure 38 a cross section through two surfaces is given, one front and one back, which are very close to each other, and which generate a thin wedge shaped volume. If the increments for these two surfaces are made in resolution sized units, then a fringe pattern is generated at the edge. It can be seen from Figure 38 that this is an interference effect between the two different stepping frequencies of the two surfaces. Only where the front surface is represented by a smaller distance value than the back surface at a pixel position does the wedge exist.

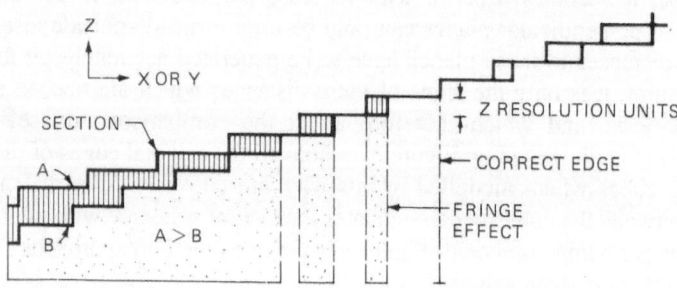

Figure 38 Fringe Effects

Vertical Wedge: Fringe Effects

Intersection of a Vertical and a Horizontal Wedge

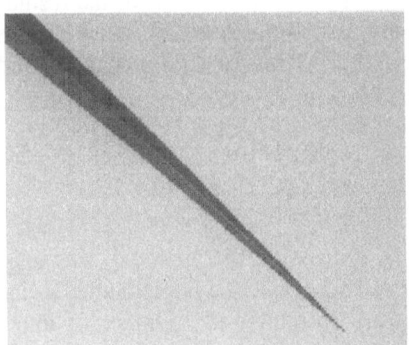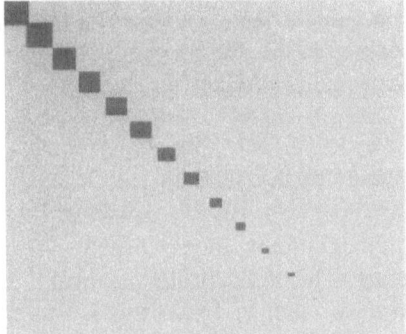

Union of a Vertical and a Horizontal Wedge

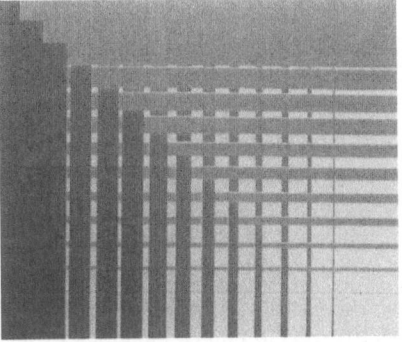

Figure 39 The Plaiding Effect

Where there is equality, gaps appear at the edge. Even if "equality" was considered to "exist"—n other words, the fact that the front surface distance equalled the back surface distance was taken to define a solid enitity—this would only move the fringe effect further out. The decision to make equality not "exist" was based on considering what would happen to a thin wedge such as an aircraft wing if it were displayed in perspective, moving further and further away. The perspective transformation would bring its surfaces closer and closer together and if equality were considered to "exist" the result would be that the wing would spread wider and wider as it moved into the distance rather than getting narrower. Figure 39 illustrates the effect shown in Figure 38.

It is clear that two facets which lie between 45 degrees and 90 degrees to the display plane will not create this effect even with steps in resolution sized units. This is because at each pixel position the surface steps forward or backwards by at least one unit. When this fact is linked with the way that straight lines are always represented by stepping sequences of m or $m+1$ units (m an appropriate sized integer) then it is clear that once one of these surfaces crosses the other, it becomes impossible for it to recross or touch the other again. The minimum non zero slope permitted for a surface is restricted by the size chosen for the resolution units. If the resolution is n bits the only way to obtain a step at each pixel position in this limiting case is to use the full $2n+1$ bits of the comparison and fractional fields taken together.

Integrated Circuits

Although the prototype display system was successful, the approach was only going to be economically practical if the processors could be implemented as integrated circuits. To do this it was necessary to reduce the number of interprocessor links. Of the four parallel schemes outline above, two permitted this reduction in a reasonably simple way: the tree structured incrementing scheme, and the pipelined incrementing scheme. The number of bits necessary for the comparison and selection stage ruled out both forms of combination into a single unit. Both the combined incrementing units could be rearranged to process their values serially, while outputs were required in parallel at the clock rate. The first system to be examined from this point of view was the tree structured processor. However, the eventual desire to implement a scheme where increments were also incremented to give curved surfaces seemed easier to accomplish with the second arrangement. The tree structured system was developed as a reconfigurable systolic array processor system, but there has not been time or resources to explore this possibility much further to date. In practice, once the systolic method of processing had been established (1975) there were a number of ways in which the internal processing of each unit could be arranged. The objective was to reduce the clock cycle time to as short a period as the technology and the architecture would allow.

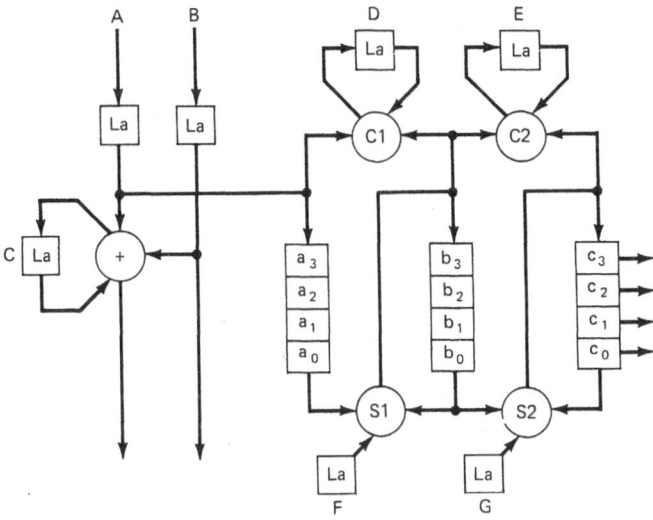

Figure 40 Serial 1 Bit Machine

The simplest scheme consists of a one bit wide input stream for depth data values, in the way illustrated in Figure 40. The shift registers are shown schematically to be four units long, in practice they would need to be the length of the comparison and fractional field which is being used. The only drawback of this arrangement was that a pipeline over thirty processors long was necessary to hold the depth value for a single plane. An alternative solution resulted from increasing the width of the incrementing unit. In this case the addition (+) and the two comparisons *(C)* require a carry to be included in the operation which has to be completed each clock cycle.

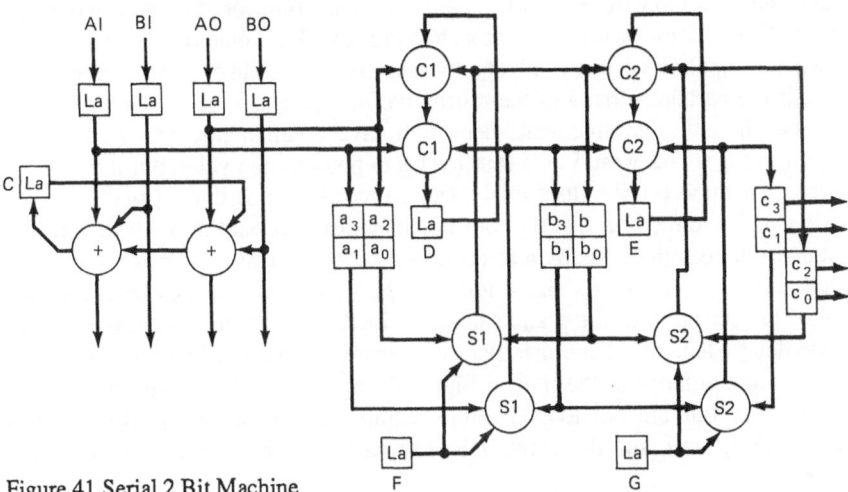

Figure 41 Serial 2 Bit Machine

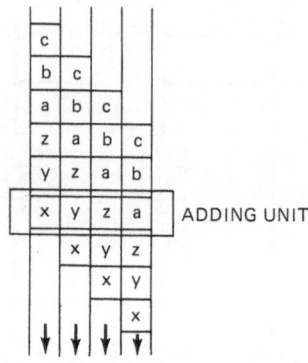

Figure 42 Systolic Processing

The result is that half the number of processing units are required to hold the value of one plane in their incrementing unit latches. This means that half the number of pixels have to be processed per plane. The limit of this approach is set by the carry chain speed. Calculations were carried out for an eight bit wide system based on data for the UK5000 cmos gate array. Using a carry look ahead circuit appeared to allow a 33 bit depth value to be processed with a clock cycle time of 100 ns, sufficient to support a display of 512x512 in real time. The layout of Figure 41 suggests an alternative way of arranging the processing. If a latch were placed between each of the one bit adders and one bit comparators, to make the operation truly systolic, then the delay time of the carry would be saved. The difficulty with this approach is illustrated if a map of the data passing down the pipeline of this kind of processor is made. Take as an example the completely parallel version of the schematic four bit system shown in Figure 42. At first sight this arrangement seemed to save components. The adding unit shown in Figure 42 would take four cycles to process one value but it would be processing three other values at the same time. It is possible to place a comparison either directly in parallel or one delay after this addition. However, it is not possible to follow this by a selection operation, at least as far as a particular depth value is concerned. The whole four bit comparison has to be completed before the selection of the plane can be decided. It is therefore necessary to include delay elements in the data path in the way shown in Figure 43, where an interesting similarity to the unit in Figure 40 appears. The only differences are where carry bits are not looped round within the unit but are passed on to a neighbouring unit, and the depth values in each shift register are not from the same plane.

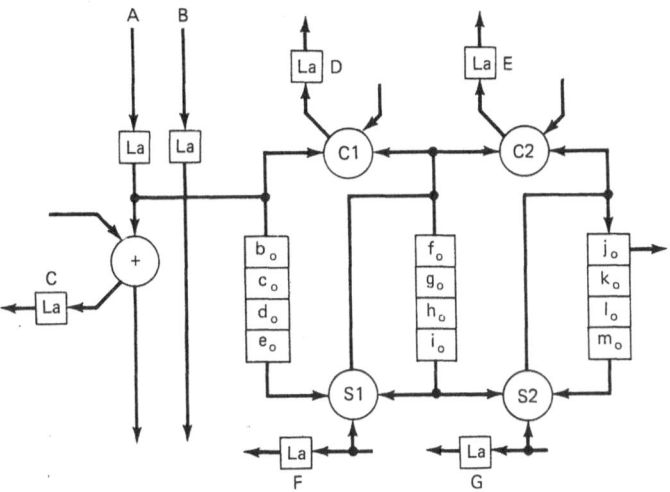

Figure 43 Parallel Systolic Processing

Although there are many ways of combining these processors in parallel, there seem to be two principles which can be applied to produce the optimum IC. The first results in the use of the scheme shown in Figure 40 rather than that shown in Figure 43, because this partitioning of the system gives a unit which can be packed onto an IC in whatever number the current technology will allow, without increasing the pin count for the IC. The equivalence between these two circuits is reflected in the way both can be arranged to give a bit sliced implementation of the pipeline. The units from Figure 40 have to be arranged as shown in Figure 44. By arranging the delays in the incrementing pipeline appropriately and passing output to fast shift registers in the same way used in frame stores it is possible to reduce the pin counts to the same number that a scheme built up from the units in Figure 43 would allow—without a cumulative increase in carry pins as the IC's processor count is raised. The second principle is that doubling the data path for the arithmetic and comparison operations halves the necessary pipe length and reduces the ratio of memory cells to logic in each processor. On the other hand it increases the addition time, though not necessarily in a linear way. There is consequently a design trade-off to be made depending on the nature of the implementation. Where register cells are relatively large a wider data path appears justifiable, where they are smaller, less so. The design for the UK5000 used an adder of up to eight bits wide by using a carry look ahead circuit. This was done because only a few units would have been produced and the number of register cells available on the gate array was limited. In contrast, the advantage of the structure in Figure 40 (developed in 1975 for the tree processor in Figure 21) was how shift registers from neighbouring processors could be stacked together as a block of memory. Mixing memory technology and control logic on a custom IC was not

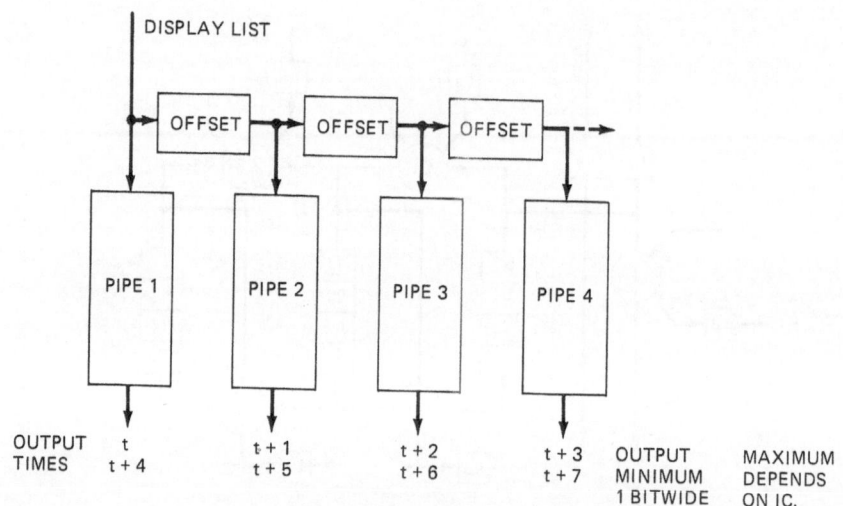

Figure 44 Equivalent Bit Slice, Multiple Pipeline Processing

a facility available to the project using SERC fabrication facilities. It was, however, a long term option since memory blocks are placed on microprocessor ICs as standard practice.

Figure 45 shows a schematic floor plan for the ultimate IC. Because the shift registers are all the same length, the access point to an equivalent set of memory

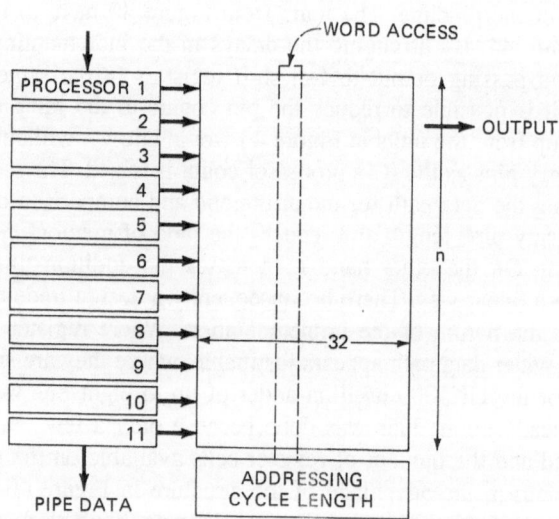

Figure 45 IC Floor Plan

registers will be at the same place at the same instant in time. This makes it possible to use a cycling addressing scheme and a standard block of memory. The particular advantage that this has is that a 32 word wide unit can be provided, but the number of words cycled through can be software selected depending on the required resolution. Although one bit wide processing provides the shortest latch to latch delays, hence the fastest clock rates (the adoption of multiple pipelines makes this less critical for speed), the arrangement shown in Figure 45 will work with one or more bits wide data paths depending on the properties of the final design. Another factor which has been difficult to assess is how long a pipeline needs to become to give the best system performance.

Pipeline Control and Priming

In concept, the simplest way of using this kind of machine in real time is to have a pipeline long enough to hold the maximum length display list likely to be encountered. In practice the scene is subdivided until the display list is the same length as the pipe. However, while the primary display algorithms were being explored the simple approach was adopted. If a technology could be found which sufficiently reduced the size of these processors then this approach would give a very simple system useful in quite a variety of applications. With this objective in mind, first CCD technology (1975-6) was investigated, then n-mos (1976-84), and finally c-mos. However, it seems that the simple approach is still some way off. When it became clear that a complex scene would require a large number of integrated circuits, particularly if the processor was extended to handle curved surfaces, then it became important to consider what facilities were necessary to allow the pipeline to be used with a scene subdivision or other scene coherence preprocessor.

Consider a display list of 50 units long, and a pipe of 25 pixel processors in length. If the display screen is divided into four quadrants and the display list is subdivided to remove elements which do not feature in each quadrant, then four new display lists will result. If the new display areas require display lists of 20 elements, 4 elements, 15 elements and 17 elements respectively then the display pipeline will be able to work in real time. Each list can be padded out to give a list 25 units long, which can then be cycled through the pipe until the required number of pixel values have been generated for each of the display lists, the lists being swapped as each section of the display screen is completed in sequence.

Where complex scene models are being processed there may well be a need to sub-divide the screen to the level of a few pixels, for parts of the image. In this case the display list must be reduced to a length which is less than the number of pixels required, as well as less than the pipe length. This means that some way of managing several lists of less than the pipe length must be found, if continuous pixel rate output is to be maintained. There were two inter-related problems which had to be resolved to make this possible. First it was necessary

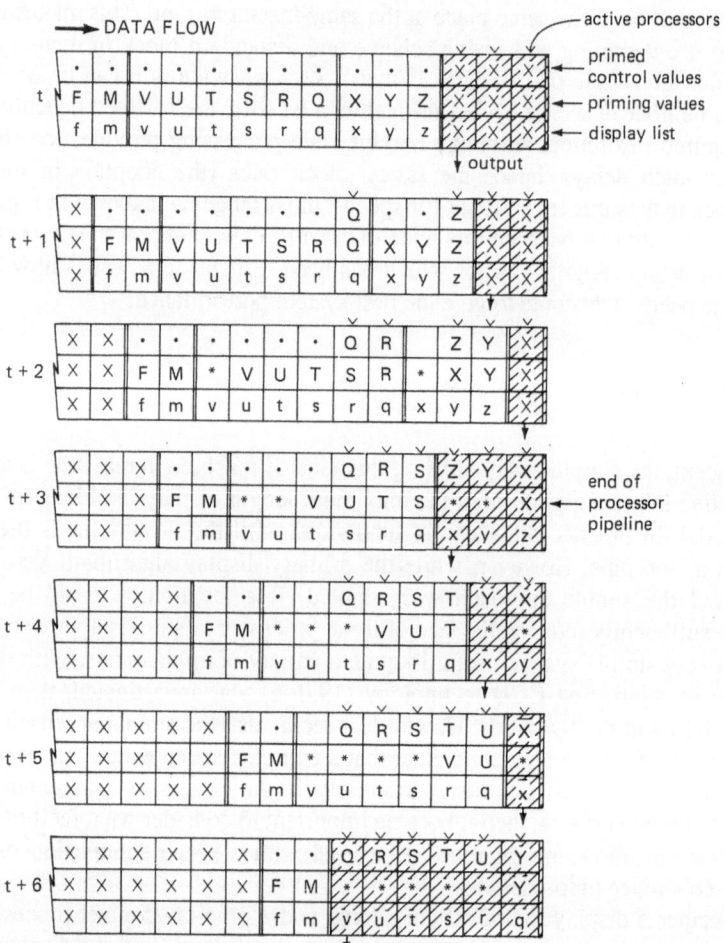

Figure 46 Multiple Lists in a Processor Pipeline

to process variable length lists and second it was necessary to prime the processor with new incrementing directions each time a new list was entered. The simplest approach found so far is illustrated in Figure 46. The first requirement is that only one list is generating output at any instant in time. A processor which is producing an output value can only do so once it has processed the whole display list. The output will always be generated, therefore, at the tail end of a list. The only way of maintaining continuous output is to allow each list to generate output, only when it is the last list in the line: the shaded lists in Figure 46.

In order for a list to be processed the processors it is entering have to be primed with control data which determine the incrementing direction. This priming information is shown in capital letters in the diagram. At time $t+1$ the two lists *(v,u,t,s,r,q)* and *(x,y,z)* are each entering the processor which is their own list length from the end of the pipe, so evaluation has to start for each of these lists. In both these cases the processors are primed with the incrementing control data Q and Z. In the next block period the primary list has moved one step down the pipeline. In order to keep up, the priming data list has to be passed down the pipeline at twice the speed, once list processing starts. This ensures that the priming data list reverses its direction in the processors in the way shown. This is the only scheme yet found which allows multiple lists to be handled, and at the same time allows the priming information to be entered with the list it controls. Clearly, before a display list reaches the "active" primed processors it has to be passed passively down the pipeline, the incrementing operation suspended, and the output instruction masked out.

It is possible to extend this priming operation. If partial results from a previous calculation are stored in a frame buffer they can be passed down the pipeline in this way to the appropriate processor where they can be used as the starting point for a subsequent calculation. It is this facility which makes it possible to use this kind of processor for ray tracing algorithms. It only seems practical at present to process the first level node in a ray tracing tree in real time. However, it looks as though subsequent levels can be processed more slowly, for example to improve the rendering of a static portion of a display. The exact way in which this kind of processing can be accommodated, given the alternative ways of partitioning the pipeline for IC fabrication, is the subject of current analysis. Primary illumination rays can already be obtained using the shadow volumes described below. Secondary reflections and refracted rays are being explored in the context of curved surface modelling techniques described below.

Patterns and Shadows

One objective for using a divide and conquer preprocessor on a scene display list is to minimise the need for a boundary expansion operation. However, the clipping phrase structure is also a very useful and powerful construct for handling patterns and shadows. Figures 47 and 48 illustrate its use to generate surface colour patterns. In order to get these results it is necessary to extend the way that the slave processor depends on the depth selection unit. In the simple examples given so far, colour has always been associated with a surface.

In pattern projection it is necessary to associate the colour of surface property with the clipping volume. In Figure 47 the flag is a plane surface which is cut into red and blue sections to give the pattern shown. Transforming such a tile is the same operation as transforming an object: a rotated flag is shown. The only difficulty encountered with this example is shown in Figure 48. When this tile was brought forward until it cut the display screen it created a shadow, which was generated by the clipping volume.

Figure 47 Pattern Tile: Colours Projected onto Surfaces

Figure 48 Identical Front and Back Surfaces

This is a property of the algorithm designed to handle boundary phrase representations of solid objects so that cross section cuts are automatically created when the object cuts the display screen. The solution is to provide a rear surface to the flag. The problem with this is that at some point a thin object such as a flag will become so thin that the front and back surfaces coincide. This is equivalent to $A.!A$ which does not exist. This problem is a variation on the problem of whether to make "equality" exist or not. Clearly in this case it must be made not to exist to be consistent with the previous discussion. The solution to this problem is to say that the flag is a two dimensional sheet like object and like a boundary has no thickness. This means that the flag is treated as the Boundary expansion of $A.!A$. In other words:

$$@A.\bar{A} \quad + \quad @\bar{A}.A$$

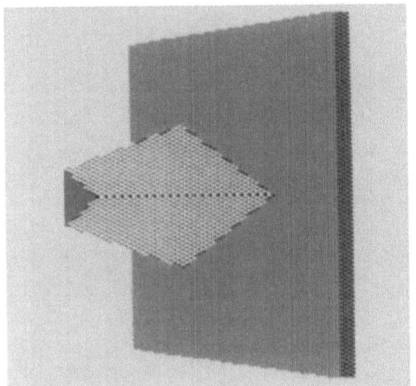

Figure 49 Shadow Volumes as Clipping Phrases

Cast Shadows, Multiple Light Sources and Facet Models

Figures 49 and 50 illustrate the use of the boundary phrase display process to create cast shadows. If the shadow volumes are assumed to have already been created, then casting shadows is a very similar process to that of projecting patterns onto a surface using clipping expressions. In the example in Figure 49 the shadow volume is the truncated pyramid which is the shadow cast by the triangle cutting off the apex of the pyramid. There are two interesting problems which are associated with casting shadows. The first is generating the shadow volumes as part of the real time exercise so that it is possible to have moving light sources. The second is generating umbra and pen-umbra, where there are extended or multiple light sources.

Consider the shadow which will be cast by the cube $A.B.C.D.E.F$ it will be necessary to define the silhouette of the object as seen from the light source. The shadow volume will be the projection of the silhouette centred on the light source. It is possible to create this volume by taking the union of the individual shadow volumes generated by the separate polygonal facets of the object.

To do this, however, it is necessary to have the edges of the polygonal facets defined explicitly. If the Boundary expansion is applied to the cube then the facet A will exist as the phrase:

$@A. [B.C.D.E.F]$ or $@A.[B.C.D.E]$

if the facet opposite to A is F, and it is removed. It is clear from examining this representation that it is not necessary to define the edges in terms of vertex pairs, it is more useful in this context to use the dual form given by facet pairs. This means that the edges of the facet can be given by the list:

$A/B, A/C, A/D, A/E$

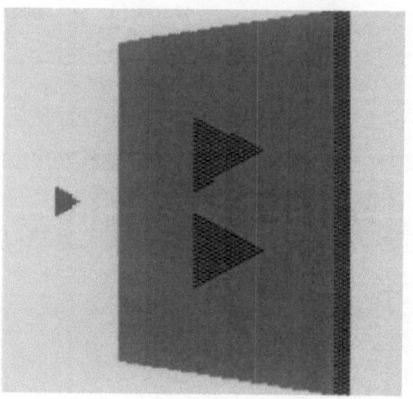 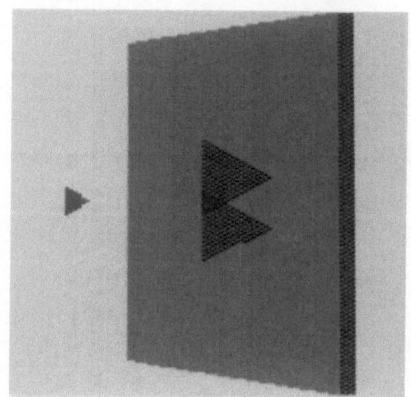

Figure 50 Multiple Light Sources

Given that edges are defined by pairs of planes it is possible to define any plane through the edge by taking the appropriate linear combination of the coefficients of the two planes meeting at the edge. If the light source is taken as a point at position P, then the shadow volume of the facet A of the cube will be the pyramid of planes passing through P and the edges of the facet A. If these planes are represented by the edge and the point which generates them then the shadow volume will be:

$$A.(A/B)p.(A/C)p.(A/D)p.(A/E)p$$

This volume can then be used as a clipping volume to create shadows on the surface of other volumes. The display lists for Figures 49 are derived from:

$$(G.H.I.J.K.L).[A.(A/B)p.(A/C)p.(A/D)p] + (A).[B.C.D]$$

The casting of multiple shadows raises an interesting problem in the treatment of the associated or property data. In simple cases of occultation, one surface and its colour is replaced by another. However, when there are multiple light sources and a point is partially in shadow, this form of simple replacement is no longer adequate.

It is necessary to combine the property data in some appropriate way. The simplest solution in this case is to form the logical OR of the two property bit strings. If each light source has a unique bit position in the illumination code then ORing together these values when a surface point lies inside both shadow volumes, permits an output to be generated which is capable of representing all the necessary combinations that will affect an illumination algorithm. Given 24 bits to hold colour or property data, this approach will allow 24 different light sources to be modelled, creating shadow effects in any combination that results from moving objects or light sources in a scene. Although the pipeline architecture limits the number of combinations because of an internal register size, it is possible to run the data through multiple pipelines, giving a form of array processing to increase the effective word size.

Clipping Local and Global

The clipping function was developed initially to process pieces of surface. In other words, if a boundary section lay outside its clipping volume then it was deemed not to exist. Once this facility was incorporated into a processor it was a relatively simple step to extend it to give projected shadows and a pattern painting capability. The illustrations demonstrate the results. However, there was one problem which appeared when the use of clipping volumes in this way was studied further. It seemed desirable to be able to project patterns onto a total volume rather than onto each of its convex pieces, for no other reason than to shorten the display list:

$$X.[P1] \quad + \quad Y.[P1] \quad = \quad (X+Y).[P1]$$

But this required the ability to apply clipping operations at the second comparison and selection stage of the processor. Since only one depth value is retained at this stage, this was not a viable option. What was possible was the equivalent of the clipping operation carried out on the property values alone, at the second stage. If the required surface in this case $(X+Y)$ had been selected to pass to the second stage, then it could be tested against the clipping volume—not to remove it—but to allow property data associated with the clipping phrase to be selected or not. If the surface $(X+Y)$ should lie outside the clipping volume, its depth value would still be retained as belonging to the visible surface at the pixel point in question.

At first sight the idea of providing a true clipping operation at the second stage of selection seemed to be a path back to the array processing solution, until the hierarchical structure of the Boolean expression was re-examined. Consider the boundary expansion:

$$@(A.(B + (C.(D)))) \rightarrow @ A.(B + (C.(D)))$$
$$+ @ B.(A.(\bar{C} + (\bar{D})))$$
$$+ @ C.(A.\bar{B}.(D))$$
$$+ @ D.(A.\bar{B}.C)$$

This can be arranged to give:

$$@(A.(B + (C.(D))) \quad + A.(@B.(\bar{C} + (\bar{D}))$$
$$+ \bar{B}.(@C.(D)$$
$$+ @ D.C))$$

This contains 13 rather than the original 16 convex units. Where the alternative boundary expansion is employed this will be reduced to 10 units:

$$@A.(B+(C.(D))) \quad + \quad A.(@B \quad + \quad @C.(D) \quad + \quad @D.C)$$

This arrangement does not appear to require much of an extension to each pipeline processor, however, depending on the scene description, a stack will be required to hold the currently active front and back surfaces of the factored out clipping phrases. For example, the processing sequences to clip the surface element @C will be:

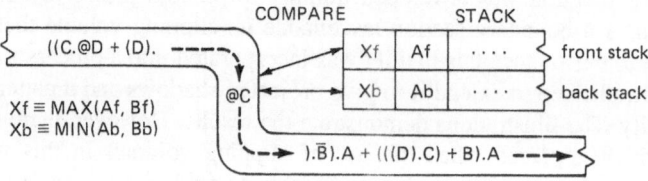

Figure 51 Stacked Clipping Phrases

The extra registers in each processor to provide the stacking facility did not appear to be justified in the earlier designs. However, when the various possibilities for implementing curved surfaces started to be explored, one option needed stacked values. If a stack existed for one purpose, it could also be used for the other. In the example given the stack is strictly speaking unnecessary, the stacked values of Xf and Xb incorporate the values of Af and Ab. Af and Ab are only retained in case there should be multiple sub-expressions requiring A to be recovered. For example: .

$$A.(B + (C.(D)) + (E)).(F + (G))$$

However, if this is partially expanded to give:

$$A.(B + (C.(D))) + A.(B + (E)) + A.(F + (G))$$

then the full boundary expansion can be avoided: a list which could contain 47 convex units being replaced by a list containing only 23 units. Should the introduction of facilities in a processor to handle curved surfaces require a stack, one of the options this would open up is a two stage true-clipping operation.

Regularised Set Operations and Two Dimensional Objects

The introduction of the back surface to the flag in Figure 48 raised a series of interesting problems. Equality between front and back surfaces had been decided to not "exist". The decision to make equality between interacting surface and clipping planes "exist" was based on the display of the boundary expansion of the simple object $(A+B)$, where A is a cube and B is the same cube translated sideways so that four of its sides remain co-planar with A and partially overlap with A.

Equality Does Not Exist
$@\ (A + B)$ $@\ (A . \bar{B})$

Equality Does Exist
$@\ (A + B)$ $@\ (A . \bar{B})$

$@\ (B + A)$ $@\ (A . \bar{C})$

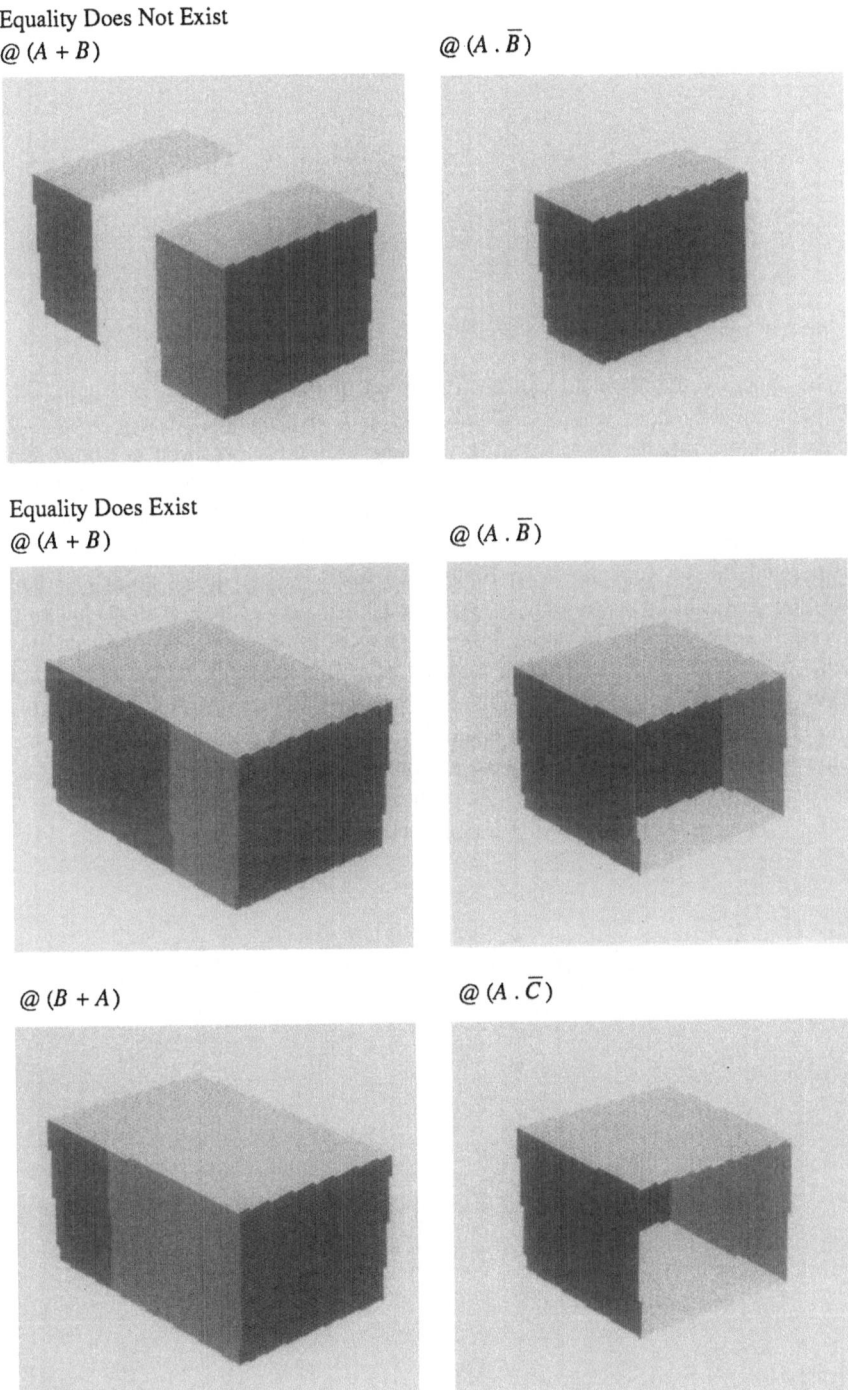

Figure 52 Regularised Sets and Hanging Faces

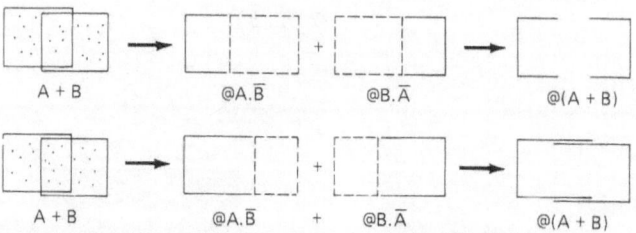

Figure 53 Clipping Phrase Equality Problem

Schematically the problem can be illustrated in the way shown in Figure 53. Where equality does not "exist" the boundary expansion can clip pieces of coincident surface to leave a gap in the way shown for $@(A+B)$ in Figure 52. The problem does not occur for $@(A./B)$. Making equality "exist" fills in the gap, depending on the order of the convex elements different final images. However, it also gives a different result for $@(A./B)$, were hanging faces are generated in the way shown in Figure 52. Each method gives good and bad results! It would be convenient to have the subtraction volume without hanging faces, it is very useful to define box-like objects given by expressions such as $@(A./C)$ where $/C$ is the cube A with its near side missing. It is essential not have holes in objects defined as $@(A+B)$, when $A+B$ does not. A solution to this dilema (so far, in that no counter examples have been found!) is provided by the alternative form of the boundary expansion. If a different swapping rule is used for expanding $(A+B)$ to give $@A+@B$ rather than the clipped pieces $@A./B$ + $@B./A$ then the result is shown schematically in Figure 54.

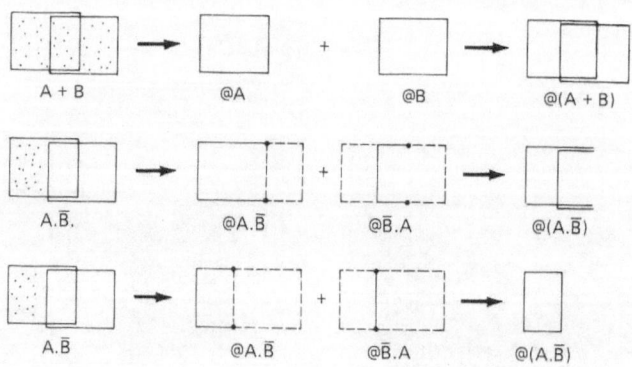

Figure 54 Regularised Set Operations and Hanging Faces

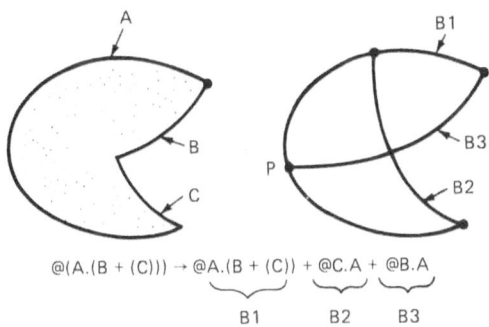

$$@(A.(B + (C))) \rightarrow @A.(B + (C)) + @C.A + @B.A$$

Figure 55 Equality and Hierarchy

This expansion allows the correct rendering of $A+B$ to be made whether equality "exists" or not. At the same time the expansion allows hanging faces to be generated or not, depending on the interpretation of equality, when using subtraction operations. This allows a choice to be made, at the level of individual components in a scene, of the kind of results that are required. By allowing an operator-type to determind the results, an implementation of regularised set operations can coexist with non-regularised set operations. This allows three dimensional and two dimensional objects to be correctly generated and displayed by the same system.

In Figure 52 the output from $@(A+B)$ and $@(B+A)$ is different. In this case, where two pieces of surface are identical, the first one entered into the register of the second stage comparison and selection unit is the one displayed. This is done to cope with the kind of problem which can appear in the form illustrated in Figure 54. Given the pieces of boundary shown, as long as $B1$ is processed first then the point P which belongs to $B3$ which could replace P of $B1$, will be discarded. If $B3$ were processed first then the surface of A with the colour red, say, could end up with a blue line across it, given the appropriate pixel spacings, and B being blue. If the expansion order is reversed then this swapping order has to be reversed.

Towards Curved Surfaces

It was clear from the start of the hardware design, when an incrementing scheme was adopted, many curves could be generated using a multiple incrementing scheme. Using a difference table for a function merely required hardware which would allow increments to be incremented themselves. The problem was how to handle the results. One possibility based on curved line work carried out in Heriot Watt University was to walk along the surface, using the value of the function, positive or negative, to determine the next increment to make. This form   of

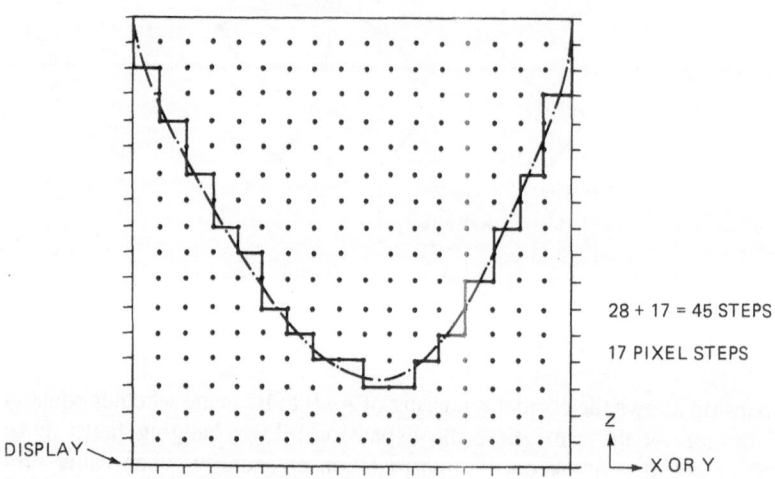

28 + 17 = 45 STEPS

17 PIXEL STEPS

DISPLAY

Z

X OR Y

Figure 56 Surface Crawling

surface crawling, tied to the scan line subdivision algorithm of Watkins, was suggested as a possible way of implementing curved surfaces. The binary sub-division of a display space—scan line, quad or oct tree—in a divide and conquer algorithm, splits the image up into units which either contain a single surface or are of a pixel cell size. Once a section of a surface has been partitioned in this way it is clear that the potential form of many surface equations can be used in a surface following scheme of the form indicated in Figure 56. The difficulty which seemed inherent in this approach was the number of steps which could be required to follow a curve. In the example shown, there are 45 incrementing steps to cover 17 pixel positions. This kind of difference is cumulative, and seemed to imply that a real time solution was impossible following this course.

During the early work, this problem was ignored, or rather postponed for later analysis. The real time display of polyhedral objects presented difficulties enough. However, once it was clear that polyhedra could be processed in real time in a general way, given the appropriate hardware, the problems of curved surfaces were re-examined. This work is incomplete but its general drift is out-line below. The reason for following this line of investigation is shown by the Mach Banding effects in Figure 57. Although methods such as the carpenter's algorithm will recursively provide as close an approximation to a curved surface as needed by cutting off corners, it is hard to obtain the fineness of grain neces-sary to avoid edge effects, in a real time system. One solution to this problem is to adopt a post processing, averaging operation such as that employed in smooth shading algorithms, another is to adopt a better form of interpolation.

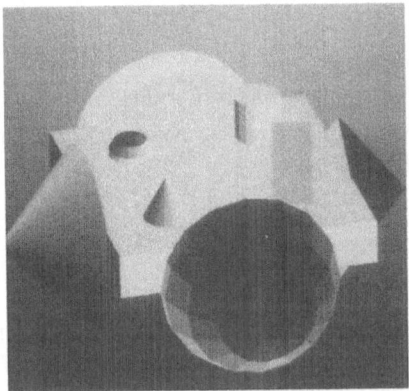

Figure 57 Mach Banding

The first method studied was one based on quadric surfaces. This was for two reasons. The first was that it had been decided in a search for real time solutions to work directly with distances from pixel positions along viewing rays. This seemed possible with quadrics. The second reason was that the maximum number of intersections with such a viewing ray was two, of which one would be a front surace and the other a back surface. This aspect has been described above in the context of the Boundary expansion and the array processor.

The general equation for a quadric surface will have the form:

$$O = a.x^2 + b.y^2 + c.z^2 + d.xy + e.xz + f.yz + g.x + h.y + k.z + m$$

For a particular pixel position x and y will be constants, which allows this equation to be reduced to a function in the variable z:

$$O = A.z^2 + B.z + C$$

where $A = c$
$$B = e.x + f.y + k$$
and $C = a.x^2 + b.y^2 + d.xy + g.x + h.y + m$

The problem is to find the two values of z which satisfy this equation. Where A is not equal to zero, the standard formula for solving quadratic equations can be applied:

$$z = \frac{-B \pm \sqrt{B^2 - 4AC}}{2A}$$

this in turn can be represented in the simpler form:

$$z = S_1 \pm \sqrt{T_1}$$

where $S_1 = -(e.x + f.y + k)/2c$

and $T_1 = (x^2.(e^2 - 4ac) + y^2.(f^2 - 4bc) + xy.(2ef - 4cd)$
$\qquad + x.(2ek - 4cg) + y.(2fk - 4ch) + k^2 - 4cm)/4c^2$

On the other hand, where A is equal to zero there will only be one value of z which will be given by:

$z = T_2 / S_2$

where $S_2 = e.x + f.y + k$

$\qquad T_2 = a.x^2 + b.y^2 + d.xy + g.x + h.y + m$

Should both A and B be zero at the same time, then the surface will be perpendicular to the display screen, and the potential form for the surface equation will have to be used, in other words:

$k = T_2$

k still has to be evaluated for each pixel position, even though it will only be the sign of k which will affect the display algorithm.

(T_1, S_1) and (T_2, S_2) can both be evaluated using the same incrementing scheme in the following way:

$T_2 = a.x^2 + b.y^2 + d.xy + g.x + h.y + m$
$S_2 = e.x + f.y + k$

$$\Delta Tx \quad = \quad a.(\Delta x)^2 + (2a.x + d.y + g).(\Delta x)$$
$$\Delta Ty \quad = \quad b.(\Delta y)^2 + (2b.y + d.x + h).(\Delta y)$$
$$\Delta Txx \quad = \quad 2a.(\Delta x)^2$$
$$\Delta Txy \quad = \quad \Delta Tyx \quad = \quad d.(\Delta x).(\Delta y)$$
$$\Delta Tyy \quad = \quad 2b.(\Delta y)^2$$
$$\Delta Sx \quad = \quad e.(\Delta x)$$
$$\Delta Sy \quad = \quad f.(\Delta y)$$

Redefining the coefficients of the equations for T_2 and S_2 in terms of the coefficients of the equations for T_1 and S_1 gives:

$a = (e^2 - 4ac)/4c^2$

$b = (f^2 - 4bc)/4c^2$

$d = (2ef - 4cd)/4c^2$

$g = (2ek - 4cg)/4c^2$

$h = (2fk - 4ch)/4c^2$

$m = (k^2 - 4cm)/4c^2$

$e = -e/2c$

$f = -f/2c$

$k = -k/2c$

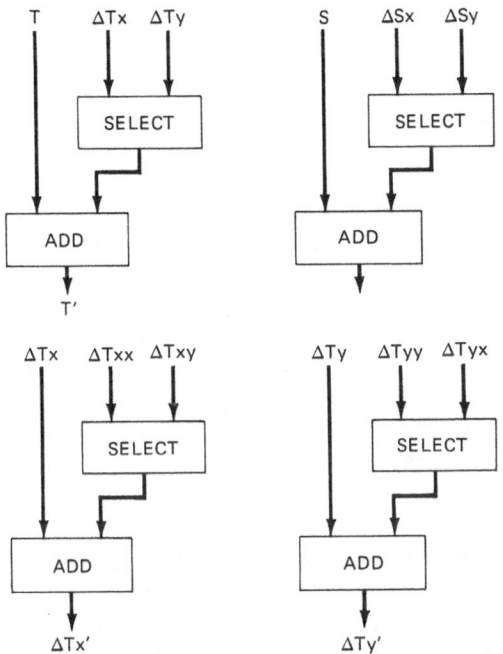

Figure 58 Incrementing Units for Quadric Surfaces

This allows the general incrementing hardware shown in Figure 58 to be used in each pixel processor in the display pipeline.

The final depth value used in each pixel processor is given by:

```
IF  A=0  THEN
        IF  B=0  THEN
              V1  :=  T
        ELSE
              V1  :=  T/S
    ELSE BEGIN
        V1  :=  S - SQRT(T);
        V2  :=  S + SQRT(T)
    END;
```

A and B in this case are reduced to 1 bit control values based on the original values of A and B. Each processor has to be able to evaluate a division and a square root function. This task was made simpler than it might have been by making T and S fixed length values. A scheme has been designed in outline, which is capable of this calculation using a shift register based processor.

The important difference between the T and S values and the Z or K values used for planes is that if n bits are used for the latter, $2n$ bits will be required for the former.

Higher Order Surfaces

Once it was realised that quadric surfaces could be processed without requiring a large increase in the hardware of each pixel processor, higher order polynomial surfaces had to be examined. A brief look at the formula for solving the cube roots of a cubic expression indicated that an alternative method had to be found for higher order surfaces! Standard approximation procedures were suggested, but they appeared to suffer from two drawbacks. The first was that a general purpose ALU seemed necessary to carry out an operation which might take a variable number of cycles to converge on the required solution. The second was that only one real root would be found where more than one existed if a viewing ray intersected the same surface in several places.

Two steps were needed to resolve these problems. The first was the use of an approximating plane for each section of a surface. This plane could be processed in real time in the way that has already been described. The second step was to define the surface in a potential form relative to this approximating plane. Taking the cubic surface as an example, there would have to be at least three approximating planes because there could be three different distances found at each pixel position. Because the starting point in the search for the intersection point is close to the surface, it is possible to use a binary subdivision process to

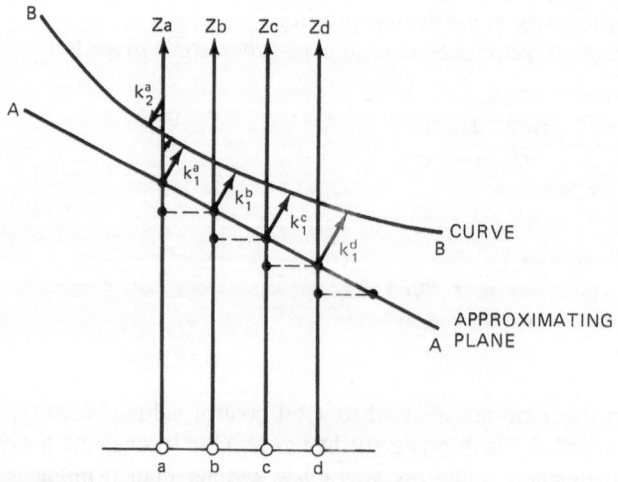

Figure 59 Curved Surfaces and Approximating Planes

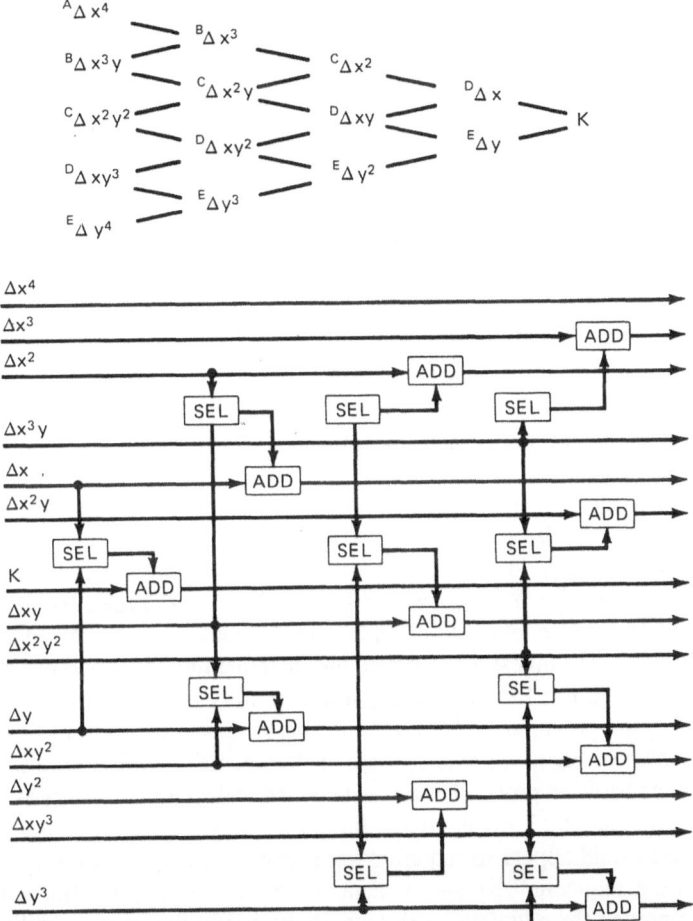

Figure 60 Forward Incrementing Processor

walk a test point along the viewing ray until it is within some required accuracy range of the surface. The incrementing steps taken in this process can be added to or subtracted from the approximating planes' depth value to give the depth value for the surface itself. The method is shown diagrammatically in Figure 59. Different strategies are being explored for walking to the surface to handle difficult cases. It appears that this operation can be carried out in a fixed number of steps, given a required final accuracy and a given closeness for the approximating plane. This approach clearly transfers difficult calculations from one part of the system to another. However, if it is viewed as the basis for a superior form of smooth shading then as long as the pixel processor size stays reasonably small then it seems to be a reasonable approach.

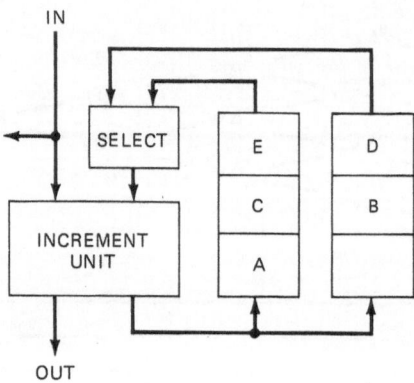

Figure 61 Sequential Processing of Increments

As an exploratory exercise consider the requirements for processing a fourth order polynomial surface. The first requirement is to set up an incrementing scheme which will provide the values for the different pixel position $a,b,c, ...$ A difference table of the form shown in Figure 60 will be necessary. A simple parallel adding scheme which will implement this table is given. An alternative method is also being investigated where the incrementing is carried out sequentially. However, in this kind of scheme it is necessary to have a series of registers in each pixel processor to hold intermediate results. The object of this arrangement, shown in Figure 61 is to process each incremental value in turn so that the difference between processing a plane surface and a curved surface is merely one of data-list length. To make the optimum use of components in the scheme in Figure 60 would appear to require several planes to be processed in parallel. At present the sequential expansion seems more in tune with the boundary expansion approach for maintaining the maximum versatility of the pipeline as a whole. This arrangement is incomplete because it only permits forward increments to be evaluated easily, although the general form of the solution seems correct. A better approach started to appear when the problem of walking to the surface was analysed a little further.

Walking to the Surface: Curve Smoothing

Once the value of k has been obtained for the surface, at positions on the approximating plane, then the z depth values of the plane can be modified by a sequence of steps, taken along the viewing ray, chosen to reduce k to zero, or as nearly as possible to zero. Where a viewing ray does not cut the surface, it is necessary to determine this fact from the changes in k. Several different strategies are being explored to cope with this problem. Where the viewing ray intersects the surface then a binary subdivision of the stepping sequence along the viewing ray—in the z direction—will give the required result in a fixed number of steps. Given the initial step-size of one resolution unit where the display resolution is 2^n pixels, then $n+1$ steps will define the surface depth to the accuracy required in plane surface displays. Whether this approach covers all eventualities is the subject of current word regarding curved surfaces.

Returning to the fourth order surface: the increments necessary to walk to the surface will be Δz, Δz^2, Δz^3, Δz^4. If these increments are renamed for convenience to be Δkz, Δkzz, $\Delta kzzz$, $\Delta kzzzz$ then the corresponding increment in z : Δz which generates these changes in k can be referred to in a consistent way. The problem with these increments is that they can only be used for a constant stepping distance Δz. Where increments correspond to steps of $\Delta z/2$ the calculations get much more complex.

Stepping in the z direction permits the surface to be considered as the equation of one variable z:

$$k = a{:}z^4 + b.z^3 + c.z^2 + d.z + e$$

The first level increment will be:

$$
\begin{aligned}
\Delta kz \quad &= \quad (4a.z^3 + 3b.z^2 + 2c.z + d) . (\Delta z) &\text{(A)}\\
&+ \quad (6a.z^2 + 3b.z + c) . (\Delta z)^2 &\text{(B)}\\
&+ \quad (4a.z + b) . (\Delta z)^3 &\text{(C)}\\
&+ \quad (a) . (\Delta z)^4 &\text{(D)}
\end{aligned}
$$

Two facts were clear from this expansion: if the direction of the increment Δz is reversed $-\Delta z$, the sign of the odd powers of Δz would also reverse. Similarly if Δz were halved to $\Delta z/2$ then the scaling of each line would be different. The simple consequence of this result is that each line will have to have its own difference table, if the ability to change the increment size by factors of two is desired. These increments would be:

$$
\begin{aligned}
\Delta kzz_A \quad &= \quad (12a.z^2 + 6b.z + 2c) . (\Delta z)^2 &\text{(E)}\\
&+ \quad (12a.z + 3b) . (\Delta z)^3 &\text{(F)}\\
&+ \quad (4a) . (\Delta z)^4 &\text{(G)}\\
\Delta kzz_B \quad &= \quad (12a.z + 3b) . (\Delta z)^3 &\text{(H)}\\
&+ \quad (6a) . (\Delta z)^4 &\text{(I)}\\
\Delta kzz_C \quad &= \quad (4a) . (\Delta z)^4 &\text{(J)}\\
\Delta kzzz_E \quad &= \quad (24a.z + 6b) . (\Delta z)^3 &\text{(K)}\\
&+ \quad (12a) . (\Delta z)^4 &\text{(L)}\\
\Delta kzzz_F \quad &= \quad (12a) . (\Delta z)^4 &\text{(M)}\\
\Delta kzzz_H \quad &= \quad (12a) . (\Delta z)^4 &\text{(N)}\\
\Delta kzzzz_K \quad &= \quad (24a) . (\Delta z)^4 &\text{(P)}
\end{aligned}
$$

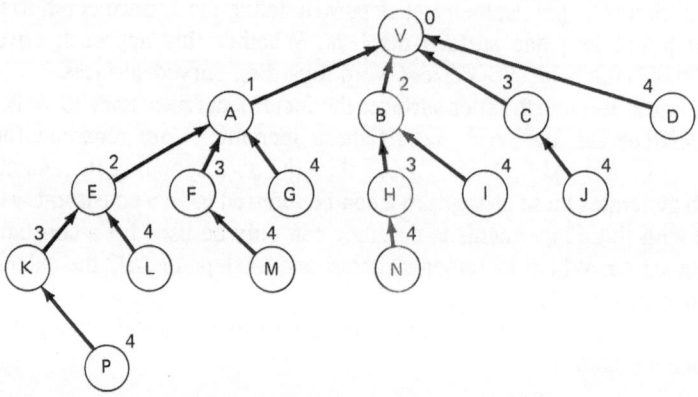

Figure 62 Binary Subdivision Incrementing Tree

This sequence of increments can be represented in a tree structure shown in Figure 62. An incrementing unit which could perform these calculations is shown in Figure 63. Where the increment halves then the power associated with each node in Figure 62 indicates how many places to the right the value has to be shifted. A rearrangement of the incrementing expressions allows an alternative scheme to be set up, shown in one form in Figure 64.

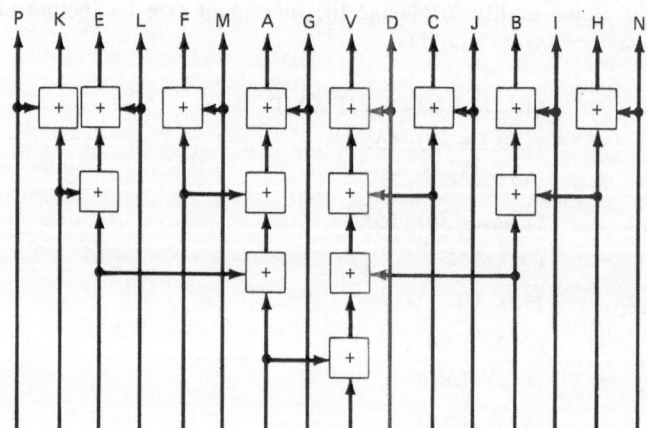

Figure 63 Incrementing Scheme: Walking to the Surface

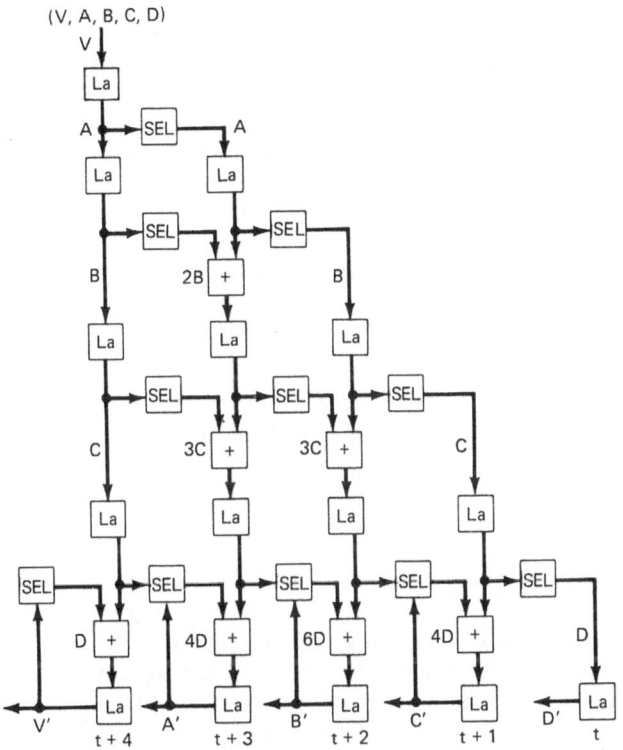

Figure 64 Alternative Scheme: Walking to the Surface

This approach appears to offer the best arrangement for systolic operation. Because of the symmetry the number of adders can be reduced even further, and the processor is predominantly latches and selectors. The rearrangement which supports this hardware is the result of expressing the increments in terms of the first level increments A, B, C and D to give:

$$V' \quad = \quad V \; + A.(\Delta z) \quad + B.(\Delta z)^2 \quad + C.(\Delta z)^3 \quad + D.(\Delta z)^4$$

$$A'.(\Delta z) \; = \quad\quad\quad A.(\Delta z) \quad + 2B.(\Delta z)^2 \quad + 3C.(\Delta z)^3 \quad + 4D.(\Delta z)^4$$

$$B'.(\Delta z)^2 \; = \quad\quad\quad\quad\quad\quad\quad + B.(\Delta z)^2 \quad + 3C.(\Delta z)^3 \quad + 6D.(\Delta z)^4$$

$$C'.(\Delta z)^3 \; = \quad\quad\quad\quad\quad\quad\quad\quad\quad\quad\quad + C.(\Delta z)^3 \quad + 4D.(\Delta z)^4$$

$$D'.(\Delta z)^4 \; = \quad\quad\quad\quad\quad\quad\quad\quad\quad\quad\quad\quad\quad\quad\quad + D.(\Delta z)^4$$

This approach can also be applied to the x and y incrementing scheme, to permit both forward and backward increments to be calculated to follow different raster patterns which result from the scene coherence processor.

The incrementing unit used to process plane half-spaces clearly has to be enlarged to incorporate these two modifications. The first stage allows the curved surface increments to be updated moving in the x and y directions on the screen. The output from this section is then passed to a second stage in the incrementing unit where the value of k is modified by moving in and out in the z direction until k is reduced to as near as possible to zero. There are many options open for the detailed implementation of this scheme and these are currently being explored. Until a substantial amount of simulation has been done the full behaviour of this kind of system will not be known. The basic approach seems sound and the architecture of the resulting processor is still capable of supporting video rate data generation. However, it is unclear just what level of curved surface representation it is worth supporting at this level in the system. Will quadric surfaces be adequate, or are quartic surfaces necessary, for example, in blending operations. The attitude at present is that a superior form of smooth shading can be provided where not only smooth illumination effects are supported but also smooth contour edges. The long term options depend on the development of the scene coherence processor, and the modelling system to include curved surfaces.

Scene Coherence Processor

There are a variety of different scene coherence algorithms which can be applied in different situations. For many simple scenes edge following will reduce the amount of calculation by an order of magnitude. Where high scene complexity, high resolution, and high speed are all objectives, then a combination of object space and image space subdivision, and hierarchical modelling techniques need to be used together. A general processor which will allow scan line binary subdivision; quadtree, four way subdivision; and octree, eight way subdivision is being developed to act as a preprocessor to the pipeline system described above, as well as a general geometric processor, which with the transformation unit will serve the modelling and analysis system.

Quadtree Processing

The input data structure consists of a tree representation of the Boolean expression model in the form:

(ABCD(EFGH(IJKL(MNOP) (QRST))(UVWX(YZ))))

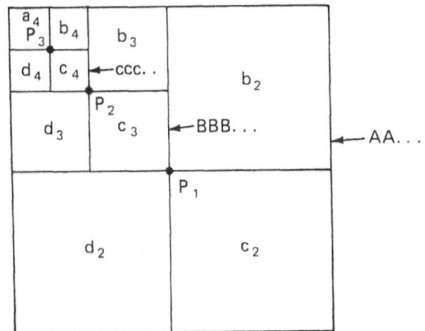

RECURSIVE DISPLAY LIST: AAAAAAAAAAAA. BBBBBBB.CCCC.DD

Figure 65 Recursive Quadtree Subdivision

This arrangement can be processed as a linear list of convex units in a pipeline processor, and at the same time it can be treated as a tree by stacking the pointers representing the various levels in the tree shown as $x's$ above, in the appropriate way.

The aim is to process the list recursively for each sub-quad in the display screen in the way shown in Figure 65. At each level the routine will have to process the whole display list for the quad in question. In Figure 65 the list AAAAA... will be defined for the whole space centred on $P1$. The first subdivision will create the new list BBB... which will apply to the quad centred on point $P2$, the second subdivison will create the list CCC.. which will apply to the quad centred on point $P3$, and so on. Processing the list in this way ensures that the amount of storage space used is kept within bounds. In the ideal situation each list would be divided down to a quarter of its length at each stage in the recursion of the level above. In the simple case this gives a geometric progression, whose limit is well within twice the original list length.

The quadtree scene coherence algorithms which have been studied so far, depend on three primary ways of reducing a display list length each time the display area is subdivided:

1. Convex Object List Reduction

2. Convex Object, and Linked Tree Pruning

3. Hierarchical Overlap or Cover Testing

The first method consists of removing plane facets which cannot affect the visible object formed in a quad by a convex unit in the tree model. The second method consists of removing convex units which lie outside the quad being

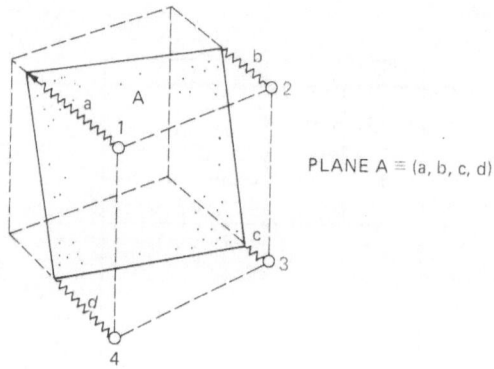

PLANE A ≡ (a, b, c, d)

Figure 66 Representing Plane Surfaces in a Quad

processed. In this case because of the hierarchical structure of the model, not only the convex unit is removed but all subtrees linked to the same node in the tree. The third is the most complex and consists of using the depth values of convex units which totally enclose a quad to test against other units. Where these units lie at a greater distance than the covering surface then they can be removed. These three options have been selected because they can be carried out using the depth values of planes evaluated at the corners of the quads in the way shown in Figure 66. If the mid-way depth value for a plane, along the edge of a quad is required then the operation is simple: add together the two depth values at the vertices of the edge and divide by two–shift the result right by one place. Given a display list of planes represented in this way, indexed by k, a new list for a sub-quad associated with the vertex number t, can be created and indexed by j using:

$$V(s,j) = (V(t,k) + V(s,k))/2$$

where j: new list index; k: old list index; s: vertex number; and t: quad number.

Where a front plane surface has depth values which are all less than the corresponding depth values for another front plane, within the same convex solid phrase, then clearly the first surface can be removed. Several variations on this kind of test can be used to prune individual planes from a display list as the display screen is subdivided.

If a convex unit lies outside a quadrant then it can be removed from the display list, along with associated sub-trees. If a convex unit does not exist at the corners of a quadrant it does not mean that it does not enter the quad in the way diagrammed in Figure 67. The test which has been developed to cope with this problem is to expand the convex unit by a sufficient amount that if it were to just be touching a corner of the quad, on expansion it would just be covering the centre point of the quad.

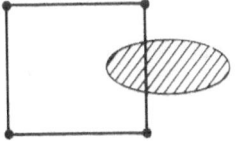

Figure 67 Quadrant Occupancy

This makes it possible to carry out a single test to see whether the convex unit should be pruned or not. Although not totally efficient, this method is safe: it never rejects an object which should be kept, though in its simplest form it will accept units which are outside the quad.

The centre point test initially seemed to require an extra value to be calculated for each plane in a quadrant. However it was found that one of the existing corner values of a plane surface would act as the expanded centre value in the way shown in Figure 68 in two dimensions for a cross section through a raster line.

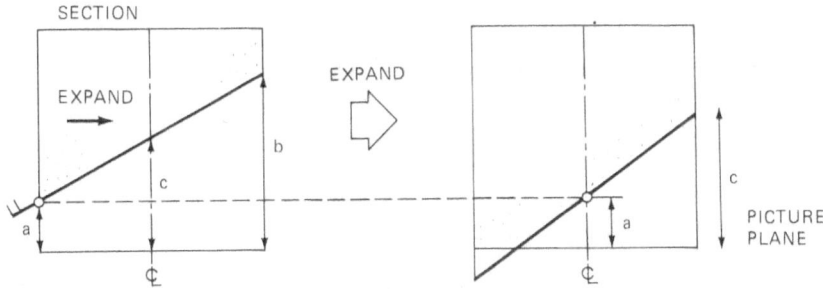

Figure 68 Plane Expansion

If V is the unexpanded depth value for a plane at the centre of a quad and dVx and dVy are the increments to move to the edges of the quad, then for a front plane:

$$V_{expanded} = V - |dVx| - |dVy|$$

and for a back plane:

$$V_{expanded} = V + |dVx| + |dVy|$$

These two values correspond to the minimum and the maximum of the quadrant corner depth values for the unexpanded front and back planes respectively. However, if the signs of the incrementing values are known then a direct addressing scheme can be set up in the following way:

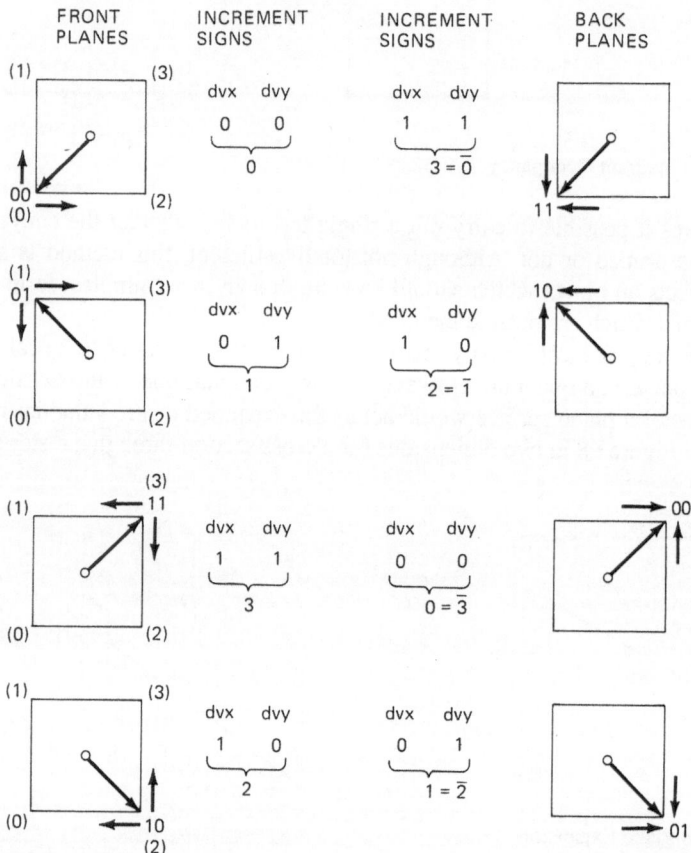

Figure 69 Expansion Value Selection

It is possible to use the signs of dVx and dVy to directly select the correct corner value of V for the expanded-volume test, if the vertices of the quad are relabelled in the way shown. The advantage that this has is that back surface expanded values can be selected in the same way by complementing the sign bits in the way shown in Figure 69.

This new labelling has no effect on the calculation of depth values. These two calculating schemes permit a simple architecture to be proposed for a divide and conquer scene coherence processor. If we consider the list of plane definitions defining a scene as made up from a list of 4-tuples $(V0, V1, V2, V3)$ and a property reference A, then a possible processor structure can be that shown in the block diagram in Figure 70. The input plane value for a given quad is defined by the index memory address k, the output memory address is given by

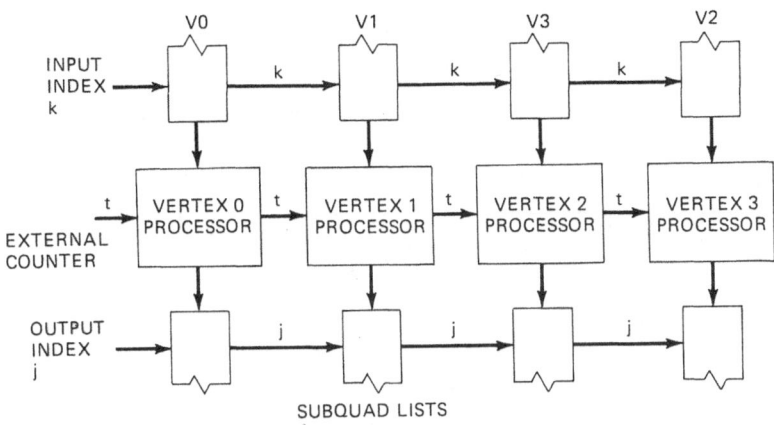

Figure 70 Scene Coherence Processor Block Diagram

the index j. The quad being processed is controlled by the value of t which selects which of the four inputs VO, $V1$, $V2$, or $V3$ will be broadcast to all the vertex processors to generate the new vertex depth values for the sub-quad t in the way indicated in Figure 71. The vertex processors themselves can be arranged in a variety of ways, which are again the subject of current investigations. Each processor tests the visibility of each convex unit in the input list for the vertex position it is managing. This makes it possible to prune the convex units of planes that lie totally outside the visible surfaces. The test for existence inside the quad for convex units is closely tied up with tests for cover. One possible arrangement is shown in Figure 72. The objective is to develop a specialised byte slice processor to implement this system. However, more work needs to be done integrating the curved surface results with this level in the system. The relationship between approximating planes and the higher level modelling scheme will have a major impact on this processor.

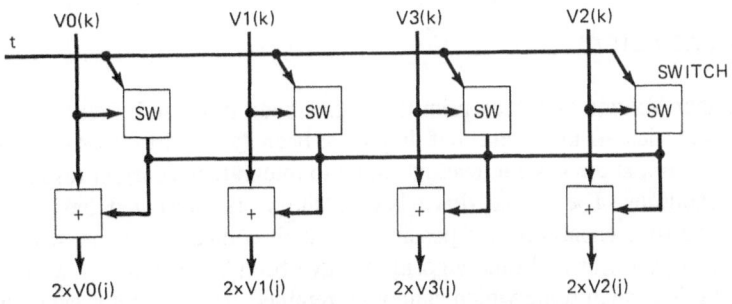

Figure 71 Incrementing Unit for Scene Coherence Processor

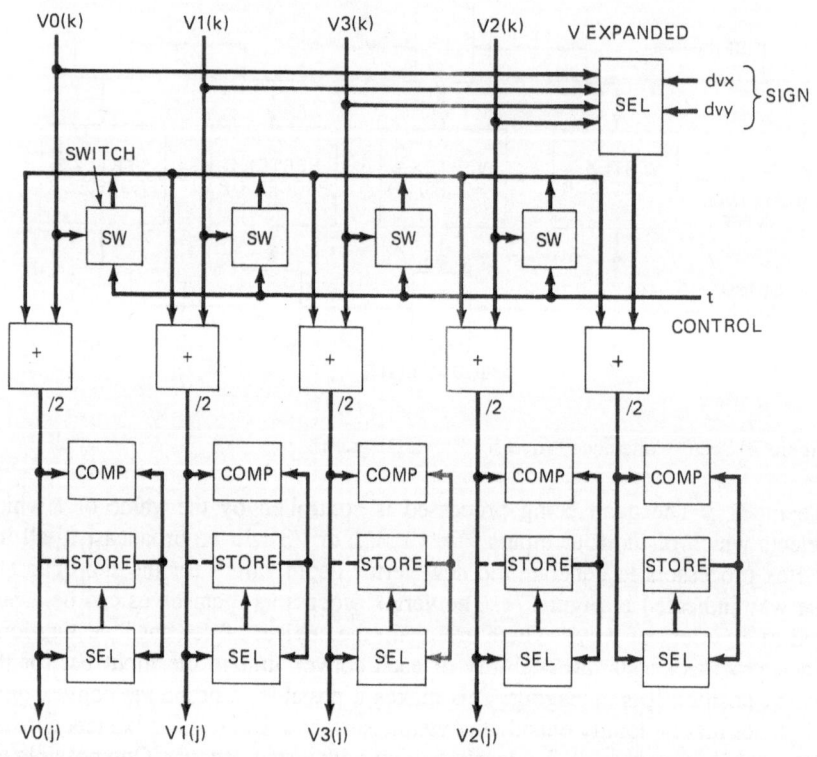

Figure 72 Scene Coherence Processor: Schematic Layout

The examples have been given for the quadtree subdivision, a similar scheme applies to octree subdivision, and part of the design of this processor will be to ensure that both kinds of algorithm are supported by the hardware.

System Structure

In this paper Volume and Area primitives have been discussed. Point and Line primitives are just as important, but they have been assumed to "already exist". Part of the work at the system level has to be to integrate the current results with existing facilities. The whole drive behind the work presented has been to produce real time capabilities, if possible, in small compact systems. It is clear that in doing this near real time algorithms have been by-passed and at the system level this is an attitude which cannot be retained. The general system structure for the Area and Volume Data is shown in Figure 73. There are several options which have not yet been integrated into this arrangement.

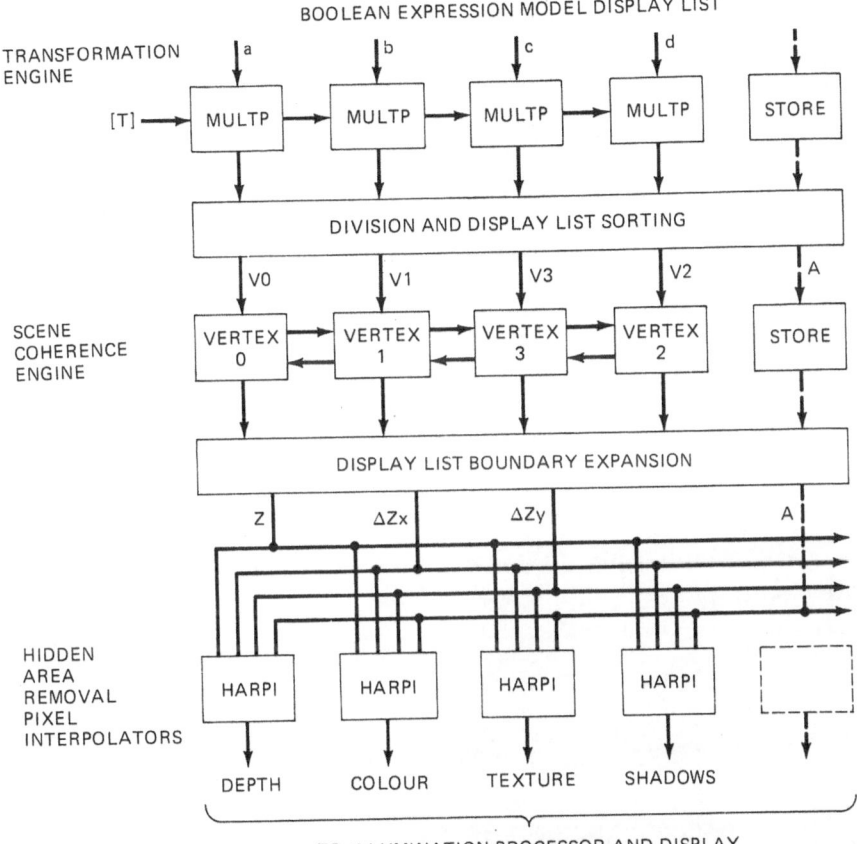

Figure 73 Volume and Area Display System

If the priming scheme is developed further, then it will be possible to cascade HARPI processors. The output from the HARPI processors will permit a limited form of ray tracing in real time. If the output of HARPI processors is passed to an appropriately designed post-processor it will be possible to represent lines and points in this system using a form of image processing algorithm. Although an incrementing scheme for the HARPI processors has been designed to process curved surfaces, the ability to prepare the difference tables in the supporting system has still to be provided. Similarly the transformation unit will have to be extended to allow the curves to be transformed. Again, though the simple flow of data to give moving images has been provided, the necessary ways of interacting with a display file for interactive work still needs more study. One aspect that looks promising is the ability to generate Boolean expression models automatically from a TV camera input, for certain kinds of objects.

(A)

(B)

(C)

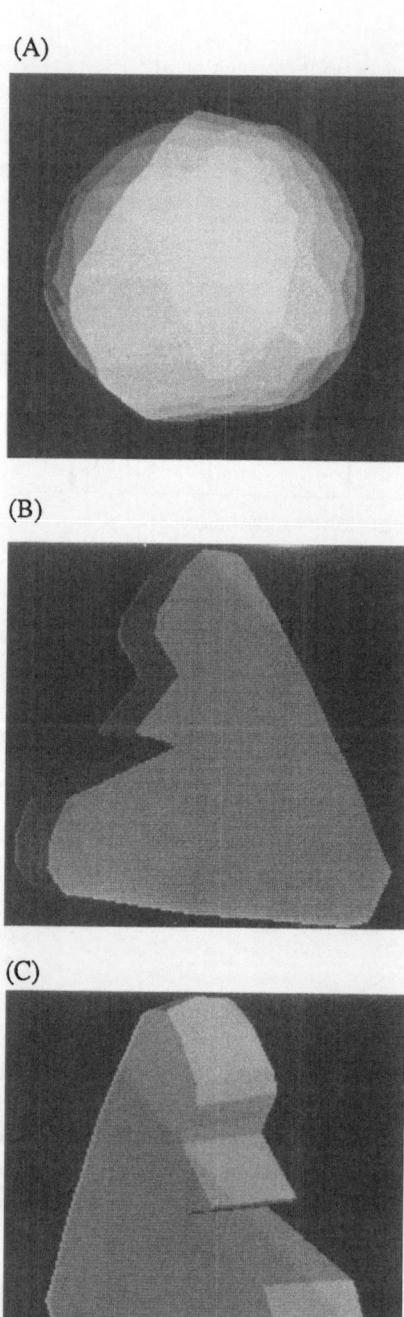

Figure 74 Volume Models Generated from TV Camera Input

Automatic Generation Of Models

If an object is rotated in front of a TV camera and a series of silhouette images are stored, it is possible to reconstruct from these images a three dimensional model if the position in which they were obtained is known. The displays of two models generated in this way are shown in Figure 74. The first object was a convex ball of plastercine, the second was a more complicated object with concave surfaces.

The first stage of this process was to define the edge of the silhouette. This was then converted into straight line segments by following sequences of pixel steps in n and $n+1$ groups. When n changed then a vertex was defined. The set of vertices was then converted into a nested collection of convex hulls. Each convex collection of vertices was then converted into a convex Boolean expression model relating the edges which linked the vertices together. The hierarchy of the convex hull model was carried over to the Boolean expression to model the whole area of the silhouette. This operation was applied to all the silhouettes.

The boundary model of each silhouette was then converted into a three dimensional model by replacing each edge by the plane through the edge and through the camera. This pyramid volume was created for each silhouette. By knowing how far the object had been rotated between each of the silhouettes it was then possible to rotate the pyramide volumes the same amount. The intersection of the resulting volumes was merely a matter of list concatenation: or rather expression concatenation. The resulting Boolean expression model of a volume could then be used for generating a display.

Conclusions

This paper presents a modelling and display system which seems to be growing in power as more and more is discovered of the underlying mathematical properties of the system being used. Initially adopted because it offered some intuitively satisfying ways of representing objects: it appears able to support powerful yet relatively simple hardware. Having said this, there still seems to be a vast amount of further work to do following the same themes.

Acknowledgements. Displays produced by J. E. Foggitt and M. Lavington. Funding provided by S.E.R.C. Key developments helped by J. Downie, J. Woodwark, M. Sabin and Prof. R. Forrest. Electronic circuit design and VLSI design help received from J. Mclean and M. Morant.

References

[COOK] D. F. Cooke and W.H. Maxfield, "The Development of a Geographic Base File and its use for Mapping". in proceedings (Urban and Regional Systems Association)

[EARN85] R. A. Earnshaw, "Fundamental Algorithms for Computer Graphics." NATO ASI Series, Springer-Verlag, Berlin, 1985

[FOLE82] J. D. Foley and A. van Dam, "Fundamentals of Interactive Computer Graphics." Addison Wesley, London, 1982

[NEWE72] M. E. Newell, R. G. Newell and T. L. Sancha, "A New Approach to the Shaded Picture Problem." in proceedings ACM National Conference 1972

[ROUG69] R. S. Rougelot, "The General Electric Computed Colour Display". in "Pertinent Concepts in Computer Graphics", ed M. Faiman and J. Nievergelt, University of Illinois 1969.

[SUTH63] I.E. Sutherland, "SkETCHPAD: A Man-Machine Graphical Communication System." in Spartan Books, Baltimore 1963

[THOM76] A. L. Thomas, "Spatial Models in Computer Based Information Systems". Ph.D. Thesis, Edinburgh University (April 1976)

[THOM86] A. L. Thomas, "Overlap Operations and Raster Graphics." Computer Graphics Forum, Vo 15, No 1, March 1986

[WARN69] J. E. Warnock, "Hidden Line Problem and the Use of Half-Tone Displays". in "Pertinent Concepts in Computer Graphics", ed M. Faiman and J. Nievergelt, University of Illinois 1969

[WATK70] G. S. Watkins "A Real Time Visible Surface Algorithm." Thesis Computer Science Department, UTECH-CSc-70-101, University of Utah, 1970 June

[WAUG70] T. C. Waugh and A. L. Thomas, "Geographic Information Management and Mapping System". GIMMS, System Manual, June 1970

[WOOD80] J. R. Woodwark and K. M. Quinlan, "The Derivation of Graphics from Volume Models by Recursive Subdivision of the Object Space." in proceedings Computer Graphics `80 Conference, 1980

Polygon Processing for VLSI Pattern Generation

A. C. KILGOUR

Abstract

The generation of masks for the manufacture of a VLSI circuit from a geometric description in standard CIF format involves among other operations the merging of all overlapping or abutting polygons in the description, and the discarding of all areas of overlap. Inflation of the polygons prior to merging may also be required, with subsequent shrinking after merging. This paper describes an efficient and secure algorithm for polygon merging and intersection, using the "plane sweep" approach. Special attention is given to the handling of concurrent edges and multiple edges incident on the same point. Details are given of the geometric calculations and data structures used, an analysis is included of the expected time efficiency of the algorithm, and some performance figures quoted for a VAX implementation.

Polygon Union and Intersection

The problems of detecting intersections between the edges of two given polygons, and of constructing the union and intersection polygons, have been widely studied. Algorithms for detecting and counting intersections have been reported by Shamos and Hoey [SHAM76], Bentley and Ottman [BENT79], and Bentley and Wood [BENT80]. Methods for constructing the complete union and intersection boundaries have been described by Eastman and Yessios [EAST72], Sutherland & Hodgman [SUTH74], Shamos [SHAM75], Sutherland [SUTH79], Barton and Buchanan [BART80], Tilove [TILO80] and Weiler [WEIL80]. Beretta and Nievergelt [BERE81] introduced the term "plane sweep" to describe the approach common to many of these methods, in which an imaginary line (either horizontal or vertical) is swept across the plane and the edges ordered according to their intersections with this line, and Nievergelt and Preparata [NIEV82] described an algorithm of this type for the polygon intersection problem. The algorithm presented here is similar to that of Nievergelt and Preparata, but was developed independently and incorporates general solutions to the problems of concurrent edges and of multiple edges incident on the same vertex [KILG82].

The worst case time efficiency for any polygon intersection or union algorithm required to produce the complete boundary as output, given two input polygons with n and m sides, will always be at least $O(nm)$, since every edge of each polygon may intersect every edge of the other. On the other hand, Shamos has shown that the intersection between two *convex* polygons with a total of n sides can be constructed in $O(n)$ time [SHAM75]. A desirable property for any polygon comparison algorithm is that it should achieve optimal time efficiency $O(n)$ when given input data representing convex polygons, and degenerate gracefully towards the worst case $O(n^2)$ as the complexity of the problem increases. Plane sweep algorithms like the one presented here achieve this property. The complexity of the problem, in so far as it affects the efficiency, is measured by the number of "peaks" (local maxima) on the input boundaries, and the number of edge intersections present.

Applications of polygon comparison algorithms include polygon clipping [SUTH74] [FOLE82], hidden surface removal [NEWE72] [WEIL77] [SECH81] [STER82], and VLSI design rule checking [MEAD80] [GRAY81]. Although design rule checking is likely to be an application in future of the method described here, its present use is as part of the Shapesmith package [LATT86] to convert from a geometrric description of a VLSI layout in standard CIF format to commands for generating masks on any of a range of pattern generation machines, such as David Mann, Varian, Electromask or E-Beam machines [HON80].

The Application Context

A VLSI layout as defined by a CIF file consists of a sequence of symbol definitions and symbol instances [MEAD80]. A two-dimensional integer co-ordinate system is used, and co-ordinate values are required to lie within 24 bit capacity. The fundamental geometric elements are boxes, polygons, flashes and wires. Wires and boxes are special types of polygon, and flashes, which are intended to be circular, may be represented as regular polygons. (Such an approximation is

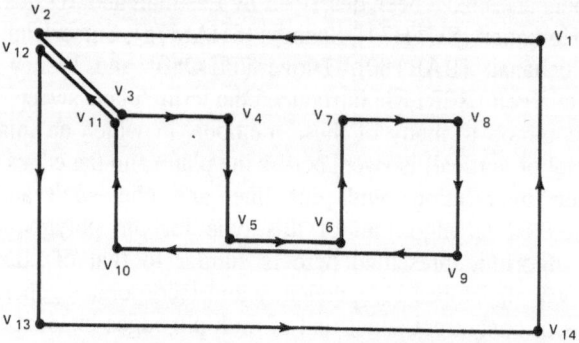

Figure 1

usually necessary in any case, since most pattern generation machines cannot generate circles.)

A deficiency of the CIF format is that there is no simple way to define holes in a polygon. Where a hole is required, a single self-touching polygonal sheet must be specified. (Figure 1 shows an example.) It is part of the job of the comparison algorithm to decompose such cases into simple sheets.

Even apart from the specification of holes, the polygons defined by the CIF input are not guaranteed to be simple. Also there is no imposed sign convention as regards the order in which the vertices are specified. There can thus be ambiguity as to which parts of the boundary represent holes, and which enclose the interior. In the algorithm described here a variation of the "non-zero winding number convention" proposed by Newell and Sequin is adopted [NEWE80]. However, a slightly different definition of winding number is used, which is associated with the polygon boundary rather than with interior points.

If a semi-infinite test line is drawn from any point on a polygon edge so as to lie entirely in the *positive* (left-hand) half plane defined by the edge, the *wrap number* or *winding number* of the edge is defined to be the signed total of the number of other edges which cross the test line, counting +1 for an edge which crosses from its positive to negative side, and -1 for a crossing from negative to positive. It is a property of any polygonal graph that the result is independent of the initial point chosen, and of the direction of the semi-infinite line.

This definition of wrap number avoids the need to consider such notions as "interior" and "exterior", but has the consequence that the boundary of an isolated simple polygonal sheet may have wrap number either 0 or 1. An isolated sheet with wrap number 0 is said to be negative, and in the system described below any such sheet has its vertices reversed, and its wrap number changed to 1, before further processing.

A control program parses the CIF input file and passes individual polygons to the polygon package, which first extracts all sheets with wrap number 1 or 0, reversing the latter as indicated, then adds them to a list of sheets belonging to the current layer. When a layer is complete, it can either be merged with itself, or with another previously built layer. The comparison algorithm in fact builds both the union and the intersection, and either may be extracted by the control program as required. The same algorithm is used both to generate the individual sheets from an input polygon and to compare a layer with itself, or with another layer.

Generating the Equivalent Simple Polygon

A single polygonal sheet may be defined as a directed graph having n vertices $V_1, V_2 \ldots V_n$ $(n > 2)$ which are points in 2D Euclidean space, and n edges $V_1 V_2$, $V_2 V_3 \ldots V_n V_1$ which are two-dimensional vectors. It is normally also assumed that no two consective vertices are co-incident, so that the edges are all non-zero vectors. The degree of all vertices of this graph is clearly zero, since each has one incoming and one outgoing incident edge. A general polygon may be defined as a collection of any number of polygonal sheets. A general polygon also has zero degree. If the graph of a general polygon is modified to include as vertices all intersection points between edges, splitting edges which pass through intersection points which are not already vertices, and combining any groups of co-incident vertices, the result is still a graph of zero degree, since every new vertex resulting from an intersection has two incoming and two outgoing edges. The result of this operation may be called the augmented graph of the polygon. The process may be applied equally well to a group of two or more general polygons (which by definition together also constitute a general polygon).

As Weiler first pointed out [WEIL80], the process of finding the union or intersection of two polygons reduces to the problem of forming the augmented graph and extracting from it sheets with wrap number 1 (for the union) or 2 (for the intersection). A general method for generating from the augmented graph the sheets of what may be called the *equivalent simple polygon* is as follows:

```
Set the status of all edges in the augmented graph to
'unmarked';
while unmarked edges remain do begin
    find any unmarked edge;
    set status of edge to 'marked';
    open a new output sheet;
    append copy of tail vertex to output sheet;
    save identity of tail vertex as start vertex;
    while head vertex of current edge is not start vertex
    do begin
        append copy of tail vertex to output sheet;
        select next edge from augmented graph;
        set its status to marked end;
    close output sheet
end;
```

To complete this description it is necessary to specify exactly how the "select next edge from augmented graph" step is carried out. The edge selected must be one whose tail vertex is the same as the head vertex of the previous edge, and if the edges incident on a vertex in the augmented graph are imagined as ordered radially about the vertex, the required outgoing edge may be determined thus:

```
set edgesum to +1;
repeat
    move to next edge in clockwise direction;
    if edge is incoming then edgesum: = edgesum +1
    else edgesum: = edgesum -1
until edgesum = 0;
```

The edge at which the loop stops is the required outgoing edge (which is guaranteed to be unmarked). Where two edges incident on a vertex have the same polar angle, the incoming edge is to be regarded as preceding the outgoing one, if the edges are of opposite sense. If the edges are of the same sense, the order is immaterial.

An alternative convention would be to go round the incident edges in an anticlockwise direction, which would in some cases give a different set of output sheets. The clockwise convention ensures that the interior of positive sheets is connected.

It can be shown that the equivalent polygon generated by the above method is simple in the sense that each individual sheet is simple (although negative sheets may have two or more nonconsecutive vertices coincident), and no two output sheets cross each other. Degenerate sheets consisting of only two vertices may be produced, but these can be discarded without affecting any subsequent application of the output. Sheets with wrap number 2 comprise the intersection of the input polygon or polygons, and sheets with wrap number 1 represent the union. Figure 2 shows two typical input polygons (each with a single sheet, but not both simple), their augmented graph, and the equivalent simple polygon generated by the given method. A total of three output sheets are generated with wrap numbers +1, +2 (inside the first and touching it at three points), and -1 (disjoint). Note that the part of Q with final wrap number 0 is not included in any of these sheets.

Applying the Plane Sweep Approach

The direct application of the above method could lead to a very inefficient algorithm because of the need to search the augmented graph for unmarked edges, even if an efficient method of generating all the intersections could be found. Also the wrap numbers of the output sheets would have to be determined individually at the end, a potentially costly operation. Adopting the plane sweep approach allows the detection of edge intersections, the generation of output sheets, and the assignment of wrap numbers to be carried out simultaneously, with the last two being provided at very little extra cost.

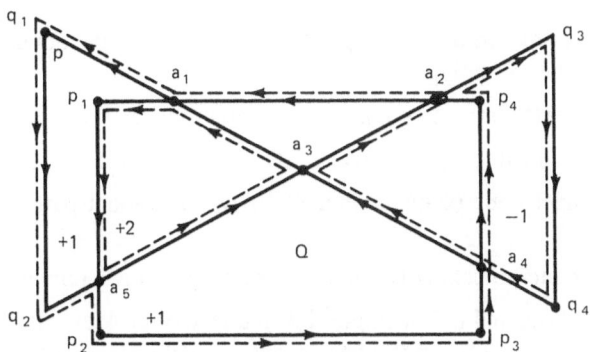

Figure 2

The description following envisages a horizontal line sweeping the plane from top to bottom as in a TV raster scan. Points are ordered from top-to-bottom in Y and from left-to-right in X.

Principal Data Structures

Before describing the complete algorithm, it is useful to consider the data structures that are required.

Representation of Polygons

A polygon is represented as a doubly linked ring of sheets, and a sheet points to a doubly-linked ring of vertices. A vertex consists of a point record (containing integer X and Y co-ordinates) together with forward and backward pointers to neighbouring vertices on the same sheet. The ring of sheets representing a polygon has a special header node, a pointer to which is sufficient to identify the complete polygon (although each polygon also has a unique integer label, a copy of which is held in all its constituent sheet nodes). Pointers to the header nodes of all polygons known to the system are held on a one-way linear list.

During the construction of the output polygon an incomplete form of sheet referred to as a path exists, in which the constituent vertices form a doubly-linked queue rather than a ring. Polygon headers, sheets and paths are all represented as variants of a single record structure. The implementation is in the Imp-77 programming language [ROBE80], but is presented here in equivalent Pascal form. The fields common to all variants are:

label: unique integer polygon identifier;

vertcount: total number of vertices in path, sheet or polygon;

wrapno: wrap number of sheet or path, or of complete polygon if all sheets have same wrap number;

sense: positive or negative (sheet or path);

knownsimple: *boolean* which is *true* if polygon or sheet is guaranteed to be simple;

boxmin, boxmax: point records giving the extremes of the bounding box for the path, sheet or polygon;

predsheet, nextsheet: ring pointers to neighbouring sheets;

status: tag field with values POLYHEAD, PATH or SHEET.

For a sheet header node (status = POLYHEAD) the variant part of the record contains:

nextpoly: pointer to next polygon header on list of known polygons;

peakqueue: head and tail of singly-linked queue of peak events belonging to this polygon (may be empty; peak events are defined below).

For the other node types the variant part contains:

entryvert: pointer to any vertex on the path or sheet;

pathends: pointers to front and rear of doubly-linked vertex queue (pathonly).

Events and the Event Queue

An *event* is defined to be any point in 2D space which lies on more than one edge of the input polygon or polygons, with the exception of non-vertex points shared by coincident or partially coincident edges. Every event is either a vertex or an intersection between edges (or both). The essence of the algorithm is the processing of events in a defined order. The position of an event is represented in the present implementation by three values:

px, py: integer x and y co-ordinates obtained by rounding true x and y values (if necessary);

yresidue: difference between true (double length floating point) y position and the rounded value py.

(It turns out to be unnecessary to retain a residue value for x.) For events derived from input vertices, *yresidue* is zero.

```
If ev1 and ev2 are two event records, ev1 is greater
than (ie. to be processed before) ev2
if
(ev1.py > ev2.py) or
((ev1.py = ev2.py) and
     ((ev1.yresidue > ev2.yresidue) or
     ((ev1.yresidue = ev2.yresidue)
     and (ev1.px < ev2.px))))
```

If all three co-ordinate fields are equal, the events are merged and treated as a single event.

As well as the position of the event, each event record contains an "upper edge list" consisting of pointers to the first and last edge in the active edge list (see below) which are incident on the event, and a "lower edge list" which, when the event is processed, will contain pointers to the front and rear of a queue of new edges which are to replace the edges in the upper edge list as members of the active edge list.

Since events are to be processed in order, and new events to be saved for later processing as they are detected, the natural data structure for holding events is a priority queue [SEDG83]. The simplest form of priority queue to implement is the array representation of a partially-ordered binary tree (usually referred to as a heap). The array elements themselves are pointers to the event records, so as to minimise the work required when entries have to be rearranged.

Although the array implementation of the priority queue is the most efficient and the simplest to code, it has the disadvantage of requiring prior allocation of sufficient space for the largest number of events likely to be simultaneously active. However, in a virtual memory system there is no great disadvantage in declaring a large array part of which may never be used in a particular execution of the program. A linked, dynamic implementation such as a balanced tree scheme might be preferable where the logical address space is limited, but would carry an additional space penalty of at least two pointers per entry.

The Active Edge List

The third major data structure to be manipulated is the active edge list. As will be seen from the foregoing, edges are not explicitly represented in the data structures for input or output polygons. Edges enter or leave the active edge list only when an event is processed, and the active edge list starts and finishes empty.

Edges on the active edge list are arranged in increasing order of the X co-ordinate of their intersection with a horizontal line through them all, though such intersections are never computed. Where the active edge list contains a horizontal edge, its position is determined by its left-most vertex.

When an event is processed, its "lower" edges, ie. incident edges whose other ends are below or to the right of the event, replace in the active edge list its "upper" edges, ie. incident edges which are already on the active edge list. Searching of the edge list is necessary only when a "peak" event has to be processed, ie. one with no upper incident edges. For maximum efficiency the active edge list ought to be organised as a balanced tree, or at least have a balanced tree index, so that the location of a peak event relative to existing active edges could be done in logarithmic time. However, in the present implementation, the active edge structure is a two-way linear list.

Every edge on the active edge list points to a path, ie. an embryo sheet of the output polygon, and is either the "left" or "right" edge of the path. Left and right edges of the same path are directly linked by a separate pointer field in the edge record. Each edge has a "sense" field which is either "positive" or "negative". A positive edge is one whose tail vertex, as defined on the source polygon, is less than (in Y), or greater than in X if the Y values are equal, its head vertex, ie. it is descending or, if horizontal, moving right. Otherwise the edge is negative. A peak on an input sheet occurs where the edges incident on a vertex are negative then positive in that order.

The record structure for representing an edge has the following fields:

source label: label of input polygon to which edge belongs;

wrapno: wrap number of edge;

sense: positive or negative;

peakedge: boolean which is *true* if the edge derives from a peak event;

lowevent: boolean which is *true* if lower end vertex has been recorded as an event;

matched: boolean used in path matching at an event;

side of path: left or right;

leftbundle, rightbundle: booleans to deal with concurrent edges (see below);

highvert, lowvert: pointers to upper and lower vertices, respectively;

delta: point record containing x and y displacements from upper to lower end of edge;

prededge, nextedge: pointers to predecessor and successor in active edge list;

otheredge: pointer to other side of path.

When an edge leaves the active edge list it is normally discarded, ie. the record returned to free storage. However if the edge derives from a peak it is retained, as peak events are saved with the source polygon to which they belong, so that if the same polygon is used again the preprocessing to find the peaks (see below) need not be repeated. In the application to pattern generation the re-use of the same polygon (or layer) is relatively rare, so the saving of peak events gains relatively little advantage.

Concurrent Edges

Any practical polygon comparison algorithm has to be able to deal with concurrent edges. In the merging of one or more layers of a VLSI layout concurrent edges are a common occurrence. Intersections are normally detected between adjacent edges in the active edge list, but if there are other edges concurrent with either of the two edges participating in the intersection, these edges must also be considered as incident on the event. The same is true when a vertex event occurs on one of a group of concurrent edges.

To facilitate handling of such cases, groups of concurrent edges in the active edge list bound together in so-called "bundles", the binding being done by means of the 'leftbundle' and 'rightbundle' fields in the edge record. The 'rightbundle' field is true for an edge if it is concurrent with its successor, and the 'leftbundle' field true if it is concurrent with its predecessor. Before an event is processed, all concurrent edges are included in its list of upper incident edges. Concurrency is initially detected when lower edges at an event are ordered (see below). All positive edges in a bundle precede all negative edges, but otherwise the order of concurrent edges is arbitrary (though fixed during the lifetime of the bundle).

Outline of Algorithm

The outer structure of the polygon comparison algorithm is as follows:

```
preprocess input polygon(s);
initialise polygon to receive output sheets;
```

```
while event queue not empty do begin
      copy top event from event queue;
      delete top event;
      while new top event coincides with first event do
            begin
            merge new top event with copy of first event;
            delete new top event
            end;
      process copied event record
      end;
```

Events are regarded as co-incident if their integer X and Y co-ordinates and their 'yresidue' fields are all equal. When events are merged, their upper and lower edge lists are combined. The upper incident edges already exist on the active edge list, and the edge record contains pointers to the first and last active edges incident on the event. Relative to the event position, these edges are ordered anticlockwise. When a new edge is added to the upper edge list, it is necessary to check if it precedes the first edge on the upper list, or succeeds the last edge. This is done by comparing its upper vertex with the relevant edge using the point-line comparison function (described below).

Similarly when a new edge is added to the lower edge list, it must be placed in the list in the correct position relative to existing edges, which are ordered anticlockwise relative to the event. However, edge records on the lower edge list are not yet present in the active edge list, so a linear search is required when adding a new edge. Again the point-line comparison function is used to compare the lower vertex of the new edge with each edge in turn on the lower list, until the correct position is found. If the lower vertex is found to be exactly on an existing lower edge, the new edge is included in a bundle with this edge.

When the top event record is deleted from the event priority queue, it is returned to free storage unless it represents a peak event, in which case it is added to the peak list for the input polygon from which it derives. This is why the top event record is copied. If retaining of peak events were dispensed with, the copying would not be necessary. Because of the ordering effect of the event priority queue, peak events are returned to their source polygons in sorted order, which minimises the work necessary if the same polygon is used again in a subsequent comparison.

Detection of co-incident events is simplest if left until the events come to the top of the event queue. A small saving of space might result from earlier merging, but earlier detection would be difficult with the priority queue structure adopted. The commonest cause of co-incident events arises where two edges in the active edge list have a common lower vertex. Because of the method of processing edges, two separate events are recorded for such vertices.

Polygon Preprocessing

A feature of the algorithm presented here is that full advantage is taken of the natural order inherent in the source polygon vertices. Only local maxima (peaks) are considered in the preprocessing step, rather than all vertices. As defined above, a peak is a vertex at which consecutive incident edges are negative (rising or left-moving) and positive (falling or right-moving). Finding the peaks involves examining all vertices, so has time complexity $O(N)$, where N is the total number of vertices, but placing the peaks on the priority event queue has complexity $O(P \log P)$ where P is the number of peaks.

In the case where there are only two input polygons, which are single-sheet and convex, each will have just one peak, so the saving compared with sorting all vertices is potentially substantial. On the other hand, if the input polygons consist of multiple sheets with small numbers of vertices (e.g. rectangles) the saving is slight.

The preprocessing procedure makes use of any existing peak lists in the input polygons. The structure is as follows:

```
if there is only one input polygon then
        record polygon peaks in event queue
else if both input polygons have sorted peak lists then
        merge sorted peak lists directly into event
        queue
else begin
        record polygon peaks for first polygon;
        record polygon peaks for second polygon
end;
```

where "record polygon peaks" is a procedure whose action is:

```
if polygon has sorted peak list then
        add peaks from peak list to event queue
else
        find peaks and record them on event queue;
```

The merging of the sorted peak lists makes use of the fact that in the array representation of the priority event queue, an ordered list in array elements from 1 upwards is also a partially ordered binary tree, so comparison of each newly-added event with its parent event is not necessary. This approach could also be used when already sorted peak events from a single polygon are being added to a previously empty event queue, but has not been implemented because a maximum of one comparison per inserted event is in any case guaranteed in this case.

Processing an Event

The main tasks to be performed when processing an event are:

(i) removing the upper incident edges from the active edge list and replacing them by the lower incident edges;

(ii) matching the paths belonging to the upper incident edges to the lower edges, or where appropriate closing paths to form complete output sheets;

(iii) recording events generated by the lower edges.

Events generated by lower edges include end events for their lower vertices, and intersection events. The leftmost (front) and rightmost (rear) edges on the lower edge list are checked for possible intersection with their new neighbours on the active edge list. If the lower edge list is empty, an intersection check is carried out between the two edges which have newly become adjacent. It is possible that edges which become adjacent in this way may already have been adjacent at some previous stage in the algorithm, so it is necessary to check for and discard any intersection event detected which precedes the current event in the defined event ordering.

The stages in processing an event are as follows:

```
if upper incident edge list is not empty then
            find neighbouring edges from upper edge list
else begin
            search active edge list to find event
            neighbours;
            if event lies on an active edge then
       add this edge to upper edge list of event
end;

if event has upper incident edges then begin
            include any bundled edges in upper edge list,
            and modify neighbour edges accordingly;
            unlink upper incident edges from active edge
            list;
            for each edge in upper edge list do
                  if lower end of edge is below or
                  to right of current event position then
                        add edge to lower edge list for event
            end
end;

if lower edge list is empty then begin
            check neighbouring edges for intersection;
            if intersection found and its position is less
            than position of current event then
                  record intersection event in event queue
                  end
```

```
    else begin
        for each edge on lower edge list do begin
            if lower vertex event has not been recorded
            then begin
                record event for lower vertex of edge;
                assign wrap number to edge
                end;
            check for intersection between left neighbour
            and first edge on lower edge list;
            check for interesection between right
            neighbour and last edge on lower edge list
            end;

        extend or merge paths of upper incident edges;
        link lower incident edges to active edge list;
        dispose of edge records on upper edge list
end;
```

Here the neighbouring edges are the nearest pair of active edges on either side of the event. These are determined simply as the predecessor of the first edge in the upper edge list, and the successor of the last edge in the upper edge list, except where the upper edge list is empty (i.e. at a peak event).

The extension of an upper incident edge which projects below the event requires a little care to ensure that the identity of the event record is preserved. This is because there may be other previously recorded event records in the event queue which refer to this edge in their upper edge list. (Such records will include the lower end event for the edge plus any previously discovered intersection events at locations below the current event.) So it is necessary physically to move the edge record from the upper list to the lower list, leaving a copy of the record on the upper list. The copy is needed for the path matching process but is later returned to free storage with the rest of the records on the upper edge list.

Assigning wrap numbers to edges on the lower edge list is very straightforward, and is summarised below:

```
if left neighbour edge exists then begin
        thiswrap: = wrap number of left neighbour
        edge;
        if sense of left neighbour edge is negative
        then
            thiswrap: = thiswrap -1
        end
else thiswrap: = 0; (* background *)
for each edge on lower edge list do
        if sense of edge is positive then begin
            thiswrap: = thiswrap +1;
            wrap number of edge := thiswrap
            end
        else begin
            wrap number of edge := thiswrap;
            thiswrap : = thiswrap -1
            end;
```

The final value of 'thiswrap' is guaranteed either to be zero, if there is no right neighbouring edge, or to equal

```
nextwrap + s
```

where nextwrap is the wrap number of the right neighbouring edge and s is zero if this edge is negative, and -1 otherwise. In other words, the effect on the wrap number of crossing the edges on the upper edge list from left to right must be the same as the effect of crossing the lower edges, so that replacing the upper edges by the lower edges maintains the consistency of wrap numbers on the active edge list.

This method of assigning wrap numbers ensures that all edges belonging to the union and intersection polygons have the same wrap number, independently of whether they are outer sheets or holes. When a new path is initiated it is given the wrap number of the first pair of edges contributing to it (see below), and it is subsequently contributed to only by further edges with the same wrap number. The simplicity and economy with which wrap numbers may be assigned to output sheets is a major advantage of the plane sweep approach.

Assigning Edges to Paths at an Event

The correct assignment of edges to paths when processing an event is crucial. A general algorithm has been stated previously, but when using the plane sweep approach it is more convenient to adopt an equivalent approach which deals separately with the upper and lower incident edge lists. The method uses the sense of each edge in the matching process, rather than the notion of "ingoing" and "outgoing" edges in the general description. (Positive edges in the upper list are ingoing, and in the lower list are outgoing, and *vice versa* for negative edges).

The function of the matching algorithm is to discover pairs of edges belonging to the same path. If both matched edges are on the upper list, each will already belong to a path. If both belong to the same path, the path closes and is added to the list of output sheets, otherwise the two paths must be merged. If one matched edge is from the upper list and one from the lower (the commonest and simplest case), the path of the upper edge is extended and becomes owner of the lower edge in place of the upper. Finally, if both matched edges are from the lower list, a new path is initiated which owns the two edges. Although wrap numbers are not explicitly used, the algorithm always matches pairs of edges with the same wrap number. An outline of the method follows:

match nested adjacent positive-negative pairs in upper list;
match nested adjacent positive-negative pairs in lower list;
match pairs of negative edges from front of upper list and front of lower list;
match pairs of positive edges from rear of upper list and rear of lower list;

match nested adjacent negative-positive edges in upper list;
match nested adjacent negative-positive edges in lower list;

When a pair of edges are matched they are marked and disregarded in subsequent searches. When nested adjacent positive-negative pairs have been matched, in either list, the remaining unmatched edges must form a sequence (possibly empty) of negative edges followed by a sequence (possibly empty) of positive edges. Matching of upper and lower negative edges from the front of the lists continues until there are no more unmatched negative edges on one or both of the lists. Similarly, matching of upper and lower positive edges from the rear continues until all unmatched positive edges on one or both lists have been processed. This must leave at least one of the lists "empty", ie. with no remaining unmatched edges. If unmatched edges remain, they consist of equal numbers of negative and positive edges, which are then matched from the inside out.

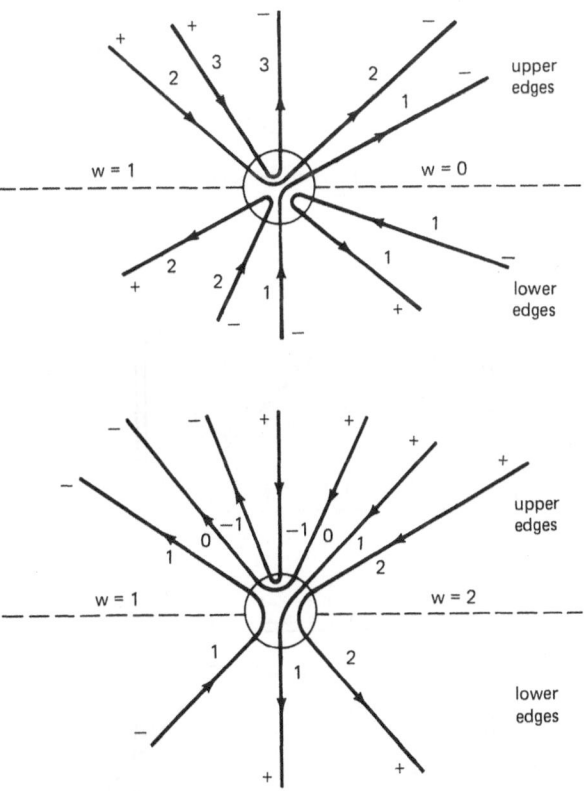

Figure 3

Although this method results in previously-matched edges being examined more often than is strictly necessary, it is straightforward to implement, and the inefficiency is not important since the vast majority of events have four or fewer incident edges. Figure 3 shows two examples of the matching of edges by this algorithm. Wrap numbers on edges are also shown, although not explicitly made use of. It can be seen that the effect of the algorithm is the same as that of the "clockwise search" algorithm given previously.

Merging of Paths at an Event

When the edge-matching algorithm at an event indicates that two edges belonging to different paths have to be joined, the paths owning these edges have to be merged. Three different cases arise (see Figure 4):

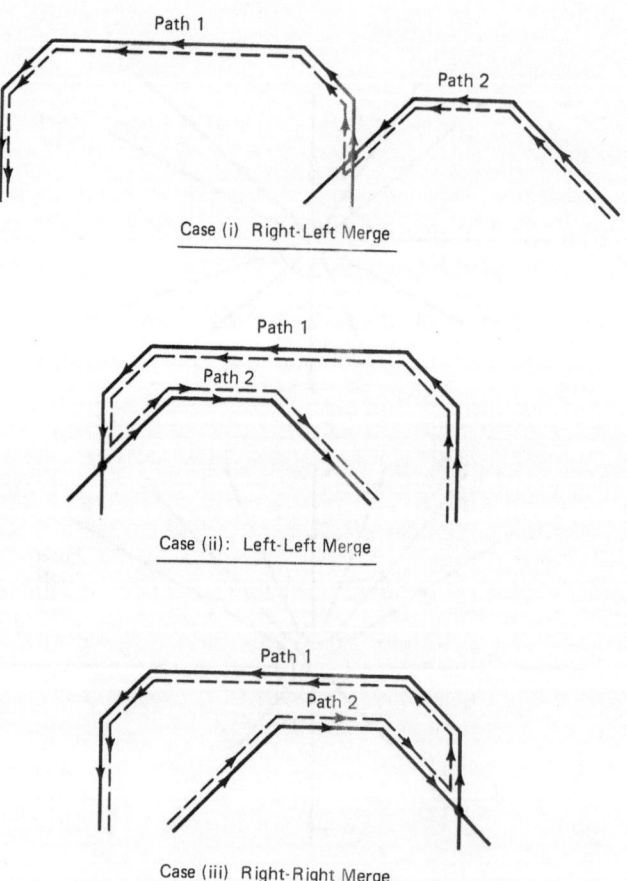

Figure 4

(i) right edge of path 1 joins left edge of path 2
(ii) left edge of path 1 joins left edge of path 2
(iii) right edge of path 1 joins right edge of path 2

In all cases one of the two path records is retained, suitably modified, and the other discarded. The vertex queues of the two paths are concatenated, with a new vertex corresponding to the position of the event, but the order of concatenation is different for the different cases.

Case (i): join front of vertex queue of path 2 to rear of vertex queue of path 1;
left edge of merged path:= left edge of path 1;
right edge of merged path := right edge of path 2;
sense of merged path: = sense of path 1;

Case (ii): join front of vertex queue of path 2 to front of vertex queue of path 2;
left edge of merged path: = left edge of path 2;
right edge of merged path: = right edge of path 2;
sense of merged path: = sense of path 2;

Case (iii): join rear of vertex queue of path 2 to rear of vertex queue of path 1;
left edge of merged path: = left edge of path 1;
right edge of merged path: = left edge of path 2;
sense of merged path: = sense of path 1;

The front vertex of the vertex queue for a path is always on the left edge of the path, and the rear vertex on the right edge. However the "forwards" link in the vertex nodes points from front to rear only if the path has negative sense. Otherwise it is the "backwards" link that points from front to rear, and the forwards link from rear to front. This convention ensures that the queue concatenation procedures for the three cases work consistently.

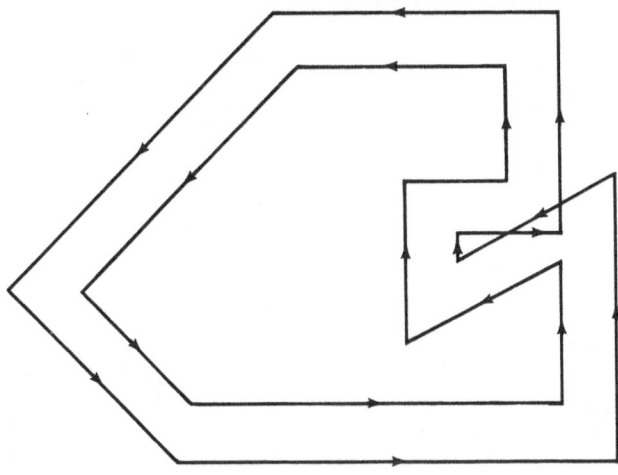

Figure 5

Inflation and Shrinking

General Approach

Inflating a polygonal sheet (sometimes referred to as "bloating") involves moving each of its edges by a given distance b say in a direction perpendicular to its length (and *away* from the polygon interior), and replacing the original vertices by the intersections of the new edges. Shrinking is just inflating by a negative distance. Inflation is illustrated in Figure 5.

A simple sheet or polygon may cease to be simple after inflation or shrinking. However, application of the plane sweep algorithm to the inflated or shrunk polygon allows the extraction of a simple output polygon. Until this self-merge operation is done, inflation is reversible in that a subsequent shrink by the same amount will restore the polygon to its original form. Extracting the equivalent simple polygon after inflation may involve irreversible loss of information, e.g. where a hole disappears.

A problem with inflation if applied in the way described is that the effective width of a sheet is increased by a factor of $\sqrt{2}b$ at right-angle corners (and more at acute corners). One solution is to use circular arcs for the inflated boundary, the centre of the circle being at the original vertex and the radius equal to b. Barton and Buchanan [BART80] describe such an approach. Circles, however, cause problems computationally for several reasons, and it seems preferable to stick to line segments if at all possible.

An alternative to rounding by circular arcs is to snip off corners by a line perpendicular to the join of the old vertex and the new intersection, at a distance from the old vertex equal to the inflation parameter b (Figure 6). If this is done the maximum distance from the old vertex (V in the diagram) to the modified inflated polygonal boundary is given by

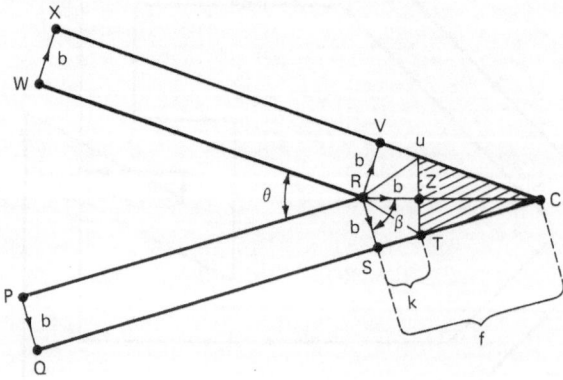

Figure 6

$$d = b \sec(\pi/4 - \theta/4)$$

where θ is the internal angle at the corner. The maximum thickening ratio is thus

$$d/b = \sec(\pi/4 - \theta/4)$$

which has a minimum of 1 when $\theta = \pi$ (edges collinear) and a maximum of $\sqrt{2}$ when $\theta = 0$ (edges collinear, but in opposite directions).

In VLSI layouts there are supposed to be no acute angles (though angles slightly less than 90° can arise due to rounding). For $\theta = 90°$ the thickening ratio is

$$\sec(\pi/8) = 1.0824$$

which is unlikely to cause any problems. The snipping method has the added advantage in the case of rectilinear layouts of introducing only 45° edges (turning rectangles, for example, into octagons after inflation). Also shrinking again after snipping the inflated boundary will restore the original shape.

It is clear that vertices with reflex internal angles should not be snipped after inflation, and for efficiency it is better to avoid snipping obtuse corners above a chosen size. For example, if corners with internal angles of 135° or more are not snipped, the maximum thickening ratio at unclipped corners will be $\sec(\pi/8)$, the same as the maximum ratio at clipped 90° corners. Choosing to clip only corners less than 135° also has the advantage that layouts including only rectilinear and diagonal edges will still have that property after inflation.

Detailed Inflation Algorithm

Consider first an individual edge E_1 of the polygon from vertex P (px,py) to vertex R (rx,ry), as shown in Figure 6. The parametric equation of the edge may be written as

$$x = px + dx{\cdot}t$$
$$y = py + dy{\cdot}t$$
$$\text{where } dx = rx - px$$
$$dy = ry - py.$$

The equation for the normal to E through P in the negative direction (ie. to the right of the line) may be written as

$$x = px + dy{\cdot}u$$
$$y = py - dx{\cdot}u$$

After inflation the edge E will pass through a point Q at distance b along this normal. The value of the parameter u at this point is

$$b/l$$

where

$$l = (dx^2 + dy^2)^{1/2}$$
$$= \text{length of } E.$$

The coordinates (qx, qy) of Q are thus given by

$$qx = px + (b/l)\cdot dy$$
$$qy = py - (b/l)\cdot dx$$

and the equation of the inflated edge is

$$x = qx + dx\cdot v$$
$$y = qy + dy\cdot v$$

To bloat a complete sheet it is necessary to inflate adjacent edges and compute the intersection C of the inflated edges. An edge comparison procedure is used for this, which is more fully described below. It returns the value, v_c say, of the parameter value on the inflated first edge (QS in figure 6) at the intersection with the inflated second edge. If this value is less than 1, the angle between the edges is reflex. If the value is greater than 1, the distance f from S, the inflated corner vertex on the first edge, to the intersection point C, is given by

$$f = l\,(v_c - 1)$$

where l is the length of the edge. Since

$$\tan\beta = f/b$$

where β is half the external angle between the edges, the value of f/b can be used to decide when to snip the corner. A value of 0.5 for f/b represents an angle of about 53° between the edges, and a value of 1 a right angle. The value above which snipping is to occur is a parameter which can be modified to suit circumstances. A value of 1 will cause only corners with internal angles of 90° or less to be snipped.

Where snipping is required, a new point T must replace C on the first inflated edge and a corresponding point W on the second inflated edge. It is not hard to show that

$$k = \text{length of } RT$$
$$= b[(1 + q^2)^{1/2} - 1]$$

where $q = b/f = \cot\beta$

and hence the coordinates of T can be found from the equation of QR. By symmetry W is an equal distance in the negative direction along the second inflated edge.

The complete algorithm for inflation may be expressed as follows:

```
choose any vertex as start vertex;
inflate edge between start vertex and its
successor;
repeat
    current vertex : = next vertex;
    inflate edge between current vertex and its
    successor;
    compare inflated edges, computing position of
    intersection;
```

```
         if distance to intersection point > critical value
         then begin
              snip corner;
              output two vertices of snipped corner
              end
         else
              output intersection point;
         .   assign second inflated edge details to first
              inflated edge
         until current vertex = start vertex;
```

The output vertices are stored in a new doubly-linked circular list. If required the inflated sheet may then be cleaned up by application of the polygon merge procedure.

For deflation or shrinking it is necessary only to use a negative value of the inflation factor b.

Primitive Geometric Operations

All algorithms in the domain now referred to as *computational geometry* depend on a small group of fundamental geometric comparison operations. The availability of correct and efficient implementations of these operations is often taken for granted (as in the recent survey by Lee and Preparata, 1984), yet published correctness proofs, even for apparently trivial geometric operations, are extremely sparse.

A typical case in point is the problem of deciding whether or not two line segments intersect, and if so, finding the intersection point. If the segments have integer end-points and double-length integer arithmetic is available, then the decision problem is straightforward. Accurate location of the intersection point, and identification of the nearest point to it with integer co-ordinates, is more tricky. The approach used in the present system is described below, but no proof of correctness is attempted.

Point-Point Comparison

This is the ordering used in the event queue, and has already been described above. It is essential that events be processed in strict Y order. The worst case arises from edges with a very small negative gradient. Intercepts on such an edge may have y co-ordinates whose fractional part is indistinguishable from zero at floating point precision. Such edges should in principle not occur in VLSI designs, but could result from small errors in the input data.

Events with identical Y co-ordinates normally occur only at exact integer Y values. For points with identical Y values, the ordering is defined by the X value. Points with the same integer part of their X co-ordinate are regarded as co-incident.

Point-Line Comparison

A directed line divides the plane into three regions: a *positive* half-plane consiting of points to the left when travelling along the line, a *negative* half-plane, consisting of points to the right, and finally those points actually *on* the line. In the present application lines are always defined by two points (vertices), $V1$ and $V2$ say, and the direction is from $V1$ to $V2$.

Provided the end-points have integer co-ordinates, and double-length integer arithmetic is available, the question, "given point P (x,y), what is its relationship to the line defined by points A and B?" can always be answered precisely (Figure 7). The sign of the quantity

$$S_{ABP} = (x_B - x_A)(y_P - y_A) - (x_P - x_A)(y_B - y_A)$$

provides the answer. P is in the positive (left) half-plane if S is positive, the negative (right) half-plane is S is negative, and on the line if (and only if) S is zero.

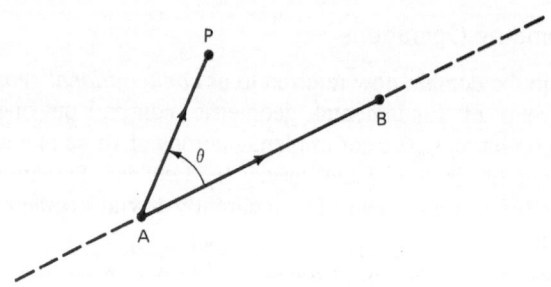

Figure 7

The computation of S requires only five subtractions and two multiplications. S is the cross-product of the vectors AB and AP, and represents twice the area of triangle ABP. It is also equal to

$$l_{AB} \, l_{AP} \sin\theta$$

where l_{AB} and l_{AP} are the lengths of vectors AB and AP respectively, and so may be used to find the angle between the two vectors (though this is not required in the present application). Rather than compute the vector lengths, it is better, if the angle is needed, to compute the quantity

$$C_{ABP} = (x_B - x_A)(x_P - x_A) + (y_{BP} - y_A)(y_P - y_A)$$

which can be shown (using the cosine rule and some simple algebra) to equal

$$l_{AB} l_{AP} \cos\theta$$

Provided the differences are saved from the computation of S_{ABP}, finding C_{ABP} requires only two further multiplications and an addition. Either the tangent or cotangent, whichever does not exceed 1, can be found from the ratio of S and C, and hence the angle (using the appropriate inverse function, or simply table look-up). The signs of S and C also allow the correct quadrant to be determined. This is a more efficient and accurate method of finding the angle between two vectors than that suggested in [BOWY83].

The computation of S forms the basis for the comparison of two line segments, discussed in the next section. The point-line comparison test is also used in two other ways in the polygon processing system. The first is where a new (peak) event has to be placed relative to existing edges in the edge list. All the edges are regarded for this purpose as pointing downwards (from "upper end" to "lower end") and the task is to locate two adjacent edges, say AB and CD, such that $S_{ABP} > 0$ and $S_{CDP} \leq 0$. (The left neighbour is null if $S \leq 0$ for the first edge, and the right neighbour null if $S > 0$ for the last edge.)

The second application of the point-line comparison is for the cyclic ordering of lower edges emanating from the same event. When a new edge is to be added to the lower edge list of an event, it has to be inserted in such a way as to preserve the anticlockwise ordering of the edges with respect to the event. This is done by comparing the lower end of the new edge to each existing edge in turn, using the point-line comparison test, until a value of $S \leq 0$ is found. The new edge is inserted preceding the first edge found with this property (or appended, if no such edge is found). The search is similar to that required when locating a new peak relative to active edges, except that the number of comparisons required is likely to be quite small.

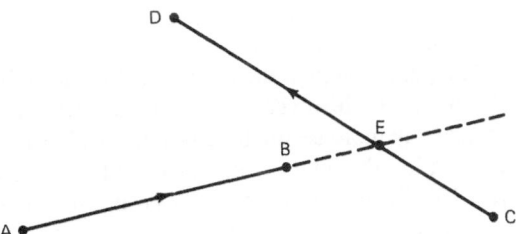

Figure 8

Line-Line Comparison

Given end points with integer co-ordinates, the question, "given two line segments AB and CD, say, do they intersect?" can always be answered correctly. (Accurate computation of the intersection point is another matter, however.)

A first step is to discover whether C and D are on the same or opposite sides of the line AB. This may be done by computing

$$S_{ABC} = (x_B - x_A)(y_C - y_A) - (x_C - x_A)(y_B - y_A)$$

and

$$S_{ABD} = (x_B - x_A)(y_D - y_A) - (x_D - x_A)(y_B - y_A)$$

and comparing their signs. If the signs are the same (and neither is zero), then no intersection is possible, because both points are on the same side of AB.

If the signs of S_{ABC} and S_{ABD} are opposite, the value of the parameter t (in the parametric form of the equation of RS) at the point E say where RS crosses the line AB is given by

$$t_E = S_{ABC}/(S_{ABC} - S_{ABD})$$

The $S_{ABC} - S_{ABD}$ may be written as S_{ABCD}, and may be shown (by simple algebra) to equal

$$(x_B - x_A)(y_D - y_C) - (y_B - y_A)(x_D - x_C)$$

and also equals twice the area of quadrilateral $ACBD$. Although its proof requires only simple algebra, the existence of this elegant and optimal (in terms of computational cost) formula for the area of a quadrilateral appears to have been unknown until given by Shamos in Appendix 1 of his thesis [SHAM78].

From the value of t_E the co-ordinates of E can be found:

$$x_E = x_C + (x_D - x_C)t_E$$
$$y_E = y_C + (x_D - x_C)t_E$$

and it then remains to determine whether E is within the line segment AB. This may be done by testing if either x_E is between x_A and x_B, or y_E is between y_A and y_B.

Because of the limited precision of floating point numbers, it is possible that roundoff in x_E and y_E could give an incorrect result, although the circumstances in which this may happen have not been fully analysed. For a guaranteed decision as to whether or not the line segments intersect, it would be possible to compute S_{CDA} and S_{CDB} and compare their signs. If they also differ in sign, the segments definitely intersect. However, it is not clear that accurate location of the interseciton is made any more secure by this additional test.

In the present application the intersection co-ordinates are reported in integer and fractional form. The fractional part of the x co-ordinate is not required for subsequent point (event) comparison, and is discarded.

Expected Performance

Let p be the number of peaks in the input polygon(s), and k the number of edge intersections. Each peak adds 2 edges to the active edge list when processed, so the size of the active edge list cannot exceed $2p$. If a balanced tree index to the active edge list is used, the cost of inserting a new peak would thus be $O(\log p)$, and the total cost of peak insertion in the active edge list would be $O(p \log p)$ at worst.

The other critical structure is the event list. Since the size of the active edge list cannot exceed $2p$, and at any time only intersections between neighbouring edges are detected, the number of events on the event queue cannot exceed $3p$. If

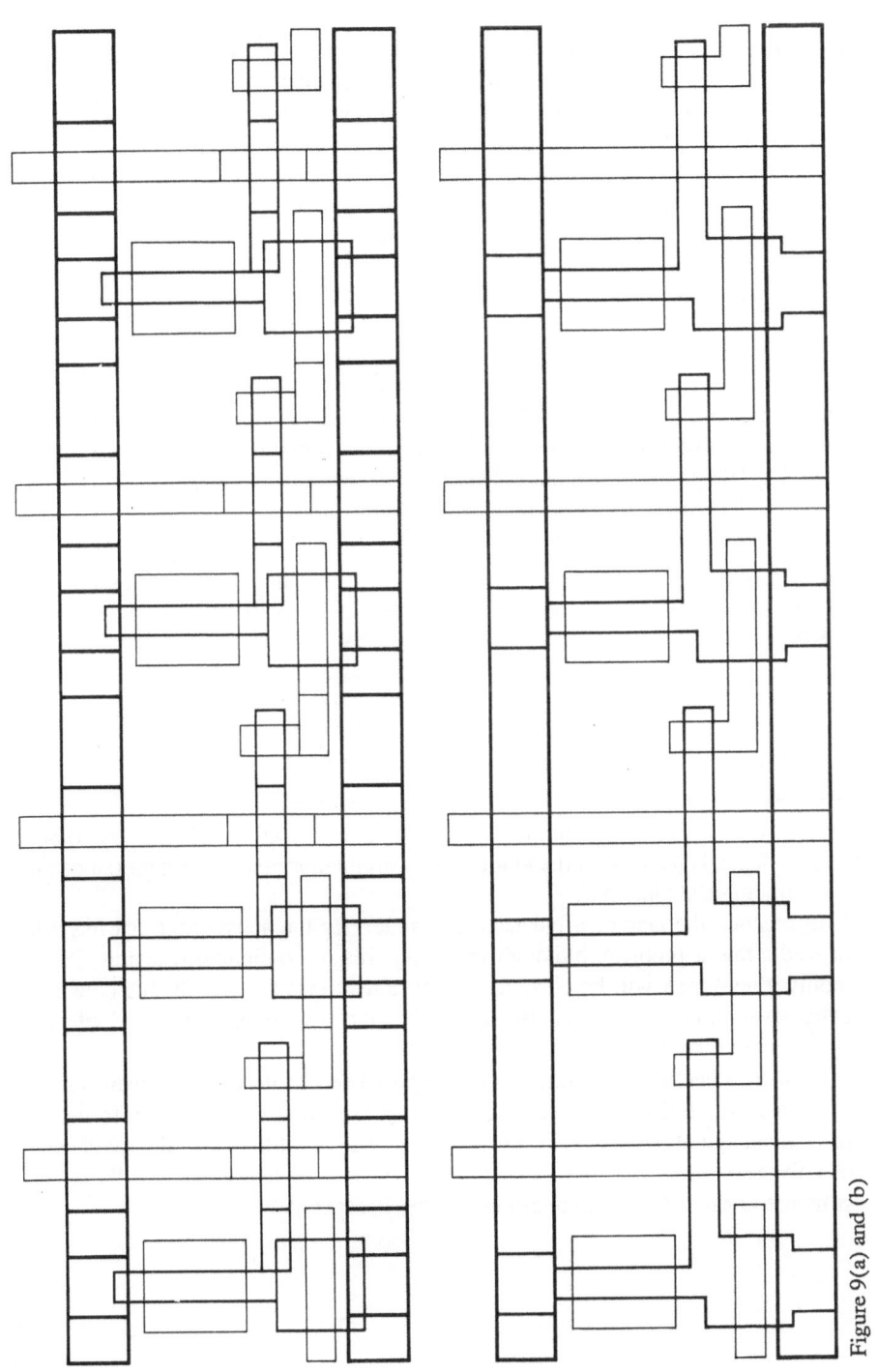

Figure 9(a) and (b)

the event queue is maintained as a heap, the cost of inserting a new event, or deleting the top event, is thus $O(\log p)$. The total number of events cannot exceed $n + k$, where n is the total number of edges (and vertices). Hence the total cost of all operations on the event queue is $O(n + k)\log p$.

Putting these two results together gives a total expected efficiency of $O((n + p + k)\log p) = O((n + k)\log p)$, since $p \leq n/2$. For two convex polygons, $p = 2$ and $k \leq n/2$, so the efficiency is $O(n)$, which is optimal.

Practical Experience

The system has been in practical use as part of the Lattice Logic Shapesmith PG package [LATT86] for over two years, without major problems. It has been carefully tuned and optimised by Neil Menzies of Lattice Logic, and appears to be significantly faster than competitive systems. The initial implementation was on a VAX 11/780 under VMS, but the system has been successfully ported to SUN, Apollo and Whitechapel MG-1 workstations.

Typical execution times for the VAX VMS implementation are given below:

No. of Polygons	No. of Vertices	CPU Time / (hrs : mins : secs)
888	3678	29
4951	19848	2:59
16099	65896	7:09
277100	1108972	1:52:57
919000	3986217	14:44:57

The final figure was dominated by paging overheads, and like the other figures depends heavily on the amount of main memory on the system (since all data structures are internal).

In practice the lack of a balanced tree index for the active edge list has not proved a major problem, although this is an area of continuing research. Commonly a new peak will be close to the previously-inserted one. If this does not apply, every tenth edge is examined, and then the precise location found when a sign change is detected.

Further research is concentrating on the possibility of using parallelism (based on an area-subdivision approach) to speed up execution times, and on trying to take advantage of the hierarchical structure of the circuit to reduce the overheads of polygon comparsion. (At present the circuit is completely "flattened", ie. all structure expanded, prior to merging or other operations.)

Acknowledgements. Firstly I would like to thank John Gray and Irene Buchanan (formerly of Lattice Logic, now with European Silicon Structures) who first inspired my interest in the polygon processing problem, and gave constant support and encouragement during the development of the system. I would also like to thank Neil Menzies of Lattice Logic who has converted my initial code into a robust and efficient commercial product. Finally, thanks are due to the University of Glasgow for study leave during which the basic ideas underlying the system were developed.

References

[BART80] BARTON, E. E. and BUCHANAN, I., The polygon package. Comp. Aided Design 12, 1 (Jan 1980) 3-11

[BENT79] BENTLEY, J. L. and OTTMAN, T. A., Algorithms for reporting and counting geometric intersections. IEEE Trans. on Computers C-28, 9 (Sept 1979) 643-647

[BENT80] BENTLEY, J. L. and WOOD, D., An optimal worst case algorithm for reporting intersections of rectangles. IEEE Trans. on Computers C-29, 7 (July 1980) 571-576

[BERE81] BERETTA, G. and NIEVERGELT, J., Scan conversion algorithms revisited. Informatik, ETH-Zentrum, Zurich (1981)

[BOWY83] BOWYER, A. and WOODWARK, J. A Programmer's Geometry. Butterworths, London (1983)

[BURT77] BURTON, W., Representation of many-sided polygons and polygonal lines for rapid processing. Comm ACM 20,3 (1977) 166-171

[EAST72] EASTMAN, C. M. and YESSIOS, C. I., An efficient algorithm for finding the union, intersection and differences of spatial domains. Dept. of Computer Science, Carnegie-Mellon Universty. (Sept. 1972)

[FOLE82] FOLEY, D. and VAN DAM, A., Fundamentals of Interactive Computer Graphics, Addison-Wesley, 1982

[GRAY81] GRAY, J. P. (Ed.) VLSI 81. Academic Press, 1981

[HON80] HON, R. W. and SEQUIN, C. H., A guide to LSI implementation. Zerox Palo Alto Research Centre Report (Jan 1980) 79-123

[KILG82] KILGOUR, A. C., A span-line approach to the polygon intersection problem. Report 82R6, Dept. of Computing Science, University of Glasgow (Dec. 1982)

[LATT86] LATTICE LOGIC LTD Shapesmith PG, Artwork Manipulation and Mask Preparation Software Suite, Reference Manual, Version 3.1.1. 9 Wemyss Place, Edinburgh (Jan 1986)

[LEE84] LEE, D. T. and PREPARATA, F. P., Computational geometry - a survey. IEEE Trans. on Computers C-33, 12 (Dec. 1984) 1072-1101

[MEAD80] MEAD, C. A. and CONWAY, L. A. Introduction to VLSI Systems. Addison-Wesley, 1980

[NEWE72] NEWELL, M. E., NEWELL, R. G. and SANCHA, T. L., A solution to the hidden surface problem. Proc ACM National Conf. (1972) 443-450

[NEWE80] NEWELL, M. E. and SEQUIN, C. H., The inside story on self-intersecting polygons. Lambda (now VLSI Design) 1,2 (Second Quarter 1980) 20-24

[NIEV82] NIEVERGELT, J. and PREPARATA, F. P., Plane-sweep algorithms for intersecting geometric figures. Comm ACM. 25,10 (oct 1982) 739-747

[SECH81] SECHREST, S. and GREENBERG, D., A visible polygon reconstruction algorithm. Comp. Graphics 15,3 (Aug. 1981) 17-27

[SEDG83] SEDGEWICK, R., Algorithms. Prentice-hall, 1983

[SHAM75] SHAMOS, M. I., Geometric complexity. Proc 7th ACM Symp. on Theory of Computing (May 1975) 224-233

[SHAM76] SHAMOS, M. I. and HOEY, D., Geometric intersection problems. Proc. IEEE 17th Conf on Foundations of Comp. Science (1976) 208-215

[SHAM78] SHAMOS, M. I., Geometric Complexity. Ph.D. thesis, University of Yale (1978)

[STEA82] STEARN, D. D., Vista: visual impact simulation technical aid. In D.S. Greenway and E.A. Warman (eds.) EUROGRAPHICS 82 North-Holland (1982) 333-337

[SUTH74] SUTHERLAND, I. E. and HODGMAN, G. W., Reentrant polygon clipping. Comm. ACM 17, 1 (Jan. 1974) 32-42

[SUTH79] SUTHERLAND, I. E., The polygon package. File no. 1438, Silicon Structures Project, California Institute of Technology (1979)

[TILO80] TILOVE, R. B., Set membership classification: a unified approach to geometric intersection problems. IEEE Trans on Computers C-29, 10, (Oct. 1980) 874-883

[WEIL77] WEILER, K. and ATHERTON, P., (1977) Hidden surface removal using polygon area sorting. Comp. Graphics 11,2 (Summer 1977) 214-222

[WEIL80] WEILER, K., Polygon comparison using a graph representation. Comp. Graphics 14,3 (July 1980) 10-18

6 Human-Computer Interface

Human Factors of
Input and Output Devices

B. SHACKEL

"A computer is like life is like a sewer - what you get out of it depends very much upon what you put into it."

— Adapted from Tom Lehrer

Abstract

For many users the computer is remote and hidden; the terminal or workstation is effectively the computer to them. This interface from the computer must be made to match well the needs and characteristics of the human user, if good human-computer interaction is to be possible. This paper outlines some of the relevant human characteristics which must be allowed for, and then discusses various human factors aspects of input and output devices and of terminal design.

Introduction

Scope

For the users of today's computer systems, the terminal is in effect the computer. What the user must input to the computer, and what the user sees and/or hears in return, is the totality of his/her human-computer interaction. So the 'human interface' through which this interaction occurs becomes the computer for the user.

This human interface comprises any feature with which the users may interact during their work. So the human interface consists not only of hardware aspects but also of any relevant software and documentation. The hardware interface comprises the displays, controls, terminals, printers, consoles and similar equipment having a fixed physical form. The software interface comprises those parts of the human-computer interaction process which are not hardware, are more transitory and are varied by program control:- for example, the format and layout of the messages between user and system, the logical structure and sequence of operation of the procedures for using a word-processor or an accounting system, etc. The documentation comprises the initial start-up guide, the detailed operating tutorial, the reference manual, the maintenance and fault-finding manual, the 'help' facilities, the memory aid card, etc., which should be supplied with any computer application to support the users during their learning and regular use of the system.

This paper is concerned with the hardware parts of the human interface; the hardware comprises the input and output devices, the terminal or workstation, and also the relevant workspace and environment features. The lecture to be presented and this paper are both drawn from a much longer text being revised for publication; only the major topics can be summarised in this shorter version, with particular attention to various comparisons.

Human	Computer
Central Processor	*Central Processor*

Storage - about 10^8 to 10^{12} 'chunks'
     - associative
     - errors of detail
	Storage - about 10^6 to 10^{10} bits
	     - literal
	     - depends on file structure

Slow - about 5 - 50 'chunks'/sec	very fast - up to 10^8 bits/sec
Much preprocessing (eg 10^8 eye receptors into 10^6 optic nerves	Accurate and excellent calculator
Adaptive and Heuristic	Depends upon skill of system designers and programmers
Self-reprogrammable	

Input ⇐ ⇐ ⇐ ⇐	*Output*
Multi-channel	Mainly visual at present
Very flexible	Limited speech mode is developing
Slow	Can be fast
Wide dynamic range (eg in intensity up to 10^9)	

Output ⇒ ⇒ ⇒ ⇒	*Input*
Multi-channel	Mainly manual at present
Multi-axis	Limited hearing mode is developing
Slow	
Very flexible	Engineering constraints limit flexibility

Figure 1 - Two sophisticated information processing entities with limited communication links between them.

Human Channels   Computer Devices

Input	Output	
Eyes	Visual displays	several basic types exist (with many different manufactured versions)
Ears	Aural displays	research prototypes and some production versions
Nose	?	doubtful use except for fault detection
Skin	Tactile displays	research on aids for the blind

Input	Output	
Hands	Manual controls	many types exist
Arms	Arm controls	several types exist but only in vehicle systems or vehicle simulators (eg steering
Legs	Leg controls	wheels, pedals, joysticks)
Voice	Voice controls	research prototypes, and some production versions with vocabulary about 50 to 200 words (isolated speech) and recently some up to 1000 words
Head	Head controls	research (some prototypes and a few military versions)
Eyes	Eye position or movement controls	research (mainly for military)
Muscle potentials	Bioelectric controls	tailored systems for direct electro-physiological control of prostheses; research on direct control by brain electric signals

Figure 2 - Summary of present status of human-computer communication links

Human Characteristics

While the discussion in this paper will primarily be in terms of hardware, we should remember that the aim must be to match the equipment to the capabilities and characteristics of the human user. When we compare the general characteristics of the human sensory and action modalities, or human input and output, with the related computer characteristics, we see a considerable mismatch. In essence, we find two sophisticated information processing entities with limited communication links between them (Figure 1).

The present position in the development of communication links between human and computer can best be illustrated by listing the various possible human input/output channels and then noting the current status of engineering development of devices to link with these channels. This summary is presented in Figure 2.

The potential for development, and the present very limited state of progress, is evident. Few of the whole range of possibilities are at present used even for special systems. However, quite a number of them are now being explored in research projects, and in some cases prototype equipment is being tested. As would be expected, much of the research is supported from military funds, but in some cases the stimulus is not military but toward the rehabilitation of the disabled.

Input Devices

Introduction

In this section and the next some aspects of particular input and output devices will be discussed. The interrelation of these devices in complete terminals will be discussed in the subsequent section on "Some Related Terminal Topics".

The Main Types of Input Device

To provide a synoptic view, summaries of the devices with their principal features and references have been written in tabular form in the longer text. Designers and users of interactive computer systems can select from a fair array of possibilities, although not all are readily available. The principal devices are too many to be summarised here; only keyboards and speech input will be mentioned and then some comparisons, especially of pointing devices, will be discussed.

Keyboards

Keyboards are the most widely used technique for inputting information to computers. The design of computer input keyboards has been greatly influenced by traditional typewriter design. Consequently the QWERTY layout for typewriters has become the de facto standard for the computer input keyboard. Moreover, evidence has been accumulating in recent years [NOYE83b] to suggest that the QWERTY layout is by no means as unsatisfactory as earlier believed.

Sequential vs Chord Keyboards

Unlike the QWERTY standard typewriter keyboard, keying on a chord keyboard is carried out by simultaneous patterned pressing of one or more keys, as with a piano or organ. This results in fewer keys being needed on a chord keyboard when compared with a sequential keyboard, where keys are pressed one at a time. The chord keyboard was first studied as a data entry device in the 1950s, but it was not until the 1970s that chord keyboards became commercially available, and within the last decade three chord keying devices have been marketed. The emphasis upon the development of these recent keyboards has been on more general purpose applications.

An excellent review by Noyes [NOYE83a], based upon her thesis [MART81], has reviewed and summarised the present situation very well. Many of the advantages of chord keyboards stem from their size, and one-handed operation, which increases their flexibility. It would appear unlikely that ease of learning would be an aspect favouring a chord keyboard when compared with a sequential keyboard, since chord keyboards require initial guidance before they can be used, followed by intensive learning of the chord patterns.

At present, there seems little justification for developing 'general purpose' chord keyboards since the sequential keyboards available fulfil the majority of the requirements of the general population. However, it could be argued that although there appears to be no immediate need for a general purpose chord keyboard, the rapid development of personal computers might create the need.

New Keyboard Developments

Probably the most significant change which could be made for standard keyboards is at last being implemented. As long ago as 1926 it was suggested (by Klockenberg) that the posture and position of the hands enforced by the keyboard was very awkward and would be much improved if the keyboard were split, so that the two halves could be placed further apart and more convenient for each hand. This concept was first implemented in a product offered for open sale in the PCD Maltron keyboard (see illustration in [NOYE83b]) on which not merely are the keys separated from the two hands, but also set at different heights so as to fit the unequal lengths of the fingers.

Recent extensive research by Zipp et al [ZIPP83] has proved the reduction in physiological strain, and therefore effort for the user, to be gained by separating the two halves of the keyboard, rotating them outwards at their nearer edge to the user, and also sloping them outwards so that the outer sides are lower than the inner. Similar research by Nakaseko et al [NAKA83] has led to the successful adoption of such a design in a keyboard being marketed now by S.T.R. of Switzerland. Similar studies have been conducted by Brunner & Kopfer [BRUN83] which will probably lead to a similar product design on the market.

Such full implementations of ergonomics results, that lead to significant reductions in the effort for the human user, and probably also in improvements in productivity, are much to be applauded.

Finally, the layout of keyboards for national and cultural groups has received much attention recently. Hanes [HANE75] gave some general guidelines; Radhakrishnan et al [RADH83] and Al-Khalili [ALKH84] have presented designs for Indian script and Arabic keyboards respectively; and the Stuttgart University I.A.O. has been studying the human factors issues in the development of a multilanguage keyboard for the European Community [FAEH83].

Speech Input

Speech recognition is suggested by some to be the ultimate step in transferring information from the human to the computer. Computer speech recognition means that a person can speak commands, read text, etc., and it will be reliably recognised and interpreted by the computer. Using speech as the form of human-to-computer communication may greatly simplify the requirement placed on the user because he or she uses a well-learned mode of communication.

If we separate speech recognition into three levels, ie. isolated word recognition, speech but with enlarged delays between words, and continuous speech recognition, we can say that quite good success is being achieved with the first, the second can be handled less well (and is not really very useful), but the third is not even within sight. Moreover, there must still be constraints on the user even to achieve the first level of isolated word recognition. Nevertheless, various successful systems are in operation, and isolated word recognition for vocabularies of 30-200 words is achieved with quite good success. Recently Kurtzweil has claimed commercial success for a machine with a 1000 word vocabulary.

Successful applications of speech recognition machines have been claimed in working situations such as baggage handling at airports, incoming goods section at warehouses, and parcel sorting. In computer-aided design, speech data entry is being used to aid text annotation on engineering drawings, printed circuit board layouts, and in the preparation of programmed tapes for numerically controlled machine tools. Finally, many groups are doing research on word-processing applications with the aim of producing the 'voice typewriter', but this goal is certainly some way into the future.

Advantages and Disadvantages

In a useful review of the present status, [LAMB84] has summarised the situation as follows. "Voice data entry offers the greatest advantage for tasks which are complex and use multiple modalities, in which the operator is very busy or overloaded and speed is important, in which the voice channel is not already saturated and in which provision can be made for verification of entries and correction of the small percentage of errors typically made by current devices.

Benefits of voice data entry include freedom of hands, eyes and thought for other tasks; mobility and general freedom of movement; no panel space requirement; compatibility with audio and visual feedback; and facilitation of simultaneous multi-model communication. It may permit sequential tasks to be done in parallel; it can be used in darkness or when the user is otherwise handicapped. It requires minimal operator training and with appropriate training of the recogniser can accommodate different talkers, languages, and dialects.

Limitations include complexity, which can adversely affect reliability and maintainability; some substitution, rejection, and false alarm errors requiring effective entry verification and error correction procedures; and critical signal level requirements, usually necessitating a properly positioned headset microphone. Vocabulary must be limited to a few hundred words; there must be specific training of the machine by the speaker with the vocabulary and in the environment which has to be used; and the system performance will usually be sensitive to changes in the speaker's voice due to stress or other factors.

Many of the current limitations of speech recognisers can be overcome in specific applications by carefully implementing necessary control conditions; constraint or limitation would be needed upon: -vocabulary size and confusability, redundancy of recognition patterns, number of training passes, speaker population and training, environmental conditions, syntax structures, possible cementing interpretations, and task-related alternatives. Nevertheless, improvements may be expected as the technology matures, and already the cost, availability, size and interface requirements of recognition equipment are certainly improving.

Comparisons

No researcher has yet been able to conduct a comprehensive comparison of all the different input devices from the ergonomics point of view. Indeed, many of the comparison studies which have been done have not first optimised the operation for the human user of the various input devices examined. There is still much ergonomic research to be done to provide valid results comparing the best performance possible from different types of input device. However, some useful data can be given from fairly recent research upon some of the devices.

Voice, Keyboard and Light-pen

One of the best studies of voice input so far was carried out by Welch [WELC80] using one of the best commercial systems available at that time. He measured the speed and accuracy of subjects entering data by either voice input or a typical keyboard or a light-pen. Only one small advantage was found for the voice input device; with it the subjects made fewer errors confusing 'O' with '0' and '1' with 'I' - probably because they could keep their eyes on the text. However, in general the subjects were slower and made more errors with voice input than with the other, more conventional devices.

In a subsequent experiment, Welch added a second task in which the subjects had to press a button while performing data input. Under these circumstances the speed of voice input was degraded much less than the speed of either keyboard or light-pen input. These results agree well with those of Mountford & North [MOUN80].

The general conclusion one can offer, tentatively, from the research done so far, is that voice input may be expected to be useful and productive, but more in special conditions and situations than in simple data entry tasks. General guidelines cannot be offered at present, and each potential application needs to be reviewed carefully to see if the ergonomic factors are such as to favour the use of voice input.

Touchscreen, Touchpad and Trackball

Whitfield et al [WHIT83] made a very thorough experimental study to compare performance with a touchpanel mounted directly in front of the CRT screen, a somewhat similar touchpad mounted on the desk in front of the display unit, and the conventional trackball. The tasks carried out by the subjects involved both rather coarse selection of items within a typical menu, rather more precise selection of cells within a large matrix on the screen, and accurate target selection of single small objects on the display. They found that both performance and subjective reaction from the subjects were no worse for the off-display touch input than for the on-display touchscreen; however, both devices were worse than a trackball for high resolution targets. For precise details reference should be made to the original paper. The interesting conclusion is that the ergonomically less 'compatible' off-screen touchpad was found to be no worse than the on-display touchscreen.

Mouse Compared with Other Devices

In the last few years the mouse input device has gained much attention in the microcomputer market place, and has almost become something of a 'gimmick'. The ergonomic evidence in its favour comes from two studies, by English et al [ENGL67] and by Card et al [CARD78]. The latter study compared the mouse with a rate-controlled isometric joystick, with the familiar cluster of five cursor keys, and with text keys similar to those of word-processing terminals (which move the cursor along to the next character, word, line or paragraph). The mouse was found to be faster than the joystick by about 10% and faster than the keys by about 30% (average movement times being 1.66, 1.83 and about 2.2 seconds respectively) and, perhaps more important, giving only about half the error rate of the other devices (5% against 9-13%).

However, it must be noted that these results were obtained from only four subjects (even though they were fully trained to reach a steady level of performance). Further, the test procedure involved the subjects in an extensive series of single trials, each of which involved pressing the space bar, moving to the control device and with it moving the cursor from its present position to a clearly marked target on the screen; this task would not successfully simulate the loss and recovery of hand location on the home keys when involved in touch-typing. For this reason, the experiment may not extrapolate fully to positioning the cursor when touch-typing the text.

The general conclusion would seem to be that the mouse has definite advantages, but for some people and some tasks (particularly touch-typing) the advantages may not be significant and individual users may have preferences for other input devices.

Output Devices

Introduction

Before reviewing output devices, a brief discussion of some human characteristics may be useful. Although detailed data will not be presented, there are two general principles which underlie and help to explain many differences in human performance. These are that (1) perception in particular, but also, action depends on organisation, and that (2) there are basic differences in functional performance between different human input and output modalities.

The basic fact about *perception* in any domain is that it is an active organising process of interpreting incoming sensory data on the basis of experience. Although different people have large amounts of experience of the real world in common, the details, even quite important details, may vary from individual to individual. And the immediate context is relevant too. This is why different people may honestly disagree in their descriptions of events and in their interpretation of situations witnessed together. The importance of this principle of perception is that it can be the key to major improvements. If the users have to reorganise complex information, then they may interpret it differently or make errors. However, if the complex information is displayed differently, in a way which better matches the organisation characteristics of perception, then the users will all interpret it similarly, faster and more accurately.

Turning to the second general principle, the basic *differences between different modalities* in their functional performance are equally important. For example, there are marked differences in speed of receiving information between silent reading and listening. Compare the impossibility of understanding an author at a conference reading his written paper at apparently breakneck speed, which in fact will never be more than 150-200 words per minute, with the ease of normal silent reading which averages 250-350 words per minute. Similarly, there is a marked difference in speed between skilled handwriting and skilled typing and other action modalities. Thus, we see that these two general principles underlie and explain many observed differences in human performance.

The Main Types of Output Device

To provide a synoptic view, summaries of the devices with their principal features and references have been written in tabular form in the longer text.

Although teletypewriters and alphanumeric CRT displays are the most common forms of output device used in computer systems, there are numerous other possibilities from which designers may choose. The principal developments, in recent years, in output devices for direct interaction with the user have been in electronic displays. The underlying display technologies have been clearly summarised, and a selection procedure oriented towards human factors aspects has been described, by Bailey [BAIL82] based upon a comprehensive report by Snyder [SNYD80].

In this Section some general suggestions are first offered about selecting and designing displays, and then various human factors aspects are discussed and illustrated - again primarily in terms of comparisons between alternatives.

Selecting a Display Technology and Designing the Human Factors Aspects

This section suggests a procedure by which a designer can select one or more CRT or flat panel display technologies for a specific application [SNYD80]. The procedure also can be used to evaluate specific display designs against system and user requirements. The procedure requires knowledge of the information to be displayed, the environment in which the display will be used, the layout of the user's work station, and any voltage/power constraints.

Define Display Functional Requirements

The first step in any display selection/evaluation process is the specification of the functional requirements of a display. In this step, it is then necessary to answer the following questions:

1. What symbology must be displayed?
2. Is dynamic presentation required? If so, at what data rates?
3. Is the displayed information alphanumeric, vectorgraphic, or pictorial, or some combination of these?

4. How much of this information must be presented simultaneously, and in what format?
5. What are the workspace layout constraints?
6. What environmental/power contraints exist?
7. What is the nature of the ambient illuminance?

These functional requirements should then be used to generate more specific design or performance requirements.

Establishing Design Requirements

The functional requirements indicate what information is to be displayed, where, when, and how often. The design requirements, on the other hand, specify the exact design variables to which the hardware (and software) must conform to assure an acceptable level of user performance.

Some of the most important human performance related considerations that should be specified in the design requirements are:

- application characteristics,
- display size,
- colour capability,
- luminance capability, and
- resolution.

Display Details

The final stage involves much design work to decide the details of the display itself, such as character size and resolution, and of the structure of the information to be presented in terms of format, layout, etc. Substantive recommendations on these topics are presented by Cakir et al [CAKI80], Damodaran et al [DAMO80], Galitz [GALI81] and Tullis [TULL83].

Comparisons

Visual versus Auditory Displays

To design good displays, a designer should know as much as possible about the tasks to be performed. The designer must analyse carefully the reasons for displaying each item of information, how the information will be used, its importance, when it will be used, and what the user is likely to be doing at that time. Different users of the same information during normal operation versus an emergency situation must also be considered. The above general recommendations apply when considering any display requirements.

Specific criteria can then be applied to consider whether a visual or an auditory display would be more appropriate. These criteria are set out as a set of recommendations in Figure 3.

Use auditory presentation if:	*Use visual presentation if:*
1. The message is simple	1. The message is complex
2. The message is short.	2. The message is long.
3. The message will not be referred to later.	3. The message will be referred to later.
4. The message deals with events in time.	4. The message deals with location in space.
5. The message calls for immediate action.	5. The message does not call for immediate action.
6. The person's visual system is overburdened.	6. The person's auditory system is overburdened.
7. The receiving location is too bright or dark-adaptation integrity is necessary.	7. The receiving location is too noisy.
8. The job requires continual movement.	8. The job allows for a stationary position.

Figure 3 - Recommendations for using auditory or visual forms of presentation (Source: Deatherage [DEAT72]).

'Windowing' versus 'Scrolling'

This issue has been debated by many over the years on the basis of personal experience and opinion; now a definitive experiment has been reported [BURY82]. The 'scroll' mode which has more often been provided on visual display terminals involves moving the data, that is, pressing the 'scroll up' key moves the data up on the screen. By contrast, the 'window' mode involves moving your window, so that pressing the 'window up' key moves the window up and thus displays data on the screen nearer towards the beginning of the file.

In their experiment, Bury *et al* tested a total of 281 novice subjects under various experimental conditions. Results showed that in most cases subjects in the window groups performed significantly faster and with significantly fewer moves than did subjects in the scroll groups. Equally, when allowed to 'self-define' the system, a significant majority of the subjects defined the system to 'window'. Explaining and demonstrating the appropriate concept had no significant effect on performance, nor did the use of key top graphic 'scroll' figures.

Display Screen Size

Finally, we should note a shortcoming of most visual displays; they are usually too small. Too little attention has been given to the maximum size, in terms of the number of character spaces available if an alphanumeric display, or of the physical size and resolution if a graphical display.

For example, typescript and book pages typically comprise 70 to 80 character spaces per line and 40 to 50 lines per display (ie. per page), totalling about 3000 to 4000 spaces. Alphanumeric CRT displays typically comprise about 24 lines of 80 characters, ie. about 1900 spaces, and the largest is about 32 lines of 80, ie. about 2600 spaces. Thus the user is presented with, at most, about one-half of the page size with which he is familiar; does this significantly affect performance, especially if turning the page is not so easy as with a book or file?

Again, sketches and drawings typically range in size from an A4 page up to a 50x30 inch drawing, but in all cases with a human visual capability of about 1 thousandth of an inch and a line-drawing resolution of about 5 thousandths. Graphical CRT displays have limited picture size and resolution so that drawings, such as circuit diagrams or architect's plans, often cannot be presented whole. Various techniques for zooming and using a movable 'enlargement window' are being used, but the question again arises, do these limitations significantly affect performance?

So far, there is very little hard evidence on these questions, and we must hope that the gap will be recognised and research stimulated. While it seems likely that engineering progress will in due course overcome these limitations, it is suggested, that, at the least, ergonomics research could lead to a better understanding of how far such developments must go to satisfy essential user needs. Moreover, since better display performance is always likely to cost more, the results of such research should help the user to make a cost-effective choice between different displays for different types of usage.

Screen versus Paper

After so much work was done in the 1970s to overcome the slowness of the printer by developing cheap VDUs, it is somewhat ironical that recent studies are revealing productivity advantages for hard copy.

Kozar & Dickson [KOZA78] compared the speed and quality of decisions in a simulated production environment, based upon presenting the same information either on paper hard copy print-out or on a CRT display. They found that the decisions made were similar in quality, but that the CRT users took significantly longer to make their decisions. They concluded that, unless the advantages of the CRT (accessibility, automatic filing, graphic techniques, etc.) are fully utilised, then it could be a costly alternative to the standard paper print-out display.

A possible objection to various studies in the literature is that they do not compare the basic difference between paper and screen, because of the different line lenghts and amount per page of text in the two conditions. This possible criticism cannot be applied to two recent studies, by Wright & Lickorish [WRIG83] and by Gould & Grischkowsky [GOUL84], which are both meticulous in their organisation. Both studies involved subjects undertaking a proof-reading and text-error detection and marking task while reading text on a screen or paper. The same line lengths, etc. of text were used for both sets of reading material, so as to present as near similar conditions and test the basic difference between screen and paper. Wright & Lickorish found a reduction in accuracy of about 10%, and reductions in reading speeds between 17% and 56%, when subjects were reading the text on the screen compared with on paper; the average deterioration in reading speed was about 30%. Gould & Grischkowsky found very similar results, with again a significant increase in errors of about 10%, and a deterioration in reading speed of about 25%, when reading on screen compared with paper. Gould has conducted a number of subsequent studies to try to determine the causitive factors, but so far does not have a specific explanation (personal communication at SID).

The implication of these studies taken together is that considerable care should be taken when specifying the type of display and terminal to be used for various tasks. With the present advantage for paper in reading speed, and the obvious value for recording and reference back, it is clear that the concept of the 'paperless office' must recede considerably into the background of technological thinking. Moreover, with the present equipment, and until the reasons are known and solutions found, the advantage in reading speed for paper is such as to justify many computer users with VDTs purchasing a printer in addition. In circles where productivity is a magic criterion for the 'bottom line', productivity improvements of 30% can surely seldom be obtained so easily.

Colour vs Monochrome

The first consideration is the colour of characters on a monochrome CRT, whether they should be green or yellow, etc.. While the colour sensitivity curve of the eye suggests that a yellow, or yellow-green phosphor would be best, and while some evidence has been reported of subjective preference for yellow displays, there are no reports of objective performance differences. Haider et al [HAID80] studied the differential strain of work with VDUs with green or yellow characters on 13 trained VDU workers with 9 office workers serving as controls. They found some indications of beneficial effects of yellow, some indications of beneficial effects of green, and some indications of no advantage for either green or yellow characters. In the absence of other data, the subjective preference results in favour of yellow or yellow-green characters are a reasonable guide, but should not be over-emphasised.

In colour versus monochrome CRT displays, there is a fair amount of evidence [LUDE84] to indicate the advantage of colour-coding, even redundant colour-coding, to improve visual search performance. However, there is very little evidence to prove an advantage of colour-coding compared with other types of coding, for identification of particular items within a display. This does not mean that colour cannot be advantageous, but it should be used with caution.In using colour on alphanumeric displays, restraint is often better than a riot of colour. Excellent advice is available in a fully illustrated 'open' report by Robertson [ROBE83].

Many other questions on the use of colour on CRT displays are essentially unresolved. For example, any possible long term effects of working with coloured

CRT displays for data entry, enquiry, or interactive dialogue, are not known. Although many people seem to like colour displays, others find them annoying and garish. The performance benefits of colour in visual search are well proven, but no other substantial performance benefits have been adequately demonstrated. More ergonomics research may provide data as a basis for decisions about the benefits of coloured CRTs versus their cost and other disadvantages.

Some Related Terminal Topics

Types of Terminals

Although many details of input and output device must be designed satisfactorily, the devices have little relevance on their own. They are always effectively part of a whole terminal and workstation for the human user.

Terminals range from the standard 'teletype' (older version only just becoming obsolete) to the 'intelligent' VDU, and from the cash/dispenser in many banks to the concept of the multi-function workstation for the automated office of the future. Moreover, as the relative cost of hardware decreases, so it will become easier to match the terminal to the specific functional needs of specific users; and the users can and will demand this.

The present position, therefore, comprises a very wide range in the varieties of terminal; a definite and growing trend towards function-specific solutions; and a gap in the industry, gradually now being recognised, between the levels of design competence for computing and for ergonomic aspects. If that gap is bridged then better designed terminals will encourage the many new types of potential user because they find the computer usable.

Terminal Design

In one sense the word 'terminal' means merely the end of a connecting link from the computer, but if designed from that viewpoint it is unlikely to facilitate good human-computer interaction. At the least, a terminal must be a combination of input and output devices designed as a complete unit for interaction. However, for good human-computer interaction the definition should be qualified by requiring the terminal to be designed as an appropriate workstation for the human tasks and optimised for human interactive usage. To do this the designer must start with the human user and his tasks, capabilities and needs.

This orientation to terminal and workplace design, approaching the whole problem from the viewpoint of the human user rather than from that of the computer equipment, sounds obvious; but is is not easily adopted by designers because of their past training and their functional responsibilities within the design process.

This orientation has been embodied in the structured procedure of 'workstation anlysis' as the basis for the human factors part of the design process - see

Shackel, [SHAC74] chapter 2 and Damodaran et al [DAMO80] for fuller discussions of this procedure.

From the general quality of terminals at present, it is clear that technical quality is good, rapid introduction of technical innovation is widespread, costs and prices are being reduced markedly, but the design compromises almost always favour the technical and economic factors. However, users are becoming much more aware of the importance of human factors, so even manufacturers are beginning to take notice. We may therefore expect significant improvements, not merely in the marketing brochures but also in the actual products, in the next few years.

When this happens, we may expect more commercial users of computer systems to gain some of the productivity improvements for ergonomic workstations reported by Springer [SPRI82]. He found both that employees put a high priority on comfort and significantly preferred the fully adjustable ergonomic workstations, and that "two of the new workstation designs resulted in significant improvements in performance - 10% for dialogue tasks and 15% for data entry tasks".

Other similar examples take us to the frontiers of technological and ergonomic research and development; for example, graphics terminals and large screen displays. With regard to the former, Davis & Swezey [DAVI83] gather all the relevant data they can to present human factors guidelines in computer graphics, but thus also point out the gaps in our knowledge and the areas requiring further research. With regard to the latter, the work of Negroponte [NEGR81] and Bolt [BOLT77] on large screen displays has shown the potential advantages but also leaves many questions unanswered, particularly cost and availability; Spence & Apperley [SPEN82] have made an interesting proposal for a 'bifocal display' to provide some of the advantages of a large screen display at much lower cost. Thus, it is evident that ergonomics ideas and research are addressed to these questions also, but the results cannot yet be codified in a set of criteria and recommendations.

Conclusion

In this paper I have aimed to draw attention to some of the problems and possibilities which will form part of the future for input and output in human-computer interaction. On the way to the future of easier, better, more satisfying human usage of computer systems, much ergonomics research has to be done. But even when the research has been done, the future will be no nearer; the results must still be applied wisely and widely if better products are to be designed. I hope this paper will have helped in some small way towards such better design procedures.

References

[Al-KH84] Al-Khalili, A. J . 1984, An Algorithm for an Intelligent Arabic Computer Terminal. International Journal of Man-Machine Studies, 20.4, 331-341

[BAIL82] Bailey, R.W. 1982, Human Performance Engineering. Englewood Cliffs NJ, Prentice-Hall

[BOLT77] Bolt, R.A. 1977, Spatial Data Management - Interim Report. Architecture Machine Group, MIT, Cambridge, Mass

[BRUN83] Brunner, D.E. & Kopfer, R. 1983, Tastaturen: von der Hanmechanik zum ergonomischen layout. Paper from IAO Stuttgart supplied by Nixdorf Computer at Hannover Fair

[BURY82] Bury, K.F., Boyle J.M., Evey, R.J. & Neal A.S., 1982, Windowing Versus Scrolling on a Visual Display Terminal. Human Factors, 24.4, 385-394

[CAKI80] Cakir, A., Hart D.J. & Stewart T.F.M., 1980, Visual Display Terminals (a manual). Chichester UK, Wiley

[CARD78] Card S.K., English, W.K. & Burr, B.J. 1978, Evaluation of Mouse, Rate-Controlled Isometric Joystick, Step Keys, and Text Keys for Text Selection on a CRT. Ergonomics, 21, 601-631

[DAMO80] Damodaran, L., Simpson A., & Wilson P. 1980, Designing Systems for People. ISBN O-85012-242-2. NCC Publications, National Computing Centre, Oxford Road, Manchester

[DAVI83] Davis E.G., & Swezey, R.W. 1983, Human Factors Guidelines in Computer Graphics: a Case Study. International Journal of Man-Machine Studies, 18.2, 113-133

[DEAT72] Deatherage, B.H., 1972, Auditory and Other Sensory Forms of Presentation. In: H.P. van Cott & R.G. Kinkade (eds), Human Engineering Guide to Equipment Design, pp 123-160. Washington DC, US Government Printing Office

[ENGL67] English, W. K., Engelbart D. C., & Berman M. L., 1967, Display-Selection Techniques for Text Manipulation. IEEE Transactions on Human Factors in Electronics, HFE-8, pp 5-15

[FAEH83] Faehnrich, K. P. & Kern P., 1983, A Study of the Definition of a Multilanguage Keyboard. Institut fuer Arbeitswirtschaft und Organisation, Stuttgart University, Annual Report, pp 43-56

[GALI81] Galitz, W. O. 1981, Handbook of Screen Format Design. Wellesley Mass, Q.E.D. Information Science Inc.

[GOUL84] Gould J. D. & Grischkowsky, N. 1984, Doing the Same Work with Paper and CRT Displays. Digest of Technical Papers, SID International Symposium, vol 15, 280-283

[HAID80] Haider M., Kundi M., & Weibenbock M., 1980, Worker Strain Related to VDTs with Differently Coloured Characters. In: Grandjean & Vigliani (1980), pp 53-64

[HANE75] Hanes L. F., 1975, Human Factors in International Keyboard Arrangement. In: A Chapanis (ed) Ethnic Variables in Human Factors Engineering, pp 189-206. Johns Hopkins University Press

[KOZA78] Kozar K. A. & Dickson G. W., 1978, An Experimental Study of the Effects of Data Display Media on Decision Effectiveness. International Journal of Man-Machine Studies, 10, 495-505

[LAMB84] Lambert D. R. 1984, Voice Control of Displays. Digest of Technical Papers SID International Symposium, vol 15, 224-226

[LUDE84] Luder C. A. & Barber P. J., 1984, Redundant Colour Coding on Airborne CRT Displays. Human Factors, 26.1, 19-32

[MART81] Martin J. M., 1981, A Study of Keying Skills and Various Alphanumeric Keyboards. Doctoral Thesis, Loughborough University

[MOUN80] Mountford S.J. & North R.A. 1980, Voice Entry for Reducing Pilot Workload. Proc. Human Factors Society 24th Annual Conference, 185-189

[NAKA83] Nakaseko M., Grandjean E., Hunting W., & Gieser R., 1983, Studies on Ergonomically Designed Alphanumeric Keyboards. Submitted to Human Factors

[NEGR81] Negroponte N., 1981, Media Room. Proceedings of the Society for Information Display, 22.2, 109-113

[NOYE83a] Noyes J., 1983a, Chord Keyboards. Applied Ergonomics, 14.1, 55-59

[NOYE83b] Noyes J., 1983b, The QWERTY Keyboard: a Review. International Journal of Man-Machine Studies, 18.3, 265-281

[RADH83] Radhakrishnan T., Atwood J.W. & Krishnamoorthy, S. G., 1983, A Multilingual Input/Output Device for Indian Scripts. International Journal of Man-Machine Studies, 19.2, 137-146

[ROBE83] Robertson P.J. 1983, A Guide to Using Colour on Alphanumeric Displays. IBM UK Laboratories, Hursley, UK, Report No. TR 12.218

[SHAC74] Shackel B., 1974, Applied Ergonomics Handbook. London, Butterworths

[SNYD80] Snyder, H.L., 1980, Human Visual Performance and Flat Panel Display Image Quality. Report HFL-80-1, AD AO92685, from Virginia Polytechnic Institute & State University, Blacksburg, VA

[SPEN82] Spence R. & Apperley, M., 1982, Database Navigation: an Office Environment for the Professional. Behaviour & Information Technology, 1.1,43-54

[SPRI82] Springer T.J., 1982, VDT Workstations: a Comparative Evaluation of Alternatives. Applied Ergonomics, 13.3, 211-212

[TULL83] Tullis, T.S. 1983, The Formatting of Alphanumeric Displays: a Review and Analysis. Human Factors, 25.6, 657-682

[WELC80] Welch, J.R. 1980, Automatic Speech Recognition - Putting It to Work in Industry. Computer, 13.5, 65-73

[WHIT83] Whitfield, D., Ball, R. G. & Bird, J. M., 1983, Some comparisons of on-display and off-display touch input devices for interaction with computer generated displays. Ergonomics, 26.11, 1033-1053

[WRIG83] Wright, P. & Lickorish, A., 1983, Proof-reading texts on screen and paper. Behaviour and Information Technology, 2.3, 227-235

[ZIPP83] Zipp, P., Haider, E., Halpern N. & Rohmert, W., 1983, Keyboard design through physiological strain measurements. Applied Ergonomics, 14.2, 117-122

HCI and Research and Development In User Interface Design

T. F. M. STEWART

Abstract

Although the terminology may be confused, there is no confusion over the objective of user interface design which is to facilitate good human computer interaction. Various disciplines have contributed to this field including psychology, ergonomics and computer science but good interfaces still owe much to the creativity or art of their designers.

A key feature of successful interfaces is that the designers have understood the users and their tasks and matched the interface to these requirements. Some of the problems of achieving this are discussed for different types of users and tasks.

Despite the growing interest in user interface design, far too many computer systems still end up with unusable or unacceptable interfaces. A number of reasons for this are explored including the difficulty of quantifying the benefit of interface improvements, the poor usability of human factors information itself, the problems of incorporating human factors knowledge at the right time in the system development process and the need for developments in the underlying technology to support some of the most interesting interface innovations.

Finally, the paper reviews some promising developments around the world in the activities of the national and international standardization bodies. It is still not clear just how much can or should be subject to standardization but certainly there is considerable scope for eliminating many unnecessary confusions and inconsistencies familiar to users of more than one system.

Introduction

It is not clear to some people which is the more all embracing term - Human Computer Interaction (HCI) or User Interface Design (UID). To some, the design of the interface between user and system encompasses all aspects of the relationship between human and computer. Interaction to them is merely one of the activities which takes place at the interface.

To others however, human-computer interaction is the total relationship and the interface merely a collection of some hardware and software features which permit two-way communication. Such territorial disputes about the boundaries of the domain are inevitable in any new discipline and may be of little significance in themselves but I suspect that the confusion generated does little to advance either cause.

For convenience in this paper, I will use the term user interface for the collection of features and facilities which permit two-way communication between user and computer power. In my view, the purpose of user interface design is therefore to facilitate good (however defined) human-computer interaction.

HCI/UID Has A Long History

Most of the press publicity and indeed most of the obvious problems were initially with the ergonomics of the hardware and this aspect of UID has been a thriving field for research and debate (although regretably not always in that order). However, from the early days of computing there has been a growing body of research on the software interface - the interface between the users and the systems within the computer. Indeed, a number of papers presented at the International Symposium on Man-Machine Systems in September 1969 addressed just this topic.

In the introductory paper of the special issue of the journal "Ergonomics", Shackel discussed the importance of the software interface [SHAC69]. This interface has always been recognized by ergonomists as important, but now that many of the hardware problems have been solved, it assumes major importance for all those concerned with making computer power useful and usable.

Whereas a good hardware interface allows people to operate equipment, it is the software which determines what the system does and often what the user does also. Indeed, many systems have been introduced in such a way that their procedures have become full-time jobs for certain of their users. These jobs were seldom designed to be rewarding or satisfying and problems of boredom and alienation have been reported [EASO74].

Working in the user interface area has not been without its problems. It proved difficult enough to provide solid cost justification for hardware ergonomics but it can be almost impossible for software ergonomics. Yet Gilb and Weinberg estimated that one designer error in the IBM/360 operating system (using a space as a field delimiter) cost in the order of $100 million in lost computer time, corrupted files and debugging effort [GILB77]. However, one of the biggest problems in justifying software ergonomics is that people are even more adept at adjusting to bad software than they were at adjusting to bad hardware. The costs of such adjustment, in terms of errors, delays, frustrations and dissatisfaction are often well hidden.

Research in software ergonomics has been growing in recent years although it is not always labeled as such. Terms such as software psychology [SHNE80] and cognitive ergnomics [SIME83] generally refer to the same area although theprime motivation of the researchers may be slightly different. The literature is growing and there are the beginnings of theories being developed [ALLE82]. In addition to the research evidence, there is a useful body of practical guidelines which have been derived over the years and which aim to provide specific inter- pretations of the research and advice to the system designer. For a particulary comprehensive set see Smith and Aucella [SMIT83] and Gaines and Shaw [GAIN83]. However, there is a gap between theory and practice. Furthermore, the practising system designer often has enormous difficulty reconciling diver- gent views reported at conferences and in the literature [MACG82a]. In some cases, the recommendations appear to conflict with each other as well as with the practical realities of system design.

One of the difficulties in reconciling theory and practice is that usability and acceptability are not exclusively features of products or characteristics of sys- tems but are judgements which people make. They therefore reflect the attitudes, experiences and expectations of the users as well as the qualities of the product.

Usability And Acceptability

Attempts to improve usability and acceptability usually focus on minimizing the effort involved in using the equipment or system. For example, this may require special hardware design to make screens easier to read or it may involve reduc- ing the complexity of the interface style of language. In addition, greater consis- tency, better training and conforming to well established population stereotypes can all help. It is possible to build in suitable cues which encourage the user to adopt a suitable model in dealing with a novel system feature. A good example of this is the Office Technology Limited IMP Work Station which uses a tele- phone handset to allow users to annotate with speech. Without a recognisable handset, there would probably have to be rather careful instructions on how to leave and receive voice messages [REMI81].

Another method of improving usability and acceptability is to reduce both the likelihood and, more significantly, the implications of errors. Gilb and Weinberg [GILB77] describe various means of anticipating input so that a certain amount of automatic checking can be done before too much damage is done. It is also possible to check the most likely errors that users will make and ensure that their consequences are not too severe. For example, forgetting to change shift is a very common keying error yet some equipment puts such significant functions as 'clear the screen' on the same key as 'home cursor' (Epson HX20 is an exam- ple).

But some of the discussion on improving usability seems to overlook the fact that most users are willing to accept rather more effort and risk of error if the system is satisfying to use and performs some really useful function for them. This has been recognised by Bennet [BENN84] and by Shackel [SHAC85] who has proposed an operational definition which reflects the complex and multifaceted nature of usability. By specifying numeric values to be achieved in each part of the definition, the formula can become part of the user requirements specification and is therefore much more likely to be taken seriously during the design process. See Figure 1.

Of course, the popular version of usability "user friendliness" is only one small part of this overall equation. Nonetheless, to improve the friendliness of the messages or at least to avoid being quite so rude and impolite, as computer systems often are, seems to be worthwhile. Certainly the obscure and unintelligible language of much computing is unfriendly and may be intimidating to many ordinary users.

Proposed Operational Definition of Usability

Usability can be specified and measured by means of the operational criteria defined below. The terms should be given numerical values when the usability goals are set during the design stage of 'requirements specification'.

For a system to be usable the following must be achieved:

Effectiveness

- The required range of tasks must be accomplished at better than some required level of performance (e.g. in terms of speed and errors)
- by some required percentage of the specified target range of users
- within some required proportion of the range of usage environments

Learnability

- within some specified time from commissioning and start of user training
- based upon some specified amount of training and user support
- & within some specified re-learning time each time for intermittent users

Flexibility

- with flexibility allowing adaptation to some specified percentage variation in tasks and/or environments beyond first specified

Attitude

- and within acceptable levels of human cost in terms of tiredness, discomfort, frustration and personal effort
- so that satisfaction causes continued and enhanced usage of the system

---

Figure 1 Definition of Usability proposed in terms of goals and operationalised criteria which can have numerical values specified and measured

Art or Science?

What is clear, regardless of the terminological confusion, is that designing interfaces which can be used successfully by people remains very much an art as well as a science. That is not to say that there is little science. Indeed there is a growing body of relevant science and even the most imaginative and creative leaps in user interface design have been underpinned by science. But the essentially innovative part of the process reflects the art.

Two of the major leaps in user interface design in widely available systems reflect this combination of art and science. The first of these was the Visicalc spreadsheet program which some would say was really responsible for the explosion of personal computers (PCs) into the office. The elegance of Visicalc came from a sound understanding of what users would want to use the package for rather than on the application of any particular theory of user interface design. The originator, Dan Bricklin, was a business school student with real requirements for doing 'what if' spreadsheet calculations. He sat down and drew up the specification for the kind of system which he would really like himself. The two strokes of genius were, first, to write the specification in terms of what he wanted to achieve and not to worry, at that stage, about what convolutions the software might have to undergo in order to achieve it, and second, to give the programming task to a very creative programmer (Bob Frankston) with extensive experience of writing computer games.

The result of the these two strokes of genius were that when the specification said that a column of numbers should move to allow a new column to be created, the programmer assumed (correctly) that the best way to do that was for it to happen directly on the screen without the user having to specify all the different transformations separately. This style of direct manipulation is now a common feature of many interfaces and the lasting tribute to Visicalc is the proliferation of 'visiclones'. (For an analysis of direct manipulation as an interface technique, see [SHNE85]). Of course, such spreadsheets cannot do everything and are not the best model for all tasks. But Visicalc represented one of the first user interfaces where the users found that once they understood it a little, the package was much more useful than they had expected. Up to that time, most computers had promised much but delivered little.

The second major leap was represented by the Apple Macintosh. Of course, the windows, icons, mice and pop-up menu (WIMP) approach was really pionieered by Xerox at the Palo Alto Research Centre but it was not until the Macintosh that it all came together into an affordable package. There are many criticisms which can be made of the Macintosh as a product and indeed its commercial success is not yet quite what the original reception appeared to promise. Nonetheless, like Visicalc it has generated a plethora of look-alikes and no self respecting user interface today would be complete without some concession to WIMPs. Although the Mac interface is a real joy to play with, and sometimes to use, it comes into its own in some of the graphics applications.

At a recent User Interface Workshop organised under the auspices of the Alvey Programme in the UK, the designer of MacDraw, Mark Cutter described the interface design process behind this package and its predecessor Lisadraw. His description of the process made it clear that considerable ingenuity and creativity had gone into the design. Many of the features were ones which he himself wanted in a drawing aid. He also went to some trouble to have colleagues at Apple try out early versions and incorporate their feedback and comments. This may seem to be a completely different process to the Visicalc example but I believe that one of the key elements is common. That key element is the knowledge of the user's requirements.

With Visicalc it was the user who was the specifier. With Macdraw, the task, ie. drawing, is one which all children and most adults understand very well. The assumptions which the designer made about what a user might need or expect at a particular point were therefore based on an implicit model of the user and his task which bore some close relation to the real world. For example, one of the features of Macdraw which is quite different from Macpaint, and which reflects this task knowledge, is that the objects which are drawn can be overlaid without losing their properties.

Much of the current scientific endeavour in the fields of user interface design and human computer interaction is therefore focussed on achieving a better understanding of the relevant characteristics of users and of their tasks.

Users And Task Profiles

In the previous section, we argued that usability and acceptability are highly user and task specific. There are three types of user/task combinations which have been the subject of a number of studies:
- The computer professional developing systems for other to use.
- The regular user of a clerical system.
- The occasional user of an information system.

1. The computer professional developing systems for others to use.

The computer professional often has two quite distinct roles with respect to computer systems. As a professional his purpose is to act as an intermediary between computer technology and end users. This role may simply involve operating equipment or systems on behalf of others or it may require the creation or development of facilities for others to use directly.

In order to act in this professional capacity, he typically uses computer equipment and systems himself. In some cases this will be exactly the same facilities as the end users, but in other cases he will use specialized control or development facilities not normally available nor necessary to ordinary users.

Whilst developing systems for others, professionals often encounter problems with the hardware or software which they solve long before ordinary users ever get near the system. In doing this they often apply intuitive human factors knowledge and this can be remarkably effective. Many potentially fatal traps and bugs have been cleaned up during system development without the computer professionals getting any credit. Such professionals, therefore, are interested in usability and acceptability both for users and themselves.

For users, professionals need to be able to predict what the system will look like to the user and what the user might do with the system at certain key points. The good professional attempts to put himself in the user's position and anticipate both types of event. This can be rather difficult. Various studies have found striking differences in attitudes between computer professionals and ordinary users, for example see Hedberg and Mumford [HEDB75].

It is too easy for the professional who has become highly proficient with a system to forget that the end users will not possess his knowledge of computing or of the system design. Of course, it is often necessary for the professional to create jobs which he himself would find totally unacceptable in terms of job satisfaction. The danger here is that he forgets that the end users may be more like him than he realises and underestimate their requirements for intrinsic satisfaction and challenge in the job.

One of the tools which could help such designers to create better interfaces is a means of making explicit the user's conceptual model of the system and the designer's model of the user. Unfortunately, further confusion is added by both of these being referred to as 'user models' in literature. However, They are both valuable design tools and represent important avenues of research (see later).

For themselves, professionals seem to be mainly interested in the performance of the equipment and the systems they use. Research into their problems frequently focuses on such issues as the unpredictability of unstructured programs with an over abundance of GO TO statements [JACK80] or identifying effective problem solving strategies for improving programmer productivity [CURT82] for a thorough review of this area. The emphasis is on programming as a cognitive activity [GREE80] and on achieving good solutions to complex intellectual problems. Computer professionals are notoriously tolerant of unfriendly systems or difficult to use hardware and can often be seen working well into the night without additional financial reward, although it should be remembered that just because they do not complain does not mean that their efficiency has not been reduced by poor interfaces.

2. The Regular User of a Clerical System

The regular user of any system rapidly acquires the necessary skills for using the subset of facilities he uses frequently. Significant effort may be involved when he wishes to change from the well worn path of familiar options. The most important issue which has been widely researched is the impact the system has on the user's job and what effect that has on his job satisfaction and motivation. One of the best known researchers in this area is Enid Mumford and she has pioneered a method of involving clerks and secretaries in the design of their own jobs as part of a sociotechnical system design [MUMF83].

However, by far the most widely publicised issue for clerical users concerns the allenged health hazards associated with the introduction of Visual Display Terminals into the office.

Various risks have been identified including eyestrain, postural problems, repetitive strain injuries, facial dermatitis, adverse pregnancy outcomes and other dramatic and frightening maladies. Many of these are unproven but a significant number are well established and ergonomics related. For a thorough review of the technical and medical issues, see Berqvist [BERGQ84].

Discomfort, temporary fatigue and other similar conditions are all too common. These are unpleasant, unnecessary and unacceptable in the modern office. However, some of the claims made in the name of VDT ergonomics are clearly rediculous. After all, the office is a place of work and much of the advertising hype about ideal environments and user-friendly equipment seems to overlook this fact. Comfortable working conditions are not the same as confortable resting conditions.

One reason why the impact of VDTs on the workplace and on the individual has often been far more negative than was necessary is that office VDT tasks may be quite different from the equivalent paper-based tasks.

Firstly, the VDT becomes much more of a focus than the equivalent paperwork or manual records. For example, even with shared manual filing systems, staff can usually choose how to work, whether to refer briefly to a file on the spot, to take it back to their desk or to take it to a colleague or supervisor. With VDT tasks, far more attention focuses on the VDT and the tendency would be to bring the work to it rather than vice versa. This makes it all the more important that the VDT working conditions are right.

Secondly, there is an interaction between the VDT and various aspects of the environment and some of these interactions pose problems for users, for example, the interaction between the image quality of the display and the illumination at the workplace.

3. The Occasional User of an Informational System.

The occasional user is a target for increasing numbers of systems. Such users may have a degree of choice over whether to use a system or not. It is therefore vital that the system presents an attractive and satisfying face to the occasional user with minimum effort and risk with the interaction. Videotex systems were designed specifically to serve such users and use simple failsafe menus and attractive colour graphics. Although videotex systems such as Prestel have been made very easy to use at the expense of real usefulness [STEW80], nonetheless they have represented a breakthrough in user interface design. The bulk of research on casual users has focused on topics such as making computers tolerant of incorrectly typed input [MACG82b], making systems adapt to naive users [THOM81] and making user interfaces more enjoyable [MALO82].

Of course, it is a mistake to imply that simply because the user only makes occasional use of the systems, its impact on his life is likely to be similarly insignificant. For example, the patient being interrogated by a computer diagnosis system is unlikely to be familiar with interface but its potential impact and therefore its acceptability can quite literally be of life or death importance to him.

What have These To Do With Graphics Users?

As an outsider to the field of computer graphics, my perception is that user interfaces in graphics systems tend in general to be better than user interfaces in other systems. The major reason for this I would suggest is that the designers of many graphics systems are rather closer to their users than is true in, for example, the office automation sector. One of the criticisms of proponents of advanced office automation systems is that many of them have not only never worked in a real office but actually have very little respect for those who do. Small wonder then that the user interfaces are poorly conceived and even more poorly executed.

The major critisism of user interfaces in graphics systems might be that they are difficult to learn in order to use them properly. This is one of the other underlying themes of HCI. There are enormous differences between people in their capacity, performance, expectations and attitudes and nowhere is this reflected more than in their behaviour in front of computer workstations. Not only do people differ from each other, but their behaviour also changes over time.

We can all accept the difference between novice and expert and some sytems have been able to cope with this transition in their interface design but what is very difficult to appreciate is the way the same person changes over time, differentially across the various parts of a system. As a result, much attention is being focussed on the possibility of adaptive systems which could tailor the interface to the current state of the user and the task he is trying to perform. This involves not only a model of the users and their task but also an ability to monitor the process of the interaction.

One of the most promising uses of artificial intelligence techniques is to create such adaptive interfaces. The Adaptive Intelligent Dialogues (AID) project funded by the Alvey Programme in the UK has as its aim the creation of just such an interface. The project is a joint effort by STC, British Telecom, Data Logic, Essex University and the Heriott-Watt/Strathclyde MMI Unit.

Adaption intuitively seems like a good idea and a major aim of the project is not so much to test whether this is true as to discover under what circumstances adaption has advantages. Elaborating the advantages is also important as part of the kind of cost benefit analysis which will be necessary to justify future investment in adaptive systems.

The most obvious disadvantage to date is the enormous overhead which an adaptive systems requires in order to monitor the interaction and change its nature. This overhead is not just in terms of the costs of the extra hardware and software but also in system complexity (which has an impact on the design process, the ease of modifying and updating the system and the response time of the system).

A less obvious consequence of the complexity is that a whole new dimension of error and misunderstanding can occur. It is all too easy to imagine reciprocal misunderstanding which gets perpetuated rather than cleared up as the iterations progess. The complexity itself gives rise to increased risk of error but it is the potentially greater consequence of errors which could be more problematical.

Another disadvantage of adaptive systems is the uncertainty for the user about what the system is doing or is about to do. This could make it more difficult for the user to learn the system and may actually inhibit early exploratory learning.

Perhaps surprisingly, naive users may not be the best target for adaptive systems. Many "professionals" would probably value both adaptive interfaces and adaptive functionality. One of the interesting things about "professionals" (eg planners, engineers, designers, accountants etc) who make extensive use of computers, is that they often tend to mould the problems they tackle to the tools they have availabe. This can make enormous sense and can be an efficient use of resources. However, it is important that someone somewhere keeps an eye on the original or 'real' problem. The possibility of such a user bending the problem to suit a system that is trying to adapt to him suggests the possibility of positive feedback with potentially disastrous consequences.

Reasons For Poor Interfaces

There is now widespread recognition of the importance of good user interfaces, yet I cannot help asking why the computer industry continues to 'shoot itself in the foot' with poor interfaces.

Some time ago, I looked at the psychological literature to find out just what we look for in a human friend to see if this gave me any ideas for user friendly features to incorporate in the interface. The qualities my brief literature search revealed are shown in Figure 2 along with some examples from real systems which seem to be almost deliberately perverse. I wish the examples were out of date. Unfortunately they seem just as common and as relevant today.

I am quite prepared to accept that no system designer actually sets out to design unfriendly interfaces (although during my most cynical periods I occasionally doubt this). Yet, it is clear that many users experience rather poor interfaces. By 'poor', I mean interfaces which are not matched to the capabilities and limitations of the users or the requirements of their tasks in ways which should have been avoidable by applying current knowledge of interface design and user psychology.

If we ask why this should be so, we may find designers arguing that user interface quality will have little importance in their specific system, that human factors knowledge is not in an appropriate form for them to use in the real world

Quality required	Typical example	Quality shown
Patience	'YOU HAVE BEEN IDLE TOO LONG' message to user of timesharing system	Impatience
Tolerance	13/04/81 not accepted as valid date because system expects month/day/year	Intolerance
Warmth	'FATAL ERROR' 'TERMINATE' 'ILLEGAL ENTRY'	Intimidating hostility
Politeness	'ERROR' –always user error, never, 'I'm sorry	Arrogance
Understanding	'REMOTE TERMINAL' – means a terminal remote from computer, probably on the user's desk!	Self-centredness
Helpfulness	'HO79 ON THE IBM 5260 RETAIL SYSTEM' The manual reads: 'The personalisation change control number on the diskette that is in the machine does not match the personalisation change control number that is in the protected totals area of the machine' – it simply means that you have put in the wrong diskette!	Obscurantism
Sincerity	'HELLO' on machine instead of a light to show the power is on	Insincerity

Figure 2 Typical examples of unfriendly dialogue

design process, that human factors concerns were raised too late for them to consider or that really the technology is not yet ready for the user interface research to be applied.

I would now like to consider each of these in turn.

1. 'User interface quality is not important in this system'

The first reason which many designers would give for not paying much attention to human factors when designing systems is that although some interfaces may be superficially more attractive than others, when it comes to 'real' use, most human factors issues make little difference to performance.

Human factors pracititioners would deny this strongly - perhaps too strongly in some areas. A recent study by Martin and Corl [MART86] reports some experimental studies of the impact of system response time on user 'productivity'. Whereas some other investigators have reported productivity enhancements of as much as 200% due to improved response time, the Martin and Corl results suggest rather less spectacular improvements. Nonetheless, for certain repetitive date entry type tasks, they did show a clear relationship between response time and productivity. Such benefits can be quantified and can be significant in real world systems. The authors were rightly cautious about their results and warned against the rather optimistic claims which others have made which can only serve to discredit the field. One of the differences between the present study and the others was that both simple data entry and more complex problems solving tasks were studied.

Of course, differences in user preferences can be 'real' too. Many personal computers are now bought by the end user and so preferences can be a sigificant component of the purchase decision. Several examples exist of user interface innovations which were treated sceptically on the basis of their performance in laboratory tests becoming highly successful products because they so obviously make sense to end users. The mouse and multiple windows can both be traced back through Xerox PARC to Englebart's pioneering work on augmenting human intelligence in the 1960's [ENGL73].

2. 'Human factors knowledge is not in an appropriate form for me to use in the real world design process'

The second reason why designers might not take enough account of human factors is that is is difficult to apply what knowledge there is to real systems. Mosier and Smith [MOSI86] reported some market research amongst the users of the Smith and Aucella compilation of 580 user interface guidelines. As might be anticipated, the guidelines have proved useful but are still too difficult to find and apply in every case. What is required is skilled interpretation of the general guidelines to make them specific to particular designs. It is often extremely difficult and more expensive to design good user interfaces and indeed there are very many more ways to get it wrong than to get it right. However, there are occasions where the choice is really quite simple and it would not be more difficult or more expensive to get it right yet the designers all too often make the wrong decision. As I pointed out earlier, the basis for this choice is or should be a model of the intended users and their tasks.

Often this model is implicit and as a result contains all manner of inconsistencies and anomalies. The advantage of the explicit model is that it is open to scrutiny, is available to other people also, can be tested and refined and by being explicit is less likely to contain inconsistencies and contradictory components than the implicit model. Such models represent valuable tools for interface designers and some promising research is being conducted in this area. [YOUN85].

3. 'Human factors concerns were raised too late for me to consider'

The next problem area is that of human factors coming in too little too late. This is frequently a valid criticism but is one area where there has been some progress. There are moves to understand the design process properly and try to match the human factors input to the needs of the designers at the appropriate stage in the design process. This represents quite a challenge to human factors professionals whose skills are typically analytical rather than creative.

A current Alvey project at the HUSAT Research Centre (in which we are collaborators and ICL is acting as 'uncle') is taking this issue a step further. The project aims to investigate the information technology design process in order to establish what kinds of human factors are needed at different stages and by different participants in the process. In a sense, this kind of market research is relatively uncommon for human factors specialists. Like many professionals we tend to be poor at taking our own advice about the importance of understanding the needs and the tasks of the user. Hopefully the results of the project which is now underway in a handful of organisations will help to improve the usability of human factors knowledge itself and allow its contribution to be more timely.

4. 'The technology is not yet ready for the user interface research to be applied'.

The fourth reason, waiting for the technology to catch up, also has some truth behind it. Curtis, in a keynote address at CHI86, argued that such user interface breakthroughs as the mouse and windows had really been ahead of their time and that it was only when some of the supporting technologies emerged such as high resolution bit mapped displays that they were able to be exploited. Certainly one of the reasons for the current upsurge of interest in user interface design amongst computer scientists is that new developments in the capability (or the price performance) of the technology have created the opportunity for major breakthroughs.

Another area where improvements in technology stimulate innovations in interface design concerns the use of artificial intelligence techniques. There are two areas where I believe AI is already making and will continue to make a substantial contribution to user interface design and I look forward to significant advances in these areas over the next few years. These include:

- intelligent front ends which contain application experts to decouple the user from the vagaries of different services and systems accessed over a network,

- user models which encapsulate key characteristics of users and act as design tools for user interface designers.

There is another class of technological developments which are having a major impact on user interface design and these are the developments in the tools and techniques available to the designer. These represent breakthroughs in interface design even though relatively few of them can really be considered as fully working tools. One of the most influential was Moran's Command Language Grammar [MORA81] which was a representational framework of the conceptual user interface. A key feature of this is the notion of levels of interface (task, semantic, syntactic and interaction) and the representation of users tasks in terms of Goals and sub-goals, the Operators for acting on the interface, the Methods used to achieve sub-goals and Selection rules for choosing between two or more alternative methods.

Another area of tool development concerns dialogue specification techniques which allow the user interface to be explicitly defined in interactive computer systems and handled by a User Interface Management System (UIMS). There are several promising specification and design tools based on transition networks including CONNECT [ALTY83], SYNICS [EDMO81], and RAPID/USE [WASS84]. These are primarily research vehicles at the moment. In the future, it is likely that fully developed, practical tools will allow the designer to build a formally described specification which is executable at least as a prototype.

But not all the problems which face the user interface designer have anything to do with technology. There are one or two areas where we appear to be waiting for technical solutions to what are essentially non-technological problems. One of these issues concerns the development of flat panel displays as an attempt to overcome the widely publicised problems of CRTs. Most of the health and safety problems attributed to VDUs have nothing to do with the radiation emitted from CRTs or the fact that the display flickers. Certainly these can be important factors in some situations but in most cases the problems have to do with the way the technology is used and this has little to do with its design per se. I believe that the search for flat panel displays to solve all VDT problems is misguided and doomed to failure.

Similarly the attempt to overcome all interface problems by replacing keyboards with speech recognisers is equally misguided. Certainly some people find it off putting to type (especially British managers) but I am convinced that the real reason for this has been that British managers have never had any computer systems worth learning to type for. The utility of the systems has been so low that the additional burden of typing has made them totally unacceptable. However, simply replacing the keyboard with a micophone and some speech recognition technology does not overcome the problem of what to say to the computers. Saying "id OAC008" is likely to be even less acceptable than typing it. What matters is what you say to the machine and what it understands about what you are trying to do. Simply replacing the keyboard with voice input is technically difficult but actually achieves very little in terms of improving the usability and acceptability of the interface unless it is matched by proper understanding of users and tasks.

Learning The Wrong Lessons

The difficulties of learning from our mistakes are well known. What is less well known is the problem of learning from success. All too often the wrong lessons are learned.

For example, some people believe that what matters about windows is being able moving them about the screen on top of one another, what matters about icons is having pictures of envelopes or trash cans and what matters about prototyping is getting the rough edges knocked off partially thought out design solutions.

In all these cases I suspect that the wrong lessons have been learned. To me, the importance of windows is that they allow you to skip context, the importance of icons is that they allow you to deal with different objects and assume many properties gathered together in a single entity, and the importance of prototyping is that it allows you to say to people that the system is under test not the users.

Some Promising Developments?

There is currently a world-wide explosion in HCI/UID research and development. It forms a significant part of programmes including the Japanese Fifth Generation Computer Systems Project, the UK's Alvey Programme for Advanced Research in Information Technology and the European ESPRIT programme. However, it will take some time for such research to influence product development. An alternative approach is to forget about trying to convince designers and simply apply brute force through imposing some form of user interface standard.

One of the most influential impacts on the hardware interface was the German DIN standard for VDTs (DIN 66 234) which despite its faults has nonetheless been taken very seriously by suppliers who wished to enter or remain in the German market. Part 8 has recently been published for discussion and this deals with principles of dialogue design. This part has generated substantial controversy and may be significantly modified before it is finalised. Nonetheless, it is not the only standardisation effort currently underway and it may well stimulate those who criticise it to take part in the other standardisation activities.

The American National Standards Institute recently set up an HCI Standards committee and this has concentrated initially on identifying three areas where HCI standards might be developed.

These are:

• **HCI Design Methodologies**

  user needs analysis, functional requirements, formal design specifications, iterative design etc.

• **HCI Interaction Principles**

  input devices and techniques, display techniques, output devices, dialog techniques, user guidance

• **Evaluation and Testing**

This work is only just beginning but by concentrating on getting the framework right initially, the group is setting the scene for making rapid progress in the straightforward areas and leaving the more complex ones till later.

One of the standardisation activities which is close to my own heart is that of the International Standards Organisation (ISO). In its main procedure manual "The Directives for the technical work of ISO", ISO identifies four distinct sets of aims for standards any or all of which may be embraced by an ISO standard.

These specific aims include:

• mutual understanding;
• health, safety and the protection of the environment;
• interface and interchangability; and
• fitness for purpose.

Despite the improvements which have taken place in hardware and software design, it is clear that there is still much to be achieved in user interface standards in terms of mutual understanding, interchangability and fitness for purpose.

What Is Wrong With Current Standards?

Apart from the problem that there are relatively few formal standards for VDUs, the main criticism to date is that those which do exist tend to be based on product design features such as height of characters on the screen. Such standards are very specific to cathode ray tube (CRT) technology and do not readily apply to other display technologies. They may therefore inhibit innovation and force designers to stick to old solutions. More importantly, the standards specify values for a range of different parameters quite independently and take little account of the immense interactions which take place in real use, for example between display characteristics and the environment. The standards can also be criticised for being more precise than is reasonable in areas where research is still continuing.

The Solution - User Performance Standards?

In our approach as a Sub-committee 4 (SC4) of the Ergonomics Technical Committee (TC159) of the International Organisation for Standardisation (ISO) , we have put the emphasis on our user performance standards. Thus, rather than specify a product feature such as character height which we believe will result in a legible display, we are developing procedures for testing directly such characteristics as legibility. The standard is then stated in terms of the user performance required from the equipment and not in terms of how that is achieved. The performance measure is a composite including speed and accuracy and the avoidance of discomfort.

Such user performance standards have a number of advantages. They are:

• relevant to the real problems experienced by users,

- tolerant of developments in the technology, and
- flexible enough to cope with interactions between factors.

However, they also suffer a number of disadvantages. They cannot be totally complete and scientifically valid in all cases. They represent reasonable compromises and obtaining the agreement of all the parties in standards setting takes time.

We have all agreed that our main focus initially should be on office tasks. This represents the area which is likely to affect most people in the short term. By mid 1986, we will have registered four parts of the proposed standard as draft proposals.

These parts include:

Part 1. Introduction to the standard.

Part 2. Task Requirements.

Part 3. Visual Requirements.

Part 4. Keyboard Requirements.

Parts 1 and 2 contain much guidance material and general recommendations. Parts 3 and 4 in addition contain draft test methods for assessing legibility, discomfort and keyboard usability. These test methods will require considerable empirical testing and refinement before they reach the status of an international standard but they represent an important step in the right direction.

The work of the sub-committee is truly international with the active participation of the following countries: Austria, Belgium, China, France, Germany, Italy, Netherlands, Norway, Poland, Sweden, United Kingdom, United States of America.

Towards Human Computer Interaction Standards

The initial focus of the work was purely on the hardware ergonomics issues as this was where the most obvious problems lay. Now that these are being tackled, attention is turning towards the software issues and the more general user interface considerations.

However, whereas most people agree that hardware standards are "a good idea", the same does not hold true for the human computer interaction standards. Indeed, we often hear a number of objections raised and in the last part of this chapter, I would like to deal with them in turn.

1. 'Not enough is known about good HCI to make a standard'

It is perfectly true that we do not know enough about what makes an interface good. But we do know a surprising amount which could aid the design process and improve interfaces. This objection usually stems from a misunderstanding about the nature and purpose of standards. It is entirely appropriate for standards to be guidelines and recommendations of good practice. Indeed, it is inevitable that human computer interaction standards will be just that. By the time we are sufficiently certain to be able to prescribe exactly, the technology will have moved on to leave us behind. One role of these standards will be to focus attention on good practice and principles, not to prescribe precise solutions.

2. 'It is too early for standards'

Clearly there can be dangers in standards which are the results of rather hasty conclusions. When the technology is very fast moving it is all too easy for the relatively slow conservative standardization process to get left behind. However, this is less likely to apply to the kind of user performance standards which I discussed earlier. In addition, one of the most important roles of standards of human computer interaction is to improve consistency between different systems so allowing users to transfer skill between systems. As a user of several different systems myself, I find it enormously frustrating that the differences between systems may be masked by their apparent similarity.

For example, not only is it likely that a key such as "delete" will be on the different places on the keyboard but the function it performs can also differ from system to system. In some cases such differences may serve a valid purpose and should be retained. But in other situations the inconsistencies are inadvertent and could have been avoided had there been clear recommendations in a recognised standard.

3. 'But a standard user interface would be very boring and unattractive'

No one is suggesting standard user interfaces. A good analogy is the telephone handset. There are certain characteristics it must possess if it is to connect to the telephone network. There are other aspects of design which can vary but which must conform to certain human characteristics if it is to work effectively with real people (eg., microphone sensitivity, key button size etc.). Within these constraints there are wide variations in functionality, aesthetics and concept which still allow product designers considerable scope for creativity.

4. 'You will never manage to get agreement; look how long it is taking to get hardware standards'

On this point I must concede that the critics could be right. But I remain an optimist that common sense and self preservation will prevail. After all, the consumer electronics industry seems to have recognised that everyone benefits from common standards across manufacturers (whether they be formal or de facto) and that user confidence in technology actually increases sales and boosts the market.

Certainly, standards themselves are a relatively "blunt instrument" in the fight for better user interfaces but I believe they can make a worthwhile and useful contribution.

References

[ALLE82] Allen, R.B., 1982, Cognitive Factors in Human Interaction With a Computer. Behaviour and Information Technology, 1,3, 217-236

[ALTY84] Alty, J.L. 1984, Path Algebras: a Useful CAI/CAL Technique. Computing and Education, 8, 1, 5-13

[BENN84] Bennett, J. L. 1984, Managing to Meet Usability Requirements, in: Visual Display Terminals: Usability Issues and Health Concerns, Bennet, J. K., Case D., Sandelin, J. and Smith, M. (eds) (Englewood Cliff New Jersey, Prentice Hall)

[BERQ84] Berquist, U. 1984, Video Display Terminals and Health. Scandinavian Journal of Work, Environment and Health, 10, Supplement 2

[CURT82] Curtis, B., 1982, A Review of Human Factors Research on Programming Languages and Specifications, in Proceedings of Conferences on Human Factors in Computer Systems, Gaithersburg, Maryland, pp 212-218

[EASO74] Eason, K.D.E. Damodaran, L. and Stewart, T.F.M., 1974, A Survey of Man-Computer Interaction in Commercial Applications. LUTERG Number 144, Department of Human Sciences, University of Technology, Loughborough.

[EDMO81] Edmonds, E.A. Adaptive Man-Computer Interfaces. in Computing Skill and the User Interface, Coombs, M.J. and Alty, J.L. (eds) (London: Academic press) pp 389-426

[ENGL73] Englebart, D.C., Watson, R.W. and Norton, J.C. 1973, The Augmented Knowledge Workshop, Proceedings of the NCC, 1973, pp 9-21

[GAIN83] Gaines, B.R. and Shaw, M.L.G. 1983, Dialog Engineering, In Designing for Human-Computer Communication, edited by Sime and Coombs

[GILB77] Gilb, T. and Weinberg, G.M., 1977, Humanised Input (Cambridge, Massachusetts: Winthrop).

[HEDB75] Hedberg, B., and Mumford, E., 1975, The Design of Computer Systems, Human Choice and Computers (Amsterdam: North Holland/Elsevier) pp 31-59

[JACK80] Jackson, M., 1980, The Design and Use of Conventional Programming Languages, in Human Interaction with Computers, Smith, H.T. and Green, T.R.G. (eds) (London: Academic Press) pp 321-347.

[MACG82] Macguire, M. 1982, An Evaluation for Published Recommendations on the Design of Man-Computer Dialogues, International Journal of Man-Machine Studies, 16,3, 279-292

[MACG82b] Macguire, M., 1982, Computer Recognition of Textual Keyboard Input from Naive Users. Behaviour and Information Technology, 1,1, 93-111

[MALO82] Malone, T. W., 1982, Heuristics for Designing Enjoyable User Interfaces: Lessons from Computer Games. in Proceedings of Conference on Human Factors in Computer Systems, Gaithersburg, Maryland, pp 63-68

[MORA81] Moran, T.P., 1981, The Command Language Grammar: a Representation for the User Interface of Interactive Computer Systems, International Journal of Man-Machine Studies, 15, 3-50

[MOSI86] Mosier, J.N. and Smith, S.L. 1986, Application of Guidelines for Designing User Interface Software, Behaviour and Information Technology, 5, 1, 39-46

[MUMF83] Mumford, E., 1983, Successful Systems Design, in New Office Technology, Otway, H.J. and Peltu, M. (eds) (Francis Pinter: London) pp 68-85

[REMI81] Remington, R. J., 1981, The Transition from Word Processing to Information Processing: Human Factors Considerations, in Word Processing: Selection, Implementation and Usage in the 80's (London: Online Publications) pp261-270

[SHAC69] Shackel, B. 1969, Man-Computer Interaction-The Contribution of the Human Sciences. Ergonomics, 12,4, 485-500.

[SHNE80] Shneiderman, B., 1980, Software Psychology (Boston: Little, Brown)

[SIME83] Sime, M.E. and Coombs, J.M., (eds) 1983. Designing for Human Computer Communication (London: Academic Press)

[SMIT83] Smith, S.L. and Aucella, A.F., 1983, Design Guidelines for the User Interface to Computer Based Information Systems, prepared by the Mitre Corporation, Bedford, Massachusetts, Report Number ESD-TR-83-122

[SHAC85] Shackel, B. 1985, Human Factors and Usability - Whence and Whither?, ACM Software Ergonomis '85, Stuttgart University, 24-26 September 1985

[SHNE85] Shneiderman, B., 1985, Overcoming Limitations Imposed by Current Programming Languages, in the Role of Language in Problem Solving I, Jernigan, R., Hamill, B.W., and Weintraub, D.M. (eds) Elsevier Science Publishers BV (North Holland)

[STEW80] Stewart, T.F.M., 1980, Human Factors in Videotex, Proceedings of the 4th International Online Information Meeting, London, pp 87-96

[THOM81] Thomas, R. C., 1981, The Design of an Adaptable Terminal. In Computing Skills and the User Interface, Coombs, M.J. and Alty, J.L. (eds) (London: Academic Press) pp 427-463

[WASS84] Wasserman, A.I. and Shewmake, D.T. 1984, A RAPID/USE Tutorial, Medical Information Science, University of California, San Francisco

7 Graphics Standards

R & D - Issues and Trends Consequent Upon GKS and Related Standards

J. L. ENCARNACAO

Abstract

Graphics standards are a "hot issue" in most conferences and workshops addressing Computer Graphics. This paper contributes to this discussion by presenting and analysing some R&D activities and by discussing the trends of Graphics Standards mainly from two points of view:

- *Harmonization of the Graphics Standards;*
- *Integration of special hardware and VLSI to increase their performance and flexibility.*

A wide spectrum of issues is presented, discussed and some conclusions for further developments in this area are taken. An extended list of references gives the possibility for further detailed readings of specialized publications addressing the area discussed in the paper.

Introduction

This paper discusses the different graphics standards and some examples for on-going R&D issues related to applications programmed with these standards. The trends for supporting their performance and flexibility by using special hardware or by bringing their functionality into silicon are also presented and anlysed.

Conceptual and Standardization Issues

There are different levels of graphics standards and/or standards proposals with a very specific functionality:

1. The graphics programming standards (GKS; GKS-3D, PHIGS and PHI-GKS) with their language bindings;
2. The interface for device drivers and graphics libraries/series (CGI);
3. The archive interface at the graphics system level (CGM and GKSM);

4. The videotex interface (CEPT-GDS and NAPLPS); and
5. The communication interface between applications or between applications
   and their databases (IGES, VDAFS, STEP, PDES, etc.).

All these standards are needed in some way they are not competitors, but necessary servers for a given functionality (constituency). Details about these standards may be taken from the literature [ISOI85] [BONO85] [ENCA86a] [EN-
CA86b] [ISOT86] [ISOT85].

But of course there are still some problems with these standards and/or standards' proposals:

Portability between graphics programming standards

The proposals GKS and GKS-3D are upwards compatible, but at the moment
(Summer 1986) no portability is possible between GKS-3D and PHIGS. In order
to achieve portability between a GKS-3D and a PHIGS environment the concept
called PHI-GKS [RIX86] [SCHO86] was defined in Darmstadt. First pilot implementations will be finished by the end of 1987. PHI-GKS aims at a consistent
"family of standards" defining a PHIGS funtionality upwards compotible to
GKS.

The main ideas and the basic concepts we propose for PHI-GKS are summarized in the following:

a) Extension of the GKS levels to a further output level for hierarchical segmentation and editing.
   The combination of segments and structures (see g) in one data structure
   leads to one additional output level with the different input functionalities.
b) Workstation control as in GKS.
   This means that output effects all active workstations. Segments are stored on
   all workstations which are active upon creating the segment. Workstation Independent Segment Store (WISS) has to be available (active) all the time, to
   guarantee a consistent editing for all workstations.
c) Extension of the state diagram.
   Basis will be the GKS state diagram reflecting the workstation control. The
   "segment open" state has to be allowed in parallel to all workstation states
   because of the possibility of editing a segment. Another extension is the state
   of archival, which will be allowed to be open whenever PHI-GKS is open.
   Therefore the state is described by a triple (Workstation State, Segment State,
   Archive State).
d) Archiving functionality in addition.
   In addition to the metafile concept of GKS the concept of archiving in PHIGS
   seems to be necessary also for PHI-GKS.
e) Extension of the deferral mode to the update state functionality.
   PHI-GKS will adopt the more elaborate functionality of PHIGS. This compatible solution results in:

- add deferral mode "WAIT"
- add regeneration modes "NIVE", "UQUM"
Note: "Suppressed"="UWOR, "allowed" "PRIN/ASAP"

f) Combined transformation pipeline.

The workstation dependent transformation (WKST-transformation and view-ing) are already identical (at least in the next versions of GKS-3D and PHIGS). For the workstation independent transformations (Normalization, Segment, and Modelling transformation) PHI-GKS combines the different concepts. The integration of segments and structures in one common data structure leads to the pipeline. Normalization transformation is executed prior to the storage in the workstation independent segment storage (WISS), and normalization clip is excuted after the segment and modelling transformation. Segment transformation is handled like a segment attribute in GKS. Only the attributes of a root segment will have an effect and are valid for this segment hierarchy. The modelling transformation concept of PHIGS will also exist. It will be executed after the segment transformation.

g) Extension of segments to hierarchical data structures.

The extension of segments needs an "execute segment" function. The seg-ment header that contains the segment attributes, will be available for each segment, but will be traversed only within a root segment. The editing functions will address the element number and labels as in PHIGS. The seg-ment header cannot be edited with these functions. The elements within a segment are conceptually 3-dimensional, but it is implementation dependent, how they will be stored within WISS.

h) Combined attribute model.

The attribute model of setting and using individual and bundled attributes will be adopted as it is defined in GKS and PHIGS. A difference is coming up, because of the binding at generation time (GKS) and at traversal time (PHIGS). To combine these two concepts we introduced a new attribute value "to be inherited" (tbi) for all modal attributes. This means: if the value "tbi" is set, the system will work like PHIGS, if it is set to any other valid valued, it will use this value within traversal process. If there is no explicit setting of an attribute the initial values will be taken from the PHI-GKS state list and if this is set to "tbi", it will be taken from the description table. Also primitives outside segments can be handled in the same manner. The segment header will be set from the PHI-GKS state list at creation time. The additional con-cept of an Edit State List allows to enquiry of the current attribute setting at the editing position.

i) Primitives outside segments.

The concept of non-retained structure in PHIGS was eliminated. Within PHI-GKS the concept of primitives outside segments will allow this functionality. The attribute values will be taken from the current PHI-GKS sate list.

k) State lists and description tables.

The state lists and description tables in PHI-GKS will be merged from GKS-

3D and PHIGS. One additional list is the edit state list, which allow enquiry of the current attribute setting at the editing position.

Following these concepts PHI-GKS will be upward compatible to GKS and GKS-3D and will include the same functionality as PHIGS do. Adopting the new concepts and some minor changes to PHIGS, the two proposals will be equivalent. The PHI-GKS concepts were defined in a workshop in Wenschdorf, W.Germany, from May 5 to 9, 1986; this workshop had 14 participants from industry and from research institutions, coming from three different countries. The results were presented at the ANSI meeting in June 1986 and have been since then a subject of discussion and consideration by ISO, ANSI, NNI and DIN experts and also by others coming from other standardization evironments. PHI-GKS does not intend to be a competitor to PHIGS; but if a concensus in the GKS context (portability; harmonization) is not possible with the PHIGS developers and standardization bodies, then PHI-GKS may develop into a standard alternative to PHIGS.

Compatibility between Metafile Standards.

There are two proposals:

a) *GKSM - the GKS Metafile*. It is an audit trail of the GKS commands that were used to produce a picture. GKSM stores the segment structure of the picture.
b) *CGM - the Computer Graphics Metafile*. It is a snapshot of the final image that a program has created. CGM stores no picture structure information.

Both are only compatible for GKS level O. For higher levels there is a compatibility problem. Some discussion is going on in standardization bodies because of this. A solution may be to define a core of required functions, which may then be extended for a snapshot functionality in the sense of CGM and for a audit trail functionality in the sense of GKSM. The standard would then incorporate three levels:

- a set of required functions,
- a slightly modified version of CGM, and
- a slightly modified version of GKSM.

The discussion on this is still in progression and alternative proposals are also been considered and discussed. Before the end of 1987 some concensus about this issue is expected.

Computer Graphics Interface (CGI)

CGI is a standard functional and syntactical specification of the control and data-exchange between device-independent graphics software and one or more device-dependent graphics device drivers.

The original intention was to have standard functions partioned into device classes. For each device class there is a set of basic required functions and an additional option set, which itself is based on required functions for that device class and on a set of non-required functions. Several companies are now announcing "their" own CGI interface (IBM, AT&T, TI, INTEL etc.), which is basically derived from ANSI's CGI-draft published in 1983/84. Since the final CGI will not be officially approved before the end of 1987, we may come to a set of "de facto industrial standards", that are not compatible with each other and also not compatible with the final standard.

A second issue in this area is the language binding of CGI. Some want to have a single entry language binding, others a multiple entry language binding. A decision in this area will be strongly influenced by the R&D work on window and user interface managers, as will as on implementation issues for flexible and efficient user models.

The compatibility between the videotex interfaces (CEPT-GDS and NAPLPS) is also a matter of argument. Here the basic issues are: concept of multiple workstations, GKS compatibility and direct programmability. Some work has to be done also in this area in order to increase the level of harmonization between the different standards [ECMA85].

Validation of graphics standards

In order to ensure that a given implementation of the standards fulfils the specification of the standards, several R&D activities have taken place and different tests centers have been or are in the process of being established in W. Germany, UK and USA [GESS85]. There are three basic levels of testing:

1. the testing based on tests suits for
   - the language binding,
   - the user operating interface and
   - the different internal tables and interfaces;

2. the reference testing based on the comparison of a (configurable) reference implementation with the candidate implementation; and

3. the proof of the implementation correctness.

The testing based on test suites is already used for GKS in the different test centers: the reference testing is in an advanced state of development. The proof method is still a subject of research.

Optimizing the implementation of graphics programming standards

If a given implementation of the graphics programming standard is modular and configurable, then there are two basic approaches to optimize its functionality and/or performance without changing the functionality at the interface specified by the programming standard. This is specially the case for GKS implementations.

The two approaches are:

• optimization of the device-independent part of the implementation and minimization of the device-dependent (device driver) part; this results in a maximal use of the functionality specified in the standard; or

• minimization of the device-independent part of the implementation and optimization of the device-dependent (device driver) part. This results in the optimization of the way the device functionality (capabilities can be used).

Both areas are subject of intensive R&D. This work is also necessary to support the development of workstations designed to improve the performance and flexibility of the standards [ENGL85].

GKS in a network environment

Most of the graphics applications today run in some sort of distributed environment. Computer networks are more and more the basis for system development and for running complex applications. WSI (the workstation interface implicitly defined in the GKS document) opens the possibility of using GKS related standards in a network environment. The GKS oriented communication protocol is based on services supplied by the T.70 transport protocol [DFNB84].

Application issues

Examples of ongoing R&D activities to study the applicability of graphics standards in an efficient and flexible way are [WILL86] [BACH86] [DAI86]:

Documentation system
    Basic R&D issues are:
    • interpretation of text and graphics,
    • metafile interface,
    • SGML interface;

Presentation graphics
    Basic R&D Issues are:
    • choice of a common set of application primitives and
    • choice of a common data structure, with the functionality organized in functional clusters (levels);

Window and user interface managers
    Basic R&D issues are:
    • how to use GKS and CGI in an integrated way, and

- how to have some sort of operating system portability (common kernel of OS functions, for example between MS/DOS and UNIX);

Using graphics standards in and/or for expert systems

Basic R&D issues are:
- how to interface graphics programming standards with logic programming languages (e.g., interfacing GKS with PROLOG or LISP),
- how to efficiently implement the corresponding picture interpreters and
- how to integrate interactive-graphics dialogues as the implementation of the man-machine-interface (operating) of expert systems;

Robot programming supported by graphics simulation

Basic R&D issues are:
- mapping of kinematic functions,
- backtracking of the parameters of spatial conflict situations and
- using the robot simulator as a special "output device" to produce the code resulting from the simulation and to load it into the "physical roboter" (teach-in-simulation);

Simulators

Basic R&D issues are:
- how to use and integrate VLSI components and special hardware architectures to support and/or optimize the GKS-3D, PHIGS or PHI-GKS based "Simulator-driver". This approach aims at an increase of the performance and flexibility, up to the real-time constraints.

basic components are:
- interpolators for trajectories,
- curve and surface generators,
- transformation accelerators and
- distributed implementations (mmp architectures).

This topic will be discussed in more detail in the following section.

Hardware and VLSI for Graphics Standards

Following [FUCH85] [STRA86] [GUTT86a] we should consider:
- Graphics processors
- Specialized chips
- Specialized boards
- GKS chips and machines
- Workstations.

Graphic processors have a functionality specially tailored to graphics processing and to the support of graphics standard functions. Examples are:

TI TMS 34010/GSP [GUTT86b]

This is a 32 bit microprocessor with 256 KByte instruction cache, video/CRT control, DRAM control, multiport Video RAM control and host processor interface. CGI or GKS implementations reside either in ROM or are downloaded into a RAM. CGI may also be implemented on the TMS 34010 CGA emulation board running in an emulation bypass mode (resulting in 2x performance increase). The TMS 34010 directly supports the following CGI functions:

- Display bitmap
- Bit BLt source array
- Transparency
- All drawing modes
- Bitmap foreground colour
- etc..

INTEL 82786 [GRIM86]

This 32 bit microprocessor supports directly multiple bitmaps and hardware windows, an instruction set designed for small and very fast CGI drivers and text processing functions.

The issue is now to find suitable graphics system architectures to make optimal use of the functionality of these graphics processors, which include also a very strong general-purpose applicability.

Specialized chips have a functionality, which is very specially tailored to a given standard. An example is the:

GKS chip [MEHL84]

This chip has three based components in silicon:

- a workstation interface processor,
- a processor for GKS-based transformations and clipping and
- a processor for symbol generation, for attribute evaluation,
    setting and for sorting.

The prototypes of these chip components have been developed in Darmstadt and are available since summer 1986; the redesign is planned for 1987.

More and more *boards* based on general-purpose microprocessors (e.g., MC 68000, 68010, 68020) have also been announced. Their functionality is build to implement the standards (Example: OMNICOMP boards for GKS and GKS-3D [OMNI86]).

Based on graphics (geometry) chips, specialized boards, and general-purpose CPU's several so-called *GKS-Machines* will be available soon, which strongly support in their architecture and functionality an efficient execution of programs using graphics programming standards (Example: SIGMEX [SPIE85]; GKS-PC's; etc.).

Increasing R&D activities exist for the development of special *workstation architectures* [ENCA84]. They are based on distribution strategies. From the point of view of GKS there are two types of distribution:

Functional distribution - here we have the input and output pipelines; Examples of special components are clippers, transformers, character generators, etc..

Object distribution - here the primitives and segments are processed by concurrent object processors.

The strategy is to combine both; the architectures are based on functional pipelines for object processing. Graphics applications may then run in multiuser mode on a network of workstations (networking) and real-time applications are possible because of the immediate picture regeneration after a modification of dynamic attributes.

The development of the Darmstadt *GKS-Workstation* [GOEB86] is based on a set of specialized modules. This mmp-architecture allows for a parallel processing of these modules:

1. *GKS Module* - builds the GKS control and the application interface to GKS; it has knowledge of number and type of workstations, configuration of the workstation, and data structures and inquiry functions.
2. *Workstation bus* - interconnects associated workstations; it is responsible for synchronization and for all merging and sorting activities.
3. *Input/output to metafiles* (WISS/GKSM module) - allows the connection to a hard disc as a local extension.
4. *Output modules* - there are several picture generation modules taking care of the workstation transformations, clipping, colour, logical refresh, etc..
5. *Distributed display file* - this implements the object distribution. Segments are buffered locally, until they get all merged into the refresh buffer. Objects are distributed at the time they are created. This module is also responsible for the harmonization of the workload among processors.
6. *Workstation control module* - it is responsible for the synchronization of the output modules, has a monitoring function and is furthermore the permanent bus master for the pixel bus (write and read "permissions"). This module also implements the request input.
7. *Input module* - is responsible for the mapping of logical to physical devices. It implements the sample and event input.

This workstation concept is based on MC 68000 and should have been ready for evaluation as a prototype before the end of 1986.

Conclusions

The R&D activities described in this paper have mainly the following goals in mind:

a) Better access to device hardware features, without loosing the advantage of a standard graphics programming interface - for this not only the "Standard bypasses" may be used, but also issues on optimization and maximization of the device driver functionality and implementation techniques based on combinations of GKS and CGI are being resolved to support this in the future;

b) Higher performance and more flexibility to integrate advancements in the technology without having radical changes of the software ("evolution instead of revolution") - for this, new workstation architectures are being developed, which, on the one side, allow for the integration of advanced VLSI components and new graphic processors, improve the flexibility and allow for the integration of special algorithms (e.g., rendering) and features, but, on the other side, still offer the advantages (from an application point of view!) of common programming and data interfaces.

Of course there are and have always been, and in all technologies, areas where you do not or cannot use standards. This is also the case for computer graphics. Standards are, in any case, defined based on the so-called "90% rule": they are there for most of the applications, most of the devices, most of the times!". . .

In the discussion and evaluation of graphics standards it is very important to consider the trade off and user's point of view: Users do *not* want to be merely *operators* of the suppliers special software, *but* mainly *programmers and users* of their own (graphic) applications. In many cases, the environments are heterogeneous (hardware and software from different suppliers) and programmers as well as users have to be able to move from one environment (device) to the other without too much effort; this "programmers' portability" also requires standards and is extremely important from an economic and an acceptance point of view.

Graphics standards are a good basis for supporting all these goals. They also have a life cycle and their functionality will be redesigned and extended in time to give better support to the underlying technology and to user needs. This will be done based on the increasing experience with their use and with applications running on them. Performance and flexibility will be reinforced by new workstation architectures using advanced graphic processors and VLSI components.

Computer graphics is on the way to become an established technology and discipline. Well established technologies and disciplines always have had "their" standards. Computer graphics also has, from an application's/user's and system integration's point of view, a strong need for standards. Standards do not have to be static; R&D activities like the ones described in this paper will guarantee a dynamic and adaptive process in the development and application of graphics standards. This will further develop, widen and intensify possibilities and opportunities in the computer graphics market.

References

[BACH86] J. Bach, L. A. Messina und C. Parra-Ramirez, GKS und PROLOG als Werkzeuge zum Aufbau von Graphisch-Interaktiven Expertensystemen. Proceedings of the Annual Meeting of the German Computer Society (GI), Berlin, October 1986 (in German)

[BONO85] P.R. Bono, A Survey of Graphics Standards and Their Role in Information Exchange. Computer, Vol. 18, No. 10, Oct. 1985, pp. 63-75

[CGFO] Several very important contributions related to graphics standards have been published.
Computer Graphics Forum. - The Journal of the EUROGRAPHICS Association published by North-Holland Elsevier Science Publ. B.V., Attn. Journals Department, P.O. Box 211, NL-1000 AE Amsterdam/The Netherlands

[DAI86] F. Dai, Roboterprogrammierung ueber vorgeschaltete graphisch-interaktive Simulation. DFG-report, Darmstadt, July 1986 (in German)

[DFNB84]Graphische Kommunikation in offenen Netzen Ziele und Loesungssaetze. Deutsches Forschungsnetz - DFN Berlin Mai 1984 (in German)

[ECMA85] Syntax of Graphical Data for Multiple-Workstation Interface (GDS). Standard E CMA - 96, Geneva, September 1985

[ENCA84] J. Encarnacao, M. Goebel and R. Lindner, HoMuK: Ein Homogener Multiprozessor-Kern fuer verteilte graphische Systeme. in Entwicklungsperspektiven mittlerer Rechnersysteme, W. Proebster and R. Remshardt (eds.), Oldenbourg, Publ. Co., Munich, 1984, pp. 111-150 (in German)

[ENCA86a]J. Encarnacao and J. Schoenhut, Interfaces and Data Transfer Formats in Computer Graphics Systems. EUROGRAPHIC Seminars, Springer Publ. Co., 1986

[ENCA86b] J. Encarnacao, R. Schuster and E. Voege, Product Data Interfaces in CAD/CAM Applications - Design, Implementationand Experiences - Symbolic Computation. Sub/series Computer Graphics Springer Publ. Co., 1986

[ENDE85] G. Enderle (Ed.), Special Issue: Computer Graphics Standards. Computers & Graphics, Vol. 9, No.1, 1985

[ENGL85] G. Englert and M. Goebel, Ein Basissystem fuer die automatische Konfigurierung verteilbarer graphischer Systeme. Technical Report, GRIS 85-4, April 1985, TH Darmstadt, FG GRIS (in German)

[FUCH85]H. Fuchs, VLSI and Computer Graphics. Tutorial Notes No.7 EUROGRAPHICS'85, Nice, France, EUROGRAPHICS Association, Geneva

[GESS85] F. Gessert, M. Goebel, W. Huebner and G. Pfaff, Validierung des Graphischen Kernsystems. Technical Report No. GRIS 85-8, October 1985 TH Darmstadt, FG GRIS (in German)

[GOEB86] M. Goebel and D. Kroemker, A Multiprocessor GKS Workstation. IEEE CG&A, July 1986, Vol. 6 No. 7, pp. 54-60

[GRIM86] J. Grimes, A VLSI Implementation for ANSI CG-VDI. Proceedings of CG'86, Anaheim, 1986, pp. 309-313

[GUTT86a] K. Guttag, Future Directions in Semiconductors for Computer Graphics. Proceedings of CG'86, Anaheim 1986, pp. 423-430

[GUTT86b] K. Guttag, J. van Aken and M. Asal, Requirements for a VLSI Graphics Processor. IEEE CG&A, January 1986, Vol. 6, No. 1, pp. 32 -47

[ISOI85] Information Processing Systems - Computer Graphics -Graphical Kernel System (GKS). Functional description, International standard ISO/IS 7942, 1985

[ISOT86] Information Processing Systems - Computer Graphics - Graphical Kernel System for Three Dimensions (GKS-3D). Functional Description, ISO/TC97/SC21 N853, 2nd DP 8805, February 86

[ISOT85] Information Processing Systems - Computer Graphics - Programmers's Hierarchical Interactive Graphics System (PHIGS). ISO/TC97/SC21 N819, November 1985

[MEHL84] M. Mehl and S. Noll, A VLSI Support for GKS. IEEE CG&A, August 1984, pp. 52-55

[OMNI86] OMNICOMP Product Specifications. Omni 1000 1200 and 2000 GDS Houston, Texas; 1986

[PFAF84] G. Pfaff (Ed.), Special Issue: Conformance and Certification of Graphics Systems. Computers & Graphics, Vol. 8, No. 1, 1984, published by Pergamon Press, Headington Hill Hall, Oxford OX3 OBW, UK

[RIX86] J. Rix et.al., PHI/GKS. Workshop/Report, ZGDV Report 6/86, May 1986

[SCHO86] J. Schoenhut, Are PHIGS and GKS Necessarily Incompatible? IEEE CG&A, July 1986, Vol. 6 No.7, pp. 51-53

[SPIE85] R. Spiers, The Realisation and Application of an Intelligent GKS Workstation. Proc. 1st Intl' Conf. Computer Workstations, IEEE-CS Press, November 1985, pp. 254-261

[STRA86] W. Strasser, VLSI-Oriented Graphics System Design. Tutorial Notes, EUROGRAPHICS'86 Lisbon, Portugal, August 1986, EUROGRAPHICS Association, Geneva

[WILL86] A. Williams, An Architecture for User Interface R&D. IEEE CG&A, July 1986, Vol. 6, No.7, pp. 39-50

8 Documentation

On-line Documentation

P. J. BROWN

Abstract

*An important potential application of graphics workstations is for display-
ing documents. This paper starts by presenting a survey of the problems
and aspirations of on-line documentation. It is argued that an on-line
document should not try to imitate a paper document, but instead should
exploit its interactive nature, thus allowing readers to tailor what is displayed to their own needs.*

*The second part of the paper describes the GUIDE system, which is an
interactive system for displaying on-line documentation. GUIDE aims to
present documents, made up of text and graphics, in a flexible way
suitable for both naive readers and naive authors.*

Introduction

There is a continuing trend to make documentation available on-line. Such on-
line documentation may supplement documentation on paper, or it may totally
replace paper. The increasing cheapness of graphics screens and the availability
of new mass-storage devices such as CD-ROMs will accelerate this trend.
Nevertheless human readers, given a choice, usually prefer paper documentation
to on-line documentation.

There is, however, hope for the future. The modern graphics workstation has
several advantages that provide a basis for displaying on-line documentation that
human readers will find pleasant. Among these advantages are:

- Interactive control using menus (pop-up or pull-down) selected by a mouse
  or other pointing device.
- Integrated text and graphics.
- Use of different fonts.
- Use of separate windows. This is especially valuable for *computer
  documentation*, i.e., documentation about the computer's own software or
  hardware, since one window can contain the documentation and another
  window can be running a sample session using the software that the
  documentation describes.

This paper analyses on-line documentation and describes a new system for displaying it in an attractive way. The system applies to any type of on-line documentation, whether it be computer documentation, documentation on office procedures, an on-line encyclopedia, or a document describing how to travel from X to Y.

Survey of Problems and Opportunities

A good way of surveying the field of on-line documentation is to present some commonly-expressed opinions, and analyse the thinking behind them.

'All computer documentation should be available on-line.'

Clearly, when a computer user has a problem, it is good if he can immediately call up on-line documentation concerning that problem. It is widely agreed that reference manuals, at least, should be available on-line, and where storage capacity allows they are indeed available. Only on today's smaller computers is the storage capacity insufficient for much on-line documentation, and the availability of cheap CD-ROM players may well soon remedy this deficiency.

'You need three manuals: a primer, a full tutorial manual and a reference manual.'

This statement highlights a wider problem which applies irrespective of whether documentation is on paper or on-line. There are many possible types of readers ranging from beginners to experts, and including a particularly difficult case: an expert in a related area, such as a FORTRAN user learning Pascal or an English lawyer learning about American law. Moreover there are also many possible types of perusal:

- Some readers want a summary.
- Some readers want a complete tutorial.
- Some readers simply want to ascertain one fact – for example, the meaning of the term 'segmentation fault'.

There is thus a spectrum of possible readers and a further spectrum of possible types of perusal. You do not need three manuals, you need an infinite number!

With manuals on paper, the only course is to produce a small number of manuals – usually it is just one – and to hope to cover as many reading needs as possible. This is an almost hopeless endeavour, which is why the vast majority of computer user manuals are held to be bad.

With on-line documentation, on the other hand, there is an opportunity for the user to interact with the program that is displaying documentation, and thus to tailor the documentation to his needs.

'. . . in addition you need a Computer-Aided-Learning script.'

This statement is more controversial. Clearly a good CAL script is worthwhile, but good scripts are hard and expensive to produce. For every good script there are ten useless ones.

'For computer documentation, the help system, the error messages, the on-line documentation, and information embedded in the program (e.g., prompts, menus) should be one integrated whole.'

Again, this is an apparently sensible comment that brings huge practical problems. Computer scientists are forever producing integrated generalised systems, but such systems usually become so complicated that no one ever uses them.

'Documentation should integrate text, graphics, images, animation, and sound.'

There are clear opportunities here, but systems are currently in early stages of development (e.g., Intermedia at Brown University [YANK85] or Microsoft's Multimedia Encyclopedia).

'Documentation should be organised around a database, with an intelligent knowledge-based front-end.'

Clearly a database is desirable for any large body of documentation, and the intelligence is a hope for the future (though ZOG [ROBE81] represents a good base). It is normally best to represent documents in a structured manner, but nevertheless they should be portable. Emerging standards such as ODA [HORA85] will help to achieve this. See Joloboff [JOLO86] for an excellent discussion of standards for document interchange.

'Only if you are really desperate do you actually read the manual.'

Sadly, this statement is undoubtedly true. Currently most of our manuals are so poor that users, rather than reading these manuals, prefer to blunder about randomly trying to solve their problem.

'On-line documentation should be in a typesetting language so that the same source can be used for all peripherals, whether VDU or typesetters.'

This philosophy is followed by the UNIX documentation [KERN78], where the same source file (called the manual page) is used to print documentation on paper or to display it on-line. The economic advantages of this unified approach are obvious, yet it is arguably wrong. If the on-line documentation is simply a replica of the paper documentation, then it has all the disadvantages of paper yet few of its advantages. Inevitably, therefore, readers will prefer the paper version. Good on-line documentation must surely take advantage of interactive communication with the reader to do things that a static medium such as paper cannot do.

'Software with a good graphical interface does not need a user manual.'

A more specific form of this message is: 'They do not provide user manuals for arcade games'. In practice, however, it has been found that, though a good graphical interface does indeed reduce the size of the user manual, it only eliminates it if the functionality offered is small.

'More projects fail through being too ambitious and too general than for any other reason.'

It is an attractive human trait to strive for ambitious goals, but developers of computer software have carried this to absurd lengths. Unfortunately an ambitious software project half completed usually turns out to be worthless. If one tried to create a system for on-line documentation that contained all the desirable features we have outlined above, the project would be absurdly ambitious even for a computer scientist. There is thus a need to tackle modest projects that can soon create a system which will attract real users. Experience of usage of this on-line documentation system—and currently there is a great dearth of such experience except with extremely simple systems—can then lead to new ideas for the next generation of projects.

Examples of Current Status

The above survey has attempted to highlight the needs for on-line documentation. We shall now give an impression of the state of current systems in the field. We shall follow a similar format to the survey, except this time we shall use facts rather than opinions.

Our local UNIX system has three levels of on-line documentation.

As an example of one way a documentation system has evolved to meet the needs of different readers, the UNIX system at the University of Kent at Canterbury has the following three levels of on-line documentation:

- **Man**, the normal UNIX manual pages.
- **How**, a subset of each manual page. Typically **how** produces five lines of explanation of how to use a UNIX command (e.g., what switches are available).
- **Help** (elsewhere often called **apropos**), a one-line summary of each manual page.

The system is therefore designed to meet three separate readership needs. (See Witten and Bramwell [WITT85] for an alternative approach to replacing the **man** command.)

None of these three commands communicates interactively with the user and thus each produces a fixed text. Indeed almost all existing on-line documentation systems are designed to display on screens the sort of material that would normally be read on paper.

An error message: 'it is illegal to type the HELP key in this state'.

The user manual for the system which produced this error message claimed that the user could always type the HELP key when he was in trouble. This was indeed true, but the response that is shown above was not helpful. Although perhaps an extreme example, it illustrates that the general integrated documentation system is a long way off.

Experience of trying to teach how to write documentation shows that 80% of students' efforts are incomprehensible.

The vast majority of those of us who were trained in a scientific or engineering discipline are incapable of producing a complete and readable user manual for the simplest software. The most common error is to explain the detail with excruciating thoroughness without letting the reader know how all this detail fits together. Often the reader will learn what an input line consisting of '\$*lplg*' means, but will never learn what overall job the software that supports this magic is supposed to do. Thus if an on-line documentation system encourages—or forces—authors to put some structure into their outpourings, then this can lead to a higher standard of documentation.It is fruitless, however, to expect too much: the author who writes really incomprehensible rubbish will produce material of the same standard whatever system he is using.

Help systems which intelligently try to tell users how to correct errors often do more harm than good.

When a computer detects an error, this is often due to two pieces of information clashing with one another. For example a programmer may have declared a variable to be a string, but is using it as if it were a number. The compiler, therefore, has two clashing pieces of information. As Horning [HORN74] points out, there is normally no way for the compiler to tell which of these two pieces of information is right and which is wrong. Thus any intelligent help system that tries to make a judgement is likely to turn out to be a 'confuse system' rather than a help system.

Mack *et al* [MACK83] quote a good example of this. A user of an editor tried to save his material and chose X as the new filename. He was told that this was impossible (the reason being that a file called X already existed). The user invoked his intelligent help system and it told him that the way to solve his problem was to invoke the command 'Delete X' and then do his saving.This piece of advice might, of course, be disastrous if the existing file X was a valuable file whose name happened to be the same as the arbitrary name chosen by the user.

Advertisement: 'Systems programmer wanted for document preparation work'.

Many of our existing on-line documentation systems are so complicated that authors need to be systems programmers—as the above advertisement highlights. Even if an on-line documentation system is a dream to use, unless the system is easy for authors there will not be any authors; in this case the system, for all its potential, will be useless.

There is little research on on-line documentation.

This curious phenomenon appears to be world-wide.

The Need

This concludes our survey of the potential applications of on-line documentation, and of the current state-of-the-art in the field—which lags far behind the potential. It is clear that there is ample scope for new approaches to on-line documentation and the rest of this paper describes the GUIDE system, which represents one such approach.

Aims of the GUIDE System

The aims of the GUIDE system can be summarised as follows:

- *To exploit a modern graphics workstation.* As some of the software for machines like the Apple Macintosh shows, screen-based software can be an order of magnitude more pleasant to use than the older glass-teletype software. GUIDE is designed to take advantage of a pointing device, which we will here assume to be a mouse, and a graphics screen of at least medium resolution. In addition GUIDE supports pictures as well as text.

- *To be truly pleasant and simple to use by both readers and authors.*

- *To be highly interactive* so that readers can tailor documentation to their own needs.

- *To cover any nature of document.*

- *To be a modest system.* Readers only need a small amount of functionality: too much functionality makes systems hard to use. As we shall see, authors do not in fact need much more functionality than readers. As a result of its modest pretensions, GUIDE does not try to offer all the typesetting functions found in, say, **troff**. Instead it just fills lines of text to fit the current window. It does not right-justify text (which normally makes the text *less* readable) nor does it hyphenate.

- *NOT to try to imitate paper.* If one could find a software designer who had never seen paper, he would produce a radically different and far superior system for on-line documentation.

In this paper we shall particularly concentrate on the user interface, and how a graphics workstation is exploited. Graphics should also be exploited within documents themselves (e.g., pictures or the use of separate fonts), but even if this is not so the gains from a workstation-based user interface can still be considerable. Following on from these aims, GUIDE has no concept of a 'page'. The idea of fixed pages is totally unsuitable for a system that may run in a window which might dynamically change in size. Instead the GUIDE reader sees a single scrollable document (like a galley proof).

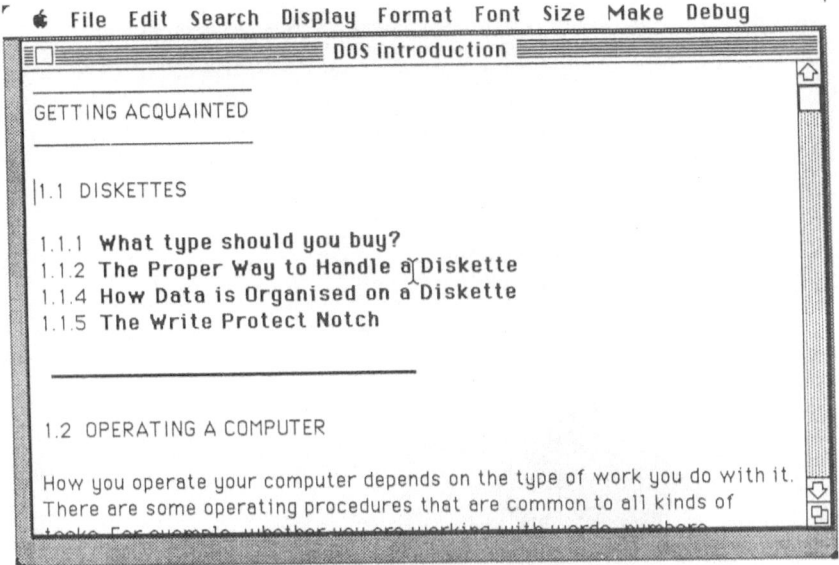

Figure 1 A sample GUIDE screen

Pages and Data Structures

Following on from these aims, GUIDE has no concept of a 'page'. The idea of fixed pages is totally unsuitable for a system that may run in a window which might dynamically change in size. Instead the GUIDE reader sees a single scrollable document (like a galley proof).

Secondly, the data structures used to represent documents inside the computer are hidden from the user. The user is not presented with the impression that he is walking a tree or directed graph, though such walking may indeed be going on behind the scenes.

Example of GUIDE

GUIDE is best illustrated by examples that show snapshots of its actual usage.

GUIDE has been implemented on several computers, partly at the University of Kent and partly by Office Workstations Ltd. (OWL). In this paper we will take our examples from the implementation of GUIDE on the Apple Macintosh. This implementation was done by OWL; their staff, in particular Gordon Dougan, deserve the credit for refining and improving the original GUIDE ideas.

Figure 1 shows a sample display of what the GUIDE reader might see. The document that is displayed is concerned with a computer operating system (DOS), and the document is focussed on the part about diskettes. It can be seen

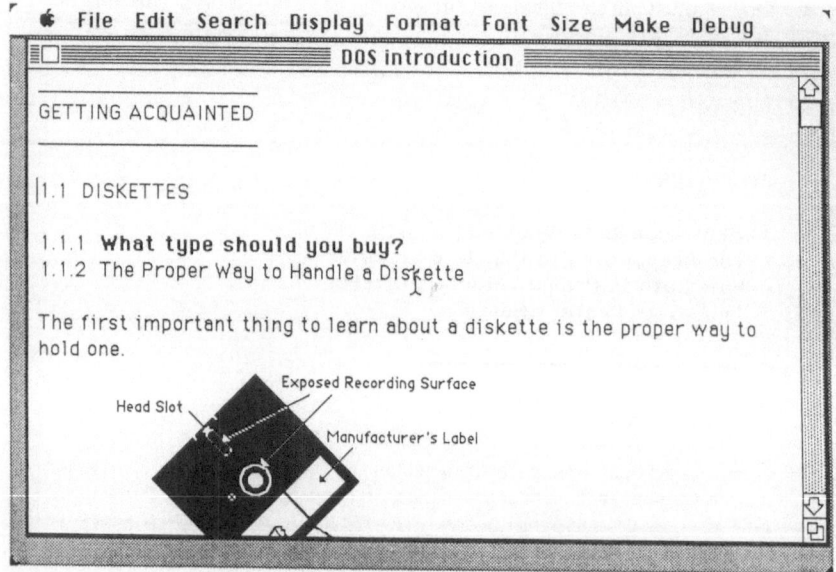

Figure 2 The result of selecting the second button

that within the document there are four phrases in bold type—the same font as
the menu at the top of the screen. These four phrases are *buttons* that can be
selected just like menu items, i.e., the user can point at any one of them and
click a mouse-button. Each button has an associated replacement, which is, like
any other part of the document, a mixture of text, pictures and further buttons.
When a button is selected its replacement appears. Both the button and its
replacement are, of course, designed by the author.

Figure 2 shows what happens after the user has selected the second button,
i.e., the button labelled **The Proper Way to Handle a Diskette.** (A close look at
Figure 1 will show that the cursor is pointing at this button.) The button has been
replaced by a mixture of text and pictures, and, since this replacement is relatively large in size, the material previously below the selected button has scrol-
led off the screen. Given that the author is not a perverse soul, the replacement
gives further detail about the topic named by the button, i.e. the proper way to
handle a diskette.

Typically a GUIDE reader works as follows. Initially a summary of the
document is presented; this summary consists largely of buttons, and the reader
selects the buttons that interest him. He continues selecting buttons until he
reaches the level of detail that he wants. If at any stage the level of detail becomes too great he can 'undo' a replacement; this prevents the displayed document being cluttered up with material that does not turn out to interest the
reader. As the user holds the mouse-button down in preparation for an 'undo',
GUIDE highlights the replacement that will be undone. If the user then changes

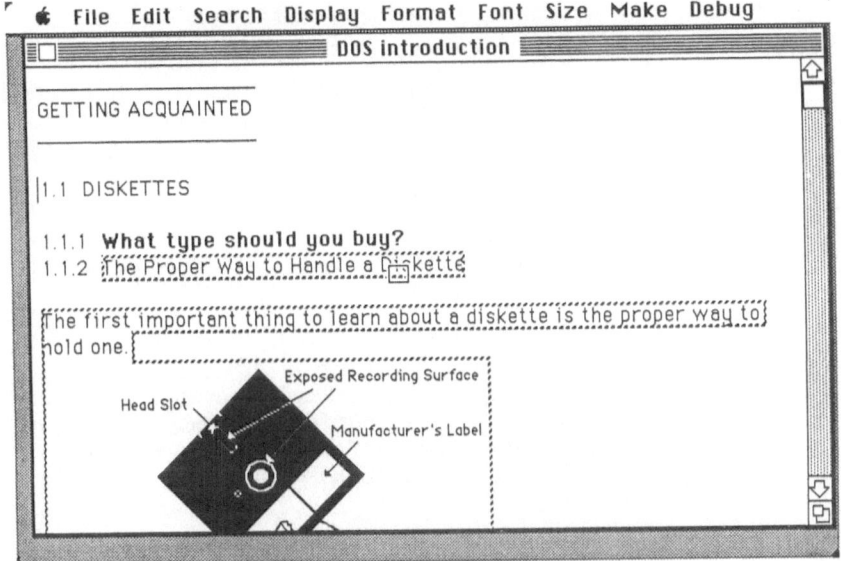

Figure 3 Feed-back before undoing

his mind, he can abort the undoing by moving the cursor away. Figure 3 shows this highlighting—a border that surrounds the blocks of text or graphics that will be undone.

This is an example of a general facility of GUIDE: providing graphical feed-back to the user about the nature of the document. The feed-back may be by means of changing cursor-patterns, temporary highlighting while the mouse-button is held down, or momentary flashing to show the appearance of a new object on the screen. Buttons can be selected and undone in any order and at any time. The end result is that the reader will have a displayed document tailored exactly to what he needs to know. If he wishes, he can save this for later use—he can even print it on paper.

In addition to the type of button that we have just described—which, strictly speaking, we should have called a *replace-button*—GUIDE offers a further type of button, called a *note-button*. Names of note-buttons are underlined to distinguish them from replace-buttons, which are displayed in bold. Figure 4 shows an example of a note-button.

In Figure 4 the user has just selected a note-button called *bytes* (as the cursor, which partly obscures this note-button, shows). While he holds down the mouse-button, a subwindow is displayed on the screen. This subwindow gives the definition associated with the term 'bytes'.

Since GUIDE is designed to offer only a few facilities, each facility should ideally cover a range of users. Note-buttons are a good example of this. As well as their use for explaining jargon, they can be used for footnotes, for citations in

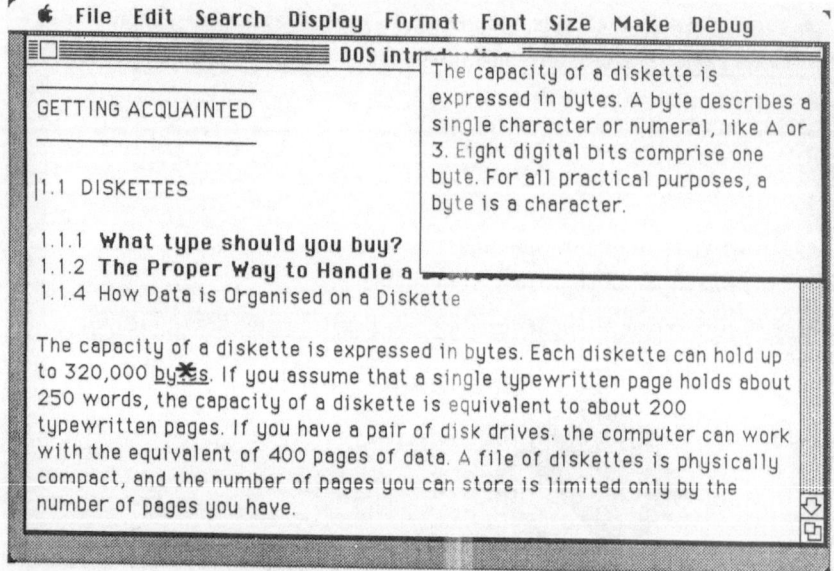

Figure 4 Selecting the 'bytes' note-button

technical papers, for annotations, or even for dealing with details that may change. As an example of the last of these, a *safety manager* note-button could have, as its definition, the name and telephone number of the safety manager within a given organisation. If this individual changed, the definition could be changed without changing the text of documents.

Editing

The reader can, whenever he wishes, edit the displayed document. Indeed GUIDE is a screen editor. To make a change the user simply points at where the change is to be made and then inputs new material and/or deletes existing material. As an example of an edit, the user might wish to add personal comments such as 'The diskettes are stored in the big green box'. Material added by the user is treated by GUIDE in exactly the same way as the existing document—indeed GUIDE keeps no record of which is which.

Edited documents can be saved, though on most systems readers will be prevented by protection mechanisms from changing the original master.

Authors and Readers

The editing capability is a facet of one of GUIDE's most important principles: *the reader is the author and the author is the reader.* In other words the rigid dis-

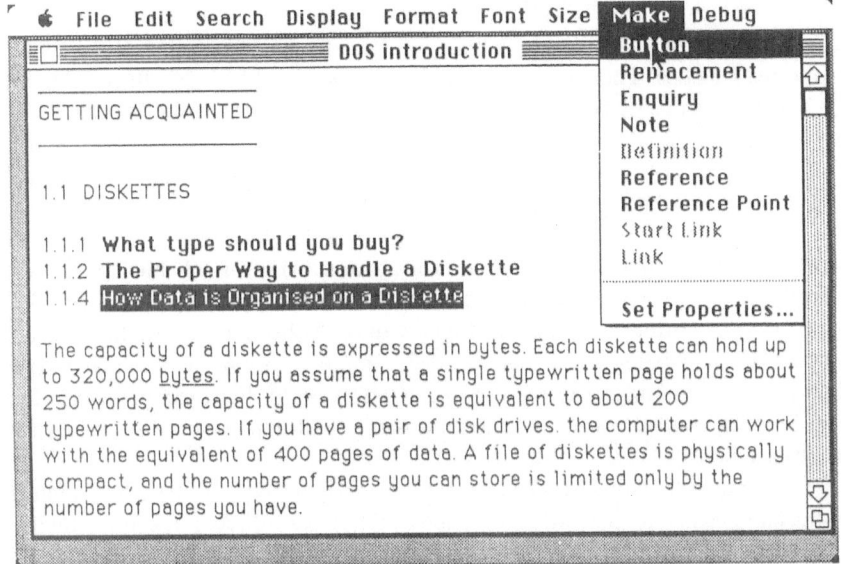

Figure 5 Creating a new button

tinction between author and reader is a relic of paper documents that need not be carried over to on-line ones.

We have seen that readers can edit documents, thus becoming authors. On the other side of the coin, the *only* way that authors can create documents is to view them as readers do. An author of a new document will start from a null document, and will then edit the new material into this null document. To create buttons the author uses the pull-down menu labelled **Make.** This pull-down menu allows the creation of new buttons and other GUIDE structures.

To be specific, creation of a new replace-button consists of:

1) Typing the button name (or drawing it if it is graphical), just as if it were an ordinary part of the document.

2) Selecting the name to be used for the new button; on the Macintosh this is done by 'dragging' the mouse over the name, holding the mouse-button down until the dragging is complete. The selected name is highlighted (by displaying it white-on-black) so that the user can easily see what has been selected,

3) Selecting the **Button** command within the **Make** pull-down menu, to turn the selected name into a button.

Figure 5 illustrates this stage. The newly created button, which is called **How Data is Organised on a Diskette,** will now be just like any other button in the document. It will have a null replacement. Assuming the desired replacement is not null, it is supplied by

4) Selecting the new button, just as a reader would.

5) Editing the null replacement.

It is an important point that the author gets exactly the same view of the button as the reader does. This helps the author to think like the reader, thus reflecting the best advice that can ever be given to any author: think like your reader.

Capturing Existing Documents

Most GUIDE documents are not in fact created from scratch but are derived directly from existing unstructured documents. In this case the author will select parts of the existing document and cause them to become the replacement of buttons. If the existing document employs some mark-up or layout conventions, then it can be automatically converted to GUIDE form. For example every Section heading can be turned into a button name, with the body of the Section as its replacement.

On an implementation of GUIDE that runs under UNIX, all the UNIX manual pages have been automatically converted to GUIDE form. As a result the readers can view the manual pages to any level of detail—thus encompassing the facilities of the **man, how** and **help** commands mentioned earlier.

Other Features

GUIDE contains a few other features, which are found in its user manual [BROW85]. The most important are:

* *Enquiries,* which allow the reader to select alternative replacements, e.g.,

     Is it **Blue, Green** or **Red** ?

  where **Blue, Green,** and **Red** are separate buttons, each with its own replacement. When the user selects a button that lies within an enquiry, the entire enquiry disappears, and the selected replacement takes its place. An 'undo' will, of course, restore the enquiry, and the user can then select another button within the enquiry, e.g. **Red** rather than **Blue.**
* *Automatic tailoring.* A certain amount of tailoring is possible before the reader views a document. For example if he is known to be a manager, certain manager's options can be pre-selected, or if he is known to be in building B then the options for building B (e.g. name of safety manager) can be pre-selected.

Summary

To summarise, we believe that the graphics workstation has provided an opportunity to make on-line documentation truly pleasant. The key to realising this opportunity is to exploit the high-bandwidth human-computer interaction that the workstation offers. In particular a simple highly interactive interface allows the user to tailor what is displayed to what he wants to see. Furthermore the use of graphics and of separate fonts makes the documentation itself easier to understand.

In the next few years, therefore, on-line documentation will prove itself not only in the field of computer documentation—where it is already widely accepted—but also for access to any kind of information that readers want displayed in a flexible way.

Acknowledgement. GUIDE has had some financial support from the Science and Engineering Research Council. I have also benefited greatly from discussions with my colleagues at the University of Kent, and with the staff of OWL.

References

[BROW85] Brown, P. J. (1985) GUIDE user manual. University of Kent at Canterbury

[HORA85] Horak, W. (1985) 'Office document architecture and office document interchange formats: current status of international standardization'. IEEE Computer 18, 10, pp. 50-60

[HORN74] Horning, J. J. (1974) 'What the compiler should tell the user'. in Bauer and Eickel (Eds.), Compiler construction, Springer-Verlag, Berlin, pp. 525-548

[JOLO86] Joloboff, V. (1986) 'Trends and standards in document representation'. in van Vliet (Ed.), Text processing and document manipulation, Cambridge University Press, pp. 107-124

[KERN78] Kernighan, B. W., M. E. Lesk and J. F. Ossanna, Jr. (1978) 'Document preparation'. Bell Syst. Tech. J. 57, 6, Part 2, pp. 2115-2136

[MACK83] Mack, R. L., C. H. Lewis and J. M. Carroll. (1983) 'Learning to use word processors: problems and prospects'. ACM Trans. on Office Systems 1, 3, pp. 254-271

[ROBE81] Robertson, G., D. McCracken and A. Newell. (1981) 'The ZOG approach to man-machine communication'. Int. J. Man-Mach. Stud. 14, pp. 461-468

[WITT85] Witten, I. H. and Bob Bramwell. (1985) 'A system for interactive viewing of structured documents'. Comm. ACM 28, 3, pp. 280-288

[YANK85] Yankelovich, N., N. Meyrowitz and A. van Dam. (1985) 'Reading and writing the electronic book'. IEEE Computer 18, 10, pp. 15-30

Document Structures for Integrated Text and Graphics

HEATHER BROWN

Abstract

For many years text and graphics have been prepared using separate systems. The results have then been stitched together at the last moment to produce an 'integrated' document. The techniques used in the text systems have not lent themselves to graphics work, and vice versa. It is only very recently that attention has been focused on the overall structure of documents that may contain many different elements: images, voice, tables, and spreadsheets as well as text and graphics.

Another interesting development is the gradual emergence of international standards for document description and interchange. Some of these standards attempt to separate the structure of the document from its contents, thereby providing an overall framework for documents containing different elements.

The Office Document Architecture (ODA) is one such standard. This paper describes the general principles of ODA, and examines its relevance to documents containing integrated text and graphics.

Introduction to ODA

The preparation of international standards is necessarily a long-drawn-out process, and one that must take account of work being done elsewhere. The *Office Document Architecture* and *Office Document Interchange Format* (ODA/ODIF) standards have been making their way through the various stages of the standards processes for both the International Standards Organization, ISO [ISOD85a-f], and the European Computer Manufacturers' Association, [ECMA 85]. The two proposals have been leap-frogging one another and, though they differ in detail, are essentially the same. In addition, the ISO draft standard contains the CCITT *Document interchange protocol for the telematic services* [CCIT85] as a subset. The discussion below describes the ISO proposal.

Strictly speaking, ODA provides a static description of a document that can then be exchanged using ODIF. However, ODA also provides an underlying architectural and processing model for documents, and it is this model that is the most interesting feature of ODA and the subject of this paper.

Before launching into details it is worth noting that the six parts of the ISO standard amount to 250 pages with almost no examples included! The description given here is necessarily much briefer. In some cases the descriptions and examples are simplified to the extent that they are not strictly accurate. The intention is to introduce the basic principles of ODA in a fairly gentle fashion, then to expand a little on the more interesting features of the document model without getting lost in too many details.

ODA provides a hierarchical, object-oriented view of a document. Documents are described in terms of a tree structure, with objects corresponding to the nodes in the tree. All the *content* of the document comes in the leaf nodes; the nodes higher up in the tree simply define the relationships between the objects (i.e. the structure of the document). This is important for multimedia documents as the higher levels of the document structure are largely independent of the content.

Information about the objects is provided by their *attributes*. These generally give information about the objects themselves, but they may also define relationships between objects that are not implicit in the tree structure. So, although it is simplest to think about the document model as a tree, it is actually a more general graph.

Logical and Layout Structures

An important feature of the ODA model is that the document is described by two structures: the *logical* structure and the *layout* structure. The logical structure divides and subdivides the content of the document into items that mean something to the human reader or writer. These may be general items which occur in many documents, or they may be items specific to a particular document type. General items are titles, chapters, sections, diagrams, and footnotes. Specific items could be logos, telephone numbers, and dictionary or catalogue entries.

The layout structure, on the other hand, divides and subdivides the content into page sets, pages, and rectangular areas within pages. These rectangular areas, which are positioned so that their edges are parallel to the edge of the containing page, can themselves be subdivided into nested rectangular areas. Subdivided areas are known as *frames*, while the lowest-level areas are known as *blocks*. A column of text, for example, could be represented by a frame which is then subdivided into blocks representing the areas used for individual paragraphs of text. Similarly, an area set aside for a diagram could be represented by a frame which is subdivided into two blocks representing the diagram itself and its caption.

In both the logical and the layout structures, only the lowest level objects in the tree (known as *basic objects*) have content associated with them. For the logical structure this could mean that content in the form of strings of characters is associated with basic objects such as titles and paragraphs. For the layout structure, by definition, it means that content is associated with blocks only.

Figures 1 and 2 show how the logical and layout structures might look for a fragment of a document representing the beginning of a chapter. A chapter is assumed to begin on a new page. It consists of a title followed by a number of sections. The fragment contains the chapter title, the title of the first section, and three paragraphs which comprise the first section.

The logical structure representing this fragment might be as shown below in Figure 1.

Document Structures for Integrated Text and Graphics

Heather Brown

University of Kent at Canterbury

Figures only from paper of the same name!

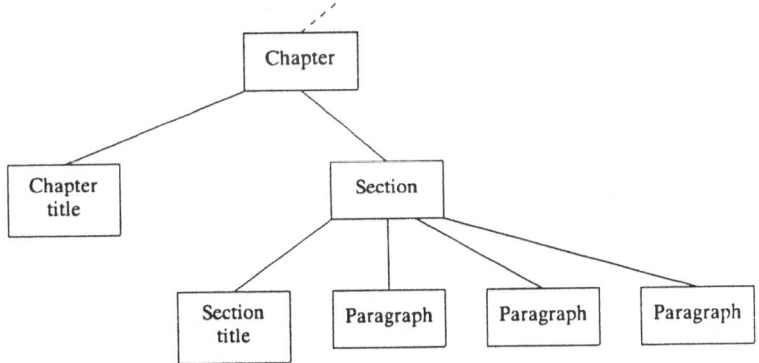

Figure 1

Only the titles and paragraphs will have content associated with them. When the document has been formatted a corresponding layout structure will exist, and this will associate the same content with pages, frames, and blocks. The two structures are clearly dependent on one another and come together at the level of the content. Figure 2 shows the combined structures, assuming that the third paragraph comes on a new page, and Figure 3 shows the actual page layout that might result.

The content of a logical object will normally correspond to the content of a block, but this is not always so. A paragraph could be split over two pages, for example, and in this case the content for the paragraph is divided into two portions and associated with two separate blocks belonging to two different pages. Figure 4 shows a simplified version of how this might be reflected in the structures. The rule is that an object can have more than one content portion associated with it, but a content portion always belongs to only one object. In particular, as we shall see later, two or more contents portions may appear in a single block.

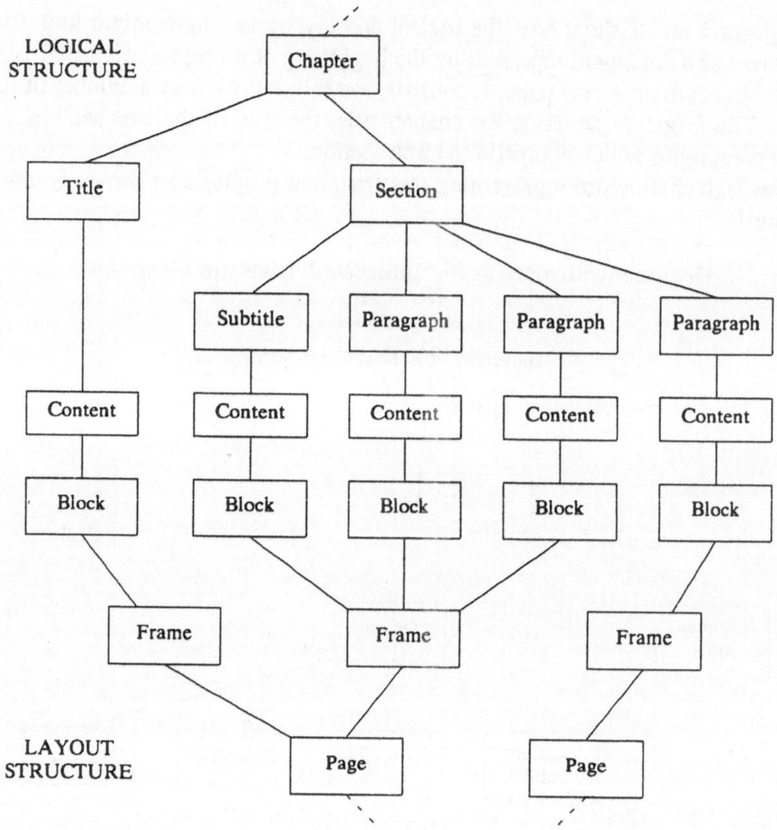

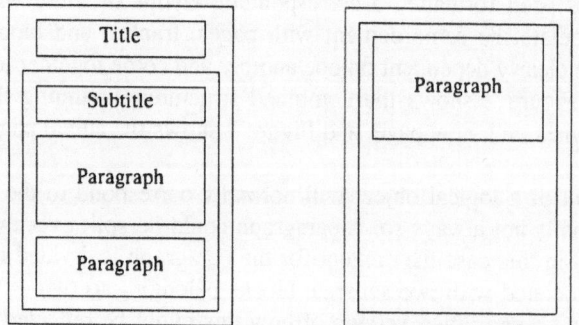

LOGICAL STRUCTURE
Chapter
Title
Section
Subtitle
Paragraph
Paragraph
Paragraph
Content
Content
Content
Content
Content
Block
Block
Block
Block
Block
Frame
Frame
Frame
LAYOUT STRUCTURE
Page
Page

Title
Subtitle
Paragraph
Paragraph
Paragraph

Figures 2 & 3

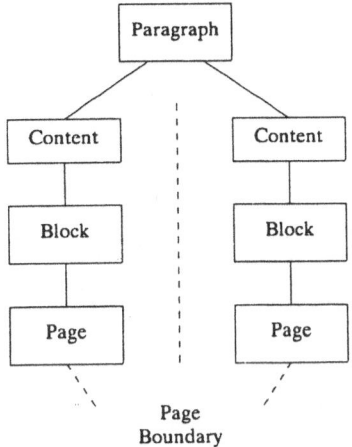

Figure 4

Generic and Specific Structures

The previous section introduced a specific example of a document fragment which assumed that a certain set of constituents could occur at the start of a chapter. ODA does, in fact, encompass four related structures rather than two. For both the logic and layout of a document there are *generic* structures, which define the types and combinations of constituents that are allowed in a document of a particular class, and there are also *specific* structures, which describe one particular instance of a document belonging to that class. (The structures in the previous section should more properly have been referred to as the specific logical and specific layout structures. It is convenient, however, to assume that 'structure' means 'specific structure' unless specified otherwise.)

The ODA generic structures are often drawn as trees, but they may also be thought of as grammars describing all possible documents of a particular class, in the same way that a grammar can be used to describe all possible programs written in a particular programming language.

Just as a grammar consists of a set of rules, the ODA generic structures consist of a set of object descriptions. Each object definition has an attribute called *generator for subordinates* which describes how it can be made up from subordinate objects.

These subordinates may be:

- optional (0 or 1 occurrence),
- required (exactly 1 occurrence),
- repetitive (1 or more occurrences),
- optional and repetitive (0, 1, or more occurrences).

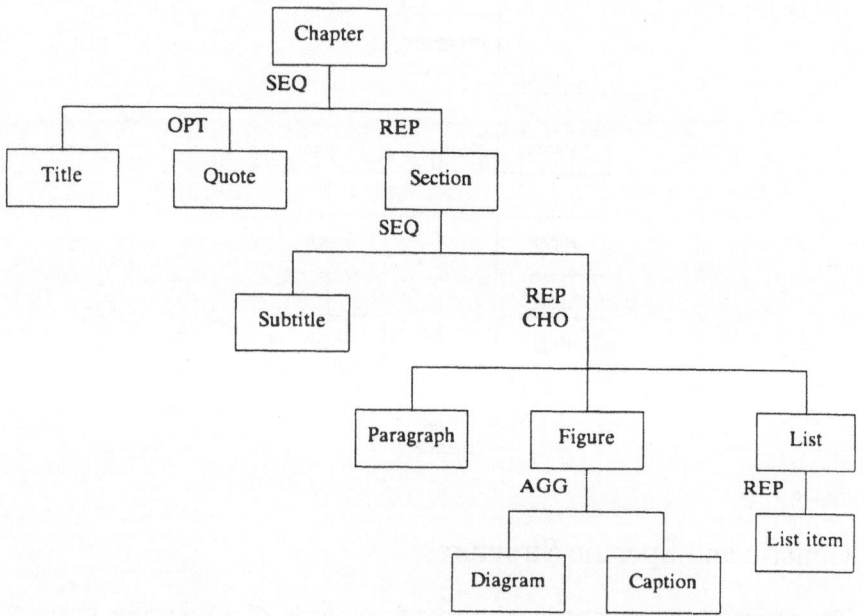

Figure 5

In addition they may be expressed as:

- a sequence (occurring in the order specified),
- an aggregate (occurring in any order),
- a choice (only one occurs).

To show how this works in practice we shall return to the chapter example used in the previous section. The generic logical structure for that chapter might have been as shown in Figure 5. This says that a chapter is made up of a mandatory title, followed by an optional quotation, followed by one or more sections. Each section begins with a subtitle and then consists of a mixture of paragraphs, figures, and lists. The 'REP CHO' construct represents a series of one or more of these items occurring in any order. Figures in turn consist of a diagram and a caption (in either order), and lists consist of one or more list items.

Specific instances of this structure could range from a simple chapter with one section of three paragraphs, as in our example, to chapters with an initial quotation and several sections containing different mixtures of paragraphs, figures, and lists.

A corresponding generic layout structure is harder to describe without getting into details of the document layout process. It might, for example, define two

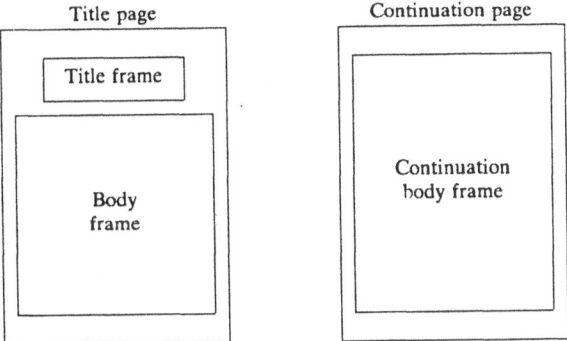

Figure 6

different page styles; a 'Title page' for the first page of the chapter, and a 'Continuation page' for all subsequent pages. Figure 6 shows these two different page styles and Figure 7 shows the top levels of the generic layout structure used to define them. The two body frames would then need to be defined as containing a series of frames and blocks corresponding to subtitles, paragraphs, figures, and so on. At the lowest level, a frame for figures might be defined with two subordinate blocks as shown in Figure 8. Attributes attached to these blocks and the frame would define the position of the blocks within the frame and might, perhaps, specify that the figure frame should be centered within the body frame. As the blocks are subordinate to the figure frame, they must lie entirely within it,

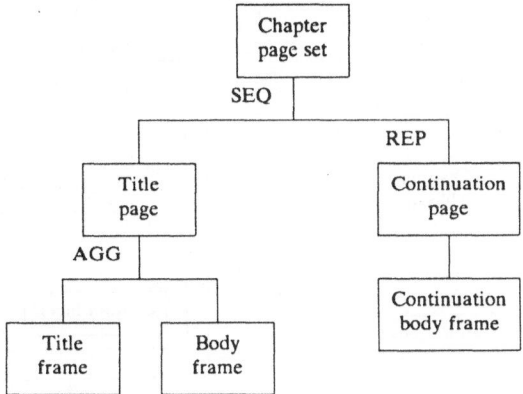

Figure 7

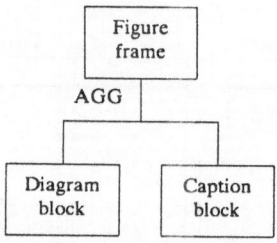

Figure 8

but the blocks themselves could either overlap or be disjoint. So the actual layout of a figure could be in either of the ways shown in Figure 9.

Content Architecture and the Layout Process

The description so far has scarcely mentioned content. It has just been something that occurs at the leaves of the specific structures. This reinforces the point that a lot of the document architecture is independent of the content, but it is now time to explain how content fits in and, in particular, how different types of content are handled.

In simple terms, each content portion is of a given type that is defined by its content *architecture*. This means that each type of content is assumed to conform to a given set of rules and that there are procedures laid down for processing the content portions.

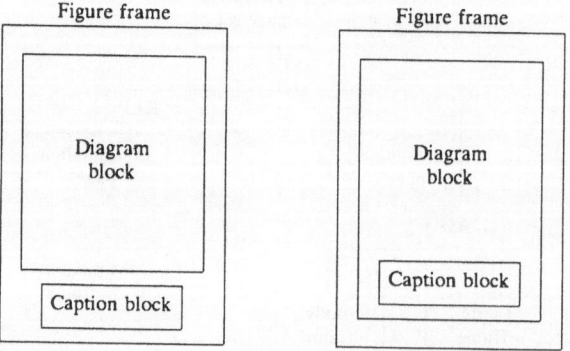

Figure 9

ODA currently defines several levels of *character content architecture*. Some of these conform to CCITT standards for Telex and Teletex; some describe higher quality text. The rules embodied in the content architecture define the internal structure of the contents and cover such items as the positioning and orientation of characters, positioning of lines and of words within lines, indentation, tabulation, and the use of different character fonts.

We have now described nearly all the parts of ODA needed to understand how a document is laid out. The only missing item is the so-called *layout style*. This is a set of attributes associated with the generic structures which gives information about the positioning of frames and blocks and defines the possible relationships allowed between logical and layout objects. The next section gives some examples showing how these relationships might work in practice for our sample chapter. For now it is sufficient to note that the combination of the content architecture and the layout style provide all the rules needed to decide how the document should be laid out.

The *layout process* is what decides exactly where each item of the document is to be placed and on which page. In ODA terms it can be defined as the process used to create the specific layout structure of the document. This starts with the specific logical structure and uses the content architecture and the layout style derived from the generic structures to decide exactly how the content is placed into pages, frames, and blocks.

If the document has more than one type of content, then the rules for the different content architectures will be used to deal with the appropriate content portions. This is, however, the only point at which the content affects the document architecture and processing.

An Example of the Layout Process

The ODA terminology is very precise, but apt to be confusing because of all the different structures and processes concerned. To show how the various pieces fit together, we shall introduce some of the most important attributes that make up the layout style and then show how they could be used in our chapter example to influence the layout process.

A crucial aspect of the layout process is to decide what type of layout object can be used for any given logical object. This is dictated by three attributes within the layout style: 'layout object class', 'layout category', and 'permitted categories'.

The 'layout object class' is used to indicate that an entire logical object (with all its subordinates) must be laid out in a single instance of a layout object derived from a given layout definition. No other part of the document may share the same layout object. In our example, a logical 'Chapter' would have its layout object class defined as 'Chapter page set'. Each chapter would then be laid out in a separate page set with a single title page and as many continuation pages as necessary. The start of a new chapter would automatically signal the need for a

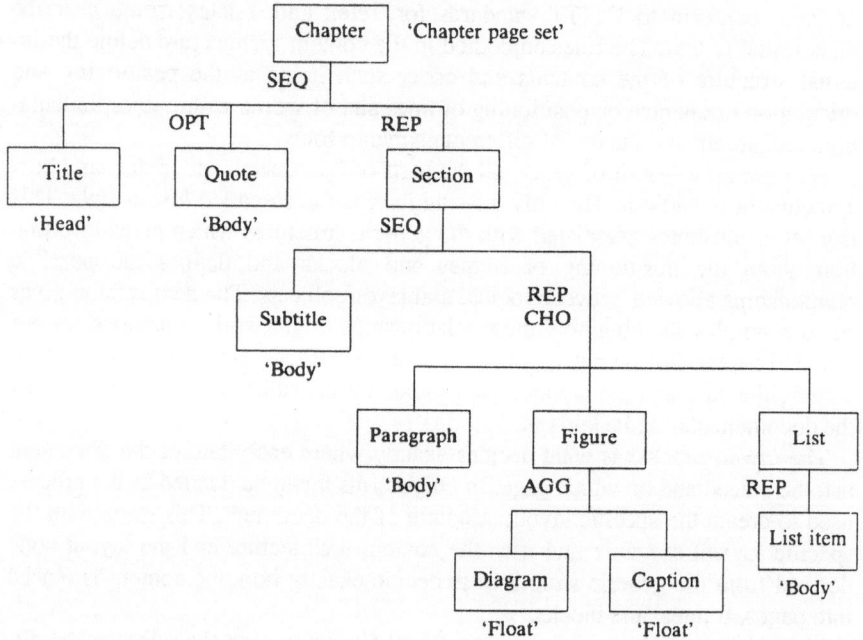

Figure 10

new page set. This attribute can only refer to page sets or pages, not to frames or blocks, so it is effectively restricted to major logical divisions of the document.

For lower-level objects the two attributes 'layout category' and 'permitted categories' are provided to associate basic logical objects with 'frames'. 'Layout category' is used to associate a name with a basic logical object. The object can then only be laid out in a frame that has the same name as one of its permitted categories. Note that a frame may have several different 'permitted categories', so objects from several different layout categories may appear within a single frame.

In our chapter example, however, we shall keep a simple one-to-one relation between basic logical objects and frames, and use only three layout categories called 'Head', 'Body', and 'Float'. Figure 10 shows the generic logical structure with appropriate layout object class and layout category names added. 'Head' appears only once as the layout category of the Title. It would also be the only permitted category of the 'Title frame', thus ensuring that only the chapter title could be laid out in the title frame.

To ensure that all the other parts of the chapter are laid out in order in the 'Body frame' of the title page and then in the 'Continuation body frames' of subsequent pages, the name 'Body' is used as the layout category of all the remaining basic logical objects (except those in the figure) and as the permitted category   of

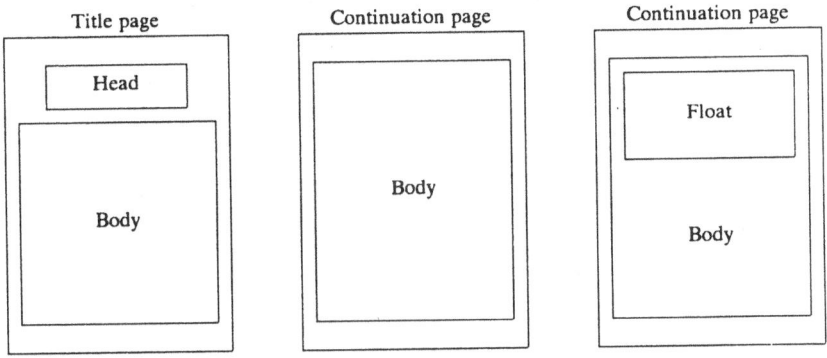

Figure 11

both the body frames. The quote, if present, and any following paragraphs and lists would then be placed in blocks within the body frames. Further attributes would control their relative positions within the frames.

The figure was not included above because it has its own frame within the body frames. So the final step is to use the name 'Float' to associate the Diagram and Caption of the figure with the 'Figure frame'. By a judicious use of attributes and facilities not described here, the figure frame could be made to float to the top of its enclosing body frame. This might lead to a specific chapter page set as shown in Figure 11. The frames are labelled with their category names.

Positioning of Blocks within Frames

The previous section outlined the method of fitting contents into pages and frames. To illustrate the final stage, fitting blocks into frames, we shall introduce a few more attributes, and then look at a variation on our chapter example to illustrate their use.

Both frames and blocks can be given a 'position' attribute to fix their position within their containing frame (or page). Alternatively, their position may be dictated by other blocks being fitted into the same frame, as described below. They may also be given a 'dimensions' attribute to define their maximum allowed size.

The actual size of blocks is influenced by their content. In the case of a paragraph of text, for example, the block would probably assume its maximum width, but would grow downwards only as far as needed to accommodate the lines of text it contained. At present ODA does not define a content architecture for graphics, but one could imagine that a graphics block might assume the minimum size necessary to display all its contents, and that the maximum allowed size would effectively define a clipping area. This sizing of blocks is one of the areas where the content architecture interacts with the overall layout process of the document.

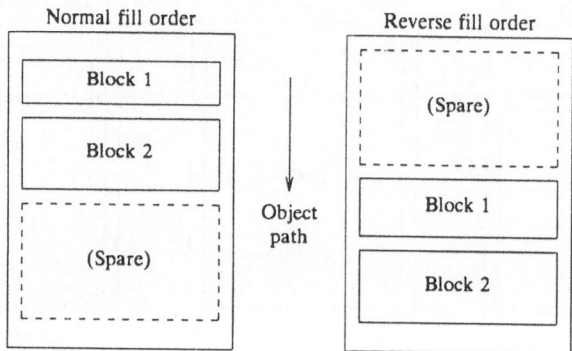

Figure 12

The process of fitting blocks into frames is influenced by five separate attributes. Four of these ('fill order', 'concatenation', 'offset', and 'separation')
apply to basic logical objects, and one ('object path') applies to pages or frames.

The object path of a page or frame gives the direction of filling. If the object
path is downwards, blocks will normally be positioned with the first block at the
top and subsequent blocks coming underneath. The fill order of the basic logical
objects can be used to alter this. If the fill order has the value 'normal order' then
the situation is as described above. If the fill order is 'reverse order', however,
the blocks will be positioned with the first block at the bottom. In this case subsequent blocks will not be placed above the first one, but will push it up to make
room for themselves underneath. The two cases are illustrated in Figure 12.

The exact positioning of the blocks is influenced by their 'offset' and 'separation' attributes, which define minimum distances between adjacent blocks or
between blocks and their containing frame.

To illustrate the use of the 'concatenation' attribute and to show a more complex version of filling of blocks into frames, we shall finish by looking at a new
version of the paragraph in our chapter example. In this variation, a paragraph
can be subdivided into strings of text and footnotes. The generic logical definition with the values of the fill order and concatenation attributes added is shown
in Figure 13.

The intention is to allow the paragraph to contain footnote text that belongs
logically within the paragraph but is to be laid out in the traditional manner at
the bottom of the page. All the strings of text, however, are to be treated as one
and to be laid out in a single block (unless a page break happens to intervene).

The desired effect can be achieved by giving the strings of text normal fill order but giving the footnote text reverse fill order. In addition, the first string of
text and the footnotes are specified as 'unconcatenated' while the subsequent
strings of text are specified as 'concatenated'. Concatenated objects share

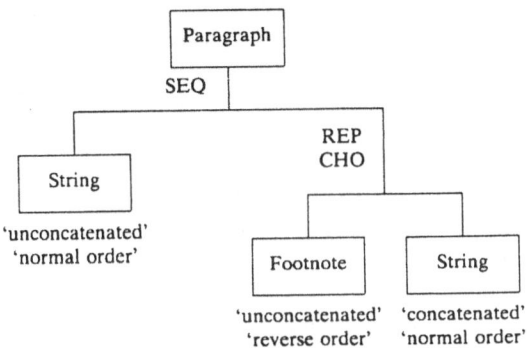

Figure 13

the same layout block as previous objects with the same content architecture, layout category, and fill order. So in this case the subsequent strings are concatenated with the initial string rather than the intervening footnotes. If we assume there are three paragraphs and that the middle one contains two embedded footnotes, the final layout will be as shown in Figure 14.

ODA and Graphics

It can be seen from the descriptions above that ODA provides a general document model that could readily be extended to encompass a graphics content architecture, and indeed other contents architectures for such things as sound or spreadsheets. The document layout process interacts with the content architec-

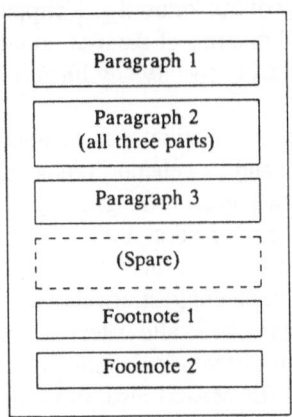

Figure 14

ture mainly at the level of deciding the size of individual blocks. The higher level decisions are effectively independent of the content.

Several extensions and refinements to ODA are expected [HORA85]. A great opportunity will be missed unless these allow existing or emerging graphics standards to be incorporated into ODA documents.

ODA and Page Description Languages

The ODA document and page layout process is relatively complex, but its use of rectangular blocks—with their edges parallel to the edges of the containing page—provides a very restricted imaging model. To put this into context, it is worth looking briefly at one other document imaging model.

The integration of text and graphics has been helped by the recent emergence of sophisticated *page description languages* whose main purpose is to communicate a description of pages containing text, graphics and images to a printing system. In addition to a range of graphics imaging operators, they are procedural languages with many of the trappings of high-level programming languages [REID86]. PostScript [ADOB85a] [ADOB85b] is a notable example of such a language.

The PostScript imaging model contains most of the facilities associated with the output from high quality text formatting systems as well as graphics systems. A page image is built up by painting ink on selected areas of the page. The ink may be black, white, coloured, or any shade of grey. It may represent letters, lines, curves, filled shapes, or halftone images.

Two important concepts are the *current path* and the *user coordinate system*. The current path is a set of points, lines, and curves used to describe shapes and their positions. The shapes may be concave, convex, or self-intersecting. Once the path has been defined it can be *stroked* to yield a line drawn along the path, *filled* to yield a solid region of ink, or used as a clipping boundary. All items on a PostScript page are defined in terms of the user coordinate system, which can be translated, rotated, and scaled to specify any linear transformation from the user space to the device space.

These concepts, used in conjunction with PostScript's comprehensive set of graphics imaging operators and its general-purpose programming facilities, lead to an extremely flexible and powerful imaging model. Characters, for example, can be printed at any size or orientation, they can be printed along any path and can be subject to all the possible coordinate transformations.

The ODA imaging model, by contrast, is relatively simple and restricted. The character content architecture does allow text to come in different fonts and sizes, but it only allows four different orientations (0, 90, 180, and 270 degrees). The ECMA ODA standard [ECMA85] also provides a simple content architecture for pixel images, and there should soon be a graphics content architecture for geometric shapes. Unfortunately, it seems likely that the integration of text, graphics, and images will be limited to the mixing and superimposing of rectangular blocks containing the different types of content.

Conclusion

Whatever its deficiencies, ODA is a coming international standard. It is being taken seriously in Europe where major Esprit and Alvey research projects are being undertaken into document creation and handling techniques based on the ODA model. It remains to be seen whether the expected graphics content architecture and other extensions will provide the necessary framework for the integration of high quality text and graphics.

Acknowledgements. I am indebted to Dr. Tony Towl and other colleagues at Kent for many long discussions on the ODA standard and for their help in unravelling some of its intricacies. I would also like to thank the SERC and the Alvey Directorate for their support of work on document structures.

References

[ADOB85a] Adobe Systems Inc., PostScript Language Reference Manual, Addison-Wesley (1985)

[ADOB85b] Adobe Systems Inc., PostScript Language Tutorial and Cookbook, Addison-Wesley (1985)

[CCIT85] CCITT Recommendation T.73 Document interchange protocol for the telematic services, Geneva (Mar 1985)

[ECMA85] ECMA/TC29/85/11 Office Document Architecture (1985)

[HORA85] W. Horak, Office Document Architecture and Office Document Interchange Formats: Current Status of International Standardization, IEEE Computer, pp 50-60 (Oct 1985)

[ISOD85a] ISO/DP 8613/1 Part 1: General Introduction Information Processing–Text and Office Systems–Document Structures. ISO/TC97/SC18/WG3 N557 (Oct 1985)

[ISOD85b] ISO/DP 8613/2 Part 2: Office Document Architecture Information Processing–Text and Office Systems–Document Structures, ISO/TC97/SC18/WG3 N558 (Oct 1985)

[ISOD85c] ISO/DP 8613/3 Part 3: Document Layout and Imaging Information Processing–Text and Office Systems–Document Structures, ISO/TC97/SC18/WG3 N559 (Oct 1985)

[ISOD85d] ISO/DP 8613/4 Part 4: Document Profile Information Processing–Text and Office Systems–Document Structures, ISO/TC97/SC18/WG3 N560 (Oct 1985)

[ISOD85e] ISO/DP 8613/5 Part 5: Office Document Interchange Format Information Processing–Text and Office Systems–Document Structures, ISO/TC97/SC18/WG3 N561 (Oct 1985)

[ISOD85f] ISO/DP 8613/6 Part 6: Character Content Architectures Information Processing–Text and Office Systems–Document Structures, ISO/TC97/SC18/WG3 N562 (Oct 1985)

[REID86] B. K. Reid, Procedural Page Description Languages, Text Processing and Document Manipulation, ed. J. C. van Vliet, pp 214-223, Cambridge University Press (1986)

Author Biographies

Biographies
Techniques for Computer Graphics

David F. Rogers

David F. Rogers is Professor of Aerospace Engineering at the U.S. Naval Academy. In 1959, he earned a Bachelor of Aeronautical Engineering degree from Rensselaer Polytechnic Institute and subsequently was awarded the MSAE and PhD degrees from the same institute. Dr. Rogers is the author of three textbooks on computer graphics, including "Mathematical Elements for Computer Graphics" and "Procedural Elements for Computer Graphics". He is a member of SIGGRAPH, ACM, the American Institute of Aeronautics and Astronautics, and the Society of Naval Architects and Marine Engineers. Dr. Rogers is the founder and former Director of the Computer Aided Design/Interactive Graphics Group at the U.S. Naval Academy. He is series editor for the Butterworth Series in Computer Aided Engineering and the editor of Computers & Education. He also is a member of the editorial board of The Visual Computer. Dr. Rogers was co-chairman of ICCAS '82, The International Conference on Computer Applications in the Automation of Shipyard Operation and Ship Design. He is a member of the International Program Committee for ICCAS. He was also Co-Chairman of the International Program Committee for Computer Graphics Tokyo '85. Dr. Rogers was Visiting Professor at the University of New South Wales, Sydney, Australia in 1982. He was an Honorary Research Fellow at University College London in England during 1977-78 where he studied Naval Architecture. Professor Rogers was one of the original faculty who established the Aerospace Engineering Department at the U.S. Naval Academy in 1964. He has both an experimental and a theoretical research background, and has research interests in the areas of highly interactive graphics, computer-aided design and manufacturing, numerical control, computer-aided education, hypersonic viscous flow, boundary layer theory and computational fluid mechanics.

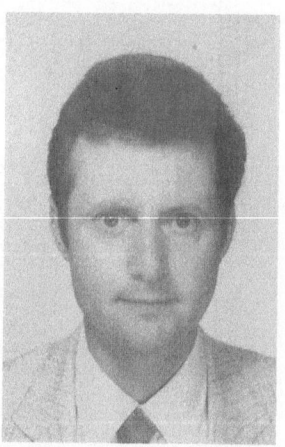

Rae A. Earnshaw

Dr. Earnshaw was born in York, England and educated at Roundhay School and the University of Leeds. He holds the BSc and PhD degrees, has been a faculty staff member for 16 years, and heads the graphics team responsible for campuswide provision of computer graphics hardware and software. His PhD was the first in computer graphics to be awarded by the University. He is a member of the British Computer Society and Chairman of the Computer Graphics and Displays Group. He has been a Visiting Professor at Illinois Institute of Technology, Chicago; Northwestern Polytechnical University, Xian, China; and George Washington University, Washington, DC. He has acted as a consultant to US companies and the College CAD/CAM Consortium and given seminars at a variety of UK and US institutions and research laboratories. He is the author and editor of many papers, monographs and proceedings, including "Fundamental Algorithms for Computer Graphics" published by Springer-Verlag in 1985. He was present at the early SIGGRAPH Conferences, including the University of Pennsylvania in 1976, the USA Bicentenary Year, and has made a number of contributions since then, including Panel Chair at SIGGRAPH 84 and 85. His current interests are graphics algorithms, integrated graphics and text, display technology, CAD/CAM, and human-computer interface issues. He is a member of SIGGRAPH, ACM, IEEE, IEEE Computer Society, an Associate Fellow of the Institute of Mathematics and its Applications, and a Fellow of the British Computer Society.

Brian Barsky

Brian A. Barsky is an Associate Professor of computer science at the University of California, Berkeley, where he is Director of the Berkeley Computer Graphics Laboratory, and he is an Associate Professor of computer science at the University of Waterloo in Waterloo, Ontario, Canada. He was an Attaché de Recherche Invite at the Laboratoire Image at Ecole Nationale Superieure des Telecommunications in Paris and a visiting researcher with the Computer Aided Design and Manufacturing Group at the Sentralinsitutt for Industriell Forskning (Central Institute for Industrial Research) in Oslo. Barsky's research interests include computer-aided geometric design and modeling, and interactive three-dimensional computer graphics. He attended McGill University, where he received a DCS in engineering and a BSc in mathematics and computer science. He studied computer graphics and computer science at Cornell University, where he earned an MS degree. He earned a PhD degree in computer science from the University of Utah, received an IBM Faculty Development Award in 1983 and a National Science Foundation Presidential Young Investigator Award in 1985, and was the technical program chairman of SIGGRAPH 85. He is a member of ACM SIGGRAPH, the National Computer Graphics Association, the IEEE Computer Society, the Canadian Man-Computer Communications Society, and the Society for Industrial and Applied Mathematics. Professor Barsky's address is Berkeley Computer Graphics Laboratory, Computer Science Division, University of California, Berkeley, Ca 94720.

Heather Brown

Heather Brown began her computing career in 1963 at the IBM Laboratories at Hursley near Winchester, where she worked on software development for the early IBM 360 computers. After a brief period at the Mathematical Laboratory at Cambridge University, she moved to the Computing Laboratory at the University of Kent where she is now a reader in Computer Science and the Head of the Computer Science Department. Her main research interests are in computer document preparation and typesetting techniques. These interests were stimulated by a visit to Stanford University in 1980 when she worked with Professor Donald Knuth's group on the TEX typesetting system. Since then she had been involved in a number of research projects concerned with techniques for document creation, manipulation and printing. She is currently working on a research project which is using ODF as a basis for developing an interactive documentation system for software engineering.

Peter Brown

Peter Brown is Professor of Computer Science at the University of Kent at Canterbury. He has previously worked at IBM (UK) Laboratories, and as visiting professor at Stanford University. His research interests have been in macro processors, compilers and VLSI. During the last three years, partly supported by the Science and Engineering Research Council, he has been working on highly-interactive software for graphics workstations, and has been particularly interested in on-line documentaion. He holds BA and PhD degrees from Cambridge University, and a Master's degree from the University of North Carolina.

Jose L. Encarnacao

Jose Encarnacao is Professor of Computer Science and Head of the Interactive Computer Graphics Research Group at Technische Hochschule, Darmstadt, Federal Republic of Germany. He chaired the German DIN activities from which GKS evolved, and was the past Chairman of Eurographics (1980-84). He is the author and editor of 8 books and conference proceedings, and has directed and chaired numerous conferences and workshops in Germany and abroad. He has lectured at numerous tutorials, seminars and advanced courses in the areas of computer graphics, CAD/CAM, and interactive systems, and also acts as a consultant to governmant and industrial organisations. He is the Editor-in-Chief of Computers and Graphics and a member of the Editorial Boards of IEEE Computer Graphics and Applications, CAD/CAM Digest, Informatica, Computer Graphics Forum, and Informatik F & E.

Robin Forrest

Robin Forrest is a Professor of computing science in the School of Information Systems at the University of East Anglia, Norwich. He has a BSc in mechanical engineering from the University of Edinburgh and a PhD in computer-aided design from the University of Cambridge. He has been an Assistant Director of Research in the computer laboratory, University of Cambridge, Visiting Professor at Syracuse University and the University of Utah, Visiting Expert at the Beijing Institute of Aeronautics and Astronautics, and Visiting Scientist at the Xerox Palo Alto Research Center. His current research interests include computational geometry, both theoretical and applied, geometric modelling, colour raster graphics, and illustration systems. He is a Fellow of the British Computer Society and the Institute of Mathematics and Its Applications, a member of ACM, and an affiliate of the IEEE Computer Society.

Henry Fuchs

Henry Fuchs is a professor of computer science at the University of North Carolina at Chapel Hill, where he has been teaching graduate courses in computer graphics and VLSI design, and directs the research of PhD students and research associates in graphics algorithms and VLSI architechtures. Dr. Fuchs is the principal investigator of research projects funded by DARPA, NIH, and NSF. He consults for a variety of industrial organizations. He is an associate editor of ACM Transactions on Graphics and was chairman of the 1985 Chapel Hill Conference on VLSI. He received a BA from the University of California at Santa Cruz in 1970, and a PhD from the University of Utah in 1975.

Roy Hall

Roy Hall is the Director of Software Development at Wavefront Technologies. He has been researching and writing image synthesis systems since 1981. Hall was introduced to computer graphics as a tool for finite element analysis. He received his MS in computer graphics from Cornell University in 1983. Since then he has worked with Robert Abel & Associates, Vertigo Computer Imagery, and Universal Studios in establishing production graphics systems. He is a member of the IEEE and the ACM.

Michael R. Kaplan

Michael Kaplan graduated with a Masters Degree from Cornell University's Program of Computer Graphics in 1979. He is the President of Kobra Graphics, the developers of the Visual:Geniszs rendering software package, and is currently a Member of the technical staff at Dana Computers, Inc., Sunnyvale, California, USA.

Alistair Kilgour

Alistair Kilgour has been involved in computer graphics since joining the Computer Aided Design Project at University of Edinburgh in 1966. While at Edinburgh he developed a satellite graphic system on a DEC PDP-7 with 340 display connected by a high-speed link to a time-shared PDP-10, and assisted other members of the CAD project in the application of interactive graphics to a range of engineering problems. In 1974 he moved to Glasgow as lecturer in computing science, and became senior lecturer in 1984. At Glasgow he has worked on graphic system design, graphical algorithms, and computational geometry, and has been involved in teaching graphics at both undergraduate and postgraduate levels. In addition to graphical and geometric algorithms, his current research interests are in interactive dialogue design and visual programming.

Tosiyasu Kunii

Tosiyasu L. Kunii is currently Professor and Chairman of Information and Computer Science at the University of Tokyo. He started work there in raster graphics in 1968, which led to the Tokyo Raster Technology Project. His research interests include computer graphics, database systems, and software engineering. He has authored and edited 25 computer science books and published 80 refereed academic/technical papers in computer science and applications areas. Professor Kunii is President of the Computer Graphics Society, Chairman-of-the-Board of the Handheld Computer Society, Editor-in-Chief of the Visual Computer: An International Journal of Computer Graphics, and a member of the Editorial Board of IEEE Computer Graphics and Applications. He is active in IFIP, has organized and is ex-chair of the Technical Committee on Software Engineering of the Information Processing Society of Japan, and has organized and is ex-president of the Japan Computer Graphics Association. He served as Vice-General Chairman of the International Conference on Computer Graphics, Pattern Recognition and Data Structure in 1975; General Chairman of the Third International Conference on Very Large Data Bases in 1977; Program Chairman of Intergraphics 83, Computer Graphics Tokyo 1984, 85, 86, and CG International 1987. Kunii received his BSc, MSc, and DSc in chemistry from the University of Tokyo in 1962, 1964 and 1967. The author's address is Department of Information Science, Faculty of Science, the University of Tokyo, 7-3-1 Hongo, Bunkyo-ku, Tokyo 113, Japan.

John Lansdown

John Lansdown is Chairman of System Simulation Ltd, a UNIX software and systems house specialising in work for designers and other decision makers. Since 1960 he has been using computers in art and design — initially in his work as an architect — but, more recently, in the fields of choreography, film-making, graphic and product design. He has been Secretary of the Computer Arts Society ever since its inception in 1968 and has organised a number of exhibitions and conferences dealing with the impact of computing on the arts. Until June 1986, he was a Senior Research Fellow and Tutor at the Royal College of Art and is currently a Senior Research Fellow at City University, London. He is also a Senior Visiting Fellow at the Department of Architectural Science, Sydney and the Department of Media and Communication Studies, Dorset Institute of Higher Education. With Gillian Crampton-Smith, he teaches a post-graduate course in Computer Graphics for Graphic Designers at St Martin's School of

Art, London. John Lansdown's publications include works on computer-aided design, architecture, art, graphics, knowledge-based systems and choreography, whilst his regular column in the Computer Bulletin, " Not Only Computing — Also Art" has been running since 1974.

Zsuzsanna Molnar

Zsuzsanna Molnar received her BA from the University of Michigan and her MFA from the Electronic Visualization Program at the University of Illinois. Her main interest and work has been in the area of real-time animation. She has been an active member of the computer graphics community, producing images and instructional media, lecturing and publishing internationally. She was involved in the development of Zgrass, an interactive graphics language designed for artists and educators. She has worked for Evans & Sutherland, and is currently Manager of Technical Marketing at Silicon Graphics, Inc.. Her group's responsibilities include education, creation of demo software and application consulting. She co-chaired the first tutorial for Artists & Designers given at Siggraph '83 and organized a panel on real-time simulation for Siggraph '85.

Mike Muuss

Mike Muuss has 15 years of experience in working with advanced computer systems. For the past 5 years, he has been leading the U.S. Army's Ballistic Research Laboratory's (BRL) Advanced Computer Systems Team in research projects concerning networking, graphics, CAD/CAE, operating systems, parallel architectures, and command and control. He is the principle architect of BRL's constructive solid geometry based CAD editing system "GED" and its advanced ray-tracing package "RT". Mr. Muuss was born in 1958, and received a BES in Electrical Engineering from Johns Hopkins University in 1979.

Peter Quarendon

Peter Quarendon joined the UK Scientific Center from the IBM Hursley Laboratories in 1982 to work on computer graphics and solid modelling. He is now Manager of the Graphics Application Group.

Brian Shackel

Brian Shackel graduated in classics from Cambridge University in 1947 and, after three years as a naval officer, returned to Cambridge to read psychology. He joined the Medical Research Council's Applied Psychology Research Unit in

1952 and, from 1954, was Head of the Ergonomics Department at EMI Electronics Ltd.. In 1969 he took up his present position as Professor of Ergonomics at the University of Technology, Loughborough. Professor Shackel is a Fellow of the British Psychological Society, a Fellow of the Human Factors Society (USA), a Fellow and past Chairman of Council of the Ergonomics Society, and currently Honorary Treasurer of the International Ergonomics Association. He has been an Academic Adviser to the Department of Employment and, in turn, Editor of the journals "Applied Ergonomics" and "Journal of Occupational Psychology". Relevant books include "Man-Computer Communication" (Infotech State-of-the-Art Report, pp 340, 1979); "Man-Computer Interaction (Ed.) (North-Holland, pp 983, 1985). He is a past Dean of the School of Human and Environmental Studies at Loughborough University, and has recently completed ten years as Head of the Department of Human Sciences.

Tom Stewart

Tom Stewart is a Director of System Concepts Limited, an independent systems consultancy based in London, England. System Concepts provides problem solving, consultancy, and information planning and marketing services to its clients. Tom specialises in the ergonomic and other human factors aspects of computer systems and consults regularly for major user and supplier organisations. He holds degrees in Physics and in Psychology from the University of Glasgow and in 1970 moved to Loughborough University as a Founder Member of the Human Sciences and Advanced Technology Research Group. His research topics included office communications, human computer interaction and VDT ergonomics. Before joining System Concepts in 1983 he worked for the international management consultancy, Butler Cox and Partners, and for one of the world's largest insurance brokers, Willis Faber. A well-known author and public speaker, his publications include the ergonomics manual Visual Display Terminals (of which he was a co-author) and the international scientific journal Behaviour and Information Technology (of which he is editor). He is Chairman of the International Standards Subcommittee which is drafting VDT standards and is currently advising the European Commission on the ergonomics of new technology. He was a member of a recent World Health Organisation working party on VDT health issues.

Adrian L. Thomas

Adrian Thomas obtained his PhD at Edinburgh University on spatial models in computer-based information systems. After a period in the Department of Electrical and Electronic Engineering at Heriot-Watt University he joined the Department of Mathematical Sciences at the University of Durham where he developed VLSI hardware in connection with real-time display systems for 3-D object models. He is now with the University of Sussex.

John R. Woodwark

Up until 1985 John Woodwark was a Lecturer in Manufacturing Engineering at the University of Bath, responsible for projects in robotics, solid modelling and computer graphics. He is now at the IBM UK Scientific Center working on Geometric Reasoning.

Index